MEMOIRS OF A SAN FRANCISCO ORGAN BUILDER

by
Louis J. Schoenstein

MEMOIRS OF A SAN FRANCISCO
ORGAN BUILDER

by
Louis J. Schoenstein

Cue Publications
San Francisco

TABLE OF CONTENTS

DEDICATION

In grateful and loving remembrance of
my father and mother, I dedicate this
effort of mine, to preserve for posterity
some of the many interesting notes,
historical data, anecdotes and experiences of my father's life as an organ
builder, and the events of the many
years I was privileged to work and labor
harmoniously with him until his death.

FOREWORD

Those seeking reading that is interesting and informative, that tells of people who built our great organs, of others who gained fame as organists, of organs of the past and of organs of our day will, I believe, find this book very satisfying, and at the same time, pleasant reading. Its author has seen organs grow from the early tracker-action instruments, requiring of the organist great strength and endurance, to the larger organs of today, which require almost no physical effort. He has actively participated in the building and installation of many of our finest and largest organs. Although his descriptive matter is accurate and detailed, he has made it both interesting and amusing by constantly giving of his vast knowledge of the history of San Francisco and of many of the people who were prominent in the earlier days of California. And through it all, there is a vein of humor and of human understanding, of love of San Francisco and of his profession.

Stanley H. Page
Los Gatos, California

PREFACE

The manuscript of this book was completed in 1962, my seventyeighth year. Although much has transpired until this happy year of its publication, I have decided to leave the book as it was then and make no attempt to chronicle events and changes that have taken place since. However, as this book will appear in the centennial year of the organ building firm founded by my respected father, I beg the reader's indulgence in my brief resume of the immediate past and future of the firm which has been the life work of my family.

After my retirement, my younger brothers and partners, Otto and Erwin, continued the firm of Felix F. Schoenstein and Sons founded by our father in 1877. Otto has since passed on to his eternal reward in 1969. After bringing the firm to the start of its one-hundredth year in 1977, Erwin who as our factory manager supervised the building of sixty-nine organs and the re-building of onehundred and twenty-nine organs, retired and sold the firm to Jack M. Bethards of San Francisco. I am proud to relate that my son, Lawrence, who has returned to the firm after twenty years with the Aeolian-Skinner Company will be in charge of all organ building under the new management and that his son, Terrence, is also serving with the firm. Therefore, not only will the name of Schoenstein continue as a tribute to my father and his father, but the fourth, fifth and, God willing, later generations will carry on with their own hands the traditions of our family craft.

Most of this book deals with the sixty-four years of my life spent as a San Francisco organbuilder. The rehearsing of the events has been a source of pleasure to me and I felt that they might possibly be of interest to others especially those familiar with the early history of our beloved San Francisco and those who, by profession or otherwise, are interested in churches, church music and choirs, organists, clergymen and in the organ itself — "The King of Instruments".

This book is not intended to be a complete nor thorough history of organs and organ building in San Francisco and its environs.* It is, rather, as the title implies, simply a chronicle of my personal recollections which I have endeavored to make as accurate as my memory would allow. I have tried to make this humble effort something of interest to all who read it and not just to those who make the organ their profession.

In the following pages there will be much intermingling of stories of my church, the Roman Catholic, with the Episcopal, Lutheran, Presbyterian, Methodist, Baptist, Mormon, Christian Science, Congregational, and the many other denominations as well as Jewish Synagogues and Temples and Masonic Lodges, etc. proving that the organbuilder's life is most unique, daily working in some church or house of worship, associating with religious people of all shades of beliefs, but reserving to himself his bounden duty of worshipping and serving God in the faith and in the Church of his love and conviction.

So many people have helped me with this book that I am sure to neglect to mention some, a fault of memory for which I hope to be forgiven. However, I wish to thank everyone I can in this limited space. First, to my late, dear wife Josephine, who never discouraged me on the seemingly endless task I undertook to write this book and to my sons and daughters, particularly Edward, who with the help of Lawrence, Bertram, Vincent and Victoria, have been responsible for taking the dusty manuscript after fifteen years asleep and bringing it to life through publication. Many others helped in the preparation of the original manuscript and the publication of the book: They include my cousin, Pauline Bartholome, Elenor Joyce McCarthy, Theresa Blease Sullivan, Vernon Gregory, and Teri Hyde and Valerie Ryan of R/H Composition Service. Many people generously provided information to help clarify my recollections and also gave continued encouragement throughout the years I toiled over the manuscript: These include Ludwig Altman, William H. Barnes, Msgr. James Culleton, Msgr. Robert F. Hayburn, Ray MacDonald, Rev. John B. McGloin, Harold Mueller, Stanley H. Page, Richard Purvis, Ernest M. Skinner, Right Rev. Charles A. Ramm, Very Rev. Francis Hubert Ward, and Rev. Arno Weniger. For the biographical notes on early builders I am indebted to Emma Hedemark, Mrs. Charles B. Andrews and Ralph Whalley. Finally, my gratitude to the members of the American Guild of Organists for their encouragement and to the Organ Historical Society, for their many efforts on behalf of the book, particularly Donald R.M. Paterson, Robert B. Whiting, Thomas W. Cunningham, Alan Laufman, and Barbara J. Owen.

I make no pretense to being an author and being fully aware of my shortcomings in this regard am surprised at myself for my boldness in attempting to write this book. After all I am a grammar school boy growing old.

LOUIS J. SCHOENSTEIN
San Francisco, California

*In order to put some limit on length I have left out many organs and events outside the San Francisco Bay Area even though our firm carried out our professional responsibilities throughout the West.

INTRODUCTIONS

The recollections of venerable San Francisco organ builder Louis J. Schoenstein add a valuable personal insight into what was probably the most quickly changing period in the history of American Organ Building — the first half of the 20th Century. The events which so dramatically changed organ building both mechanically and tonally were magnified in San Francisco as most of the City's 19th Century organs had to be replaced quickly after the Fire of 1906. Mr. Schoenstein's recollections of the builders, organists and clerics whose lives made the organ business so interesting for him bring warmth and humanity to a subject too often treated only in technical terms. It is, indeed, a shame that more organ builders have not made the effort to record their experiences as Mr. Schoenstein has. As far as I know, this volume stands alone to fill that space in organ literature.

William Harrison Barnes, Mus. D.

Evanston, Illinois

We all know people who have lived full and interesting lives, and who have a storehouse of entertaining tales. How often we wish those stories could be committed to paper — and how rarely it happens. How fine it is that we know so much about organs and organbuilding of the nineteenth century (after much painstaking research, to be sure!) and how sad it is that we know so little about organs and organbuilding of our own period — or rather, that so little is in print. Too often, we see in print detailed accounts of past events, meticulously researched by a reputable scholar, only to find the events of the 50 years immediately preceding the writing "of too recent occurrence to be of interest" and ignored altogether.

Oral history is both entertaining and instructive; much would be lost without it. That memory is sometimes faulty is perhaps irrelevant: far better to have *something* set down as a starting point, than to have nothing at all. If we wait to publish until we have all the facts, we never will publish, for never will we have all the facts. What we have here is a splendid accumulation of organ lore, rich in anecdote. Mr. Schoenstein writes out of his own experience, and future generations will thank him for recording his recollections. Would that more organbuilders and organ enthusiasts would emulate him!

The era of which Mr. Schoenstein writes is one of major importance to the history of the organ, a period of ferment, encompassing a revolution and a counter-revolution in organbuilding. His perspective as a westerner is unique; very little about organ history on the west coast has found its way into print before now. Much research remains to be done, of course. Perhaps this volume will inspire such research.

Alan M. Laufman, President
Organ Historical Society

Harrisville, New Hampshire

Chapter I

THE GREAT FIRE

It can truly be said that the earthquake and fire of April 18, 1906, closed a period of the history of San Francisco. The San Francisco after the fire was the San Francisco of a new era. Gone were the pioneer days, the days of '49, the days of the Bonanza Kings, the days of the Gay '90s. Yet, in this transition, something fundamental, something undefinable, typically San Franciscan, lingers on. The spirit of old San Francisco has not died. Rebuilt, readjusted, rearranged, chastened by fire and calamity, afflicted with more than its share of trouble and woe, yet always cheerful, tolerant, jovial, hospitable, kindhearted and gay, the City by the Golden Gate faces the future undaunted, unafraid, conscious of its glorious past and of its destiny to be a gem in the diadem of cities of our fair land.

As this period of 1906 was the termination of an era in the history of San Francisco, so, likewise, it might also be considered the close of a chapter in the history of the pipe organs of San Francisco. Such familiar names of organ builders, mostly from the Atlantic Seaboard, whose organs were at one time erected in San Francisco, as Simmons, Appleton, Erben, Wilcox, Johnson, E.G. Hook, Felgemaker, as also our Western pioneer organ builders, Mayer, Bergstrom, Andrew and son, Felix F. Schoenstein, Murray M. Harris and Thomas Whalley, are now mostly but a memory. Most of these firms have dissolved or, in the course of time, passed into oblivion.

After the fire a few of the above mentioned builders were again represented in supplying the city with new pipe organs — among them Hook and Hastings, Kimball, Whalley, Bergstrom and Schoenstein, but the greater number were from builders heretofore not represented, the names of which are now household words in the litany of contemporary organ builders of our country, such as Austin, Ernest M. Skinner, Hope-Jones, Pilcher, Jesse Woodbury, Hall, Aeolian-Skinner, Estey, Wurlitzer, Robert-Morton, Moller, Tellers Kent, Seeburg-Smith, Johnston and Wicks organs. The depression years of 1929-1936 further helped to eliminate some of the above firms, or caused reorganizations among them.

The tragic World War II, following closely on the heels of

the depression, almost completely paralyzed the noble industry, but as indispensable as church and religion are to mankind, so is the genuine pipe organ an indispensable requisite in the house of worship and its wants will always somehow be supplied for the well being of mankind, and the greater honor and glory of God.

Details of the earthquake and fire can be found in the many splendid articles and books written about the event, so I will not go into further detail here. Suffice to say that a total of 442 city blocks were destroyed and a casualty of 500 lives were lost. Undoubtedly, one of the most stupendous catastrophies recorded in modern times.

On that eventful day, I was living with my parents and family at 2306 Bryant Street, near the corner of 21st Street, in the Mission District. The great conflagration did not spread to this neighborhood, notwithstanding that an isolated but serious fire started at 22nd and Mission Streets on that fateful morning. This, fortunately, the fire department or available citizenry succeeded in extinguishing. However, on the third night of the conflagration, a tongue of the downtown fire did work its way out into the Mission District as far as 20th and Dolores Streets, and on this night we, in company with many neighbors, fearing the destruction of our homes, evacuated and camped for the night on the hillside above Vermont and Army Streets, expecting that by morning our homes would be reduced to ashes. Fortunately, on this Friday night, the third night of the conflagration, the fire was brought under control and we were not burned out.

We returned to our home, which had been shifted from its foundation by the earthquake, reinforced it temporarily until permanent repairs could be made later, arranged emergency living quarters in an old unused barn to the rear of our property, built a temporary shed to serve as kitchen on the sidewalk curb, and made ourselves contented and comfortable as did many others of the thousands of San Franciscans who lived through this period of suspense and uncertainty.

Gradually came the light of a new dawn. The quaking earth finally subsided. Order was restored out of chaos, and life began to flow again in its normal channels. The thought of a Divine Providence, which perhaps had never been taken too seriously by carefree, jovial San Franciscans, took on a new significance. The people had again learned how to pray. The churches that escaped destruction were reconditioned for future use, and were patronized as never before.

Undaunted by the catastrophe, even before the flames were completely extinguished, San Franciscans, the sons of the Argonauts, again set to work to rebuild and rehabilitate their destroyed metropolis.

The business section of Fillmore Street, overnight, became the new center of trade. Then Van Ness Avenue usurped the distinction of being the new Market Street, or the center of the shopping district — but not for long.

With superhuman courage and confidence in the future of their beloved city, the merchants of the larger business establishments proclaimed that they would rebuild and reestablish their businesses at the same locations in the so-called downtown area. This unbounded faith in the future of their beloved city was contagious, with the result that in a short space of time a greater and more beautiful San Francisco was built on the ruins of the old.

Market Street, with its "Path of Gold" is again its incomparable main artery. A jingle oft quoted in those eventful days when Fillmore Street thought it would be the permanent Market Street comes to mind, and I quote — "Market Street was Market Street when Fillmore Street was a pup; Market Street will be Market Street when Fillmore Street is grown up."

With the turbulence of the earthquake and fire gradually quieting down and with too much leisure on our hands, we approached our neighboring St. Peter's Catholic Church, on 24th and Alabama Streets, with the suggestion that we put their organ into condition again for future use. With this, our first organ work after the fire and earthquake commenced.

At the close of this eventful year, we were privileged to have a distinguished visitor in San Francisco in the person of the noted Organ Architect, and author of the "Art of Organ Building", Ashdown Audsley, L.L.D. My father had the pleasure of visiting and interviewing him on December 17, 1906.

In a following chapter I will make reference to the pipe organs erected in the churches and institutions of San Francisco located in the area ravaged by the fire only. Forty-two pipe organs were thus consumed by the conflagration. Undoubtedly, there were other churches in the fire area, mostly of the Protestant denominations, that were destroyed, but had no pipe organs. Churches that at one time had been located in the fire district but had moved to other locations before the fire, I shall refer to in another chapter, as well as the organs and churches which were destroyed by the effects of the earthquake only.

Chapter II

THE WRATH OF FIRE

Pipe Organs Erected in San Francisco, Prior to
1906 and Consumed in the Great Conflagration.

St. Patrick's

In recalling the establishment of my father's business on August 5, 1877, in a small shop at 512 Birch Avenue, St. Patrick's Church and its pipe organs undoubtedly must receive first mention, as his first private business activities in the pipe organ field were associated with this church.

Previous to my father's arrival in San Francisco in 1868, St. Patrick's Church was already established and occupied a small frame building on Market Street between Second and Third Streets, where the Palace Hotel now stands. This church was built in 1854, with Rev. John Maginnis as the pastor.

In 1864, Joseph Mayer, San Francisco's veteran organ builder, constructed a 16 stop, two manual pipe organ, with a gothic case, for this church. In 1870, the new St. Patrick's Church, now located on the north side of Mission Street, between Third and Fourth Streets, was begun. The Mayer organ from the original St. Patrick's Church on Market Street was then moved to the basement of the new church, where it remained for some time in use, until the church edifice above was completed, the dedication of which took place on March 17, 1872. Rev. Peter J. Grey was the pastor and Rev. Thomas Larkin was his assistant at this time.

My father's notes state that in 1876 the old Mayer organ was removed from the basement church by Mayer and erected in a Catholic Church at Virginia City, Nevada, where it was later destroyed by fire. However, another version of the final history of the old organ may be the following.

In the early part of my career in 1909, on being called to repair an old Mayer organ in the Catholic Church at Colusa, California, for Rev. Michael Wallrath, I was told it was the old original St. Patrick's pipe organ. It was in such a dilapidated condition at the time that I did not deem it worth repairing.

Referring again to the old original St. Patrick's Church, the frame building which formerly stood on the site of the Palace Hotel, before the site on Mission Street was selected, was eventually moved to the north side of Eddy Street, between Octavia and Laguna Streets, opposite Jefferson Square, and was called St. John's Church. As children we often attended services there. In later years this old church was again moved farther west on Eddy Street, near Scott, where it now stands alongside the imposing Holy Cross Church, I, therefore, believe that this church can justly be singled out as San Francisco's oldest frame building, now 112 years old.

The new St. Patrick's Church was a beautiful and imposing Gothic brick structure, with a tall, graceful spire, containing a set of Carillon Bells, the gift of Peter Donohoe. It was also deserving of having the best pipe organ then obtainable. Therefore, Rev. Peter J. Grey, pastor of the church, secured an organ imported from Europe. It was purchased from a firm named Ibach, of Barmen, Germany, and was shipped to San Francisco by tramp ship via Panama, costing $10,000. It was dedicated June 20, 1876.

Mr. John H. Dohrman, who had functioned as organist on the Mayer organ in the original church on Market Street, also served as organist on the new organ and, after a period of 35 years as Organist of St. Patrick's, terminated his eventful career.

As the story was related by my father, two employees of the firm came from Germany to install this large new instrument. This, on arrival, they partly did, but not satisfactorily complete the work. The "City by the Golden Gate" was at that time at fever heat with the lure of the gold mines, the one absorbing topic of the day, and these artisans deserted their appointed work before entirely completing it for the diggings of the elusive gold in the Sierras.

Joseph Mayer, the local organ builder, had, evidently, according to my father's version, been similarly affected and had returned to Marysville, where he formerly lived.

My father was then approached by Father Grey, who undoubtedly knew that he had formerly been in the employ of Joseph Mayer, and asked if he would, or could, proceed with the work and bring the installation of the organ to a satisfactory completion. This opportunity to demonstrate his skill as an organ builder was accepted, with the result that thereafter he established himself in business, as previously mentioned, on August 5, 1877.

John H. Dohrman, a native of Germany, as stated, was the organist. I recall him in his declining years. Mr. Dohrman was rated by my father as the organist par excellence, and as the most efficient organist San Francisco had ever had, barring none of the celebrities that came in later years. He held sway at the organ of St. Patrick's until the retirement of Father Peter J. Grey in 1898, who then passed away in 1907. He was succeeded by a Miss Marie Short, who played the organ until its destruction at the time of the earthquake and fire in 1906.

During a period of fifteen years, under the pastorate of Father Peter J. Grey, my father was, in addition to being custodian of the organ, also a member of the choir, a paid quartet. From notes obtained from a book written by a contemporary authoress of that period, I noted a reference was made to St. Patrick's quartet in that it sang for the first time in San Francisco, Bach's Mass in B Minor on April 17, 1869. Members of the quartet were: soprano, Miss Brandle; mezzo soprano, Signora Bianchi; contralto, Mrs. M. R. Blake; basso, Felix Schoenstein. My father had a sonorous bass voice which he had cultivated under the tutelage of Mr. Bianchi, a tenor of note at the time, and also a member of the choir. My father's musical talents were likewise sought by others, and at times he sang in the choruses of the Handel and Hayden Oratorical Society, under the direction of Humphrey J. Stewart, then recently arrived from England. He also sang with the Glee Club of Sacred Heart College under Brother Hosea. Being musically inclined, he also directed an amateur brass band affiliated with one of the societies of St. Boniface's Church. He related also having furnished the music at the cornerstone laying of the first Mission Dolores Church, the brick edifice alongside the old Mission.

St. Patrick's choir under the able direction of John H. Dohrman set a high standard in church music in its day. This was before the Mortu Proprio by Pius X had gone into effect. Mozart's Twelfth Mass and others of this type were the favorites. Music of a highly theatrical nature was the rule, and although it was lauded and admired from a musical and artistic standpoint, it did not meet with the approval of my father, even though he was paid for singing it, as music befitting the house of God.

While commenting on St. Patrick's choir, several recollections mentioned by my father come to mind. He recalled certain peculiarities of the organist. Mr. Dohrman, evidently realizing his virtuosity, assumed that others should be like him. Since the members of the paid quartet were also professionals, they should be treated as such. Therefore, no rehearsals were had, practicing was to be done at home or elsewhere, and when they came to sing, they, as professionals, were supposed to know what they were singing. And, as if this severe attitude was not sufficient, he would at times seem to delight in ensnaring his singers by transposing the music in a different key then usually sung, or distract them by other means, possibly to test their ability, or should I say to humiliate them and to exhalt his own importance. Whatever the motives of his idiosyncrasy might have been, my father always spoke highly of him, revered him as a great musician and enjoyed his friendship until he passed away.

Another celebrity my father often spoke of, was Karl Formes, a basso. I do not recall my father mentioning whether or not he sang in the choir, but he spoke of him often and he was evidently associated with him in some capacity or other; if not in St. Patrick's choir, it was in the Handel and Hayden Oratorical Society, of which my father was a member. Humphrey J. Stewart, organist of the Church of the Advent, then at Second and Mission Streets, was musical director of the organization at the time. Karl Formes must have been a famous basso. He was idolized by my father and was his ideal of what a bass singer should be.

In recalling the organist, John H. Dohrman, my father's association with the choir, and his esteem of Karl Formes, I have digressed from the subject which I intended to deal with more minutely, namely, the organ.

To my knowledge, St. Patrick's organ was the only imported or foreign made, organ in San Francisco at the time. Its specifications and appointments were drawn up by Mr. John H. Dohrman. It was a large three manual of about sixty stops. It had an ornate case of typical European or medieval design, made of black oak, with a Gothic tower in the center which held five large sixteen foot pipes, two fields of smaller pipes on either end, with a double group of small pipes one above the other between the center tower and the end groups. All front display pipes were made of pure English block tin, highly polished. All front pipes were speaking pipes. The keyboard, as most organs of that time were made, was set in flush with the case. Huge draw stop knobs, with a pulling motion of about six inches on square shanks were arranged in double rows on both sides and above the keyboard. The compass of the manuals was fifty-eight notes and thirty on the pedal. The key action was tracker. The Great manual, or "Hauptwerk" as it was called, was the lowest manual. This was provided with a pneumatic auxiliary action to help relieve the tension on the keys. The second manual was the Swell manual, or Oberwerk, and the third, or upper one, the choir. Strange to say, the second, or Swell manual, was not enclosed in a swell box. The choir was the only enclosed section. The pipes on the Swell manual were all exposed. The building of a suitable Swell box to enclose the pipes on this chest, which was laid out in chromatic arrangement with the tallest eight foot pipes on one end and the small trebles on the other, was one of the improvements my father made when he first took charge of the organ. He prided himself on this accomplishment, as it consisted of oscillating shades on both sides, front and top, all operating simultaneously on traces. The blinds were made of double thickness lumber, filled with sawdust to make them soundproof, and were so arranged that any individual blind could be readily removed for convenient access for tuning.

With all this care and thoughtful planning and laborious work, my recollection of it is that it was not an over-effective swell box, due, undoubtedly, to the many joints to be controlled, and the sound, on being emitted, going in all directions instead of in one general forward direction.

One other improvement my father prided himself on was the revoicing of the Oboe 8' reed stop on this chest. In fact, all the reeds of the organ, the Trumpet 8', the Clarinet 8', and the Oboe 8' were exceedingly blatant and strident. The Oboe 8' was as loud as an ordinary Trumpet. By applying an inverted leathered cone, resting lightly on top of each pipe on a threepoint support, and possibly by diminishing its supply of air, he subdued its sonority and secured a pleasing Oboe horn effect.

The revoicing of the string stops, which were never too

satisfactory, also required much of his skill and patience, and he succeeded admirable in making these stops usable. What intrigued me most was the mounted Cornet elevated over the 12th and 15th stops, next to the Trumpet. These were of a rather large and generous scale, especially the treble notes. The Great manual had two chests, the C and the C# side. The choir manual was chromatic and was the smallest of the three divisions, and was the only division of the organ originally under expression, as previously stated. Tonally, the organ was exceedingly brilliant, with a superabundant array of Mixture, Sesquialtra and mutation stops, on the baroque type. The Diapasons, although of good quality, seemed to be smothered up entirely by the Trumpet and Mixtures. At least that was my impression in those, my youthful days. That the ensemble was out of balance must have been an established fact, as, aside from a general tempering down of a super-brilliancy and stridency in the organ, one of the further improvements my father made was the addition of a large Open Diapason sixteen foot Pedal stop to secure an adequate foundation tone. These pipes were made of heavy two and a half inch Puget Sound cedar, and were placed in the lofty, narrow arch behind the organ and were voiced on four inch to six inch pressure. So effective was the result of adding these pipes, that the windows in the clerestory of the nave of the church rattled violently when they were used, and the organist was cautioned thereafter to use this stop sparingly on that account.

I remember my father building these pipes in 1889, in his first shop at 512 Birch Avenue, in the Hayes Valley. I was then about five years old, but ever since, the fragrance of freshly planed or sawed cedar wood recalls to my mind the time when I was in his shop while he was making these pipes.

The organ was originally planned to be pumped by foot power, requiring two men to operate it, each one operating two feeders connected on a rocker shaft. Here, again, my father's skill and ingenuity was brought to the fore. He installed a Pelton water-wheel, belted to a crankshaft which operated the four feeders of the bellows. This was the first water motor of this type applied to an organ in San Francisco. Not only did this water motor do its work satisfactorily, but the device he arranged to control the valve to make it respond to the demands made upon the organ was most uncanny in its operation. A large, vertical lever pivoted at the end near the floor, with a left and right motion, was provided, one direction controlling the water valve, the other connected by a rope to the top of the bellows, governed the speed of the water motor. My father was proud of this achievement, and he promised us little children at home that, as a reward if we were good, some day he would take us to St. Patrick's Church and show us the machine blowing the organ.

It was in fulfillment of this promise that one day he took me, for the first time, into the mysterious insides of this large pipe organ. I was then about seven years old. The dark, dusty interior with all the pipes and mechanism, the ladders and walk boards, was most interesting. What fascinated me most was going back into the recess under the Pedal, Open Diapason 16', that my father built, where the water motor was located, and watching the clock-like lever controlling the water motor as it operated the feeders of the bellows with as much delicacy as if it were operated humanly.

In this dark recess was a dim gas jet. It was the apparent hideout for the organist during the sermon, as I recall that Mr. Dohrman was not a Catholic. The fragrant aroma of a fine cigar usually betrayed to what purpose it was often put.

Three outstanding events always come to mind when I recall St. Patrick's organ. After the organ had been in use for thirty years, dust had accumulated to such an extent that a general cleaning was necessary. This was done by my father and myself in 1899. It was one of my first jobs, as I had, but a year before in my 13th year, terminated my schooling at St. Boniface's School. All pipes in the organ were removed, including the large front tin pipes, and the organ, in general, given a thorough cleaning. One of my special jobs was the polishing of the front tin display pipes to a bright luster, as they evidently originally were. During the course of years they had become badly tarnished. This polishing being finished, we proceeded to lift the pipes into place again. They weighed considerable. This we were made fully aware of when we tried to lift the largest, or center pipe, into place. After getting it into an upright position on the floor and then placing it on the organ bench, where I stood holding it temporarily against the pipe rack, my father hastened to the upper level of the organ to secure a good hold on the upper end of it. At a given signal we both hoisted the pipe, with the expectation of placing it in its designated spot, but lo and behold, I came to realize that I was just a trifle too short to raise it to the edge of the pipe sill, upon which it was to rest. Likewise, the original grip my father had taken on the pipe above was dissipated to its fullest extent. Being at the bottom with the heaviest end of the load, and my strength waning, the large pipe seemed momentarily poised in midair, making no progress either up or down. Its weight became increasingly heavy. Panic seized me, and I was about to give up when, by a superhuman effort, my father got a fresh hold and hoisted the recalcitrant pipe to its final inch onto the safe and solid pipe sill of the organ case. The tuning and voicing of the organ then followed the cleaning.

It was during the month of July that this work was done. I distinctly remember a little incident that occured on the Fourth of July. I naturally expected to celebrate the day as young American would do, but evidently the organ had to be completed and ready for use the following Sunday. My father, accordingly, found it necessary that we continue with the work, and the special objective of the day was the tuning of the Mixtures and Cornet, at best a slow and tedious job. Although I was very reluctant to comply, obedience to our parents was a matter of strict policy in our family, and so instead of shooting off fireworks, I was at the organ bench all day, listening to the shrill discordant notes of the Mixtures until they finally came to a perfect blend, or tune, with the accompanying stop.

During these long and wearisome hours, seeing the sun shine through the large Gothic Windows on the east side of the nave during the morning hours, and then gradually set in the afternone, flooding the western windows with rays of crimson light indicating that the day's work was reaching its completion, one had to do something to break the monotony of the ordeal. I recall resorting to some perspective drawing of the vaulted ceiling of one of the naves of the church, one hand holding the keys, the other wielding the pencil.

One period of intermission, which I looked forward to with much pleasure, was the noon hour when we had our lunch, invariably at the "Pioneer Restaurant" on Fourth Street and Pioneer Place, a landmark of San Francisco, known far and wide for the huge doughnuts and good coffee served there. The interior of the establishment was adorned with frescoes on the walls. I recall the cold marble tops on the tables, the white sand on the floor, and the rotund and gray haired proprietors, "Volz and Gall", behind the counters taking the cash, greeting and directing customers and waiters.

Later in the afternoon on the same day, we had unexpected visitors. The Moroscos Opera House was a few doors east of St. Patrick's Church. It being a holiday, undoubtedly a special matinee program was being given there. Mr. Marshall Geiselman, a prodigy at the organ and a protege of Robert Harrison, organist of St. Mary's Cathedral, was passing the church and, acting as good Catholics do, entered and paid their respects to the Divine Presence in the Holy Eucharist in the tabernacle. On hearing the organ being tuned, and that on a holiday, they came up to the organ loft to see who was working, and greeted us. Mr. Geiselman's regret on my behalf at my being compelled to work while he could attend the opera, gave me little consolation. Later on, while holding the keys, waiting for the customary shout of "next" from my father, I playfully placed my fingers under the keys (there were no finger boards over these manuals and the keys evidently had no adequate bumpers on top of them either). I touched some foreign, hard substance under the keys. Knowing it should not be there I finally wiggled it out. At first it appeared as though it were a piece of glass but, on closer examination, and on rubbing off the dust, it proved to be a precious stone, a garnet. Evidently it had fallen out of someone's ring and remained hidden there for years, until I uncovered it. So after all, for complying with my father's command to help him tune the organ on the Fourth of July, I received my reward.

With the retirement of Father Grey in 1898, a new pastor, or administrator, was appointed - also a new organist....the aforementioned Miss Marie Short, who later became Mrs. O'Brien.

My last recollection of Mr. Dohrman was seeing him at the William Dingee residence on Washington and Franklin Streets, where, in the presence of Mrs. Dingee and my father, he demonstrated some music on the piano which he had previously arranged for my father, to be placed on a cylinder for the orchestrion which had been installed in the Dingee residence. (For further particulars of this visit see William Dingee Residence.) Mr. Dohrman was well along in years at this time. I did not see him again after that, and he passed away in 1899.

(I might mention here that Miss Marie Giorgiani, organist for many years at Old St. Mary's, and Miss Desmond, organist for an equally long period at St. Patrick's Catholic Church, were former pupils of Mr. Dohrman.)

One other incident in my recollections of old St. Patrick's Church and its organ is the following: From practically the inception of the installation of this pipe organ, we had a contract with the pastor for the maintenance of the instrument, making regular monthly visits, and it was on one of these visits, during the month of March 1906, that the incident occurred. Our former procedure, as related previously, was now reversed, and my father sat at the organ bench while I did the tuning. After playing some extemporaneous chords on the manuals, with some pedal accompaniment, which my father delighted to do to demonstrate his agility with his feet on the pedal board, he noticed that some of the Trombone 16' notes were not sounding. We thought nothing unusual of it at the moment. I prepared to enter the interior of the organ to investigate. Going through the usual door on the north side, I entered the deep recess in the organ chamber to the rear, where the water motor was located. There I lit the gas jet and my candle, and proceeded further up a ladder to an elevated chest, where the Trombone pipes were located. To my great surprise, I was horrified to see that a great number of the pipes were missing. On the floor and walk board were others, flattened and neatly pressed into packages of about 10" square. Similar packages were wrapped in paper and neatly tied. The plot and evidence clearly proved the case - a burglar had been systematically visiting and looting the organ. He made his entrance to the organ through a small door that led to a narrow passage between the gallery stairway and the organ chamber walls, in which was hanging the rope from the belfry above, used by the sexton to ring the bell. A door leading from this dark passage led into the organ chamber. Its existence was practically unknown to anyone, so at least we thought, besides ourselves, who used it occasionally when we found the main gallery door locked. The burglar could enter here unobserved, take a package or two under his arm and casually leave again unnoticed, undoubtedly assuming this proceedure could be continued indefinitely. Our monthly visit, however, upset his plans. We immediately notified the pastor, and the case was turned over to the police for investigation. The last report we heard was that the thief had been apprehended and his case set for trial. However, justice was defeated. The earthquake and fire of April 18, 1906, intervened. The evidence, police records, courts and jails, all were temporarily effaced. The slate was again clean.

After the fire, St. Patrick's Church was again rebuilt on the same site. The old foundation and walls were retained and reinforced with a steel frame, and the old type of architecture followed, with the exception that the former lofty spire was replaced by a low, square Tudor Gothic tower. The "South of the Slot", however, was not the South of Market as before the fire. What had once been a densely populated district of the working class had now become a commercial and industrial district with a generous supply of transient workmen's hotels and boarding houses. The more affluent parishioners who had once supported St. Patrick's, were gone, and, owing to this difficulty, the lack of means, the restoration of St. Patrick's Church made slow progress.

However, these difficulties did not discourage the indominitable pastor, the Right Reverend John Rogers. It was his dream to make this church, which was dedicated to the Patron of Ireland, St. Patrick, the shrine and mecca of the Irish Catholics of San Francisco. At first, only the walls and roof sufficed for the holding of divine services. Later, the finished inside plastering was done, and temporary benches on a hard, coarse concrete floor served for many years. Finally, art glass windows, depicting the saints and legends of the Irish were installed. A set of chimes were placed in the belfry as of yore.

a gift of Mrs. Mary Hourihan in 1954, and were frequently played to the delight of the passerby. A small reed organ, or harmonium, answered the purpose where once the thundering tones of the old organ filled the nave. Subsequently, the finished columns of imported Connemara marble, from Ireland, and the wainscoting were installed, and beautiful altars were added at a later period.

Though other items were still to be provided, such as a proposed marble floor, permanent benches, and the completion of the exterior of the church and tower, it was Monsignor Rogers' idea that his parishioners should not be deprived, meanwhile, of the joy and inspiration that a pipe organ would lend to divine services. He, accordingly, sought the services of Arnold Constable, a local architect who had distinguished himself in the designing of many local church edifices, and who was recognized as an authority in Gothic design, to lay out the facade of a proposed new organ in the Gothic style for the lofty nave of St. Patrick's Church. The contract for the organ was awarded to the Skinner Organ Company of Boston, in 1928. It was to be a three manual and pedal electric pneumatic action organ, with thirty-four stops and a detached console. That both organ builder and architect achieved noteworthy success can best be demonstrated by a visit to St. Patrick's. The organ was installed by John Saul and Harry Law, with Stanley Williams assisting.

Rev. Monsignor John Rogers passed to the great beyond before the church was entirely completed. His tenure lasted from 1905 to 1935. After his demise, his successor, Father James J. McHugh, instead of installing the marble floor, put in a wooden floor with inlaid linoleum tiling in the aisles, the light fixtures and other necessary accessories and the new permanent pews, He also completed the tower and the exterior of the church. The reconstructed St. Patrick's Church, now again restored with its pealing chimes which, as of old, bring back memories of a glorious past.

The care and maintenance of the beautiful new Skinner organ was finally placed in our hands, under the pastorate of Rev. Msgr. Leo Powleson, who served as Pastor from 1935 to 1953. Mrs. Teresa Grubb, a professional organist of many years practical experience, was organist of this historic and

revered church. Mr. Mayo Brolan not only ably assisted her as
second organist, but also served as master carilloneur of the
bells, for which St. Patrick's Church was always known.
During the Lenten season, at Christmas and the Easter Holidays, and especially on the patronal feastday of the church,
St. Patrick's Day, its bright and cheerful silver tones float over
the air in defiance of the din of traffic on the streets below,
invariably lifting one's thoughts from the sordid and material
things of life to those of eternal happiness.

Mr. Mayo Brolan passed away in 1945. Mrs. Grubb, the
organist followed him to the eternal reward in 1946. Miss
Kathrine Rattigan, a former parishioner of St. Patrick's, was
Mrs. Grubb's successor for a time, also carilloneur. The bells
are now rung from an electrically controlled chimes keyboard.

After Miss Rattigan's demise, the position of organist made
many and frequent changes. Among them, as far as I can recall, was Mr. Robert Hayburn, who played from 1931 to
1933. Subsequently, he entered the Seminary for the Priesthood. After his ordination, he was stationed at several locations and now holds the office of Consultant and Director
of the Archdiocian Music Committee. He is an able organist
and an authority on organ design. Others following him were
Mr. Seymour Snare, Mr. Paul E. Fitzgerald, and the present
organist, Robert R. Vaughn.

As in many another Catholic church of the city, and especially in the good old days before the fire, so also here in
St. Patrick's the position of sexton is an honored and respected one, with the result that the incumbent, James Maher,
now 70 years old and who has held the position for 45 years,
a typical son of Ireland, is proud of his long term of faithful
service. Aside from being an efficient and faithful worker, he
is a character to behold when walking through the aisles of
the church in a slow, measured pace, swinging his broad,
athletic shoulders in a defiant mood, challenging, as it were,
anyone not toeing the mark to a rude awakening. With
"Skid Row", formerly but a block distant from St. Patrick's,
a stalwart guardian as James Maher was indeed desirable.

St. Patrick's Church, again rebuilt and restored, with the
Reverend Msgr. McCarthy, the present pastor, seems to link

a glorious past — the San Francisco that was — with the future — the San Francisco to come.

ST. FRANCIS DE ASSISI
Vallejo and Dupont Sts.

Before referring to the organ and related material, some data on this historic church may be in order. It is the oldest Catholic Parish Church in San Francisco, and was named after its Patronal Saint, St. Francis of Assisi. An adobe structure was first built on the present site in 1849. The present edifice was then built, in 1859, over the adobe chapel. When the former was completed, the adobe structure was removed. St. Francis Church also served as San Francisco's first Cathedral for Archbishop **Sadoc** Alemany, O.P.D.D. until the dedication of Old St. Mary's Church in 1854.

It seems that in the beginning of my career as an organ builder, in assisting my father, our work brought us more often to the North Beach, South of Market, and the Hayes Valley sections of the City than elsewhere. The North Beach section with its European atmosphere and the foreign tongues spoken there, intrigued me. It often made me think of my father as a young man of 19 arriving in San Francisco, a foreigner himself, unable to speak the English language, and erecting, with his brother, their first musical instrument — a large orchestrion — in "Bottle Mayer's" famous resort on Jackson Street near Kearny. With this work completed, a total stranger among strangers, he accepted, temporarily, the menial job of bottle washer. He later worked in a furniture factory on Hayes Street, near Polk Street, until he got acquainted with San Francisco's pioneer organ builder, Joseph Mayer.

While at "Bottle Mayer's", he logically wanted to be near his work and lived in a place at the foot of Telegraph Hill, on Montgomery Street, above Columbus Avenue. When going to St. Francis Church, I would often recall the events my father related of his early arrival in San Francisco, and his early days spent in this district. From my father's notes regarding the first pipe organ at St. Francis Church, I conclude that it was a two manual and pedal organ, built by Joseph Mayer of San Francisco.

This organ was originally built by him for Grace Episcopal Cathedral in 1862. Later, possibly 1866, it was removed and installed on a rental basis in St. James Episcopal Church, on Post Street between Taylor and Mason Streets, on the site where the Olympic Club now stands. When dissension disrupted this congregation, however, the edifice was sold to the St. John's Presbyterian Church. Evidently, at this time, the organ was moved to Joseph Mayer's Shop on Page Street, for disposal. A Pedal stop was added to it while there, and the organ was eventually sold to St. Francis Catholic Church on Vallejo Street, where it was installed and gave service for many years.

In 1866, or thereabouts, it was moved to Vallejo, California, and installed by my father in St. Vincent's Catholic Church, where it served for many more years. In 1940, our firm installed a new modern electric pneumatic pipe organ there to take its place. Relics of this old organ, a few old pipes made by Mayer, delapidated, fragile, patched and worn, are still retained in our office as examples of "organ pipes, as they should not look."

Coming back to St. Francis Church on Vallejo Street, John Bergstrom of San Francisco was awarded the contract to build the new organ, in 1891. It was a large three manual and pedal, tracker action, and attached console. Two outstanding features of this organ, I clearly remember. It was the only organ I recall, excepting St. Patrick's, that was equipped with gas jets for illumination. It was quite an improvement over the humble tallow candle, with its dim light, its dripping wax, and the danger of dropping it some time in between the maze of inflammable trackers. The other feature was a large fly wheel on the right side of the organ, connected with the crankshaft operating the feeders of the bellows, that had to revolve to pump the organ. It was a man's size job, but with some effort and getting up some momentum, I was able to manipulate it, at least sufficiently for the purpose of tuning the organ. I do not recall the name of any organist playing on this organ.

Father Terrence Carraher was the pastor of St. Francis

Church for many years, a kindly, old, white-haired gentleman.

I recall a little incident that happened in 1903, when the organ was in urgent need of a general cleaning and over-hauling. My elder brother, Leo, who had spent a number of years previously in New York City working for the Muller & Abel Organ Company, Odell, and the Aeolian Company, had just returned to San Francisco to claim his bride. I was very proud of my brother. He was tall, well-built, manly looking, and just coming from New York, I thought he was "it", to use a slang expression. However, Father Carraher, coming on the scene one day when much of the organ was open and apart, looked wonderingly at the dismantled parts and asked my brother if "he was able to do it." This was, of course, quite a humiliation to my brother, just returned from New York after working with some of the Country's leading firms in organ building. It is, however, not an uncommon happening to youthful organ builders. I met with a similar incident in later years.

In former years, it seems an organ builder was thought of as an elderly, experienced man, graced with a venerable beard and bespectacled. These qualifications my aged father fully acquired in the course of time. However, at the age of 19 or 25, he would have had as little chance as his own sons later had, had he been judged and appraised by the above standard.

A habit and practice of mine as a youngster, when making the rounds and assisting my father in his work, was to make exploring visits up into the towers and belfries of churches we visited, whenever the opportunity permitted, and if they were left open for access. It was always a thrill to see and touch the bell in the tower, to see the frightened pigeons flutter and fly away, their privacy distrubed by an intruder. The vistas from the towers of most of San Francisco's churches, owing to the topography of the city, with its many hills and the Bay often in view, as was the case from the to-wers of St. Francis Church, were always romantic and fas-cinating to me. Many a belfry I have climbed, many a time I have walked the catwalks in the dark attics of the churches. In time, this diversion and hobby passed. When responsibility later rested on my shoulders, time was too valuable and limited to indulge in this pastime, and work was too absorbing to wander around where the pigeons dwelt.

I recall one incident while erecting a blower and motor, with my elder brother Leo, in an exposed portion of a belfry in a corner of the roof a few feet away from a large bell. It was in St. Vincent's Church at Vallejo. From its lofty location there was a most beautiful view of Mare Island and the Navy Yard. We were busy working on the blower, which was located in the belfry, with our backs to the large bell, forgetting that the noon hour had arrived. The conscientious sexton, however, had not forgotten the hour, and at the stroke of twelve pulled the rope of the bell, not knowing that we were up almost alongside of it. Its sudden, unexpected motion, the clang of the bell, almost floored us momentarily, but then we enjoyed the sight of the swaying bell at such close range, and listened to its wonderful harmonics.

Another incident I may relate in connection with the climbing of church towers, occurred but a few years ago in making our regular monthly visit to one of our city's Catholic churches. The organ there was a fine modern one, three manual electric pneumatic action. In making my inspection, I noticed that the ceiling over the organ was badly marred and stained from an evident recent leak in the roof above. It was during the wet season. Knowing quite well that the reporting of such damage does not always result in immediate action, I climbed to the roof and tower of this church to see if I could find the cause or location of the leak myself, before reporting it. I was soon rewarded. Looking down from the tower, I saw a veritable pond of water that had accumulated in the lower level between the tower and the gable roof, and this was spilling over the flanging and penetrating the ceiling over the organ. By agile, if not dangerous climbing, I managed to get to the gutter, and by reaching arm's length through the water, found the outlet to the leader pipe securely sealed and blocked by a large tennis ball, evidently thrown onto the roof of the church by some boy and finally lodging in the gutter. A screen placed over this opening would have prevented this accident.

Referring again to St. Francis Church, another favorite pastime, if I may so call it, while in the neighborhood of the Church at noon time, was eating lunch at the Royal Cafe, then located at the intersection of Columbus Avenue, Broadway and Dupont Streets. Coffee and snails of excellent quality was the standing order at this place.

The Bergstrom organ at St. Francis Church, and the church itself, were destroyed in the fire and earthquake of 1906. After the fire, St. Francis Church, the oldest parish church in San Francisco, was again rebuilt, the same foundations and walls being retained. A steel frame was installed and an edifice again erected, resembling and closely following the lines of the old church. For many years after the fire only a reed organ served the purpose for musical accompaniment at church services. However, during the pastorate of Father Patrick Collopy, in 1926, a new modern electric pneumatic organ, divided on both sides of the large Gothic window, with detached console and chimes, was installed by our firm.

This organ consists of six units, with couplers duplexed and unified, and is of exceptionally good tone quality. Only the north side of the organ is occupied. The south chamber is still vacant, except for the display pipes, and will provide the space for future additions which the organ should have. Miss Ryan, a most pleasing and lovable soul, was the organist presiding at the organ from its installation until 1939, when she was called to her eternal reward.

On the morning of Sunday, November 4, 1945, at 5:30 a.m., a disasterous fire broke out in the north end of the church, consuming the entire sacristy and seriously threatened the destruction of the venerable old edifice. Flames finally broke through the roof and gutted the attic in the section over the sanctuary, but due to the very efficient effort of the San Francisco Fire Department, little damage was done to the interior of the church, as all the fixtures were covered in time with tarpaulins — the organ included.

I arrived on the scene when the Fire Department were mopping up, and met the organist, Chester Farrell, bemoaning the contents of his music cabinet, which was thoroughly drenched by water.

The damage to the church was again repaired and the old venerable edifice stands as imposing as ever.

TEMPLE EMANUEL

My earliest recollections of Temple Emanuel go back to about 1890. As youngsters, I recall my father telling us children that a few years later he would give us a playhouse for our enjoyment. This turned out to be a discarded part of the organ of Temple Emanuel, being made available due to a rebuilding which was then being completed.

It was the old bellows of the organ, a most unusual type, consisting of two boxes about five feet square, and open on one end. These boxes telescoped one inside the other, similar to a piston in a pump, and a compression ring or gasket was provided to make the moving joint air-tight. By raising one box and letting it sink into the other, it would act as a pump and force the air into the organ. There was no reservoir or auxiliary bellows in the organ, as is usually the case, This pumping device was discarded at that time for a more modern one which I shall refer to later.

The two discarded boxes were brought to our back yard at 1202 Fillmore Street, to make the playhouse my father promised us children. One box was placed above the other, representing a two story house, and doors and windows were cut into them, and a ladder applied instead of a stairs. It was an ideal playhouse for us, and the envy of all the other children in the neighborhood, so much so, that it generated some rivalry and they tried to build better and larger playhouses, however, without success. This discarded bellows playhouse held its superiority and reputation as the best in the neighborhood until the winter rains set in, and the glue sizing, colored with Venetian red, used on the inner walls became soft and tacky and the glued joints opened up and fell apart, making the house unsafe and uninhabitable.

At about this time, I remember also my first visit to Temple Emanuel. Evidently Temple Emanuel was often the topic of discussion at home between my father and elder brother Leo, who referred to it as the "Turnip Church" because of the two large inverted turnip-shaped adornments forming the tops of the towers.

In 1864, when Temple Emanuel was built on Sutter Street, between Powell and Stockton Streets, it must have been an outstanding structure in the young and growing city. As early as 1865 an organ was already installed in this edifice. It was built by Joseph Mayer, California's pioneer organ builder, in his workshop on Dupont Street. It consisted of three manuals and pedal and had 28 speaking stops. The console faced the congregation, and the action was partly tracker, with the Weigle "Kegel Lade" palet chest, the system used by Walker of Ludwigsburg, Germany, in their larger organs. Mr. Mayer, having served his apprenticeship with this firm in Germany, was the first organ builder to build an individual valve chest for an organ in San Francisco. The name "Kegel Lade" denotes chest of small cones. From a description of it, as related to me by my father, each pipe had its own individual valve. It was a small round leathercovered cone resting in an orifice leading to the pipe. The individual cones or "kegels" were actuated by a fine wire passing through the stop channels, operated by the square of the tracker action when the key was depressed. This principle, more or less, has been used in later years by our contemporary builders of the Universal Air Chest System, the trace or tracker, however, being now operated electro-pneumatically. The scale of the manuals was 58 notes and the pedals 27 notes.

The first organist of Temple Emanuel was Mr. K. Herold, one of San Francisco's prominent musicians and organists in the early days. Mr. Wolf was one of the cantors, and Jacob Varrsanger, Rabbi, served from 1886 to 1908.

In 1892, while Louis Schmidt, Sr., was organist, my father remodeled the old Mayer organ by removing the tracker action and applying his patented outside pneumatic action to the key mechanism. He also provided a new blowing arrangement by discarding the old box type bellows, previously referred to, and replacing it with a standard bellows and feeder arrangement. Subsequently, a water-wheel was attached to this bellows, thus dispensing with the necessity of pumping the organ by hand. Edward Crome, then a young man who had recently come from St. Louis and accepted work with my father, and Peter Mueller, an old friend of my father, assisted him in this alteration work, which must have required several months time.

One day while organist Louis Schmidt, Sr., was seated at

the organ, he was overcome by a heart attack, and succumbed. Shortly thereafter, Wallace A. Sabin, a young and prominent organist from England, succeeded him. I remember making a visit with my father to the old Mayer organ before he rebuilt it. However, I do not recall anything about the specifications of the organ, or any details of its interior construction, as I was too young then to comprehend.

I did not enter into the inside of the organ, for at my young age, being about eight years old then, even an organ builder's son was not permitted to roam around in the sacred precincts of an organ unguarded. I do recall, however, seeing the console and taking a peek inside the organ, which to me then was a maze and a mystery.

Temple Emanuel was an imposing edifice and awed me by its massiveness. The organ, with its beautiful front high up over the ark, or tabernacle, as is customary in the Jewish Synagogue, was most impressive. The case of the organ consisted of three towers, with front pipes decorated in gold. The two large ones were on either end, and the small one in the center of the case, exposing to view as much as possible a large rose window in the north wall in back of the organ. The detail and design of the case, or woodwork and paneling, were in keeping with the Romanesque architecture of the edifice. It was made of walnut, with raised panels of laurel wood, with moulding and trim of cedar, and made an imposing appearance. A free reed, Vox Humana, with short length resonators and square wooden feet, was an unusual stop of this organ. All tone work was voiced on three inch pressure. There was originally no bellows in the organ, the air coming directly from the square feeder boxes referred to in the beginning of this chapter. I believed this was the largest organ Mayer had built.

One of the pleasant memories of Temple Emanuel that I recall, was my interest, as a youngster, in the circular or spiral stairway that led up to the organ loft, a distance of about two stories, beginning in the dark and dank basement. A dimly lit gas jet was the sole illumination. In 1898 this Mayer organ was replaced by a new modern electric pneumatic instrument, built by Hook and Hastings Company of Boston, Mass. It consisted of three manuals and Pedal and had 38 speaking stops. Opus 1789.

The old organ was dismantled by my father and was stored in the basement of the Temple, where it remained for many years, and was finally acquired by Byron Mauzy, a piano dealer on Post Street. He later had it converted into several small pipe organs. Louis Schoen, a musician and amateur organ builder, assisted Mr. Mauzy in this work.

The new Hook and Hastings organ was installed by a Mr. Merrwagen, of Boston, assisted by my father. As the new organ was larger than the old one, the entire width of the organ loft had to be used. The original case was retained and additions made to it on either side. The new console was in the same location as the old one, except that the organist now faced the organ. The principle of the slider chest with the usual pallet valve was used, but operated electrically. The organ had a large bellows with a pair of horizontal feeders on a rocker arm operated by an electric motor in the basement through a connecting rod to the rocking arm under the bellows. Centrifugal blowers were not yet in use at that time. A specially designed rheostat was installed, to control the action of the feeders, consisting of about six to eight mercury cups into which contacts arranged on a revolving drum would dip consecutively. This drum was connected by a cord to the top of the bellows, which would rise and fall as the air was consumed, thus regulating the speed of the motor. The splattering of the mercury when it came in contact with the hot points, also the unresponsiveness of the whole device to increased or decreased air consumption made it unwieldly and unsatisfactory and was later replaced.

The furnishing of the low voltage current for the key action of the electric pneumatic mechanism was also a problem, as in all other electric pneumatic organs of early vintage. A low voltage generator driven by a motor, or the more recent rectifier as now commonly in use, were not on the market then. Batteries of some type or other had to be used. In this organ six large Leclanche batteries were installed requiring replacing of elements and solution at least once a year. This task I remember doing a number of times. Wallace Sabin was the organist at Temple Emanuel from the time the new organ was installed until his death in 1945.

One incident that I shall never forget occurred on one of the Jewish holidays. Regardless of how well the organ behaved during the year, there was always a feeling of suspence when the holidays arrived lest something go wrong at a critical time. We, therefore, made it a practice to be present at the services in case of emergency. These holidays were celebrated with the greatest solemnity, and the best of music was prepared and arranged by Cantor Edward J. Stark, a musician and composer of note. On this particular holiday, as usual, the best professional singers were engaged, and an orchestra of five or six musicians was stationed in the already crowded organ loft. Wallace Sabin was at the console.

After a successful introductory number, a look of consternation and despair came over the organist, I was told. Word was passed to my father, who was up in the loft, that the Trombone 16' stop on the Pedal section had stuck and could not be shut off. Due to the already crowded gallery, and to the fact that a large, hinged panel door, which was the only means of entering into the organ, had to be opened out toward the singers and musicians, immediate access to the interior of the organ was impossible. And then, of course, the trouble had to be located first before being corrected. With Cantor Stark noticing the turmoil and commotion above, and Sabin dismayed and distracted, my father, in a state of frenzy, called for me. I was stationed in one of the lower rear rooms. We consulted. Something had to be done quickly, but what? My father concluded to leave them to their fate and make the best of a bad situation. However, knowing Cantor Stark's irritability, especially when aroused, and Sabin's nervousness and his displeasure at having his musical program spoiled, and, being aware of the discredit this incident would be to our reputation, I hesitated to do this.

With all the courage I could muster I decided to face the music, and entered the loft. During a short intermission and prayer I had the singers and musicians vacate their places and, opening the large panel door, I crawled into the organ. There, I disconnected the slider of the 16' Trombone stop and shoved it into an off position, which temporarily silenced it. Undoubtedly, due to dampness, it had become swollen and stuck tight. This ended our dilemma on that occasion.

Cantor Stark took especial offense if we came to tune or correct any trouble on the organ shortly before services, particularly after he had his music arranged for the singers on the organ loft. We had the greatest deference for his wishes, especially myself, only a youngster, who, in fact, had a holy fear of him lest we would ruffle his calm or disturb his peace of mind. However, frequent emergency calls were made by Mr. Sabin. The electric action organs were not so reliable in those days as now, and each time we called, which was mostly on short notice and with little time to spare, it was with fear and dread of meeting Cantor Stark in the choir loft. If Mr. Millet, the Sexton, was aware that Cantor Stark was occupied up in the choir loft he would forewarn us to be careful, which advice did not make us feel any more comfortable.

On one of these occasions we all accidently met in battle array, as it were. The atmosphere was surcharged with dynamite. I refrain from quoting here the language that was used by both Cantor Stark and my father. Both spoke German, their native tongue. Epithets and cuss words were freely passed. In normal, peaceful times, when the organ behaved and we called on schedule, there were no better friends than Cantor Stark, Wallace Sabin and my father.

On April 18, 1906, when the terrible earthquake and fire devastated San Francisco, the old landmark, Temple Emanuel fell victim to its wrath. Only the scarred brick walls remained. After a period of some months, when the rebuilding of the city was under way and the old locations were again being occupied, Temple Emanuel was also reconstructed, using the massive, buttressed walls that had remained standing. This time the edifice was constructed on a more conservative plan, minus the lofty towers. An organ was installed in the latter part of 1907, a two manual tubular pneumatic Kimball, installed by Mr. Max Hess of the Kimball Company. Wallace Sabin was again organist, but the position of cantor was now occupied by Reuben Rinder, as successor to Rev. E.J. Stark, who had since been called to his eternal reward. Rabbi Jacob Voorsanger, who passed away during 1908, was succeeded by Rabbi Meyers.

This new Kimball organ was blown by a modern centrifugal blower. It gave very satisfactory service, aside from the ill effects of dampness which seemed to be an inherent feature of the rebuilt, as well as of the old building. Ascending the same spiral staircase again always reminded me of my early visits to this old landmark.

One of the pleasant Sextons stationed at Temple Emanuel at this time was Frank Rhodes. After his death, he was succeeded by Charles McKenna, who was also sexton later at the new Temple Emanuel. He passed away in 1943, having served the Temple faithfully for a period of 33 years. His successor was, I believe, Bill O'Connor.

Temple Emanuel, realizing the need of a more permanent and worthy edifice, and in a more desirable neighborhood, in 1925, began construction on the new Temple Emanuel at its present site on Arguello Boulevard at Lake Street. The old Kimball organ was removed by an amateur organ enthusiast and installed in the North Brae Methodist Church in Berkeley.

Plans were drawn for the new Temple Emanuel by the architects Blakewell-Brown and Schnaidecker. We were frequently consulted by them regarding the general layout of the new organ, space to be required, etc., and Cantor Reuben Rinder interviewed us often in regard to the merits of the various makes of organs, as the new Temple organ would have to be in keeping with the dignity and high standard for which Temple Emanuel was known in the past. As we were entirely neutral and disinterested in the purchase of the organ, at that time not being under obligation to any firm, we unhesitatingly and strongly advocated a Skinner organ as the best on the market. Undoubtedly, our advice was appreciated and accepted, and also coincided with that of Wallace Sabin, for, in 1925, the four manual organ of 50 speaking stops, with echo organ, was installed by the Skinner Organ Company of Boston, Mass. It has proven to be one of the outstanding organs in San Francisco.

Wallace Sabin, who, for forty consecutive years had been organist of Temple Emanuel, passed to the great beyond in 1937 while conducting the Lorin Club, mourned by all who knew him as a gentleman and a musician of the highest order. A short time previous to his demise, a new face was becoming familiar around the console at Temple Emanuel.

On one of our regular visits for tuning the organ, we were introduced to the newcomer, a young man recently arrived from Berlin, Germany, Mr. Ludwig Altman, as the assistant organist to Wallace Sabin. Having the same given name as my own, Ludwig (German for Louis), and being able to converse with each other in the German language, we soon found a mutual warm friendship developing between us. Mr. Altman's evident high musical training, his knowledge of the organ, his virtuosity, and his affable and pleasing manner, soon made him a worthy successor to his illustrious predecessor and a respected member in the organist fraternity. With the approach of World War II, in 1943, Ludwig Altman joined the armed forces, his place being temporarily filled by Harold Mueller of St. Luke's Episcopal Church.

In recent years on the recommendations of Ludwig Altman the tonal qualities of the organ have been greatly changed and enhanced, by certain exchanges and addition of new stops, to bring the instrument more in line with the modern Boroque trend, very evident at the present time.

It might be of interest to note that it has been our good fortune to continuously service the four pipe organs that have been in use in the Temple Emanuel edifices during the last 90 years. We believe this is a record to be proud of. We are appreciative of those in authority who have placed their trust and confidence in us these many years, and as father, sons and grandsons have now served the same institutions faithfully, we hope future generations may continue to do so.

OLD ST. MARY'S
(Now Paulist Church)

Old St. Mary's Church, built in 1852, where San Francisco's first Archbishop, Joseph Sadoc Alemany, O.P., D.D., resided, was the first Cathedral of San Francisco. It is located at California and Dupont Streets and brings to mind many recollections of my early youth. Sentimental attachment also made my father, as well as many other San Franciscans, revere the place, as he recalled as a young man attending meetings of the St. Peter's Benevolent Society in the basement of Old St. Mary's. The Society was founded in 1864, and was a German Catholic organization affiliated with St. Boniface Church, and is still functioning: the latter Church was then located on Sutter and Trinity Place near Montgomery Street. Being temporarily deprived of their own church and meeting place due to the building having become unsafe, they were allowed the use of the basement of Old St. Mary's as their temporary meeting hall.

From the beginning, Old St. Mary's had a small two manual Willcox pipe organ of about 8 stops; compass of manuals was 48 notes and that of the Pedal was 12 notes. It had a mahogany case with gold pipes, with the keyboards built in flush with the case. It had a beautiful tone. An 8' Trumpet on the Great was, for some reason, later converted to a Clarion 4'. It was built in the New England States and was believed to have been shipped around the Horn to San Francisco, according to my father's notes. It was located on the organ loft in the tower room in the gallery, the front case fitting in between the Gothic opening or arch facing the church. The pump handle protruded from the north side. Originally, it had an attached keyboard, as above noted. At a later date, however, it was altered to a detached console by Joseph Mayer, with the organist facing the alter. It must have been an old instrument, for I distinctly remember that the large wood screws were hand made. It was evidently a used organ when brought to San Francisco.

Professor John Knell was the first organist, and was later succeeded by Professor Eimer, who functioned at the organ for many years. It was during his term as organist, in 1870, that the console was detached. I often heard my father speak of Professor Eimer, but am in doubt whether his references to him included the new Cathedral position of Van Ness Avene, or only at Old St. Mary's on Dupont and California Streets. A Professor Topke succeeded him in 1876. This old Willcox organ was used until 1903, when it was removed by us to the Gentlemen's Sodality Chapel in the basement of St. Ignatius Church.

Referring again to Professor Eimer, I do not recall him personally, but I do distinctly remember, however, the organist who was stationed there when I first helped my father work on the organ, in 1896. It was none other than Miss Marie Giorgiani, a former pupil of Professor John H. Dohrman, a charming, young and beautiful woman, and no less competent and proficient in her chosen calling than she was good to look upon. Her reputation as a musician was known far and wide, and she was, in fact, considered the most efficient and accomplished woman organist in San Francisco and the Bay Region. The fact that a woman successfully held this position was a tribute to her ability, as most positions of note at that time were filled by men. At times her musical temperament would clash with that of my father's, and, womanlike, she would always have the last word. Nevertheless, overlooking these little tiffs, I must say that a fine regard and loyal friendship always existed between Miss Giorgiani and my father, and ourselves. Miss Giorgiani served Old St. Mary's continuously for the long period of 45 years.

On the occasion referred to above, in 1896, when I helped my father work on the organ, if I recall correctly, the interior of the church had just been redecorated, and the organ was to be tuned for the reopening of the church. It must have been a Saturday, as it was a day on which I was free from school and could therefore assist my father. My particular function was to pump the organ. My elder brother, Leo, was at the keyboard holding the keys, while my father tuned the pipes in the organ. Father was so engrossed in his work and, undoubtedly, desirous of getting through with it, that he completely forgot about lunch time and worked on and on. An empty stomach told me it was long past the noon hour. Possibly a light breakfast in the morning aggravated the situation, and the physical exertion of the continuous pumping of the organ did its part. At any rate, if ever in my life I felt the pangs of hunger, it was on that day. I recall, in later years, when tuning the organ at Old St. Mary's of often eating lunch with my father in an old, rather dilapidated boarding house on the north side of California Street, a few doors up from Kearny Street. It evidently was table d'hote style, as a large bowl of soup was placed on the table and all customers helped themselves. A generous supply of crisp French or Italian bread, with the other delectable entrees, including a helping of claret wine, all for twenty-five cents, was served. A visit to this place was always a treat.

Up to this time Old St. Mary's Church had been in charge of the secular clergy. In 1898, the Paulist Fathers took charge, and a new life seemed to permeate the parish. It was under the pastorate of Rev. Father Smith, in 1901, a newly arrived priest from New York City, that a peculiar incident occured in connection with the organ.

Father Smith had scarcely had the opportunity to get acquainted with us when he was approached by one of those notorious nomads who, without reference or reputation, or at best only fictitious ones, are always willing to tune, repair or improve your organ for you — not, however, without first obtaining a substantial down payment and an agreement providing frequent payments on account before the job was completed, if it ever reached that stage. And this is just what happened to the organ at Old St. Mary's. This knight of the road, undoubtedly more proficient with his tongue than with his hands, induced the priest to let him overhaul the organ, notwithstanding the fact that my father had a contract for regular maintenance of the organ, calling every month. Though the organ was old and antiquated, it was kept in good tune and working order. It was in making one of our regular visits to the organ that we were greatly surprised to find that someone else, other than ourselves, was working, or had been working on the organ. We saw no trace of the individual. A most disagreeable odor of burnt rubber filled the edifice, and all indications pointed to the fact that the self-styled organ builder was a charlatan. No professional work had been done on the organ, rather harm and damage, and the little activity he had shown was merely a stall to make believe he was earning the down payment he had already received. The man never returned to complete his work and left the organ in a deplorable condition. We also learned that he inveigled the pastor of St. Patrick's Church to similarly rebuild their large organ, but here he evidently did not have the opportunity to do much mischief as he had to make a hurried exit from town.

After this incident we became well acquainted with the pastor, Father Smith, to our mutual benefit, and a warm friendship ensued which continued until his demise in later years.

As Old St. Mary's Church, under the direction of the Paulist Fathers, was exhibiting new and vigorous life, and with Marie Giorgiani, now in her prime, as organist, the question of a much needed new and modern pipe organ came to the fore, especially after the incident related above.

In 1903, the old Willcox organ, which undoubtedly had been brought around the Horn was sold or given to the Jesuit Fathers of St. Ignatius Church, or to be more specific, to Father Calzia, S.J., the spiritual director of the Gentlemen's Sodality at that time. The organ was placed by us in their large chapel in the basement of the Church, and was modernized to the extent of installing a pneumatic action and a centrifugal blower to it.

Immediately thereafter, Old St. Mary's Church procured in place of its old instrument, transferred to St. Ignatius Chapel, a small, modern electric pneumatic action pipe organ, which was temporarily used until the larger and more imposing permanent organ could be installed. These transactions were conducted with the Murray M. Harris Organ Company of Los Angeles, California, which was then forging ahead with rapid strides as one of the country's leading organ builders. After several months of use, the temporary organ was replaced by the larger and permanent new organ.

It was my good fortune to assist Charles W. McQuigg, the voicer, in the final tuning and tone regulating of this instrument. The organ was completed and in use but a few months. On the morning of April 18, 1906, it fell prey to the flames and destruction that devastated San Francisco on that fateful day.

Old St. Mary's was one of the first churches in the downtown section to rebuild. The old walls, sacred to the memories of early San Franciscans, were retained. The old granite steps, imported from China, were again put to use. A steel frame supporting the floor and the roof was cleverly and securely concealed in the walls, and the result was a remarkable replica of the old church. Again, the clock, with its pealing chimes, strikes the hour and, below it, we read the same impressive text from holy writ embossed in the stone that passed through the scourge of fire and earthquake, still exhorting the passerby, the idle lounger in the square opposite, and especially the youth of the day passing the church, with these significant words: "Son, observe the time and fly from evil." In years gone by, where St. Mary's Square, with its green sloping lawns, tall trees and fragrant flowers, stood, and where in more recent times the modern statue of the Chinese Reformer "Sun Yet Sen" was erected, notorious houses of ill repute stood and operated brazenly. No doubt, many a hesitant youth, on hearing the bell in the church tower strike the hour, had looked up at the clock and observed the inscription below, with its admonition, saved his honor and the purity of his soul for a better life.

Shortly after the fire Miss Giorgiani, I was informed, was delegated to go back East to select a suitable new pipe organ for the reconstructed church. An organ from the Hook and Hastings Company of Boston, Mass., was her choice.

During 1907 and 1909, I also sojourned to New York and Boston, which visit I shall relate later. While there I also called at the factory of Hook and Hastings Company, at Waltham, Mass., shortly before my return to California. I was shown an organ in their erecting room and was told that it was the new organ for Old St. Mary's Church in San Francisco. It was my intention on going back to New York to remain there for a number of years, acquiring knowledge and experience in the organ business. But fate seemed to have destined it otherwise. On leaving San Francisco after the earthquake and fire, at which time we lost the servicing of most of the organs we formerly had, I thought it would be many years before San Francisco would again be the city it had been before disaster struck. But, with the indominatable spirit of the argonauts of old, San Francisco arose phoenix-like again, from its bed of ashes and, with zeal and energy, began to build and reconstruct a greater city. My father, therefore, found himself swamped with the arrival of new organs from the east, or contemplated new ones to be installed in the near future, and importuned me to return home again and accept the opportunity to join with him in a co-partnership and secure my future with him. On April 9, 1909, I returned to my native city, "San Francisco, the incomparable."

The new organ for Old St. Mary's, that I had seen in the course of construction at the Hook and Hastings factory in Boston, was installed by our firm in 1909, and was one of the first organs to be installed after the fire. It was a three manual, tubular, pneumatic action organ with a detached console, and had 34 speaking stops. This organ, the fourth pipe organ installed in Old St. Mary's during its hallowed career, has now satisfactorily served the church for the last 60 years. Although a number of organists have filled the position in recent years, the name of Marie Giorgiani, now deceased, is still lovingly remembered wherever Old St. Mary's is mentioned.

Another faithful character of Old St. Mary's, whom I do not want to overlook, was the sexton, Mr. Pat Casey. From my earliest recollections, he was connected with the church until he passed away in 1936.

In 1945, we were given the contract to releather and electrify the organ, also to enclose the choir manual and to rebuild the console to conform with the standard of the A.G.O. With these improvements completed, Old St. Mary's organ is now again one of the ideal and model church organs in San Francisco.

Organists who held the position following the demise of the late Marie Giorgiani were Richard Weismueller, Gordon L. Wilson and Robert E. Noonan, the present organist, a musician of note who ably upholds the reputation of Old St. Mary's Church for its edifying and liturgical music.

ST. IGNATIUS

I remember my father relating that shortly after his arrival in San Francisco in 1868, he was desirous of affiliating himself with a German Catholic Church, if there was one in San Francisco. He finally located St. Boniface Church, which was then located on Sutter Street at Trinity Place, near Montgomery Street. He evidently became acquainted there with Joseph Mayer, one of their parishioners and organist of the church. Incidentally, he was also the veteran organ builder of California and San Francisco. My father eventually became his forman and worked and lived with him for seven years.

Owing to the decrepit condition of the church, if it could be called such, as it was originally used as a warehouse and was constructed only of galvanized iron which, in time, had rusted so that the stars could be seen through the roof, it became necessary to seek other quarters until a new permanent location could be found, or a remodeling of the old church could take place. If I remember my father's statement correctly, a lawsuit was instituted at this time by certain trustees of the church, undoubtedly with good intent, opposing the disposal of the Sutter Street property.

During this period of uncertainty and strife, a temporary use of other churches was sought. Among these was St. Ignatius Church, then on Market Street where the Emporium building now stands. At this location the Jesuits already had a large three manual E. & G.G. Hook tracker action organ, built in Boston. Opus 453-1868. Mr. John Mueller was the organist. One of their chapels was graciously loaned to the German Catholics of St. Boniface Church until they could again establish themselves. I remember my father relating having made temporary altars out of packing cases for this chapel. Being young and still single, and evidently devoted to his religion, he also voluntarily did the janitorial work.

He also often referred to the German Jesuit Missionary Rev. Father Weninger, S.J., who at that time was visiting in San Francisco and the far west. This missionary, who since then has become famous, must have been an outstanding man, an exemplary and saintly priest, a fine orator, and an author of note. One book my father received from him was entitled "Ostern im Himmel" — Easter in Heaven. I remember reading this book, at least in part, as a boy. It was later loaned to some friend of the family and has since disappeared. My father stated that the Mission given by Father Weninger, at that time in the German language for the benefit of the many German immigrants that were flocking to San Francisco, made a deep impression on him with lasting and benificial results.

Later, St. Boniface German parish bought its own property on Golden Gate Avenue (then called Tyler Street), between Leavenworth and Jones Streets, and built a church on that site.

The Jesuits, in 1880, left their Market Street property and located in the Hayes Valley district, buying the block bounded by Hayes and Grove Streets and Van Ness Avenue and Franklin Street, where the beautiful St. Ignatius Church and St. Ignatius College were built. Being born in the Hayes Valley district myself, on Linden Avenue, in 1884, almost within the shadow of this magnificent and imposing edifice, and living at different periods later in nearby locations, its grandeur, its great towers, the immensity of the structure and its pealing bell always impressed me. When I was five years old, we moved to the Western Addition section, at 1202 Fillmore Street.

That St. Ignatius Church always had an appeal to me may be shown in an incident that occurred which I shall never forget.

One of our neighbors, a Mrs. Freeman, must have taken a fancy to me. My head was then adorned with a luxurious growth of golden curls, which my mother related, were the envy of one of my aunts, whose boy's hair was straight and commonplace, and who always insisted that my mother cut my hair and not make a girl out of me. My locks were eventually cut off, shortly before I began school at five and a half years. Our good neighbor, Mrs. Freeman, asked my mother, one day, if she could take me out sometime, and having an engagement with the dressmaker, who was located on Franklin Street opposite St. Ignatius Church, she took me along on this particular afternoon. When we arrived at the place, instead of taking me into the house, she told me to wait on the front steps until she returned, which would be but a short time. In my childish simplicity I obeyed, and did not notice into which of the several doors of the building she had entered. I waited, and waited, and waited. To me it seemed an eternity. Childlike, I finally concluded that she had forgotten all about me. Then the impulse struck me, for some reason or another, to go over to St. Ignatius Church and wait there on the steps of the church for her. Of course, this was my undoing. I waited there in vain for her, also, watching closely the many people who were constantly entering and leaving the church, as there was probably no church in San Francisco more frequented than the Jesuit Church at this time.

Finally, my patience here also became exhausted, and becoming alarmed I determined to find my own way home. A few blocks from our home on Fillmore Street was Jefferson Square, a public park dear to us children. It was practically our playground every Saturday and Sunday. I must have concluded that if I could find the park, with its tall trees, which could be seen for several blocks distant, I would be safe and find my way home. What led me to walk one block farther west toward Gough Street, where I noticed the trees of the park several blocks away, I cannot say, but that my guardian angel led me there. I headed straight for the park and, while walking through it, was surprised to be intercepted by my older sisters and their girl chums, just returning from St. Boniface School. That they were surprised and startled to find me alone in the park, is to say the least. They hastily led me home and informed my mother that they had found me in the park. I, however, undoubtedly to hide a guilty conscience, went to my father's shop on Fillmore Street, where I tried to make myself useful, not telling him of my escapade. I remember he was turning some wood at the time on the lathe, an operation we children always enjoyed watching. It was a foot-powered lathe, and I put my foot on the treadle also, apparently thinking I was assisting him. When I got home later my mother and sisters, as well as the neighbor, Mrs. Freeman, confronted me with my ill behavior. I was severely reprimanded. I regretted the intense anguish and distress I had caused this good neighbor, who incidentally, solemnly vowed never again to take me out, a promise she faithfully kept.

The Jesuits, being always progressive and farseeing, were evidently not backward at the Market Street location either, for here they had already installed a large three manual tracker action "Hook" organ, built in Boston, as previously stated. This organ was later moved by my father at or about 1880 and installed in the new church on Hayes Street. Some additions were made, the case extended and an auxiliary bellows applied. My first connection with this organ was when it was removed, in 1897, from the Hayes Street church, after it was sold to Father Nugent of St. Rose's Church, on Fourth and Brannan Streets, where my father, assisted by my brother Leo and some hired helpers, again installed it there.

This sale and removal of the old organ from the Hayes Street church was made in preparation for the arrival of a new, modern and colossal instrument, that was soon to adorn and enhance the beauty of St. Ignatius Church. Through the beneficence of Bertha and Andrew Welch, who donated a sum of $50,000 to the church for an organ and choir fund, ($30,000 to defray the cost of a new organ and $20,000 for organist salary and a suitable choir) St. Ignatius, already the mecca of religious activity, was to be further enhanced in its charm by the installation of one of the finest organs in the country.

The new organ was a four manual and Pedal instrument, the first four manual to be installed in San Francisco, and was built on the electric pneumatic system, the first of this type to be used here. It had 84 speaking stops, among them a 32' full length Pedal Open stop. The lower octave of these pipes were made here in the church. It had a very intricate but dependable combination action, adjustable from the console. The Solo or high pressure reeds, I am informed, were secured from the French builder, Caville-Coll of Paris. All in all, the organ was so outstanding at the time, mechanically, tonally, in its proportions, in the excellence of the workmanship and the quality of materials used, that it was epochal and proved to be the forerunner and worthy model of the organ of today. The immensity of its proportions, the beautiful case of polished ashwood, with its two carved angels of 8' height adorning the top, were most impressive. The organ was built by the Farrand and Votey Organ Company of Detroit, Michigan, and installed under the direction of Col. William D. Wood and a Mr. Whitehead. My brother Leo and others assisted in its installation.

During the progress of the installation of this large organ, a smaller two manual pneumatic pipe organ of about six stops was provided by the Farrand and Votey Company, and temporarily used for services until the large organ was completed. The small organ was later sold to Father McGinty of Holy cross Church on Eddy Street near Scott.

The installation of the new St. Ignatius organ, with its 6,000 pipes, and its approaching dedication which was set for Christmas Day of 1897, had attracted city-wide interest. I do not recall any organ, including the Festival Hall organ of the Panama-Pacific International Exposition, receiving so much attention and thoughtful consideration. And, when it became known that the famous organist, Clarence Eddy, was coming from Paris where he was sojourning, specifically to dedicate the organ, enthusiam was boundless and the desire to be present at the dedicatory services was so great that the church could not accommodate the crowds that were present that early Christmas morning at 5:00 a.m.

Dr. Maurice O'Connel, a young man, a former student of the College, possessing great talent and genius as a musician, later occupied the position of organist. Father Edward Allen, S.J., then stationed at St. Ignatius also, a musician of note and an apparent authority on the organ, a performer on the instrument, who also had evidently been instrumental in drawing the specifications for the new organ, was an interesting and lovable character, whom I shall always remember.

Some further points regarding the construction of this organ may be of interest. The blowing plant was located above the organ in the east tower room. It consisted of a series of feeders actuated by crankshafts driven by an electric motor. Only once was I up in the bellows, or pump room, and as I recall, there were about four groups of four feeders each. There was a separate motor and set of feeders for high pressure stops. The low voltage current depended on a series of storage batteries. Although my father had the care and supervision of this organ after its installation, the care of the batteries, motors and bellows was under the supervision of an electrician. For that reason we seldom saw this apparatus. The organ held up remarkably well, until later when the steel springs on the pneumatics of the high pressure stops of the Solo manual began to break. Each time that occurred it meant a severe cipher. Dust accumulated rapidly in this organ, marring the immaculate and superb appearance it had when new. St. Ignatius, as previously stated, was one of the most frequented churches in San Francisco, and therefore sweeping and dusting by broom and duster, a necessity before the advent of the vacuum cleaner, was a daily routine.

By 1906, nine years after its installation, there was more

dust in this organ than in many others after a period of twenty-five or thirty years. This excessive accumulation of dust later interfered with the reliability of the key contacts of the organ. A movable butterfly spring, resting in a counter-sunk hole, on a metal strip where dust easily gathered, which was to act as a conductor for the electricity for the key circuit, often proved faulty. Other troubles also, commonly referred to as short circuits, developed. With all respect to my dear old dad, brought up in the old school of the mechanical and tracker action, the new electric pneumatic action of the modern organ was something new and mysterious to him. Although he acquired a general knowledge of it in time, it was still mostly unfathomable to him. It was left to younger minds, who grew up with this development, to more fully grasp and understand its functions.

Even so, younger minds also had their troubles to contend with, but from another unpleasant source. One day while engaged in some work on the console, I had the pedal keyboard removed and was lying in the pit below adjusting some faulty contacts when D. Maurice O'Connell, the organist, happened to come along. On seeing that I was doing the work alone, he expressed his displeasure at having such a young, inexperienced man work on such a costly organ, he not being aware that right along it was I who was correcting mechanical troubles, and not my father. Had I been a gray-haired, bewiskered, patriarchal-looking gentleman, as my father was, the slight very likely would not have been given me.

Another experience I had with this organ, I will always remember. One afternoon when I had the console panels removed and was delving into the maze of wires looking for some particularly troublesome contact, I noticed a beautiful cherry red glow on some of the wires. Being late in the afternoon, I thought it was a ray of the setting sun, shining through a piece of glass of that particular color in one of the art glass windows which adorned the church. At the same time, however, I detected an odor as if something was getting hot, and to satisfy my curiosity I placed my finger on this red glow to see whether it was merely a reflection of the sun's rays through the colored window, or whether it came from some other cause. On touching the spot, I readily perceived that it was a hot wire, cherry red, a short circuit, one of those accidents that may happen to an electric organ. I hurriedly pulled off the motor and battery switches, and then proceeded to locate the cause of the short circuit and corrected the trouble.

The fire of 1906 eventually spelled the doom of this beautiful church and wonderful organ, as it did to many another. To the best of my knowledge I have been informed that, although the downtown fire of early April 18th had already bypassed the site of St. Ignatius Church and it was felt it had definitely survived the threat of destruction, yet, due to a later fire originating in the Hayes Valley district, at Hayes and Laguna Streets a few blocks west, the so-called "Ham and Egg Fire", caused by a woman insisting on making a fire in her stove when her chimney was destroyed, and also due to lack of water, the fire swept down Hayes Street. In the intense heat of the on-rushing flames, the tall spires of St. Ignatius Church first became ignited, and finally the entire building was consumed.*

A few days after the fire, on visiting the ruins, the only things I recognized that were left of the wonderful organ were the twisted crankshafts lying in the debris in the basement. With this grand, impressive 84 stop Farrand and Votey organ also went its more humble partner, the first pipe organ formerly in use at Old St. Mary's which was, a short time before during 1904, modernized and placed by us in the basement of St. Ignatius Church for the use in the Gentlemen's Sodality Chapel.

Typical of the farsightedness of the Jesuits, they envisioned a greater and better San Francisco for the future, and built again accordingly. Disposing of their property on Hayes Street and Van Ness Avenue they secured a new site on Parker Avenue and Fulton Street, a considerable distance farther west, on an eminence overlooking the city, for their future permanent home. Adjacent were several of the old cemeteries no longer used for burial purposes, and the neighborhood, in general, was but sparsely populated.

---

*The above stated information, however, would be contradicted by a statement I recently heard from a eye witness, a Mr. Brainard, who stated the spires of St. Ignatius Church caught fire in the afternoon of April 18th, and that this was not caused by the so called "Ham and Egg Fire" of the Hayes Valley.

As a start, however, a temporary church and college, built of wood, was erected shortly after the fire two blocks below on Hayes and Schrader Streets, and they remained there until 1914. To again supply the musical requirements, even for this temporary church, a two manual and pedal pipe organ, tubular pneumatic action, was purchased from the Murray M. Harris Organ Company of Los Angeles. My brother Leo, I believe, installed this instrument. It rendered excellent service until the new imposing church on the hill, which was meanwhile in the course of construction, was completed. We then moved this organ to the upper gallery of this imposing new structure, and it was remarkable how well and adequate it sounded in its spacious interior.

The new St. Ignatius Church was very much a replica of the old St. Ignatius in general appearance, excelling it, however, in many regards, making it in fact a better built and a better designed building. For the time being, some of the refinements and adornments of the old church are still lacking, the interior decoration and frescoes and the many large oil paintings that adorned the old church. Recently, a Baldochium altar has been installed and art glass windows are gradually filling in the plain glass windows. One item, however, is again put to its old accustomed use, and that is the faithful old church bell, the only surviving article of the former Jesuit church, which for years pealed forth its mellow tones calling the worshipers to service, ringing from the belfry on high. Silenced temporarily by the cataclysm that destroyed San Francisco, the bell, defying the elements, though cracked and scorched has been placed in the new lofty campanile on St. Ignatius Heights, blown there by the winds and fog coming in from the mightly Pacific, again giving forth its hallowed tones, although less melodious than of yore, yet reverently heard and welcomed by those who recall its beckoning tones in their youth.

With the ever expanding and progressive activities of the Jesuits on the Pacific Coast, in conformity with a plan of expansion for their University at Santa Clara, the Jesuits purchased the old grounds and buildings of the College of the Pacific at College Park, San Jose, the latter institution having secured a new site at Stockton, California. In the music hall of the old College of the Pacific building stood a large 3 manual Kimball pipe organ, which was included in the sale of the property. St. Ignatius Church, by mutual arrangement with the superiors of their Order, secured this organ for use in the new St. Ignatius Church, it being larger and more suitable for the large edifice than the two manual Murray M. Harris organ originally built for the temporary church.

Originally, this organ at the College of the Pacific was installed by my brother Leo, in 1912, while in the employ of the Eilers Music Company, who were then the agents for the Kimball Company. It was at first a tubular pneumatic action organ, and was later electrified by Thomas Whalley of Berkeley. We removed this organ from the old College of the Pacific building and erected it in the new St. Ignatius Church, where it is giving excellent service to this day. True, it is a smaller organ than its wonderful prototype in the old St. Ignatius Church before the fire, but one that fills the building admirably and apparently answers all their musical requirements.

In its new location, we applied to the organ an entire new electric action, a new console, also a set of chimes. This Kimball organ sums up to the total of five pipe organs that the Jesuits have had since their beginning in San Francisco, a record for any church. The Murray M. Harris organ that was used in the temporary church on Hayes and Schrader Streets, and then in the new St. Ignatius Church on Fulton Street, until it was replaced by the present Kimball organ, was sold in 1928 to St. Joseph's Church in Mountain View, California, where we had the pleasure of installing it.

The church was a large frame building of the old type. One night a pyromaniac, who later was apprehended, applied an incendiary torch to the edifice and it was practically destroyed. However, the fire department seemed to concentrate their efforts on saving the organ, which they did with excellent result. The next day, on being summoned to appraise the damage, the scene that confronted us was one of complete wreckage. A few blackened girders were swaying precariously over the organ. Wet muck and debris, a foot deep, covered the gallery floor. Fortunately, the main parts of the organ had been covered with tarpaulins.

Owing to the excellent reputation of this organ, its good tonal qualities and high class workmanship, also to the fact that the Rev. Father Galvin, pastor of the church, valued it highly, we recommended that it be salvaged and restored for the new, modern church that was to be built immediately. The organ was removed to our factory, all parts thoroughly gone over, an electric pneumatic action applied in place of the former pnuematic action, the former attached keyboard made into a detached console, and the organ arranged in two units placed behind suitable grills. If ever an organ was resurrected from certain doom, it certainly was this organ, and it is functioning today as satisfactorily as if it were a new instrument.

In concluding my recollections about St. Ignatius Church and its pipe organs, I am sorry to have to relate an incident of tragedy. Several years ago a fire, due to some mysterious cause, originated in the attic of the new church, just about over the organ. The new St. Ignatius Church, although an excellently built edifice of steel frame and brick, is still not absolutely fireproof. In fighting the fire in the lofty, dark and hazardous place in the attic, a fireman evidently lost or misjudged his footing and plunged through the plaster ceiling down to the organ loft alongside the organ, to his death.

Many musicians occupied the coveted position of organist of this famous church during the course of the years, among them being Dr. Maurice O'Connell, Mr. Martinez, Harry Brown, Mrs. Teresa Grubb, Leo Horvorka, who served for many years and was retired as emeritus organist, succeeded by Mrs. Miller, substitute organist.

The present organist is Mr. John E. Klobucar.

ST. BONIFACE
(German National Church)

As early as 1852 a Benedictine priest named Fr. Florian Schwenniger. O.S.B., and a Very Rev. James Motter were in San Francisco and administered to the spiritual needs of the German speaking Catholics flocking to this city. It was not until 1860 that St. Boniface Parish was duly organized.

The first church was located on the north side of Sutter Street, between Montgomery and Kearny Streets, at Trinity Place. According to my father's data and other reliable sources, it was originally a jewelry store, of wood and galvanized iron construction, moved to the site acquired by the German Catholics and remodeled for church purposes. Several secular priests served as pastors of the church after its founding in 1860, but the outstanding one, the one who served St. Boniface Parish for thirty years, either as pastor or assistant, was the beloved and revered Father Sebastian Wolf. He was a young priest, newly ordained when appointed, having just completed his studies at St. Bernard's Seminary at old Mission Dolores. Under his pastorate, in 1862 Joseph Mayer built a two manual and pedal tracker action organ for the church.

Other names of assistant priests often heard mentioned were: Fr. Kaiser, Fr. Herder and Fr. Mailer.

On September 30, 1868, my father and uncle arrived in San Francisco. Shortly thereafter, on October 21, 1868, a very severe earthquake rocked the city, the most severe one prior to the earthquake of 1906, a rather unpleasant welcome for the newly arrived emigrants. I remember my father relating how he and his brother, in search of a German Catholic Church where they could attend and comply with their religious duties, first entered Trinity Episcopal Church, then located on Post and Powell Streets, assuming they were in a Catholic Church. Here, he heard his first pipe organ in America. Shortly thereafter, they came across the galvanized building serving as St. Boniface Church.

It was then in a very decrepit condition, with the roof rusted and in such bad shape that the stars could be seen through it at night, as related by my father. This made a sad impression on my father and uncle, accustomed to the substantial and beautiful churches in the old Fatherland. Soon, however, they realized that they were in a new land, pioneering and paving a way for a better future.

In 1869, this old building had to be abandoned as unsafe and unfit for services, and arrangements were made to temporarily hold services in one of the chapels of the old St. Ignatius Church on Market Street, and in the Notre Dame des Victoires Church, the National French Church on Bush Street. The organ, built for the old galvanized iron church by Joseph Mayer, California's pioneer organ builder, in 1862, was then temporarily removed to the organ shop of Mr. Mayer, on Page Street, and stored there until 1872 when it was reinstalled by Mr. Mayer in the new St. Boniface Church located on Tyler Street (now Golden Gate Avenue) between Leavenworth and Jones Streets.

From 1871 to 1877 my father was in the employ of Joseph Mayer, and lived with his family on Page Street. He, therefore, must have assisted Mr. Mayer in the moving of the organ to the new church. Shortly thereafter, during 1879, undoubtedly during the interval when Mr. Mayer was temporarily away from the city, my father was commissioned by the acting pastor, Father Mailer, to make some alterations on the organ. He added an octave couplet to the Great, changed an 8' Open Pedal Flute to a 16' stop, completed the scale to 27 notes, it being only 13 notes previously, and provided a very unique combination pipe for the Pedal, consisting of an 8' open wood pipe, with its fifth a stop pipe, both speaking simutaneously from one pipe hole. It might be of interest here to note that the bellows of this organ was unique. It consisted of only one diagonal feeder, pumped by foot, and one diagonal fold above serving as the bellows or reservoir.

Joseph Mayer, builder of the organ, was organist and choir leader at St. Boniface Church for about sixteen years, beginning with the installation of the organ in the old Sutter Street church. This service he gave gratis to his parish church. A Mr. Buettner followed him as organist, for a short time. Then John Knell took the position, and he was succeeded by Professor John B. Mayle, who came from Fort Wayne, Indiana, to fill the position of teacher of the boys in the higher grades of the parochial school and serve as organist in the church as well. Both of these positions he held until 1906.

I might add here some of my own personal recollections of this, my favorite church, this hallowed spot that meant so much to me personally, and to our family. In other words, it was our "Parish Church" which, if properly understood and appreciated, should invariably mean that, next to home and family, it should be our most cherished place on earth. Here, among its parishioners, my parents became acquainted with one another, were married, and all the ten children of the family were christened. Here most of them attended the parochial school and received the sacraments, and here, my eldest brother was married. Here the happy days of my youth were spent and friendships made that have endured through the years to the present time. Many a romance of former school chums found its culmination at the altar, where loving hearts were united as one in matrimony. Here many a faithful friend, or dear relative or acquaintance was brought to receive the last blessing of the church before being laid to rest in the cemetery.

My earliest recollection of St. Boniface Church is as early as 1887, when I was three years old. This may seem incredible. My parents took me with them to some evening devotion. I distinctly remember walking up Leavenworth Street from McAllister Street toward Golden Gate Avenue. The cable slots and the roadbed for the Leavenworth Street cable line were just then being put in. On entering the church, I recall seeing some statues around the high altar. One figure held a wafer over a chalice. In my childish fancy, I thought he was offering me something good to eat — a cookie or something. In later years I realized that the four statues represented the four Evangelists, and that particular one with the wafer represented the Evangelist St. John.

A later recollection of St. Boniface, when I was about five years old, recalls a visit I made with my mother to the school, which was located on the lower floor, below the church. The purpose of the visit evidently was to see one of the Dominican Sisters, who was teaching, in regard to one of my sisters or brothers who was attending the school. This was my first visit to a school or classroom. I remember the Sister in charge of the class placed me on top of her desk and asked me if I could find and point out my sister Frances, who was a pupil in that class. I remember the many faces looking at me, but evidently that did not disturb me, as it did not take me long to locate her and gleefully point her out, to the amusement of all the pupils and the teacher.

My first recollection of the organ was later; while attending school I saw the organ in the gallery above. It was a moderate-sized two manual and Pedal tracker action organ, with attached console, with 8 speaking stops. The case, made of Spanish cedar, was ornate, with considerable carved moulding work on the top. I have been reliably informed that this wood carving was done by an uncle of mine, named Lawrence Hofman, who, sometime after doing this work, disappeared from view and was never heard from again. (To compliment my mother, whose brother he was, and to perpetuate his memory, I named my first born son Lawrence.)

And, if my memory serves me right, and the description of the organ, as related to me by my father is not incorrect, the front pipes were made of pure tin.

In time, as necessity required, the church on Tyler Street was enlarged by building a new facade with enclosed stairways, and a spire. The rear of the church was also extended, forming a sort of transept.

Organ music and singing fascinated me from my early childhood. I recall how my brother Frank and I would often remain for the 10:30 High Mass on Sunday, after attending the 9 o'clock children's mass. We would take our seats in the gallery, where children ordinarily, at the children's mass, were not permitted. The organ was in the center of the gallery and was separated from both sides by partitions which went clear to the ceiling. Seated in one of the gallery pews alongside the organ, although we could not see the organ and the singers, we were close to them and, at times, we would lustily sing along with them, unobserved and unnoticed and, I assume now, also unheard. At any rate, I am certain there were no discordant notes from us. We were always careful not to overlap or to let our voices be heard when a pause was made by the choir. Undoubtedly, musical qualities, such as a good ear for intonation, rhythm, etc., inherited from our father, precluded the possibility of our committing any such serious breach against the rules of harmony or music. True, we fashioned our own words or sounds, if the Latin words sung by the choir were not discernible or understood by us. This childish prank, on our part, I am sure annoyed no one and gave us much pleasure. In later years I had the privilege, with other boys, of singing in the boys' choir.

Professor John B. Mayle, as stated, was the organist as well as the teacher for the older boys of St. Boniface Parochial School. He was an interesting character and a most likeable soul and had a great influence on my character in its formative years. He was meticulous in his personal appearance, a strict advocate of order and discipline and, a firm believer in doing all things systematically and well. He demanded obedience and respect for authority but, with all his severity, he was human and sympathetic and won the love and affection of his pupils.

The job of organ pumper was one of the coveted jobs of the older boys during school days, as it would mean a little compensation in some form or other and an hour or two respite from attending classes. I was never favored with this privilege, as undoubtedly I was always too small and did not have the physical strength to hold up under the ordeal. The organ was pumped by foot, as I have stated, a "one lunger", and the result, even from the most efficient pumper, was a jerky and unsteady supply of air. Tonally, the organ sounded sweet and mellow, typical of all the Mayer organs. The wind pressure was about two and a half inches. Mr. Mayer, being the builder of the organ and a member of the parish, was evidently chosen, rather than my father, also an organ builder and member of the parish, to tune and service the organ when needed. This work was done a few times during the year and required the services of two boys, one to hold the keys and the other to pump the organ while Mr. Mayer was inside the organ tuning it.

In 1887, Rev. Sebastian Wolf retired and returned to Germany, and the parish was placed in charge of the Franciscan Fathers. A new life seemed to take hold of the congregation. Being established for the German speaking Catholics of the city, primarily, with the constant influx of these nationals to this country, especially in the '80's and '90's, it was soon found necessary to build a larger and more commodious group of buildings. The old rectory was razed and the large wooden church, with the organ, was bodily moved to a temporary location about 100 feet east to clear the space for the new church. For the dedication of the new church, on its completion in 1902, the organ was brought over from the old church building and installed in the new church by Joseph Mayer. Then came the earthquake and fire of 1906, and the new buildings were all destroyed, and "finis" was written to one of the oldest organs in San Francisco. This event also terminated Professor Mayle's career as teacher and organist, a position he held at St. Boniface for many years.

Undaunted, reconstruction of the church that had been in use but a few years was immediately started, and early consideration was given the matter of procuring a suitable pipe organ for the rebuilt church. My uncle, Ferdinand B. Schoenstein, an active and loyal member of the parish, with the approval of the pastor, Rev. Maximilian Neuman, O.F.M., a priest of musical training and talents, started a subscription list to gather funds for this purpose. Through the instrumentality of my brother Leo, then employed by the Eilers Music Company, and Mr. William B. King, at one time one of the most promising organists in the Bay region who evidently acted as their representative, induced Father Maximilian to purchase the two manual tracker action organ formerly in use for many years in the old First Presbyterian Church on 13th and Webster Streets in Oakland, California, as that church was soon to be sold and the building razed, preparatory to moving to their new location on Broadway and 28th Streets.

The organ was bought and installed by my brother Leo, and solemnly dedicated. Mr. Celestine Winger was the new organist. This old organ was one of the few imported from Europe. It was built in Soho — London, England, by Bevington & Sons in 1875, and was of excellent tonal quality. Mechanically, it was made with that high regard for professional quality, typical of the European craftsman. The console was attached, with large faced draw stop knobs. The organ was rather high, with quite an ornate case. It answered the purpose for St. Boniface Church for a number of years until, in

1914, with the arrival of the Rev. Florian Zettle, O.F.M., a musician of note, and also undoubtedly through the energetic and persuasive tactics of Fletcher Tilton, then agent of the Austin Organ Company of Hartford, Conn., who convinced him a better and more modern instrument was needed and deemed desirable for St. Boniface Church. A deal was made to procure a new Austin organ, but to retain and combine with the new organ all the pipes of the old English organ. This plan was carried out successfully, with the result that a new, modern 3 manual and Pedal organ was installed, Opus 1112, with a total of about 45 speaking stops. Our firm of Felix F. Schoenstein & Sons installed this instrument, under the supervision of Otto Schoenstein. Mr. Winger, the organist who functioned at the Old English organ, passed away about this time and a Mr. Clarence Schu succeeded him for a short time.

The organ, which cost $18,000.00, was dedicated on April 23, 1923. A recital was given by Uda Waldrop, Municipal Organist, and Fletcher Tilton, Representative of the Austin Organ Company.

With this fine organ now available, it became imperative to secure the services of some other competent and virile organist. A young man possessing all the necessary qualifications was found, in the person of the present organist, Mr. Arthur Luis. Mr. Luis, then a new arrival from the old country, well versed in the spirit and rudiments of true church music, a talented and thoroughly schooled organist and a choir and chorus leader of distinction, has successfully and satisfactorily held the position since. It is commonly stated that the organist of St. Boniface Church is the most occupied and engaged organist of any in the city, due to the many services being almost constantly held.

After about 37 years of use, the pneumatics of the organ needed replacing, at which time Austin's Unit actions, consisting of magnet, primary and power pneumatic, were applied to the trackers of the Universal air chests, and is giving excellent service since.

After 105 years, St. Boniface Church still holds its charm and interest, not only for the writer because of the sentiments attached, but for all who visit it and attend its services, the church of the kind Franciscan Friars, the sons of our Father, St. Francis of Assisi, San Francisco's patron saint.

NOTRE DAME DES VICTOIRES
(French National Church)

One of the old established churches of San Francisco is the Notre Dame des Victoires Church, commonly called the French Church, located on the north side of Bush Street, between Stockton and Grant Avenue. The cornerstones of the structure was laid in 1856.

I remember my father speaking often of this church, as he evidently spent many a day there working on the pipe organ, which was built by Joseph Mayer in 1875. It was a two manual organ with 18 sets of pipes. My father was in the employ of Mr. Mayer at this time.

This organ was built of a type unusual in America. The console, which was detached, was placed to the rear of the organ. The center part of the organ was built low, with the chest and smaller pipes resting on the gallery floor, thereby enabling the organist, who was facing the altar, to look over the organ in the central section. On either side were the larger, or bass pipes. Due to lack of sufficient height on the organ loft, the large front pipes of the organ, placed in two bays on either side of the low part of the center, protruded below the gallery railing. Each bay contained a group of five pipes. The Pedal pipes were placed on the rear wall of the choir loft, on either side of the console, and were enclosed in cases with scrolled panels. The organ case was of Romanesque design and made of black walnut, and, on the whole, made an impressive and pleasing appearance. Mr. John Knell was the organist at this time. A Mr. Koekel and Mr. Vogt also functioned as organist for some time.

My first visit to this church and organ must have been many years ago, as the occasion seems so remote. I remember crawling through a small floor with my father to the bellows room behind the organ, which seemed to be over the vestibule of the church. There was strong odor of fish oil, a lubrication used frequently then, so I concluded that some machinery was there and that the bellows must have been driven by a centrifugal water motor. The appearance of the interior of the church was different from that of most churches. I recall it was very dark, and what struck me as most unusual was that the entire floor of the church was covered by a red carpet, something quite out of the ordinary in a Catholic Church. Here I might state, that if I correctly remember, my father informed me that the church was originally built for a Protestant denomination. The dimly lighted edifice, the ever present fragrance of incense, the flickering sanctuary lamp, the carpeted floor making the quiet and solitude more noticeable, always gave me the impression of entering some old European church.

This church also held some interesting recollections for my father of his early manhood days. He related an incident that occured in 1870, at the time the members of St. Boniface Church, the German national church, of which my father was a member, were temporarily using the basement of the French Church for Sunday afternoon vesper services, as their own church on Sutter Street, had become unusable. As the congregation assembled for services on this particular Sunday afternoon, they found themselves locked out. They were thus made aware that they were not welcome there. A committee reported the matter to Archbisop Sa doc Alemany, and he, in his wisdom, well aware of the hostile feeling that existed at that time between the French and the Germans, during 1870, advised them to forget the incident and suggested to them that the time had come for them to buy a new site and build and occupy their own church. This they did, and the new St. Boniface Church was built on Tyler Avenue, now Golden Gate Avenue.

I remember some of my school mates who lived in the neighborhood of the French Church mentioning the fact that in later years they also served mass there. One of these boys later became the Rev. Clement Berberick, O.F.M., who for some years was pastor of St. Anthony's Church, but has since passed away.

Father Guibert, S.M., was the pastor of the French Church in 1899, a young, energetic priest, one evidently interested in music. I had just about left school at this time to work with my father permanently, and I recall visiting the French Church with him to see the new organ that was being installed by a Mr. Wiener, of the W.W. Kimball Company of Chicago, Illinois. It was the first Kimball organ to be installed in San Francisco. What became of the old original Mayer organ, I do not know.

The new organ was a two manual tubular pneumatic organ, with detached console. I recall how I admired the beautiful, lustrous, tinned pneumatic tubing, the neatness of its arrangement, the shellacked or varnished finish of all the woodwork, and the general heft and thickness of wood used in the construction of the organ throughout. It made a great impression on me. The tone, I recall, was different too, from that of most organs around here, somewhat bold and assertive, undoubtedly due to a higher pressure being applied than that commonly used.

A new organ was deserving of a new organist, and a very appropriate choice was made in securing the services of a young and brilliant organist just returned from Paris, France, Mr. Achille Artigues, who had just successfully completed his course of study at the Conservatory of Music, with high honors. After a few years of active service, his tenure was suddenly interrupted by the fire and earthquake in San Francisco, on April 18, 1906. The beautiful and historical church and the fine organ were destroyed in the general conflagration.

In keeping with the indomitable spirit manifested by all the churches of San Francisco, the Church of Notre Dame des Victoires was soon rebuilt on the same site. As I recall it, the interior of the new church resembles the old church very closely, with the exception that the former mystifying gloom is no longer there, nor is the floor carpeted as before. The exterior facade of the church, however, now made of pressed terra cotta brick, with its tall windows in circular form, and the towers topped with small spires, is quite a change from its former design.

Shortly after the new church was completed we learned that a new three manual and Pedal electric pneumatic organ had been bought from the Johnston Organ Company of Van Nuys, Calif., and was to be installed in the church. I am under the impression that my brother Leo installed this organ for the Eiler's Music Company, who were agents for the Johnston Organ Company at the time. A small Echo organ with chimes, placed near the high altar, is also part of this organ. Our firm has serviced the organ ever since.

Raymond White was organist at the church for many years. Later, Miss Wesling, and others, followed him as organist. Loyal sons and daughters of France, famous organists, such as Joseph Bonnet, Madame Coci, and others invariably performed or gave sacred concerts at the organ whenever their national tours brought them to San Francisco. The present organist is Charles Shatto.

This organ has been in constant use since its installation without any alterations.

THIRD BAPTIST

The Third Baptist Church was established in 1852. When I first visited it, it was located on the east isde of Powell Street, between Sutter and Bush Streets. It had a Mayer one manual tracker action organ, of ten stops. The organ was originally installed in the gallery and then, at some later date, was placed on the auditorium floor in the front of the church in the left hand corner. In 1900 we moved the organ from this location again to the center of the rostrum and made further alterations by removing the keyboard from the front and placing it on the side of the organ, to give more room for the pulpit. This required the designing and making of a unique rollerboard arrangement between key and pallet. Father was quite proud of being able to surmount this difficulty. I believe a new bellows was also put in.

The organist was a Charles Pearson, an amiable gentleman and always friendly to my dad.

In early years when I was quite small and my dad had his shop on Fillmore Street, more than once holy fear entered my being, especially when it was dark, when a colored gentleman from the church called at the shop to see my father regarding some work to be done on the organ, which seemed to be quite frequently. This fear, however, passed away in later years, quite naturally.

In 1906 the church and the organ were destroyed in the great fire, with so many others.

Shortly after the fire, in 1908, a new church was built on Clay and Hyde Streets, and a new Austin organ was installed, Opus 223. Rev. Kelley was the pastor at this time and Mr. Tyrell was one of the trustees. Another familiar figure was old Mrs. Anna Martin, the caretaker.

The new organ was the third Austin organ to be installed in San Francisco, and was erected by Edward L. Crome of Los Angeles. It was a two manual 12 stop, tubular pneumatic organ, Opus 223, and functioned satisfactorily for many years. Finally, due to the corrosion of the lead tubing and the practical impossibility of conveniently replacing the damaged tubing, we electrified the organ and placed a motor generator set in the universal air chest on a platform mounted on springs, for the low-voltage current, which proved to be quiet and satisfactory. With these improvements a new lease of life was granted the organ, which gave additional good service for many more years. However, after 37 years, the pneumatic leather used in the organ became in urgent need of replacement.

During this period, on the occasion of a Mother's Day celebration, because the organ had been giving trouble from ciphering, and fearing that this might happen during the concert, in order to allay their fears, I agreed to be present at the service and take care of any emergency that might arise. I thought I had an inconspicuous seat in the gallery, and possibly I did, but finding myself the only white person among the blacks, I became selfconscious. However, the music and services were touching and impressive, proving that, regardless of color, we are all children of the same Father with much the same human qualities.

The organ was not releathered at this time, 1944, and we terminated our work with the church, due to some unpleasant difficulties.

In 1952, the church edifice, with the organ, and site were sold to the Chinese Baptist Church.

In 1960, however, after the Chinese Baptist Church took over, we were again called to service the organ. After we relinquished our service on the organ in 1944, the pneumatics of the electric action was applied thereto. Evidently working satisfactorily in its inception, it was found in much need of a general overhauling when we again took over.

The former Third Baptist Church then bought the property owned formerly by Captain Charles Goodall, located at the corner of McAllister and Pierce Streets, and built an imposing new edifice there. Here again, under the management of new people, we were called upon by the pastor, the Rev. F.D. Haynes, to try to locate a suitable used, modern pipe organ to give them service for a limited number of years only. Eventually, however, an electronic organ was finally decided upon.

FIRST CONGREGATIONAL
Post and Mason Streets

The first Congregational Church, founded in 1850, was originally located on Jackson and Trenton Streets, a crude, frame building. In 1854, a brick building was erected on the southwest corner of California and Dupont Streets.

According to the data left by my father, this church had a two manual pipe organ of 10 stops. Its builder was unknown to him. It was a rather low, squatty instrument, evidently built to fit into the space requiring these proportions. Organists at the time were Mr. Douglas, Mr. George Powers and Samuel D. Mayer.

Later, the church acquired the property on the southeast corner of Post and Mason Streets, where a large, beautiful Gothic brick structure was erected. A graceful, lofty spire adorned the edifice. The first services in the new church were held on May 19, 1872.

Mr. John Bergstrom removed the organ from the old church, remodeled it, built a larger and higher case to harmonize with the interior of the new Gothic structure, and erected it in the new church.

In 1891 this old organ was removed from the First Congregational Church of San Francisco and was installed in the Plymouth Church of Oakland, Calif. In 1900 it was modernized and several stops added to it by Thomas Whalley, of Berkeley,

California.

The scaling of the pipes and voicing of this organ I always considered exceptionally good. Although voiced on a light pressure, probably 3½, it was full toned and pleasing. A 42" scale Open Diapason, the bass pipes of which form the display pipes, had a rich and dignified tone. All the stops harmonized perfectly. The mutation stops corroborate and blend especially well with the foundation stops, do not stand out singularly as seems to be the vogue at the present time, but together they produce a grand, rich, pleasing ensemble. (Author's Note: According to my father's notes, he stated 'builder of organ unknown.' In Mayer's biography, it states he built the organ. From my observation, I would decidedly say it was not a Mayer organ. The pipe work is not a sample of his handy work; it is more probably an Erben, Appleton or some eastern make organ, and may have been erected only by Mayer for the builders of the organ. From reliable sources I have been informed that the organ arrived in San Francisco in 1852, and was shipped around the Horn. Mr. William Carruth played this organ for many years.)

This old organ was removed from the First Congregational Church at Post and Mason Streets at or about 1890, to make room for a larger and more modern organ, the generous gift of Mrs. Harriet C. Alexander in honor of her parents, Charles and Mary C. Crocker, of Union Pacific Railroad fame. The contract was awarded to the George Hutchings Company of Boston, Mass., Opus 206-1891.

The new organ was a large 3 manual and Pedal, tracker and pneumatic Barker lever organ. It consisted of about 45 stops. The console was detached, the organist facing the congregation. The case was quite lofty, of imposing design, and was made of rich black walnut. I remember the impression it made on me the first time I saw it. The panels in the lower part of the case were recessed about four inches from the front surface of the case. Two overhanging towers on either side, which held the large 16' pipes, supported on carved brackets, with groups of pipes between them, completed the facade. The inside of the organ was a labyrinth of trackers, levers, squares, roller boards, pipes and mechanism. Only the best of materials were used. I especially recall the excellent high grade felt used on the valves and pallets. Workmanship was unexcelled. Any amount of dovetailing was done, mouldings were shaped on unessential parts, all wood shellacked, showing that skill and craftsmanship had been lavishly expended and was appreciated.

My first visit to the church was in the company of my father, who had been summoned there by the organist, Samuel D. Mayer, relative to taking over the regular maintenance of the organ. This was in 1901. The proffer of this work to my father was a compliment to him, and he was fully aware of it. Due, undoubtedly, to the lack of proper maintenance, the organ had been left to disintegrate and it required many hours of painstaking work on our part to get it working satisfactorily again. I recall when we were being shown the blowing apparatus in the basement, the organist, Mr. Mayer, introduced us to the sexton, and elderly gentleman named Mr. Pike, and my father jokingly remarked, "Well, I will get along with him." Mr. Mayer replied, "I know you will." Sixty-eight years have passed by since. We have seen sextons and organists come and go in the course of the years, but we are still servicing the organ.

Much of the regulating of the mechanism of the organ was left to me at that time, as there were places in the organ where a full-sized man could not navigate to advantage. Father would sit at the console and direct me as best he could what to do. I had to do my own thinking and planning, and make my own decisions and, I admit, working on this splendid organ awakened in me the first real desire and determination to master the organ business. I remember there was some mechanism working the Pedal stops and keys that was very intricate, being partly pneumatic and partly tracker, that was not operating satisfactorily. It had me stumped, as I was at that time lacking the necessary experience. My father was equally baffled, especially as he could not get access to it for close inspection.

At this time my brother Leo, who had been in New York for a number of years in the employ of the Muller & Able Company, and the Odell Company of New York, returned to San Francisco for the happy event of his marriage to Sophia Vetter, who he had courted for some years. We were naturally overjoyed to see him again, for his own sake and in anticipation of the joyous occasion that was to take place. However, we also induced him while here to give us a helping hand in regulating the mechanism of that particularly troublesome Pedal stop. It was interesting to see how he mastered the difficulty, and showed us how to proceed to get the entire organ into satisfactory working condition again. I most certainly was proud of my eldest brother and looked up to him as a master, and regretted that only too soon he would be leaving us again for the East. We finally got the organ in fine tune and working order, to the entire satisfaction of Mr. Samuel D. Mayer. Our relations with him were always very pleasant and cordial.

This happy situation was rudely interrupted and terminated by the earthquake and fire of April 18, 1906, which, early in its devastating progress, destroyed the church and the beautiful organ. After the fire, in 1907, the church was rebuilt on the same site. The old brick walls were retained, but the imposing spire that had adorned the old structure was not replaced. The interior of the church, however, was still quite lofty and impressive.

A new three manual Austin pneumatic organ was secured at this time. Opus 184. It had an imposing front with two towers, in which the Diapason 16' was placed. This organ was installed by Edward L. Crome and Roy Tolchard of Los Angeles, and we assisted them in doing this work. It was the second Austin organ installed in San Francisco, at that time.

After the completion of the installation of the First Congregational organ, by mutual agreement all future Austin installations in this territory were carried out by our firm.

The organ was quite satisfactory tonally, but never gave me that feeling of superiority and excellence that made the former Hutchings organ so outstanding.

At this time, 1913, rapid progress was being made in the rebuilding of San Francisco, and plans were being laid for the holding of an International Exposition to commemorate the completion of the Panama Canal in 1915. The First Congregational Church decided to erect a new permanent edifice. A prominent local architect was engaged, and plans were drawn and accepted for the proposed building.

On July 7, 1913, we signed a contract with the church to remove the large Austin organ from the temporary church and store it in a warehouse awaiting the time when the new edifice would be ready to receive it. We also, in the interim, did the necessary preparatory work at our shop for the electrification of the organ, when installed in its new location. We were consulted by the architect on several occasions regarding the arrangement and disposition of the organ parts in the new church, but were never able to get a definite statement, as to just what had been decided upon. Finally, we learned that the architect's plan was to make a divided organ, placed behind a grill or opening on either side of the rostrum. The details of this organ layout were not fully drawn and determined upon until the construction work on the building was far advanced. On one of my visits to the architect I expressed my disapproval of the arrangement and the location of the organ as tentatively decided upon, but in a most supercilious manner, with a wave of the hand, he set my objections aside, saying, "tut, tut, answer my questions."

When the organ chambers finally took shape, and they were, by the way, the last part of the church to be finished. I was astounded at the place provided and the inadequacy of proper openings for the egress of tone into the auditorium of the church. In the old church the organ was installed as an entirety in the center of the nave and its tone had uninterrupted opportunity for filling the auditorium, which it did admirably. In the new arrangement, with the organ divided and the organ chambers having insufficient and indirect openings into the auditorium of the church, I had my serious misgivings as to what the outcome would be.

As I feared, when the organ was finally tried, it proved a dismal failure. The full organ ensemble sounded like the Swell-manual only, with the expression shutters closed. This unsatisfactory condition was, after some buck passing, admitted. However, the architect tried to pass the responsibility on to us, as my father, in my absence, had been induced to sign a large batch of blueprints relating to that part of the church where the organ was to be located, not fully realizing the importance of this act and certainly not knowing the details of what he was signing and not knowing that I had previously objected to the vague and incomplete layout of the organ chambers as far as they were then actually shown on the blueprints.

This disasterous blunder caused quite a bit of unpleasant publicity in the daily press. It also made it exceedingly trying for the organist, Uda Waldrop, to perform on an organ that could not be heard, and, for the congregation and its world-renowned pastor, the Rev. Charles F. Aked, who had hoped to present to San Franciscans the very best in religious services and church music, it was a sad disappointment. Consultations on how to correct the situation were then held by the trustees of the church, and the services of a Mr. Mann, an acoustical expert of the Johns-Manville Company, were secured.

On his recommendation, certain plaster walls were removed; in other places baffle boards were constructed of cedar wood and placed advantageously to throw out the tone; all unnecessary corners catching the tone were eliminated; openings in the grill of the proscenium arch were enlarged; all wall surfaces were shellacked to get a hard, reflecting surface. All these expedients had their good results and the tonal output of the organ was considerably improved.

At this time, Edwin Lemare, the famous organist, was holding the position of mucinipal organist at the Civic Auditorium, San Francisco. He apparently intended to make San Francisco his permanent home. In his capacity as municipal organist, he also let it be known that he was an organ consultant and architect, and his valuable services and advice were secured by the First Congregational Church in their dilemma with their large, but still inadequate, organ. In addition to the acoustical improvements achieved by the Johns-Manville expert, Mr. Lemare tackled the tonal source directly itself, and recommended that the first open Diapason be replaced with one of a larger scale with a more powerful and pervading tone, and that the pressure of the organ be raised somewhat, which required a re-voicing of the pipes. This was done by Mr. King and Mr. Gallagher of the Austin Organ Company. Mr. Lemare also finally advised the adding of an echo, or antiphonal, organ on the opposite end of the church over the gallery, not so much for the delicate and ethereal effects normally sought for, but to increase the full organ ensemble by adding another Diapason and other desirable stops for accompanying the congregation in chorus singing.

We installed this Echo, or antiphonal, organ in 1922, Opus 184 A. These improvements were carried out with marked success and the organ answered all necessary requirements. At what cost all these alterations and improvements were made, I do not know. I do know that if the eminent and learned architect in his line had taken a little advise from a humble, but practical organ builder, the expenditure of much money and a very unpleasant situation could have been avoided. It was through the generosity of a Mr. I. E. Morse, a retired and affluent gentleman, who was deeply interested in the church and the organ, and who was loyal to us throughout, and understood the organ builder's point of view and his difficulties, that this troublesome situation was finally satisfactorily adjusted.

In 1914, Rev. Chas. F. Aked became interested in the Peace Expedition to Europe, sponsored by Henry Ford, and resigned from his charge at the First Congregational Church. Rev. James L. Gordon was appointed his successor. With him new ideas in church management were also introduced. The peace and serenity that had reigned in the church choir under the able and much advertised leadership of Uda Waldrop was disturbed by serious disagreement. As an able, efficient organist, and choir leader, he did not see the need of an independant choir leader, and resigned in 1926 to become organist of the First Unitarian Church.

Just previous to his resignation, a new three manual console and a harp had been added to the organ. The displaced console was then acquired by the Sixth Church of Christ Scientist who, at that time, were building their new church and needed a console for their pipe organ, which was the former Austin organ of the First Church of Christ Scientist.

It seemed a pity that after having weathered all the disagreeable incidents of the unsatisfactory installation of the organ in the first place, going through the period of reconstruction, putting up with the inadequacies of the old console and, just as all of these obstacles were being overcome and surmounted, with the outlook placid and satisfactory, Uda

Waldrop should find it necessary to resign. Other changes of ministers and organists took place.

Raymond White presided at the console for a number of years. During his term and under the pastorate of Rev. Jason Noble Pearce, the console was removed from its location on the choir loft, the cable extended, and the console placed on the auditorium floor. Being movable, it could be placed in any location desired.

In 1937 the First Congregational Church joined with the Methodist congregation of the former William Taylor Hotel venture, with the Rev. Edgar Lowther representing the Methodists and the Rev. Jason Noble Pearce representing the Congregationalists, both acting as joint pastors for what was then called the Temple Church. In 1942 this union was dissolved and both units again assumed their former identities. Mrs. Elizabeth Fotheringham presided at the organ during 1947.

In 1958, Rev. William E. McCormack was serving as Pastor, and as of 1959, Dr. Leonard Beck was the organist.

In 1959 it was decided to remodel the entire southern interior of the church to give it a more ritualistic or ecclesiastical aspect then that of the puritanical severity of a meeting hall it formerly had. An altar in the center at the top of ascending steps was installed with a huge cross in the background. Choir stalls flanked the altar on both sides, Pulpit and Lecturn in front of the Choir stalls. The former convexed, concaved plaster ceiling that was but slightly perforated to permit the tone of the organ to diffuse into the auditorium was removed entirely, and an open ceiling of arched baffles about 18" apart were installed, only obstructing the view of the interior organ parts from the audience, but for the first time releasing all the organ tone from its confinement behind constructed walls, etc. to its natural right of freedom of expression, sounding as it never had before — a grand and glorious ensemble.

In 1960, further tonal additions and alterations were made by adding a Mixture, other Mutation stops, some brighter reed stops to give the organ the more classical or Baroque aspects so prevalent at the present time.

At this time, the antiphonal, or Echo organ, from the gallery was combined and placed with the remaining parts of the organ below, with good results.

In 1960, a near tragedy occurred at the church. A fire broke out under the Sanctuary floor, charring the wood and consuming some of the organ cables connecting the console above. Fortunately, the fire was contained in the confines where it originated and no harm was done to the organ proper or the building.

The First Congregational organ is one of San Francisco's noteworthy organs now, worth hearing, but especially to see and hear its accoustical rejuvenation from an organ that was dead, but has now been brought to life again.

Our firm has been proud of bringing about this transformation, in conjunction with the organist, Dr. W. Leonard Beck, and the architect to a final and successful conclusion.

ST. JOSEPH'S
Tenth & Howard Streets

St. Joseph's Church is one of those parishes established in the early days of San Francisco. The church is located at Tenth and Howard Streets in the "South of Market" district. The edifice, before the fire, was a frame structure and stood on the west side of Tenth Street between Howard and Folsom Streets. This neighborhood, in the early days, was covered with sand dunes and swamp land, and my father recalled when the hill at Tenth Street was removed, the street cut through, and the land graded for the building of the church.

The neighborhood in early days was traversed frequently by most San Franciscans on their way to the Woodward Garden, located between Mission and Valencia, 12th and 14th Streets, nearby.

St. Joseph's Church was commonly referred to as the "Gallagher's Church", as the Rev. Cornelius Gallagher was the first pastor. After his demise, his brother Rev. Hugh P. Gallagher, functioned as pastor, to be followed by his nephew, Rev. Joseph A. Gallagher and, finally, to be succeeded by Rev. Patrick Scanlon.

The church had a very old two manual and pedal organ. My father's notes refer to it as a Simmonds organ which, in 1888, my father gave a general cleaning. It had a mahogony case. The keyboards of the G G Compass 49 notes were set into the case, with draw stopknobs on either side, and sliding doors, as was customary in the organs built in that time. The Pedal Open Diapason 16' pipes, of generous scale, were made of about 7/8 inch material and were ribbed or reinforced with diagonal cleats on the outside of the pipes. The bass manual pipes in this organ were not made of zinc, as is customary now, but of soft pipe metal, from the lowest note up. This practice undoubtedly produced a better and richer tone, but its drawback was that many of the bass pipes, including the front pipes, settled in their feet or telescoped from their own weight. This organ was hand-pumped, and it was my particular job, while assisting my father, in addition to holding the keys to also keep the pump handle going.

We serviced this organ from 1877 to 1906.

I recall the intersection of Tenth and Howard Streets was a busy location. On the northwest corner was the large power and car house of the Market Street Cable Company for the Howard and Leavenworth Street lines. It was a transfer corner, and I remember as young children whenever we made trips with our parents to the Mission District and transferred there, while waiting for the cable car, we would look in at the power house and watch the huge wheels and drums whirl around drawing the cables which were driven by the steam engines. There was always a constant din about the place, and the peculiar odor of greased cables and warm oil filled the air. Being a transfer corner, restaurants and other business establishments had located there. Nearby, on Tenth Street near Howard, was the Lick Public Baths, frequented by many San Franciscans. One eating place we patronized often was the Anchor Restaurant, where we had our meals when in this neighborhood. The proprietor I especially remember, on account of his long handle-bar whiskers. My father jokingly referred to him as "Garibaldi." On the opposite side of the street, on the southwest corner, was St. Joseph's School and auditorium, and farther down on Tenth Street was the parochial residence and then the church.

The lamp post at Tenth and Howard Streets, in front of St. Joseph's School, in time became famous as it was the rendezvous for several young men who, in 1883, met to discuss the founding of the Young Men's Institute, a Catholic organization still in existence, which since then also embraces the Young Ladies' Institute, with branches in all of the larger cities of the Pacific Coast.

Reverend Patrick Scanlon was the pastor of St. Joseph's when I was a youngster and visited the church with my father, on our regular calls to tune the organ. I always had a holy fear of him when I called at the priest's house to collect the bill for our regular maintenance work, on account of his severe and grave countenance. Undoubtedly, under this outwardly severe demeanor, there was a kind and generous heart. I also still have a vivid picture of the housekeeper who admitted me at the door, and asked me to take a seat in the parlor. She was a tall, slim, stately, middle-aged Irish lady, always dressed in black, trim and old-fashioned looking, with ruddy cheeks. Invariably, I would make my collection on the first visit, and never had to call a second time.

Sometime in 1903, a Mr. Laviolette, who was in the electrical business, applied an electric motor to the pump handle of the organ. As I recall it, through some misunderstanding or other, my father was not consulted in the matter, otherwise he would not have approved of the installation, or would have arranged some device for the regulation of the motor. However, though inexperienced in this matter, the electrician succeeded in figuring out the transmission for the proper speed of the counter shafts and pump handle to sustain full organ demands, but at what a price. Since there was no regulating device, the motor, running continuously at top speed, would thump and thump. The air in the bellows was always throbbing and the noise of the loose connecting joints on the pump handle could be heard, and caused the greatest annoyance throughout the church. Later on, my father had a rheostat applied to it with good effect. As I recall it, this was the first electric motor driven pump handle installed in San Francisco.

Early organists of this church were a Mr. Weber and a Mr. Kessels. Later, a most unique and interesting gentleman functioned as organist. His name was Sullivan, a man of extremely feminine characteristics, lavish in the use of cosmetics, always immaculately groomed, dressed in the height of fashion. And, to top it all, very loquacious and possessed of a charming Irish brogue. He and my father were apparently good pals. I believe he received his instruction in organ playing from John H. Dohrman, organist of St. Patrick's Church, as did others, including Miss Desmond, for many years organist of St. Peter's Church, and Miss Marie Giorgiani, who, in later years, became the dean of women organists in San Francisco.

The old church, rich in pleasant memories and associations of San Francisco's early history, was completely destroyed in the fire and earthquake that devastated the city on April 18, 1906.

Rev. Mulligan, an energetic young priest, former chancellor of the archdiocese, had succeeded Father Scanlon as pastor some years before the fire. I remember the morning of the earthquake when the people living in the South of Market District were being driven from their homes by the fire, and were moving enmasse toward the southern part of the city, Father Mulligan, with a group of nuns from the school, haggard, grimy from soot, carrying a few personal belongings, passed our home on Bryant and 21st Street, enroute to St. Peter's Church, his neighboring parish, for temporary shelter. St. Peter's, fortunately, was not destroyed. With a fatherly greeting of "God bless you all", he and his company trudged along to their destination.

A few months after the fire I happened to meet Mr. Sullivan, the former organist of the church, on the street. I was amazed at the change that had taken place in him. Gone was the vim and vivacity, the buoyancy and charm of former days. His face was thin and pale, and I could clearly discern the telltale marks of a malignant disease bringing him to an early end. However, for old times sake we had a little refreshing smile at his favorite corner. When asked by the barkeep what it would be, the answer was, "the same as I have always taken." We parted, bidding one another goodbye, which, in fact, it proved to be. Shortly after he passed away, a victim of cancer.

Father Mulligan continued as pastor of St. Joseph's Church after the fire, and set to work rebuilding the parish properties. At first a temporary wooden church, rectory and school were built. Being a very energetic and determined worker he endeavored especially to induce his former parishioners to return to their old homesites. Through the influence of the South of Market Promotion Association, he strove to stop the establishing of business and industrial plants around the church, but to no avail. The former populous district of South of Market was a thing of the past. The people did not return to make their homes there, but settled in the newer outlying districts of the city, and the South of Market District, in time, became almost exclusively industrial and commercial. Yet, the beautiful church stands at Tenth and Howard Streets, a monument to his loyal parishioners and a memorial to the energetic pastor, who shortly thereafter passed away.

A somewhat unique feature of St. Joseph's Church is the inclined floor, affording better visibility for those in the rear pews. The interior of the church is most artistic and edifying, with its frescoed walls and stained glass windows, its excellent, well-voiced two manual and Pedal Pilcher organ with attached console adds further charm. The instrument was sold and installed by Mr. Augustus Clark, a gentleman of high caliber, in or about 1910, representing the Pilcher firm.

Monsignor Richard Collins, a worthy successor to the former pastor, Rev. Mulligan, had done fine work in sustaining and directing a parish and school that was once populous and thriving, but now is used mostly by transients and people of the hotel district as a convenient place for attending services.

Mr. Lucette, sexton, pioneer and old standby of the parish, has been part and parcel of St. Joseph's for many years. Its present pastor is Rev. James A. McGee.

Aside from a releathering of the pneumatics, no tonal or mechanical changes have been made.

PRESENTATION CONVENT

I recall, before the fire of 1906, of often hearing of the Presentation Convent, which was then located at Lombard and Powell Streets, in the North Beach District of San Francisco. Being an old institution, it must have been located there for many years, but I do not remember ever seeing it.

From notes left by my father, they had a one manual tracker organ, made by Bergstrom. It was installed some time between 1868 and 1878. After the fire, which consumed the organ, the Presentation Sisters located their new convent on Masonic Avenue and Turk Street, in the Western Addition, in the section where the old cemeteries had been located. The front of the convent property faces what was formerly the rear of the old Calvary Cemetery. To the south of it was the old Masonic Cemetery, and to the west is now the new San Francisco Women's College, located on top of what was once called "Lone Mountain", an old landmark of the city. To the north was located Ewing Field, used for baseball and other sports. This, however, was built sometime after the convent was erected.

In the 1880's this part of the city was considered the outskirts of the town, and burials took place in the several cemeteries located there. I recall attending one of these funerals one day by chance, as we children were taking a hike up Lone Mountain. At Turk Street and Masonic Avenue we saw a funeral cortege enter the cemetery opposite from where the convent now stands. In the procession we spotted a company of uniformed soldiers. That was enough to arouse our curiosity. We raced down the hill and followed the cortege to the grave. Here taps were sounded and muskets fired in a last military salute.

This part of the Western Addition was rather sparsely settled until after the fire of 1906, and, when the Sisters built their new convent in this district, it was considered quite a way out of town.

Our first introduction to the new convent was in 1914, when we installed a Hook and Hastings pipe organ in their chapel, which is still in use. It is a coincidence that at about this time we installed four small Hook and Hastings pipe organs in Catholic institutions in the diocese, and I have been informed since, on good authority, that they were the gifts of the Most Rev. Archbishop Patrick W. Riordan D.D., to the respective institutions. They were the Holy Family Convent, Presentation Convent, Our Lady's Home, Oakland, and the Newman Hall, Berkeley.

The Presentation Convent organ consists of 2 manuals and Pedal, with 9 stops, pneumatic action, a detached console, and oak case with gilded front pipes. It makes an ideal organ and enhances the beauty of the chapel. This organ arrived during our busy period at the 1915 Fair, and due to lack of help, the installation was entrusted to my brother Frank, ordinarily not active as an organ mechanic. However, being the son of an organ builder and a machinist and mechanic par excellence in his own right, he succeeded admirably with this job. The tonal work was left to us to complete.

Since then the convent and institution has expanded and a new, modern high school for girls has been erected. The Masonic Cemetery property opposite has been acquired by the Jesuit Fathers for the buildings and campus of the San Francisco University, The Ewing Field structure and venture proved to be a financial failure, and one day during a very severe windstorm, it was destroyed by one of the most dangerous fires San Francisco has experienced, which threatened the entire Western Addition. With its elimination, the entire district was soon transformed. Beautiful and substantial homes and dwellings abound there now . . . the San Francisco College for Women was built atop Lone Mountain and, what was in 1915 a sparsely settled district, is now in 1965 one of the ideal and growing districts of the city.

Presentation Convent is today in a most desirable locality.

GREEN STREET FOURTH CONGREGATIONAL

Green Street Congregational Church was located on the south side of Green Street, between Stockton and Powell Streets. I believe it was a frame building and I remember the interior as being always dark and gloomy. It had a very old organ, either a Simmons, Johnson or Erben.

In my father's notes, he refers to it as possibly a Simmons. It undoubtedly came from the Eastern states and was probably erected by Shellard and McGrath. It had two manuals and Pedal, with console recessed and sliding doors, and contained about ten stops. My father serviced the organ regularly from 1896. The tone was sweet and pleasing, as it was in all the old organs.

A Mr. Wilson, I recall, was the treasurer of the church in late years. He was engaged in the tailoring business. I remember this fact for the reason that my father and Mr. Wilson undoubtedly had agreed upon a trade and barter basis for servicing the organ. For servicing the organ for a period of one year, Mr. Wilson would make my father a suit of clothes to order. The last one so made was of very light color, cadet blue, of material such as the mail carriers uniforms were formerly made of. My father, being dark complexioned with black hair and beard, wearing at the time a large brimmed slouch hat, looked odd and queer to us children, and we advised him not to have a suit of that hue and material made again.

During the early part of 1902 we received the contract to make certain alterations on the organ, one of which was to extend the mechanism so as to bring the keyboard out from its recessed position, common to many of the old organs. I remember helping my elder brother Leo with this work. He had shortly before returned from New York to make his permanent abode again in San Francisco, and joined in partnership with my father. I do not recall the outcome of this work, whether it was completed or not. The church and the organ were consumed in the holocaust of 1906.

After the fire, the North Beach District very quickly reestablished itself. The church, in line with the general trend, built again on the same site. This, evidently, was a mistake, as most of the English speaking people formerly living in this district had moved to other sections of the city, leaving the district almost exclusively to the Latin races, which, before the fire, had already predominated there. I recall working several times on a large two manual reed organ in the new church, but after a few years the congregation evidently concluded it was better to move out of the district.

A substantial brick edifice was then built at the corner of Cumberland and Dolores Street in the Mission District. A two manual Wicks organ, with detached console and about 8 stops, was provided for this church.

The vacated church, after standing idle for a number of years, was then rebuilt.into a theatre and called the Green

Street Theatre, in which a burlesque show held forth for a time, catering to a clientele quite the opposite from the previous church goers.

This type of entertainment did not hold for long either, and the church building, which had been closed much more than being occupied, was finally razed and the property put to a more profitable use.

FIRST UNITED PRESBYTERIAN CHURCH
Originally called Central Presbyterian Tabernacle

The First United Presbyterian Church was originally located on the north side of Golden Gate Avenue, between Jones and Taylor Streets. It had a large three manual Johnson organ, Opus 661-(2-32), tracker action, with attached console and was hand pumped.

In 1884, my father moved it from this location to a new church they had built on the northeast corner of Golden Gate Avenue and Polk Street. For this work he received the sum of $200.00.

The new church was a large square, 75 x 75 feet, frame structure. A broad stairway led up from the main entrance on Golden Gate Avenue to the church auditorium on the upper floor. The organ was located on the Golden Gate Avenue frontage. It had about 32 stops with the usual inter-manual couplers. The tone was rich and brilliant, yet pleasing and reserved, being voiced on 3" pressure. The organ was rather lofty, with the upper portion overhanging the lower section. The case was made of black walnut, with panels in herring-bone pattern, tongue and grooved. Large 16' and 8' open Diapason pipes served as the front display pipes. A centrifugal water motor, located in the basement and belted to a crank-shaft in the organ, furnished the air for the organ. This apparatus was applied by my father when he moved the organ to this church.

We serviced the organ from 1904 until it was destroyed in the fire of 1906.

I remember it was while holding the keys in assisting my father to tune the organ that I succeeded in playing, or formulating, my first chords on the organ, and that he commended me for it and encouraged me to further strive to develop a proficiency at the keyboard.

The treasurer of the church, a Mr. Bennett, seems always to remain fresh in my memory, possibly for the reason that when I called to present our quarterly bill, I was always sure of receiving payment from him, with a smile and a solicitous inquiry regarding the well-being of my father. He had a stand, or place of business, in the old California Market on California Street, between Kearny and Montgomery Streets, and a visit to the Market was always fascinating to me.

Here, at the First United Presbyterian Church, we also became acquainted with the organist Johannes Raith. It was about 1904 or 1905, and he had but recently arrived from Mexico. He was a native of Germany and spoke little English at the time.

Arriving at the church one day, on one of our regular tuning visits, we heard a note on the organ sounding continuously while he was playing. We thought a cipher had developed, and that he had decided to endure the nuisance rather than give up his practice. On reaching the console, however, we were surprised to find that he had deliberately fastened down the key because, he told us, the composition called for it and the harmonies of the piece were arranged and interwoven around this deliberate cipher, as we thought it was. The fire and earthquake of 1906 destroyed the church and its large Johnson organ.

In 1908 the church was rebuilt on a new site, farther west on the south side of Golden Gate Avenue between Steiner and Pierce Streets. This location had formerly been occupied by St. Rose's Academy, a large three-story frame building.

When I was a small lad, probably during 1892, and living at that time at Turk and Fillmore Streets, the convent was consumed by fire. It was a spectacular fire and, undoubtedly, a dangerous one owing to the high frame structure and the strong west wind, so prevalent in San Francisco. I thought San Francisco was doomed that night. The new edifice built by the First United Presbyterian Church is on the site now making it the third location this church has occupied on Golden Gate Avenue.

Shortly after completion of the new church we installed a two manual and Pedal electric pneumatic Austin organ of 10 stops, Opus 980. The structural part of the organ was, for the most part, installed by Harry Doyle, a young man then in our employ, recently graduated from the University of California. He took a deep interest in organ building and, undoubtedly, wanted to make this profession his life's work. Later, he went to the Eastern states and accepted employment with some of the larger organ building firms there. He kept in contact with us for a number of years and, I believe he eventually married. I have often wondered if he put the knowledge he acquired at the University to good use in the organ business.

During 1944 the console was detached, the cable extended and placed several feet from the organ, with the church choir between the organ and console.

Since then the congregation has disbanded and the church has been renamed, and is being conducted by the black people, now quite populous in the Fillmore Street District. The organ has never been altered tonally.

ST. MARY'S HOSPITAL

Rincon Hill, located at the foot of Harrison Street, in the early days of San Francisco before Nob Hill had acquired its fame for its sumptuous mansions, was one of the favorite residence sections of the elite and wealthy. Close by was the dock of the Pacific Mail Steamship Company, at the foot of Main Street, the spot where many an immigrant first set foot on San Francisco's soil.

Located on Rincon Hill at this time was also one of the prominent hospitals of the city, St. Mary's Hospital, conducted by the Sisters of Mercy. It fronted on the north side of Harrison Street, between Fremont and Beale Streets.

As I recall the building in later years, when it was no longer used as a hospital but had been converted into a home for sailors, the huge brick pile on the hill always looked sinister and foreboding. At no time, while it was used as a hospital or later, had I occasion to enter the building, but from data I have from my father, the chapel contained a small Bergstrom pipe organ. Whether this organ was destroyed in the fire of 1906, or what disposal was finally made of it, I do not know.

The new St. Mary's Hospital erected in 1927 by the Sisters of Mercy, on Hayes Street between Schrader and Stanyan Streets, is now one of the finest in San Francisco.

Its beautiful chapel had to function without a pipe organ until 1948, when we were fortunate enough to secure for them a very appropriate and satisfactory Aeolian pipe organ of 10 stops. It was co-incident that the Sisters of Mercy in locating their Mother House in Burlingame, California, in purchasing the old Frederick Kohl estate, containing a beautiful mansion, also came into possession of an excellent Aeolian pipe organ of about 20 stops, with an Echo division. This organ we later removed from the old mansion and installed it in the chapel of their new Convent, then recently built a short distance below the residence.

So pleased were they with this new organ that the determination was made if ever they purchased an organ for St. Mary's Hospital Chapel in San Francisco, it would have to be an Aeolian organ. As stated, this opportunity came in 1948 when we were made aware that a Mr. Roscoe Oakes, of Washington Street, San Francisco, residing on the eleventh floor of a sumptuous apartment house, was the owner of a splendid Aeolian organ and wanted to dispose of it. Suitable arrangements were made; it was purchased by the Sisters and installed by our firm in a very satisfactory manner in St. Mary's Hospital Chapel.

The organ, being placed at the south end of the chapel, rather high and near the ceiling, sounds beautiful, refined and ethereal and is of a very religious and devotional type. The console is placed on a gallery below, also to the rear of the chapel.

(For details of the organ see Roscoe Oakes Residence organ.)

CENTRAL METHODIST EPISCOPAL CHURCH

All I remember of this church was its location on the north

side of Mission Street, between Fifth and Sixth Streets. I never entered it and have but little data concerning it from my father, with the exception of a notation that they had a two manual Bergstrom organ.

In my father's notes he states it was a Bergstrom organ, 2 manual, tracker action, hand pumped with a walnut case, as usual. In the biography of John Bergstrom, however, no mention is made of this organ built by him. I personally am inclined to give the statement of my father credence in this instance.

The building was destroyed in the fire of 1906. After the fire, the church was located on the southwest corner of Leavenworth and O'Farrell Streets where a considerable part of a substantial edifice was built, with the hope of completing the structure in the future. The church, however, was never fully completed.

A fusion of the Wesley Methodist Church, the Howard St. Methodist Church and the Central M.E. Church was arranged in conjunction with the William Taylor Hotel venture. The lofty William Taylor building on Leavenworth and McAllister Streets was then erected and housed the Temple Methodist Church, as the combined churches were then called.

This functioned for a few years, but later, during the depression, it found itself in financial difficulties which finally put an end to this undertaking. The church was abandoned and the hotel was taken over by a company and conducted under the name of the Empire Hotel.

A splendid four manual Skinner organ had been installed in the Temple Methodist Episcopal Church and, on disbanding of the church units, we dismantled the organ and shipped it to the Occidental College of Los Angeles, which had purchased it for their own use. Since our firm did not reinstall it in its new location, we do not know if tonal changes or additions were made to it.

NOSTRA DE GUADALOUPE
(Spanish National Church)

The Spanish Church, as we most frequently called it, was

located on the north side of Broadway, west of Powell Street. Broadway, at this intersection, begins to make a steep incline up to the top of Russian Hill. It is located in the North Beach section of San Francisco, fringing on the Italian Quarter. Possibly, in this district, there resided more Spanish people than elsewhere in the city in the early days, or the church would not have been built there.

In 1898, when I began my career, we visited the church monthly to service the organ, and had been so doing since 1892.

The church, at that time, was a frame building and the rectory was alongside of it. In going up to the organ we had to pass a door that led to the priest's house. Invariably, when we passed it, we detected the strong aroma of cigarettes. This was suprising and unusual to me. I knew of priests in their leisure moments smoking fragrant cigars, but for anyone especially a clergyman to smoke cigarettes seemed to me, and I do not doubt to my father also, something shocking. My father and I were never addicted to smoking. The one at the Spanish Church who indulged in this, his favorite weed, was our good old friend, The Right Rev. Antonio Maria Santandreu.

Rev. Antonio Santandreu and my father were good friends and, in later years, whenever they met they would recall their first meeting in 1877, when Father Santandreu was stationed at Mission San Jose and my father had been summoned to repair a reed organ in the Old Mission Church.

As I recall the conversation, my father was not yet married at the time, but was courting my mother. A trip to the country he undoubtedly felt, would be a most enjoyable outing for both, so he took her along and she enjoyed looking through the old adobe Mission building and its surroundings while he repaired the organ. Father Santandreu would remind me of this occasion and tell me he knew my father and mother before they were married, and before I was born.

The organ in the Spanish Church, which we tuned and serviced, was a two manual and Pedal Bergstrom tracker action organ. My particular job, besides holding the keys, was to pump the organ. This was done by manipulating the long pump handle on the right side of the organ. As was frequently the case where organs were hand pumped, the pumper, to while away the time and break the monotony of his tedious job, would resort to writing or carving his initials on the wall and drawing pictures and cartoons. I, too, was not immune from this habit. That I was quite youthful at this time, just emerging from boyhood to young manhood, is evidenced by the fact that I was still engaging myself in drawing or designing on the wall an improved coaster, with brake attachments, for coasting and safely navigating the steep hills of our city, a sport we boys delighted in. I recall that shortly after these visits these boyish ambitions and desires were supplanted with other thoughts and activities more in keeping with my advancing years. In fact, it was here in the basement of this old church where I tuned my first note on an organ.

True, it was not a pipe organ, but a reed organ. My father was requested to tune the organ, but the job must not have been very urgent as he insisted that I try my skill and endeavor to tune it. I had been with him and observed him do this work on various occasions, so the procedure was known to me, but the practical experience was lacking. I hesitated at first, admitting that I was fearful of not succeeding and, secondly, more apprehensive that the Reverend Pastor would come upon me while at work, observing a mere boy trying to tune his reed organ, and would protest at this procedure. Hesitation, fear and a lack of aggressiveness seemed to be my weak points, but I have since given credit to my father for insisting that I tune the organ, thereby inculcating in me needed self-reliance and courage.

I remember there was one note in particular that was badly out of tune, so much so I was bewildered. I tried tuning it. I do not recall now whether it was sharp or flat. At any rate, I did not seem to improve it at all, as it went further out of tune. Being uncertain in my course, I continued with some more scraping on the reed, with still more violent discordant vibrations. In my fear of making the organ worse than it was, and of being caught trying to tune it, I finally decided hurriedly to try tuning in the opposite direction, as a last resort, flat or sharp as the case may have been, and, to my great satisfaction and peace of mind, I noted that, by that procedure, the two tones were improving, or coming closer in tune. A few more scrapes on the reed in the same direction brought the tones in perfect unison, or tune. I had successfully and unaided tuned my first note. An indescribable feeling of ease and triumph came over me. Fear disappeared, and the rest of the job of tuning the reeds, instead of being a mental torture, became an unforgettable achievement.

About this time we also gave the Bergstrom organ a thorough cleaning, I do not know how old it was then, suffice to say that sufficient dust had accumulated to warrant this cleaning.

It was after one of these tedious days in cleaning out the dusty organ, without the use of our modern vacuum cleaners, while waiting at the corner for the Powell Street cable car to return home, that my father, evidently feeling very thirsty, suggested that we enter the corner saloon and have a glass of cool refreshing beer. Needless to say, the beverage hit the spot. I recall this incident as it was the first time I had entered a saloon to have a drink over the bar.

Speaking of cable cars, I always enjoyed riding on them, especially the Powell, Jackson and Sacramento Street lines. Transportation was not as rapid then as now. At the time we lived at 21st and Bryant Streets in the Mission District. That we often came home late for supper is explainable when I contemplate the car connections we had to make to get home. From the Spanish Church on Powell and Broadway, or any of the churches in the North Beach District, we would take the Powell Street cable car, then transfer down Ellis Street and across Market to Fourth and Bryant Streets, and there transfer again out Bryant Street to 21st. At the corner of Fourth and Bryant Streets there was also a favorite watering place, the usual water trough for the horses outside but inside the refreshing bar for those desiring a drink. As stated, my first and only visit to a saloon, until years later, which took place at Powell and Broadway, must be considered in the light of an exceptional emergency visit only. I remember, while waiting for the car at Fourth and Bryant Streets, often after the evening rush, how long and endless the wait seemed. My father, at times, would pass through the swinging door and have his glass of beer. I would be outside on the alert, watching for the car. If the headlight on the car turning the corner at Second and Bryant Streets appeared, father would have to hurry, and I would give him the high sign through the swinging door. If no car was in sight, he could have his drink in peace and comfort, undisturbed. My reward for watching would be a handful of salted pretzels, when he came out.

In 1906 the fire and earthquake destroyed the Spanish Church and the Bergstrom organ. In 1910 a new concrete structure was built on the same site, more pretentious and beautiful than the old church.

About 1912, the First Unitarian Church bought a new Skinner organ, and their old organ, a Hook organ, tracker action, Opus 1380, of two manuals and Pedal, was for sale. (See First Unitarian.) A deal was made with the First Unitarian Church and the old Hook tracker organ was bought and installed by my brother Leo in the new Spanish Church.

It is an imposing organ of 21 stops, built in 1888, with an ideal church organ tone, according to the old school. Mr. Leo Arrillaga was organist at the time. The blower was placed up in the tower. It had to be placed out of hearing as it was unusually noisy in operation. In later years we put in a large slow speed blower, nearer the organ, the one formerly in use in the organ at St. Mary's Cathedral, which had to be replaced with a larger blower when its organ was remodeled and modernized. This new blower has given excellent satisfaction ever since. The "Hook" tracker organ, formerly in the First Unitarian Church, has never been enlarged or altered and is being used regularly.

So, after about 76 years of tuning and servicing the organs in this church, things have changed. The old hand-pumped Bergstrom has disappeared. The saloon on the corner, where I had my first drink, is gone. It had to be razed to make room for the new Broadway Tunnel entrance, directly in front of the church. We no longer service the organ regularly. New pastors and organists are serving the church now. But there still remains the old Powell Street cable line, with its clanging bell and antiquated cars, climbing the hills. The aroma, noticed when ascending to the organ loft, seeping its way through the door leading from the rectory, from the cigarettes smoked by the good old padre, has now ceased.

Death has claimed the old veteran Monsignor, known as

the oldest priest of the Archdiocese of San Francisco. He entered his eternal reward at the age of 91 on September 14, 1944. In addition to the title of Monsignor he received from Pope Pius XI, he was also honored by King Alphonse of Spain, by being named Commander of the "La Real Order de Isabella La Catholica."

GRACE EPISCOPAL CATHEDRAL

San Francisco's famous Nob Hill was not only the citadel of the "Bonanza Kings", with their mansions, but it was also the location of the cathedral of the Episcopal Church, Grace Cathedral.

Although passing the large brick edifice often, which was erected in 1860, I never had occasion to enter its portals, as evidently in the years following 1898 when I began my active career as an organ builder, assisting my father, he did not have the maintenance of the organ that was there. According to records left me by my father, however, and substantiated by those of Joseph Mayer, the latter, in 1862, installed a 2 manual and Pedal pipe organ in the edifice. This, however, was only on a rental basis. Professor H.M. Boswick was organist.

This organ was later sold by Mr. Mayer, and according to my father's records, was erected in St. James Episcopal Church, which was then located on the north side of Post Street, between Taylor and Mason Streets, where the Olympic Club building now stands. Later, this congregation disbanded and the church was taken over by the Presbyterians and the name changed to St. John's Presbyterian Church. The latter then procured a large three manual Johnson organ, Opus 394 (3-38), in 1873. A Mr. Katzenbach presided at this organ.

The Mayer organ, which had been removed from the above named church to Mayer's shop, where a Pedal stop was added to it, was then installed in St. Francis Catholic Church, on Vallejo and Dupont Streets, on or about 1873, where it was in use for a number of years. When this church eventually secured a new three manual tracker action Bergstrom organ, in or about 1877, the old Mayer organ was finally sold and erected in St. Vincent's Church in Vallejo, California. Here we added a new bellows to it, also a blower and, finally, due to its worn out condition, replaced it in 1940 with a new organ of our own make. And so, after having given good service for 107 years in a number of churches, this organ finally came to its end. We have a few of its old battered pipes as souvenirs.

Coming back to Grace Cathedral again, my father's notes state that after the aforementioned Mayer organ was removed, they secured a two manual and Pedal organ, what make the writer cannot establish, with console attached and a high walnut Gothic case. What eventually became of this organ, I do not know. It is possible that it was sold to the First Christian Church of Oakland, which had a two manual organ, whose history I never had occasion to establish.

The first mention my father makes of working in Grace Cathedral was in 1890, when he was commissioned to remove the old pipe organ, above referred to, to make room for a new and modern organ built by Cole and Treat of Boston, Mass. Robert Searles was the donor of the organ, if I have not been misinformed, or his name was in some way connected with its installation.

As stated, my father had, in this particular case, the rather unpleasant task of removing the old, dusty organ, a job at best disagreeable and grimy. As I recall my father relating it, the new organ had already arrived and had been uncrated and was waiting to be placed in the location occupied by the old organ, and naturally was receiving all attention and solicitude from every one. The builders, naturally proud of the high class finish of their product and wanting to make a good impression, incessantly, and with much ceremony, kept brushing and wiping off the dust accumulating from the old organ and settling on the new organ parts that were lying about. This superior attitude of these Bostonians installing the new organ, and their apparent contempt for the old organ and the party removing it, evidently riled my father, or he would not have mentioned it to me on several occasions.

The new organ was, of course, the subject of much interest and discussion throughout the city. It functioned pneumatically. It had an elaborate, richly carved walnut case and was blown by a large water motor, placed in the basement. My father spoke very highly of its superb workmanship and design, but tonally it must have been lacking in power and sonority and was disappointing, either due to location or to inferior scaling, or because of lack of an adequate specification for the Cathedral. The fire of 1906, which leveled the hovels of the poor as well as the mansions of the rich, in its almost unchecked sweep, also completely destroyed Grace Cathedral and its beautiful organ.

Mr. Holt presided at the organ at this time. Rev. Foote was the rector, and Rt. Rev. W. Ford Nichols, bishop.

After the fire the property, bounded by California, Sacramento, Taylor and Jones Street, one square city block on the top of Nob Hill, where once stood the magnificent Charles Crocker mansion, was donated to the Episcopal Diocese of California for its new cathedral site.

First, a small, temporary, wooden frame chapel was built on the northwest corner of Sacramento and Taylor Streets. A contract for an organ was let to Thomas Whalley of Berkeley, who provided an excellent toned instrument of two manuals and Pedal, with attached console, tracker action, also partly pneumatic, of 12 speaking stops.

The first unit of what was to be the permanent cathedral was built in 1910. This consisted of the so-called Founders Crypt, or the basement of what was to be the future nave of the cathedral. This crypt was opened for services on January 27, 1914. At the solemn laying of the cornerstone, the President of the United States, Theodore Roosevelt, was present, adding much dignity to the occasion.

In 1914, the Cathedral contracted for a new organ with the Austin Organ Company of Hartford, Connecticut, Opus 472, through the office of Robert Fletcher Tilton, their local agent. It was to cost $17,000 and was a gift of Robert Searles, the donor of one of the previous organs.

The new organ was a large three manual, of 43 stops, with electric pneumatic action, divided on either side of the chancel. An ornate overhanging case with front pipes added dignity to the chancel, with its long choir stalls, lectern, bishop's throne and altar. It was our good fortune to install this splendid organ. My brother, Leo, also assisted in erecting it. This proved to be a very successful installation, a find sounding organ, a typical cathedral organ.

Mr. Chaplin Bayley, a young man of most pleasing personality, was the organist, and also the founder of the Cathedral
Choristers, a true Liturgical Choir of men and boys.

I recall, on a solemn feast day, either Christmas or Easter,
it was arranged as a compliment to the organist emeritus,
Mr. Holt, then an elderly gentleman, that he play the organ at
one of the early services. Those familiar with an Austin console, in which stop keys are used, will recall that the unison
"on and off" stop keys are, in many cases, placed on the left
side of the finger board in the console, as they were in this
case and, being colored black against a black background
finish, they are hard to see, especially if the console is not
adequately lighted. On this occasion, Mr. Holt, arriving at
the console, started the motor, selected his stops, but could
not get any response from the organ. Bewildered and dismayed at his predicament, we were finally called and responded as quickly as we could.

On arriving I must admit, momentarily, I was as much baffled as was Mr. Holt, as to why the organ would not play.
While hesitating to make a display of myself before the congregation, which was already assembling, by opening the console, a bright thought flashed through my mind to look first
at those inconspicuous black unison stop keys, which the
regular organist usually left in an 'on' position. Sure enough,
they were in an off position, or possibly put in that position
unconsciously by Mr. Holt in preparing for his numbers. Some
casual comment on unnecessary modern gadgets was about
all Mr. Holt said, and went on with the services.

Dean J. Wilmer Gresham, D.D., always active, pleasant and
affable, deeply interested in the organ and religious services,
was a living part of the Cathedral for many years. After the
crypt of the new Cathedral was completed and the temporary
wooden chapel was no longer needed, the Whalley organ that
had been installed there was erected in the chapel of the
Good Samaritan, on Potrero Avenue and 25th Street.

Services were held in the crypt of the Cathedral until 1933,
when the plan of using the crypt was a nucleus of the permanent Cathedral was abondoned, due to the inadequate
strength of its foundation and the added length required for

the proposed new Cathedral. Architect Walter Hobart drew plans for a new, more pretentious and imposing cathedral to crown the summit of Nob Hill, one in size and style — a replica of the old European cathedrals, to be the Bishop's seat of the Episcopal Church in California.

The first unit built was the Chapel of Grace on the northwest corner of California and Jones Street. It proved to be a little gem of Gothic architecture, well proportioned, with vaulted ceiling and stained glass windows, manufactured by Connich, a prominent Boston firm. The altar, an antique imported from Europe, gave the chapel charm and dignity. A two manual and Pedal pipe organ of 18 stops and 21 ranks was provided, and built by the Aeolian Company of New York. Colonel William D. Woods, then a white-haired man who, forty years before, had installed the large 84 stop Farrand and Votey organ in St. Ignatius Church, was in charge of the installation. This was the last organ he installed in the Bay region. (He passed away in June, 1945, in Hollywood, California.)

The exterior case of this organ was made of imported oak from England, to harmonize with other interior furnishings of the chapel. Mr. J. Sydney Lewis presided at the organ. The maintenance of the organ was entrusted to our care.

In 1951 it was found expedient to substitute all of the stops of this organ. This work was done with products of the Aeolian Skinner Organ Company, under the direction of Donald Harrison of Boston, by Otto and Lawrence Schoenstein of our firm, to his entire satisfaction, and it also gave me the pleasure of a friendly conversation with Mr. Harrison. This alteration work was undoubtedly also the first time an extensive organ shipment was made by air — this to facilitate the completion of the work for a demonstration of the organ to guests and delegates of the National A.G.O. Convention convening in San Francisco during that year, 1952.

With the new chapel now in daily use for divine services, a large part of the old crypt was razed and the large Austin organ that was there was removed by Mr. Charles B. Hershamn, who, through some connection, received the contract from the contractors of the new cathedral and not from the Vestry, with whom we had had very satisfactory relations since installing the first Austin organ. The organ had to be removed in a hurry. We noted that the roof over it was being taken off while the men were still at work removing and packing the pipes. It was finally stored in the basement of the new Cathedral, which was already making considerable progress, until 1957 when it was finally disposed of.

On completion of the chancel and transept and part of the nave of the new Cathedral, plans for the future permanent Cathedral organ were considered and discussed. One plan was to use the old Austin organ and make necessary additions to it: the other was for an entirely new organ. Bids were received from many builders. Representatives from eastern factories made personal visits to San Francisco to be on hand to negotiate to better advantage and, if possible, obtain the coveted contract. Through the beneficence of the Alexander family, a substantial sum was allotted the Cathedral for this memorial organ and the contract was finally awarded the Aeolian Skinner Organ Company of Boston, Mass. Mr. Donald Harrison personally supervised the installation of the organ.

It is a divided instrument, on either side of the chancel, consisting of four manuals and Pedal, with about 100 speaking stops. Two ornate cases of beautiful design, with tall, graceful pipes in keeping with the loftiness of the chancel, add charm, grace and dignity to its appearance.

On its completion, I had the pleasure of meeting Mr. Donald Harrison of the Aeolin Skinner Organ Company, who happened to be in San Francisco and who expressed his approval of our work.

Tonally, the organ might be said to represent a new school in the voicing of pipe organs, or rather it is a reversion to the old cathedral type, the traditional type used in the old cathedral organs of Europe, of the classical style, with its superabundance of mutation and mixture work. Yet, fortunately, moderate pressures were also used for the diapason choruses, although some of the reeds are on high pressures. All told, the organ is a masterpiece in tonal appointment, with possibly a little too strong emphasis on the brilliant or two-foot tone in full organ ensemble.

Unfortunately, in the present unfinished state of the Cathedral, with the blank wall on the east end abruptly terminating the uncompleted nave, the acoustical effects are impaired, there being too much reverberation. Rapidly played passages on full organ, such as Bach fugues, lose all clarity and terminate in one grand jumble of tone. When the Cathedral is finally completed, with an interior length of nave of 400 feet, with its transepts and high vaulted ceiling, the organ will undoubtedly sound as a true cathedral organ should sound, heavenly and inspiring.

Sydney Lewis occupied the position of organist at the Cathedral from 1924 until his death in 1942. Mr. Hugh McKinnon succeeded Sydney Lewis and remained until 1946, when he was followed by Mr. George Fairclough, interim organist, and then by Richard Purvis, its present encumbent.

Since, undoubtedly, Grace Cathedral's organ is one of the outstanding organs of the country and tonally typifies in a high degree the current trend of again reverting to the classical or traditional tonal design, we have appended its specification in full.

Unfortunately, as fate would have it, our firm had no part in the installation of this splendid instrument. In fact, when it was completed, we were also deprived of our connection with the Cathedral in servicing the organ of the Grace Chapel, being informed that they did not want two rival firms servicing the organs of the Cathedral.

A recent addition to the Cathedral has been the placing in one of the completed towers of a 44 bell carillon, the gift of Dr. Nathaniel Thomas Coulson. These had been temporarily exhibited and used at the Golden Gate International Exposition on Treasure Island, San Francisco Bay, in 1939.

When this imposing plan is finally completed, Grace Cathedral of San Francisco will be the third largest cathedral in the country, with a seating capacity of 3200 people.

It is stated that Grace Cathedral of San Francisco is the only Episcopal Cathedral in the United States where the exterior is fully completed. Mr. Louis P. Hobart of San Francisco was the original architect. In the early stages of design, the firm of Cram and Ferguson acted as consultants to Mr. Hobart. After his demise, the firm of Weihe-Frick and Kruse carried out his plans, making the necessary modifications. Messrs. Gardner — Dailey and Alec Yuill Thornton were the architects of the interior alterations, involving the new High Altar and the Chancel.

The Consecration Services of the Cathedral were held on Friday, November 20, 1964. The music was composed and arranged by Richard Purvis. Mr. Hazelton presided at the organ. The Choir of St. John's, Ross, California, Mr. Robert Hunter Organist and Chorister; and St. Mark's, Palo Alto, California, Thomas Rhodes Organist and Chorister, joined forces with the Grace Cathedral Choir Choristers. The presiding Bishops of the Episcopal Church of the United States, presided at the services at the final close.

SPECIFICATIONS OF GRACE CATHEDRAL ORGAN

GREAT ORGAN

16'	Dbl. Open Diapason	61	pipes
8'	Open Diapason I	61	"
8'	Open Diapason II	61	"
8'	Open Diapason III	61	"
8'	Stopped Diapason (Metal)	61	"
8'	Flute Harmonique	61	"
5 1/3	Quint	61	"
4'	Octave	61	"
4'	Principal	61	"
3 1/5	Gross Tierce	61	"
2 2/3	Octave Quint	61	"
2'	Super Octave	61	"
1 3/5	Tierce	61	"
IV	Fourniture 15, 19, 22, 26	244	"
III	Cymbal 22, 26, 29	183	"
16'	Double Trumpet	61	"
8'	Tromba	61	"
4'	Clarion	61	"
	Chimes (Prepared for)		
	Blank Stop Knob		

SWELL ORGAN

16'	Lieblich Gedeckt	73 pipes
8'	Geigen	73 "
8'	Stopped Diapason	73 "
8'	Gamba	73 "
8'	Voix Celeste	73 "
8'	Echo Gamba	73 "
8'	Flauto Dolce	73 "
8'	Flute Celeste	61 "
4'	Principal	73 "
4'	Harmonic Flute	73 "
4'	Spitz Flute	73 "
2 2/3	Nazard	61 "
2'	Fifteenth	61 "
1 3/5	Tierce	61 "
VI	Plein Jeu 12, 15, 19, 22, 26, 29	366 "
8'	Vox Humana	73 "
8'	Oboe	73 "
16'	Posaune	73 "
8'	Trompette Harmonique	73 "
8'	Cornopean	73 "
4'	Clarion	73 "
	Tremolo	
	Harp) Prepared for from Choir	
	Celesta)	
	Blank Stop Knob	

CHOIR ORGAN

16'	Gemshorn	73 "
8'	Diapason	73 "
8'	Viola	73 "
8'	Melodia	73 "
8'	Lieblich Gedeckt (Metal)	73 "
8'	Erzahler	73 "
8'	Kleine Erzahler	61 "
4'	Gemshorn	73 "
4'	Lieblich Flote	73 "

2 2/3	Nazard	61 pipes
V	Sesquialtera 12, 15 17, 19, 22	305 "
8'	Clarinet	73 "
8'	Trumpet	73 "
	Tremolo	
	Harp)	
	Celeste) Prepared for	61 bars
	Blank Stop Knob	

SOLO ORGAN

8'	Open Diapason (Prepared for)	73 pipes
8'	Flauto Mirabilis	73 "
8'	Gamba	73 "
8'	Gamba Celeste	73 "
4'	Octave (Prepared for)	73 "
VI	Grand Fourniture (Prepared for)	
	12, 15, 19, 22, 26, 29	366 "
8'	English Horn	73 "
8'	Tuba Mirabilis	73 "
4'	Clarion	73 "
	Tremolo	
	Chimes (Prepared for)	25 bells
	Blank Stop Knob	

PEDAL ORGAN

32'	Diapason (Open FFFF lower	
	5 resultant)	7 pipes
16'	Open Bass (Wood)	32 "
16'	Diapason (Metal)	32 "
16'	Violone (Wood and Metal)	32 "
16'	Bourdon	32 "
16'	Gemshorn (Choir)	32 notes
16'	Lieblich Gedeckt (Swell)	32 "
10 2/3	Quint (Metal)	32 pipes
8'	Octave (Metal)	32 "
8'	Flute (Wood open)	32 "

8'	Cello (from Violone)	12 pipes
6 2/3	Grosse Tierce (Metal)	32 "
8'	Still Gedeckt (Swell)	32 notes
5 1/3	Octave Quint (Metal)	12 pipes
4'	Super Octave (Metal)	32 "
4'	Flute (Metal Harmonic)	12 "
III	Sesquialtera 17, 19, 22	96 "
16'	Posaune (Swell)	32 notes
32'	Bombarde Contra	12 pipes
16'	Bombarde	32 "
8'	Trompette	12 "
4'	Clarion	12 "
	Chimes (Prepared for)	
	Blank Stop Knob	

COUPLERS

Swell to Great)		Swell to Pedal)	
Choir to Great)		Great to Pedal)	
Swell to Choir)		Choir to Pedal)	
Swell to Solo)		Solo to Pedal)	
Solo to Great) Unison		Swell to Pedal 4') Pedal	
Solo to Choir)		Solo to Pedal 4')	
Solo to Swell)		Choir to Pedal 4')	
Choir to Swell)		Pedal to Pedal 8')	

Also by reversible pistons

Swell to Swell 4')	Solo to Solo 4')	
Swell to Swell 16')	Solo to Solo 16')	
Swell to Great 4')	Solo to Great 4')	
Swell to Great 16')	Solo to Great 16')	
Swell to Choir 4')	Great to Great 4')	
Swell to Choir 16') Octave	Solo to Swell 4') Octave	
Choir to Choir 4')	Solo to Swell 16')	
Choir to Choir 16')	Solo to Choir 4')	
Choir to Great 4')	Solo to Choir 16')	
Choir to Great 16')	Choir to Swell 4')	
Choir to Great 5 1/3)	Choir to Swell 16')	

Intermanual Octave Couplers to be by Stop Knob
Solo, Swell, Great and Choir Unisons off by on and off
pistons in treble cheek of respective manuals

COMBINATIONS
(Visible and adjustable at the organ bench)

Swell	8 and cancel Pedal to Manual on and off)	by on and
Great	8 and cancel " " " " " ")	off pistons
Choir	8 and cancel " " " " " ")	in bass
Solo	8 and cancel " " " " " ")	cheek of
Pedal	8 and cancel " " " " " ")	respective
General	8 (Lettered) (to, include couplers,	manuals
	duplicated by pedal	
	pistons)	

Couplers 4

Choir Pedal to Solo Pedal reversible with indicator light)
Choir Pedal to Swell Pedal reversible with indicator light)
Intermanual Octave Coupler Cancel
General Cancel to include Crescendo and Tutti
All Couplers Off
Manual 16' Stops Off
Tremolo, Celestes, Harp and Chimes cancel on Crescendo
    and Tutti
Pedal 32' Stops Off
Toggle touch on Manual keys
Prepared for Harp and Chimes Dampers on and off

PEDAL MOVEMENTS
Swell Expression
Choir Expression
Solo Expression
Crescendo
Tutti reversible pedal and piston
Music rack (solid)
Light indicators for all blind movements
Special signal light for organist

FIRST METHODIST CHURCH

The First Methodist Church, the oldest church of the Protestant denomination in San Francisco, was founded in 1847. The first edifice was built on Powell Street, between Clay and Washington Streets. Several buildings, in the course of time, were erected on this site; the one previous to the fire was a frame building, with a spire.

My earliest recollection of this church and organ was on a visit there, with my father, in 1903, to make some repairs on the organ—a one manual Bergstrom tracker action instrument.

After the fire of 1906, in which the edifice was destroyed, my next connection with this church was in 1908, when I assisted my brother Leo in making some adjustments on a new two manual and pedal Kimball organ he had recently installed in the new church — now located on the northwest corner of Clay and Hyde Streets. The console of this organ was attached and was played by tubular pneumatic action.

Rev. Samuel Quickmire was pastor at this time.

In or about 1912 the choir loft arrangement was changed, and we made the console detached by extending the pneumatic tubing. Some years later a new relay mechanism was installed by other parties, undoubtedly with the purpose in mind of speeding up the attack and repetition of the organ, and also to eliminate the original Kimball coupler stacks—the pouches of which were made of rubberized silk which, in the course of years, had hardened and stiffened, causing much grief by constant ciphering.

The new mechanism, although it eliminated the old trouble, brought new troubles of its own of a different nature. At this time we were again given the regular maintenance of the organ and, in due time, with much adjusting, skill and perseverance we got the organ to be dependable.

Mr. Lucius Downer was organist for a number of years, and during his term we also installed a Vox Humana 8' and a set of chimes.

Rev. F.H. Buscher was pastor until 1942.

In later years, the chest pneumatics and primary actions showed signs of needing replacement. This was finally done in 1961 and at the same time the entire action was electrified, thereby eliminating the troublesome behavior of the pneumatic relay mechanism installed years previously. The organ has been giving excellent service since that time.

ZION AFRICAN METHODIST EPISCOPAL CHURCH

Among the black people of San Francisco, before the fire, two Protestant Congregations seemed to predominate, the First Baptist Church on the east side of Powell Street above Sutter Street, and the Zion African Methodist Church on the west side of Stockton Street, north of Jackson Street.

There was also a third black church, called Bethel African Methodist Church, which was located on Powell Street, near Pacific Street. This latter church, to the best of my knowledge, had no pipe organ before the fire era, but secured an organ for their new church after the fire. (See Bethel African A.M.E. Church.)

Referring to Zion African Methodist Episcopal Church on Stockton Street, I have a faint recollection of a visit to this church, with my father, to tune and service the organ. It was a very old organ, possibly an Appleton, or some other eastern make, of two manuals and Pedal, tracker action, with keyboard set flush in the case. It had about 10 or 12 stops. What I distinctly remember was the large Pedal Open Diapason 16' pipes placed in the back of the organ. These pipes were ribbed on the outside with cleats, in a sort of herringbone design, the same as were applied to Ped pipes in the old "Hook" organ at St. Joseph's Church, 10th and Howard Streets.

The organ and the edifice of the Zion African Methodist Church were destroyed in the earthquake and fire of 1906. After the fire they built a new edifice on the south side of Geary Street, between Laguna and Buchanan Streets.

For many years thereafter we had no dealings with the church until one day, in 1930, we were summoned to tune and adjust their organ. On calling, we were surprised to learn that they had a pipe organ.

It proved to be an old Johnston organ, that had been secured from some previous installation. It was a two manual and Pedal electric pneumatic action organ of about 8 stops, with detached console. Judging from the slipshod manner in which it was installed, it was evidently the work of an amateur, an inexperienced or indifferent organ mechanic.

After much work and perseverance we got the organ in presentable and usable condition. In 1945 we changed the location of the console and finally secured the regular maintenance of the organ, thereby further preserving and improving an otherwise sweet toned instrument.

In 1960, due to a Redevelopment Project in which twenty-seven blocks of the Western Addition of the city was cleared of its old homes and residences, the Bethel African Methodist Episcopal Church was also razed. What became of the old organ I do not know.

Recently, I accidently came across the new church they have since built further out in the Western Addition, on Turk Street near Masonic Avenue. I do not know if they have a pipe organ. Reading the inscription on the cornerstone, I observed the following: Founded 1852 — Rebuilt 1960.

MARK HOPKINS RESIDENCE

On the crest of Nob Hill, on the southeast corner of California and Mason Streets, where now stands the Mark Hopkins Hotel, there once stood, before the fire, an impressive mansion. This was the former home of one of the founders of the Central and Union Pacific, later the Southern Pacific Railroad Company. It was built of a dark, hewn stone, on the type of an old feudal castle, with towers and turrets and a slate roof. A heavy retaining wall surrounded it. There was a massive gate at the lower wall on Pine Street, which is still there, and a broad marble stairway led up to the main entrance from California Street.

In this mansion there was a pipe organ, built by Odell of New York. It was on one of the upper floors, as I recall it, on a landing of the main stairway.

Sometime previous to 1901, or thereabouts, the house was no longer used as a home but was converted to a museum of art and a music center, and was called the Mark Hopkins Institute of Art.

My father had been summoned by Sir Henry Heyman who, I believe was in some way connected with the management of institution, to tune and adjust the organ. I accompanied him to assist in the work.

It was a small one manual 10 stop tracker organ. One feature of the organ that impressed me, and one that my father strongly stressed, was that the front pipes were made of pure English tin. One visit to this place was all that was my good fortune to enjoy.

The earthquake and fire that came along in 1906 destroyed this impressive pile. All that remains of it today are the stout retaining walls on Mason and Pine Streets, still kept for their present use. Where once stood this glorious mansion, a relic of the past, now rears its towering height of fifteen stories, the beautiful Mark Hopkins Hotel, one time the crowning point of Nob Hill and one of the show places of San Francisco.

In 1961 the Fairmont Tower of twenty-five stories, an annex to the famous Fairmont Hotel, was completed, which now outranks the Mark Hopkins as the highest point of observation from Nob Hill.

LELAND STANFORD RESIDENCE

On the southwest corner of Powell and California Streets stood another of the famous mansions that adorned Nob Hill in the early days of San Francisco, the home of Leland Stanford, co-builder with Mark Hopkins, the Crockers and others of the Central Pacific Railroad. Leland Stanford was also, at one time, Governor of the State of California, and later founder of the institution of learning that bears his name, Stanford University, at Palo Alto, California.

In their beautiful mansion on Nob Hill the Stanfords had installed an orchestrion in their large reception room. It was an instrument imported from Switzerland.

My father, who was a specialist in this line, had provided the Stanfords with new cylinders, upon which the music for this orchestrion was produced, and was also called at frequent occasions to manipulate the instrument.

On this particular visit he was called to make some adjustments. As a treat he took me along on this visit. I do not recall whether we entered through the main entrance or through the servants' entrance; neither do I recall, strange to say, much of the interior of the mansion except that it was impressive. Possibly, I was so overawed at being in the place that I dared not look around or be too inquisitive. However, I do remember being told that a large party had been given in the house the evening before, and that something had gone wrong with the orchestrion, which was the reason for my father's visit there the next day. That the party was an elaborate and extraordinary affair, I knew from the statement of my uncle, Mr. Ernest Ludwig, of the firm of Wheeler and Ludwig, caterers who enjoyed the patronage of the elite on Nob Hill at this period.

While my father was at work on the orchestrion, Mrs. Stanford entered the room and, after discussing some matters with him, she inquired if I was his son. I am most certain my father told her I was one of his ten children. I was about fourteen years old at that time. Mrs. Stanford was evidently much interested, as she had been, shortly before, bereaved by the death of her only son, a young lad of eighteen years, over whose passing she was quite inconsolable. After a few minutes conversation Mrs. Stanford left the room, soon to return with a plate of delicious cake and pastry for me to eat. Not many years later, on February 28, 1905, she passed away while on a trip to Honolulu.

To more readily depict this fine, noble woman, I am quoting part of an article by Susan Smith of the San Francisco Examiner, March 25, 1949:

"Mrs. Frances Stent, reminiscing on old times, tells most interesting stories of the Leland Stanfords. The Stanfords were married more than twelve years before their son, Leland, was born. When he was eighteen years of age they took him to Europe, where he died in Rome of typhoid. On their return to America, the heartbroken parents built Stanford University in his memory. So crushed was his mother by his loss that she wore mourning the rest of her life.

"After the Senator's death their house at California and Powell Streets was practically closed and Mrs. Stanford estalished an office on the garden floor where she transacted all of her business.

"On the site of this house now rises Stanford Court, opposite the Fairmont Hotel.

"These were the days long before telephones, so Western Union boys were in and out all day. Mrs. Stanford's kindness to children was well known, but her heart went out especially to boys, who reminded her of her son. So, every Christmas Day, from noon to five p.m., messenger boys were entertained for Christmas dinner. They arrived in groups at the main entrance and departed by way of carriage entrance, where the old coachman gave each boy a two-pound box of Haas candy. After the messenger boys had been treated royally, boys from the orphanage arrived."

MASONIC TEMPLE

At one of San Francisco's busiest intersections — Market, Post and Montgomery, was located the Masonic Temple, built in 1860. The ground floor was occupied by stores. The main entrance to the lodge halls upstairs was on the Post Street side.

I remember accompanying my father on a visit he made there to service their organ. This was a Mayer two manual and Pedal organ, built in 1867, and located on a little loft in one of the lodge rooms. It was the first time I had entered a Masonic Lodge Hall. I remember the dimly lighted place and the thick, stale odor of cigar smoke, undoubtedly a leftover from the meeting of the evening before.

I especially remember tuning the clarinet stop. It is to be noted here that Mr. Mayer made the reed stops of his organs as well as the flute stops.

The earthquake and fire of 1906 destroyed the imposing building. According to records I have from my father, there were two pipe organs in this Masonic Temple, a one manual and a two manual Mayer pipe organ. I recall working only on the two manual organ.

After the fire the Masons acquired new property at the corner of Van Ness Avenue and Oak Streets. An imposing steel frame, stone structure was erected, consisting of several stories with many lodge rooms, offices, assembly halls, spacious corridors and stairways, and all the necessary appurtenances for a building of this type. Stores are on the ground floor. The building is of a very imposing design, made of white Caen stone. Especially impressive is the rich carving of the main entrance, and the heroic figure in marble of King Solomon, poised on the corner of the building, supported on a carved bracket and surmounted by a beautifully carved canopy. The lodge rooms, of which there are seven, differ in their design and decoration. The most outstanding is the Commandery Hall on one of the upper floors. The ceiling of this lodge room finishes off with the huge dome that is atop the building. The general design of this room consists of four equal rectangular walls containing arches, on which are superimposed the large dome referred to above. A huge double cross design chandelier, studded with electric lights, is suspended from the ceiling. A heavy carpet covers the floor and some beautiful frescoes adorn the walls. Undoubtedly, due to the concavity of the dome, the acoustics of this hall were over rich, so in later years a transparent, almost flat ceiling was placed in the dome immediately above the arches to correct this and eliminate the excessive echo.

In 1952 a rather severe fire occurred in one of the stores on the ground floor, and it appears that in repairing the damage other improvements and alterations were made to the building, among which the huge dome over the Commandery Hall was removed.

It may be a surprise to know that in October 1913, when the new Temple was completed, we had installed six two manual and Pedal pipe organs in this building at one time. They were all tubular pneumatic organs, built by the Austin Organ Company of Hartford, Connecticut, Opus 429-439-431-432 and 433. Mr. Fletcher Tilton was the agent. The smaller organs vary in size from four to six stops, some have attached consoles, others are detached, and all are placed on small balconies overlooking the lodge hall. The organ of Commandery Hall is the largest and consists of 23 stops, Opus 428. It has an imposing, classic front, harmonizing perfectly with the interior of the hall. The ensemble of this organ is most impressive. The tonal effects from its individual stops are delightful. Undoubtedly, its surroundings have also much to do with it but, nevertheless, this organ is one of the finest of the Austin organs in San Francisco.

The job of installing these six Austin organs at one time was no small matter. The building was in course of construction at the time, and there were no permanent stairways available, no elevators to be used. All the corridors were blocked with scaffolding. Plasterers working overhead, littered the floor below with grit and dirt. Several truck loads of organ material were unloaded and deposited on the ground floor in a hugh hall on the west end. Here all material was sorted and from here each case and heavy piece had to be carried by a crew of men up the flight of temporary stairs, cutting their way at times through obstructing scaffolding, to get to their respective floors to deposit their load.

These organs have held up remarkable well. Commandery Hall, in recent years, has also been used as the temporary church for the Eighth Church of Christ Scientist. We have been servicing these organs since their installation.

In making an improvement to the organ chamber of the Commandery Hall organ, we had a rather unusual experience. Directly over the organ in the Commandery Hall was a large airshaft. It seemed that all the heated air in the hall eventually found its way up this shaft. A constant draft was perceptible; also a lot of grit fell into the reeds. To remedy this situation, we advised that this opening or shaft be closed with panelling to conform to the semicircular arch directly above the organ, and a carpenter was engaged to do the work.

It had always been our assumption that the wall at the rear of the organ, although furred out from the concrete wall, was the outer or exterior wall of the building. In fastening his supports to this rear wall, the carpenter used large spikes to penetrate the furred out expanded metal lath and plaster. The forms had been nailed to the walls to fasten on the ceiling there. Scarcely had this been done, when a secretary from the office on the floor above came hurriedly to inform us that we were wrecking the walls in the hallway above. On investigation we found that the rear wall of the organ chamber was not the exterior wall of the building, as we had believed, but was only three inches thick and made a passageway between the organ and the outer wall of the building leading to the offices above. Each nail had penetrated the finished plaster of the wall of the passage way with devastating results.

Commandery Hall was also the scene of the funeral of the late Robert Fletcher Tilton, our friend, co-worker and Western Representative of the Austin Organ Company, of Hartford, Connecticut, to whom we were indebted for much of our organ activity in erecting the many Austin organs on the West Coast.

HOWARD STREET METHODIST EPISCOPAL CHURCH

Recollections of my first visit to this church seem very vague, yet I remember the church being on the south side of Howard Street, between Second and Third Streets. (My father's notes designate it as being between First and Second Streets.)

I accompanied my father on a visit he made to the church to keep an appointment he had with the organist who, I am quite certain, was Humphrey J. Stewart. No work was done on the organ at the time. It was simply an interview with the organist, and for this reason I also have no recollection of the details of the organ as to size, specification, etc. In my father's notes he refers to it as a large two manual tracker organ, builder unknown. It had a Gothic case with keyboards recessed, and a large 16 foot Open metal front.

This visit occurred quite a few years before the fire of 1906. I probably was attending school and it must have been on a Saturday, or other free day, when I at times assisted my father. The earthquake and fire of 1906 destroyed this church and organ.

In 1912 the congregation built a new church, this time on the southwest corner of Howard and Harriet Streets. Mr. Fletcher Tilton, agent of the Austin Organ Company, sold them a two manual, and Pedal Austin pneumatic action organ with detached console, which we installed, Opus 339.

This organ was provided with a set of the ordinary organ tubular chimes, probably the first set I had heard or seen.

Much ado was made about them by the agent of the company, who made great promises that they would be heard several blocks distant. The pastor, Rev. Swan Wilkinson, equally hopeful and expectant, had leaflets printed announcing the dedication of the church as "The Church of the Chimes." We placed the chimes outside up in the belfry of the tower, as requested, and they were played from the Great manual of the organ. On trying them for the first time, we were very much disappointed. Inside of the church they could not be heard at all, and outside, due to the din and noise of the traffic on the street below, they could just about be heard. The installation of the chimes, therefore, in this location was a failure. We soon thereafter placed them inside of the swell box of the organ, where they originally should have been placed and where they gave satisfactory service for many years.

There was considerable case work with ornamental pipes in this organ, all dummy display pipes. A Mr. Head from Los Angeles, formerly employed by the Murray M. Harris Company, an expert in the painting and decorating of display pipes, was specially engaged to decorate these pipes and made an excellent job of it. The organ functioned satisfactorily for many years.

The decline of population in this district south of Market Street after the fire, however, which was likewise experienced by other congregations, seriously affected the financial status of the Howard Street M.E. Church. Its continued functioning seemed imperiled. To produce some revenue, the lower part of the building was then leased to the Good Will Industries, and eventually the church consolidated with the William Taylor or Temple M.E. Church venture.

Even prior to this arrangement we had noted a general decline in the upkeep of the property, the careless and untidy manner in which especially the boiler room in the basement of the church was kept, where the motor and blower of the organ were located. More than once we reprimanded those in charge for this careless and dangerous condition.

One morning during 1940 the church was destroyed by fire, which terminated the existence of the Howard Street Methodist Episcopal Church. We were not surprised.

ODD FELLOWS HALL

The original Odd Fellows Hall was located on the west side of Montgomery Street, between Sutter and Bush Streets and, from records I have, it contained two Mayer organs. One evidently was only a one manual organ, the other a two manual with ten stops. The latter was built in 1866 and the former in 1868.

In 1885 the Odd Fellows moved to their new location on the southwest corner of Seventh and Market Streets. This edifice was a well built red brick building of several stories, superimposed with a tower on the corner. My memory of it goes back to my school days, when I attended St. Boniface School on Golden Gate Avenue and Leavenworth Street. There was no more beautiful sight to see than this building illuminated at night, indirectly from the lights and glare of Market Street. Golden Gate Avenue, always in comparative darkness, contrasted with the well illuminated Market Street. This contrast would show off the Odd Fellows Building to advantage in a white, ethereal light, always beautiful and impressive to behold.

I remember visiting Odd Fellows Hall on several occasions with my father to tune and adjust some reed organs, but never did I see or work on a pipe organ there that I can recall. Whether the organs referred to above in the old building were moved to the new building on Seventh and Market Streets, I do not know. The fire and earthquake of 1906 destroyed this building and all of its contents.

It was rebuilt again in 1907 on the same site, and probably without a pipe organ. I have never been in the building since. The ethereal illumination at night is also no longer the same. The new building is constructed of buff stone instead of red brick, and undoubtedly the lighting on Golden Gate Avenue is now more bright and luminous than formerly, and taller buildings obstruct the view, making this beautiful sight of former days no longer possible.

FIRST BAPTIST CHURCH

From records I have seen, the first church erected by the Baptists in San Francisco was built in 1855 and was located on the north side of Washington Street, between Dupont and Stockton Streets, in the vicinity of Portsmouth Square. My father's notes mention that they had a two manual organ, builder unknown. A further interesting note states that in warm weather the keys of the manual would drop down to nothing.

In 1888 a more pretentious edifice was built further up town, on the north side of Eddy Street, between Leavenworth and Jones Street. I remember when attending school at St. Boniface on Golden Gate and Leavenworth Street, observing a church with a spire a block or two away, but at that time I had no reason or occasion to visit it. Likewise, my father has made no mention in his notes of any pipe organ being installed there, so I cannot say whether they had one or not. At any rate, whatever musical instrument they might have had in this church was destroyed in the conflagration of 1906.

After the fire, the First Baptist Church located on the northwest corner of Octavia, Waller and Market Streets. Here they erected a substantial, well constructed rectangular building. A few years after its completion, in 1911, the Austin Organ Company, through its local representative, Robert Fletcher Tilton, secured the contract to build a three manual and Pedal tubular pneumatic organ, Opus 367. It was our good fortune to install this instrument, as was the case with practically all the Austin organs sold in this territory. It proved to be a very successful installation.

The console was detached, the organist sitting with his back to the organ. The front design of the organ, with its oak case, two large towers and gold pipes, was unusually well balanced. Tonally, the organ pleased me very much. That it also impressed others I know from the remark made by one of America's foremost organ builders, Ernest M. Skinner, of Boston, who was in San Francisco and my guest at the time. He stated that it was the best voiced Austin organ he had ever heard.

The dedication of the organ was a gala event. With an appropriate little talk, the Acting Pastor, Rev. Burlingame, introduced the esteemed and venerable dean of American organists, Clarence Eddy, then residing in the Bay Area, as the recitalist for the dedicatory service. A packed edifice and an appreciative audience greeted Mr. Eddy, who on persistent demand, played many encores in addition to his prearranged program. The organ gave excellent service. H.K.H. Mitchell was its first regular organist, a very pleasant, estimable gentleman for whom it was a pleasure to work.

Later, other organists and also ministers followed. One of the prominent ministers was the Rev. West, who had the honor to officiate at the obsequies of the late Warren G. Harding, President of the United States, who met his final summons staying at the Palace Hotel, while visiting in San Francisco.

After thirty years of constant use the lead tubing in the organ began to crystalize and disintegrate. The time had come for a general overhauling. We advised the electrification of the organ, which would eliminate all lead tubing. As the church also had plans for changing the arrangement of the choir loft, the work of modernization of the organ was given to us, which we carried out very successfully.

The console was lowered and reversed, i.e., the organist now facing the organ and choir, and an entire new electric mechanism was installed. Also both swell expression shoes were made to operate electrically. Strange to say, however, although nothing was changed or altered in the voicing or pressure of the organ since the console had been reversed, the organ did not seem to have that same mellowness Ernest M. Skinner and I once commended it for. This phenomenon, I am sure, might be compared to what we refer to as an optical illusion, only in this case, it is an aural illusion.

The organ of the First Baptist Church remains, notwithstanding, a splendid instrument, and when under the magic touch of its capable organist, Professor Nicols, and with the spiritual leadership of the active and able pastor of the church, Rev. Julianel, it will sing divine praises for many years to come.

Since writing these lines several other ministers and organists have filled their respective posts.

PALACE HOTEL

One of the outstanding landmarks of San Francisco in the days before the fire was the old Palace Hotel, situated on the same site as the present Sheraton-Palace Hotel, at Market and New Montgomery Streets. It was an imposing structure of seven stories, with bay windows, and was built by Ralston. The main entrance and carriage driveway was on New Montgomery Street and led into a beautiful, large court, from which one obtained a view of the balconies of each succeeding floor up to the glass skylight of the roof.

In 1905, or thereabouts, it was decided to eliminate the carriage drive and convert the space to restaurant purposes. A decision was also made to install a pipe organ on one of the balconies nearby, and to offer the patrons of the restaurant and cafe on the ground floor excellent programs of chamber music, rendered by an orchestra of about six pieces in conjunction with the organ.

The organ was placed on the west end of the balcony on the second or third floor. It was a two manual Aeolian pipe organ of six or eight stops. I do not now recall whether the complete installation was made by my brother Leo, who was in charge of the work, or whether he just put the finishing touches to it. I remember working there several times with him and listening to the exquisite music at the noon hour, rendered by the musicians. I do not recall the name of the organist, however.

The console was provided with an automatic player, and it was here that I first observed the small orifices of the double tracker board of the Aeolian automatic player. The job was quite interesting to me. We usually entered the hotel by the rear driveway on Jessie Street, walked through the basement and took an elevator to the required floor. I was always captivated by the delicious aroma from the kitchen and from the freshly baked pastries in the bakery.

The fire and earthquake of 1906 destroyed this landmark of San Francisco. The pipe organ installed in the hotel was probably the forerunner of the future theatre organ, introducing the organ for other purposes than church use alone.

PENNY ARCADE

San Francisco was always known for its wealth, for the generosity of its people, for its gaiety, luxury and carefree abondon. Although gold was not picked up on the streets, as some of the argonauts were told to believe before they began to arrive by the thousands, gold did flow freely from the hands of the newly rich, from the successful merchants and traders, and from the carefree and reckless miners who came to the City for a bit of tinseled pleasure. No wonder San Francisco looked askance at the paper currency prevalent in the East, and with more disdain on the copper penny. Time, however, brings changes.

It was about in 1904 that some business men, the name of one I remember as a Mr. D. Hallahan, with an eye on making money by other means than the almighty silver dollar, or the royal five, ten and twenty dollar gold pieces, but by enticing the lowly penny, or copper, then practically unknown or in little use in San Francisco, from the pockets of their patrons. They opened the Penny Arcade, or Fair, an amusement palace in a store on the south side of Market Street, east of Fourth Street. Customers could obtain copper pennies at the window in exchange for silver or nickel coins. All kinds of machines were provided in which the pennies could be spent. A penny in the slot would give one innumerable surprises and pleasures. There were illuminated, animated pictures, good and bad, boxing matches in action, ones correct weight, stenciled name plates, Edison phonograph records providing music, recitations, etc.

Since music is always an attraction to draw crowds and hold them interested, the owners conceived the idea of securing an automatic pipe organ which could deliver modern, up to date music. A Kimball pipe organ of about 6 stops was installed. I do not recall whether my father erected it, but we later serviced it regularly. It also had two manuals and could be played by hand if desired. I recall, however, that only the automatic player was operated by one of the attendants. I believe this was one of the first automatic players I heard perform on a pipe organ.

The assertion was made that this "Penny Arcade" establishment introduced the general use of the modest copper coin in San Francisco. A thriving business was done, with many other similar establishments opening later elsewhere.

The large department stores and other businesses and enterprises followed suit in the use of the penny, as did the newspapers, which is now a common medium of exchange in San Francisco, and throughout the country. I often recall the life and activity of this Penny Arcade, and how a flourishing business was developed on the lowly copper penny.

From available records I note that my father removed and packed this organ during February 1906, for storage. Apparently the building was to be razed and a new building erected, but the earthquake and fire of April 18, two months later, did a better job of razing buildings and their contents than was ever planned. This Kimball Organ was consumed in the conflagration.

THIRD CONGREGATIONAL CHURCH

A peculiar aspect of the great fire of 1906 was that the devastated areas were, for the most part, adjacent to each other, and the many fires that started simultaneously in the various sections of downtown San Francisco and the fire that originated in Hayes Valley finally merged and swept as one conflagration through the whole area, from the waterfront out to Van Ness Avenue, and from the North Beach sector to the railroad yards at Townsend Street in the southern end of the City. However, like a creeping and hissing serpent, a tongue or narrow prong of the fire forced its way into the Mission District and burned a large area extending south to Twentieth Street, and running between Howard Street on the east to about Church Street on the west.

In this area was located the Third Congregational Church, which was situated on the south side of Fifteenth Street, between Mission and Bartlett Streets. It was a frame building, with church auditorium above and Sunday School rooms below.

The church had a two manual and Pedal Bergstrom tracker action organ of about 10 stops, which was installed in 1891.

We had called here monthly to service the organ. I especially remember the sexton, a sort of religious crank, always argumentative, whom we tried to avoid, and who was presumed to be an expriest.

I believe a Miss Hutchinson was organist of the church. She lived in a large old mansion at the southwest corner of Fifteenth and Howard Streets. I had to call there occasionally to get the key for the church and the organ. I remember it was a large stately home surrounded by a beautiful garden.

Another party I recall was one of the trustees of the church, undoubtedly the treasurer, a Mr. Ede, on whom I called to collect the quarterly fee for the maintenance of the organ. He also lived in a beautiful home with an exquisite garden around it. I do not remember its exact location, but believe it was on Seventeenth or Eighteenth Street, near the James D. Phelan mansion on Seventeenth and Valencia Streets. Mr. Ede was a friendly, exceedingly gracious gentleman. It was a pleasure to collect from him, the money was always forthcoming, and he was always most appreciative of our work.

I recall my father telling how my brother Leo one day, while he was tuning the organ with my father, lost his footing and fell into the long trackers of the swell action, causing considerable damage.

Rev. William Rader was pastor at the time of the fire in 1906. One of San Francisco's famous military organizations was founded at this church, I have been informed, the California Grays, always popular in parades and pageants, and receiving much acclaim for their natty uniforms and the precision and skill demonstrated in military drills.

It might be mentioned here that of the four Congregational Churches once organized here in San Francisco, only the First Congregational Church on Post and Mason Streets remains. The Second, or Plymouth Congregational Church was located on Post Street, near Buchanan, and was later occupied by the Japanese. The Third Congregational Church is the one here referred to. The Fourth Congregational Church was located on Green Street, near Stockton, and was known as the Green Street Congregational Church. After the fire this church reorganized and built a temporary church at the same site. Eventually, they bought other property and erected a new brick edifice at the southeast corner of Cumberland and Dolores Streets.

It was a very pleasing structure, located opposite Mission Park. A two manual and Pedal Wicks organ was procured for it. Apparently, the congregation did not prosper at this location either, and a consolidation was effected with the Grace United Church on 21st and Capp Streets. The property and building, with the organ and all the furnishings, were later sold to the Norwegian Lutheran Church, which recently has changed its name to Ascension Lutheran Church, now the owners and apparently a very live and prosperous congregation.

ST. JOHN THE EVANGELIST EPISCOPAL CHURCH

Another church, located in the Mission District and consumed in the great fire, was St. John the Evangelist Church, located on the southwest corner of Julian and Fifteenth Streets. It was a low structure built of buff brick, trimmed with terra cotta and designed on the old Norman style, similar to the Church of the Advent that stood on Eleventh Street, near Market.

According to notes left by my father, St. John's Episcopal Church had a two manual tracker Bergstrom organ with console attached. It was hand pumped and was later rebuilt by Thomas Whalley of Berkeley. I was never in this church and I do not recall whether my father ever worked on their organ or not.

After the fire, the church was rebuilt on the same site. This time, however, a wooden structure was erected, on the Gothic plan, considerably loftier than the old church. I remember the the contractor on the job very well, not that I was intimately acquainted with him, but because of his striking resemblance, in my opinion, to the portrait and figure of King Henry the VIII of England. With his accent and the English atmosphere of the Episcopal Church about him, the likeness seemed to me to be accentuated.

The rector of St. John Evangelist Church at the time was a Rev. Benson. A contract for a new organ for the church was awarded to the Austin Organ Company of Hartford, Connecticut, Opus 270, and it was our good fortune, in 1910, to install it.

The organ consisted of 12 stops, had a detached console, and was played pneumatically. What I especially remember of this installation was placing the blower in its location behind the organ, in a pit below the floor. It was a large, slow speed "Orgoblo" of considerable weight. In fact, we misjudged its weight, as we learned later. The carpenters and plasterers had previously erected a scaffolding over this pit for their own use, and we arranged to use it and thus avoid the necessity of building a new scaffolding on which to fasten our block and tackle in placing the blower. After adding some supporting braces to this scaffolding, we moved the blower into position over the pit, resting it temporarily on some planks and, with the rigging all attached and the men at the ropes, we expected to gradually lower the blower into its place. However, when we removed the two heavy planks on which we had temporarily rested it, and the full weight was thrown on the scaffolding, there was a sudden lurch, a crashing of timber, and the blower landed precipitately at the bottom of the pit, about six feet below — none the worse for its sudden drop which, fortunately, was somewhat impeded by the crumbling timbers which had given way under the excessive load.

In making deadening walls for this blower chamber, we, for the first time, used mineral wool, stuffing it between the studs and the two surfaces of the walls, to good advantage. Considering the size of the blower and its close proximity to the organ, this installation was unusually satisfactory. Mr. Edgar Rheinhold was organist at the church at the time of the installation and dedication of the organ.

St. John the Evangelist Church was frequently referred to as the parish church of the late Honorable James Rolph, for many years the popular Mayor of San Francisco and later Governor of California.

We serviced this organ for many years until the depression and hard times made it necessary for the church to curtail even this necessary outlay for maintenance.

In later, more prosperous times, we again assumed the regular maintenance of the organ. In 1953 due to the deterioration of the lead tubing, especially under the console; we were authorized to electrify the organ, which was done. At about this time a set of chimes were added to the organ, a gift to the church from its loyal and faithful organist, Phoebe Cole, a devoted member of her church and one whose friendship we have cherished.

NOTRE DAME CONVENT

Among the early pipe organs manufactured by Joseph Mayer was one of unusual construction, built in 1876 for the Notre Dame Convent, located opposite the picturesque and famous landmark in San Francisco, the old Mission Dolores at Sixteenth and Dolores Streets.

The convent was a large and imposing structure on the east side of Dolores Street. I believe it was a three-story building originally, or two-story with mansard roof and dormer windows. In my early youth while still attending school, I remember my elder brother Frank, who somehow had not followed the organ profession but who, on this particular occasion had to assist my father, probably by pumping the organ for him while he was tuning, related how a kindly old nun, who usually answered the doorbell, befriended him by giving him a large delicious apple to eat. As I became old enough, the job of pumper was turned over to me, and I remember on many occasions my father tuned this organ.

The organ was located on the gallery of the chapel. It was a one manual, tracker action Mayer organ of about 16 stops. The ceiling of the gallery being somewhat low, no more than about ten feet high, the organ had to be specially arranged to fit into this low space. The bellows was, therefore, placed outside of the organ against the rear wall on the gallery. The chest of the organ was placed practically on the gallery floor, and the large 8' diapason pipes, which were used as the display pipes in this organ, extended below the gallery railing. The Pedal pipes were on both sides of the organ and could be played in the usual manner from the Pedal keys or from the manual keys, if preferred. This was arranged by a specially designed roller board. The console being attached, the organist looked over the central part of the organ, toward the altar, which was made as low as possible. The plan of this organ was a duplicate, in general, of the one adopted by Mr. Mayer in the organ he built for the Notre Dame des Victoires Church on Bush Street. The case was quite artistic, with graceful, curved mouldings, all made in black walnut. Tonally the organ sounded pleasing, being voiced on the light pressure of 2½ inches.

Like many of the Mayer pipes, however, they were not too sturdily made and, in time, from many years of tuning with a tuning cone, the pipes of the Piccolo and Octave 4 sets became badly damaged. My father induced the Mother Superior, Mother Julia, to have new pipes installed, and I remember after they arrived from the East and we had placed them in the organ, what a decided contrast there was between them and the pipes made by Mr. Mayer. The cost of installing these new pipes was $50.00.

It was in 1901, or thereabouts, that I began making the rounds at the end of the month to collect the bills due my dad, and I was getting to be quite proficient at this work, at least so I thought. On calling at the convent to collect the aforesaid bill of $50.00, I asked for Mother Julia and was directed to one of the large parlors, after presenting my bill to the sister who had opened the door.

After waiting some time, Mother Julia appeared and, hearing the jingle of money in her hand, I knew that she was going to pay the bill. She was well pleased with the new pipes and graciously handed me the coins. I do not recall the denominations. Most certainly there were some gold coins, but I definitely do remember receiving a quantity of large silver dollars, also. Paper money was not looked upon favorably at that time in California.

I was delighted to receive such a large cash sum, thinking how pleased my father would be when I turned in my cash at the end of the day and proving thereby my efficiency as a good collector. I counted the money and let the coins drop into my pants pocket. Thanking the sister very kindly for her prompt payment, I gave her a receipt and started to leave, when suddenly the lining of my pants pocket, evidently not accustomed to such a heavy strain, gave way and ripped and the fifty dollars rolled down my pants leg and scattered all over the polished floor. This was indeed one of my most embarrassing moments. The good Mother Superior chided me and told me I should be more careful in handling such a large sum of money. My estimation of my ability as a collector dropped very low at that moment. On my hands and knees I gathered up the rolling coins, counted them again and hurriedly took my departure, a rather subdued and chastened collector.

Pumping the organ was always one of the necessary evils connected with having a pipe organ. In churches it was usually an easy matter to procure an organ pumper, although this tedious job was often shirked, especially by the younger generation. In a convent, where no masculine help is available, and the pumping, a man's job at best, had to be done by one of the nuns, it was quite a problem. So it was no wonder that Mother Superior consulted with my father to find some way of pumping the organ mechanically.

I do not know whether it was the Mother Superior or my father who suggested that a Mr. Hicks, a builder of gas engines, be engaged to attach a gas engine to a centrifugal blower to pump the organ. I am inclined to believe it was Mother Superior's suggestion as Mr. Hicks was engaged at the time in applying a gas engine to a water pump on the convent property.

At any rate, in 1900, a gas engine and a Sturdivant blower were rigged up in the basement and the air pipe was led up and attached to the bellows in the organ. After much coaxing, some sputtering and backfiring, with a strong arm pulling the flywheel, and the magic touch of the manufacturer operating the spark and the gas valve, the engine would finally get off to a good start, puffing and snorting so loudly that it could be heard all over the neighborhood. As the starting of the engine was so difficult and uncertain even for the one who built it, I wondered how the sisters, once alone, without the aid and advice of such experienced experts, would ever manage to operate it. And so it was, that although the engine adequately supplied the air for the organ after it got started, the big problem always remained, how to get it going. The gas engine blowing apparatus was, therefore, not a success.

The Sturdivant blower was then placed in the attic and an electric motor was provided to operate it and gave good results thereafter.

Shortly afterward the earthquake and fire of 1906 came along and destroyed the convent building. Fortunately, the venerable old adobe Mission Dolores, founded in 1773, standing on the opposite side of the street, escaped all damage. The fire did not cross the street at this location. The adjoining lofty brick structure of the Mission Dolores Church was, however, badly damaged by the earthquake, with gaping fissures through its Gothic arches and walls and had to be razed.

Notre Dame Convent was rebuilt on the same site, with possibly a story less in height. In later years we installed a large two manual Vocallion in the chapel, and subsequently added a blower to it. This reed organ had previously been in the new Mission Dolores Church, and prior to that time had been in the Swedish Lutheran Church on Fifteenth and Dolores Streets.

In 1941, the Notre Dame Sisters secured a new, modern two manual and Pedal Skinner electric pneumatic organ, a worthy successor to the pioneer organ first installed by Joseph Mayer.

ST. ROSE'S CHURCH

St. Rose's Church was one of the churches established in the early days of San Francisco. It was located on Brannan Street, between Fourth and Fifth Streets, in the South of Market District near the railroad yards and depot, and was almost surrounded by lumber yards and planing mills.

My memory of this church is associated with the disastrous fires and conflagrations that frequently occurred in this neighborhood in my early boyhood days. In fact, the first time I saw St. Rose's Church it was a burnt out shell, having fallen prey to one of those big fires which we boys went down to see after school hours. This was about 1896 or 1898.

My first recollection of actually working in the newly rebuilt church was when my father and my brother Leo removed the old E.G. Hook organ from St. Ignatius Church on Hayes Street and Van Ness Avenue, and erected it in St. Rose's Church. Rev. Terence Nugent was pastor at the time. St. Ignatius Church was making ready for the large 4 manual Farrand and Votey organ, a gift of the Andrew Welch Family.

This was the third time the old E.G. Hook organ Opus 453 of 1868, was moved and erected in a San Francisco Church. The first installation was in St. Ignatius Church when that church was located on Market Street where the Emporium now stands. It was probably originally erected by a representative of the firm from Boston, or by their agents in San Francisco, Shellard and McGrath. When the Jesuits moved to their new church and college on Hayes and Van Ness Avenue, my father removed the organ from the old St. Ignatius Church and re-erected it in the new church. He also made some additions to the organ at that time. In 1897 or 1898, he moved the organ to St. Rose's Church and installed it there.

This organ was a large three manual tracker action, with attached console. Evidently in its former locations in St. Ignatius Church, there had been difficulty in getting access to repair broken trackers or stripped leather nuts on the roller boards of the Pedal action, which were placed on the floor under a huge bellows. For better accessibility for future repair work and evidently to give the organ, which was rather broad and low, a more lofty appearance in this high Gothic Church, the organ ground frame was placed on blocks or stilts about 10" x 10" and raised about a foot from the floor. The front of the case, if I am not mistaken, was also altered from the Romanesque to the Gothic to conform to the Gothic architecture of the church.

The pitch of the organ was also lowered by my father, as I remember it was the first time I had seen sliding tuners applied to pipes in an organ. They were not made of metal or tin, however, as is customary now, depending on the resilience of the metal for the tuners to cling to the pipes, but were made of rather stiff fiber paper, rolled and glued together, with just sufficient friction to hold and yet loose enough to adjust for tuning. I know that later on in tuning this organ these proved to be unsatisfactory. With the changes in temperature, some would loosen and drop, putting the pipes horribly out of tune. The pitch was the so-called high pitch then, possibly a little higher than our 440-A today. My father brought it down to low or International pitch, our 435 today.

For some reason or another, the architecture of this church never appealed to me. The building seemed too short and broad for its height; its columns seemed so frail and out of proportion; the gallery on which the organ was placed vibrated noticeably and gave me a feeling of insecurity.

What happened to the church the morning of the earthquake in 1906, I do not know. If it were shaken down the evidence was obliterated by the fire that destroyed the entire building. After the holocaust of 1906, the church was again rebuilt, retaining the outer brick walls.

The rebuilt church never had a pipe organ installed. My father tuned a reed organ there in 1914.

In common with the other churches in the South of Market District after the fire, it had hard sledding on account of the lack of population to support it. The parishioners of former days had now settled in new districts. Factories and industrial and commercial enterprises had moved in and taken their places.

With this situation to face, it was deemed expedient, in time, to disband the parish and combine it with St. Patrick's parish. The edifice was cleared of its furnishings and stood idle for a long time. Then for a while it was used as an atelier by a scenery artist and a storage place for a local theatrical concern.

Finally, in 1940, it was decided to tear down the old gaunt brick pile. Newspaper clippings at the time showed pictures of an old console in the debris, purporting it to be from the pipe organ erected there. This, however, was erroneous as there had never been a pipe organ installed in the rebuilt church after the fire of 1906. As stated, after the edifice was no longer used for church purposes, it was used as a storehouse by a theatrical company which was having its scenery painting done there at the time, and they had evidently stored an old console and some organ parts there for possible use some day — a day that never came.

ST. PETER'S EPISCOPAL CHURCH

My first association with St. Peter's Episcopal Church was in 1911 in connection with the installation of an Austin pipe organ, which they had purchased for their new temporary church, built to take the place of the one that had been destroyed in the great fire of 1906, which was formerly located at Stockton and Filbert Street. Rev. W.M. Bonns was Rector and Miss Lila Maxwell organist.

This temporary church was erected on Jones Street, near Lombard Street. I do not recall my father mentioning that they had a pipe organ in the old original church prior to the fire, but from an old photograph I have seen, and the record received from Mr. Chas. B. Andrews, it was one built by his father in 1891.

In 1910, Mr. Fletcher Tilton, agent for the Austin Company, signed a contract with the church for a two manual and pedal tubular pneumatic organ of 12 stops, to be installed in the temporary church. It was our good fortune to erect this organ, Opus 294. My brother Leo, at that time associated with us, assisted in the installation. A Rev. Malone was the rector at the time. He was an Irishman, and as is common with his countrymen, quite witty.

On one occasion, while we were installing the organ, he came in company with Mr. Tilton to see the job. Mr. Tilton invited him to take a look at the interior of the Universal air chest, a patented feature of the Austin organ. There were no permanent lights in this organ. Rev. Malone was in the vanguard and, followed by Mr. Tilton, they passed through the vestibule doors into the air chamber, preparatory to lighting a match. Amidship of the air chest is a heavy iron rod placed to strengthen the chest when the pressure is on. In this instance, it was located about five feet six inches from the floor, just in line for Rev. Malone to strike his nose violently on the protruding rod as he entered. A severe laceration was left on his features for some time. Mr. Tilton was most apologetic and tried to assuage Rev. Malone's discomfort, but the witty clergyman replied: "I should have known better and kept away from the 'bar.' "

We had an unusual experience with this organ shortly after it was installed. To get a quiet motor installation, the blowing plant was placed in a concrete pit especially built for it outside of the church. The pit walls were about eight inches thick. During the rainy season following the installation, on one of our monthly visits, on going to oil the blowing apparatus we were surprised to find about a foot of water in the pit. Seepage from the hill alongside had penetrated the porous concrete. In the organ chamber we saw the effects of the moisture on all metal parts, but we marveled at the immunity of the action to the effects of this dampness, as there was not a single note sticking. Possibly no other type of organ than an Austin could have stood such a test. Miss Maxwell was organist of the church at the time.

In 1913, when the First Congregational Church on Post and Mason Streets built their present permanent church, St. Peter's Episcopal Church also decided to build a new and permanent building. This time they located in the rapidly growing Richmond District, on 29th Avenue and Clement Street. The material of the old Congregational Church was utilized in their new church to good advantage, and a beautiful, small but substantially built edifice was the result. Rev. C.L. Miel was the rector of this new church. We removed the organ from the temporary church in 1914 and erected it in the new edifice. The case of the organ was raised to give it more height.

Rev. John Alfred Collins succeeded Rev. Miel and has been rector of the church for many years now, and would be entitled to the sobriquet "The Marrying Parson", for in the year 1942 St. Peter's Episcopal Church had the record for the greatest number of marriage ceremonies and weddings of any Protestant Church in San Francisco. In accord with this distinction, it seemed natural that a set of chimes was an absolute necessity for an organ that was used so frequently to play the wedding march.

Deeply interested in her parish church, Miss Phoebe Cole, organist at the church at the time and for a number of years later, generously donated a fine set of Deagan chimes, which our firm installed.

Another peculiar experience we had with this organ was a severe vibration that would develop at times in the blower. It was one of the old type Orgoblos of rather hugh size, with three or four fans running at slow speed. It was a three point bearing affair, two bearings on the motor, then a coupling to the blower shaft with one bearing at the outer end of the blower. The motor was practically surrounded by the housing of the blower, common to the old type blower. The motor was placed on a cast iron swivel base for adjustment. Originally, it worked well and even smoothly, without undue vibration. However, later, especially in the new church, a heavy vibration developed which shook the motor violently. We naturally assumed that the motor and blower shaft were out of alignment and eased up the motor cradle to let it adjust itself. The vibration continued, so we assumed the blower shaft was sprung. As a temporary relief, we fastened the motor with some 2 x 4 lumber, wedging it between the housing and motor base frame.

Finally, due to the constant annoyance, we recommended the purchase of a new type modern blower, simple and accessible in construction. The depression came along and a new blower was out of the question. Strange to say, with this crude, temporary expedient, the motor seemed to find its place, the vibration ceased, and it has functioned satisfactorily ever since — albeit with the temporary and unprofessional appearance of the expedient applied to remedy the evil.

After many years of service Rev. John Alfred Collins retired. New rectors and organists followed.

After fifty-one years the organ, with its tubular pneumatic action, functions perfectly without having undergone any drastic rejuvenation.

Indeed, a credit to the reliability of an Austin Organ.

FIRST PRESBYTERIAN CHURCH

The first church of this congregation was located in the downtown district of San Francisco, on Dupont Street near Clay. It was built in 1849. In later years, they built a rather imposing Gothic frame edifice, with a tall spire, on the southeast corner of Sacramento Street and Van Ness Avenue.

I remember seeing this church, but as far as I can recall I never entered the building and, therefore, have no information on the organ except what I have received from my father and others.

It was my father's belief that the organ installed in this church was the original Boston Music Hall organ. Whether it had previously been in the original church on Powell Street, I do not know. Evidently it was a three manual and Pedal tracker, possibly an Appleton organ.

After this organ was removed from the Boston Music Hall, sometime prior to 1863, and shipped to San Francisco, it was replaced by the famous Walker organ of Ludwigsburg, Germany. This latter organ, in recent years, came into the possession of Ernest M. Skinner for a time, and was erected in Methuen Hall at Methuen, Massachusetts. The organ and property later became the property of Edward F. Searles.

The church on Sacramento Street, with its three manual tracker action organ, was destroyed by the fire of 1906. A Mr. George Pettinos was organist at the time.

A new, substantial steel frame, brick building has since been erected on the same site and soon after its completion a splendid four manual organ was secured from the Hutchings Organ Company of Boston, Massachusetts.

The selection of this organ was carefully made after a thorough investigation of some of the leading makes by the organist of the church, Dr. Otto Fleisner, who made a special trip to the East for this purpose.

The organ, at present, is actually a three manual, with the solo or echo on the fourth manual yet to be installed. The console is detached.

A unique feature of the console is that it has draw stop knobs arranged on either side of the manuals on jambs fulcrumed on the inner end. To put the console in playing condition, these stop jambs are opened like the covers of a book, and through a latch automatically lock themselves. To close the roll-top cover, the stop jambs are unlatched and closed, or brought together close to the manual keys before the roll-top cover can be lowered. Another feature of the organ is that the piston combination action is of the blind type, i.e., not moving the stop knobs on and off visibly. Small numerals indicating the number of the piston last pushed are registered on a small recorder board.

The organ is divided, with the swell and part of the pedal on one side and the great, choir and part of the pedal on the other side. The console was in the choir loft, originally on the right side between the two divisions of the organ. Some years ago we extended the cable for the console and placed it at a lower and more forward position to conform with a general plan and arrangement of having choir singers, console, altar and pulpit in a more closely assembled group.

The organ was originally installed by a Mr. Frank Bowen, who came from Boston for the purpose. We serviced the organ for many years and we consider it one of the fine organs of San Francisco.

Dr. Otto Fleisner, a native of Germany, served most efficiently and faithfully as organist of the church for many years. In 1958 he retired on a pension and was awarded the title of organist emeritus. Dr. Fleisner also rendered notable service at the School for the Blind at Berkeley, California, where he was instructor of music, specializing in the pipe organ, teaching the blind students the art of organ playing through the American Braille Notation System. Dr. Otto Fleisner passed away in 1944 at the ripe age of 85, himself practically blind, beloved and mourned by many.

He was succeeded by Joel Anderson and, in turn, by Walter B. Kennedy.

Reverend John Hayes Creighton was pastor of this church for 23 years.

ST. LUKE'S EPISCOPAL CHURCH

St. Luke's Episcopal Church is located on the southeast corner of Clay Street and Van Ness Avenue. The Parish was founded in 1868 and the first church was located on Pacific Avenue between Polk and Van Ness Avenue. The second church built was a frame structure. It had a George A. Andrews and Whalley organ, which was installed in 1882. It was a two manual tracker action, with attached keyboard and walnut case.

In 1900, a brick and stone church was erected and dedicated at the present site. I do not have any record of a pipe organ being installed in this church, but for good reasons presume the Andrews-Whalley organ, above referred to, from the old frame church, was moved into this building.

This structure, the brick and stone church, with all its contents was destroyed in the fire and earthquake of 1906.

Finally, in 1908, the present edifice, built of steel and concrete, with a limestone exterior of Tudor Gothic, was erected on the present site. On completion of this edifice in 1909, a new pipe organ was installed, an organ that undoubtedly has been the subject of more comment and discussion than any other organ in San Francisco. It was a three manual and Pedal Hope-Jones organ, electric pneumatic action, built at Elmira, New York.

Hope-Jones, a native of England and an organ builder of note at this time, due, undoubtedly, to the revolutionary ideas he introduced into the art of organ building, was idolized and hailed by many as the man of the hour, and condemned by others as the desecrator of the noble art of organ building.

St. Luke's organ was installed by David Marr, from the factory in New York.

The first thing that attracted the attention of organ people here was the preparatory work done for the reception of the organ — the building of the much talked of cement organ chambers. This was a new venture in organ construction, as heretofore all swell boxes were generally made of wood and by the organ builder at the factory as part of the organ. Here, however, it was built by a building contractor on the premises, as part of the building, before the organ arrived. This heavily constructed swell box was necessary, it was stated, on account of the high pressures to be used in the organ — a revolutionary introduction in organ building, especially in comparison with American built organs where, heretofore, the lighter pressures of three to six inches were commonly used. With the high pressures of six to twenty-five inches utilized in the Hope-Jones organ, pipes of unusual weight, scaling and voicing were necessary — certainly not comparable to the usual organ pipes ordinarily seen.

The specification of the organ was most unusual also, consisting of sonorous leathered-lip open Diapasons, tubby Tibias, exaggerated narrow-scaled strings, a unified Tuba unit on 16-8-4 on 25" pressure, of tremendous power, yet not over brilliant, an Orchestral Oboe 8', typically Oriental, a Clarinet 8' and Tromba 8' normal and of fine quality, and a Vox Humana 8' exceedingly nasal in character. It will be noted that the organ completely lacked the usual Diapason chorus, with mutation stops and Mixtures. No wonder this organ aroused so much interest and was so talked about at this time. Fortunately, the swell blinds that were installed, making the entire organ expressive, were made of laminated wood of about four inch thickness, and although worked mechanically, and that with surprising ease, produced a most wonderful diminuendo and fortissimo effect, making it possible, notwithstanding the exaggerated tonal qualities, to yet secure any desired gradation of tone.

To say that St. Luke's organ was not a good organ, or was musically unbalanced or unsatisfactory, would be debatable, depending on one's point of view. It was an unconventional organ, untraditional and decidedly revolutionary and contrary to the principle that every good organ must have the tones of mutation and Mixture pipes to be satisfactory. These essential tones, necessary in every good organ, are replaced here by those of the rich harmonic producing, keen string stops, the brilliant, powerful reeds, and the super octave couplers; also by the unification of certain 8' stops in various pitches. The proof of the pudding was the hearing of this organ. At the time of its installation it was lauded and applauded by all our prominent organists. It was the popular thing to do then.

Likewise, now that the pendulum has swung the other way, back to the old tradition of classical organ, with a lack of the fundamental 8' Diapason tone, with its abundant supply of mutation stops, Mixtures and super-brilliant 2' tone, St. Luke's organ was considered all wrong, unconventional and traditionally a misfit.

Mechanically the organ was as revolutionary as it was tonally. In the first place, the console was the so-called horseshoe or circular type, exposed, or without a roll-top or hinged cover. This, undoubtedly, was the forerunner of the conventional theater type console. It was supplied with stop keys or tongues, instead of the usual draw stop knobs for control of the registers. The suitable base device was certainly most unusual and extraordinary. The adjustable combination piston setter board in back of the console. All these features were new and had never before been seen in a pipe organ in San Francisco. The gang switch, or stop switch, engaging the copper ribbon buss bars, the small magnets used throughout the organ, the relay mechanism, all were novel.

It was not surprising, therefore, that soon after the organ was installed small maladjustments developed that needed correction. The materials used and the workmanship on the organ were of the highest order but, notwithstanding this, troubles developed which, I believe, were aggravated by lack of experience on the part of those who were given the maintenance of the organ.

Rev. Elie Morgan was rector of the church for many years.

As stated in the beginning of this article, St. Luke's Church was well built, in fact, too well built. A cross on the east end of the church, directly over the altar, was made of solid stone. An earthquake occurred one day and toppled this heavy stone cross from its mooring. Fortunately, it fell in the direction away from the church, onto the adjoining roof. It was then replaced by a lighter metal cross.

In 1912, the regular maintenance of the organ was entrusted to our care. Failing notes were the general complaint of the organist. We found the supply of current inadequate and increased the size of the leads from the generator, which was located in the basement. Buss bars and switches, we found, had been cleaned with some preparation, undoubtedly Brilliant shine, certainly with good intent but with bad results, for when it dried or evaporated it left a white sediment on the surface of the buss bars which caused the contacts to fail and notes to miss.

Wallace Sabin was organist at the church when the Hope-Jones organ was installed in 1908, and served for many years thereafter. In 1937 Uda Waldrop succeeded him as organist, and at that time desired that some alterations be made to the organ.

The Tromba 8' stop of the swell was softened or subdued somewhat. The Orchestral Oboe, which was a monstrosity and never did stay in tune, was replaced with a more conventional Orchestral Oboe. Mr. Waldrop, who had previously held the position of organist at the First Congregational Church, was very pleased with an Austin Vox Humana that was installed in the Echo organ there. Along with the alterations above mentioned, he also wanted a new Vox Humana, which was urgently needed. He wanted a duplicate of the one at the First Congregational Church. This we supplied, but on hearing it he was much disappointed, stating it was not satisfactory. We had this set exchanged for the usual type Austin Vox Humana on its own separate chest with individual tremolo. This is in use now and is very satisfactory.

An interesting character we came to know at the church was a Mr. Branchflower, the sexton. I believe he also held this position in the old church before the fire. He was exceedingly painstaking and meticulous in his work, in which he took great pride. He was succeeded by Gustave Louis Minch, a young German refugee.

Gustave Minch served St. Luke's for 27 years. During the Second World War he worked for the Government on the docks where he injured his foot. This left him permanently crippled. His faithful wife, Rosa, took over his work at the church, with his feeble assistance. He passed away on June 13, 1953. This devoted and faithful couple were always an inspiration to me.

Another faithful soul, part and parcel of St. Luke's is Mrs. Florence Stone, long time secretary and able assistant organist, when circumstances required her skill.

Brigadier General Noble was also a frequent visitor to the church and always shown great interest in the organ. Rev. Jennings was pastor for a number of years and we found him a most agreeable and pleasant gentleman to get along with.

In 1935, Harold Mueller, a former pupil of Wallace Sabin and an organist of high repute and ability, succeeded Uda Waldrop as organist at the church and filled that position for many years.

Rev. John C. Leffler, formerly of St. John's Episcopal Church at Ross, was rector of St. Luke's during this period.

During the years we had the maintenance of the organ in our care, the usual replacements had to be made, such as re-leathering the penumatics, replacing worn out contacts, etc. A major improvement undertaken was the installation of a new seven h.p. electric motor, changing from direct current to alternating current, with a convenient start and stop push button.

That St. Luke's organ is one of distinction would seem to

be proven not only by the varying and conflicting statements made and opinions expressed about it, but also by the fact that the name plate, which had a conspicuous place on the console, was stolen one day for reason unknown, probably as a souvenir of a genuine Hope-Jones organ, an instrument no longer being built. Fortunately, through a friend, John Swinford, also an organ expert, a new name plate, a duplicate of the original, formerly attached to the old St. Matthews Episcopal organ in San Mateo, was procured and applied to the console. However, this substitute plate has again disappeared.

An innovation we had introduced in this organ, and which we have since seen copied at several churches, was to make the music rack of glass plate to secure more vision of the singers opposite the organist.

During 1952, St. Luke's made a substantial addition to its edifice, mostly for social use. Possibly the next major improvement will be a new, modern organ.

Several years later, Rev. Carl Norman Tamblyn, formerly of St. Luke's Episcopal Church, Woodland, California, was made the new rector of St. Luke's. Harold Mueller then accepted the position of organist at Trinity Episcopal Church, San Francisco, and Robert Whitley, a prominent organist, succeeded Harold Mueller.

With professional luminaries always occupying the position of organist in this church, it became self evident that a larger, more modern and up-to-date, tonally designed and voiced organ would have to be obtained without delay. After due deliberation the choice for a new organ fell to the lot of the Aeolian Skinner Organ Company of Boston, Massachusetts. The old Hope-Jones organ that had served the church for fifty years was sold to the Carlmont Methodist Church at San Carlos, a suburb of San Francisco.

Our firm removed the old organ and have since erected it in the aforementioned church, where it again has a new lease on life.

During 1961, the new St. Luke's organ, a sixty-four stop, three manual organ arrived and was installed by my son, Lawrence L. Schoenstein, now the Western Representative of the Aeolian Skinner Organ Company. His son, Terrence Schoenstein, a fourth generation Schoenstein, assisted his father as also did Richard Harger, of Honolulu, Hawaii.

Needless to say, the organ is a gem of perfection as regards to its installation and appearance, and tonally meets all expectations of the classical type of organ now riding the wave of popular acclaim.

The new organ was dedicated in 1961. Organ recitals and sacred concerts are being held frequently and I am certain that under the able manipulation and direction of its gifted organist, Robert Whitley, the musical services of his church will be enhanced and the music loving citizens of San Francisco will be given an opportunity to hear and enjoy the latest acquisition of an excellent pipe organ, added to the list of organs already a credit to our city.

During 1963, Robert Whitley resigned as organist and was succeeded by Kenneth Mansfield, the present organist.

CHURCH OF THE ADVENT — EPISCOPAL

According to the records left by my father, the first Church of the Advent was located on the south side of Howard Street, opposite New Montgomery Street. It was founded in 1859. Reverend Gray was the rector. Other available notes place the location at Mission Street near Second Street.

The church had a two manual and Pedal tracker action organ, undoubtedly of some Eastern builder. The key desk was attached and it had a high Gothic case. An unusual feature of the manual keyboards was that their fronts were covered with black walnut and not ivory or celluloid, as is usually the case. Evidently, as the church wanted a more modern and better organ, the old organ was disposed of in 1882 and sold to some church in Victoria, British Columbia. My father dismantled the organ, packed it and had it shipped to its destination.

The church then procured a new Odell organ from New York, Opus 143, a two manual tracker action, 22 stops, with console attached. It was the first organ in San Francisco that had combination pistons between the keyboards. These worked mechanically. The stop slides of the chest which they operated worked pneumatically. It had a high Gothic case made of walnut.

The organ was first erected on the choir gallery, but was subsequently moved by my father and erected in the chancel near the altar. When the church later contemplated a new building farther out on the east side of Eleventh Street, between Market and Mission Streets, it was again moved by my father and stored until the new edifice was ready to have it installed.

I recall my father stating that at the old church on Howard Street Humphrey J. Stewart held his first position as organist on his arrival in San Francisco from England. While holding this position, Dr. Stewart composed an oratorio, which was given its first rendition in this church. The congregation was Anglican and followed the English High Church ritual.

The work of reinstalling the organ in the new church was not done by my father as he expected, to his chagrin, but by Wilhelm Bros., former employees of my father, who then applied a pneumatic action to it.

I have been in this church on Eleventh Street on one occasion, as I have a faint recollection of observing the wood screen that separated the chancel from the nave of the church. Its exterior was of unique design, made of buff terra cotta. The fire and earthquake of 1906 destroyed this church.

After the fire a new church was built on the south side of Fell Street, between Franklin and Gough Streets. A two manual tracker pneumatic organ was secured from Thomas Whalley of Berkeley.

As we have never worked on this organ, only visited it once, I am not in a position to comment on any special features of its design. I can only assume that, in common with all the Whalley organs, this organ also fulfills the traditional requirements of a typical church organ.

During 1955 the organ was remodeled and revoiced by John West, one of our employees, in collaboration with my son Lawrence, from the conventional to the Baroque type, reducing the wind pressure to two and one-half inches making some substitutions of scales and pipes.

NORWEGIAN LUTHERAN CHURCH
formerly called Scandinavian Church

One of the last pipe organs built by my father was for the Norwegian Lutheran Church, in 1899. Incidentally, I note from his records that he was fifty years old at this period.

At this time the church was located on Howard Street, between 12th and 13th Streets, at the point where the street makes a large bend. The building was a frame structure and the organ was placed on the loft at the front of the church opposite the altar.

Rev. O. Gronsberg was pastor at the time and John T. Lindtner was organist and choir leader.

The organ had two manuals and Pedal, an attached console, and an oak case with front pipes painted in a pale blue pastel shade. It was hand pumped and, I recall, it was my job to be pumper on several occasions when my father tuned the organ.

This organ was built by my father in his shop in the basement of the family home on 21st and Bryant Streets. He had then already practically abandoned the idea of manufacturing organs extensively, but at the strong solicitation and urging of his friend, Mr. John Lindtner, to undertake the work, he consented to build this organ. It was very satisfactory, well-toned instrument, but it was not in use many years when the fire and earthquake came along and destroyed it.

Mr. Lindtner was a most estimable, venerable old gentleman, tall, with bent shoulders, silvery white hair and a flowing beard, invariably with a fragrant cigar between his lips, walking always slow in gait, cane in hand and a violin box under his arm, a square stiff hat on his head, sometimes a flowing cape over his shoulders. He was a picture to behold and one would unconsciously stop and look back when passing him on the street. He gave my younger sister, Clara, violin lessons, and I remember calling for her at the church evenings after rehearsal, which was always a joint affair in which all his young pupils participated. He also conducted and successfully directed an amateur orchestra for the young men of St. Anthony's Church, which originally had been led, for a short period, by Louis Schoen. The group consisted for the most part of young men who did not know one note from another and had to begin, so to say, with their a, b, c to learn their music.

Mr. Lindtner, through a superabundance of patience, skill and endurance, and after laboriously writing out and arranging simple melodious parts for the different players and instruments, succeeded in producing a remarkable and gratifying ensemble that delighted the embryo musicians and encouraged them to strive for greater achievements. In later years, Louis Ritzau conducted the band and orchestra. He was followed by Professor Zech, at which point the orchestra reached its zenith of proficiency.

After the fire and earthquake, the Norwegian Lutheran Church was rebuilt on the same site. We installed a large reed organ in the new church, which gave service for several years, when it was transferred and installed in the Catholic Church in Martinez, California.

The congregation found it expedient in time to sell its property on Howard Street, undoubtedly due to the encroaching of industrial plants which were gradually surrounding the church and, in 1930, succeeded in buying the edifice and property of the Mission Congregational Church located on the very desirable corner of Cumberland and Dolores Streets, opposite beautiful Mission Park.

This well built and fully equipped church also contained a Wicks pipe organ, to which we later added a set of Deagan chimes.

UNION SQUARE BAPTIST CHURCH

As stated in a previous article, it seems that the churches of early San Francisco, at least the greater number of them, all clustered around Union Square, or within a block or two from the Square.

Union Square Baptist Church, according to data given to me by my father, was located on Post Street, between Powell and Mason Streets, and undoubtedly derived its name from its close proximity to Union Square. They later moved to their new location on the south side of Bush Street, between Polk and Larkin Streets.

It was a frame structure and they had there a one manual

tracker action organ. I do not know if this organ was already in use in the old church and, if so, who moved it to the new church. The keyboard was attached. The case of Corinthian design did not have the usual hardwood finish, but was painted. I do not recall the make of the organ, but assume it came from the Atlantic Seaboard. My father had the regular care of the instrument and serviced the organ from 1892 until it was destroyed in the fire of 1906.

Due to some faulty design there was considerable "robbing" or dropping of pitch, when full organ was used. Possibly the pallet, channels, or the air supply from the bellows were too small. At any rate, the task of getting this organ in tune must have been trying. I remember my father finally resorted to tuning the "temperament", or laying his bearings, on the Oboe reed stop, an unusual procedure.

DR. BAZET RESIDENCE

Before the fire and earthquake of 1906, I frequently went with my father to tune and adjust a large Orchestrelle reed organ in the residence of Dr. Louis Bazet, a physician in a three-story buff brick building on the north side of Geary Street, west of Larkin.

As I recall the layout, the two lower floors were arranged for offices, operating rooms, laboratory, etc. On the top floor were Dr. Bazet's rather luxurious living quarters. He was a native of France, a pleasing, middleaged man, rather dark complexioned, typically Gallic in his bearing and characteristics. His reputation as a physician and surgeon was of the highest in San Francisco. I recall his handyman about the place, who was also a Frenchman with a decided accent, always wearing a white apron. In fact, the whole atmosphere of the house, the decorations in his home, the fixtures, the bronze bust of Napoleon, his crest and the fleur-de-lis of France woven in the tapestry and upholstery, all gave proof of a profound respect and love for his native land. Beside the French cultural atmosphere, there was also present, at least to my keen sense of smell, the sickening and nauseating ether odor of the hospital or sickroom that seemed to permeate the whole house.

Dr. Bazet evidently enjoyed music as a diversion from his arduous duties as a physician and surgeon, and took pleasure in using the automatic player of his Orchestrelle. However, he objected to the constant foot work that was necessary to keep the organ supplied with air, so he asked my father if he could arranged some electric blowing device.

In 1900, or thereabouts, being still the era prior to the introduction of our present type centrifugal electric blower, my father devised and planned a three feeder pump with a regulator arrangement, belt driven from an electric motor. This was placed on the lower floor on a ledge over a passageway and proved to be very quiet at the organ and satisfactory in every way.

I recall, while placing the bellows in its designated place, which was somewhat confined, some cutting of wood had to be done. My father did not happen to have a wood saw with him. "Dematies", the handy man I referred to above, was watching the progress of our work and, seeing our urgent need for a saw, offered to get one at once. He soon returned, producing, however, the Doctor's saw, remarking jokingly, "If it cuts human bones, it will also cut your wood." Gruesome thoughts of operations on humans thereafter occupied my mind.

The fire and earthquake of 1906 destroyed this home and I have never since heard of the Doctor.

CHURCH OF THE NATIVITY
(Slavonian Church)

From my father's records, I note that in 1905 the Slavonian Church, located on the north side of Fell Street, between Franklin and Gough Streets, had a small pipe organ. My father mentioned it was a "Mayer Organ." I believe this statement could be erroneous, because it is not to be found on the list of organs built by Severin Mayer.

This church and organ were destroyed in the fire of 1906. I recall that after the fire and earthquake a large number of Slavonians had settled in the Potrero Hill section of the city, in the vicinity of 18th and Vermont Streets.

While they were congregating in this district, the desire to have their own parish church, if only a temporary one, took form again and Reverend Francis V. Turk, one of their countrymen and former pastor, took matters energetically in hand.

A site was secured in the neighborhood, where divine services were temporarily held. I recall my youngest brother, Erwin, served as altar boy for the priest. Later they returned to their former location where, in time, a new church with rectory was built.

The ground floor was used for meeting purposes, and the church proper was on the upper level. Father Turk was a young and active man and enjoyed the respect and confidence of his people. The church was beautifully adorned interiorly, with a splendid high altar and all necessary fixtures.

Since a new pipe organ was desirable and necessary, arrangements were made to secure a small one from Byron Mauzy, a piano dealer on Post Street, who, at the time, was also interesting himself in the manufacture and sale of pipe organs. It appears that when the old Mayer organ of Temple Emanuel was disposed of, Byron Mauzy secured the old pipes and, it is my belief, on good authority, that this material was used in the construction of several small organs. Evidently, they were stored in the interim in some secure place outside of the fire district, and so were not destroyed in the big conflagration.

The organ at the Nativity Church that I worked on after the fire which was about in 1909 was a two manual, mechanical action organ, console attached, with about 8 stops, some beginning only at tenor C. The pipes seemed to be a varied assortment of used material, good and bad. The Pedal pipes were distinctly Mayer pipes. The front display pipes were deplorably made. The chest action was rather novel as it consisted of individual valves operated by a slender steel wire passing through the stop channels, coming in contact with the valves. These wires were operated by a square at the end of the chest, which was operated mechanically from the key. Outside of the chest mechanism, the key action was poorly made and designed and had every indication of an amateur's work. We considered the organ very unsatisfactory from every standpoint.

This, however, was not the case with Father Turk, who

valued the organ highly and considered the purchase he made a very good one. We spared his feelings as much as we could, though we personally reluctantly repaired and adjusted the organ, being called frequently in the course of the years to service it.

Undoubtedly, comment from other sources, from organists who had to play it and those in a position to judge, especially our reluctance to work on it later, induced him in time to alter his view, and he intimated that when conditions were more favorable he would secure a new organ, one built by a reputable firm, strongly hinting that we would be the parties. The depression, with its aftermath, followed. Father Turk's health failed, and quite unexpectedly he was summoned by sudden death, mourned by his faithful parishioners, who still hold his name in reverence and benediction.

Father Turk's successor, Father Verdusek, was not long in noting the necessity of securing a new and dependable pipe organ, and, at a comparatively early date, he carried out the wishes of his predecessor and gave us the contract in 1940 to install a new modern electric pneumatic organ to replace the old unsatisfactory instrument.

The organ was installed, through smaller in contents, consisting of only three sets, unified and duplexed, on 4' pressure, and with its modern facilities, light and responsive action, its very efficient Swell effect as the entire organ is enclosed, easily out-classed the old organ in volume and tonal quality, and it is now a very desirable, but above all, a most trustworthy organ.

ST. JOHN'S EVANGELICAL REFORMED CHURCH

In 1915 we were called to service the organ at St. John's Evangelical Reformed Church, on Larkin Street near Vallejo.

We found a two manual and Pedal Hinners organ of 8 stops, tracker action with the Pedal action pneumatic. It was an excellent toned organ in all respects. After putting the organ in condition, we serviced it regularly thereafter.

Reverend Johannes Kroehnke was pastor at the time, a most pleasant and agreeable gentleman, a picture of health and vitality. A short time after one of our visits in 1916, we learned, to our sorrow, of his untimely passing. In one of the parlors of the church there was a life-size portrait of Reverend Kroehnke, a remarkable likeness of him, a work of art painted by an unknown artist.

A further contribution of this artist for the adornment of this church was a large painting, possibly ten feet by fifteen feet, located on the stair landing, depicting Christ preaching to the multitudes from a boat on the Sea of Galilee. Both paintings I admired very much and I believe they would do justice if placed in any art gallery.

The first St. John's Evangelical Reformed Church was located at Franklin and Broadway Streets.

On good authority I was told a pipe organ was located in the gallery of this church. What make it was I have not been able to ascertain. The church was in use but a few months when it was destroyed by the fire of 1906. It was rebuilt on the location stated above, with the Hinners organ installed.

Mrs. Robert J. Hill, a daughter of Reverend Kroehnke, was organist of the church.

A set of Chimes was placed in the organ some years ago but, for the present, requires the services of a Carillonneur to play them. Undoubtedly, some day they will be made playable from the organ keyboard.

It seems in 1944 the St. John's Evangelical Reformed Church disbanded and the edifice was taken over by the "Church for the Fellowship of all Peoples."

Chapter III

THE ORCHESTRION

Its origin, its development, music arranged by Felix F. Schoenstein and some of the early installations in San Francisco and vicinity, 1868-1925.

Here is the early history of the orchestrion as recorded by my father in his notes.

"The first orchestrion installed in San Francisco was purchased by Mr. J. Wittmeier, nicknamed Bottle Meier, as he was the first one to introduce bottle beer in San Francisco, at his establishment on Jackson Street, near Kearny.

"The instrument was built by Lukas Schoenstein, my brother, of Germany, in 1868. It had a compass of about 60 keys, called a clavis, or clavier, and played two manuals. That is, the music did not play only in unison, but played on two separate organ manuals, each independent of the other. The clavis, however, was in one straight line across the instrument. The orchestrion consisted of six sets of pipes, divided in their respective compasses. It also had drums and the other usual percussion instruments. Twelve cylinders were furnished with the orchestrion. One power unit, driven by a 400 lb. weight suspended on strong gut cords, which had to be raised by winding a crank in the rear of the orchestrion, was the driving power which made the orchestrion play.

"The case was a rather high structure, the woodwork beautifully made and polished. The front was divided into three movable doors, the panels of which were lined with blue silk, on which as a background were painted musical instruments, and portraits of Mozart, Beethoven and Haydn. Some of the compositions it played were the overtures Zampa, Jubel, and Oberon, The Blue Danube Waltz, German folk songs, etc. Later on this instrument was moved to Woodward's Garden, where I made a number of new cylinders for it with American tunes and melodies. When Woodward's Garden went out of business, the orchestrion was moved to Sutro Baths, where it remained for a number of years, and where it was also overhauled by me.

"The second orchestrion to arrive in San Francisco came in 1874. It was erected in the shop of my brother, F. B. Schoenstein, on Fulton Street, where it was put on display for future sale. I made my first cylinder for this instrument. One of the numbers was the "Magic Flute", by Mozart. The third orchestrion was ordered by Mr. Koenig, also owner of a popular resort on Pacific Street near Dupont. It was, however, smaller than the one owned by his rival, Mr.

Wittmeier. Soon after, however, Mr. Koenig secured a larger orchestrion.

"Thereupon Mr. J. Wittmeier changed his place of business from Jackson and Kearney Streets to Pacific Street, between Kearney and Montgomery, and also ordered a much larger orchestrion then he previously had, this one containing 120 clavis or keys.

"This instrument was also made by Lukas Schoenstein of Germany. It required two cylinders or rollers to be inserted at one time, as one long roller would become too heavy and inconvenient to handle. One was inserted from the right, the other from the left side of the orchestrion. In the center they would engage the main driving machine. There was also on either end additional pumping units, which started and stopped automatically as the demands for air for the music required. There was besides an additional machine unit which operated the drums and percussion.

"Shortly after this improvement had been completed by Bottle Meier, Bottle Koenig, his rival, enlarged his place on Pacific Street and ordered a still larger and more imposing instrument, his third one, also from Lukas Schoenstein in Baden, Germany. Although it was on the same style as the former instrument, the music was of a more elaborate order and was arranged to play as a three manual organ. I made two sets of new cylinders for this instrument.

"With the introduction of numerous orchestras in the theatres and the attendant popularity of the theatre as a place of amusement and entertainment, as compared with the more plebian beer or music hall, this mechanical type of music was put in the shade and was soon found obsolete.

"These two marvelous instruments, mechanical wonders for their artistic music and mechanical perfection, were then removed from their former locations. Bottle Meier's orchestrion was installed in the famous Cliff House, and Bottle Koenig's was erected in the Beach Pavilion or Seal Rock House. The Cliff House orchestrion was later modernized by Mr. de Nike by installing an electric motor to it, and applying perforated paper music rolls thereto, impairing, however, its musical possibilities of contrapuntal and polyphonic music in preference to unison playing. Both of these instruments were finally junked, as was also the instrument at Sutro Baths.

"Between the years 1870 and 1890 there was also a small orchestrion in an establishment on Clay Street, above Kearny Street, and one in the Schwaebische Halle on Kearny Street, near Pacific Street. Also, one on Market Street, near Sixth Street, and one in an establishment on Market Street, between Kearny and Montgomery Streets, owned by a Mr. E. Hacquette in the Palace of Art.

"Leland Stanford had a large one cylinder orchestrion in his mansion on Nob Hill. In his travels in Switzerland he saw the instrument, bought it and had it shipped to his San Francisco home, where it was erected in his picture and art gallery. I made four new cylinders for him containing American and religious tunes. This orchestrion was destroyed in the great fire of 1906. I had the privilege to know Leland Stanford, Jr., when he was about 18 years old, before he went to Italy, where he died.

"The James G. Fair residence also had a one cylinder orchestrion. It was smaller than the Stanford orchestrion. The Fair residence orchestrion had an ebony veneered case. I made a cylinder for them also. One of the pieces was "The Mikado."

"About 1900 this James G. Fair orchestrion was acquired by William J. Dingee for his residence on Washington and Franklin Streets. At this location I made six more cylinders for this instrument. William J. Dingee also had a summer home at Redwood City, where the orchestrion was eventually moved. The building in which it was standing was shoved from its foundation in the 1906 earthquake, but fortunately the instrument was unharmed and was then shipped by us to New York.

"Still another orchestrion erected in San Francisco was for a Mr. Paru, for his establishment on the east side of Dupont Street, between Bush and Pine Streets. He had me make several new cylinders for it. An establishment in Astoria, Oregon, gave me an order for six cylinders for their orchestrion, containing mostly Swedish music.

"With the advent of the perforated music roll for automatically operated musical instruments, the usefulness and further development of the old type of orchestrion, which was often the only source of high class orchestral music available for the masses, after 80 years of development finally came to an end."

"In 1903, I took out a patent, No. 740993, to improve the then prevalent one manual perforated music roll arrangement to one that could play on two or three manuals, thus greatly augmenting the musical effects. It was also planned that with the use of my patent, the registration could be likewise included with the music. My patent rights were granted on all points, without opposition or infringement on the ideas of others."

In the foregoing notes my father evidently overlooked mentioning several orchestrions. First, the one in the Elvisa Hayward mansion at San Mateo, on which he worked occasionally. Another was in the Claus Spreckels mansion on Van Ness Avenue and Clay Street, which was finally junked when no buyer could be found for it when the mansion was razed. There was one in Idora Park which I helped my uncle tune in 1912; and another one on J Street in Sacramento, where I called at one time with my uncle.

There was still another very ancient, small orchestrion in a private home on the corner of Steiner Street and Broadway. It was made in Paris. I assisted my father and uncle working on it. Evidently, this was the last orchestrion they worked on.

There was also a Welte orchestrion in the Eilers Music Store which my father tuned in April 1906 after the fire. I believe this orchestrion was eventually sold to the E. D. Connolly's residence in Menlo Park.

The orchestrion referred to in F. B. Schoenstein's shop on Fulton Street was originally made by my uncle, Lukas Schoenstein, in Germany, as my father stated. He failed to mention, however, that it was only the complete interior part of the instrument, without the exterior case. This exterior case my father built here in San Francisco, in his Birch Avenue shop in 1874. It was made of walnut and beautifully designed and executed — a fine piece of work. The orchestrion was then sold to an establishment in San Luis Obispo, but later found its way back again to F. B. Schoenstein's shop. When, as children, we would visit our uncle on Sunday afternoons, he would invariably play the orchestrion for us, to our great pleasure and delight. In 1912 I assisted my father and my uncle in modernizing the instrument by applying a pneumatic action and the modern perforated music roll system to it.

After the demise of my uncle in 1931, having been appointed executor to settle his estate, and realizing there was no market for this obsolete type of musical instrument any more, I donated it to the DeYoung Museum in Golden Gate Park, San Francisco, as a sample or type of musical instrument once in great favor and demand. I doubt if there is a specimen of this type or size left, or to be found hereabouts in the Bay cities.

It remained in the museum on exhibit for some time. Later, on an occasion when all the musical instrument exhibits were rearranged to other parts of the museum, it was removed and not again replaced. The reason given was that it was too large and took up too much space. It was then placed in the museum warehouse where it ignominiously remained for some time until sentimental reasons urged me to remove it to my home and possibly use parts of it, especially the handiwork of my father, as a remembrance to him. In the latter part of December 1947, I succeeded in removing the instrument from the museum warehouse and brought it to my son Lawrence's home, where some day he hopes to utilize the pipes to make a small residence organ.

Now that there are practically no orchestrions left for visual observation to demonstrate their construction, especially the tedious work that was involved in applying the music on its cylinders, it might not be amiss to describe here the latter procedure in detail, as well as to give a general description of their mechanism.

The small Swiss music box, with its small metal cylinder and protruding pins coming in contact with a steel comb, might be the closest replica in miniature of what a full sized orchestrion with its organ pipes and mechanism would be. The pipes used in an orchestrion are identical to the ordinary pipes in a church organ, however, in scale and construction, favoring the orchestral tone in every possible way; hence its name "orchestrion", derived from orchestra.

The mechanism from key to valve, and the slides controlling the various stops are identical to the mechanical action used in pipe organs of that period. The blowing arrangement was also of the feeder type, filling a reservoir with air from which the pipes drew their supply, the only difference being that the feeders were more numerous and of smaller capacity than used in ordinary church organs. In fact, this pumping mechanism, which was operated by cams having about a 2½" lift, was given special consideration, for to observe the cams in motion was most interesting. For this reason they, and the pumping unit, were usually open to view behind a glass panel in the front and in the lower part of the orchestrion.

The average size orchestrion had only one driving unit, containing the necessary transmission gears operating the above-mentioned cams, and the governor that controlled the descent of the 400 pound weight, the driving force that operated the orchestrion, usually placed in the back of the instrument, and which had to be wound up by a crank. The larger orchestrions, as those of Bottle Meier and Bottle Koenig, had three or more of these power units. The governor, a revolving fan with adjustable blades, which was necessary to regulate the tempo of the music, and which revolved at a high rate of speed, making it appear as though it were almost stationery, was most fascinating to watch, especially in the larger instruments with several units. It was uncanny to observe these governors go into action and again stop, depending on the supply of air that was required or consumed in the rendition of the music being played.

In referring now to the part from which the music originated, I will call it, for uniformity sake, the cylinder. In my father's notes he mostly referred to it in the German term "Walzer", denoting revolving or moving. He also referred to it in the American term of music roll or roller. Some refer to it as barrel, as in a barrel organ. This latter term, however, was anathema to my father, as the type of music played on the latter type of instrument was entirely different and not to be compared to that used in the orchestrion.

The size of the average cylinder was about 8" in diameter and from 5 to 6 feet long. The cylinders were hollow to make them as light as possible, and were usually made of poplar wood, glued together on maple wood octagonal end blocks, smoothly turned, stained to a walnut finish and then highly French polished. Two metal pins were then inserted on either end of the cylinder, on which it would revolve. Over the highly polished surface would then be fastened a clean white paper, somewhat moistened, glued to itself only and not onto the cylinder. When its glue joint, as well as the paper in general had dried, it would shrink and cling securely to the cylinder.

On one of the end pins of the cylinder, a series of grooves or notches, usually seven in number, were turned into the pin about one-sixteenth of an inch apart, each groove representing a given piece or composition, or a number of pieces, according to the arrangement of the music. By lifting a jacknife lever which would ordinarily run in one of the grooves to give the cylinder its lateral position, and by sliding the cylinder until the lever registered with another groove any of the desired numbers could be played. The clavis, or keyboard, which came in direct contact with the pins on the cylinder would automatically rise or become disengaged when the composition or number was finished.

Bearing horizontally against the end pin of the cylinder was a low pitched worm gear under constant pressure in one direction. The purpose of the worm gear was to give the cylinder a lateral motion of about a half inch, the distance between two keys on the clavis, during a specific number of revolutions of the cylinder, which was mathematically calculated so that when the worm gear reached a certain position, the required number of revolutions of the cylinder had taken place and the piece of music arranged on it had come to its conclusion. The clavis, as previously stated, would then automatically lift and the cylinder would move laterally to its starting position, ready for a new selection if desired, and the driving mechanism would stop.

Referring again to how the cylinder is made, after the blank white paper was fastened to it, it was rotated in a machine representing an orchestrion, which was provided with a set of sharp pointed clavis keys duplicating the keys of the orchestrion for which the music was to be written. The driving power in this case was the hand of the artist arranging the music, operating a dial on which was indicated the various speeds, or using the music term, the beats and bars of music as arranged on the manuscript that was being translated into music on the cylinder. The indicator on the dial was moved one space, equivalent to one beat of the bar, say 4/4 time. On the first beat, all the notes indicated on the manuscript, and for the specific instruments indicated, had to be indented into the paper on the cylinder by pressing the clavis key of the given notes by hand. Again the dial would be moved for the next beat, and so on. After each indentation on the paper had been made, by a series of code marks it would then be marked whether it was a 1/32, a 1/16, a 1/8, or a 1/4 note, a half or a whole note.

After this preliminary work of marking the music in code form on the paper was completed, which often required several weeks time for one cylinder, the cylinder was removed from the improvised clavis and was then placed on a convenient work bench and was ready to have the brass pins inserted. They, in turn, were all made by hand of hard brass. The wire was first passed through a roller to flatten it somewhat and then wrapped tightly on square iron mandrels in sizes according to the value of the notes they were to represent, in lengths up to two inches. The square formed wire was then cut through with a chisel, in the center. This would produce the sharp pointed, staple-shaped or "U" shaped pins. Single pins without the "U" shape were used for short notes. These were then driven into the wooden cylinder in the indentations made in the paper as previously described.

A series of quick staccato 32nd notes would be very close together, just sufficient space for the clavis key to make a clean cut repetition. These, of course, would be the single pins, with their ends sharpened to a point. A 16th note would be a single pin of thinner gauge, a quarter note of heavier material. If a note was sustained for over a quarter beat, or a half beat, or a whole bar or several bars, as was often the case, the "U" shaped pins up to a half inch in length would be used or, if necessary, bridged together, giving the notes their required value. After these thousands of pins were inserted, the sharp notes properly filed, all others carefully tested for proper height and vertical position, and a general check made to see that there was a sufficient space allowed for clearance at the end of the piece to disengage the clavier, the paper covering the body of the cylinder was then ready to be removed. This was rather easily done provided no glue had come in contact with the polished surface. The masterpiece was now completed — something beautiful to behold.

Yet, the music that was to be heard from this mechanical process was not to be enjoyed until the cylinder was placed in the orchestrion for which it was designed. If the job was accurately done, it was a success — if errors were made, it was almost beyond human skill to correct them.

The process of arranging the music for these cylinders reminded me much of the work of the great composers arranging their operas and symphonies on paper, yet visualizing and hearing every note, tone color and combination in advance, before hearing the finished product. The preliminary work of arranging the music from a given score, to the notes, pitches and available registration, was also no small matter. I am not enough of a musician to fathom the intricacies of this branch of music, as my father was. Yet, in special instances where he wanted something exceptionally good, he had this work done by some of the outstanding musicians of San Francisco, Mr. K. Herold, Mr. J. Knell and Mr. J. H. Dohrman.

To summarize, there were a total of 20 orchestrions installed in San Francisco and environs, to the best of my knowledge, from 1868 to 1925.

I have given this topic of the orchestrion, a general description of its functioning, and the making of its music cylinders, the space and attention that I have because I consider it of historical value, being one of the lost arts, probably never again to be revived or utilized.

Chapter IV

PIPE ORGANS OF SAN FRANCISCO

Pipe organs erected in San Francisco prior to 1906, but located outside of the fire area and organs of special interest erected since 1906.

ST. PETER'S CATHOLIC CHURCH

In observing the climate of San Francisco, it is not to be wondered at that the early Franciscan Padres, in establishing Mission Dolores in the heart of what is today known as the "Warm Belt of the Mission District", did so by choice and deliberation. Here, during the summer months, when other sections of the City are blanketed in a heavy pall of fog, billows of fog are seen rolling down the slopes of "Twin Peaks" and adjoining hills, attacking as it were, the Mission District, seeking to envelop it, if possible. Due, undoubtedly, to a warmer temperature, the result of being protected on the west side by the high hills and sheltered from the direct ocean breezes, the Mission District invariably continues to bask in warm and glorious sunshine, while other parts of the city are shrouded in gloom. Quite naturally, therefore, it became a favored section where many thousands later made their homes.

As the city developed, Sixteenth Street, Valencia Street and Twenty-Fourth Street became busy shopping centers of the Mission District. At the intersections of San Bruno Avenue, Potrero Avenue and Twenty-Fourth Street, the horse drawn car lines terminated. The Twenty-Fourth and Howard cable line continued from there down to the Ferry. Large tanneries were located along the lowlands of Army Street, car barns and the San Francisco County Hospital were located in the vicinity. The old California Woolen Mills were at Nineteenth and Bryant Streets, and other factories found it expedient to locate near desirable living quarters for their employees.

It was quite natural that in this thriving and favored district, there should also be located a Catholic Church to care for the spiritual needs of its children, mostly of Irish birth or descent. In 1877 St. Peter's Church was built on Alabama Street, between 24th and 25th Streets, with Rev. Thomas Gibney its first pastor.

My first recollection of St. Peter's Church goes back to about 1892. My father had received an emergency call to repair the organ there. It was on a Sunday afternoon and, evidently with the thought in mind of killing two birds with one stone, he took us small children along to give us an outing on nearby Bernal Heights after he had repaird the trouble.

We were a group of about six children. We were living at Turk and Fillmore Streets at the time, so the ride out to the Mission District was in itself an event for us. I recall boarding the Ellis Street cable line, transferring again to the Leavenworth and finally to the Howard Street cable line, at Tenth and Howard Streets, where the huge power lines were located. I remember being shown the large wheels and machinery of the power-house while waiting there for the car. I also recall that on reaching the church I was car sick from the peculiar odor of the coal oil lamps in the car and the smell of the grease from the cable coming up through the cable slot. There were no paved streets in the district at this time, as I recall, with the exception of 24th Street, which was surfaced with basalt blocks. Alabama Street and all the smaller streets were simply macadamized.

St. Peter's is a large Gothic Church, of wood construction, on the east side of Alabama Street, between 24th and 25th Streets. It formerly had a tall spire on its south corner, and the interior of the church was finished in plain white plaster.

The organ, located on the gallery, was a two manual and Pedal tracker action, Bergstrom instrument of 21 stops, with attached console. The church was large and lofty and the organ filled the edifice admirably. The Trumpet of the organ was rather strident, and the Vox Humana somewhat nasal in tone, but on the whole the tone was rich and dignified. It was a typical church organ.

After making the necessary adjustments on the organ that Sunday afternoon, my father took us for a hike to the top of Bernal Heights, stopping on the way to visit a friend living on the hill, a former employee of my father's, named Mr. Kellar.

My next visit to St. Peter's Church was with my brother Leo, who went there to collect the bill for the regular care of the organ. The priest's house at that time was an old two-story dwelling, located on 24th Street. It was later moved to Florida Street where it was used as the Christian Brothers home. Father Peter C. Casey was the pastor of the church at the time. On the way out my brother had an excuse for first calling at Ninth and Brannan Streets at a blacksmith shop conducted by August Vetter, to see his friend Louie Vetter. (Later, however, when August Vetter, Sr., became Leo's father-in-law, I realized the real purpose and intent of this side visit.) From Vetter's Blacksmith Shop we walked out Potrero Avenue, a broad, muddy thoroughfare, with rails for the horse-drawn cars in the middle of the street. I recall passing the old St. Catherine's Home and the old frame building of the San Francisco City and County Hospital. Little did I realize then that soon thereafter this district would be our future home. The family located at 2306 Bryant Street, corner 21st Street, in 1896, and lived there for forty consecutive years. At this favored spot, called home, both my father and mother passed on to their eternal reward. Here we children grew to manhood and womanhood, establishing in time our own homes. The old home was finally sold, but remains for us a fond memory of many happy days spent there, also of many heartaches, sorrows and disappointments, which are part and parcel of every mortal's life.

We have serviced St. Peter's organ continuously since 1884 when the organ was built. During that time, I had many a visit to my credit to repair and tune the organ; in the early years with my father, in later years with my own helpers. I recall on the occasions of my quarterly visits to collect the bill for the maintenance service (checking accounts were not generally used as they are now, and it was the custom to call personally to collect a bill), waiting in the parlor for the pastor, or rather waiting to be paid. There was a large oil painting on the wall that always interested me. It depicted the body of some young saint, or martyr, a young maiden floating with hands tied, eyes closed in peaceful death, on the surface of the water. I often thought of that picture when, to my surprise, some years later, I found that it had been placed by someone on the wall of the baptistry of the church where we had to pass it each time we entered the organ loft to tune the organ.

A Miss Desmond, a former pupil of John H. Dohrman, was organist at St. Peter's for many years.

At the time of the fire and earthquake in 1906 St. Peter's Church was not destroyed by fire. However, it was severely shaken and a lot of the plaster ornamentation of the interior had to be repaired and firmly secured. Previous to the earthquake, the church had been beautifully frescoed, or decorated. This work was retouched and brightened up during this overhauling. The Bergstrom organ on the loft evidently went through a severe shaking up. When we first entered the church after the earthquake, two of the large front pipes were lying down in the pews below, and the case showed cracks in several places. The organ was never too rigid. I remember when crawling about it to do repair work, how it would sway and creak. Through the convulsions of the earthquake, it must have rocked violently.

As stated, this was the first job we undertook to overhaul after the fire. It was completed on May 29, 1906. We replaced the damaged pipes, repaired and glued up the cracks in the case, and above all, we reinforced the main structure with diagonal braces. I recall an incident that I think might be worth relating in connection with this particular item. Those who lived through the earthquake period will recall that it was not only the initial or major shock that was experienced, but that for a long period of several weeks thereafter there were frequent shocks, consisting of 52 in all, of lesser intensity, until they finally subsided. My father and I had just completed the main bracing of the organ. I was high up on the 16' pedal open diapason pipes applying some additional bracing. My father was below, and to test the effectiveness of the bracing we had applied, he, with a strong grip, gave the organ a sudden jolt. People's nerves were still jittery and on edge from the terrible ordeal they had gone through, and it required little provocation, such as a deep rumble, a shaking or vibration of the floor even if caused by the passing of a heavy vehicle on the street, to get them panicky. This sudden shock startled me. I thoght it was the recurrence of another severe earthquake. Panic gripped me and I scampered pell-mell down from my lofty position in the organ and rushed out into the street expecting to see others as frightened as I was. I found no one excited. My father, realizing what he had done, came out after me with reassurance that he was the cause of that artificial earthquake, which, of course, pacified me. The scare I had, however, was real and I shall never forget it.

A few months after the earthquake a severe windstorm swept through San Francisco and in its progress and fury, the tall spire of St. Peter's Church was blown down and crashed into the street. Undoubtedly in years gone by, the old spire had withstood many a strong wind, possibly worse than this particular one, but the severe shaking of the spire during the earthquake had evidently weakened the structure and it fell an easy prey to the fury of the wind. The spire was not rebuilt, but was replaced by two smaller, modified towers on either side of the gable roof adding beauty and grace to the building, yet preventing the possibility of future mishaps.

After the death of Father Peter C. Casey, the beloved pastor, the famous and renowned priest and orator, Rev. Peter C. Yorke, assumed charge of the parish and remained until 1929. During his pastorate we installed an electric blower to operate the organ, and also set the Pedal keys further in to make the organist more comfortable at the keyboard. We also, with the same purpose in mind, made the sharp keys of the Pedals radiate.

Rev. Ralph Hunt succeded Rev. Peter C. York and Rev. Timothy J. Hennessey is the present pastor. Mr. Peter Doyle, a familiar figure at St.Peter's Church, was sexton for many years.

In the course of time the bellows of the organ became so worn out, with gussets blowing out and bellow folds parting, that the bellows would not rise any more. The time had come, if further satisfactory use of the organ was to be had, to undertake a drastic renovation of the old venerable instrument. After consulting with the pastor, Rev. Timothy Hennessey about the condition of the organ and the urgency of immediate action to which he readily consented, and also receiving the approval of Fr. Robert Hayburn, Director of the Diocesan Music Committee, our contract was accepted to remodel the 75 year old organ. This occurred in 1958.

The organ was originally built in one unit placed in the center of the gallery, closing up the greater part of a huge Gothic window. We removed the organ entirely, then separated it into two sections, one on either side of the window, retained part of the old Gothic case and made new additions thereto, applied new bellows for each division thereof, a larger blowing plant, a new Console, and applied an electric pneumatic action to the slider chests. The following additions were made: On the Swell manual — Trumpet 8' and Prestant 4'; on the great manual — Gemshorn 8' and Mixture 3 ranks; on the Pedal — Trumpet 16' extended from the swell.

The remodeled organ has received the highest praise, both for its appearance, its tonal quality and the practicability of its installation. Fr. Hayburn was the Recitalist at its dedicatory service.

HOWARD PRESBYTERIAN CHURCH
San Francisco's Oldest Pipe Organ

One of the most interesting organs of San Francisco is undoubtedly the organ that has the distinction of being the oldest pipe organ in use, and possibly the first pipe organ installed in San Francisco. This is the organ of the Howard Presbyterian Church, located on the southwest corner of Oak and Baker Streets, alongside of the Panhandle of Golden Gate Park. The claim that it is the oldest pipe organ in San Francisco at present is substantiated by records and information I have obtained from reliable sources; whether it was the first pipe organ installed here is debatable and I am not in a position to make a definite statement as to that. The pipe organs of Old St. Mary's Cathedral on Dupont Street, St. Joseph's Church on Tenth and Howard Streets, Green Street Congregational Church, and the African A. M. E. Church were all equally as old, if not of an earlier vintage, and may have arrived earlier — but in the absence of any proof of their prior arrival, and since they were all destroyed in the fire of 1906, the Howard Presbyterian Church organ can without doubt lay claim to being one of the first and, at the present time, the oldest pipe organ in San Francisco.

From data I have received from an esteemed friend, a gentleman at this writing in his 81st year, Mr. William Frederick Hooke, organist at Howard Presbyterian Church for many years, the church was first located in the Rincon Hill District of early San Francisco on Second Street, and was dedicated on June 15, 1851. In 1852 the organ was installed.

It had been shipped by sailing vessel around the Horn. Whether it was a new organ at the time, what the cost of it was, and who installed it in the church here, I have not been able to learn. As its arrival preceded the coming to the Coast of Joseph Mayer, California's first organ builder, who located in Marysville in 1856, it is probable that some organ builder from the eastern seaboard accompanied the organ on its long voyage for the purpose of installing it, or that it was erected by some organ mechanic in the employ of the music firm of Shellard & McGrath, San Francisco's early music dealers. Mr. Shellard, whom my father knew personally, lived on Montgomery Street at the foot of Telegraph Hill.

In the course of time, undoubtedly due to the rapid growth of the city and the shifting of the population to other sections, the Rincon Hill location on Second Street was abandoned and a substantial brick edifice was built on the south side of Mission Street, between Third and Fourth Streets. This new church was dedicated on January 6, 1867. The organ was moved to this new location, possibly by the same parties who originally installed it, or by Joseph Mayer, who was then established in San Francisco. In the event that the organ was a used instrument when it arrived, it could have been about 25 or 30 years old before it had been discarded for something larger and better. Its present age, therefore, could be around 146 years. If it was a new instrument when it was installed here, over 116 years have already passed since it was used to sing the praises of God for the pioneers of San Francisco.

There is an engraved notation on the top of the low C pipe on the Oboe marked (San Francisco). This would ordinarily indicate that that particular set of pipes was made and voiced for this particular organ and it could, therefore, be assumed that the entire organ was new or built for this particular church.

In 1891, Mr. William Frederick Hooke became organist of the church and served in that capacity for many years.

In 1896 the church was again moved further west to its present location at Oak and Baker Streets. The new edifice was dedicated on March 6, 1896. My father moved the organ from the Mission Street location, and erected it in the new church alongside the east wall of the auditorium, in a recess provided for it. The pulpit and rostrum were placed before it, with the seats of the auditorium parallel with it. The entrance to the auditorium was on the north end. The church was evidently arranged in this way with the thought in mind of using this auditorium later as a Sundayschool room, and building the main auditorium on the vacant lot adjoining to the east. Evidently, also, with this thought in mind, the organ was placed on four heavy casters running on metal tracks so it could be moved intact when the time for moving came. Sometime during 1904 the interior of the church was rearranged and the organ was moved by my father to the south end of the church. Whether the organ was dismantled entirely, or left intact and rolled on the casters to its new location, I do not know. The seating arrangement of the church was then altered again to suit the new location of pulpit and organ.

At this time my father made some improvements and alterations to the instrument. Like all old organs of that period, the manual keys were set in the organ flush with the case, with draw stops on either side. Two sliding doors when closed, concealed the keyboards and stop knobs entirely. There was a miniature Pedal board of only 12 keys, to be played with the left foot. The position and relation of manual and Pedal keys was most uncomfortable, so the organist had my father bring the manual keys forward as much as possible and make the Swell manual keys overhang the Great keys, similar to the modern keyboard. The 12 note Pedal board was discarded for a 30 note concave radiating Pedal board, still retaining only the 12 pipes, the same repeating at their successive octaves. A new bench was provided and the old hook-in Swell Pedal lever was replaced with a balanced Swell Pedal. The exterior of the organ was painted and the pipes redecorated. Fortunately, the painter left the original inscription of the builder of the organ intact, which reads: "William B. D. Simmons & Co., Boston, Mass"

Other interesting features of the organ are that the Swell stops begin at tenor C, with one stop labeled "Swell bass" sufficing as a suitable bass for all the Swell stops. Also the interior of the Swell box was originally padded, but this was removed and it is now lined with some fiber board to confine the tone in the box when closed. From all indications no zinc was used in the construction of the larger metal pipes; they are all made of so-called pipe metal, a composition of lead and tin, which accounts for its rich, pleasing tone. Even the pipe conductors are made of the same material. The scale of the manual keys is 56 notes, and the Pedal, as stated was originally only 12 notes. The pressure of the organ is about 3", and it was hand pumped until 1918 when we installed a modern blower. That the tone of the organ is pleasing and mellow, yet rich, goes without saying. The specification of the organ, as given below, will be of interest to organ students:

Compass of manuals, 56 notes.
Compass of Pedal originally 12, now 30 notes.

GREAT

Open Diapason 8'	Flute 4'
St. Diapason Treble 8'	Twelfth 2 2/3'
St. Diapason Bass 8'	Fifteenth 2'
Clarabella 8'	Cornet 3 rks.
Dulciana 8'	Trumpet 8'
Principal 4'	

SWELL

Dbl. Stopped Diapason 16'	Principal 4'
Open Diapason 8'	Fifteenth 2'
Viol de Gamba 8'	Haut boy 8'
Stopped Diapason 8'	Tremulant

PEDAL
Sub. Bass

COUPLERS

Swell to Pedal 8'   Bellows signal   Swell to Great unison

Great to Pedal 8'

ACCESSORIES

Great forte pedal
Great piano pedal
Pedal check
Bellows signal

CALVARY PRESBYTERIAN CHURCH

The first Calvary Presbyterian Church was built in 1854 and was located on Bush Street, between Sansome and Montgomery Streets. Later, in 1868, they moved several blocks farther West and located opposite Union Square at the northwest corner of Geary and Powell Streets, where the St. Francis Hotel now stands. It was a classic and substantial brick edifice.

Union Square and its vicinity, in the early days of San Francisco, seemed to have been a focal point for most of the churches. Temple Emanuel, with its two lofty towers, although one block distant on Sutter Street, could readily be seen from the Square; likewise the tall spire of the First Congregational Church at Post and Mason Streets, one block west. Trinity Episcopal Church was located at the northeast corner of Post and Powell Streets. Opposite the Square, in the middle of the block on Geary Street, was the St. Mark's Lutheran Church. On Post Street, on the south side between Dupont and Stockton was the Unitarian Church, with its famous Pastor, Starr King.

The general outline and design of the old Calvary Church was very much reproduced in the architecture of the new or present church, now located on the corner of Fillmore and Jackson Streets. In fact, the frames and sashes of the present windows, the iron fence surrounding the church, the pews and other material were salvaged from the old downtown church. Whether this was for economic or sentimental reasons, I do not know, but would incline to the latter assumption, since the case of the old organ was also retained for the new organ in the new church. My father evidently did not have charge of the old organ and I, therefore, never had occasion to enter the interior of the church.

From records I have and from information received, the organ in the old church was a three manual Erben organ, with attached console, built in New York in 1858. Mr. Gustave A. Scott was organist at the time, and was later followed by Mr. Robert Burness.

In 1901 the cornerstone for the new edifice on Fillmore and Jackson Streets was laid, and a contract for a new organ was awarded to the Murray M. Harris Organ Company of Los Angeles, California. It was a three manual and Pedal organ of 35 stops, with attached console, tubular pneumatic action. Most of the wood pipes of the old Erben organ and some of the diapason sets were retained. All other pipes and mechanism were entirely new. The old classic case, with the large scale open diapason pipes, was retained. Two new large bellows, with crankshafts operating 3 feeders each, were provided and placed in the room below the organ, while the motor itself was placed in the basement below, belted to the crankshafts above. Mr. Edward L. Crome, of Los Angeles, an old acquaintance who had served his apprenticeship in his early manhood with my father, installed the organ and we assisted him.

Later, in 1904, we received a contract for the regular maintenance of the organ.

On meeting Mr. Crome at the church on the above occasion, he recalled an incident of my early youth which I vividly remembered. While in the employ of my father, Mr. Crome made a tool chest for himself. As small children, I remember we would go to my father's shop, and being curious about everything, we would ask the men employed there what they were making. In this instance, on questioning Mr. Crome, he told me he was making a tool chest. When he had it completed, he put me into it, locked it and rolled it several times across the floor. I was always rather small of stature, but on seeing this tool chest again, I fully realized how diminutive I must have been as a child.

I recall another unusual incident in connection with the installation of the organ. Centrifugal organ blowers were not in use when this organ was installed. Direct current was preferred for its practicality in controlling the speed of the motor. In this district, at that time, there was no direct current available from the power company. The only direct current power available was the 500 volt current from the street car line. Possibly, because he did not have a suitable rheostat for 500 volts available, Ed Crome devised a temporary expedient by using a huge jug filled with water, connected to the leads of the line, one with a moving contact connected to the top of the bellows which would rise and fall, and the other touching the water permanently to complete the circuit. This expedient worked satisfactorily after a fashion until a permanent rheostat was obtained.

In 1906 the new Calvary Presbyterian Church, then only a few years in use, came through the earthquake that ravaged the city practically unharmed. Cracked walls, broken plaster and fallen chimneys were the only damage. The organ was unharmed. As the fire did not reach this neighborhood, there was no damage from that source.

Organists who played at this time were Robert Burness, Marshall W. Geiselman, Walter B. Kennedy and Ben Moore. The maintenance of the organ was under our supervision most of the time, except for the interval when Mr. Whalley had charge of it. During this time it was found necessary to replace the lead tubing used for the pneumatic action with new material.

An interesting character of the church was a Mr. George Radcliff, the faithful sexton who served the church for a period of 32 years.

In 1929, through the beneficence of Mr. and Mrs. John A. McGregor, a substantial sum of money was left to the church for a new, larger and more imposing organ. To house this instrument properly and to make other desirable improvements to the church, the property to the west of the church was acquired and the edifice was extended an additional 25 feet.

At about this time, or in 1928, St. Mary's College was erecting the buildings on its new campus at Moraga, California, with a beautiful chapel building as the central point. Through our recommendation and negotiation, the old organ of Calvary Presbyterian Church was sold to St. Mary's College and we erected it in their chapel. It is ideally located in the organ loft, and its beautiful tone and impressive appearance make it a fortunate acquisition for the College

Calvary Presbyterian Church then secured its new four manual Welty-Aeolian organ containing 72 stops, with Echo organ. This entire organ is under expression, beautifully made and voiced. Tonally it apparently did not quite come up to the expectation of organ critics, as shortly after its installation tonal changes were undertaken, stops changed and substituted, pipes revoiced. Undoubtedly, the desired results were achieved. Calvary Church organ is unquestionably one of the most impressive large church organs in San Francisco.

Beginning with 1946, the maintenance of this large organ was again entrusted to our firm, as it had been in years gone by.

Mrs. Jollie Bengsome was organist at the new organ most of the time. She was preceded by a few years by Mr. Robert Bossinger and more recently by Raymond White and following him quite a category of organists.

FIRST UNITARIAN CHURCH

The original location of the First Unitarian Church was on the south side of Geary Street, between Stockton and Dupont Streets.

In 1864 Joseph Mayer built for this church a two manual tracker action organ of 24 stops. It had a beautifully carved case with deep recessed Gothic panels. The console was set into the case, as was customary at this time. The front pipes were richly ornamented and decorated. From notes I have from my father, it seems that some years later, while he was in the employ of Mr. Mayer, and assisting him in tuning this organ, a severe earthquake occurred while he was pumping the organ. Mr. Louis Schmidt, Sr., was organist of the church at this time.

In 1888, the Church realizing the steady encroachment of business establishments in its immediate environment, in common with many other churches in the downtown district, moved out further west and located in the residential section at the southwest corner of Franklin and Geary Streets, where a substantial stone structure was built. On vacating the old property, the Mayer organ was sold to the Brooklyn Presbyterian Church of Oakland, and installed there by Mr. George Andrews of Oakland. It remained there intact, unchanged for many years. Later, we installed a modern, kinetic blower. In 1930 it was finally electrified and modernized by adding a new detached console and making some other alterations on it. This work was done by Mr. Oliver Lowe of Berkeley. This organ is still giving a good account of itself, after 104 years of active service. A visit to this organ to view the quaint design of its case, with the highly ornate, decorated front pipes, would be interesting and worth the effort.

In 1888, on moving to its new location on Geary and Franklin Streets, the Unitarian Church secured a more modern and better built two manual and Pedal tracker organ of 24 stops, a Hook and Hastings organ from Boston, Opus 1380, which was located in the front of the church in an alcove to the left of the chancel and pulpit. My first recollection of this church is connected with a childhood incident.

As small children, we were often in this neighborhood, and whenever we passed the stone church on the corner of Franklin and Geary Streets we would stand in awe and reverence and gaze at the white marble tomb behind the iron fence enclosure, near the entrance to the church, which, we were informed, contained the mortal remains of its pastor (1860-1864) Thomas Starr King, the famous patriot and orator of the Civil War period. It was largely through his efforts, that San Francisco supported the Union cause.

In 1912 the Unitarian Church was the recipient of a gift of a new pipe organ, which was secured from Ernest M. Skinner of Boston, Mass. A bronze plaque placed on the organ case indicates the donor, and reads as follows:

To remember

George Williams Hooper

June 29, 1847 — Feb. 4, 1911

Gift of

Sophronia T. Hooper

his wife

April Nineteen Hundred Twelve

The organ is a three manual and Pedal electric Pneumatic organ, detached console, of 34 stops.

On being told that they were to be the recipients of a modern organ, the Unitarians sold the old Hook and Hastings organ to the church of Nostra de Guadalupe, the Spanish Catholic Church, which shortly before had built its new edifice in the North Beach District. The old Unitarian organ was dismantled by my brother, Leo, and installed in the Spanish Church in a most desirable location in the choir loft. From all appearances and from every practical standpoint, it would seem as though the organ had been built for the place. To this day, it is giving excellent service, a gem of the old art of organ building.

At the First Unitarian Church where the organ formerly stood is now an artistic and elaborate baptismal font, one quite distinctive from any I had ever seen before.

After the removal of the old organ, preparations were immediately begun for the installation of the new Skinner organ. Contrary to the usual procedure of the organ builder providing the swell boxes or chambers for the different divisions of the organ, these were built into the choir loft on the rear gallery by a local contractor, according to plans submitted by the organ builder. When the organ arrived, it was installed by the Linhares Brothers and Charles Atkins, employees of the Skinner Organ Company of Boston.

After the installation of the mechanical part was completed, and the organ wired and functioning, ready for the tone work, voicing, regulating and tuning, Mr. Ernest M. Skinner came out from Boston to put on the finishing touches. As I had but a few years before, in April 1909, terminated my employment with his firm in Boston to return to San Francisco to again take up work with my father (forming the partnership of Felix F. Schoenstein & Son), Mr. Skinner and I were both delighted at the opportunity of again working together. Mr. Skinner sat at the console and I was up in the organ carrying out his instructions. In due time the organ was completed.

Meanwhile, many visitors, organ enthusiasts and critics,

called at the church to get a preview of the first Skinner organ erected on the Coast. Their comments varied, ranging from the extremely favorable and laudable to those of criticism of some of its features, especially in regard to its tonal structure. The lack of a diapason chorus, with its accompanying Mixture and Mutations on the Great and the placing of a Bourdon on the Great manual, were criticized. Others commended the beautiful strings and orchestral reeds on the Choir, the Erzaehler, the large-faced draw stop knobs on the console, something new at the time, and the generally excellent ensemble tone of the organ. True, depending on what school of organ tradition, design and specification one was brought up in, criticism could be made that the organ was not conventional. It was decidedly distinctive and different, yet I consider it one of my favorite organs.

The dedicatory recital was played by Ben Moore and Wallace Sabin. Mr. Clarence Bretherick (a typical Englishman with sideburns and a skull cap) a congenial and thorough church organist of the old school who had already held the position of organist on the old organ, functioned at the new organ for many years. He passed away in 1944 at the advanced age of 92 years.

His successor as organist of the church was San Francisco's popular organist, the late Uda Waldrop, who assumed this position in 1926. Several improvements had been made on the organ at his request. The Choir Tremolo had never been quite satisfactory. We installed a new one and in conjunction therewith also changed the Choir regulator. We also removed the Vox Humana from the Choir and placed it in the Swell manual.

I remember from the time the new organ was installed, a middle-aged Japanese, named Suzuki, served as sexton of the church. In time I noticed he was being assisted by several of his young sons, each one being assigned a bit of work according to his ability to perform it. In time they grew up to be strapping lads and young men, but always loyal and in kind consideration assisting their aging father. In conversation with them, I learned they were converts to the Catholic faith and attended St. Francis Xavier Japanese Mission Church. With the coming of World War II, they and their entire family were obliged to evacuate the City, in common with all Japanese. I often wondered what became of this old, faithful Japanese and his loyal sons, until one day in 1946, after hostilities had ceased, I was surprised to unexpectedly meet one of the boys doing janitorial work in one of our local Synagogues, where we served the organ monthly.

In 1966 I was saddened to learn this Ernest M. Skinner organ was disposed of for some Baroque type organ and sold to the First Methodist Church of Huntington Park, California. I trust the new owners will appreciate and enjoy its beautiful tones as I did.

ST. MARKUS GERMAN LUTHERAN CHURCH
(Now commonly called St. Mark's)

From data I have available, the first pipe organ for St. Markus Church was built by Joseph Mayer, San Francisco's veteran organ builder, in 1867. It was a two manual tracker action organ. A Mr. Schluetter was organist.

The church was located on the south side of Geary Street, between Stockton and Powell, opposite Union Square. In 1890 the church evidently wanted a better and larger pipe organ, and the old Mayer organ was, therefore, sold to the St. Mark's Lutheran Church of Oakland. The records show that my father in 1891 made a contract with the church to build them a two manual and Pedal organ of 23 stops, installed complete for the sum of $3,100.00.

This was the largest organ my father had built, and it was his pride and joy until he died. I remember in my early youth, the organ in course of construction in his shop at 1202 Fillmore Street. At the time we lived in the rear of the place, but as more space was now required for his shop, the family moved to more spacious quarters on Turk Street, around the corner. I remember when the organ was advanced to the extent that the Great chest, the large bellows below it, both Pedal chests on either side, and part of the solid black walnut case were erected to the chest level. I was then seven years old. My father led me up the ladder and let me stand on the protruding center tower base just above the keyboard. The organ could not be erected any higher, due to lack of height in the shop.

My next recollection of St. Markus organ was its dedication. It was finished February 6, 1891. At that time we children attended St. Boniface Parochial School. On Sunday morning we attended the 9 a.m. mass at St. Boniface Church. The building of St. Markus organ was evidently my father's masterpiece, and its final dedication was an outstanding event in his career. He wanted his children also to remember it and, if possible, to be present on this auspicious occasion. We were, therefore, instructed, after attending our regular religious services at St. Boniface Catholic Church, to proceed to St. Markus Lutheran Church opposite Union Square for the 11 a.m. dedicatory services of the organ. Evidently, my elder brother, Leo, must have taken us in charge as at that time I was unfamiliar with the downtown section of San Francisco. At any rate, we arrived somewhat late. The church was already filled with people. However, I recall we marched reverently up the main aisle, genuflected, as we were taught and accustomed to do in our Catholic Church, took our seats and remained for the service. Whether the parishioners recognized that we were in the wrong church or not, I do not know. Certainly, they could not have been scandalized by our action or behavior.

I remember seeing the organ, in the rather dimly lighted church, in the loft above when we left the edifice. Mr. Werner, a heavy set gentleman, was organist, and well that he was, as it required some masculinity to play the organ with vim and vigor. I remember, also, my mother speaking of the organ at table time and expressing her fear that the organist, due to his rotundity and strength, would break the instrument.

The pastor was Rev. Fuendling, one of the most prominent clerics of the German Lutherans in San Francisco. Other pastors who followed him were the Reverends Feix, Raun, Ortlundt, Smith and Dr. Geo. Dorn, D. D.

St. Markus Church, in common with many of the other national churches, seemed in the course of time to lose its national identity. The use of the German language was gradually curtailed or eliminated, the German appelation of St. Markus changed to the English version of St. Mark's, and the final Anglicization took place when one of its later pastors, bearing the name of Smith, took over the pastorate of a once purely German congregation.

Coming back to the organ again, the contract price was $3,100.00. So conscientious and thorough was my father in building this organ, that he spared himself in no way, but gave everything for his ideal. Nothing was too good for this organ. Note that the organ case, or exterior, was made of black walnut throughout, and not only the front of the organ that was visible — but also both sides to the rear of the organ which, at that, were standing in a dark gallery unobserved by most people. His contemporaries would simply have applied a redwood paneled case, stained to match.

In the tonal aspects my father also exceeded ordinary prudence. The Trumpet stop had to be extra good, so he imported one from his brother's factory in Germany, who were builders of orchestrions. A free reed Trumpet with brass resonators was installed. The three rank Cornet on the Great was a replica in scale from some European organ he had read of and became enthusiastic about. An Octaviant 4' stop in the Swell, rich in harmonics, seemed to give him a special delight. A strong Violin Cello in the Pedal was his pride, as there was none other of that type hereabout at that time. A fixed composition piston button, piano and forte, for the Great manuals and Swell, which worked pneumatically, drawing out and returning the slides with gusto, was also something to be proud of. One thing he did not install in the organ was a tremolo. With all these super-fineries, it is evident that my father proved to be a better organ builder than a business man, with the result that after paying all his contracted bills and obligations, he found himself to be the loser in the venture. So pleased were the church officials, however, with the organ and their dealings with my father during the transaction, they presented him with a gratuitous bonus of $100.00, and also gave him a testimonial and recommendation of the highest order.

My next recollection of the organ was thirteen years later, in 1904, when my father and my brother, Leo, reinstalled the organ in the new church built on O'Farrell and Franklin Streets. This new church, of a more modernistic design in its exterior, was especially so in its interior. In place of the dark dismal aspect of the old building, the interior of the new church was finished in a light cream or buff color, highlighted with gold. Altar, pews, furnishings all were treated in the same way. A flood of light penetrated the pale amber-shaded windows. In this cheerful setting, it was obvious that the exterior of the organ, made of rich black walnut, and now being located in the front of the church over the altar, presented a most striking contrast to the rest of the church.

There must have been some heated discussions as to whether this beautiful black walnut case should be painted to match the rest of the interior of the church. I do not know how the dissenting opinions were finally brought into agreement, but I do know, however, that to my father it would have been sacrilege, unprofessional conduct, unethical behavior to paint any beautifully made and finished hardwood product. Probably his antipathy to the suggestion won out. The black walnut case was not painted a cream or any other color, but was highlighted in gold. Artistic tastes may differ, but one must agree on seeing this classic organ front, with its imposing center tower, gold pipes and dark walnut case trimmed in gold, that it made a striking appearance.

In both locations of the church, the organ was pumped by hand. The senior Mr. Crome, father of the late Edward L. Crome, organ builder of Los Angeles, pumped this organ for many years.

Other interesting characters at this church were a Mr. Wehrenberg, an elderly gentleman bedecked with a little skull cap and always smoking a fragrant cigar, who evidently was the sexton emeritus and lived at the church; and the more active and energetic janitress, the lady with a scowl, always complaining, adorned with a work apron and her head wrapped in a cloth as though she had a headache. Old Mr. Wehrenberg passed away in 1900.

In 1906, the earthquake and fire which destroyed most of the church edifices in San Francisco graciously spared this brick edifice, being just beyond the fire limits. Aside from cracks and fissures in the masonry and other minor damage which was soon repaired, it was unharmed. The fire came, however, within one block of the structure.

In 1920 a motor and an auxiliary blowing plant were installed in the room below the organ by Thomas Whalley of Berkeley. This helped greatly to improve the steadiness of the air and, above all, it relieved the necessity of having an able-bodied human organ pumper.

I have never learned the reason why the applying of the blowing plant was not entrusted to my father, the builder of the organ and custodian from the time of its installation. I remember he always referred to it as "his" organ. This attitude of cocksureness and proprietorship was probably the reason. There is a possibility that an estimate for this improvement was desired and not acted upon immediately — or he may have had some other plan of procedure. I know he was much disappointed and chagrined at not getting the work. At no time, however, did he criticize its merits or efficiency, as he recognized it as an improvement to the instrument and a much needed one.

Johanes Raith, a prominent musical character of the city, was organist at St. Markus for many years, until incapacitated by an accident. His wife, then took over as organist and served until 1945. She was succeeded by Douglas Peterson, a recent arrival from Minneapolis, Minnesota.

Extensive improvements to the church were contemplated at this time as a fitting climax of the centenary of the founding of St. Mark's, the oldest Lutheran Church on the Pacific Coast. In keeping with this program a contract was signed in 1946 with the Moeller Organ Company for a new three manual organ, which has since been installed and was placed in the chambers on either side of the newly arranged chancel and altar. Mr. Richard Purvis, one of the young, prominent organists of San Francisco, was organist at the church and was, undoubtedly, deserving of a new and modern instrument.

The old organ, built by my father 71 years ago, which had served the church faithfully without any major alteration or improvement since its installation, with the exception of the application of a blowing plant, was finally purchased by our family, with the hope of modernizing it to further perpetuate its usefulness and serve as a memorial to its builder.

On January 6, 1947, with a crew of workmen, among

them Peter Derrick, an old friend, we began dismantling the organ, but not before he played the final and last tune thereon — "Holy God We Praise Thy Name."

Shortly thereafter, we signed a contract with St. Peter and Paul Catholic Church, of the North Beach District in San Francisco, to rebuild, electrify and rearrange this old organ into a divided organ to be located on either side of the large Rose Window, and to combine it with the present Johnston organ, making it a three manual instrument of 34 stops. The rebuilding of the old organ was not only a matter of faithfully carrying out a contract, but also a labor of love to preserve a masterpiece for posterity, made by my father 71 years ago.

Since then under the sponsorship of the late Rev. Bartholomew Pellegrino, S.C., a musician of note and an admirer of the organ, several additional stops and a set of chimes were added, further enhancing the tones and the full ensemble of this superb organ.

ST. JOHN'S PRESBYTERIAN CHURCH

In the early days of the City there stood on Post Street, between Taylor and Mason Streets, where the Olympic Club building now stands, the former St. James Episcopal Church.

Mr. Joseph Mayer, the local organ builder, rented them the use of one of his pipe organs, which had previously been in use in Grace Cathedral, at California and Stockton Streets. It was a two manual and Pedal tracker action organ with attached console and about 10 stops of 58 note compass. It had a pleasing, artistic Gothic case made of white cedar.

Dissension arose in the congregation and the church disbanded. The property was then taken over by St. John's Presbyterian Church, which was organized on March 6, 1870.

The old Mayer organ was then removed to Mayer's shop where some improvements were made — among other items another Pedal stop was added. This organ was then subsequently sold to St. Francis Church on Columbus Avenue, near Dupont St. where it remained in use for a number of years. When St. Francis Church, in later years, secured its large three manual Bergstrom organ the old Mayer organ was sold to St. Vincent's Church, Vallejo, California, where it was again put to use for many years, until finally, in 1940, after an eventful career of 78 years, we replaced it with a modern electric action organ of our own make.

When St. John's Presbyterian Church took over the St. James Episcopal Church property they also decided to get a larger and more imposing instrument and, in 1872, bought a three manual and Pedal Johnson organ of 30 stops, Opus #394 from Westfield, Mass. It had a rich brilliant tone, yet pleasing, as it was voiced on 3½" wind. The lowest octave of the Great manual was supplied with a Barker pneumatic lever action to help relieve the heavy tension on the keys. Mr. Fred Katzenbach was organist of the church during its early period.

In 1889 St. John's Presbyterian Church moved to a new location on the southeast corner of California and Octavia Streets. I do not know who moved the organ on this occasion, as my father made no mention of it.

It is from this new location on California and Octavia Streets that my first recollection of St. John's Presbyterian Church and its large Johnson organ begins. My brother, Leo, and I assisted my father in tuning and adjusting the organ on several occasions. It was pumped by revolving a large wheel which operated a set of two bellows connected to a crank shaft. Mr. Fletcher Tilton was organist at the time.

I recall a window at the rear, or south end of the church, overlooking the Western Addition and the southern part of the city, with the San Bruno Hills in the distance. The church being on the southwestern slope of Nob Hill afforded an interesting view of the city. I also recall the old sexton with a white goatee, an inveterate cigarette smoker, his fingers stained from nicotine, tremblingly holding the weed.

About 1905, the church decided to build a new edifice farther out in the Western Addition, and selected its present fine location on Arguello Boulevard and Lake Street. The cornerstone of this structure was laid in 1905.

On completion of the new church my father did not receive the contract to dismantle and move the organ. It was given to Mr. Byron Mauzy, a local piano dealer, who, at the time, was showing some interest in the pipe organ field.

However, after the large organ was dismantled and lay scattered all over the floor of the old church, preparatory to being moved and re-erected in the new edifice, Mr. Mauzy evidently lost heart, doubting perhaps whether he would be able to put it together again. Whatever the reason, we were called to the scene and given the contract to install the organ in the new church.

That the work of dismantling the organ was very amateur-ish, was most evident, since every pipe was numbered and marked with a blue pencil to assure its replacement in its former position. We installed the organ in the new church in the Fall of 1905. The installation work was made more difficult for us as we had not dismantled the organ and the markings were so much Greek to us, however, it was eventually completed with most of the work being done by my brother, Leo.

An incident lingers in my memory concerning the organ bellows. After we were assured of the contract to re-erect the organ in the new church on Lake Street, we considered the re-leathering of the bellows with new material the most necessary improvement required. The old leather had become dried out and cracked, and the bellows and feeders leaked like a sieve. As the organ had to be pumped by hand, an airtight bellows was of vital importance. We, therefore, had the bellows removed from the church to our shop and it was my pleasant job to re-leather them. I took great pride in doing this job as expertly as I could, as I had always admired the wonderful workmanship on some of the organ bellows made in the East and I tried to equal that as much as possible. To move the bellows from the church, we engaged our usual expressman, a Mr. Feldhaus, who had a large express wagon with two husky steeds. The two bellows were quite heavy. We placed them edge way or upright on the wagon, evidently thinking they were so heavy there was no need to tie them down securely. At any rate, on descending the steep decline on Nob Hill, down California Street, and on reaching the small intersecting street between Webster and Fillmore and California and Pine Streets, in which he turned south toward Pine Street, the bellows lost their equilibrium and almost fell out of the wagon — the wagon tipping dangerously to the low side. Aside from giving the express-man and me, his lone passenger, a good scare, no damage was done and we finally arrived safely at our destination.

The organ had scarcely been completed for the dedication of the church on April 14, 1906, when, on the fateful morning of April 18th, San Francisco was visited by the devastating earthquake and fire. St. John's Church, lying far beyond the fire limits, was not threatened by it, but the earthquake did its destructive work. Just behind the organ on the interior of the west wall was a large brick chimney leading from the basement to the roof. This had crumpled completely and fallen right into the back of the organ. What a sight we beheld on our first visit to the church after the disaster — brick and mortar all over the organ, trackers, squares, roller boards broken, and pipes crushed. The building was otherwise not seriously damaged, and had it not been for the fallen chimney the repairs would have been nominal.

The repairing of the damaged organ was again entrusted to us. The repairing and replacing of broken trackers, squares, etc., was this time mostly my particular job. I recall it was a matter of several weeks before the organ was again in first class working order.

What changes have occurred in the past 56 years! While engaged in doing the above-mentioned repair work on the organ, I would at times go to the nearest restaurant on Point Lobos Avenue — now Geary Street — for lunch. At other times I would take my lunch and sit under a Lupine bush in one of the many vacant sand lots, of which there were many in the neighborhood at that time. (Now a vacant lot is hard to find anywhere in the Richmond District.) The old sexton with the white goatee and unfailing cigarette again took up his post at the new church. As the pumping of the organ was undoubtedly one of his many duties, and as age and infirmity came upon him, it was not a difficult matter to induce the church authorities to have a modern blower installed. This we did, and it was a great improvement to the organ in having a steady and even flow of air.

Mr. Robert Burness, for many years organist of Calvary Presbyterian Church, and one of the pioneer musicians of San

Francisco, became organist of St. John's Presbyterian Church shortly after the organ was installed in the present edifice, and filled the position for 38 years until his death, which occurred on December 26, 1945.

In 1910 some improvements to the organ were made by us. The pitch was changed to 440-A. The choir manual which heretofore was open, was enclosed and made expressive, giving the organist further facilities for suitable accompaniment purposes. An Unda Maris, 8 stop, was added to the choir and a Vox Humana 8' was put on the swell manual, in place of the Cornet. During 1941 a set of chimes was added to the organ by Louis Maas of Los Angeles, still further improving and adding to the resources of the organ. St. John's organ was the largest three manual tracker action organ in San Francisco and, undoubtedly, on the West Coast. Certainly, the largest Johnson organ I have come across.

After many years of servicing the organ, it was finally showing signs of disintegrating. Leather nuts on tapped wires of the wooden trackers would become pulverized when adjusting, the frail trackers would break by the slightest touch and were often inaccessable for repair. We found it necessary to complain and urged the church authorities to undertake a drastic modernization of the organ, an otherwise ideal tonal instrument.

Years passed by, and there always seemed to be more important improvements and additions required on the church property. Eventually, when our work became unbearable and unprofitable, and we threatened to discontinue our regular service contract, action was taken.

Finally, in 1954, a campaign was authorized to gather funds for a modernization of the organ with the result that our firm was awarded a contract to undertake the work. The beautiful and massive black walnut case was retained. The slide and pallet chests and all of the old pipes which were still in excellent condition, were preserved and used. An entire new electric pneumatic action was applied to the organ. Several new bellows were installed. A new three manual and Pedal console, with all necessary combinations — pistons, couplers, etc., was provided. Six new additional sets or ranks of pipes were added and a necessary larger blower was installed, resulting in a better and larger organ than ever before. This rebuilding work, of which we were justly proud, was mostly done by my brother, Erwin Schoenstein, performing all the factory or construction work with his son, Leonard. The installation and erecting work was under the supervision of my brother, Otto Schoenstein, with my son, Lawrence Schoenstein, ably assisting him.

The organ was finally re-dedicated on March 10, 1957, at which time I was invited to be seated on the rostrum to represent our firm, with several of the officials of the Organ Committee, each one giving a verbal report of their activity. I spoke briefly on the history of the organ and complimented the congregation on their decision to retain their old historical instrument as a reminder for future generations of the genius of the American Organ Builder.

During the 92 year history of the organ, only five organists presided at the organ, to our knowledge: Fred Katzenbach, Robert Fletcher Tilton, Robert D. Burness, his daughter, Marion Burness, Miss Dora Schively and Sol Joseph, the present organist.

Following is a copy of the dedicatory remarks made by the Rev. Lloyd R. Carrick, on that occasion:

"In a few moments we will come to the high point of our Service — the actual dedication of our re-built Johnson Pipe Organ at Saint John's. As we approach this sacred ritual, I ask you to have in mind a passage of scripture which has come to my mind in this connection. I refer to Mark 14:3-9. It reads, in part:

"'And while Jesus was at Bethany in the house of Simon the Leper, as he sat at the table, a woman came with an alabaster jar of ointment of pure nard, very costly, and she broke the jar and poured it over His head. But there were some who said to themselves indignantly, 'Why was the ointment thus wasted? For this ointment might have been sold . . . . and the money given to the poor.' And they approached her. But Jesus said, 'Let her alone; why do you trouble her. She has done a beautiful thing for me. . . .She has done what she could. . . .Truly, I say to you, wherever the gospel is preached in the whole world, what she has done will be told in memory of her!

"Early in our consideration of our Pipe Organ we had to face the same practical question which the disciples raised that day. Was the $27,000.00 we proposed to spend a waste of money? Were we justified in doing this when so many needs of the world stared us in the face? We could, of course, have put in some kind of an organ for about one-tenth of what we have finally spent. Should we have done that?

"My answer is this: I am convinced in my own heart that we are today on MARY'S SIDE of this Scripture, rather on the side of the Disciples. I believe our Living Lord is looking down on us this hour and saying, "The people of Saint John's have done a beautiful thing for me. . . .They have done what they could. . . .Whenever the Gospel is preached in this Church in the years to come what they have done will be told in memory of them."

"From the very first the challenge of this Organ Campaign has been this: To do in our day what our forefathers did in their day. In the year 1872 our forefathers 'did what the could!' They placed in this church one of the best organs they could then buy — an organ which has served us for 85 years. They handed on an instrument of worship which has brought uplift and inspiration to generations then unborn. All of us have felt the 'beauty of holiness' which this organ has brought to us — some in this congregation have heard its voice for over 50 years!

"When this old instrument became obsolete the question then confronted us: Would we in our day pass on an instrument which would inspire worshipers for another 85 years? Or — would the quality be cheapened in our hands?

"I, for one, rejoice that our answer has been in the AFFIRMATIVE! I rejoice that 'we have done a beautiful thing', that'we have done what we could.' I rejoice that we are passing on an organ which is not only 'just as good' but one which is MUCH BETTER than the one we received from the past!

"Today we praise the memory of those who gave so spontaneously in 1872. It is a satisfaction to know that in the years ahead our children, and our children's children, will THANK US for what we have done in 1957.

"In the Scripture Passage Jesus said, "She has done a

beautiful thing FOR ME." I am sure all of us feel that we have done this FOR CHRIST, whom we love and worship. Our motive has been to make our worship of Him more effective in the years that lie ahead. It is with that thought in mind that we would now humbly come to this Dedication — in which we set aside this instrument to the GLORY OF GOD and to the uplift of His children here below."

TRINITY EPISCOPAL CHURCH

Trinity Episcopal Church, the first organized Episcopal Church in San Francisco, was founded in 1849, was located at the corner of Jackson and Powell Streets. Later a second building was built on Pine Street, between Montgomery and Kearny Street. The third, a more pretentious edifice, was erected on the northeast corner of Post and Powell Streets.

I recall my father relating that this was the first church he entered on landing as an emigrant in San Francisco in 1868, in search of a Catholic church where he could attend to his religious duties. Its similarity with that of the Catholic church first baffled him, until he was made aware of its identity. He finally located the German Church, St. Boniface, at Sutter and Trinity Place, of which he later became a loyal member.

In its edifice at Post and Powell Streets, Trinity Church had a pipe organ. It was a two manual and Pedal tracker action Jardine organ, with a case of Gothic design. This was the first pipe organ my father heard in San Francisco. Professor Gates was the organist.

In 1892 Trinity Church moved to its new edifice on the northeast corner of Bush and Gough Streets, and I believe the old organ was also moved to this edifice and used for a number of years.

My first connection with Trinity Episcopal Church was in 1897, when they secured their new 55 stop Hook & Hastings pipe organ, Opus 1772 evidently, replacing the old pipe organ above referred to.

The old organ was then sold to the Trinity Methodist Episcopal Church of Berkeley, California, located then at the

north end of Ellsworth Street near the University of
California campus, where it remained in use until the old
church building was razed to make room for the present
athletic field. What became of the old organ, I do not know,
but believe some amateur organ enthusiast secured the pipes
to build an organ.

The new Hook & Hastings was a three manual electric
pneumatic organ of about 21 stops. The Swell was enclosed,
the Choir and Great unenclosed. It had a detached console,
and, incidentally, was the first movable console applied to
any organ in San Francisco. Mr. Anderson, an employee of
the Hook & Hastings Company, came from Boston to erect
the organ. My father and my elder brother, Leo, assisted in
its installation. It was the first electric action Hook &
Hastings organ in San Francisco. Although made on the
electric action system, it still retained the slider chest and
pallet valve. There was a large reservoir bellows in the organ
above, with hand pump for emergency purposes, and an
auxiliary bellows with feeders, in the basement below. My
father's notes state that these bellows were first operated by
a water motor of some type, but that its functioning was
unsatisfactory. Whether this was because of excessive noise,
uncontrollability, or for some other reason I do not know.

Eventually, the services of an expert electrician, Mr. Frank
Broily of the California Electric Works, were secured and he
devised a plan of blowing the organ by a centrifugal blower
instead of the feeder pump arrangement. He installed a
Sturdivant or American blower, directly connected to the
motor, which gave very satisfactory results. The motor ran at
one continuous speed, and its supply of air into the bellows
was controlled by a regulating valve connected with the top
of the auxiliary bellows.

I have read a report at one time in "The Diapason", stating
that the first centrifugal blower used to blow an organ was
introduced to the organ trade in a church in Detroit,
Michigan. However, I believe this blower installed in Trinity
Church, San Francisco, preceded the above stated claim by
many years.

The console of the Trinity Episcopal Church organ was
first located on the west side of the organ. It was later moved

to the south side, and choir stalls arranged accordingly. Mr. Townsend, a contractor, was in charge of the work. He arranged with an electrician to splice the cable, which had to be extended.

Mr. Humphrey J. Stewart was organist and music director.

I recall while the organ was being erected, a visitor of note called to inspect it. Mr. Willis Davis was a gentleman of leisure and wealth, an organ lover who, at that time or possibly later, had a splendid Aeolian pipe organ in his residence on Scott Street and Pacfic Avenue.

Trinity Episcopal organ, like many of the other eastern made organs that were shipped to San Francisco, gave us considerable trouble for some time until it became acclimated. The swelling of the apparently excessively kiln dried wood, as used in the eastern states, after arriving in the damp San Francisco climate caused untold trouble. The wood absorbed moisture, joints opened up, grooved primary boxes loosened, etc. Also, the furnishing of a proper current supply for the low voltage for the key action was a problem. At first six Edison-Lalande wet cells were applied. However, every year these batteries had to be refilled and recharged. The fluctuating output was a continuous source of trouble with the action, and it was no wonder that the first electric action organs were criticized as unreliable and undependable — a stigma it took many years to disprove and eradicate.

I quote here a statement made to my by one of our early California organ builders substantiating this charge. "Electric organs are good when they work, but tracker organs always work." This insinuation of the electric action in the stages of its development may have been justified to an extent. However, in the course of years, with constant improvement and perfection of the electric action, it has now become the standard of almost every organ made, large or small.

Another reason for the uncertainty of the action was the intricate design and wiring system of the slider chest stop action. To avoid the constant drain on the batteries when a stop was continuously on, a cut-out circuit was arranged on the stop for it to consume current only at a given point in its motion of "on and off," and always be prepared for the next motion. Due to some disarrangement at the most inopportune time, some loud and boisterous stop would often remain on. We would hurriedly be called for to adjust it. We were not always able to locate the trouble quickly and had to resort at times to the temporary expedient of disconnecting the slide entirely. Another weakness of the organ was the exceedingly fine wire used on the electric magnet terminal wires, which frequently were severed due to corosion, causing a broken circuit.

Humphrey J. Stewart was undoubtedly in his prime while organist of Trinity Episcopal Church, and his music and that of his choir was hailed as the best in the city. Rev. Frederick Clampett was the beloved and revered pastor of the church for many years.

Other familiar names I recall connected with Trinity Church are those of some of the sextons. First, there was a Mr. Westfield who, I have been told, served many years in the old church on Powell and Post Streets. After his death, a Mr. Beard held the office for some time, and he was followed by the dean of the church sextons of San Francisco, Mr. John Goman who, in his old age, acquired the title of sexton emeritus after serving Trinity Episcopal Church for 36 years. He passed to his eternal reward in 1942 at the ripe age of 86 years. Mr. Harry Forster, his erstwhile assistant, then carried on.

The fateful morning of April 18, 1906 arrived. Trinity Church being two blocks west of the fire line was unharmed by either earthquake or fire. The edifice must have been built exceptionally well and sturdily. I do not recall seeing a crack in its masonry, and do not know of any damage done to it. The organ was also unharmed. After the earthquake a large circular chandelier suspended from the ceiling, about 15 feet in diameter and evidently of considerable weight, was removed. Whether this was injured in the earthquake, or removed as a safeguard in the event of a similar visitation in the future, I do not know.

At this time, also, a double set of twine nets were suspended from the rectangular space over the nave of the church to kill or absorb an overabundance of echo, or of reverberation, that heretofore had been quite annoying. This expedient proved very effective and is still doing good service at the present time.

Mr. Louis Horton Eaton, a prominent organist of Boston, succeeded Humphrey J. Stewart as organist at Trinity Church, and following him came Benjamin A. Moore, a young man with high ability, a master at the organ and a gentleman in every sense of the word. His tenure outranks that of all of his predecessors. His devotion to his work, his integrity and pleasing personality made him many friends. Such an able musician as he was deserving of having an instrument that would give him full scope for his musical abilities.

As evidence of the high esteem in which Ben Moore was held in Trinity parish, nothing being too good for their favorite son, it was deemed proper to secure a new modern four manual electric pneumatic Skinner organ, designed according to his own specifications. A divided organ was decided upon, Great, Choir, Solo, and Pedal, on the north side of the chancel, and the Swell and some Pedal stops on the south side. The organ chambers were specially built for the organ. The Great manual was unenclosed. There were 52 speaking stops and some unifications in the organ, voiced on various pressures. The tone was rather rich and brilliant, typical of the Skinner organs built in recent years. The high-class workmanship and voicing of the individual stops throughout make the organ one of distinction. Each section of the organ had an ornate, harmoniously designed exterior case in which the front display zinc pipes are left in their original color and material. I believe this was one of the few organs in San Francisco where this innovation was followed.

The organ was installed by John Saul and Harry Law and was dedicated on February 15, 1924.

In 1925, through the beneficence of the Lulu Gullixson family, an Echo organ was added to the instrument and placed on the west wall of the church, adding more facilities to an otherwise complete instrument. The old Hook & Hastings organ that was installed in 1898, preceding the Skinner organ, was sold to the Trinity Episcopal Church of San Jose, California.

On February 12, 1951, Ben Moore died after a long illness, mourned by his friends. His successor, and present organist, is none other than the equally prominent and much liked gentleman and revered musician, Harold Mueller, F.A.G.O.

PLYMOUTH CONGREGATIONAL CHURCH

Plymouth Congregational Church, also known at one time as the Second Congregational Church, an offshoot of the First Congregational Church, was originally located on the east side of Taylor Street, between Geary and Post Streets. In 1882, a new site was acquired at Post and Webster Streets, where the congregation built the present large frame edifice.

I remember this structure, as it was a landmark to us children, and we spent a good part of our childhood in this neighborhood. Originally, the structure had a tall, graceful spire, but I believe it was removed shortly after the earthquake of 1906.

I often worked there assisting my father. It was an old Mayer organ of two manuals, built in 1868, with 12 or 16 sets of pipes. Evidently, it had first been erected in the old church on Taylor Street. I presume my father moved it to the new church on Post and Webster Streets.

This church was apparently in a flourishing condition at one time. Leading members of the church, whose names I often heard mentioned by my father, were a Mr. Steadman, the organist, and a Mr. Bufford. Mr. Delipiani, who was organist at Temple Ohabai Shalome, succeeded Mr. Steadman as organist at Plymouth Congregational Church and functioned for many years. In time, the popularity of the church seemed to wane. The congregation finally disbanded. The old Plymouth Church was eventually taken over by the Japanese in 1913. Since then we have not worked on the organ.

Several years ago out of curiosity and sentimentality I entered the church. The organ as of old was still unchanged — in its original condition, with a pump handle protruding from the inside, which I pumped often as a youngster when tuning the organ with my father. The organ, however, was not in playing condition. An electronic instrument was in use. I believe this organ, now 94 years old, could claim the distinction of being the oldest and possibly the only Mayer organ left intact and unchanged in San Francisco.

MISSION DOLORES CHURCH

The most famous of the churches of San Francisco is, of course, the beloved and revered old adobe structure, Mission Dolores, founded by the early Franciscan Padres Crespi and Palou on June 29, 1776, five days before the signing of the Declaration of Independence took place. It was the sixth Mission established in Upper California under Padre Junipero Serra, O.F.M. Built by the Indians of adobe, and designed to withstand destruction by the forces of nature, it is today one of the landmarks of San Francisco. The cornerstone of the Mission was laid by Padre Palou on April 25, 1782.

In the early pioneer days of San Francisco, Mission Dolores and St. Francis Church were the only two Catholic churches in the city. Old St. Mary's and the many others followed later. From about 1853 to 1866, one of the old Mission buildings was also used as a study house for Diocesan priests, called St. Thomas Seminary, from which a number of priests were ordained. Among them, Rev. Sebastian Wolf, who became the first Pastor of St.,Boniface Church and who happened to christen me in 1884.

As the old adobe Mission, in time, became inadequate to fill the needs of the congregation that settled around it, a new large brick parish church, in the Gothic style, was built in 1869, north of the old Mission. Sometime previous to this, 16th Street had been cut through, necessitating the removal of an adobe extension to the Mission proper, called "Mansion House." I recall seeing pictures of it, and remember as a boy seeing some of the remnants of the old adobe walls in the northwest corner lot of 16th and Dolores Streets.

The laying of the cornerstone of this new brick church must have been quite an event. I recall my father relating that he conducted an amateur brass band on the occasion. The band was called the "St. Cecilia's Musik Verein", an organization of the German St. Boniface Church on Tyler Street, now Golden Gate Avenue. A little Erben pipe organ, built in New York, presumably used in the old Mission

Church, was then installed in the new brick, Gothic structure.

I have a faint recollection of seeing it at one time, high up in the gallery of the lofty Gothic church. I remember my father relating that after one was through playing the organ the entire keyboard was shoved into the organ and the opening then closed by two sliding doors. It evidently was a one manual and Pedal organ.

The earthquake of April 18, 1906 caused severe damage to the new church but, by the grace of God, the old Mission Dolores adobe structure adjoining it was unharmed. The fire, although it leveled several blocks from the opposite side of the street eastward, did not injure either the old adobe Mission or the new brick edifice. The damage to the new brick church by the earthquake, however, was so severe that it was condemned as unsafe and was razed. Someone other than my father evidently removed the organ before the building was torn down, as many years later when Rt. Rev. Msgr. William J. Sullivan was pastor of the new church, that had since been built, I was asked to look at some stray organ pipes he had stored in the basement of the parochial residence. These proved to be, I am certain, the remnants of what was once the little Erben organ.

Shortly after the fire and the demolition of the brick church, a temporary frame structure was built somewhat to the rear of the former church, and was used for a number of years, preparatory to the building of a new permanent edifice. Rev. Father Cummings was pastor at this time. A reed organ was used in this structure.

The old adobe Mission building, which had come through the earthquake unscathed, was nevertheless thoroughly gone over. It was reinforced with steel girders and otherwise strengthened and preserved for future generations. This work was done with the greatest care and skill, and defies detection.

On completion of the new church in 1913, we first installed a large Vocallion reed organ, which had formerly been used in the Swedish Lutheran Church. It was logical, however, that in time a better and more permanent instrument be installed and Rt. Rev. Msgr. Sullivan, then pastor of the new church, decided to buy a new organ, as we had all other organs of this Boston firm, sold heretofore in this territory. This organ was installed in the early twenties.

It is a three manual and Pedal electric pneumatic action divided organ, all under expression, placed in alcoves in both tower rooms. The organ has 43 stops. The Choir manual is practically duplexed from the Great manual.

Not satisfied with the gallery organ alone, Rt. Rev. Msgr. William Sullivan had us later, in 1924, build a small sanctuary organ of 5 stops, which we placed in a niche behind the high altar on the opposite end of the church, concealed by a beautifully designed and executed grill. The console for this organ was placed in the North transept of the church and its chief purpose was to accompany the children in congregational singing at the early Mass on Sunday mornings. Rt. Rev. Msgr. Sullivan, however, also being deeply interested in a boys choir, succeeded in having one established in his Church. Miss Frances Murphy, a pupil of Wallace Sabin, was the organist.

To lead and direct the choir boys more directly, whose seats or stalls were located in the Sanctuary on either side of the high altar, visible to the congregation, he had us build another small console, which we placed directly behind the high altar, connected with the transept console. The organist was thus completely concealed from the congregation, but was plainly in view of the choir boys.

Since provision was made in the gallery organ console to play the small Sanctuary organ eventually, as an Echo or Antiphonal, but not visa versa, we connected both by a cable placed over the ceiling of the church.

Miss Frances Murphy was organist for a short time after the installation of the new organ, later accepting a position as organist at St. Dominic's Church. My sister, Miss Cecilia Schoenstein, who for many years had been organist at St. Anthony's Church, then became organist at Mission Dolores. She held this position for about six years, when she returned to her old position at St. Anthony's. Robert Hayburn, a promising young musician, succeeded her as organist at Mission Dolores and, on deciding later to enter the seminary at Menlo Park, he relinquished the position to the present organist Mr. Herbert Bergman.

Mission Dolores became the parish church of the auxiliary bishop of the Diocese at that time, The Right Rev. Thomas J. Connally, D.D., and since then one of the present auxiliary bishops in the person of The Right Rev. Merlin J. Guilfoyle. In concluding, a word of appreciation is due its faithful sexton, James Milholland.

Mission Dolores is now one of the flourishing parishes of the Diocese in its own right, as well as by reason of its romantic and historical background. It has also since been given the title or distinction of a Basilica. It is a church that must be visited and attended if one's pilgrimage to San Francisco's churches is to be complete.

TEMPLE OHABAI SHALOME

The organ at Temple Ohabai Shalome was an old Joseph Mayer tracker action organ with attached keyboard set into the walnut case. It was built in 1872. The Temple was originally on the east side of Mason Street, between Post and Geary Streets, and, in 1896, was moved to the present site on the south side of Bush Street between Laguna and Octavia Streets, where my father reinstalled the organ. A. Mr. Delipiani, an old friend and acquaintance of my father, was the organist. I recall his characteristics vividly. He reminded me of some European ambassador or diplomat, tall and slim in stature, a rather nasal voice and foreign accent, bespectacled, with a black cord attached to his glasses. He was constantly fidgeting and replacing them on his nose. He had a thin, dark moustache, was well dressed in black cutaway suit and wore a stiff derby hat, and was always smoking a fragrant cigar.

My first recollection of working on the organ was in 1899, the year after I left school, when I assisted my father. I remember the day perfectly. The Spanish-American War had been terminated, and on this particular day the first United States transport was due to arrive in San Francisco harbor, returning the first contingent of California volunteers from the Philippine Islands. San Francisco had prepared a royal welcome for them. The downtown streets had been festooned and decorated and a triumphal arch was built over Market Street. All the people who could possibly do so, hurried to the hilltops and other vantage points overlooking the bay to witness the naval parade that was to escort the transport through the Golden Gate down the bay to its unloading pier.

Although I had planned to witness the parade of the soldiers up Market Street later in the day, I did not feel that my father could spare me in the morning when the transport was due to arrive — as he needed me to hold the keys while he was tuning the organ.

As I recall, it was about 10 o'clock in the morning when Mr. Delipiani happened to drop in. We, of course, began to discuss the absorbing topic of the day, the expected arrival of the soldiers and the celebration to be held in their honor. He was surprised that we were working. I told him that dad was concerned about getting his work done. He obviously observed, however, that my heart was not with my work. Just then loud cannonading was heard and the whistles started to blow — a signal that the transport had been sighted far out beyond the heads. Mr. Delipiani noticed my excitement and my evident longing to see the ship enter the port, and shouted to my dad: "Mr. Schoenstein, let your son go to witness the celebration; I will hold the keys for you. I was a boy myself once and know how he feels." Needless to say, after a hurried thank you, and without further asking my father's consent, I dashed off for the hilltops on Pacific Heights, where I had a fine, unobstructed view of the Bay and the notable event, as the transport, with its array of decorated craft escorting it, glided through the waters to its pier.

On my return to San Francisco from New York, the first job I worked on was again at Temple Ohabai Shalome. It was on April 9, 1909. In fact, this date marked the beginning of my partnership in business with my father, forming the firm of Felix F. Schoenstein & Son.

The special work my father had contracted to do on the Ohabai Shalome organ was to replace the original Mayer metal pipes, which were in bad condition, with new pipes of standard make; to extend the lowest octave of the open

Diapason 16' on the Great with a stopped 8' wood pipe; and to quiet and rebush the action in general.

The designing and making of this chest on the pneumatic system applied to the tracker action system was my first constructive job on my return home. The experience of again working with my father proved to be most pleasant to me, and I am sure it was comforting to him, also, to have me with him again. My father was especially interested in this organ, as he informed me it was his particular work while in the employ of Joseph Mayer, the organ builder, in his early career, to make the walnut case. He carefully called my attention to the hand-carved Gothic mouldings encasing the panels in the front of it. He also made the manual keys for the organ.

The Synagogue was evidently being redecorated at this time, so the organ was also getting this special attention, not only the interior of the organ, but also the exterior of the case. A Mr. Stern, one of the directors of the Temple, evidently a retired gentleman, did the work of highlighting the mouldings and ornaments of the case with gold. The combination of the dark walnut with the gold trimming made a very effective contrast. I recall the leisurely pace in which he did his work, and the never-failing fragrant cigar he continuously smoked while so engaged. Another interesting character who was a daily visitor while we were at work on the organ was the cantor, Reverend Solomon. Many a pleasant conversation we had together.

We made one additional improvement to the organ, and that was to install a kinetic blower, eliminating the hand-pump arrangement formerly in use. Speaking of the hand-pump, this organ had the unique feature of having two pump handles, or, to be more explicit, one pump lever fulcrumed in the center with a handle on either end.

Finally, in 1929, the congregation disbanded and the property was taken over by the Japanese for a Buddhist or Shinto Temple.

Subsequently, during World War II, the old Synagogue became the church of a black congregation.

One day in May 1944, we received a call from a Reverend Ogborn of a Macedonian Baptist Church on Bush Street, to look at an old pipe organ they had there, to report on its condition and the cost of the repairs.

We had never heard of this church, but soon found that it was the old Temple Ohabai Shalome, christened with a new name. On examination of the organ, we found that the new pipes we had installed 25 years before were intact and unharmed. Aside from some broken pedal trackers that had been trampled on, and a split fold in the bellows that let the air rush out when pumped, the organ was none the worse for its many years of disuse. After spending several days working on it, the organ was again in good condition.

The edifice is doomed to be razed in the near future to complete a Redevelopment Project in the Western Addition of the city. The organ, we understand, was recently, in 1968, reconditioned and revoiced, to make it a more Baroque type instrument than it originally was. The work was done by two former employees of our firm.

TEMPLE SHERITH ISRAEL

Sherith Israel was the second Jewish congregation to have a substantial building erected in San Francisco. It was located on the northeast corner of Post and Taylor Streets, before the fire. The synagogue was located on the upper story, and a religious instruction school, parlors and offices, were on the lower floor.

For some years and up until 1901 we serviced the old tracker action Bergstrom organ they had there. It was a two manual organ with about 12 stops and an attached console. Reverend Jacob Nieto was the Rabbi at the time and Mr. Davis was the cantor.

About 1903 the Temple planned to build a new structure, so through our instrumentality the old Bergstrom organ was sold to St. Bridget's Church at Van Ness Avenue and Broadway, of which Father Cottle was then pastor. It was installed by my brother Leo Schoenstein. This Bergstrom organ supplanted a one manual Kimball organ, then in use, which was moved to the Methodist Church in Palo Alto. In 1906, at the time of the fire and earthquake, St. Bridget's

Church was badly damaged by the tremor. The front brick wall of the church with granite facing fell on the Bergstrom organ and damaged it beyond repair. The fire did no damage to the edifice as it did not cross to the west side of Van Ness Avenue at this point.

In 1904, the cornerstone for the new Temple Sherith Israel, located on the northeast corner of California and Webster Streets, was laid. The building is an imposing limestone structure, rather rectangular in shape, surmounted by a huge dome. The interior of the Temple is most impressive. The whole north end, containing the altar, the ark, the pulpit, and above it the organ and choir loft, was finished in polished mahogany, since subdued, a masterpiece in design and workmanship. The pews are made of the same material, and a beautiful red carpet covers the floor. The walls are artistically frescoed, the work of some Italian artists. The huge dome, which forms the ceiling of the Temple, and which seems to fade away in the azure sky, is intercepted by a partial lower ceiling with a large opening in the center, making the upper or final ceiling of the dome visible from below. Over the upper surface of this first ceiling is a passage way on which is located the echo organ. Art glass windows, white marble stairs in the entrance and vestibule give this edifice an appearance of wealth and affluence. It is, indeed, one of the show places of San Francisco.

The organ is a large three manual and Pedal Los Angeles Art (Murray M. Harris) organ, built in Los Angeles in 1904. It contains 55 stops and is one of the excellent organs of the city. Although the tone is somewhat smothered in a large pocket over the organ chamber above the opening arch, the tonal qualities in the organ are of the best and its ensemble is one that pleases me very much. The voicing was the work of the famous John W. Whitely, formerly of England. There is a splendid Diapason Chorus in the Great unexpressive which gives the organ its character and dignity. The Swell and Choir manuals and part of the Great manual are enclosed.

I have always admired the full Pedal in this organ, and could never quite account for its grandeur and sublimity, except that it has an octave coupler, coupling up good material already present in the bass. As to the stability and satisfactory functioning of this instrument at all times, I would refer to this organ as the "Rock of Gibralter", always reliable and dependable.

During the past 58 years practically no major improvement has been made to the organ, with the exception of installing an Eck generator in 1913 to dispense with the wet cell batteries originally installed. A notice still there, written on the wall of the blower room, reminds one of the horse and buggy days when the wet cells were in use. It reads: "Do not sweep while blower is running. Keep battery cells filled with clear water, so that plates are well covered." There is also this note referring to the first generator installed, later followed by the present Eck generator: "Keep generator oil cups well filled with vaseline, *never use oil.* Keep brushes well cleaned with gasoline, *nothing else will do as well.*" A large American blower, driven by a huge belt about 8" wide and 15' long from a seven h.p. motor, furnishes the wind. This equipment is now obsolete, but its dependability is in keeping with the general trait of the organ. The combination action of the organ is the blind system. The console is arranged with the stop knobs in tiers on either side, with the "straight" Pedal board of 30 notes. The interior of the organ is high and lofty, the Swell organ over the Choir and Great, and the latter about 12 feet from the floor.

The echo organ in the dome consists of three stops. It was the first echo organ installed in a church in San Francisco, and we expected to hear something ethereal and heavenly, sound floating down from above as it were, but we were sadly disappointed on hearing it the first time. Although there is a very soft string, a vox humana, and flute in it, due to the excessive reverberation and amplification of tone caused by the dome, which seems to magnify every sound in the edifice, the tone was so loud as to make the echo organ practically useless. The entire echo organ, already enclosed in its swell box with expression shutters, was then put in a second enclosure with marked improvement. From the location of this echo organ I have learned a valuable lesson, which has been borne out by many other successful echo organ installations that I have seen and heard since during my career, and that is, not to place the echo organ over or above the main organ but preferably opposite it, so that the tone comes from some other direction. In the Sherith Israel organ the soft stop of the Swell manual with blinds closed, although closer to the organist, sounds more distant than the soft stop of the echo organ in the dome 50 feet above the organ.

We have serviced this organ, as stated, for a period of 57 years and admire its durability, dependability and staying qualities, both mechanically and tonally, and that is why it merits the analogy of "The Rock of Gibràltar."

Shortly after the fire, Temple Sherith Israel, being one of a few suitable and substantial buildings left that had not been destroyed in the catastrophe, was used as the courtroom for the jury trials of the then famous graft cases of Abe Ruef, Calhoun, Eugene Schmitz, etc. Here the accusations and charges of the Prosecuting District Attorney, Francis J. Heney, and the late Hiram Johnson, his assistant, were wont to fill the dome with their vehemence, and answered again just as vehemently by the attorneys of the opposition. Although cigar smoke and the usual clamor and commotion of City Hall or courtroom scenes permeated the air and gave the Temple the usual atmosphere of a court house, on Friday evening and Saturday morning services were again held with the usual decorum and reverence.

The Police Chief, William J. Biggy, who attended many of these trials, was shortly thereafter found dead aboard a boat on the Bay.

Reverend Jacob Nieto, Rabbi of the Temple, was a most unusual personage, one who would be picked out of a million. He had a dark moustache and a little Van Dyke goatee and invariably wore a large-brimmed, dark slouch hat. Typically Hebraic features made him one of the outstanding clerics of his day. Benjamin Liederman had held the office of Cantor for many years, until he retired and finally died on October 3, 1961.

Organists who held positions here were: William King, Dr. Humphrey J. Stewart, Benjamin Moore, Warren D. Allen, Dr. Achille Artigues, and William W. Carruth. The latter held the position from 1919 until his death on August 27, 1954. Harold Mueller is the present organist.

Music at the Temple has always been highly featured, and a paid quartet serves throughout the year. At the holidays the choir is augmented, rendering music unexcelled anywhere.

LEBANON PRESBYTERIAN CHURCH

Out in the Eureka Valley District on Sanchez and 23rd Street is an old frame church with a tall spire. It was built in 1883. In 1903 they procured a John Bergstrom two manual and Pedal organ of 8 stops and three couplers. Some shipping notations on the inside of the case marked "Petaluma, California" would indicate that possibly it was first installed in some church in that town. Mr. William Barr, under whose supervision the organ was procured, was its first organist and remained until 1910.

I recall before I could work on the Pedal trackers under the Pedal chest, I had to first do some general housecleaning as the organ pumper evidently had the habit of throwing all his newspapers over the partition into the organ when he was through reading them.

In later years we were called more frequently to service the organ and always enjoyed the mellow tones of this old organ.

Organists who functioned in addition to the aforementioned were: Mrs. Ella N. Mellars, from 1910 to 1925; Mrs. Sydonia McKinlay Irvine, 1925 to 1940; Mrs. Ruth Wallace, a short period during 1944; and again the elderly veteran organist, Mrs. Ella N. Mellars who assumed the position again in 1944.

About this time agitation began about improving and rearranging the Sanctuary layout, in which the old tracker action organ with its attached keyboard did not fit well into the picture. About 1949 the old organ was sold and a modern Moller organ was installed in its place.

The old Bergstrom organ finally found a new abode in the old historic Mission San Carlos Borromeo, Carmel, California. It was installed by a Mr. Martin, a local maintenance man.

METROPOLITAN TEMPLE ORGAN
Fifth St. bet. Market & Mission Sts.

My first recollection of Fifth Street, where the Metropolitan Temple was located, was the imposing United States Mint Building. In going to St. Boniface School on Golden Gate Avenue and Leavenworth Street, we would at times go to Sixth and Tehama Streets to visit a relative. Sixth Street also being a busy shopping center for the South of Market District, my mother would go there often to do her shopping. I remember seeing the two large square towers located at the rear of the Mint Building, near Mint Avenue. When we saw yellow smoke coming from the chimneys we were told, and believed it, that gold was being melted and that gold money was being coined or made. When I was older I would pass the Mint often on my own accord. However, to this day I have yet to enter its portals. Opposite the Mint, nearer Market Street, was the Lincoln School. I looked upon this place with reverence, as it was the school where my father, as a young emigrant to San Francisco, attended evening classes to learn to speak, read and write the English language. To the south of this school, or opposite the U. S. Mint Building, stood the Metropolitan Temple Building.

It was built with the purpose in mind of being a community, or union, church for various Baptist denominations then in the city, but failed eventually in this regard and was thereafter converted to a music or public hall. I recall distinctly attending one meeting in this building, and that was a political meeting, the first campaign of Eugene E. Schmitz, running on the Labor Party ticket for Mayor of San Francisco. I must have inherited this trait of interest in political issues from my father. At the earliest possible date he took out his citizenship papers and voted at every election that he was able to, until his death. He took the privilege of suffrage seriously and set an example to many a native born American who carelessly neglects his privilege and duty to vote.

The mayorality campaign was getting exciting. I believe it

was the first time the Labor Party put up its own candidate. I did not favor Eugene Schmitz' candidacy, but attended the meeting to hear and see what the opposition party had to offer. My favorite was John Partington. The election was that of the year 1904. I was not even eligible to vote at that time, not having reached my majority. Politics were taken more seriously by the youth of my day.

While attending the above political rally, I remember I sat in the gallery, opposite the large organ. It seemed quite lofty and appeared to have an attached console. Strange to relate, I do not recall if I heard the organ at any time previous, or at this meeting. I often heard my father speak of it, and it must have received quite a lot of popular acclaim in the early days of San Francisco.

To my best knowledge, it was a three manual and Pedal organ, tracker action. It was built by John Bergstrom & Company of San Francisco, in his factory at 29th and Mission Streets. I recall my father's statement that, at this time, Bergstrom was financed through the music house of Sherman, Clay & Co., and therefore used the word "Company" following his name.

Some time before the fire and earthquake of 1906, the Metropolitan Temple Building was razed, for what purpose I do not know. At any rate, novices or inexperienced help dismantled the organ and had it stored in the old St. Mary's College buildings on Mission Road. The organ had evidently been donated to His Grace the Most Reverend Archbishop of San Francisco, Patrick Riordan, for future use in the contemplated chapel that was to be built at St. Patrick's Seminary at Menlo Park, California.

When the time became ripe for considering the matter of the organ, a committee called on my father and asked him to inspect it. I recall my father describing his horror on seeing the organ, on how it was stored and in what deplorable condition it was. It was piled up like fire wood, pipes, mechanism and all in one heap. The report and verdict was that the organ was unusuable. Therefore, what was once the great Metropolitan Temple organ was now only useless junk, and finis was written to its career.

GRACE METHODIST EPISCOPAL CHURCH
(Now Grace United Church)

One of the flourishing Protestant churches of the Mission District was Grace Methodist Episcopal Church, located on the northwest corner of 21st and Capp Streets. It was built in 1886. Its stately spire and beautiful Gothic lines give it the typical church atmosphere, usually lacking in many of the newer Protestant church edifices.

About 1900, my father had the regular maintenance of the organ. It was a typical Bergstrom two manual and Pedal tracker action organ, attached console, with about 12 stops. It was pumped by hand.

I recall on one occasion, either the Christmas or Easter holidays, something went wrong with the organ, some notes were continuously sounding. Evidently my father was summoned, but must have been out of town. The case must have been very urgent as my mother, who was much concerned over the welfare of my father's business, induced an old acquaintance, Mr. Peter Mueller, a former employee of my father, to at least try and give temporary relief until my father returned. I accompanied Mr. Mueller to the church.

When we arrived a choir rehearsal was in progress. Mr. Robert C. Husband, the choir leader, and Mr. Wittich, the organist, discussed the trouble with Mr. Mueller, who seemed perplexed and apparently did not know how to go about locating the trouble. In my youthful ignorance, I knew much less and could not help him. Possibly my father arrived home later that evening and was able to correct the trouble before the morning services.

The earthquake of 1906 severely damaged the interior of the church. Practically all of the plaster on the ceiling of the lofty nave came hurtling down. The great fire that followed the earthquake and destroyed such a large portion of the downtown section of San Francisco, did not reach the church, but its southernmost extremity was not far away. The old ceiling was cleared off and the open, beamed trusswork was partly covered with wooden panels, lowering the height of the ceiling considerably. The church was redecorated and again presented its former stately, although somewhat altered, appearance.

In the course of time the popularity of the church waned, due mostly to the change of population and the encroaching of business in the now populous and thriving Mission shopping district. A new, energetic, and likeable pastor was secured, Rev. Newton E. Moats, who, with new, progressive ideas promised to revivify the failing activities of a formerly active congregation. He was a man of wonderful personality, undoubtedly most sincere, but his extreme confidence and unchecked enthusiasm proved later to be his undoing, as the church was burdened with a heavy debt that was most staggering.

Among the innovations and improvements he made and attempted, were the laying of a new, heavily padded soft carpet, from the front of the vestibule of the church to the upper auditorium floor; the installation of a new pipe organ; the formation of a large augmented choir with a prominent soloist, with programs broadcast over the air and the publishing of a monthly periodical called "The Spire."

Eventually, a merger of the Mission Congregational Church and the Trinity Presbyterian Church with the Grace Methodist Episcopal Church was entered into, forming the new Grace United Church. After some time, the Trinity Presbyterian unit withdrew from the coalition and resumed services at their former location on 23rd and Capp Streets. The Congregational unit still retains its affiliations.

Coming back to Dr. Moats arrival at the church, a new and modern organ was an important item in his plan of rejuvenation. The old Bergstrom organ was dismantled by us and was shipped to Mexico, where it was installed by local parties. Several years later, from a returning visitor, we heard of its successful functioning.

To replace the old Bergstrom organ a deal was made with the owners of the old Murray M. Harris organ, formerly in the Methodist Church at California and Broderick Streets, which was acquired by the Seventh Day Adventists. This organ was entirely rebuilt by our firm, only the Pipes, Pedal Chest, Swell boxes, and the exterior were retained.

We built a new modern console, installed new Pitman chests with individual valves, primary actions arranged, and applied three new bellows and a new motor and blower. This installation work was done mostly by my nephew, Leo G. Schoenstein, and his helper, John Strathaus, and I completed the work.

The organ, which was always of excellent tone, with the new modern appointments, proved to be exceptionally satisfactory. Uda Waldrop gave the dedicatory recital and demonstrated the organ to very good advantage.

In 1928, a set of Deagan chimes was added, a gift of Dr. Arnsby in memory of Ruth Prescott by J. E. and L. F. Prescott.

Reverend Moats was transferred in 1932 to other fields. Other ministers have come and gone.

After fifty years of satisfactory service, we began to experience trouble from deteriorating leather and from the moths eating through the pneumatic pouches of the organ, which were made of Zephyr leather, causing much ciphering. A general overhauling was urgently needed, but due to the limited resources of the church a complete job of reconditioning could not be made at one time and we had to resort to a piecemeal schedule.

Miss Helen Larson, their faithful and devoted organist, who, notwithstanding the annoyance of playing on a worn out instrument, cheerfully carried on her musical duties. She was also the spark plug continuously gathering the necessary sheckles to complete the restoration of the church organ. We admired her for her perseverance and patience.

An incident related to Grace United Church may be of interest. Years ago I was called upon to repair an old Pierce and Company #16967 Spinet Melodian for an elderly lady in a residence on 21st Street near the church. She told me it was the first organ used by Grace M. E. Church (as it was originally called). Years later, on May 26, 1953, while servicing the pipe organ above described, the Sexton asked me if I would do him a favor and look at an old Harmonium he had apart in the Sunday School below. On seeing the old instrument, I recognized it at once as the Spinet reed organ I worked on some twenty-five years before, only this time a placque with the following inscription was fastened thereon: "In memory of Henry Thomas and wife, nee Mary Forster, who presented this, the first organ, to Grace M. E. Church in 1866. Mr. Thomas was Chorister and Martha Beaumont first organist." This plate was furnished by their children in loving remembrance. The Sexton had taken the organ apart to repair it. How he succeeded, or what became of it, I do not know.

The congregation has since combined with the Epworth M. E. Church, and the property on 21st and Capp Streets has been sold to the Federal Government, and the original Murray Harris there has been sold to the Christian Bros. Novitiate at Mount La Salle, Napa County.

ST MARY'S CATHEDRAL

In the early days of San Francisco, "Old St. Mary's Church", on California and Dupont Streets, was the cathedral of San Francisco. Undoubtedly, with the expansion of the City westward and the extension of Chinatown to the very walls of Old St. Mary's Church, as well as other objectionable developments that took place within the shadows of Old St. Mary's, it was found expedient and necessary to build a larger and more adequate cathedral elsewhere, one in keeping with the dignity and character of this growing and developing City.

Accordingly, a site was secured on Van Ness Avenue and O'Farrell Street. It was a high, wind swept sand-dune, as the greater part of the Western Addition was at that time, according to notes made by my father. Van Ness Avenue, being one of the broadest avenues in the city, soon became a show street. Beautiful mansions, with their mansard roofs, soon adorned the acacia lined avenue. The broad macadamized roadway was a parade ground for the finest specimens of horse drawn equipages and vehicles.

In 1887 the cornerstone of the new cathedral was laid and the solemn dedication took place on January 11, 1891. His Grace, Archbishop Sadoc Alemany, being well along in years and wishing to be relieved of his arduous duties, retired to his old home in Vich, near Barcelona, Spain, where he died on April 14, 1888. The young and energetic Reverend Patrick W.

Riordan, a Canadian by birth, then became the Most Reverend Archbishop of San Francisco, the confines of his diocese embracing all the western states of the United States. The city developed rapidly to the west, south and north of the cathedral, and for many years it was centrally located and enjoyed all the prestige and advantages of the Cathedral Church of the City.

My earliest recollection of St. Mary's Cathedral, strange to relate, is connected with a very irrelevant and mundane matter. Sometime in one's life small, inconsequential things or incidents leave deep impressions. It seems rather incongruous to associate a cathedral with nonpareil candies, nevertheless the two are closely connected in my first recollection of St. Mary's Cathedral. I was five or six years old at the time and was out walking with some doting relative or friend of the family, as we were not ordinarily treated to candy when we went out with our parents. At any rate, I remember passing down O'Farrell Street, approaching Van Ness Avenue, alongside the iron fence, by the Cathedral tightly holding a bag of the nonpareil candies in my hand, and munching the delicious brown chocolate wafers with the white speckled dots sprinkled thereon, to my heart's content.

My next remembrance of the Cathedral was in 1892. I was attending the first grade in St. Boniface School. The 400th anniversary of the discovery of America by Columbus, was being fittingly celebrated at the Cathedral, and a special service was held on a particular weekday during the afternoon. A selected number of pupils from all the parochial schools of the city were invited to attend and occupied seats on both of the side galleries flanking the main body of the Cathedral. The main nave of the church was reserved for the grownups. Why I was so fortunate in being selected, I do not know. I do know we considered it an honor to be so privileged and remember marching in a body from St. Boniface School to the Cathedral on Van Ness Avenue. I distinctly remember the very seat I had and could point it out at any time. It was on the south gallery in the center tier near the front of the Church. I had a fairly good view of the sanctuary and also of the organ loft at the opposite end of the church. The sanctuary was crowded with the clergy and altar boys, and His Excellency the Most Reverend Archbishop Patrick Riordan, D. D., was seated on the bishop's throne. The high altar and sanctuary were decorated with tapers, flowers and ferns, the whole gorgeous setting making a wonderful impression on me.

Curiosity made me occasionally look also to the rear of the church where the large cathedral organ and choir were located. A constant movement or commotion seemed to be evident among the singers and very likely other visitors ordinarily not present there. This arrangement of the cathedral, with its side galleries running parallel with the main body of the church, giving the occupants of the gallery seats full view of the entire church, the organ loft as well as the sanctuary, proves oftentimes more distracting than edifying. Instead of concentrating one's attention on the altar, it is often diverted to observing the organist and singers, who, to help maintain a decorous and reverent congregation, would often be better only heard and not seen. I remember on this occasion hearing for the first time, that old familiar tune "Come Holy Ghost, Creator Blest."

Aside from this one objectionable feature of the Cathedral, its interior always fascinated and inspired me — its great curves and arches, its massive columns and groins of polished wood, its frescoed walls, its priceless art glass windows that were made in Munich, Germany, its oaken pews and impressive white marble altars. The broad, inviting granite steps arranged in three tiers of twelve steps each, leading to the main entrance of the edifice, gave all the prerequisites of a grand cathedral in word and deed. The large organ on the east gallery, partly concealing a large stained glass rose window, with the overhanging loft of richly designed and carved oak, made a beautiful impression on leaving the church.

The cathedral organ was a large three manual and Pedal tracker action organ, originally built by the Hook and Hastings Company of Boston, Mass., Opus 1431 in 1889. It had a Barker lever pneumatic action on the Great and Swell manuals. The console was detached, the organist facing the altar. The organ consisted of 55 speaking stops with the usual proportion of Diapasons, Mixtures, Acutas and Cornets, and all the usual and desirable variations of flutes and strings, and the indispensable reed choruses. The ensemble tone of the organ was typically traditional, or classical, and it was an ideal cathedral organ in every sense of the word. Being voiced only on 3½" to 4" pressure, the reed tone was somewhat blatant, due to the thin reeds and light metal used in the resonators, giving the organ a generally bright and brilliant tone, an ensemble assiduously being sought for at the present time.

An unusual stop on the Pedal organ was the Contra Bourdon 32' produced by adding stoppers to a 16-foot open pipe of large scale, the first one heard in San Francisco, and also the Quint 10-2/3 foot stop. It was the first organ in San Francisco to also have a Crescendo Pedal. I recall I was timid about using it. Although it had a balanced foot Pedal, it had a tendency of racing and getting beyond control, finally bringing on full organ with noise and commotion, that was very noticeable and distracting. Originally, the Swell manual was the only manual that was under expression, the Choir and Great manuals being unexpressive.

My father assisted in its erection and our firm has been the custodian of it ever since.

A peculiar incident occurred in the designing and building of this organ. As stated, most of the interior woodwork of the cathedral was of oak, red cherry and the light colored California sugar pine, highly finished, a color scheme that was harmonious and blending. The organ case, however, was made of Redwood from California. The builders, undoubtedly, thought they were complimenting Californians by using their native wood, and as the color matched with the cherry wood, the harmony was satisfactory. The craftsmanship and the finish of the case were of the highest order, but the thought of using California redwood, our cheapest wood on the West Coast market at the time, the wood we used for backyard fences, seemed to shock my father's sensibility to such an extent that whenever he saw the case it would be the occasion for some rebuke from him on the sin of omission, in not using a hardwood.

In later years, through scientific research conducted by State authorities, it was proven that California redwood was one of the best woods for pipe organ purposes, not so much for the exterior cases, but for the interior structural parts, and even for the wood pipes themselves. The Murray M. Harris Organ Company of Los Angeles used it at one time almost exclusively for the construction of the interior parts and wood organ pipes.

Back to the description of the Cathedral organ . . . resting upon this well-designed and proportional organ case were mounted a large number of display pipes. Most of these were speakers, beautifully decorated in pleasing and harmonious colors, as was customary at that time. The blower was located in the North Tower room, and consisted of a single piston type water motor, with an up and down stroke, and was supplied by a four inch water main from the city service. The piston was about 8" in diameter, and connected with a heavy rocker arm connected with two square horizontal feeders, which would force the air into two large auxiliary bellows inside of the organ. It was manufactured in Boston.

In the course of time the valves of the water motor controlling the piston, which were of a revolving type similar to that used in the old type Tuba or Cornet, or other brass musical instrument, wore out and undoubtedly due to some maladjustment caused by this, often refused to operate, and with all of its tremendous power, like a stubborn mule, would not budge at times. Plumbers, machinists and other mechanics were often summoned to correct this cause of unreliability and obstinacy. Also the high cost of the water service was making the blowing end of the organ a problem. Finally, as a solution to the difficulty, in 1913, we eliminated the entire water motor arrangement and installed a modern electric Kinetic blowing plant, which was quiet and economical in operation, and satisfactory in every respect.

The building of this Cathedral organ by the Hook and Hastings Company of Boston, coupled with the high integrity of the firm, proved to be the forerunner of many other sales of smaller Hook and Hastings organs to other Catholic churches and institutions in the Diocese.

The fire and earthquake of 1906 did not seriously damage the Cathedral edifice. It was not reached by the fire, as that was checked at this point on the opposite side of Van Ness

Avenue, but the earthquake did some damage to the main supporting trusses of the roof, which became dislocated, and some of the brick supporting the walls were cracked.

From a reliable source (a Mr. Brainard) I have been informed that on April 19, 1906, at two a.m., the wooden cross on the top of the tower ignited, due to the intense heat whereas the other exposed portions of the tower, the slate roof, metal trimmings and brick walls, withstood the heat. Two firemen, Ohlsen and Smith of Engine Company No. 34, with the assistance of Father Chas. A. Raam and Father Phillip O'Ryan, fought the blaze with buckets of water and wet sacks, finally checking the fire by sawing off the burning cross and topling it down to the pavement below.

Reference to the Cathedral cross, appeared in the San Francisco News of January 5, 1955, "the two buildings referred to felt the heat of the flames and miraculously escaped, as did St. Mary's Cathedral to the south. The golden cross atop St. Mary's did catch aflame and was extinguished by a heroic priest."

A constant reminder to me of the earthquake and fire days were several heavy welts and a split panel left in the door entering the choir loft, which the firemen made in trying to get access to the locked organ loft.

Our inspection of the organ after the earthquake showed that the edifice was severely shaken. Although none of the large front pipes were thrown from their places, they must have been dangerously close to losing their equilibrium, as all supporting stays were ripped from their moorings by the swaying they endured. A general restrengthening of the front pipe supports and a thorough cleaning of the organ, which was made necessary because of the ceiling plaster that had fallen on it, was all that had to be done to the organ to put it in condition again. The damage to the edifice was also soon repaired, and the interior redecorated, but in a more simple color scheme than before.

Organists who played the organ were Mr. A. C. Eimer, the first Cathedral organist who was still playing in 1889, and Mr. Robert J. Harrison, the latter an elderly gentleman who was quite intimate with my father. My father related, however, that this mutual good will manifested then was not always present, and that in earlier years Mr. Harrison severely condemned and ridiculed my father as a foreigner, and accused him of incompetency in building a certain organ then under consideration. Certainly, time brings changes and heals many woulds. I recall at one of our weekly visits, the discussion centered on the question of the superiority of the electric over the tracker action. At that time my father suggested that sooner or later the Cathedral organ should be electrified. Mr. Harrison, however, expressed his disfavor of the electric action and expounded the merits of the direct or tracker action. Regardless of its heft or heaviness to play, he insisted there was some personal contact or intimacy between the organist and the pipes, and that he could, therefore, interpret or communicate his feelings by certain pressures or attacks applied to the keys, as in piano playing. This argument is even today being revived, in this enlightened age. How erroneous and prejudiced he was in his view is shown by the fact, unknown to him, that both the Great and Swell manuals were applied with a Barker lever pneumatic, between the manual keys and the pipes on the chest. The touch of his fingers, therefore, regardless of how delicately or how forcefully he pressed them, did not open the pipe valve directly, but opened an auxiliary valve which, in turn, operated the chest pallet valve.

An interesting and likeable person frequently to be found about the Cathedral organ at this time was young Marshall Geiselman, a protege of Mr. Harrison. He performed brilliantly at the organ, substituting often for Mr. Harrison, and certainly a great future was destined for him. In later years, he became organist at some of our leading churches, but this luminous star of great promise, in the course of time, gradually faded into total oblivion.

After the demise of Mr. Harrison in 1908, Dr. Achille L. Artigues, a pupil of the Conservatory of Music in Paris, a young and brilliant organist, was selected for the position. He served the Cathedral in that capacity for 35 years. In 1947 he retired and in 1953 he died, at the age of 75.

In 1930, after the organ had given forty years of faithful service, and the action was getting exceedingly noisy so that it could be heard in the Cathedral below, and lacking the many refinements and improvements of the modern organ in the line of couplers, combination pistons, accessories, etc., and especially still being equipped with the old fashioned straight Pedal board of 27 notes, and the manual compass of 58 notes, it was decided to modernize the instrument by applying an electric pneumatic action to the mechanism of the organ throughout, completing the scales of all stops to conform to the new standard, to enclose the Choir manual of the organ, to apply a larger blowing unit, and to build an entirely new detached console with all the necessary couplers, combination pistons and accessories as recommended by the American Guild of Organists. This contract was awarded to our firm, after a thorough investigation, through the kindness of the Administrator of the Cathedral, Reverend Msgr. Charles A. Ramm.

I remember the first day we began to clear out, or better said, eliminate or annihilate the old tracker action in the organ. This was done with a vengeance. In the forty years preceding, whenever we worked in the maze of dry and brittle trackers to make adjustments, or in trying to turn some leather nuts for the same purpose, which later became securely rusted on the wires and pulverized if pressure was applied, defying any adjustment, trackers were often broken, requiring great delicacy in repairing them without damaging the adjoining ones. In other words, extreme caution and delicacy of touch and agility was required to climb or crawl around in this mass of frail trackers, levers, etc. On this day, however, caution and care were thrown to the wind. With a ruthless hammer in hand, with strokes right and left, what was once almost reverently treaded upon, and with the utmost caution, was now wrecked and junked as useless. The new electric action was to take its place. It was well that my father was not present at this orgy. What once, undoubtedly, had taken months of patient and skillful work to make, by the hands of master craftsmen, was now destroyed as useless in a few minutes. Such is progress with a rapid stride.

In reminiscing on St. Mary's Cathedral, several characters always come to my mind — first, the Very Rev. John J. Prendergast, V.G., who resided at the Cathedral residence; the Pedro Gomez, the sexton; and also an unknown visitor who frequently was seen passing through the choir loft.

When I was about fifteen or sixteen years old, my father entrusted me with the collection of the quarterly bills for the maintenance of the organs he then had in his charge. There were not many at the time, and the amounts varied according to the size of the organ and the frequency with which we visited them. The Cathedral organ was a large one and required weekly visits, so that bill was larger than most. At that time the issuing of checks or the keeping of a checking account was not in vogue as it is today. Cash payment in coin was the medium of exchange, even the dollar bills (paper money) was frowned upon, at least in the far West, but the large shiny silver dollars were welcomed. Many a time I called at the Cathedral residence and, announcing my mission, would be directed to the parlor where I waited with baited breath for His Reverence to appear with the cash.

Two large steel cut etchings of the City of Jerusalem adorned the walls of this parlor. I must have explored them so thoroughly that even today I see them as vividly in retrospect as if they were before me. Finally, Rev. Father Prendergast, V.G., would appear, a tall, slim, elderly man of sublime dignity, with a slow and measured step, his head wavering slightly, a voice deep and rich. He would give me the cash and I would receipt the bill. A few kindly words, inquiring how my father was, with a word or two to put me at my ease, he would lead me to the door and excuse himself. Father Prendergast was one of the first teachers at St. Bernard's Seminary at Mission Dolores, where students for the priesthood were taught before there was a St. Patrick's Seminary.

The other character, Pedro Gomez, the sexton, is unforgettable. He was of Mexican birth, dark complexioned, with a long handle-bar moustache, always wearing a frock coat. His face was pockmarked, and he limped on one leg, walking with a shuffling motion. He spoke with a stammering staccato, owing to an impediment in his speech. No more faithful and loyal soul could be found than Pedro. Forty years of faithful service he gave to the Cathedral, when finally he was laid to rest.

The third character I referred to was a gentleman past

middle age, one undoubtedly in some clerical profession. He evidently had a key for the organ loft and undoubtedly had business of some nature or an office in the tower room above the organ. During the many years we saw him pass the organ while we were working there, aside from a greeting, we never conversed with him, nor did we learn his name or what his business was in the tower room. Although I was often curious, I never did intrude in his precincts, and only in later years, going in search of a piece of wood or something, and noticing he was around no more, did I venture into the room which he had frequented and concluded it had been used for an office of some kind. I will conclude by referring to him as the "mystery man", as he still is that to me.

Archbishop Patrick W. Riordan, D.D., a man of noble character, of dignity and stately appearance, beloved and revered by all, passed to his eternal reward on December 27, 1914. His successor was the then much discussed and popular Rev. Edward J. Hanna, who became Archbishop on June 1, 1915. I recall a chance meeting I had with him one day in the Cathedral office, while visiting the Right Rev. Msgr. Charles A. Ramm, relative to discussing the alterations that were to be made to the Cathedral organ. He entered the parlor unannounced. I was introduced to him by Rev. Msgr. Ramm, and I recall his friendly and democratic bearing. A discussion of the reports of a serious earthquake that had just visited Santa Barbara and environs was had. He especially deplored the damage done to the old historical Mission Santa Barbara.

Archbishop Hanna retired on March 2, 1935, and finally passed to the great beyond on July 10, 1944 in the Eternal City of Rome, mourned and beloved by all.

St. Mary's Cathedral, with the advent of His Excellency the Most Reverend Archbishop John J. Mitty, D.D., who succeeded his predecessor on March 2, 1935, not only became a Cathedral in name, but also became a Cathedral in fact. Alterations, a short time after his appointment, were undertaken in enlarging the sanctuary to better accommodate a larger number of clergy for ecclesiastical functions, which were held now more frequently than ever before. A new bishop's throne was erected in the sanctuary, and the seating arrangement in the body of the church was changed so as to provide a large center aisle, which it lacked formerly, for processionals and recessionals. New stations of the cross and new side altars were also installed. Choir stalls were placed in the sanctuary for the use of the Seminarians, who sing at certain festive occasions.

In 1937, St. Mary's Cathedral celebrated fifty years of its existence.

On October 17, 1947, Dr. A. L. Artigues, after serving as organist for 35 years, relinquished his position due to ill health and finally died on November 20, 1952 at the age of 75 years. Rene Sarazen, his foster brother, succeeded him as Director of Music, and Mr. George Liddle, the former assistant organist, became organist of the Cathedral. Following Mr. Liddle were Brother Columban, F.S.C., and Dennis J. Desjardins, the present organist.

In 1930 the interior of the Cathedral was again redecorated, this time in a more colorful style than the previous severe treatment. The basement floor of the Cathedral was also altered. The large Chapel was reduced in size and assembly halls built therefrom.

On September 7, 1962, a disastrous fire, of unknown origin, destroyed the Cathedral, a revered and beloved landmark in San Francisco. Five months before this disastrous occurrence, the newly appointed Archbishop of the Archdiocese of San Francisco, the Most Rev. Joseph T. McGucken, D.D., was solemnly installed within the walls of this revered edifice. Undaunted, with courage and determination, he promised to immediately set about to build a new Cathedral on another site nearby, one that would uphold the prestige and grandeur of the destroyed edifice and serve as a worthy Temple to the All High.

WESLEY METHODIST EPISCOPAL CHURCH

About 1889, our family moved from the Hayes Valley District to the Western Addition, locating at 1202 Fillmore Street, between Turk and Eddy Streets. One of my earliest recollections of going to any of the neighboring churches was to the Wesley M.E. Church on Hayes and Buchanan Streets, sometime about 1892. Evidently, my father was working on the organ, and had instructed my elder brother, Leo, to go to the church after school to assist him.

Leo was then but a lad of about fourteen years, still very much interested in coasters, and I was about eight years old. On this occasion he took his coaster with him and gave me a ride as his passenger. (A coaster is a small wagon, a toy popular with the boys of San Francisco due to its hilly terrain. In my time, they were mostly homemade, consisting of a flat board, varying in length and width, with a firm rope fastened to the front axle for steering. Two or three lads would seat themselves upon it, as on a sleigh, the front boy doing the steering by firmly holding the ropes and placing his feet on the front axle — pull the coaster to the top of the hill and descend. With proper design in regarding width, length and height from the ground, they were quite safe from spilling the occupants and considerable speeds were obtained.)

I remember arriving at the church and being shown the large wheel Leo had to turn to pump the organ. Many a time, in later years, I pumped this organ in assisting my father tuning it.

The organ, a two manual and Pedal tracker action of 21 stops, was built by John Bergstrom in 1887. In fact, it was first installed in the Mechanics Pavilion for some religious convention, then it was later moved to the church.

It had a pleasing, typical church organ tone, the specifications containing all the fundamental stops, consisting of the usual Diapason Chorus with a three rank Mixture, a Dulciana, Melodia and Trumpet on the unenclosed Great, and a suitable array of stops for the Swell manual, which was under expression. It also had the customary three Pedal stops, a large 16' Open Diapason, a Bourdan 16' and Cello 8'. The console was attached. The front of the case was made of black walnut and the front pipes were rather gayly ornamented, as was customary at the time.

Interesting personages connected with the church were Rev. Stevens, who was pastor for many years; a Mr. Strange, who was treasurer of the church and from whom I collected the quarterly bills; and the sexton, a Mr. Clark. In later years,

Mr. Humphrey was one of the trustees with whom we had dealings. The organist was Miss Mable Jones, who, being very critical, was inclined to find fault and gave us much concern and kept us on our toes. Features of this church that I recall were the vivid and contrasting colors in the glass of the windows, and the groans and creaking sounds that would come from the rafted ceiling when a strong gust of west wind would hit the building.

In addition to this, the organ was not braced too solidly, and I often experienced a swaying sensation when high up in the organ tuning the oboe of the Swell manual. I recall my father telling us how he once got caught between the top of the bellows and the rails supporting the tracker action, while trying to make some repairs or adjustments. He worked his way into the narrow space all right, but when he tried to crawl out again he found himself jammed and could not move either forward or backward. He must have become frightened as it left an impression on his memory and he recalled the incident on several occasions. The fire and earthquake of 1906 did not injure the organ.

We had the care of the organ for many years, but as the fortunes of business vary, sometimes favoring one party, sometimes another, so it was with us and, at one period, the work was taken from us and given to our competitors, then entrusted to us again.

In the course of time, as was the case in many of the churches, attendance seemed to drop off and the financial status of the church was not as satisfactory as it had been in former years. When the consolidation of several of the Methodist churches with the William Taylor Hotel and Church venture was arranged, Wesley Church was one of the churches joining the combination. Church services were discontinued in the Hayes Street edifice and the building was turned over to some organization to use as a Community Center, eliminating the need of our services.

Calling at the center out of curiosity sometime later, I found the front of the organ entirely covered by a heavy drape, forming the background for a stage or rostrum in front of it. Evidently the organ was no longer being used.

However, some time later, someone must have thrown on

the operating switch activating the blower, and the caretaker of the building did not become aware of it. The motor and blower, located under the organ and accessible only through a trap door, not easily noticeable must have run for a considerable length of time without anyone detecting it. Then when the lubricating oil in the motor was consumed it ran dry and finally started to burn. When the fire department arrived they found clouds of smoke issuing from between the front organ pipes. Not being acquainted with organ construction and not knowing which panels could be easily removed to get access to the inside of the organ, they pulled down a number of the front pipes and stepped over smaller ones to get into the organ, causing considerable damage. Having finally determined that the cause of the smoke was not in the organ itself, but below, they located the burning motor and extinguished the fire.

When the consolidated churches, then called the Temple Methodist Church, bought its large four manual Skinner organ, we made an agreement with the church to service the new large organ for a number of years and take the old Wesley organ in exchange for such services. We removed the old Wesley organ to our factory and installed it in our erecting room. Here we modernized it by applying an electric action throughout, new bellows and a new detached modern console with all the necessary appurtenances. The result was very satisfactory. However, it remained standing in our factory for a number of years, as its huge size, 20 x 40 x 10, was a handicap. Most small churches wanted only a moderate sized organ. Finally, in 1942, it was sold to the San Bruno Methodist Episcopal Community Church, where we erected it in a somewhat altered style from what it had been, that is, we eliminated the exterior case and placed the entire organ in one general chamber, making the entire organ expressive. At this location the organ has again been given a new lease on life. May its tones and pleasing harmonies resound to inspire and edify future generations.

In 1952 we made some minor changes to its tone work on the suggestion of the organist, Mr. Sterling Wheelwright, by removing the Viola 8' from the Swell and placing it in the place of the 12th of the Great, thereby having it undulate with the Great Dulciana 8' as an Unda Maris 8', a soft accompanying stop, very desirable. The Great 12th was placed in the pipe holes of the Swell Piccolo. The latter were discarded, as its scale and voicing was such that it would never stay in tune on full ensemble. Then the Swell Bourdon 8' from Tenor C up was removed and rebored and in its place two sets of new modern Strings were installed, formerly from an aeolian organ, to serve as Sal. 8' and Vox Celeste 8'. The change proved to be very satisfactory.

Shortly before this work was done on the organ, the interior of the church was also completed.

ST. PAUL'S CATHOLIC CHURCH

The St. Paul's Catholic Church that I recall of years ago, was a large Gothic frame structure, located on the northwest corner of 29th and Church Streets in the Mission District. In my early youth, I had often heard my father speak of this church, and there was evidently a reason for it. In later years, I better understood what had taken place and why his recollections of the organ installation at St. Paul's were not so pleasant.

Rev. Michael D. Connolly was pastor of the church at that time, in 1890, evidently then a young man in his prime. Father Connolly, it seems, bought a rather large used three manual pipe organ from some Presbyterian Church in Buffalo, New York. The organ arrived and the various parts were lying scattered over the floor waiting to be assembled when my father was called in to bid on the installation. At the same time, he was asked to sign a statement that the complete organ was delivered and at hand. This request was evidently made for the purpose of forestalling any additional charges for extras in supplying parts that might be missing. To this my father demurred, as he had never seen the organ before, and to require such an assurance, even from an experienced organ builder who may at one time or another have seen the organ erected, would be asking a great deal.

However, a satisfactory agreement must have been reached, and my father began with the erection of the organ. A lurking suspicion remained, nevertheless, that possibly some parts were missing, and this proved to be the case. Some Pedal chests were missing. My father planned to provide these missing parts by building new ones, and, in fact, had his drawing tacked to a wall, as he related the incident to me, intending the next day to carry out his plan. Undoubtedly some disagreement developed. When he arrived the next morning, his drawing was missing and he was told he couldn't proceed with the work. It was given to a competitor, John Bergstrom, who had his factory on California Avenue. What the disagreement was, I do not know, but it was evident to me whenever my father mentioned this incident, that the memory of it was an unpleasant one for him. I do not recall if, in the following years, my father worked on the organ but "time heals many wounds", and it is very likely that it did, for in later years, Rev. Connolly spoke very highly of my father and held him in great esteem.

My first connection with the old organ was in 1913 when Rev. Connolly had his new church nearing completion, and put the old organ up for sale as the old church was to be razed to make room for other parochial improvements. A Rev. Wallrath, an estimable and venerable old priest of Woodland, California, known as the "Church Builder of Northern California", called on us at the time requesting a bid to remove the organ from St. Paul's and install it in the new Holy Rosary Church he was building in Woodland, California.

At this point it might be well to describe the organ. It was a large three manual tracker action organ of about 20 stops, and like all of them, the action was heavy and hard to play, especially when coupled. It was an old used organ, Opus 533 built in 1879, for the North Presbyterian Church in Buffalo, New York, and must have been 60 or 75 years old, judging from its specifications, construction and other telltale marks. It had a large, rather cumbersome case of three Gothic fields, console attached, with keyboard set in the case, richly ornamented front pipes and a rather rich, brilliant tone. It was hand pumped.

We submitted our bid, as requested, but Rev. Wallrath evidently thought the figure too high, and decided to move the organ himself with the aid of some carpenters, Keehn Bros., whom he brought down from Woodland. I was told the Reverend Father donned overalls and climbed into the dusty organ himself to assist with the work. Finally, the organ was dismantled and shipped to Woodland. It was an unusual procedure for a priest, especially one of his years, as he was white-haired at the time, certainly in the late sixties.

After some months he called on us again and quite humbly admitted that although he had the organ erected, he could not get it to function satisfactorily. When we asked him whether he thought he had made a bargain in purchasing the old antiquated organ and installing it himself, he replied: "Are not some of the organs in Europe hundreds of years old and still in use — why should not this old organ be good and serviceable also."

Not wanting to see his hopes of having an organ for his new church shattered, and the time and money already spent on it wasted, we consented to complete the organ and put it in tune and working condition, provided he would have a new modern blower applied to the organ so the abominable and inadequate hand-pumping arrangement could be eliminated. To this he readily agreed.

We spent about two weeks getting the organ in shape. The lack of experienced and professional workmanship was discernible all around and complicated our work and made its completion a laborious job. At any rate, Father Wallrath got an additional 18 years of service from the organ. Due to its inherent defects, the stiffness of its action, the excessive summer temperature to which it was subjected, the lack of proper care, it was condemned and shunned by all who had to play it, until finally a new pastor decided to eliminate the old useless, space-taking organ and install a modern new electric pneumatic, divided pipe organ in its place.

What actually became of the old organ I do not know definitely. I believe some of the old pipes were salvaged and given to some amateur organ builder. I believe the rest of the organ was junked. Such is the end of what undoubtedly was once a noble instrument, one that gave joy and inspiration to many and which also was a cause of worry, disappointment and chagrin to others.

To get back to my subject of St. Paul's Church on 29th Street — after the old organ was removed, the old church was torn down and a large three-story brick school building was erected on the site. Meanwhile, the new St. Paul's Church was completed and proved to be one of the most beautiful churches in San Francisco. It seemed to be Rev. Connolly's ambition to build a church and parish plant that would be a model and the pride of all San Franciscans. Indefatigably he worked and gave of his time to the project. He was to be found practically at all times somewhere about the building, inspecting, directing and managing. His right-hand man on the job was Mr. Otto Knobel, who acted as foreman or superintendent, as there was no general contractor engaged.

As the wherewithal to build such a fine structure was, as in most such cases, one of the severest obstacles to overcome, notwithstanding that his faithful parishioners, mostly of the working class, supported him loyally, every opportunity for economy without sacrificing quality was resorted to. The granite facing of the church was, therefore, mostly made out of the discarded, roughly hewn flag and street-crossing stones, at that time extensively used on San Francisco's cobble-stoned or basalt covered streets. A severe set-back was experienced during the construction of the church when a heavy wind storm blew down the tall Gothic spire that had just been erected. It was restored to its place, and rebuilt, but taking a lesson from this sad experience, this time it was anchored more securely to the granite substructure so as to defy any future inclemency of the weather. St. Paul's Gothic spires are indeed a landmark in the Mission District.

Needless to say, a completed church needed a pipe organ. After consulting with other of his fellow clergymen, and being especially impressed with the organ at St. Mary's Cathedral, which had been built by Hook & Hastings Company of Boston, he decided that the firm would be the one to build an organ for his church, also. A contract was therefore entered into with Hook & Hastings Company for a two manual and Pedal divided organ, with detached console, pneumatic action. Our firm was entrusted with the installation of this organ, which occurred in 1910.

Father Connolly was a daily and much interested visitor

while we were doing this work. He was extremely concerned that no damage be done to the edifice. In erecting the organ we noticed that one of the large 16' Pedal Open Diapason pipes intercepted one of the plaster capitals of the rear column on the gallery. We felt certain that if we asked him to remove it, the answer would be "no". However, at an opportune time it was removed, the organ erected and the column with its missing capital is now concealed by the height of the organ.

While erecting this organ an incident occurred that gave me much concern. It was quitting time and we had just completed installing the large 16' front pipes on the corner towers of the divided case. True, we had braced them but I began to wonder if the bracing I had applied was really sufficient, having in mind the possibility of another severe earthquake. We had left the church and were waiting at the corner for a car to return home when, all of a sudden, a deep rumbling sound was heard and the ground trembled under our feet in the throws of a rather sharp earthquake. My first thought was of the pipes in the organ and whether they were still intact and had withstood the shock. I looked over to the church with some trepidation, but seeing the tall spire was still in its place, I concluded the organ pipes must also have remained in position. This proved to be the case when we investigated the next morning on returning to the job. Nevertheless, additional bracing was applied, and any doubt as to the sufficiency of the bracing of the pipes never again entered my mind.

Father Connolly prided himself, and with justice, on the beautifully designed and richly carved oak woodwork and finish in his church, of which there seemed to be a greater abundance than in most churches. All the wainscoating, the organ gallery rail, communion rail, pulpit, confessionals, and above all the many ribbed, tall columns supporting the Gothic arches were all made of the finest oak, highly finished and polished. We noticed when the organ arrived that its oak case, especially its design, also its finish, did not compare with the surrounding high class finish. During the weeks that followed, in the course of the erection of the organ, we noticed that the oak panels of the organ case were beginning to warp badly. This gave us much concern at the time, but we thought it would correct itself during the interim of our completing the organ. The organ otherwise proved satisfactory in every detail, tonally as well as mechanically.

Finally, one morning when I went over to the priest's house, which was still the old residence on 29th Street, to notify Rev. Connolly that the organ was finally completed and make arrangements for its acceptance and regular maintenance, I was utterly surprised and dismayed at the reception I got. In a loud and sharp voice, certainly audible out on the sidewalk, he berated the organ company for the inferior wood they had used in the organ, for the poor workmanship and the unsatisfactory manner in which it withstood the climatic conditions. I tried to reassure him, but to no apparent avail. He threatened to sue the company, make us remove the organ, etc. Finally, he calmed himself, and after I evidently satisfied him that the trouble would be corrected, we parted, I much awed and cowed, but not beaten, for I knew that while his complaint was to an extent justified, the matter he was complaining of was but of a temporary nature and could and would be corrected.

We set to work at once and removed the oak panels, had heavy saw cuts made upon the back of them, or unfinished side of each one, gave the same unfinished side a coat of paint so that each surface was equally coated, screwed supporting ribs on the back of the panels and fastened all the panels back into place again. A noticeable improvement was soon discernable, and within a few months thereafter the wood panels, which had become acclimated, were again as true as a straight edge.

This episode with Father Connally reminded me of the incident my father experienced with him twenty-five years before. But, with all his domineering and forceful manner, Father Connally was kind-hearted and just. A rather severe exterior belied the most sympathetic, generous and kindly soul. The wonderful parish unit, built through his untiring efforts, will be a lasting monument to his memory.

Miss Ammelia Quinn, was organist of St. Paul's and played the old organ for many years. She also functioned for some time at the new organ, but evidently it became apparent that a more experienced and virile organist was needed to do justice to the new organ. Miss Quinn was, therefore, graciously retired and pensioned by Father Connolly, and a Mr. Thomas P. Nowlan, a recent arrival from Australia, was selected as her successor. Shortly thereafter Miss Quinn passed to her eternal reward. In the declining years of Father Connally's life he had the satisfaction of knowing that his work was appreciated, by being honored and elevated to the position of a domestic prelate, with the title of Monsignor. In 1932 Right Rev. Monsignor Michael D. Connolly died. Rev. Cornelius E. Kennedy, who had acted as assistant pastor to Monsignor Connolly before his demise, was appointed pastor of St. Paul's parish and held this position until 1951.

Father Kennedy, always interested in music and desiring to have some organ accompaniment closer to the children when singing at the children's mass on Sundays, had a small sanctuary pipe organ installed behind the high altar. The console was located at the left side of the sanctuary, and the organist, when seated, was visible to all the children. The organ was supplied and installed by the Kilgen Organ Company of St. Louis.

During 1962, under the pastorate of Rev. Monsignor Falvey the console of the Sanctuary organ was removed from its former location and placed in the nave of the church near the transcept.

An interesting character associated with the church was Mr. Mullin, better known as Tom, the sexton, who held that position for many years. He was succeeded by H. A. Kelley, a man of similar traits and a worthy successor.

One other incident I recall occurred shortly after the end of World War I, when the serious flu epidemic was raging. It was the time when we were all compelled to wear the flu masks, and the churches were closed for the usual divine services to prevent the congregating of large numbers of people. In most cases, services were held out of doors. At this time we were making some improvements to the Hook and Hastings organ on the gallery, by removing the usual ballast from the bellows and substituting springs for the weights in order to get more steady pressure. While thus engaged one morning, we were interrupted by three funerals. The service for each was very brief, but evidently permission had been granted to hold them in the church. This was that particular day's record, but I was informed that it averaged that number each day during the height of the epidemic.

Each time I call at St. Paul's Church I am reminded of an incident that makes me think sympathetically of my dad. Working around organs in narrow spaces, it was his custom to arrange everything for convenient access. If some panel was too large for handling and could be divided into two, he would do it. If a small ladder or stepping block could be used to good advantage, he would supply one. At. St.Paul's each time we entered the organ a large panel had to be removed. Being made of oak and quite large, its weight was considerable. In addition, some pews for the choir members were placed close to the panel, further impeding its easy removal. One day in his chagrin at the "stupid arrangement" as he called it, he took out his screwdriver and with a straight edge scratched a sharp line on the newly varnished leaner and seat of the bench where, if he had his way, he would cut off the bench to get more room for manipulating the heavy panel. The scratch in the bench is there to stay. He never cut the bench, and I have gotten along all these years without doing so, but yet when I see the scratch mark, I am tempted to complete the unfinished task for him.

St. Paul's Church, with its complete parochial plant, consisting of several buildings, proved to be what Monsignor Connolly wanted it to be, a model of beauty and efficiency for other parishes to follow. St. Paul's Church with its lovely interior, marble altars, beautiful art glass windows made in Munich, its divided organ set between a huge, dimly lighted rose window with St. Cecilia its central feature, will be an inspiration for anyone to see.

On September 19, 1945, after 31 years of faithful service to his church, Thomas P. Nowlan, organist of St. Paul's, passed away. Just two weeks previous he had summoned me to the church to adjust some difficulty about which he referred to jokingly.

After the Hook and Hastings organ was in service for 53 years, it became evident that the leather of the pouches and pneumatics was deteriorating. Also that the lead tubing was corroding and that the time for a remodeling and modernizing of the organ was at hand. We, therefore, were authorized to electrify the mechanism, apply a modern new Console, a larger modern blower and a general cleaning and overhauling of the organ, which we did with excellent results.

ST. PAUL'S EPISCOPAL CHURCH

St. Paul's Episcopal Church was located on the south side of California Street between Fillmore and Steiner Streets. It was a frame structure, surrounded by a garden and shrubbery, with a rather high iron picket fence. This church was built in 1890.

As I recall the layout, the length of the church paralleled California Street. The church possessed a small two manual and Pedal tracker action Hook & Hastings pipe organ of about 8 stops, Opus 1407 built in 1889. The console was attached. The organ had an oak case with decorated pipes and made a pleasing appearance. Tonally the organ met all the requirements of a typical church organ, and was built and voiced on the high standard always upheld by the Hook & Hastings Company.

I have no record of who originally installed the organ, but I presume it was my father as he usually did all the installation work for the Hook & Hastings Company in this territory. He also serviced the organ, as you will note from an incident related below.

In making his monthly visits to service the organs entrusted to his care, there was no trouble in most cases in getting access to the edifices as usually my father was supplied with his own private key. However, at St. Paul's Episcopal Church he not only had no key, but, in addition, was expected to scale the high picket fence in order to get into the church. The latter was probably always unlocked, therefore the extra security of the locked gate on the picket fence. This acrobatic stunt my father objected to perform in public, for obvious reasons, with the result that he got into an argument with the vestry and lost the future servicing of the organ.

I also recall an incident that possibly occurred about this time. The church owed my father some money for services rendered. I am in doubt as to whether this indebtedness was directly chargeable to the Vestry of the Church or to the organist personally. At any rate, my father directed me to call on the organist to try to collect the bill. It seemed to be one of those bad debt accounts, long overdue and impossible to collect; at least this was my father's experience. Realizing the task before me and aware that it would be an unpleasant one and, knowing that I did not have the qualifications of a hard-boiled bill collector, I must have approached my client with some trepidation and hesitation.

I recall it was a wet and dismal day. I had on a raincoat, but no rubbers. My shoes were evidently soaked, my features picqued, and I must have looked pale and frightened. On ringing the doorbell of the house, instead of seeing the organist personally, a kind, amiable, motherly woman answered the bell and, on telling her my mission, she bade me enter. Somehow or other my appearance or attitude made her sympathetic and understanding. She not only admitted that the bill should be paid, which she forthwith did, but told me I needed a hot cup of coffee and a little snack, which she gave me, putting me very much at ease. I thanked this good angel graciously on leaving. On returning home my perplexed father could not understand how I collected the bill so easily when he heretofore was unsuccessful. I did not know either.

Some years later, a new red sandstone church was built on the same site. The old church was moved to the rear and was used as a Sunday school and social hall, and was connected with the new church. Who moved the organ into the new church, I do not know; no doubt it was my father as I know amicable relations were again established after the aforesaid unpleasantness. Proof of my assumption is the fact that at this time I made frequent visits with my father to the church to tune and service the organ.

The Reverend Boyd was rector for some years, and seemed to be the man who introduced the Divine Healing Movement locally in the Episcopal Church. Succeeding Reverend Boyd came the popular rector, Rev. Leslie C. Kelly, also erstwhile Commissioner of Boxing of the State of California. With the parish under the rectorship of these much-talked-of divines, and possibly from other causes beyond their control, life in the parish seemed to ebb rather than improve.

One sign of progress was evident about this time, when we were requested to install a blower to the organ that had been pumped laboriously by hand all those years. This improvement in furnishing a steady and adequate supply of air, and the convenience in having the organ at one's disposal at any time without requiring the presence of the "official pumper" was a blessing.

In 1935 a fire occurred in the old original frame structure in the rear, consuming it completely and also burning part of the new edifice. The organ was part of the prey. On inspecting the damage we found the only thing left to remind one of the organ was the charred motor and blower we had but recently installed, lying among the debris in the basement.

The remaining part of the church was again rebuilt as the forward part of the church was practically undamaged. The tower and gable of the church, were removed, altering the facade completely. Hereafter St. Paul's Episcopal Church contented itself with a small hall on the east side of the church as a chapel, and the church was converted into a community center.

This venture seemed to prove unsatisfactory in time and, in 1938, the buildings were completely razed and the property leveled down to mother earth. Now a large food mart occupies the site.

The remnant of what was once undoubtedly a live and active parish functions now modestly and inconspicuously in a former flat or residence dwelling at Sacramento and Scott Streets.

The former rector, Rev. Leslie C. Kelly, passed away on September 29, 1945.

ST. PAULUS LUTHERAN CHURCH

St. Paulus Lutheran Church was originally located on the south side of Mission Street, between Fifth and Sixth Streets.

In 1890, the beautiful Gothic church, now standing at the southeast corner of Gough and Eddy Streets, was erected. I recall this church as opposite it is located Jefferson Square, a public park where the children of the neighborhood were wont to gather after school hours and during vacation time. Our home being only a few blocks away, we, also, were frequent visitors to the park and spent many happy hours there.

Reverend Buehler was the popular pastor of the church for many years. His congregation consisted of a fine and sturdy stock of German Lutherans, mostly immigrants from the Old Country, with the younger generation born here.

True to their tradition, and with a firm belief in the need for religious instruction for their children, St. Paulus Lutheran Church maintained and successfully conducted a parochial school, where, in addition to the three R's, in which they were thoroughly instructed, religion was also taught, and a knowledge of the German language imparted.

My earliest recollection of working on the pipe organ in St. Paulus Church was assisting my father tune and do some repair work on it. The instrument, as I recall it at that time, was a two manual and Pedal tracker action organ of about eight or ten stops, built by a firm in the Middle West. It was crudely built, compared with the standards of the day, or at least with organ construction work I saw in other instruments. It had a Trombone 16' reed on the Pedal, with wood resonators; certainly an unusual stop for a medium-sized two manual organ.

The organist at the time was Mr. Beskow. In later years Mr. Hargens acted as organist and school teacher.

The old organ had been in use already in the old church on Mission Street. My father removed and installed it in the new edifice at Gough Street, when they moved there in 1890. After the old organ was installed in the new church and had been in use for sometime, a better and more modern instrument was desired. The old organ was later sold, and removed, and I have a faint recollection of it being shipped to some church in the San Joaquin Valley.

In 1909, a new organ was secured, a larger and more modern instrument with tubular pneumatic action, from

Kilgen & Sons of St. Louis, Missouri.

We serviced this organ intermittently. It had 21 speaking stops. During the pastorate of Rev. Bernthal, we serviced it regularly for many years, while Mr. Hargens, the teacher of the school, was also serving as organist. Later on, during the period of 1923-1928, Harold Mueller, now one of San Francisco's prominent organists, and at present organist of Trinity Episcopal Church, also served as teacher of the school and assistant organist.

During the depression years we lost the maintenance of the organ to other parties. Rev. Gustav Kirchner was pastor at this time, and Mr. Gruber organist and school teacher. The former died in 1967 at the ripe age of 86 years.

In 1940 a serious fire occurred in the edifice and it appeared as though the structure was doomed. However, due to the efficient work of the San Francisco Fire Department, the fire was for the most part confined to the roof, but the damage to the organ was extensive. When I called at the church the next morning the water was still dripping from the roof rafters and ceiling, and rivulets were gushing from within the organ. The damage to the church was repaired and, when the organ was thoroughly dried out, it also received due attention. This work was done by John C. Swinford, who rebuilt, electrified and enlarged the organ by adding a Choir division to it and a four manual Austin console, formerly in the use in the outdoor organ at Balboa Park, San Diego, California.

In 1952, still another console was exchanged for the former and further additions were made to this instrument by Mr. William N. Reid.

EMANUEL BAPTIST CHURCH — Also MISSION BAPTIST

Emanuel Baptist Church was located on the west side of Bartlett Stteet, between 22nd and 23rd Streets, out in the Mission District. It was a rather tall frame structure.

The church was much spoken of and received wide newspaper publicity in the late 90's due to a sickening and revolting murder that was committed under its roof. It was in the year 1895 when the newspapers, with glaring headlines, reported the gruesome find. The Sunday School superintendent, Mr. William Durrant, a young man who had been studying for the medical profession, slew two young women members of his choir and hid their bodies in a vacant room in the church tower. After a prolonged and exciting trial, he was convicted on circumstantial evidence and sentenced to death, and paid the supreme penalty by hanging at San Quentin prison.

It was many years thereafter, about 1914, that I was called upon to inspect the organ, and to quote, I believe, on its removal. That was the first time I had entered the church. Undoubtedly, since the heinous crime that had been committed there, with its attendant notoriety, the future of the church and congregation were doomed, as a stigma apparently rested upon the edifice, notwithstanding that the name of the church had been changed. It was, therefore, logical and to the best interest that this landmark, associated with such gruesome memories, be razed.

The work of moving the organ was not entrusted to us. According to my father's records, it was a Bergstrom organ. It was a one manual and Pedal tracker action organ of about 10 stops, with attached console. At the time I inspected it, it was in a rather deplorable condition, indicating that it had not been in use for some time. To the best of my recollection, the organ was removed and secured by one of the local piano concerns, and rebuilt and altered. I am quite certain that eventually it found its way to one of the churches in our city. I recognized the organ later when called upon to repair it.

BETHANY CONGREGATIONAL CHURCH

Out in the Mission District, on the west side of Bartlett Street, near 25th Street, stood the old Bethany Congregational Church. Up on its gallery stood an old Bergstrom two manual and Pedal tracker action organ of about 10 stops. It must have been built sometime about 1896, or earlier, since the inscription of the name of an Oscar Bahlinger, June 4,

1896, was found written on parts of the organ.

In 1905 my father received the regular maintenance of the organ and we used to call there regularly to tune and service it.

There seemed to be little life about the place. The only parties we came in contact with were one of the trustees, Mr. A. T. Ruthrauff, who engaged us, and the organist, whom we met occasionally. Seldom did we even meet the pastor or encounter any meetings or socials being held. Our summing up of the social activities of this church proved to be correct, as the church disbanded, and the organ was donated to the Chinese Congregational Church, located at Benham Place, Chinatown, opposite the old Portsmouth Square.

We dismantled the organ at Bethany Church and installed it in its new location, and provided the organ with a blower. It is still functioning. We call occasionally to tune it and make adjustments, and always think of the lonely old church where earlier this organ stood so silently.

What a change of environment, now in Chinatown it was again helping people sing the praises of God, Father of us all.

This organ, in 1959, was electrified and modernized by us.

Again in 1963, it was rearranged, evidently due to a plan of enlarging the Church Auditorium to meet the needs of the growing congregation.

SWEDENBORG JERUSALEM CHURCH

For many years our family lived at Turk and Fillmore Streets. There were ten children in our family. We older children, together with children of the neighborhood and friends, took great delight on Saturday and Sunday afternoons in hiking over the hills. We especially liked to walk to the top of Fillmore Street hill, at Broadway, to look over the Bay and the Marin hills and, enroute, to look in all the store windows on Fillmore Street.

I remember the tall spire of the Swedenborg New Jerusalem Church at O'Farrell and Fillmore Streets, and recall how I first learned to tell the time by the clock high up in the church steeple. A classmate of mine and chum of my sisters, Ella Schoen, who accompanied us on these excursions, taught me how.

Shortly after the church was built, during 1891, they secured a pipe organ from George Andrews, organ builder of Oakland, who also serviced the organ.

My first connection with the church took place when we were called upon by a Mr. Barto, one of the trustees, to install a blower for the organ and otherwise put it in good condition. This was in 1929. Mr. Barto called at our place of business, and I remember him as a neatly dressed, tidy looking business man. Later, while at work on the organ one day, I was accosted by a man at the church, clad in overalls, covered with grit and grime, whose untidy appearance repelled me. I had always felt that no matter how grimy a man's hands might get while at work, he could at least keep his face reasonably clean. Therefore, the rather domineering manner in which he approached me, questioning what I was doing, together with his filthy appearance, irritated me and caused me to be, I must admit, none too courteous or obliging. He noticed my chilliness, and rather approvingly reproached me by saying, "You evidently don't know me today! I am Mr. Barto who called at your shop and gave the order to install the blower and repair the organ." He apologized for his appearance, saying he had just come from the furnace room where he had been repairing the boiler, and this accounted for his untidy appearance. I likewise made sincere apology for my error, and recalled the falsity of the slogan we so often hear that — "Clothes or appearance make the man."

Shortly after the installation of the new blower, the Swedenborg congregation left the edifice and established themselves in their new location at Lyon and Washington Streets. The old church was leased out to other denominations. However, we secured a contract from the owners of the church to regularly service the organ for the lessees.

I remember a few years ago I was called there on an emergency summons to repair some trouble. I believe the church was conducted then by some Greek denomination. My youngest son, Edward, then about seven years old, often asked me to take him with me on some job. Here, I thought was an opportunity. I remembered how I also had begged and looked forward to going with my father on similar occasions.

When we arrived, I noticed several people in the church, especially a woman on her knees at the communion rail in front of the pulpit. She was praying aloud, sobbing, moaning, and gesticulating. My son, with fear in his eyes, asked me what was the matter with her. Her behavior could not help but be noticed, but I drew his attention away from her, explaining that she was praying. I went to work to correct the organ troubles and then left as quickly as possible. This incident made an impression on my son's memory, as he has since referred to it on different occasions.

The organ is a two manual and Pedal tracker action organ, with console attached. It has 10 stops voiced on the light pressure of 3", and has a pleasing, sweet tone. A rather unusual feature of the organ, but not uncommon with the Andrews organs, is that there are some wood pipes among the front display pipes, also that the remaining metal zinc pipes are in their natural color, possibly lacquered, but not decorated. The interior of the church is also unusual, somewhat circular in form, with choir, organ, pulpit and rostrum on the east side, and a half encircling gallery on the west side. With its heavy beamed ceiling, it has the quaintness and all the earmarks of a product of the 1890's when San Francisco was in its bloom.

During February 1946, a disastrous fire occurred in the edifice, possibly the effects of flying sparks of a nearby chimney igniting the shingles of the roof. Almost the entire roof of the building was burned out. Fortunately, the organ was covered by tarpaulins by the underwriters in due time, and no serious damage was done.

In 1954, the tall steeple, with the clock from which I first learned to tell time, was removed, considerably altering the appearance of the old landmark.

ST. BRENDAN'S CHURCH

Shortly during and after the depression in 1929-30, and through the kind recommendation of Charles Bulotti, a prominent tenor singer of San Francisco, we were privileged to secure the contract to build a small two manual electric action pipe organ of four stops for the new church, recently built in the thriving St. Brendan's Parish in the West of Twin Peaks area.

Strange to say, this parish, before the fire and earthquake of 1906, was located in an entirely different area of San Francisco, on "Rincon Hill", near South Park, at one time considered the elite section of San Francisco for the wealthy, even before "Nob Hill" became famous as the abode of the "Bonanza Kings." However, in time, when Nob Hill took over the ascendency, the district around South Park rapidly deteriorated and became an industrial and warehouse district, and was stigmatized as "South of the Slot", indicating the slot of the cable cars running on Market Street, and the neighborhood where the working people and the very poor lived. The need for a St. Brendan's parish was found to be no longer expedient and was absorbed by the nearby St. Rose's Parish.

After the fire and earthquake of 1906, however, the "tables were turned." The parish of St. Rose was eliminated for want of parishioners and was integrated with nearby St. Patrick's Parish, and now the former St. Brendan's Parish was re-established in the new and thriving district west of Twin Peaks.

One incident I will always recall when servicing the organ here, was the fact that we first had to secure a tall stepladder to get access to a trap door overhead for access to a loft in the tower where the motor, blower and generator for the organ were located. Fortunately, no one has recorded a mishap so far in carrying out this stunt. The organ is giving continuous satisfaction.

ST. BRIGID'S CHURCH

St. Brigid's Church was at one time called the "Servant Girls' Church", because it was built mostly from the contributions and support of the girls doing domestic work in the homes of the wealthy people in the neighborhood.

It is a very beautiful edifice, located on the southwest corner of Van Ness Avenue and Broadway. Its outer facing of rough hewn granite, came mostly from the same source as the material used in St. Paul's Catholic Church, i.e., discarded granite street crossing flagstones, formerly much used in the city. Reverend Father John E. Cottle was pastor of the church at the time it was built.

The first pipe organ installed, according to my father's notes, was a small one manual Bergstrom tracker organ, hand pumped. A Mr. Rockel was the organist.

My first recollection of St. Brigid's Church was around 1905, when I was assisting my father or elder brother, Leo, to adjust and tune a small one manual Kimball pipe organ of four stops that was installed at the time. Later on, undoubtedly desiring something better and a more complete instrument, they bought from the Temple Sherith Israel, located on Post and Mason Streets, their old two manual tracker action Bergstrom organ, as that congregation was then preparing to move to its new edifice at California and Webster Streets.

The one manual Kimball organ at St. Brigid's was then sold to the First Methodist Church of Palo Alto. The work of moving this organ, as well as the installation of the Bergstrom organ from the old Synagogue, which occurred during 1905, was done mostly by my brother, Leo.

The Bergstrom organ, after being erected on the loft of St. Brigid's Church, made a good appearance and the volume and pleasing tone of the organ was a great improvement over that of the small Kimball organ.

This organ had not been in use many months when, on the fateful morning of April 18, 1906, the earthquake severely damaged the edifice. The high gable on the facade of the church, which was made of brick with granite facing, was shaken down and crashed into the organ loft. The organ was a total wreck. The church, however, was not damaged by the fire.

After the church was restored in 1909, a Kimball organ was again secured, and this time it was their usual stock organ, a two manual and Pedal, attached console, pneumatic action organ with about 6 or 7 stops. The Eilers Music

Company, located on Market Street in San Francisco, were the agents at the time for the Kimball Company and, judging from the number of Kimball organs sold here in this period, they certainly were successful.

Father John E. Cottle, pastor of the church for many years, passed away in 1926, and was succeeded by The Right Reverend Msgr. James P. Cantwell.

In the same year, through the beneficence of some generous donor, St. Brigid's Church was presented with a large, fine, modern organ, one suitable for all needs of the church and a credit to the congregation. At this time, major alterations were also made to the facade of the church, to the entrances, vestibules and tower. Special chambers on either side of the gallery were built, concealed by artistic grills, for the new organ.

Meanwhile, St. Vibiana's Cathedral of Los Angeles, California, had signed a contract for a large new organ with the Wangerin, Weickhart Organ Company of Milwaukee, Wisconsin. As the Bishop of Los Angeles, Right Rev. John J. Cantwell, D.D., was a brother of Msgr. James P. Cantwell, the pastor of St. Brigid's, it seems quite logical and probable that they conferred with one another on this important matter, as to the integrity, reputation and satisfactory product of the Wangerin, Weickhart Company, with the result that that company also received the contract to build the new organ for St. Brigid's Church. I have been informed that the late Richard Keys Biggs, of Hollywood, California, drew up the specifications for the organ. Our firm installed the organ under the personal supervision of my brother Erwin.

At this period, Father Norbert Feely, who was stationed at Sacred Heart Church, and who was deeply interested in pipe organs and an authority on them in his own right, was delegated to supervise the correction of certain tonal defects in the new organ, as there was a general complaint of an unbalanced tone in the organ ensemble. Individually, the stops were excellently voiced, but in groups and in divisions there was certainly room for improvement. We know that individual tastes differ, but granting this human diversity, the designer of the specifications for this organ must have had strange ideas as to what a church organ should sound like.

One of the most offending stops was a bright, snarling French Trumpet, with flaring resonators on zinc tubes. As there was already a Tuba in the organ, and a pleasing and agreeable one, the extreme contrast was deadening and atrocious, lacking any blend whatsoever. This stop was removed and in its place was added a Second Diapason. Many other changes were also made. The Vox Humana was enclosed in a separate box. It was a full year after the organ was installed before it was finally accepted.

The instrument is a three manual organ of 24 stops. The Swell division and part of the Pedal are located on one side, and the Great, Choir and Pedal on the other. The entire organ is under expression. As stated before, aside from a proper blending or balance of tone, the individual stops are of fine character, well voiced and made. The reed stops are all excellent, especially the French Horn on the manuals, which continues as a 16' reed through the Pedal. The Flutes are luscious, and Strings warm and exhilarating. Enclosing the Vox Humana made a one hundred percent improvement. The organ also had a set of Chimes, and a Harp which we acclaim as the most realistic and true to its prototype that we have ever heard in an organ. The diminuendo and pianissimo effects obtainable in the organ are especially praiseworthy. The pressures used are 6" and 15".

This being the only Wangerin-Weickhart organ in San Francisco, it received quite a bit of attention and comment. Mrs. Joan Marie O'Donnell, who received her musical education abroad, ably functions at the organ, in conjunction with her work as choir leader.

Aside from having troubles caused by moisture in the walls, over which we had no control, we had another annoyance which made us resort to unusual action. One of the most important and essential employees in a church, or any institution for that matter, is the sexton or caretaker. Without him, conditions would soon lapse into untidiness, disorder and disintegration. The sexton at St. Brigid's Church, whom we usually called Michael, a pleasant Irish gentleman, with red curly hair and a stammering impediment in his speech, had his living quarters in one of the tower rooms. His sanctum sanctorum was, of course, always securely locked. Unfortunately, the only way to get to the Great and Choir section of the organ was through a trap door in the ceiling of his living room. Each time we needed access we first had to look up Michael. At times this proved unsuccessful. We asked and pleaded for a key, assuring him that his privacy would not be unceremoniously disturbed, but to no avail. To make connection with Michael readily, or to have him open the door with a smile when we found him, got to be quite a rarity, so we concluded to forget about Michael and solve our problem in our own way. There was a high attic in the church, we noticed, and access from the Swell chamber over the attic to the Great and Choir chamber on the other side would be easy if a trap door were cut through both respective organ chamber walls and a catwalk placed over the plaster ceiling. This was done without much effort, without the knowledge of anyone, and thereafter we did not have to trouble Michael. We did notice a shy, inquiring look on his face thereafter, as if he wanted to ask why all of a sudden, after having at first been so persistent in getting access to his room we now would do without it and still tune the organ, as he saw us do on our monthly visits.

The two manual Kimball organ that the Wangerin-Weickhart organ displaced, was sold to the new St. Emydius Catholic Church in San Francisco, where we installed it and where it gave good service for many years.

In 1947 St. Brigid's Church made further improvements by completely redecorating the interior and extending the west end of the church. A noteworthy improvement made with very satisfactory results, was the application of a new kind of accoustic material to the ceiling of the church to reduce the over-abundance of reverberation that previously existed.

CROCKER OLD PEOPLES' HOME

At the corner of Pierce and Pine Streets was a large institution for the aged called the "Crocker Old Peoples' Home." I had often passed the building as a youngster, but was not aware that they had a chapel, much less a pipe organ until many years later. An old friend of my father, Harandon

Pratt, a venerable and lovable old gentleman who later earned the title of "The Dean of Organists of San Francisco", owing to the fact he was the oldest living organist hereabouts, called on my father to tune and repair this organ.

It was a small two manual and Pedal George N. Andrews tracker action organ of about 6 stops, built in 1891, blown by a Pelton water-wheel driving a crankshaft operating the feeders. It functioned in a fashion, depending often on the supply of water pressure available.

There was always something to adjust; either the belts would break or jump off the pulleys, or the controlling valve would not regulate, or the crankshaft was squeaking. As late as 1939, this relic of a blowing apparatus was still in use and, to my knowledge, it was the last surviving specimen of a water-wheel driven organ pumping apparatus in San Francisco. We finally induced the management to discard it for their own sake, as well as for the good of the organ, and to install a modern blower.

After the death of Mr. Harandon Pratt, at the age of 87, Mrs. Madden assumed the position of organist.

Since then the Institution was dissolved and the property was acquired by the Dominican Nuns operating St. Rose Academy for Girls across the street as an annex to their institution.

TRINITY CENTER or TRINITY-PRESBYTERIAN

In 1915 we were called to service an organ in Madera, California, and got acquainted with a revered gentleman, pastor of the church, named Homer K. Pitman. Not long thereafter, in 1919, he was transferred to the Trinity Presbyterian Church on 23rd and Capp Streets, San Francisco.

He was so pleased and delighted with our work and dealings with him in his former charge, that no sooner was he established in his new position, then he called on us relative to the rebuilding and modernizing of the Geo. Hutchings tracker action organ, Opus 256, built in Boston, Massachusetts in 1892, which he had in his new place. A detached console was especially desired to fit in with a new plan for an enlarged and augmented choir. Also, certain desirable additions were to be made to the organ. Shortly thereafter, we received the contract to carry out this work.

The Hutchings organ, originally installed by my father in 1892, excellently built and preserved, readily lent itself to this improvement. We retained the old case and pipes, but made an entirely new console, chest and bellows. It was also one of the first jobs where we applied an individual magnet and valve unit for each pipe, the latter being accessible and removable by removing a bottom board. The entire organ was altered to be completely enclosed, except the Great Open Diapason. The latter was placed on top of the Swell box. The double set of Swell blinds was retained and proved to be very effective. A set of Chimes, a Vox Humana 8', a Tuba 8', a Tibia 8', and a Cornopean 8' were added to the organ to good advantage. The Diapason 8' stop above the Swell box did not prove to be too satisfactory. Its supply pipe was too lengthy, causing the air to be unsteady, and secondly, its elevated position with a higher temperature above than below where the rest of the pipes were, caused it to be out of tune often and made it desirable to put it closer to the bellows and somewhat below the main chests. This was later done. The general outcome of the modernization of this organ proved to be very satisfactory and received the praise and commendation of all who heard or played it.

The name of the church, about that time, was changed to Trinity Center, and its scope and field of work greatly enlarged. Rev. Pitman enjoyed the good will and cooperation of his congregation, which was but a deserved tribute to as fine a gentleman and minister as could be found.

After the organ was in use for a number of years, a serious fire developed in the rear attic of the church one night, but thanks to the efficient work of the San Francisco Fire Department, and especially the Underwriters who covered the organ with heavy tarpaulins in time, no serious damage was done to it. Rev. Homer K. Pitman retired in 1940, and his work is being ably carried on my his successor, Rev. Benjamin N. Adams.

Many organists and choir leaders have filled the position in the past years. One did especially good work, our old friend Mr. C. C. Howard. Mrs. Rossi also served for some time. Mr. and Mrs. Fulton fill the respective positions of organist and choir leader.

One Sunday morning while I was attending mass at my own parish church, word was passed to me to fix the organ at Trinity Presbyterian Church before the late morning service. It was stated the organ would not play, although the motor was running. Being in my Sunday clothes and not prepared for any grimy work, I hoped to be spared that eventuality. On trying the organ at the console, I found the organ dead. My next move was to the basement where the blower and generator were located.

Seeing the motor running and in apparent satisfactory condition, I turned my attention to the generator, assuming that the commutator was dirty or the brushes making insecure contact, but found these also in their usual satisfactory condition. Finding the generator belt rather loose which, incidentally, was an endless belt, I concluded that was the cause of the trouble, that the belt was slipping. As the generator was on a sliding adjustable base but had previously been moved to the farthest extent possible, I decided to reset the generator so that the regulating screw would again be operative. A borrowed screwdriver did the trick, however, only after messing up my hands with the oil and grit of the belt and generator.

Feeling confident now that the trouble was solved, I returned to the console for a final test, complimenting myself on being able to correct the trouble in time for the approaching morning service. To my dismay, however, there was no response from the organ, it was still as dead as ever. Some quick thinking and rapid action was now necessary. I had not entered the interior of the organ as yet and concluded to do so, to see if there was possibly something wrong with the bellows. To my surprise, I found both bellows deflated, with the Blower running full blast. I then and there concluded the fans had loosened on the motor shaft and again went down to the basement for further examination.

The sexton, who was by this time becoming interested and

an anxious onlooker, fearing that I could not correct the trouble in time for the service, reassured me that the organ was in perfect condition the Friday night previous when it was last used for choir rehearsal.

Following my clue that the fans were loose on the shaft, I prepared to go to the rear end of the Blower where the intake valve is, to make a closer inspection. This Blower, which was placed in the corner near a wall or partition to keep a passage way clear, had the intake valve protrude through an opening cut into the wood partition into an adjoining closet in which the sexton stored material, etc. Here, to my surprise, I found a large placard shoved tight up against the intake of the Blower, preventing the Blower from drawing in any air whatsoever. On showing this to the sexton, he recalled some time during Saturday storing this material there, not knowing that it would cause any trouble. With the sexton promising never to do it again, and the organist starting the Interlude for the morning service, I mused to myself as I brushed and cleaned up, "Well, here's another Sunday morning gone to the dogs." Yet, it taught us both a lesson.

An interesting character I recall in connection with this church years ago, was a former sexton, an old gentleman whom we, for some reason, called Santa Claus. Another pleasant event I remember was attending a service there arranged for the Golden Wedding Club, of which my parents were members. On this particular occasion, as my mother had already passed on, I accompanied my father to the church. Rev. Homer K. Pitman spoke most fittingly to the visitors present, and gave them their deserved words of praise and encouragement, also asking my father to rise in recognition and take a bow.

The present organist, Ray Macdonald, F.A.G.O., a most affable gentleman and able musician, appears to have succeeded in reviving the use of this excellent organ, by arranging for periodical concerts and recitals.

ST. MARY THE VIRGIN EPISCOPAL CHURCH

From about 1889 to 1896 our family resided in the

Western Addition of San Francisco, and, for the greater part of that time, at Turk and Fillmore Streets. Almost every Saturday and often on Sunday afternoons we would go hiking over the hills and sand dunes to the foot of Fillmore Street at the Bay, or to Harbor View Park at Scott Street, near where the Fulton Iron Works was then located, or trek to the Presidio over the old wood flume to Fort Point at the Golden Gate; or we would make a visit to Mountain Lake, which we were told at the time, was so deep it had no bottom. All these hikes and adventurous expeditions would invariably lead us first to the brink of the Fillmore Street hill at Broadway, overlooking the Bay. In the valley below, to our left, which was then sparsely settled, was a small gabled church. I remember the first time we passed it. We entered it as was customary then for us children to do, assuming it was a Catholic church as a cross adorned its roof and from its name, St. Mary the Virgin, we concluded it could be none other. I remember the comments of the older children on the similarity of this church with that of our own. I believe at that time a Rev. Father Innes was rector. His name was frequently mentioned in the press and, if I am not mistaken, he later left the Anglican Church and became a Roman Catholic priest.

This church, nestling in a valley, surrounded by shrubbery, fascinated us. On entering, the fragrance of incense always seemed to be discernible; the candles and crucifix on the altar, the fixtures, all looked familiar to us. I do not recall whether they had a pipe organ at that time or not. It was always so dark in the church, especially on entering from the bright sunlight, that one could hardly distinguish an organ up in the organ loft.

It was only in later years, when I worked with my father and we received the regular maintenance of the organ, that I realized they must have had a pipe organ for many years previously. It was an old two manual and Pedal George Andrews pipe organ of 10 stops, a sweet-toned, pleasing instrument, built in 1893. Mr. Harandon Pratt was organist at that time. The blower was placed in the basement under the front porch. It was always damp and wet down there, and I marveled how the organ functioned with this damp, chilled air being blown into it.

Later, when we came to service the organ, a Miss Postell was organist. She was devoted to her work and remained at her post for many years. I also recall the old verger, an aged man, tottering along, who lived in the rear of the church. He fitted in perfectly with his surroundings, which seemed quaint and ancient, but withal, there was a hallowed reverence about the place.

Later, a change was made in the organist's position. I do not recall who took the place of Miss Postell, but I recall how bitterly she deplored and lamented her dismissal. I sympathized with her, as she seemed so attached and devoted to her work.

Through the instrumentality of Col. Robert Noble, U.S.A. Retired, who was a leading personality in local Episcopal Church circles, and a man deeply interested in and conversant with pipe organs, we were asked to submit a proposal to enlarge and modernize the instrument by electrification, etc. We made plans and submitted our proposals, but it seems our fate was to be similar to that of the former organist and, before we were aware of it, after many years of faithful service, we were again on the outside looking in at the "little Church at the corner".

About 1930, plans were discussed for building a new church, or retain the old hallowed one and rehabilitate it. The latter plan was carried out years later by making drastic renovations.

After the demise of Col. Robert Noble, U.S.A. Retired, and with a new rector and vestry, work was begun on the aforesaid undertaking. The main entrance and the location of the altar were reversed, with the latter now located on the east end and the main entrance on the west end of the church. Everything that needed remodeling seemed to have been accomplished.

In 1950, the old Andrews organ that had to be dismantled previously and stored in a warehouse during the period of alterations, also got its needed rejuvenation by being modernized and electrified, with three new stops. A new console and blower were also added. The organ was installed in suitable chambers provided for it. In later years four additional stops were added, several mutation stops and a Trumpet, making the organ a most desirable instrument - more on the modern Baroque style.

Mr. I.W. Smith was organist at this time and the Rev. Keppel W. Hill its rector, who functioned from 1948 to 1966.

It might be interesting to note that before you enter the church on the west end now, you pass through a rustic court. Forward and to the right is a brick enclosed pool, with a constant stream of crystal clear spring water spilling into it. This water, I am told, was the spring that trickled down the gulch of the Pacific Heights into the Bay when we, as children 73 years ago, made our weekly hikes of adventure into this neighborhood.

ST. CHARLES CHURCH

At 18th and Shotwell Streets, opposite a large malting concern of Zimmerman and Company, and surrounded by a general manufacturing district, was the first St. Charles Church. It was a frame structure, with the church on the upper floor and a parochial school on the lower floor.

I always recall the large circular opening in the tower over the entrance to the church. My father visited this Church since 1895 to service the Vocallion organ they had in use at that time. It had a persistent weakness of the reed tongues breaking. Before they actually broke, they would be badly out of tune. It was hand pumped, and my job, when going with my father, was to be the pumper.

I recall an incident that happened here about 1904. My father had an inventive mind and showed quite some ingenuity along that line. In his later years, when 87 years old, he was still making designs and planning a method for an individual to fly, as he had great expectations for the future of aviation. Another pet idea of his was to find a means to produce an artificial or mechanical smoking device for non-smokers, as he happened to be one, that they might enjoy the fragrance of a good cigar as smokers do. The piece de resistance this time was a so-called miner's lamp for organ tuners. Electricity was not available in all the churches at that time and the use of candles while working in an organ was extremely dangerous. So he conceived the idea of constructing a small oil lamp with a sharp point on one side that could be jabbed into the wall, and an eylet on the other side to serve as a handle, or place to put your finger in when carrying the lamp about. In this particular lamp he used salad oil as a fuel and, as the ventilation of the lamp was evidently not the best, the flame in time would gradually fade out if not often readjusted.

He had used the lamp in this particular organ. It was standing on a ledge and about seven inches above it were other wooden parts. Somehow, on completing his work he forgot to remove the lamp, undoubtedly due to its subdued radiance. Screwing the panels shut, we left for our next job some distance away in the Western Addition. On arriving there, in looking for his lamp, he realized he must have left it in the organ at St. Charles Church, evidently still burning. We immediately returned as fast as we possibly could. Street cars were the only means of transportation.

Meanwhile, in my mind I visioned a fire beginning to burn in the organ and smoke issuing from the organ loft. The nearer we got to the church, the more we feared to hear at any moment the clanging of the fire apparatus rushing to the blaze. On reaching 18th Street, still several blocks distant from the church, the first thing I did was to look for the tower with the round opening to see if it was still intact. Thank God, it was. On coming closer to the church, we saw there was no unusual commotion around it and that no smoke was billowing from its windows. Feeling greatly relieved, we nevertheless rushed up to the organ and unscrewed the front panel. Sure enough, there was Dad's patented miner's lamp still feebly burning, but fortunately no damage had been done. The wood above it had a pleasant warmth, but not sufficient to ignite. Luckily the unperfected and unsatisfactory feature of this lamp, of gradually fading out, was its redeeming feature in this case and avoided a possible calamity. The oil lamp was discarded as unsatisfactory after that.

Rev. Father Patrick J. Cummings was pastor at that time.

The old church had a quaint, yet very ornate chandelier hanging from the ceiling. As I have stated, there were many large manufacturing plants in the neighborhood of the church. One of these was the Pacific Illinois Glass Works. I was told that one of his parishioners working there made this masterpiece and generously donated it to his church.

The Illinois Glass Works was often heard of and made memorable by a horrible accident that occurred there on a Thanksgiving Day afternoon when people crowded on the roof and ventilators of this building to view the football game taking place in the ball park opposite. The roof, with its load of humanity, collapsed and hurtled its occupants on to the hot glass furnaces below, killing and maiming many.

Father Patrick Cummings was transferred as pastor to Mission Dolores Church, and Father Joseph A. McAuliff succeeded him later as pastor of St. Charles.

In 1918 it was decided to build a new church at the corner of 18th and Howard Street (now called Van Ness Avenue South). It might be mentioned that the fire of 1906 did not reach to the confines of the old church but came dangerously close to it. It was the effects of the earthquake on many of the dwellings in this particular neighborhood that caused the havoc it did, of buildings sinking to the ground, crevices appearing in the streets, etc. This was due, undoubtedly, to the ground in this area on which they were built, being filled-in or made ground.

The new church which was erected was again a frame building of Spanish design, in stucco finish. The old malt house, which was formerly opposite the old church, has been subsequently removed.

A new pipe organ was one of the items that was acquired shortly after the dedication of the new church. An elaborate high altar, unique and distinctly different from any in San Francisco, graces the entire east wall of the sanctuary. The organ we installed about 1918, was an Austin electric pneumatic organ of 8 stops, Opus 774, with an oak case and detached console. It has a pleasant tone and is satisfactory in all respects.

Rev. Joseph McAuliff, the beloved and kindly old priest, affectionately known as "Father Joe", passed away in 1939.

Since Father McAuliff's demise, Fathers of the Marist Order have taken over the pastorate of the Church. What was predominantly an English speaking Church, is now, many years later, mostly patronized by Spanish and Mexican Nationals.

RESIDENCE ORGAN JOHN J. SCHOEN

One of the small pipe organs build by my father about the year 1882 was one for an old friend, Mr. John J. Schoen, who lived in a residence on the west side of Webster Street, between McAllister and Fulton Streets.

At one time, undoubtedly previous to being sold to his son, Louis Schoen, the organ was rented for a time to the Japanese Consul, Dr. Eastlake.

It was a small so-called parlor organ, consisting of two stops with divided compass, a stopped Diapason and a Geigen Principal. The bass of the Geigen Principal served for the front display pipes. An unusual feature of this small organ was the appliance for the control of these front pipes. When pianissimo was desired and the Swell blinds were closed, a slide would also close off the front pipes or bass of the Geigen Principal and only retain the soft bass of the Stopped Diapason. The Pedal board of 27 notes, which was radiating, acted only as a coupler to the manual keys. It was pumped by foot like a reed organ and its case was made of walnut.

Mr. John J. Schoen was a pioneer of San Francisco. In later years, he moved with his family to Twenty-Sixth Street, and attended services at St. Anthony's Church, to which parish our family also belonged after 1896.

The organ was acquired principally for his son, Louis Schoen, who, in later years, made music his profession. What became of the organ, I do not know. Evidently it was an incentive for Louis Schoen to interest himself in the art of organ building. In time, for Byron A. Mauzy, a piano dealer on Post Street, he did some pipe organ work, if not of a professional nature, at least to the best of his ability, making small organs out of the remnants of some large pipe organs that were discarded for more modern instruments.

One product of this work was the organ built for the Slavonian Church on Fell Street, and this was far from the standard of perfection expected of a professional organ builder. In later years he built a creditable organ in his residence on 26th Street, a two manual and Pedal tracker action organ of about 14 stops. He sold this organ eventually to St. John's Lutheran Church on 22nd Street near Capp, where it remained for a number of years giving excellent service. We were called upon frequently to tune it and make necessary adjustments. Mr. Louis Schoen, who found fascination in the organ profession, passed away at a comparatively early age.

In 1930 St. John's Lutheran Church decided to buy a more modern organ and secured a Moeller electric pneumatic organ. The old organ, built by Louis Schoen, was then sold by us to the "Albertinum", a boys school at Ukiah, California, under the direction of the Dominican Sisters. We installed the organ in their chapel after making necessary alterations to the exterior case, due to lack of proper height.

Mr. Peter Derrick, who was largely instrumental in securing the organ, and who at the time was Director of the boys of the institution, also performed the duties of organist and gave high praise to the pleasing tones and excellent ensemble of the organ. In 1960 the organ was again moved, and placed in a new Chapel that was built on the same site. We electrified and modernized it and today it is still giving satisfactory service.

ALL HALLOWS CHURCH

As a small boy, when about ten or twelve years old, one of my greatest pleasures on Saturdays and Sundays was, in company with my sisters and brothers and sometimes with neighbor's children, to make exploratory tours and pick wildflowers on the various hilltops crowning beautiful and romantic San Francisco. One of our favorite hilltops was Mount Olympus, on Parnassus Heights, where stood the allegorical statuary group depicting the original on Mount Olympus in Greece. This hill was our favorite for several reasons. It was in the Ashbury Hieghts District, reasonably close to our home on Turk and Fillmore Streets. It was also the only hill where we were sure to find wild daisies. The other hills we roamed had, for the most part, only the usual buttercups, wild marigold, silvery fern and the popular white and blue lupins.

In addition, when we ascended Mount Olympus and looked down in an easterly direction, we beheld a panorama of a section of San Francisco with which we were not familiar. Lying before us was the Eureka and Noe Valley and beyond the Mission District, with the old adobe Mission Dolores nestling in its center, part of the South of Market District, the Potrero Hills in the foreground and, in the distance in a more southerly direction, was Butcher Town, connected by a long trestle, now Third Street, to the adjoining locality known as the Bay View District.

The most outstanding structure in this Bay View District was the beautiful Gothic tower crowning the church on the hilltop. This proved to be All Hallows Church. As children, not knowing the meaning of the name of the church, we often laughed and joked about it. Later, of course, we learned it signified "All Saints."

Many years passed and I was probably in my twenties when I first was called upon to visit this church to repair the organ. I was amazed at its antiquated appearance and the general deterioration of the neighborhood. I was told that this had been one of the early settlements of San Francisco, before the Western Addition was developed, but that the new cable car transportation facilities offered by the Western Addition attracted the residents to that new and desirable area.

The organ was a two manual, tracker action organ of four stops, with attached console, and had a pleasant tone. It was built by Geo. Andrews of Oakland in 1896. The usual reason for calling us to service this organ was to correct frequent ciphering. This is readily explained when I state that I know of no other tracker action organ as small as this one, that has as many couplers. I have often marvelled and wondered at the intricacies of a modern electric pneumatic organ, and have given their designers and originators their just due, but I believe to properly design and execute a tracker action organ with a varied number of couplers, especially sub and super couplers, requires no less genius; in fact, it requires a greater knowledge of physics and applied mechanics than do our complicated modern actions.

In due time a blowing system was installed, but outside of this no changes have been made on the organ to date. Its old ailment of frequent ciphering is still present and inherent. An organist friend of mine, who visited the church one day, told me that on hearing the organ cipher he went up to the organist and asked her why she did not have the nuisance corrected. Her answer was that by letting it cipher during services seemed the most effective way of calling the pastor's attention to the necessity of having the trouble corrected. Even this plan, we find, does not always work. Pastors will endure and inflict this musical torture on the congregation rather than call in the service man to correct it.

SACRED HEART CHURCH

For about seven years, from 1889 to 1896, our family resided at Turk and Fillmore Streets. At the top of the Fillmore Street hill, at Fillmore and Fell Streets, stood the Sacred Heart Church, built in 1885. I remember the pealing of its bell on Sunday mornings and at the Angelus hour. I also remember my parents often speaking of the pastor of the church, the Reverend James Flood, and later I learned that the frequent mention of him was undoubtedly due to the fact that my father had built a small pipe organ for his church at that time, in 1890.

I am referring to the old frame structure. The organ was a small one manual and Pedal tracker action organ, with keyboard built on the side to provide space for the singers on an evidently none too spacious choir loft. Notes available from my father state that Mr. James Paine, made the keys for the organ and, I presume, also the metal pipes, which he did for other organs my father built.

We attended this church at times, and I recall attending an evening devotion with one of my brothers when, through some accident, the decorations on the high altar became ignited by some lighted candles and, quite a disturbance ensued until it was extinguished.

In 1909 the old frame church was moved back and the present large brick edifice, with its square tall tower, a landmark in the city, was erected. The organ my father had built for the old church was not used again. I believe he salvaged the old pipes. I recall them lying around for some time and finally, the Pedal Bourdon pipes were placed in a rebuilt organ we installed in the Pioneer Memorial Church of Oakland.

Joseph Mayer, San Francisco's pioneer organ builder, then well advanced in years and almost blind, with the assistance of one of his sons, installed a small organ in the new church. It was one of the last organs he had built and was probably previously installed in the Catholic Church at Mission San Jose. In all respect to the old and venerable organ builder, my judgment was that this organ was not a credit to his reputation. It was not up to the standard of his other work, but considering his infirmities, he certainly was deserving of much credit.

Reverend Father James Flood, the beloved pastor of Sacred Heart Church, died in 1889 and Rev. Hugh Eagan was his successor. In time, evidently the church realized a better and larger organ was necessary, and Thomas Whalley of Berkeley, California, built them a splendid toned two manual and Pedal organ of 18 stops and erected it in the gallery. Thomas P. Nowlan and Dr. Maurice O'Connell were organists at the church for many years. What became of the old Mayer organ, I do not know.

During the pastorate of Rev. Msgr. John Cullen, who succeeded Father Joseph P. McQuaide, and while Father Norbert Feely was assistant pastor, one of the parishioners of Sacred Heart Church donated a new modern electric pneumatic, divided organ to the church. On good authority, I was informed it was Msgr. Cullen's family.

The old Whalley organ was then sold to St. Thomas Catholic Church, on 43rd Avenue and Balboa Street, in the Richmond District. We erected it in its new location and it is giving excellent service there.

Father Feeley, of Sacred Heart Church, being much interested in pipe organs and an authority in the matter, was entrusted with making the specifications and the selection of the new organ. He consulted us freely in the matter, and we gave him our wholehearted cooperation. The contract to build the organ was awarded to the Hook and Hastings Company of Boston, Mass., in 1938. During one of his visits to our office while working on the preliminaries, he expressed his general idea of a divided organ. I extemporaneously made a sketch of the proposed new organ for the church and gallery, which I thought would be desirable. Surprisingly, with little ado, this plan was carried out in general, barring a few minor details.

As to the details, Father Feeley was much concerned. The number of panels, the grouping of the front pipes, the design of the openings in the side panels, all had to have some bearing on or be symbolic of the liturgy of the church. As to the tonal aspect of the organ, it consisted of three manuals and Pedal, all under expression except the Diapasons. The Great, Choir and part of the Pedal were in one box, the Swell and remaining Pedal stops in another. An excellent array of colorful stops adds to a fine ensemble, rather on the mellow and pleasing side than on the bright and rich, which latter is now so prevalent in the newer organs.

There is a uniquely constructed set of pipes in the organ that probably would be of interest to mention. It is the Concert Flute 8' on the Choir manual partly made of metal and wood. The Bass are stopped wood pipes, then follows the Octave of open wood. The remaining treble notes of the set are made of metal on the principle of the genuine Orchestral Flute, the instrument held horizontally and blown by the lips of the performer by blowing over the aperture. These pipes stand naturally in a vertical position, as most organ pipes do. There is, however, no wind way in the languid. By means of a small tube properly fastened to the foot of the pipe and directed to blow over an aperture on the body of the pipe, a good flute quality is acquired; however, not having outstanding characteristics. I have heard equally as good flutes made on the ordinary pattern of organ pipes.

The front display pipes in this organ are all silent. They

were made in San Francisco of galvanized iron, as fine a piece of metal work as I have ever seen. Of course, this might sound scandalous to an organ pipe maker, to make organ pipes of galvanized iron, regardless of whether they are speakers or not, since in accord with tradition and custom the organ pipe maker would make them of zinc. Nevertheless, these iron pipes answer the purpose, and after being gilded and decorated, they defy detection by anyone.

A unique feature of the exterior design of the organ was the connecting of the two sections of the organ, which were placed on opposite sides of the gallery at a considerable distance, with a continuous case work. This was done, and parts thereof were used for music cabinets. Resting on this connecting case work, are two clusters of pipes, suitably spaced between three windows, which helps to bind both organ sections into one continuous whole.

The exterior oak case was made by Behm Bros., of San Francisco. A direct electric relay was used in this organ, something rather new in organ mechanism design at the time, barring, of course, the Wicks organ which is direct electric action throughout. The Chimes and stop keys in the console also worked on the direct electric system, which now has become quite common. There is a blind system of combination action in the console, as well as the usual type affecting the tablets.

On the whole, the Sacred Heart Church organ is one of distinction in San Francisco. It was practically the last pipe organ built by Hook and Hastings Company of Boston for San Francisco, as the company has since gone out of existence, after a notable career of one hundred years.

One of the unfortunate situations relative to the organ, is a most unsatisfactory reverberation in the church, one consisting of ten seconds when the church is empty, when only three seconds duration would be desirable. This should be corrected some day by accoustically treating the walls or ceiling of the church.

The organist, Matilda Kellar, has the proud record of being stationed here since the present organ was installed.

HOLY CROSS CHURCH

It is most probable that the oldest frame structure in San Francisco today is the little church alongside Holy Cross Church, located on the north side of Eddy Street, between Scott and Divisadero Streets. This small frame church was the original St. Patrick's Church, when it was located on Market Street where the Palace Hotel now stands. About 1887, it was moved to the north side of Eddy Street, between Octavia and Laguna Streets, opposite Jefferson Square.

I have pleasant recollections of this location. We frequently attended Sunday mass here as children, when we were prevented from attending our regular parish church of St. Boniface. Curious, as children are, we invariably selected the first seat in the gallery, which paralleled the length of the church. From this elevated front seat we had an unobstructed view of the altar, and could observe practically every movement of the priest at the altar, see the sacred vessels, and sacred species, etc.

The rustic little church, surrounded by a beautiful garden, with Jefferson Square opposite, and an unobstructed beautiful view of the southern part of the city, with the outline of the distant St. Bruno Hills, or Black Hills, in the background, was always a favored spot to me.

In 1894, St. John's Church, as it was then called, was moved a second time to a new location on Eddy Street, between Scott and Divisadero Streets, and now stands alongside the newly built Holy Cross Church. There it has remained and has been used as a Sunday School and Parish Social Hall. I believe in later years some alterations have been made in the interior of the old edifice. The long galleries on either side of the church have been removed. Its outward appearance, however, still resembles its original contour.

The new Holy Cross Church was built on classic lines and is one of the many beautiful churches of San Francisco. The cornerstone was laid in 1896. Rev. John F. McGinty was pastor at this time. It is claimed that in the early days the old road connecting Mission Dolores with the Presidio Reservation traversed by the Spanish soldiers and the padres, passed over this site.

In 1898 Holy Cross Church acquired its first pipe organ. It was the small Farrand and Votey organ that had temporarily been used in St. Ignatius Church, while the large new four manual Farrand and Votey organ was being installed. My father and elder brother Leo installed it. It was on tuning visits that I first got acquainted with the pastor, Father McGinty. Father was certainly proud of his beautiful church and took a deep personal interest in all that concerned it. Music and the pipe organ seemed to be his special hobby and consideration. It was, therefore,not surprising, that as soon as he found it possible, he secured a larger and permanent organ for his church. His choice, and a good one, was an organ from the Murray M. Harris Company of Los Angeles, California. It was a three manual and Pedal electric pneumatic organ of 33 stops, with detached console and a beautiful, hand carved oak case. It was a high grade, excellently voiced instrument, true to the standard of Murray M. Harris organs, that could not be excelled by anyone. That this organ was the chief concern of Father McGinty, and that it was the apple of his eye, was evidenced by the interest he took in it and the great solicitude he had for it. At no time were we ever able to work on the organ without him being present, observing, asking questions, etc. In time, of course, this attention became annoying, because of its persistency and regularity. In all my years in the organ business, I do not recall any clergyman who showed so much interest in the pipe organ as did Father McGinty.

The new organ was installed in 1904 by Mr. Ed. Crome, an employee of the Murray M. Harris Company, (then called the Los Angeles Art Organ Co.) assisted by my father and my brother Leo. After the new organ was installed and completed, the small Farrand and Votey organ was sold to the Santa Clara University for use in the Students Chapel on their campus. This chapel, a brick building, was distinct from the old Mission Church. In 1910 it, and its contents were consumed in a fire. In later years, the Mission church was similarly destroyed.

The new Holy Cross organ had a blowing arrangement that consisted of a bellows with three feeders, connected to a crankshaft belt, driven by an electric motor, with some type of idling device for regulating it.

In the fire and earthquake of April 18, 1906, the facade of the church was severely damaged by the earthquake. Although the structure was securely built with a steel frame and as a whole was undamaged, nevertheless the sandstone facing and brick on the facade, especially that on both imposing towers, was shaken off and toppled to the sidewalk below, with many of the stones falling through the roof and ceiling, particularly from the west tower, and landing in parts of the organ.

After removing the debris, it was found that considerable damage had been done to the organ. A new Choir and Great chest were then furnished by the Murray M. Harris Organ Company, and damaged pipes were replaced and repaired. My brother, Leo, was given the contract to rebuild the organ, which required several months work. The case of the organ on the west end was also severely damaged. The work of repairing this damage was given to Joseph Maichen, a cabinet worker, by whom I was employed for a short time, temporarily after the fire.

My particular job in this restoration was to make the lattice panels which replaced the solid ones previously installed. Along with this restoration work, the blowing arrangement was improved by removing the feeders and crankshaft and installing a Kinetic blower, however, one not directly connected, but belt driven. At this period, due to some misunderstanding, the maintenance work of the organ was given to Thos. Walley of Berkeley. After my return from New York in 1909, the work was again entrusted to my father and me.

This organ, like most electric action organs at the time, was run on storage batteries. Different types of batteries were tried, the ordinary wet cells that had to be refilled annually, and, finally, a storage battery that was charged on the premises by the 110 current run through some resistance. All proved more or less unsatisfactory. Finally, a large mercury rectifier lamp was installed, connecting with the 110 AC current and producing 10 volt DC current. This lamp cost about $15.00, as I had occasion to learn later, due to an accident I had with it.

Each time the organ was used it was necessary to go to the tower room and manipulate this lamp, a huge multi-global affair pivoted on its axis. It had to be swayed gently to and fro until the mercury, located in a small appendixlike glass tube on the main tube, would pass over a given point, creating a bright blue arc. The light would then flicker and fluctuate as long as the organ was in use. In swaying it to and fro in an endeavor to get the arc to light, which at times was difficult to do, I somehow gave the lamp the wrong twist and broke off the small glass tube containing the mercury. The fluid ran all over the floor and the lamp was ruined. Father McGinty and I compromised on the cost of a new one, each going fifty-fifty.

Having a distrust and dislike for operating this delicate apparatus thereafter, which feeling was equally shared by the organist, it did not require much persuasion, once the merits of the direct current generator were demonstrated, to have one installed. It was a belt driven generator connected with the motor operating the blower.

Miss Ruth Austin, a charming young lady, became organist of Holy Cross Church shortly after the organ was installed, and seemed to be a protege of Father McGinty. Later, as Mrs. Bruce Cameron, she still retained her position, being wedded not only to an able musician, but it appears also to her faithful organ, on which she performed continuously for many years.

In 1915 Father John F. McGinty passed to his eternal reward and Right Rev. John W. Brockhage became pastor, and, although he did not take that personal interest in the organ that his predecessor had by being such a persistent observer, there was nothing about the church that did not receive his minute attention, and there were few parish churches that could equal Holy Cross for its tidy and spotless condition.

After 27 years of efficient service as pastor of Holy Cross Church, during which time he received the signal honor of having conferred upon him the title of Right Rev. Monsignor, in addition to also being a Diocesan Consultor and a member of the Building Committee, Right Rev. Msgr. John W. Brockhage passed to his eternal reward on Nov. 1945.

HOLY FAMILY CONVENT

Probably unknown to many is the fact that the religious order of the Sisters of the Holy Family was founded and established here in San Francisco in 1890. The Most Rev. Archbishop of San Francisco, Sadoc Alemany, gave his approval, and from a small beginning, with Mother M. Dolores Armer, its first superior, the order has grown to surprising proportions, with branches in many of the larger cities of the State.

Their special work is the care of children of the poor, especially of working mothers, and catechetical instruction of the young. Their "Children's Day Homes" are well-known and recommended throughout the City. The mother house is located at the northeast corner of Hayes and Fillmore Streets.

The convent consists of a group of buildings. Undoubtedly, the first building was one of the old homes of the neighborhood. My first recollection of the place is when my father and I called to repair the small but compact Felgemaker pipe organ they had, a beautifully toned pipe organ of about 4 stops, mechanical action. If I am not mistaken, it had two manuals and Pedal, divided stops and, when coupled, was rather hard to play. It was pumped by hand or foot. The stops consisted of a rather large scale Diapason 8', a luscious Stopped Diapason 8', a soft Dulciama 8', and a Violin 4'. The Stopped Diapason 8' was extended down an octave to provide the Pedal Bourdon 16' notes.

I remember a visit I made to the Convent shortly after the earthquake and fire in 1906. I was called to repair a reed organ. The Jesuit Fathers of St. Ignatius Church, who were burned out at their location on Hayes Street and Van Ness Avenue, found temporary shelter at the Holy Family Convent. Undoubtedly, the organ was to be used for religious services in a temporary chapel on one of the lower floors. With the approach of the noon hour, I became conscious of a fragrant aroma coming from the kitchen and I was invited to have lunch there before I left. I remember how upset and confused things were under the trying conditions. People going to and fro, the hallways clogged with furniture and personal belongings and baggage of refugees, that had been temporarily stored there. But these were the earthquake and fire days, and the Sisters were doing their noble share in succoring those who had lost their homes.

In 1908, through the munificence of His Excellency the Most Rev. Archbishop Patrick W. Riordan, the Sisters were presented with a new and larger instrument, a Hook and Hastings organ, for their beautiful chapel. This was a two manual and Pedal organ of 8 stops. My father removed the old Felgermaker organ and erected it in a room on the lower floor of the building. He also installed the new organ, which added great beauty to the chapel and was commensurate with their needs for chapel services and community singing.

The organ was first pumped by hand, but soon after its installation, a Sturdivant blower was applied to it by my brother, Leo. The organ is tracker action, but its touch is remarkably light. It has an Open Diapason 8' and Dulciama 8' on the Great manual, unexpressive, and a Viola 8', Gedeckt 8', Harmonic Flute 4' and Oboe 8' in the Swell box. The Pedal Bourdon 16' pipes are on either sides of the organ.

I have made brief reference to the beautiful chapel where the organ is installed. I believe it is the most ornate, impressive and edifying chapel I have ever seen. The beautiful art glass windows, the frescoed walls and ceiling, the master work of the artist Morreti & Samman, the polished hardwood parquet floor, the white, immaculate altars, with always a few choice flowers, the hardwood pews, and the organ with its gold decorated front pipes, all combined to make a perfect picture.

In recent years, the chapel was renovated and the frescos on the walls and ceiling refreshed. This was, possibly, a needed renovation, however I preferred the former appearance of the chapel with its walls mellowed with time, giving it a serene and dignified appearance. A small change was also made at this time on the Pedal keyboard of the organ, by shortening the length of the keys to get better access to the main aisle, and the Diapason 8' stop on the Great was considerably subdued and softened. Both improvements were desirable.

In 1939 the old Felgemaker organ that was standing idle on the lower floor of the Convent was acquired by Robert Hayburn, a friend of the Sisters. We erected the organ in his home on Tenth Avenue, in the Richmond District and, at the same time, also installed a blower for it. The quaint old organ makes a beautiful appearance, and its mellow tones on a light pressure are a pleasure to hear. Mr. Robert Hayburn was at one time organist at St. Patrick's Church, and also at Mission Dolores Church, but since we installed the organ in his home, he and his brother Edmund have studied at St. Patrick's Seminary at Menlo Park, preparatory to entering the priesthood. Since then they have been ordained and are located in parishes in the Archdiocese.

Father Robert Hayburn was appointed Archdiocesan Director of Music in 1957. He won the F.A.G.O. in 1956.

Coming back to the Sisters of the Holy Family, I believe there is no order of Sisters more beloved or respected in San Francisco than these familiar nuns, our very own, going to all parts of the City and surrounding territory doing their noble work in caring for God's little ones and instructing them. Their interest in our family's welfare was always strongly manifested, and I am personally grateful to them for many a kind favor received. May God bless and reward them.

ST. DOMINIC'S CHURCH

We children occasionally went to St. Dominic's Church. My earliest recollection of the church was in an unfinished condition, with only the main body of the building constructed. At that time it was not adorned with its two imposing towers. It was of plain red brick, unplastered and unfinished on the outside. Adjoining the church, facing on Steiner Street, at the corner of Pine, was the Priory, a rather ancient-looking, mansard-roofed building. The original church, built in 1873, was still standing on Pine Street, around the corner, and was used for a parish hall.

I remember St. Dominic's Church, particularly, for several

reasons. First, it was conducted by the Dominicans, an ancient order of the Church founded about 700 years ago, the friars wearing the picturesque white woolen habits prescribed by their founder, St. Dominic. Another feature I shall always remember was the annual Rosary Sunday procession, in which the clergy, altar boys, the girls dressed in white, and the whole congregation reciting the rosary, marched around the block surrounding the church.

Another point of interest was the beautiful, and at that time the only, baldachin altar I had ever seen - a well proportioned domed cupola, supported on four columns surmounting the altar table. The interior of St. Dominic's was huge, finished in plain white plaster of classic design. It was conceded to have the largest unobstructed span of any church in the west. It was entirely devoid of any interior supporting columns. Owing, undoubtedly, to its design, its hard wall finish, and no intervening obstruction, the reverberation of tone or sound could be counted for ten seconds, which was more than three times as much as is desirable for satisfactory requirements. This excessive echo, or reverberation, proved to be very annoying and distracting, and experiments were made in stretching wires across the nave of the church to correct this defect, but without success.

Until the year 1898 St. Dominic's was without a pipe organ, a reed organ being used - and a Mr. Merrigan was the organist. In that year a more intimate connection began for me with St. Dominic's Church. A contract was awarded to the Mueller and Abel Organ Company of New York for a three manual and Pedal tubular pneumatic action organ. My brother, Leo, assisted the builders, who had come out from New York to install it.

It was during the progress of this work that I, in company with my father, visited the organ on several occasions. The organ front was made of oak of a beautiful design and of broad expanse. With its towers and gilded pipes, it made a beautiful impression. The console was detached, the organist facing the organ. I recall that although the action was tubular pneumatic, the coupler mechanism in the console was, nevertheless, still mechanical. The organ consisted of about 34 stops, was well voiced and substantially and beautifully made.

I believe that shortly before acquiring this organ, the exterior of the church was completed and the two inspiring towers were added. These towers had some bearing on the organ and, therefore, in continuing my story I must add that the organ was pumped by two Ross water motors, placed in the basement and connected by rods to the bellows equipment on the floor above, on the north side of the vestibule of the church. The Dominicans had their own water supply, which they pumped from an artesian well on their property by means of a gas engine, to a large tank about eight feet in diameter, twelve feet deep, high up in the north tower. At times, the Brother in charge would forget to stop the engine and there would be a deluge of water from above when the tank overflowed - or again he would fail to see that sufficient water was pumped, and there would not be enough to play the organ at a funeral or some other service during the week.

One of the first improvements we made, therefore, was to install a water gauge to indicate the quantity of water in the tank. This gauge was placed near the organ loft, where it could easily be seen by the organist and the Brother, who were thus kept informed of the supply of water in the tank. This was accomplished by placing a float on the water, to which was attached a rope going over a series of pulleys to a gauge at the organ loft level, marked to a half scale. Unfortunately, owing to the length of the rope and being made of cotton or hemp, with considerable stretch to it, contracting and expanding with the weather, it often did not prove as accurate as it should have, with the result that some of the former complaints of uncertainty as to the quantity of water in the tank were again experienced.

The organ was started by unwinding a hand screw on a threaded shaft about 10" long, which released the valves controlling the water motors. As there were two units of motors, bellows and feeders, but both working simultaneously, and the control being complicated and not responsive enough, it was not quite satisfactory. At times they would not begin pumping soon enough, and at other times they would race and get beyond control, creating such commotion that one would think the church was falling down. By making each unit independent, we got the blowing plant working to a nicety, and it was a pleasure to watch it function.

After installation of the organ at St. Dominic's had been completed, Mueller & Abel induced my brother, Leo, to accompany them to New York to further serve his apprenticeship with them. This, he gladly did and remained with them until the dissolution of the firm, later working for the Odell and Aeolian Company of New York.

After the builders and my brother had left, the future servicing of the organ, as we had expected, was entrusted to us. We began to experience endless trouble in constant and frequent ciphering. Mr. Hamilton Howe was the first organist, an accomplished musician and a very reasonable man, judging from his patience in bearing the inconvenience of the trouble we were experiencing. He realized that a new organ would take some time before it was finally acclimated, as he called it. A Mr. Rhys Thomas was director of the choir and Father Samuel John Jones, O.P., was in charge of the organ, music and choir of the church. As music was more extensively featured in Catholic Churches at that time than now, even to the extent of holding sacred concerts at intervals, St. Dominic's certainly was in the limelight musically.

That the organ should function properly always was, of course, our big concern. I remember at one time the keys in the console were sticking persistently. We were aware it was San Francisco's damp, foggy weather doing its mischief, and that joints and bearings had to be eased up a bit. I was at the organ loft somewhat early that day, and was to wait for my father who intended, on his arrival, to correct the aforementioned trouble. I thought it would be a great idea to surprise him by going at it myself immediately, and have the work finished when he came. This plan was carried out. It was the first time I had tackled anything of this nature and of such importance - to disassemble a three manual console, correct the trouble and reassemble it again and have everything in first class working order. This I achieved, and when my father arrived and learned I had taken the console apart, corrected the trouble, and put it together again, he complimented me on my daring. This adventure gave me confidence for further developing and mastering the art of organ building.

Another of our persistent difficulties, as mentioned previously, was frequent ciphering. The valves of this organ were made of a type I have never seen before or since in my organ building career. Each pipe had its individual valve, consisting of a felted and leathered disc glued to a round diaphragm, made of light pneumatic leather, which were directly glued to the bottom boards, but fitting opposite a wooden nipple above, which directed the air to the pipe on the chest. There were no springs in these pouches, and it appears that the resiliency of the leather in the round punched form, with the neutralizing of the air on both sides of the diaphragm, was the sole force to return the valve against the seat of the nipple. While the leather was new, this worked satisfactorily, but later from use the leather limbered up and the valve discs would not close firmly, causing frequent ciphering. This was especially noticeable when starting and stopping the organ. We corrected the most offending notes quite successfully by applying a fine spring, but realized that this was not the logical remedy, or the builders undoubtedly would have applied it originally.

This piecemeal applying of springs was tiresome, laborious and seemingly an endless job, and we realized some more permanent cure had to be devised. The thought of heavier pressure inside of the diaphragms entered our minds. After we had thoroughly diagnosed the planning and distribution of the wind trunks connecting the primary boxes, and noting therefrom for the first time that all the action was arranged to be provided with a heavier pressure than the tone pressure used, a gleam of light opened our troubled minds - why not increase the pressure slightly on the action side! This was done at once, with immediate satisfactory results, eliminating further ciphering for all time. The difference in pressure was evidently overlooked by those who installed the organ, and no mention of it was made to us. The new resilient leather which functioned satisfactorily for a time, had evidently spared them from trouble that was bequeathed to us, to solve and to correct.

Following the rather short term as organist of Hamilton Howe, Dr. Franklin K. Palmer succeeded him. Now that our unusual mechanical troubles with the organ were over, we thought we would be able to enjoy a much deserved reprieve. The new organist, Dr. Palmer, however, seemed to delight in tormenting us with picking out notes slightly out of tune, amongst the thousands of pipes, and marking them painstakingly and minutely on a long list every week. This hounding of us with his eccentricity, though annoying, was endured.

Worse things were soon to happen to the organ and to all of those interested in it. The fateful day for San Francisco, April 18, 1906, had arrived. A scourge from God, as it were, visited San Francisco. The awful cataclysm of earthquake and fire struck the City. St. Dominic's Church, being located beyond the limits of the fire, was unscathed by it, but the earthquake completely and hopelessly demolished the massive and well-built building. Undoubtedly, it was the fact in which St. Dominic's took great pride - the architectural feature of having the largest unsupported span of any edifice in the West - that was its undoing.

My first visit to the church a few days after the disaster presented me with a sad sight. The entire facade of the church had fallen out into the street. The steel skeletons of the towers were standing with the copper cupolas on top, but devoid of any brick or stone facing, which was all on the ground. Walls and roof were down in a hopeless mass. The beautiful organ was lying all over the front steps - pipes, chests, console, motors, bricks, huge pieces of stone, and steel girders, all one mass of debris.

As the edifice was not destroyed by fire, but only by earthquake, and certain insurance companies welched on their policies, the debris was left lying in this condition, later soaked by heavy rains which shortly followed, until a settlement could be reached. Meanwhile, the neighborhood boys helped themselves to the organ pipes, and outdid Peter Pan playing with his famous pipes, roaming the streets. Eventually, the debris was removed. I have never learned what settlement was finally made in regard to the insurance situation. The general and common comment was that the Dominican Fathers were hard hit and had suffered an appalling loss.

However, true to the laudable San Francisco spirit that material loss can be replaced and that spiritual values must continue and be upheld, the planning and building of a new temporary church was immediately begun. This time the church was located on Pierce Street, the west end of the property. Pews from the old church and some fixtures were the only items that were salvaged. True to the high ideals of their musical traditions, the Dominicans secured a new and larger pipe organ than the one installed in the old church that had been destroyed. This time they contracted for a three manual and Pedal organ of 58 stops, electric pneumatic action, to be built by the Jessie Woodberry Company of Boston, Mass. This organ was installed in 1909.

It was during the month of April, 1909, as I was about to return home to San Franciso from New York, that I paid a visit to the Jessie Woodberry factory in Boston, Mass., and was informed that Mr. Woodberry and a Mr. Frazee were in San Francisco completing the installation of the new St. Dominic's organ. My return to San Francisco just at this time seemed to be providential, as there was a question whether to entrust this large new modern organ to my father's supervision or to some other parties better versed in the modern electric action. The clergy, being informed by my father that I had just returned from New York, where I had been in the employ of Ernest M. Skinner for some time, and that I would rejoin him in business, dismissed all doubt and the future maintenance of the organ was entrusted to us.

The organ was, unquestionably, too large for the temporary church, and reaching very close to the ceiling because of insufficient height to the building, seemed somewhat strident and strained. Being intended, however, for eventual use in the new permanent church that was to be built later, it was felt that under favorable environment and proper location these objections would be eliminated and the organ would prove to be a most worthy instrument.

Mechanically or tonally we had no unusual experiences with this organ. It behaved as a well-designed and well-built organ should, barring the minor repairs and adjustments every organ requires. I believe this was the first stop keyed and partly semi-circular console that I had seen in San

Francisco. It also had a unique dual arrangement of combination action, one selective and adjustable from the console by operating a series of small pistons under each stop key, and the other fixed or adjusted in the interior of the console.

The first organist at this organ was Humphrey J. Stewart, who presided for a number of years. Mr. Stewart, an Anglican heretofore, we were reliably informed, joined the Roman Catholic Church while organist here and composed several masses. Miss Hortense Gilmore, a pupil of Dr. Humphrey Stewart, followed him. Later Maurice O'Connell played for some time, then Mr. Brushweiler.

During this period from 1909 to 1925, the fond hope of a new and permanent church for St. Dominic's was not dormant. In time, plans were drawn for the new edifice by Beezer Bros., Architects.

Soon the foundations were laid and the superstructure took shape. Tudor Gothic was the style selected, and all indications promised that on its completion it would architecturally be one of the outstanding churches in the Bay Region. We were consulted by the architects regarding the disposition of the organ parts and their arrangement in the organ chambers, that were to be provided on the north wall of the sanctuary. A vested choir with the necessary stalls for the choir boys was also to be provided in the sanctuary, and the console had to be located in close proximity to them. This whole scheme of having the organ and the choir in the front of the church was something new and novel for a Catholic church in San Francisco.

Another unusual feature in the construction of the edifice was the method of casting the interior stone facing which covers the walls. Each block was cast separately in the basement of the church and, so I was told, was made of a combination of plastic material and wet sawdust. The latter, by later drying out, would present a firm yet porous surface, producing an accoustically perfect surface, avoiding all excessive echo and reverberation. The ceiling of the lofty nave of the church between the roof girders was paneled with celotex. Fortunately, these precautions to acquire accoustical perfection were successful, resulting in a decided contrast to the unfortunate situation that prevailed in the old church.

On moving the organ from the temporary church to the new church in 1929, it was decided to secure a new four manual console, one that would be ample in size to contain all future additions that might be made to the organ. This console was secured from the Estey Organ Company and was donated by the late Senator James D. Phelan. The old original console was, however, retained and placed on a small gallery facing the transept of the church. Possibly some day, the fourth manual, or Solo division of the organ will be completed.

We applied new Swell shades with individual motors to the Swell and Choir division, and releathered all of the pneumatics of the organ at this time. The Great still remains in the open or unexpressive. The latest improvement made on the organ was the placing of the ornate grills or casework in front of the organ. This was designed by the architect, Arnold Constable, an authority on Gothic design, and an associate of Beezer Brothers, architects of the original plans for the church.

The four manual Estey console, installed in 1928, did not give entire satisfaction, especially its combination piston action which was practically inaccessible for making adjustments.

In 1953, through the beneficence of the Rubia family, whose son was a member of the Boys' Vested Choir, and who lost his life in the surf at Ocean Beach, they presented to the church, in his memory, a new three manual Moller Console, which is now in use and giving good service.

In the new church, Marshall Geiselman was organist for sometime, followed by Miss Frances Murphy who played for many years. Then followed Mr. Corson, Chester Wiltzie, Robert Fitzgerald, Leonard Fitzpatrick, and Mr. Johnson, the present organist. St. Dominic's is one of the few Catholic churches in San Francisco that has a permanent Boys' Choir functioning.

The noted organist and composer, Sigfried Karg-Elert, visited San Francisco in 1931 and gave a sacred concert at the church. We received a summons from Miss Murphy, the organist, asking us to come to the church and meet Karg-Elert at the console, as he had some complaints to make about the organ. As he could not adequately express himself in English, and she knowing I could converse with him in German, she felt that I would be able to learn his difficulties and possibly satisfy him. On meeting him I was surprised to learn that he had no complaint at all about the mechanism or the tuning of the organ but that it lacked in general a "certain something" that the organs in Germany had. He wanted more Mixtures, Mutation stops, etc., things, of course, that I could not give him. Personally, I had always thought that St. Dominic's organ had plenty, and an abundance, of these essential corroborative stops, but evidently they did not come up to the expectations of Karg-Elert.

I remember telling him in our conversation that followed, that I had never been to Europe or heard of any of the much-discussed European organs, but that I had read many organ specifications and the descriptions of their tonal qualities, and had often wondered, with all their Mixtures, Mutation stops, and high-pitched pipes, if the organs were not over-sharp and penetrating, and inclined to be screechy and over-brilliant. He, however, assured me this was not the case, but that they sounded well balanced, clear and bright, yet as pleasing and harmonious as the tones of a large bell.

Later I attended his recital, and judging from the numbers selected and rendered, in which there was nothing of massive grandeur or dignity, music to which the organ, the King of Instruments, should have first claim, but rather a series of selections of a light, piquant, crispy, two foot tone range, with the most unusual tone coloring produced in combination with the Mixtures, Twelfths, Fifteenths, I had ever heard I realized it was a dish of tidbits rather than a substantial he-man's steak. I then understood his need and desire for more and more Mixtures and the sparkling effervescent tones of the higher ranged stops of the organ.

During the years we have serviced the organs of St. Dominic's Church, we have become acquainted with many of its Priors, Pastors and Priests of this venerable Order, founded over 700 years ago. One outstanding character that I would like to comment upon was the faithful Sacristan, Brother Bernard Connelly, O.P., whom I recalled from my first connections with St. Dominic's fifty years previous. At that time he was a young man, performing his duties in the large church, which he kept meticulously clean polishing and wiping the leaners and seats of the pews in a most scrupulous and conscientious manner. I had often thought of his harrowing experience that early Wednesday morning of April 18, 1906, when, after opening the large church at 5:00 a.m. and while occupied at one of the side altars in preparation for a mass to be said, the earth began to quake and heave, the marble altars collapsed, walls crumpled and havoc and ruin reigned where, moments before, peace and tranquility pervaded in these sacred precincts.

As the years passed on, Brother Bernard showed the effects of passing time, but still his interesting characteristics remained until his end, the quaint drawl of his speech, his shuffling walk, his rounded, stooped shoulders, as he did his accustomed work. One day during March 1948 I missed his presence, and inquired of his whereabouts. I was informed he passed to his eternal rest at the ripe old age of 89 years.

May the new St. Dominic's Church, with its innate grandeur and medieval setting, with its Gothic windows gradually being filled with art glass, resplendent with the beauty of the Cathedrals of Eurpoe, and let us hope, with a completed 4 manual organ in the not too distant future, with its vested boy and male choir, unique in San Francisco, be an inspiration and edification to all who visit it.

CALIFORNIA STREET METHODIST CHURCH

One of the first jobs I worked on, was assisting in the installation of the Murray M. Harris organ, in 1900, at the California Street Methodist Church which was erected in 1892, located at the southeast corner of California and Broderick Streets. I had finished school about two years before and I remember my old friend, Mr. Edward L. Crome, a former employee of my father and later associated with the Murray M. Harris Company of Los Angeles, calling at the house and inviting my father and me to assist in the installation work.

My first particular job was to unscrew the caps on the large 16' Pedal open Diapason pipes to clean out any shavings that might have been left therein, as the toe holes were evidently bored after the caps were screwed on. After the initial heavy work was done, requiring considerable extra help, the remaining work was done, mostly by Mr. Crome, another helper, my father and myself. At the start the work progressed rapidly and uneventfully.

It was a large two manual and Pedal organ, with attached console of 24 speaking stops. The Swell and part of the Great were enclosed. The Open Diapason 16' and Open 8', the Octave 4, Twelfth and Fifteenth were unexpressive. A beautiful oak case, richly carved, with ornamental front pipes, made an imposing appearance. A Mr. Ellsworth was the donor of the organ. The blowing apparatus consisted of a large bellows with three feeders placed in a room below the organ. It was belt driven by an electric motor. As centrifugal blowers were not in use at that time, uncertainty existed as to how to operate the blowing arrangement. Evidently a loose pulley or idling device on an alternating current motor was not deemed satisfactory, so arrangements were made with the United Railroads Company to extend their power line from their nearest connection to the church, with the result that 500 volt direct current was obtainable. A large Rheostat was made and connected by pulley arrangement to the top of the bellows, which regulated the speed of the motor. I recall the bellows were so large that they could not be brought in through the available door, possibly also on account of the location of the door. At any rate, at the top of a landing on a stairway leading from the rear Broderick Street entrance, the wall was cut through, so the bellows could be brought into the room.

The action or mechanism of the organ consisted of a combination of the tracker action and pneumatic systems. The keyboard, including the action to the chest, was the old-fashioned tracker or mechanical action. At the chest, the tracker opened a double acting exhaust and supply valve, which supplied or exhausted the grooves in the bottom boards. These, in turn, connected with the individual valves, one for each pipe in the organ. As soon as the air was turned on, it became evident that something was not right. There was a multitude of ciphers, caused by the individual valves in the chest not seating accurately. Accessibility to the valves was not one of the fine points of the organ. The groove boards, consisting of a total of only six, three to one side of the chest, were large and heavy and required a great number of 4" wood screws to hold them securely. The chief difficulty with the hinged type pneumatics that were used, was the fact that they were too close together, all on one side of the rail and not staggered. In addition, a pin and spring protruded on one side of the pneumatic, further encumbering the already cramped space, with the result that they would rub on one another. Furthermore, the valve itself, a leathered and felted disc, which was precariously supported on a threaded wire screwed into the pneumatic, would, in time, from its own weight settle and miss the valve hole. At any rate, after weeks of tedious and laborious work in opening and closing bottom boards incessantly in trying to correct and improve the ciphering, the bottom board screws became stripped and additional and longer screws had to be applied. Naturally, the day of dedication of the organ had to be postponed. What excuses were offered, I do not know.

Mr. Harris, the builder of the organ, was a frequent visitor from Los Angeles. That he was disturbed and worried could be discerned on his countenance. Finally, after much work with untold patience and perseverence, and undoubtedly with pressure being exerted by church authorities, a date was set for the dedication of the organ. If I am not mistaken, William King of Oakland, one of the most promising organists in the Bay cities at the time, was recitalist.

The dedication and opening recital must have been a dreaded ordeal for Murray M. Harris, who was present, as well as for the organist playing the organ and the congregation listening to it. On reliable authority I was informed that men had to be stationed in each chamber of the organ during the service to pull out pipes that would insist on ciphering, thus making it possible to continue and complete the program, after a fashion. By the same authority I was informed that after the recital and dedication service, Mr. Harris was found to be in tears, as the ordeal he went through had completely unnerved him. Instead of being a crowning achievement and a successful inaugural of his first pipe organ in San Franci co, it proved to be an apparent failure, at least a temporary one. I might mention here that the stop action of the organ also worked pneumatically, that is on the exhaust system, and this also gave considerable trouble.

Tonally, the organ was of the highest order, and in workmanship and material it could not be excelled. After the opening recital, additional weeks were spent on the pneumatics and valves, making certain improvement - finally getting the organ to function satisfactorily and dependably.

Mr. Harris must have been made of some unusually fine fiber and stamina as this apparent set-back did not seem to discourage him in the least. At this time he secured the services of Mr. William B. Fleming, an organ builder and designer of repute, with a crew of efficient, practical and experienced workmen, among them Mr. O. W. Orcutt, Anton Rokus, Tommy Ross and F. Bolton, as the Murray M. Harris organs manufactured after this one, and they were numerous, were of an entirely different design and worked most efficiently and reliably, and were built in a manner to conform to the highest professional standards. It was no coincidence that the name, later adopted by the firm, "Los Angeles Art Organ Co.", could not have been more deserving or appropriate.

I recall one day while we were still battling with the recalcitrant ciphers in the organ and when, if I had been the builder or designer of the organ I would have been worried and humiliated at my apparent Waterloo, Mr. Harris, in a jubilant mood, told the assembled workmen of his good fortune in securing the contract to build the large organ for the new Leland Stanford, Jr. Memorial Chapel at Stanford University, Palo Alto, California. I remember him describing the dimensions and details of the new chapel, telling about the mosaics that were to be installed, the marble that would be used, the carving in wood and stone that would be undertaken, and that the front pipes of the organ were to be made of pure English block tin. Mr. Harris, not long after, built this, his dream organ and, at the time, also the mammoth organ for the St. Louis "Louisiana Purchase"

Exposition in 1904 - and many others. All of these organs that he built were the acme of perfection. In later years, I believe financial difficulties beset the company and I recall Mr. Harris passed away at a rather early age after a short career.

California Street Methodist Church functioned and carried on for a number of years. Rev. A. C. Bane was pastor during this period and a Mr. Hollowell was organist. In time, Mr. Ellsworth, the donor of the organ and a staunch supporter of the church, passed away, and it seems the flourishing condition of the church also began to recede. In 1926 the church disbanded.

I was reliably informed that after the fire of 1906 the church property was acquired by the late Abe Ruef, a noted character in San Francisco. In 1927 the church and property were bought by the Seventh Day Adventists Central Church. In 1930 they procured a Wurlitzer organ, which is now in use. The original Murray M. Harris organ was moved by our firm to the Grace Methodist Episcopal Church in San Francisco and from there to the Christian Brothers Novitiate in Napa, California.

BETH ISRAEL TEMPLE

In 1898, at the time I became actively engaged in the organ business, Beth Israel was located on the south side of Geary Street, between Octavia and Laguna Streets. Undoubtedly, like many of the churches and synagogues then existing in the Western Addition, they had their origin in the lower, or older part of the City.

I remember this Synagogue was quite an imposing frame building. I had called there on several occasions with my father to tune and repair the organ. It was a two manual and Pedal Bergstrom tracker action organ of 18 stops, with detached console, the organist facing the congregation.

One particular incident I shall never forget occurred when I was trying out my young wings as an organ builder. It was an emergency visit. When I arrived, the choir was still assembled around the organ. The organist was a young chap, apparently not much older than myself. He upbraided me rather severely for either not arriving sooner, or not being able to locate the trouble immediately, I do not remember which, and passed some uncomplimentary remarks which, if they had come from an older person, I probably would not have resented, but as he was young and apparently inexperienced himself, I did resent the criticism. However, time brings changes. This youthful organist was none other than our genial friend and distinguished artist, Uda Waldrop.

About 1905, Beth Israel Temple built a new brick edifice a few blocks farther west on Geary Street, between Fillmore and Steiner Streets. It is a rather imposing edifice, with the organ up in the loft over the ark, as is customary in synagogues. The old Bergstrom organ from the old Temple was moved and erected in the new location, most probably by one of the Bergstrom family. At the old location the organ was pumped by hand, and the only improvement made at the time of its removal to the new Temple was the installation of a Sturdivant blower. Later we removed the Clarinet from the Great, transferred the Swell Aeoline to the Great manual to undulate with the Dulciana and added a new Viola in its place.

The earthquake and fire came along and the building was cracked and damaged in places, but it was not of a serious nature. The interior was then gone over and redecorated - as I recall the whole of the auditorium being filled with staging. In 1907 we took over the regular care of the organ again.

Many organists functioned here during the following years, as a synagogue job in addition to a Sunday position, was "butter on both sides of the bread" for the average under-paid organist. Wallace Sabin functioned here for some time and, I recall, he wanted us to arrange to have the organ seat padded. It was finally done by some upholsterer. It was the first organ seat I saw thus cushioned. I was always under the impression that the ideal organ bench was one that was broad enough, with rounded edges and highly polished. Undoubtedly, the reason for asking for this improvement was not so much the hardness of the bench, but the exceedingly awkward position the organist had to maintain while playing the organ. The pedal keys, a straight pedal board at that, was much too far out from the manual keys, a common error in design in all old organs, giving the organist a feeling of off-balance, or falling over the manual keys, with resultant severe back strain. This error we corrected partly in time for some succeeding organist, when we substituted the old straight pedal board for a concave radiating one, and placed it forward as much as conditions would permit, making it nearer standard A.G.O. requirements. At this time we also installed two fan tremolos, and placed a full-scaled Gamba on the Great manual in the former location of the Clarinet. A noisy pneumatic, fixed combination, pedal action was also removed. Otherwise the organ is very much as it has been during the last 65 years.

Mr. Edgar Thorpe and Louis Flint were organists for a considerable number of years. Mrs. Elizabeth Laing also presided as organist for sometime and others followed her.

An outstanding character of Beth Israel was Cantor Rabinowitz, who served the Synagogue for over 50 years. He passed away in 1943, mourned by many friends. He was especailly liked by my father, and when the two met they always had a pleasant chat together.

WEST SIDE CHRISTIAN CHURCH

West Side Christian Church, one of the churches of the Western Addition, located on the north side of Bush Street, between Scott and Divisadero Streets, is one of the churches that interested me for years. We lived for a short time within a block of the church during 1894. I recall, while living there, attending a political meeting held in a tent on the vacant corner lot of Divisadero and Bush Streets on behalf of the then incumbent mayor of San Francisco, Adolph Sutro.

West Side Christian Church was built in 1895. In 1904 they secured the Murray M. Harris pipe organ, now in use. It was installed by Mr. Frank Frame and Mr. Dowdell of the Murray M. Harris factory, and my father and I assisted. This was the second Harris organ installed in San Francisco, and was a vast improvement over the first one built for the California Street Methodist Church.

The West Side Christian Church organ consisted of two manuals and Pedal, 15 stops, pneumatic action, a detached console and a beautifully executed, paneled oak case. The console being extended a considerable distance from the organ, the action, if anything, was not too responsive. Originally, it had a relay placed in the tubing between the console and the organ to overcome this difficulty, and apparently it answered the purpose so far as attack and repetition was concerned, but evidently it also complicated the mechanism and for some reason or other was a source of constant ciphering. Being placed under the rostrum platform, in an almost inaccessible location, a cipher was always a serious matter, making the organ, for a time, unusable. This situation could not remain for long, so the relay was removed and the console moved closer to the organ, with beneficial results both ways. The action performed more satisfactorily and the singers were closer to the organ.

Miss Gardner was organist for many years. Dr. Rigdon was one of the leading members of the church, the person with whom we had our business dealings.

Due to some change or upheaval in the church we lost our status and Mr. Thomas Whalley of Berkeley secured the maintenance of the organ. During that period he found it necessary to retube the organ with new lead tubing. The old tubes would split near where they were fastened to the chest and, being designed on the exhaust system, any small leak would cause a cipher. In later years, we again secured the regular care of the organ and have maintained it every since. Rev. Shaw was the popular pastor of the church for many years, and Mrs. Maury held the position of organist.

In or about 1950, West Side Church moved to new quarters in the Forest Hill Section under the name of Forest Hill Christian Church, and the old church was taken over by the Philadelphian Seventh Day Adventists.

STANFORD MEMORIAL ORGAN
(Temporarily installed in the Mechanics Pavilion)

A large three manual pipe organ that had only temporary

abode in San Francisco was the Murray M. Harris organ, built in Los Angeles for the Stanford Memorial Chapel at Stanford University, Palo Alto.

When the organ was built and ready for installation, it appears the Memorial Chapel was not quite complete enough to receive it. At that time a national convention of the Christian Endeavor Society was scheduled for San Francisco, with the large Mechanics Pavilion at Larkin and Grove Streets as its headquarters. As no better medium than a pipe organ could be selected to accompany a large assemblage in the singing of hymns and impart a religious atmosphere to the convention, arrangements were made to secure the temporary use of the organ for this purpose.

The publicity the organ received certainly compensated its builders for their efforts in installing it for only temporary use. I have a faint recollection of seeing the divided organ on the west end of the pavilion. I did not hear it while it was installed here.

Mr. Scott Brooks, I believe, functioned as organist during the convention.

WILLIS DAVIS RESIDENCE

Early in the years of my apprenticeship as an organ builder, I heard the name "Willis Davis" mentioned by my father. In the first place, he was evidently a gentleman of means and leisure, and secondly, he must have been a genius in the matter of applied mechanics and physics, and a lover of music.

At the time the Hook and Hastings organ was being erected at Trinity Episcopal Church, in 1897, Mr. Willis Davis paid my father and the other gentlemen erecting the organ a visit at the church, to see its installation.

From 1903 on I recall making frequent visits with my father to Mr. Davis' home on the northwest corner of Scott Street and Pacific Avenue to tune and service the beautiful Farrand & Votey organ he had installed there. It had been built in 1896 or 1898, I believe. It was a two manual and Pedal organ of 18 stops, electric-pneumatic action, with attached console. A beautiful case in harmony with the surroundings, added beauty and charm to the living room in which it was located.

Mr. Davis, as I have said, had a special aptitude for mechanics and built for himself a beautifully fashioned and well constructed automatic player console, which was located in a corner of the room opposite the organ, from which he played the organ automatically. It functioned very well. One fault, I recall however, common in most automatic players, was the slowness of the rewind mechanism - at least it appeared that way to me. He probably had the same complaint and, therefore, contrived some other means to more speedily rewind the music roll after the number had been completed. He rejected the ordinary pneumatic driven crankshaft power drive for a small electric motor drive arrangement, evidently run on the direct current of the organ generator, as its speed could be controlled and regulated. This was done by operating a foot pedal. With a little practice it could be deftly manipulated.

The first time I worked on his player, however, being unfamiliar with this rewind gadget, I rested my foot too heavily on the pedal. The motor shot off at full speed, and the music roll unwound in a jiffy, clattering and making a noise and uproar in the spool box. I recall this incident when I consider the finesse with which one operates the foot treadle of an automobile to control the gas. That also requires some practice to operate gently and smoothly.

Another gadget Mr. Davis had in the organ was a finely executed imitation of a mechanical canary bird in a gilded cage. The deception, as far as appearances were concerned, was most realistic. However, on hearing the songster warble, the imitation became unbelievable. At certain parts of a given music roll the bird would start warbling and again stop as prearranged, to the evident delight and amusement of his guests.

The blowing apparatus of the organ was in the basement, consisting of a bellows with feeders on a crankshaft driven by a horizontal Ross duplex water engine. Batteries were also in use at first to provide the low voltage current. However, later a motor generator unit was installed. In this basement, Mr.

Davis also had his workshop, with a fine work bench, a large chest of tools and many half-finished pieces of handicraft and organ parts.

Some years later we were informed that Mr. Davis had gone on a trip abroad. He was known to have embarked on the steamer at New York for Europe, but had never made his appearance on the other side.

Thereafter, the house, with its contents was taken over by Mrs. Henrietta DeWitt Kittle, a charming elderly lady. This was sometime during 1911 or 1912. We called occasionally at the old mansion to service the organ, and always thought of its original owner who so unhappily disappeared from the scene. Mrs. DeWitt Kittle passed away a few years later and the organ was procured by the St. Francis Episcopal Church, to which location we removed the organ and reinstalled it. (See St. Francis Episcopal Church, page 285.)

The old residence was finally razed. The canary bird in the gilded cage was sold to one of our employees, and the huge tool chest, with what tools were left in it, and the automatic player cabinet came into my possession. Later on, my dad, in his declining years, more as a matter to occupy himself and not liking to destroy this reminder of the handicraft of his old acquaintance, Willis Davis, made a small writing desk out of it for my use. The empty tool chest still lays in my basement.

MOST HOLY REDEEMER CHURCH

With the growth of the section of San Francisco known as Eureka Valley, on the eastern slope of Twin Peaks, it soon became necessary to establish a Catholic parish there. This was given the name of Most Holy Redeemer Church.

The first pipe organ that the church procured was, strange to say, the last pipe organ the veteran California organ builder, Joseph Mayer, had built, which was sometime about 1894-95. It was in 1900 when Father McQuaide, a friend of Mr. Mayer, rented this organ for use in his church.

Mr. Mayer was then over 82 years old and almost totally blind. With the aid of his son, Fred, who at intervals assisted his father, he succeeded in getting the organ installed and completed. Considering the age and physical infirmities of the veteran builder, and the rather inexperienced help he had, the result was fair, however, no match for the work being done by contemporary organ builders at the time.

The Mayer organ was in use for a number of years, when a better and more modern organ was desired. It was during the pastorate of Father O'Neill, sometime during 1907, when the organ was removed and a new two manual and Pedal Kimball tubular pneumatic organ, with an attached console of about 7 speaking stops, was secured from the Eilers Music Company, who were agents for the Kimball Co. My brother Leo, in their employ at the time, installed the organ.

The old organ was sold to a church in Oakland, St. Andrew's Episcopal Church, at 12th and Magnolia Streets, and was installed there by my brothers, Leo and Erwin. I recall working on it several times thereafter. Later on the church was abandoned by the Episcopalians and it became Simpson Methodist Church.

After the death of Father O'Neill at Most Holy Redeemer Church, Right Rev. Msgr. William P. Sullivan was appointed pastor. He made many improvements in the church and parish equipment. The Kimball organ, by this time some 25 years after its installation, needed the pneumatics replaced. The pneumatics themselves were removed readily enough from their places and taken to the shop to be releathered. A peculiar feature, however, of some of the Kimball organs at that time was that the rails on which the pallets would strike were also felted and leathered to make a soft cushion seat. The moths had destroyed this felt, as well as many discs on the pneumatics. The discs, where needed, were replaced in the shop, but the felt on the pallet rails had to be replaced on the job, as the rails could not be removed. This work was done with the aid of our loyal helper, Fred Walti. In 1946 we detached the console from the organ, discarded the tubular pneumatic action and electrified the organ throughout.

Mr. Martinez, a familiar figure among church organists, played the organ for many years. Rene Sarzen functioned successfully as choir leader.

I recall an emergency call we had early one Easter

morning, that the organ was dead and could not be used. On arriving we found that a chain applied to a regulating valve behind the organ had become dislodged, cutting off the supply of air to the organ. On leaving, my son Lawrence left the usual service slip with the statement, "Organ Resurrected." How true and appropriate it was. The organ was brought to life again.

In 1960, under the pastorate of Rev. Fr. Thomas extensive alterations were made to the lower part of the church. At this time, a larger, more suitable organ — an Austin, two manual and Pedal organ, Opus 2326, was installed, by our firm.

The old Kimball organ found a new location in a private home of an organist enthusiast living in Pacifica, California.

ST. JAMES CATHOLIC CHURCH

Another beautiful Gothic Church of the Mission District is St. James Church, at Twenty-Third and Guerrero Streets. Although a frame building, its beautiful lines make it a stately edifice. I first recall working in the church when my father and I assisted in installing its W. W. Kimball pipe organ. Oddly enough, for a church of its moderate proportions, it has two galleries where one, in most cases, is the rule. Rev. Father Patrick R. Lynch was pastor in 1901 when the Kimball pipe organ was installed. Mr. Frank T. Milner was the agent of the Kimball Company of Chicago at the time. I do not recall whether he was permanently located in San Francisco or whether he was touring the western states for them. At any rate, we saw quite a bit of him at the time. He was a pleasant gentleman, somewhat short in stature, and rather loquacious.

During 1901 the Kimball Company was selling a small stock organ, all built in one pattern. It was a two manual and Pedal organ with attached console, and had 7 stops, all enclosed except the front speaking pipes and the Pedal pipes. The case was made of oak, with the front pipes decorated. A novel and unusual feature of the organ was that all the pipes, except the pedal and front pipes, were securely fastened into place on the chest enclosed in the Swell box. In fact, the organ would be completely assembled and tuned in the factory. When shipped, it would consist of only a few major parts, the bellows, the chest, with pipes and Swell box, the keyboard with most of the lead tubing, and the pedal chest with pipes. These few units would be combined at the church, some tubes attached, and the organ would be in tune and ready to play. Owing to this compactness, it had the disadvantage, especially the chest with pipes and Swell box, of being exceedingly heavy for its size and bulk. A rigger had to be engaged to hoist the organ at St. James to the upper gallery. A rather tall gin pole was used. I remember distinctly the afternoon when it was hoisted. Father Lynch was present, also Mr. Millner, the agent of the Kimball Company, my father and I, watching the rigger and his helpers at work. The gin pole was erected on the Church floor, the tackle secured thereon and the guy ropes fastened, all in readiness to hoist the heaviest part of the organ to the first gallery level. This was readily accomplished. The gin pole was then transferred to the first gallery level and made ready to hoist it to the second gallery. After pulling the rope taut to its extreme limit, it became evident that either the pole was too short or the sling and tackle were too generously applied. At any rate it was shy about one inch in clearing the upper gallery railing. The pull rope was then lashed securely, with one man attending and all the other available help proceeded to the upper gallery to try by hand power and by the use of some leverage to lift it over the obstinate hurdle, the upper gallery railing. It was exciting and, in my eagerness to try to help, I also laid hands on the organ. I admit my feeble efforts did not amount to much, as I was then a frail lad of 14 or 15 years, yet my intentions were the best and so I resented being singled out by Father Lynch, from among the brawny men, who, with a loud voice, shouted, "Get a man, get a man." Finally, the case was inched over the railing and placed on the floor, to the great relief of everyone.

If I recall correctly, I never met Mr. Millner again, since his visit on this occasion. He passed away in 1920 and we had a visit from his son some years later, at our factory. In 1923, a serious fire occured in the church but no damage was done to the organ. In the course of the years we have worked on the organ intermittently and now service it regularly. In 1927 Father Lynch passed away and was succeeded by Rev. Msgr. Patrick J. Quinn.

ST. JAMES EPISCOPAL CHURCH

St. James Episcopal Church, on California Street in the Richmond District of San Francisco, was located there for many years and satisfied all their needs for accompanying the choir and congregation by using only a reed organ or harmonium.

However, in 1950, they hired our firm to build them a small 4 stop, two manual, electric action organ, which was placed on the gallery over the front entrance of the church, with the console in the forepart of the church near the chancel, opposite the singers in their choir stalls.

Evidently, this arrangement of having the console and choir a considerable distance from the organ did not work out very satisfactorily due to accoustical difficulties, and later we placed a small chest of two sets of pipes, a Dulciana 8' and a Genshorn 8' on an overhanging bracket close to the singers in the choir stalls to enable them to hear organ tone simultaneously with the organist, playing the organ.

This improvement proved to be satisfactory and no further complaint has been heard since.

ACADEMY OF THE SACRED HEART

On Franklin and Ellis Streets, on the southwest corner, stood a stately frame structure that was formerly the Convent and Academy of the Sacred Heart, conducted by the Madames of the Sacred Heart.

My first occasion to work there was in 1901 when the Sisters procured a small pipe organ for their chapel, which was located on the second floor of the building. My father and I installed the organ.

It was a two manual and Pedal tracker action, Hook & Hastings organ, with 8 stops and attached console. At first it was hand pumped, but later a motor was belted to the crankshaft. I remember installing the organ; the material was delivered in the yard, or garden, of the convent, from where we carried the parts up to the chapel. The Sisters, undoubtedly sympathizing with us for the laborious work, suggested that we use the elevator, which was hand-powered or, in other words, a large dumb waiter.

I recall we filled the elevator with a considerable load, not knowing its capacity or its peculiarities. On reaching the top floor we removed some of the material and, while we were in the chapel, we heard a terrific roar. The elevator with the remaining load had broken loose and was rapidly descending the shaft. The clutch had given way. In desperation, I grabbed the heavy hemp rope by which we had hauled up the elevator and finally succeeded in stopping its descent before it struck bottom; not, however, without burning the skin from my hands, which were badly blistered.

Another more pleasant incident occurred that I often recall. I believe it is a fine demonstration of self denial. The organ was practically completed, except for the front display pipes. That the eventual finish or exterior appearance of the organ would be of interest to woman, I can readily understand, especially so to the nuns who take such pride in the adornment and beautification of their chapels. Everything must be just so. We were about ready to unwrap the front pipes when the Sister standing alongside anxiously awaiting the first glimpse of the color and finish of the pipes, suddenly checked herself saying, "just because I was so curious, I will desist and wait until I see them installed in the organ", and turned away. I admired this evidence of self control and mortification of one's desires.

The organ sounded very well, but the nuns were very particular that only heavenly music and no extraneous noises and groans should emanate from the organ. Unfortunately, the panels of the feeders, which were tenoned on a frame, had shrunk and each time the feeder worked there was a creak or a crack from below the bellows. By applying a longer connecting beam fastened on both ends of the frame, we eliminated this annoying noise. The Sisters were more than kind and thoughtful of us, while we were installing the organ. More than once at the noon hour a fine warm lunch awaited us in one of the lower rooms.

The organ was not long in use when the earthquake and fire of April 18, 1906, struck San Francisco. Practically no damage was done to the building by the earthquake, and the fire was halted one block from the convent. The Sisters later vacated the convent and established themselves in a new home, a former residence on Pacific Heights, on the corner of Scott and Jackson Streets. The old Convent building was taken over by the Pacific Gas & Electric Company, undoubtedly a most convenient structure for their purpose.

During the turmoil and excitement of readjustment after the earthquake, one of our first jobs was to remove the Hook and Hastings organ from the chapel and store it in the basement of the Sisters' new home. Quite a different scene and atmosphere greeted us while thus at work in the old chapel. The serenity and devotional aspect of the chapel was gone. The quiet tread of the nuns was now replaced by the laughter and gaiety of the women clerks for whom the chapel was being converted into an office, and who could not resist the allure of the highly polished oak floor to enjoy a waltz or a two step.

The organ remained for several years in the basement of the Sisters new home. Finally, a new chapel was built alongside the old residence, which was one of several buildings comprising the Academy group. This chapel was larger and more pretentious than the chapel in the Franklin Street building. It also had a gallery in the rear. Here we again erected the pipe organ and this time added a new modern blower to it. The only other change made in the organ during the course of the years was to apply a Tremolo to it.

In 1904, the Madames of the Sacred Heart received as a gift the large Flood mansion located on the north side of Broadway, between Fillmore and Webster Streets. The huge mansion was easily altered to suit the purposes of their institution, but I doubt if the chapel there is as spacious as the one the Sisters had at the Scott Street location, as they stated they did not have the space to erect the old Hook and Hastings organ. A new, smaller Wicks organ was procured.

We then made an arrangement with the Sisters and had the

old chapel organ erected in our factory. There it remained for some time on display, until we sold it to the Trinity Lutheran Church at Palo Alto, California, where we erected it in the organ loft of their little church. It fitted into the scheme of things splendidly, as though it had been built for the church. Tonally, it more than satisfied the new owners, having a genuine, typical church organ tone which was ideally suited to their Lutheran services.

So, after 62 years, the organ has had four different habitations and a varied career.

JAMES G. FAIR RESIDENCE

Not far from the other prominent residences of Nob Hill, although not on the crest of the hill itself but one block below on the north side of Pine Street, between Leavenworth and Hyde Streets, stood the James G. Fair residence. I do not recall the exterior design or the type of architecture of the building. I do remember that there was a large stone retaining wall immediately abutting the sidewalk, with a stairway leading to the main entrance of the mansion.

My father and I visited this residence on one occasion in 1902 relative to the moving of an orchestrion that was also part and parcel of the furnishings of the house. It was a beautifully built instrument, with ebony veneered panels. In years past when the Orchestrion was in use, my father provided them with several new Cylinders; one of the pieces contained thereon was the "Mikado." Apparently on this visit the family was no longer living in the house, as all the rooms were practically vacant except for the Orchestrion. I believe it was the intention of the owners to raze the building.

The caretaker, Mr. S. F. Hughes, showed us the Orchestrion standing at one end of the large ballroom. There must have been a question of how to move the instrument. I recall trying to assist my father without success.

The organ was eventually acquired by William J. Dingee in 1902, and installed by my father in his residence. ·

WILLIAM DINGEE RESIDENCE

William Dingee was one of those fortunate Californians who, with apparent ease and in a remarkably short time, amassed a fortune. He was called the "Slate King." He had a large home on the northeast corner of Washington and Franklin Streets. Although it was a frame building, it was well built. A glittering substance was added to the paint, with the result that when the sun shone on the building it glittered and sparkled like a match box, by which name it was known. Each room in the mansion was of different design, representing a different period, finished in various hardwoods, bronze, marble, onyx and stone.

In 1902, in this sumptuous mansion, Mr. and Mrs. Dingee placed an orchestrion, and it was through the installation of this instrument that we became acquainted with these charming people. This instrument was secured from the James G. Fair mansion on Pine and Leavenworth Streets, which was shortly thereafter razed. In the Dingee residence the orchestrion was placed on a balcony on the second floor, a semi-circular room with many windows from which one had a beautiful panoramic view of the Bay. The orchestrion itself was a beautiful piece of work, and an ornament to any residence, and fitted in perfectly with the ornate surroundings.

When it was decided to provide some suitable place to store the cylinders on which the music was arranged, and yet have them within easy reach of the instrument, it was suggested by Mrs. Dingee that they be placed on exhibit, as it were, rather than conceal them in a closet. She marveled at the work and skill entailed in making one of these cylinders, with its thousands of pins. There were about a dozen of these cylinders each measuring about 8" in diameter and 5' long. They were placed in a vertical or standing position in specially built cabinets with glass doors, behind the orchestrion and along the wainscoting of the room. As these cylinders, made of dark polished walnut, had become dusty during the course of years in their former abode, lying horizontally, it was my particular job one day to brush them with a stiff brush to remove the dust between the many small pins, so that the original polish on the wood of the cylinder would again give its lustre — when displayed in their new racks — the cylinders would look attractive and in keeping with their environment.

It was while I was ·thus engaged that Mrs. Dingee passed by. She made some pleasant comment, complimenting me on my work, and on leaving, pressed into my hand a little token of appreciation, at least that is what I felt it was and I accepted it hesitantly. After she left the room I took a furtive look at the gift she had given me, which I knew by this time was currency and I thought probably a dollar bill. However, to my great surprise, I saw that it was a ten dollar bill, the largest tip I ever received in my life.

My father was to make six new cylinders for the orchestrion, for which Mr. John H. Dohrman had arranged some of the music, and he was to give Mrs. Dingee a demonstration of these musical numbers on the piano that day. Mr. Dohrman, then quite an elderly man, evidently considered the demonstration of great importance, and desiring to make a good impression, seemed to be exceedingly nervous. I noticed his feet resting on the piano pedals were in a continuous quiver. On completion of the rendition, he was graciously complimented by Mrs. Dingee, and my father received the order to make the cylinders.

The music for the cylinders that Mr. Dohrman was to arrange, was to have seven distinct and separate compositions, the usual number on a cylinder. Some time later, when the cylinder was completed and tried in the orchestrion, it turned out to be not quite as satisfactory as anticipated. It was, undoubtedly, Mr. Dohrman's masterpiece in composition, as he outdid himself, as it were, in putting as much music and harmony into a given piece as was possible, with the result that the theme or melody was almost unrecognizable, due to the elaborate embellishment and figurative style of this arrangement. I was almost twenty at this time and, although I was always fond of music, my father told me later that after working on this orchestrion and hearing its classical music and the exquisite quality of tone emanating from its pipes, I was all enraptured with music. It was especially the "William Tell", "Traviata", and the "Semiramide" overtures that captivated me.

At about this time, for some reason or other, unknown to us, the Dingee's decided to vacate this beautiful mansion and reside at a so-called cottage on a large estate down the Peninsula in Redwood City, where the Sequoia High School is now located. This residence, very modest in comparison with the sumptuous city residence, nestled amidst beautiful trees, shrubs and flowers. It was a one story frame structure, with the floor level about five or six feet above the ground.

My father moved the orchestrion from the Franklin Street mansion to this new abode. Haverside and Company did the rigging and hoisting for the job.

On the morning of the earthquake, April 18, 1906, which, incidentally was not only local in San Francisco but extended through the whole Coast area from San Luis Obispo in the South to Santa Rosa in the North, strange to relate, the studding from under the building was flattened out by the swaying of the earthquake, due undoubtedly to the lack of any diagonal bracing, with the result that the upper portion of the building was deposited intact on the ground about five feet from where it had been standing. It was practically undamaged except for the basement under the building. The orchestrion, installed a year or two before, was not damaged in any way. However, we were called upon to dismantle it at once, pack it and ship it to New York where, I believe, the Dingees had another domicile.

Mr. and Mrs. Dingee were exceedingly charming people, democratic and most likeable. Mrs. Dingee passed away previous to Mr. Dingee's demise. On his passing there were many references made in the public press to his distinguished career, his great wealth at one time, and high position held in former years, contrasted to his sad ending as a poor man.

KING SOLOMON HALL

It seems that the Masonic Lodges of San Francisco from the earliest days were always pipe organ minded. The old Masonic Temple at Post and Montgomery Streets, before the fire, had its two Mayer pipe organs. The Odd Fellows building on Seventh and Market Streets, likewise had its organ. The Scottish Rite building on Sutter Street and Van Ness Avenue, the Pike Memorial Association on Geary Street, the Golden Gate Commandery on Sutter Street, all have their pipe organs, and the Masonic Temple on Van Ness Avenue and Fell Street, has the distinction of having six pipe organs.

One of the lesser lodge halls, located in the Western Addition on Fillmore Street near Sutter, was the King Solomon Hall or Temple. This building was erected in 1905, shortly before the great fire. I believe it had a pipe organ from its inception. Some time after its installation, we were called to tune and repair it. I do not recall who sold or who originally installed the organ, possibly Mr. Augustus Clark. It was an Estey, two manual and Pedal organ, with attached console, pneumatic action, of about 7 stops. The coupler action was mechanical and the stop control by "on and off" key control, similar in design to the manual keys. I believe originally it was hand pumped, and that later a blower was installed in the attic. I recall working on the latter during 1912. In time, the pneumatics of the organ deteriorated and we recovered them with new material.

It is possible that this was the first Estey organ erected in San Francisco. Other Estey organs of about the same vintage were those of Westminster Presbyterian Church, the Holt residence and the Markus Koshland residence on Washington Street. King Solomon Hall continued its activities until the latter part of 1945 when it was disolved. The organ was removed and sold to some party in Oakland, California.

GOLDEN GATE COMMANDERY HALL

Shortly after the fire of 1906, Golden Gate Commandery Hall, on the south side of Sutter Street, near Steiner, was one of the most popular halls in the city. It was always rented or occupied. Many a social function I attended there, and I recall my first introduction to a "Twilight Scottish" dance was there.

It was also the hall selected temporarily by the Sixth Church of Christ Scientist for holding their services until their permanent church was built. Here I became acquainted with Mrs. Ella Ball, organist of the church, who played the two manual Estey reed organ, which we frequently serviced.

On the upper floor was the Commandery lodge room, containing a splendid Murray M. Harris pipe organ of two manuals of about 10 stops, pneumatic action. Its weakness seemed to be its unsatisfactory blowing apparatus, which we, in time, replaced with a modern kinetic blower. We last serviced the organ in 19ll. In recent years the entire building and equipment has been taken over by the Macedonian Missionary Baptist Church.

DANISH LUTHERAN CHURCH

Immediately after the earthquake and fire of 1906, I made it a point to observe and scrutinize the buildings that remained intact and note what effect the earthquake had upon them. There were many buildings and edifices unharmed.

The Danish Lutheran Church on Church Street, near Market, built in 1905, was one of them. I distinctly remember when they built it, as I passed it frequently riding on the street car which passed the place. It was a frame building with only a brick facing. I had seen solid brick walls, at places six feet thick, as in the old St. Dominic's Church and the City Hall, crack and fall to pieces, and had never expected a thin veneer of brick against a wood background to hold up against the rigors of a tremblor. This it did, however, and it has been a marvel to me ever since.

Some twenty-five years ago this church secured a small Kimball pipe organ, a one manual, four stop organ, divided into treble and bass, pneumatic action. I believe my brother Leo installed it for the Eilers Music Company. We occasionally called to service it. Finally, as the years passed, the pneumatics began to give out and a major repair job was necessary.

We then suggested that while this repair work had to be done, they go a little further and modernize the organ by electrifying it and making it into a two manual organ. Also, that the stops be made straight; that is, each stop to run through the whole compass, and, furthermore, to duplex it by making each stop playable from either manual. We also suggested the improvement of placing the console, if it were electrified, on the church floor below. This plan also required that the choir also be downstairs with the organist.

The whole undertaking turned out very satisfactorily. It sounded like a new and larger organ. A remarkable thing about this installation is the fact that there is not the slightest lag in the response between the organist striking the key and the response from the organ above in the gallery, although the distance is about sixty feet. In fact, several organists who tried it said it was an exemplary organ for playing Bach, as its response was so prompt and clean cut.

For the dedication of the organ, we engaged the services of Mr. Glenn Goff, for many years the popular organist at S. H. Kress Company's store. We were told he was delighted with the organ and from comments heard from the pastor, he discharged his obligation creditably. After the service he returned to his home in Burlingame, and, while working in his garden, that afternoon was summoned by death. We regretted his untimely passing, and whenever we visit the church to service the organ we always recall his memory.

WESTMINSTER PRESBYTERIAN CHURCH

Westminster Presbyterian Church was located on Page and Webster Streets. I believe for a long period this congregation carried on without a pipe organ. Later, they secured a two manual and Pedal pneumatic action Estey pipe organ of about 10 stops. It was one of the first, if not the first, Estey pipe organ erected in San Francisco.

In 1933, the congregation decided to alter the interior of the church structure, using the church auditorium proper for social purposes and building a small chapel to the rear of the edifice for holding their religious services. The church attendance had dwindled, making this move imperative. We secured the contract to remove the organ from the main auditorium and reinstall it in the new chapel.

In the new installation, the old case and display pipes were eliminated. The console was made detached, and the whole worked out very satisfactorily both tonally and mechanically. It might be stated that the stop control in the console is the type that was used by the Estey Company at the time, i.e., the manual key type stop control, depressing a natural key with stop name inscribed thereon for the "on" position, and depressing a black or sharp key alongside to put it in the "off" position. The coupler action in the console was mechanical, notwithstanding that the connection between console and organ was pneumatic. My brother, Otto, did this removing and alteration work.

I recall a little incident that occurred to me shortly after this work was finished. I was waiting on the street corner by the church for one of my assistants, who was to help me do some work on the organ, when I was approached by a rather well dressed man who glibly accosted me and proceeded to try to persuade me to purchase some mining stock which he was selling. I felt chagrined that he had the audacity to seriously approach me with such a gold brick scheme. I must have looked like a yokel, or easy mark, to him and, therefore, I resented his approaching me and, most emphatically, denounced his attempt to deprive me my money. I indignantly gave him the cold shoulder and felt rather annoyed.

While musing over this episode after he left, another gentleman approached me from the opposite side of the street. He had no hat on and had rather long, bushy gray hair. He seemed to be a prematurely aged man. On coming closer, I noticed that he was minus an arm. The limp, empty coat sleeve being folded back. I thought to myself, here I am being approached again, not by a slicker this time, but by a mendicant, or down-and-outer, panhandling for a handout. My disposition and demeanor, therefore, were not too agreeable when he came up and spoke to me. He said he noticed that I was waiting around the church and wanted to know if I had any particular business there and if there was anything he could do for me, as he was the pastor. Needless to say, I was very much embarrassed and changed my hostile demeanor. We formally introduced ourselves, and I explained my mission, which I later carried out.

Instead of the mendicant I first thought he was, I found this pastor to be an estimable and kindly gentleman, one undoubtedly a credit and honor to his high calling. I mused thereafter, clothing and appearance do not always make the man.

FIRST CHURCH OF CHRIST SCIENTIST

My first knowledge of the Christian Science denomination in San Francisco was about 1907, when I heard they were building a chruch of their own and were to have an Austin pipe organ installed. The building was located on the southwest corner of Sacramento and Scott Streets, in the Western Addition. It was, from all appearances, to serve only as a temporary structure, as its interior was made of unfinished lumber, painted or stained.

The organ was located at the south end of the church. It was a large two manual and Pedal organ, Opus 183, of about 21 stops, pneumatic action on the universal air chest system, with a detached console. I recall that this organ impressed me as something distinctive and different from any other organ I had every heard before. Undoubtedly, it was the voicing on higher pressure, the generous supply of sub and super couplers, and the rather exaggerated scaling of the various stops, rather large scale Diapasons and Flutes, extremely narrow scales for the String stops, a rather bright and brilliant Reed, that attracted me. The steadiness of the air, derived through the principle of the Universal Air Chest, proved also to be remarkable. On the whole, this organ, the first Austin organ installed in San Francisco, made a decidedly favorable impression on me.

The erection of the organ was under the supervision of Mr. Edward L. Crome of Los Angeles, assisted by Mr. Roy Tolchard. My father, brothers and I helped with the work of installation. The organ remained in this church for a number of years. William Carruth, a prominent musician of the Bay Area, was organist at this time.

Meanwhile, a new permanent edifice was built at the northeast corner of Franklin and California Streets. Mr.

Thomas Whalley of Berkeley later moved the organ. I believe at this time he also electrified the organ and added a Vox Humana 8' to the Swell and a Viola d'Amore 8' to the Great.

Following William Carruth as organist was Mr. Wallace Sabin who filled that position for a period of thirty-five years. He gave many a lesson to his pupils on this organ. Evidently in appreciation of his valuable services to the Church, and to satisfy his own desire to perform on a new and more modern instrument, First Church of Christ Scientist decided to buy a new organ. That the selection was up to Mr. Sabin was obvious.

I recall at the time he asked us to show him some of the latest Hook and Hastings organs that had been installed in the City. We had, a short time previously, installed a new Hook and Hastings organ in St. Anthony's Church, at Army and Folsom Streets, in the Mission District, and we arranged for him to see this organ. Evidently Mr. Sabin was not acquainted with this church. It was about 4:30 in the afternoon when we met him. He commented on its exterior beauty, but was more surprised on entering the church to behold its ornate interior, with its columns and arched ceiling, in the soft light of the setting sun shining through its stained glass windows, and remarked that he had not thought such a beautiful church existed in San Francisco.

After seeing the beauty of the church and the organ from below, we took him up to the organ to try it. He expressed himself as greatly pleased with it, and from comments I heard later from reliable sources, he considered it the best Hook and Hastings organ hereabouts. I also recall him making the statement that although he had been using an Austin organ and that many were installed in San Francisco at that time, he saw no reason why San Francisco should have nothing but Austin organs, and that he would like to see other makes also installed. Therefore, judging from his decision, which was finally in favor of a Kimball organ, he helped to change this situation to an extent.

The old two manual Austin organ in use in the new church for a number of years, was then sold to the Sixth Church of Christ Scientist, at that time erecting a new permanent edifice of their own on the southeast corner of Clay and

Divisadero Streets. This work was again secured by us.

The new Kimball organ for the First Church of Christ Scientist was a four manual organ of 24 stops, all under expression. It was installed by John C. Swinford, a local organ expert, and, as we have never serviced the new organ, we are not familiar with it. We have heard it on a few occasions, and undoubtedly it is in keeping with the high standard set and maintained by this Company.

Mr. Wallace Sabin, one of San Francisco's most revered and beloved organists, spoken of in the highest terms of esteem by his many pupils as a most successful teacher and friend, answered his last summons in 1937, while conducting a rehearsal at the Lorin Choral Society. He was not only mourned by the local musical fraternity, but by the city, State and Country at large, as his fame as a teacher, composer and performer on the organ had spread over the nation.

Mr. Leslie Harvey, a young man of ability, was then selected as his successor as organist at First Church of Christ Scientist. The present organist is Dwayne Gramly.

PIKE MEMORIAL TEMPLE

One of the Masonic Lodges of San Francisco occupying the brick building on the west side of Geary Street, between Fillmore and Steiner Streets, has a splendid pipe organ in one of its lodge halls. It was built and installed by Thomas Whalley of Berkeley, in 1904, shortly after the building was erected. It is a tracker action organ of 17 stops, and like all Whalley organs, has a splendid tone.

In 1965 plans were made to build an entire new edifice in some more suitable or desirable neighborhood, farther West. It is the intention of the Lodge to retain this excellently toned Whalley organ, but to modernize it by electrifying it and replacing it in a more auspicious location, where it will be better heard because of more satisfactory accoustical conditions than where it is presently situated.

CHURCH OF GOD
formerly
ARMY STREET GERMAN METHODIST CHURCH

One of the earliest recollections of my childhood was a visit made by the whole family to an acquaintance of my father, a Mr. Goetz, a painter and decorator by profession, who lived in a small cottage on the north side of Army Street, between Guerrero and Dolores Streets, out in the Mission District. I remember riding out there on the Valencia Street cable line. What I recall especially is that the main line of the Southern Pacific trains at that time, running on their private right of way on the diagonal cutoff through the streets of the Mission District, passed the rear of this gentleman's property.

As small children living in the Western Addition, we had no opportunity to see a steam locomotive. Often on a clear day I heard the whistles from the distance, and from pictures and toy locomotives had a good idea what a steam locomotive and train looked like. However, to see the real article and, at close range, was to be my privilege for the first time on this visit. It must have been about 1889 or 1890, as I doubt that I had begun attending school. The greater part of that Sunday afternoon we children played outdoors in the back yard of our host, while our elders were conveniently inside.

Beyond the fence enclosing the property was the Southern Pacific right of way. A block below was the 25th and Valencia Street Depot. At that time, especially on Sundays, trains did not run as frequently up and down the Peninsula as they do now. At any rate, no train passed the house during the entire afternoon. However, one was scheduled to pass toward evening going south. It was getting dark. My parents intended to leave earlier, but we children were determined to see the train go by. Our host undoubtedly enjoyed our childish expectancy and induced my parents to remain so we children could see this mighty spectacle of a locomotive and train passing within a few feet of the backyard fence.

As the time arrived for the approach of the train, young and old took their places along the fence. We small ones were held up to get a good view. I remember the red signal lights on a nearby post flashing. Fear and trembling seized me. I heard the whistle and rumble of the approaching train. Then it stopped — it had reached the Valencia Street Station. Again the shrill whistle and the mighty puffing of the locomotive pulling the train of cars up the steep grade toward Ocean View. Louder and louder became the noise of the puffing engine, the beam of the headlight lit up the roadbed, the earth trembled as the mighty monster, with sparks and smoke issuing from its funnel, roared past us. I was frightened, yet it was great and inspriring. The train rumbled on over the Dolores Street bridge southbound to its destination, the noise fading away in the distance. Soon thereafter we left for home. I feared crossing the railroad tracks — the red signal lights appeared as something sinister to me. For years, that experience left an indelible imprint on my memory.

In 1896 our family moved to the Mission District and located at 21st and Bryant Streets. It was then a pleasure and delight to see the long freight train at 9:30 p.m., with three engines pulling the heavy load of cars up the steep Mission Cut grade, with a red glare belching from its smoke stack illuminating the night sky. Fear had now left me, but I would always again relive the sensation I experienced as a child when I first saw the mighty locomotive pass.

It is a strange coincidence that in the early years of my career in the organ business, in 1905, my father was called upon to install a Hinners two manual and Pedal tracker action pipe organ on Army Street. The installation was at St. John's German Methodist Church as it was then called, which is located about two doors away from the home of Mr. Goetz where we, as children, had our wonderful experience of watching the train pass by at close range. On going to the church I would look over to the fence on which I was perched as a youngster and would again enjoy the same thrill of days gone by.

The church organ was one of those genuine, may I call it, "German Lutheran" organs. It had a Diapason and ensemble that could not be beat, necessary and essential in accompanying the congregational singing of that sturdy old German stock that helped build up this country.

I recall later, through the efforts of my brother, Leo, we installed a Sturdivant blower to the organ. It was placed in a small shed outside of the church building. There was an objectionable hum to it, however. As this wind pipe was made of wood, we lined its interior with pieces of old carpet to deaden the noise. This procedure proved to be very effective and was done in other installations thereafter. I believe this was one of the first blowers of this type we installed.

We called occasionally at this church in the future to tune and make adjustments on the organ. Many a time since have I walked the railroad track passing the rear of this church, but it was not the organ that I would be thinking of, but the cherished memory of that Sunday afternoon when, perched on the back fence, I watched the train go by.

The old 25th and Valencia Street Passenger Station has been gone for a long time and in recent years the ties and tracks of the roadbed itself were torn up. Soon the entire right of way will be laid out in building lots and occupied with dwellings, and the memory of a steam train running through the Mission District will be a hard fact to believe.

The scene has changed — time passes on.

FIRST CHRISTIAN CHURCH

Before the fire of 1906, I recall often passing Twelfth Street and admiring a beautiful tree-lined street running off the south side of Twelfth Street, with well-built homes and lovely gardens on either side. I do not remember its name. It was possibly between Market and Mission Streets, or Mission and Howard Streets. The old Eintracht Hall, a rendezvous for the German people, where they held their festivities, was at Folsom and Twelfth Streets.

On the north side of Twelfth Street, north of Mission Street, was located the First Christian Church. I never was in it and, for that reason, I assume it had no pipe organ or my father would at one time or other have worked on it.

After the fire, the First Christian Church located at Duboce Avenue and Noe Street, on the southeast corner and there, in 1909, they procured a two manual and Pedal Kimball pipe organ of about 12 stops, with an attached console. Mr. Hess, a representative of the Kimball Organ Company, through the local music store of Eilers and Company, made the sale. I believe my brother, Leo, then in their employ, installed the organ.

After a few years of service, a "malignant disease", if I may call it such, attacked this new organ. Many concerns and institutions disintegrate from old age or senility, or from want of progressiveness. In this instance, however, the builders of this organ could not be accused of this shortcoming, but rather of the contrary fault of being too progressive. A new type of chest pallet was designed, one in which the valve was a punched aluminum disc, fastened to the pneumatic with an iron screw superimposed and resting on an alum tanned leather washer. The face of this disc would in turn strike against the channel bar, the latter being felted or padded at the valve hole, instead of the valve itself being padded. Apparently moisture, or possibly the chemical reaction of the alum tanned leather washers in contact with the iron screw and aluminum disc caused a corrosion which, in a very short time, ate a hole completely through the aluminum disc, subjecting the pipe above to an unwanted supply of air, and causing the baneful sound called a "cipher."

To make the organ dependable and serviceable again, all these discs had to be removed and replaced with the ordinary type cardboard discs, covered with leather and felt, the tried and proven valve disc which was first discarded because evidently the newer valve seemed to be more economical in construction and installation. These valves that we put in to replace the old ones have now been in service for about 51 years, and are still functioning splendidly.

Another innovation I saw for the first time put to practical use, was the installation of the motor belt driven blower. As there was no basement available in this church, the selection of a suitable location for the blowing plant, to assure its quietness, seemed to be quite a conundrum. Finally, someone had the bright idea of placing it in a vacant room in the attic. A sound-proof room of about 5' x 6', with 6" walls, filled with sawdust or some other deadening material, was built. Instead, however, of placing the motor and the blower on the floor, it was suspended on four heavy springs fastened to the roof rafters, to float as it were in the air, the springs checking or absorbing all vibration otherwise communicated to the building. Since then we have used this principle very successfully elsewhere.

The organ at the First Christian Church, after 54 years, has gradually become the victim of old age and senility. This time, however, not the chest valves of the organ but the pneumatic pouches used in the coupler stacks, which were originally made of rubberized silk, these becoming hard and stiff, failed to function properly. We, therefore, urged the church people to eliminate the original tubular pneumatic action entirely from the organ and convert it to electric pneumatic action. This we did finally, and also at the same time made a modern detached console for the organ.

ST. THERESA'S CHURCH

St. Theresa's Parish, atop the Potrero Hills overlooking the Bay and the Union Iron Works, had its modest frame church erected at the corner of Nineteenth and Tennessee Streets. It was a typical workingman's district. At one time it probably had prospects of successful development. However, due to the constant encroachment of factories, extensive railroad and freight yards, and the like, people began moving away rather than settling in the immediate neighborhood of the church. To overcome this drawback and to establish the church more in the center of population where the greatest number of its parishioners lived, it was decided to do a most unusual thing — move the church to the people.

Property was secured at the northeast corner of Nineteenth and Connecticut Streets, about eight blocks farther west. The church edifice was cut into two parts, and each section moved separately to the new location. There they were assembled and joined together again as one unit. I believe this procedure would be a fitting story for Ripley's "Belive It Or Not" column.

Previous to the time the church was moved, the pastor, Rev. Patrick O'Connell, had purchased a one manual Hook and Hastings pipe organ of five stops, divided in treble and bass, a sweet-toned, excellent organ. My father, with the assistance of my brother, Otto, erected this organ in 1908. The church, with the organ intact, was moved to the new location in 1925.

Sometime after the church was moved, we installed a blower for the organ. In 1938 a disastrous fire occurred in the church. The organ was badly damaged by water and debris, and we decided to remove it to our shop for a thorough going over. While this work was being done, the damage to the church was also being repaired. We again installed the organ in the church, and this one manual pipe organ, one of very few in San Francisco, continues to carry on and function uninterruptedly.

UNITED GERMAN M. E. CHURCH

As stated in a previous article, there was, at one time, quite an influx of Hinners Pipe Organs to San Francisco and, during October 1909, the United German M. E. Church, on Page and Laguna Streets, also secured one, which we installed.

It was a two manual and pedal tracker action organ of 10 stops, and was a good sounding typical church organ.

This is one church that seemed to fade from our horizon. Either the organ was holding up remarkably well, or, in the course of years, the present presidium has forgotten us — a gentle reminder that after 92 years there are still "New Worlds to Conquer" even in one's home town, and soliciting patronage is again in order.

Strange to relate that, after writing the above lines, one evening during March 1945 my next door neighbor, Mrs. Wienke, paid us an unexpected visit. We were always on friendly terms, though we did not exchange visits with one another frequently. Sensing that her visit surprised us, she relieved us of our curiosity by briefly stating the main object of her visit. (Then we enjoyed the pleasure of her company the rest of the evening.) She and her husband, being members of the United German M. E. Church, which was undergoing during these properous war times, a series of improvements, told us it was deemed necessary to give the organ a general tuning and checking over. When this work was proposed she suggested that her neighbor, Mr. Schoenstein, an organ man, be selected.

An appointment was arranged and after we told the Trustees we originally installed the organ and that we further learned the organ had not been thoroughly tuned since its installation 24 years ago, we were authorized to do the necessary work, thanks to our kind neighbor.

The name and denomination of this church has changed frequently; was later called St. Johns German M.E. Church and at present, Pleasant Hill Baptist Church.

MISSION GOOD SAMARITAN

I recall that before the fire of 1906, there was located on the west side of Second Street, north of Folsom Street, some religious Center called the "Cannon Kip Center." In this Center, evidently, they had a Chapel containing a small organ which, however, was consumed in the great fire. My father or I, as far as I recall had no occasion to ever work there. However, from the records of George Andrews, of Oakland, it appears that his father had built an organ for the chapel in 1904. The Center, at times, was also known as Cathedral Mission.

In 1910 a large building of very simple design was erected on Potrero Avenue, between 24th and 25th Streets. It proved to be the new Mission of the Good Samaritan, under the auspices of the Episcopal Church. As a mission center, it also devoted its efforts to all humanitarian endeavors, such as a free clinic, kindergarten, and the usual activities of a community center. In time, it also built and conducted the St. Andrew's Inn, a home for boys. The religious aspects were not overlooked, as within the building was arranged a pleasing and edifying chapel, which served as parish church for the Episcopalians of the district.

At about this time, in 1910, the crypt of the proposed Grace Cathedral on Nob Hill was completed, and we had just finished installing a large three manual Austin organ there. Up to this time, since the fire of 1906, Grace Cathedral had been holding services in a small temporary chapel at the corner of Sacramento and Taylor Streets. In this chapel they had a pipe organ, built by Thomas Whalley of Berkeley. On completion of the crypt, the little chapel was no longer used, and the organ was moved and erected by Mr. Whalley in the small chapel of the Good Samaritan Mission, on Potrero Avenue. Some alterations were made on it at the time to fit the new location. Rev. J. P. Turner was the rector then and remained in that position for many years.

After the installation of the organ we were called upon to service it regularly. It was a two manual tracker action organ of 15 stops, slider chests, with attached console. The Pedal key action was on the pneumatic system, as was also the stop action and combination piston action. The organ gave a little trouble at first, but in time it became acclimated and behaved well. Tonally, the organ was excellent, typical of all the Whalley organs.

As the activities of the Mission were constantly developing on a broader scope and tending toward a Community Center project, and as it was receiving financial aid from the Community Chest, it was found expedient and necessary to separate the religious from the purely social functions. It was, therefore, decided to build on the adjoining lot a distinct and separate church for the conduct of the religious services. This plan was carried out and a splendid modified Gothic church was built. Mr. Hobart was the architect.

We thereupon moved the organ. Some changes to the exterior front were again necessary. At the time we were moving the organ to the new church, I was taken seriously ill with pneumonia and had to remain for several weeks in St. Mary's Hospital. On my return home, while I was convalescing, I recall Rev. Turner was much worried as to whether the organ would be completed in time for the dedication of the new church. However, with the able assistance of my brothers, everything was in readiness for the occasion.

A number of organists performed at the organ during the 53 years it has been installed here, the most notable among them being Mr. Henry Bickford Pasmore, an esteemed elderly gentleman associated with the Passmore Trio, a musical unit highly rated in the musical annals of San Francisco.

Mrs. Turner, a most kind and gracious woman, wife of Rev. J. P. Turner, passed to her eternal reward. Several years later, in 1940, Rev. Turner retired from active service, and in 1945 he also answered his last summons.

Mrs. Fredericks functioned as organist for many years and was succeeded by the Rector's wife, Mrs. Silverlight.

On the evening of November 28, 1958, a disastrous fire took place in the chapel. Living on the western slope of the Potrero Hill, with an unobstructed view of the whole Mission District, I detected a large column of smoke and flames in the distance — also simultaneously heard the sirens of the Fire Department nearby responding. I judged its location to be in the neighborhood of 24th Street and Potrero Avenue. My youngest son, Edward, immediately jumped into his car to see where and what was burning. He returned shortly and informed me excitedly that the Mission of the Good Samaritan was on fire and that the source of the fire seemed to be just where the organ was located, on the left side of the Sanctuary.

Since we had the maintenance of the organ, he felt I should be there to help salvage it, if possible, or be of assistance in any way. It was impossible to get immediate access to the building, but as soon as the flames were actually extinguished, and after getting permission from the Fire Chief to enter, I was shocked at the sight I beheld. Three burly firemen, with faces besmudged, with helmets on, standing on top of the Great Chest hacking away with their axes at the Swell box behind them. The Ped Open Dia. 16 foot pipes, standing along the east wall, were laying precariously toward the Great Chest on which the firemen were working, ready to fall. Water was dropping down from the ceiling and the floor was a mass of burned debris. Immediately I noticed that the panel to the right of the keyboard, the only place that we entered the organ to service it, was closed, and that the panel on the opposite side which we never used was unscrewed and open. Here, to my surprise, were laying a number of empty beer cans. Immediately I surmised the cause of the fire — vandals had entered the organ and hidden in this secluded spot and most certainly must have set the blaze.

The organ was a total loss. The church was restored and they later secured a new Moller organ.

SCOTTISH RITE TEMPLE

During a certain period of our business there seemed to be a cycle in which we almost exclusively installed Austin pipe organs. Not that we specialized in their organs to the exclusion of those of other builders, but the fact is that no sooner had we completed the installation of one Austin organ, than we were notified by their energetic and successful representative, Mr. Fletcher Tilton, that he had signed another contract.

It was at such a time, in 1910, that we began the installation of the Austin organ Opus 265 in the Scottish Rite Temple, then being erected at the northeast corner of Sutter Street and Van Ness Avenue. An exceedingly strong steel frame was erected here, undoubtedly necessary because of the large spans required to provide free, unobstructed space for the several large, spacious public halls and lodge rooms. The exterior of the building is of classic design. It is faced with white Caen stone, and indeed makes an imposing appearance. We had to begin installing the organ before the building was completed, so the organ could be ready for the dedication. Under the supervision of Mr. Tom Muirhead, representing the contractors, Mahoney Bros., the building made rapid progress.

Being an old friend of mine, having made his acquaintance years before while he was erecting the Chas. E. Green residence in San Mateo, Mr. Muirhead was very considerate of us and made our work of installing the organ, under the chaotic conditions of a huge building in the course of construction, as agreeable and convenient as possible. The Overland Freight and Transfer Company, which invariably did our heavy hauling, also handled the job. As the elevators were not yet installed and only temporary stairways available, it was necessary to have all material hoisted to the fourth floor, where the organ was to be located. The Overland Freight people had an employee who specialized in rigging and hoisting, a Mr. Louis Goebals. We got to be very well acquainted and quite friendly with him, as his skill as a rigger was often in demand for the handling of the many organs that were arriving and which needed special rigging facilities.

I remember an experience we had on this job, where his skill and experience seemed momentarily to fail him. Our only means of hoisting the material up to the fourth floor was through the vacant, or incompleted elevator shaft. As there was a scarcity of strong planks available, we placed three or four of the large packing cases containing the pipes across the elevator shaft at the ground floor to serve as a temporary flooring. We were just hoisting the large side panels of the Swell boxes, which in the Austin organ are usually of one piece, double thickness, made of eatern white pine, very heavy in weight and shellacked or varnished on both sides. I believe two were being hoisted at one time. Slings were properly placed. Several strong-armed men were pulling with steady heaves on the tackle rope below. I, and some of my partners, were on the upper floor ready to receive and remove the panels. Somehow, midway, the panels in their ascent struck some obstruction which threw the sling out of center, causing the smooth, slick panels to shift and finally fall out of the sling, dropping about two stories edgewise onto the pipe boxes below.

Fortunately, we above who saw the panels in their revolving and oscillating motion come in contact with the obstruction, shouted a warning in time for those below, who evidently had felt that some projection had been struck, to clear out of the path of danger. Down came the hurtling panels. They landed on edge on the center of the packing cases, cutting about half way through them. We were grateful that no injury was done to life or limb, and as to the damage that was done inside the packing cases, we were greatly surprised on opening them to find how fortunate we were that they happened to contain a few of the large diameter zinc pipes that could easily be rounded out again.

The Scottish Rite organ was a two manual and Pedal tubular pneumatic action organ of 26 stops. Only the Swell was expressive. The Great manual was unenclosed. The console was detached, and a beautifully designed heavy oak case with gilded front pipes made an impressive appearance. The organ was placed on the loft in the west end of the lodge hall. The whole room, with its beamed ceiling, its oak paneled wainscoating and plush-lined walls, its soft colored art glass windows, had the appearance of some medieval council chamber. The organ, with its powerful and full ensemble, as well as its soft and exquisite tones, was impressive and most satisfactory.

MRS. JEANETTE JORDAN RESIDENCE
and
TRINITY M. E. CHURCH

What is probably the first tract of land in San Francisco to be laid out as a restricted residence section is that parcel on the eastern fringe of the Richmond District, extending from Geary Boulevard to California Street and from Parker Avenue to Arguello Boulevard, known as Jordan Park.

In 1898 a hugh army camp was located there for the volunteers who enlisted for service in the Philippine contingent of the Spanish-American War. Subsequently, this tract was developed and Mrs. Jeanette Jordan, a kind, elderly lady, had a large, beautiful, home built for herself in this district on the west side of Commonwealth Avenue, surrounded by lawns and a garden.

In 1911 Mrs. Jordan purchased a two manual and Pedal automatic Austin pipe organ Opus 338 of about 17 stops for her home. To properly house the organ, a special music room was added to the house. The organ was located on the northern end of the room, concealed behind an ornate case. At the opposite end of the room was a large fireplace, with old-fashioned lovers' seats protruding into the room, and along the sides of the room were bookcases which had been built in. The flooring of the room was made of Japanese oak planks, about six inches wide, with a specially designed open joint. I recall after the floor was laid the boards warped badly and became as round as "elephants' backs", causing a great deal of trouble and annoyance to the contactor for some time, defying his attempts to correct the difficulty. In time, undoubtedly after the wood had become acclimated and after being more securely fastened, this trouble was overcome. I also recall the new gray finish of the redwood interior, an innovation in interior decorating at that time that was applied to the California redwood. The whole room, after being furnished, was indeed homelike and comfortable.

Mrs. Jordan liked music and seemed to delight in playing the old popular church tunes. The automatic player was used undoubtedly when company was present, for the entertainment of her guests. Some recitals by leading organists were also given.

I recall operating the automatic player. There was one lever or gadget to operate it, aside from the tempo lever. It was for the start, stop and reroll action. This was in line with the general principal of the Austin Organ Company for simplicity and for a minimum number of moving parts in the mechanism of their organs. In this particular case, however, it was carried to the extreme to the extent that the controlling device was almost uncontrollable. The slightest digression in movement from a given point would upset what one had in mind to do, and proved often embarrassing when trying to demonstrate the organ to an audience.

The organ had been installed for a number of years when Mrs. Jordan passed away. The home was then secured by Mr. Chester Weaver, well known automobile dealer of the City. Later the organ was sold to the Trinity Methodist Episcopal Church, which was then erecting its new structure at the corner of Market and Noe Streets. We removed the organ and erected it in the new church. The automatic player was removed and the organ was placed behind a screen.

The tract that bears the name Jordan Park is now completely built up with fine homes. The old Jordan residence still stands and is a reminder to me of a gracious and amiable matron, and the organ in its new location still peals forth those old tunes that once brought peace and comfort to its original owner.

SAINTS PETER AND PAUL CHURCH
(Italian National Church)

In 1884 on the western slope of Telegraph Hill at Filbert and Dupont Streets, in the Italian quarter, was located the old original Saints Peter and Paul Church. The church at that time, before the fire of 1906, had no pipe organ, but only a small harmonium. A Mr. Andrea Spadina, director of the famous Golden Gate Park Band, was either organist or director of the choir at the time.

Even small harmoniums, or reed organs, need attention occasionally, so one day my father was called upon to repair it. I do not recall if I helped him work on it, but I certainly do remember he sent me to the rectory later to collect the bill. The amount was $7.50. It was one of my first experiences in bill collecting and one that was not too pleasant at that.

On presenting my bill at the door, with the explanation that I wished to collect it, I was informed by the housekeeper that the pastor was not in but that he was expected soon, and if I wanted to wait for him I could sit in the parlor until he came. As I had plenty of leisure time on my hands then, and not wanting to lose the advantage I had gained so far of at least being invited to wait, I entered the parlor, took a seat and waited. It must have been about 10 a.m. when I called. After my first interest in surveying the room and its contents had been satisfied, the time began to drag and I finally took to studying the design of the wall paper and the carpet — anything to occupy my mind. Still no priest appeared, and also, to my confusion, no housekeeper. I had expected she would have pity on me, waiting so unsuccessfully so long, and advise me to leave and call at some other time. On the other hand, I did not have the courage to leave unannounced, or to ring the bell to tell her of my proposed departure, so I continued my vigil and waited.

Soon I perceived the fragrant aroma of the noonday meal

being cooked, and true to Italian custom, it must have been good and wholesome food that was being prepared. Hope for success of my mission revived. It was inconceivable that the pastor would miss such a repast, so he should be making his appearance very shortly now, I thought. It was now almost noon and I had been waiting patiently for two hours on the same chair in the parlor.

Then, all of a sudden I heard someone approach the front door, insert a key in the lock, open the door and enter the hall. It evidently was the pastor. I had never met him before. He was just about to pass the parlor door, which was ajar, when he saw me and inquired what I wanted. I delivered my message briefly, hoping that in addition to receiving the amount of the bill which I presented, I would also receive a little word of pity for the long wait I had endured.

The dark complexioned priest, instead of being kindly and amiable as I had expected him to be, flew into a rage and berated my father for the (in his opinion) excessive amount of the bill, stating he would never pay it and dismissed me abruptly. The pastor no doubt enjoyed that well-prepared meal, so I hoped as I left the place heavy hearted and dejected.

After the fire of 1906 a new church was built on the west side of Filbert Street, but further west between Dupont and Stockton Streets, opposite the picturesque Washington Square. At first only the foundation and the basement were completed. These were of huge and heavy proportions, intended to support the massive and beautiful church that was at some later date to be erected, with the lofty spires that were to adorn it. The large basement was used as a temporary church for a number of years.

A two manual and pedal, detached console, electric pneumatic Johnston organ, built in Los Angeles but previously placed in some building of the P.P.I.E., was purchased for $1800.00. My brother, Leo, installed the instrument.

In 1915 the upper part of the structure was completed, with the exception of the two tall spires, and the exterior finish of the facade of the church. On this occasion our firm removed the organ from the basement and installed it in the center of the upper organ loft of the new church. Finally, the two inspiring towers were added and completed, but the finishing of the front facade was further delayed. It was originally planned to make this a masterpiece of mosaic work of Italian art, but evidently this dream could not be realized, as in 1941 it was finally completed in a very simple, yet pleasing and harmonious manner. A set of Deagan tower chimes were also placed in the lofty spires.

A view of this beautiful edifice, with the green lawns and trees of the park opposite as a setting, with Coit Tower surmounting Telegraph Hill on the right, and the tall apartment buildings on Russian Hill on the left, is one of the pictures of San Francisco, beautiful and romantic to behold.

Saints Peter and Paul Church also figured in a most amazing and baffling mystery. Three times the edifice was severely dynamited. The perpetrator of the crime could apparently not be apprehended until drastic measures had been taken. Guards were stationed day and night at strategic points in the edifice. Early one morning the villain was apprehended approaching the church to try again to do his nefarious job, and paid for his crime with his life. Saints Peter and Paul Church stands securely and serenely today, a landmark of Italian art and culture.

In 1948 further developments took place in improving the organ situation. Being aware that the 12 stop Johnston organ was inadequate for the church, the acquisition of a larger organ was always looked forward to. This opportunity was made available by a combination of circumstances.

During 1947, the two manual organ of 21 stops, built by my father for St. Marks Lutheran Church in 1890, was replaced with a new modern 3 manual Moeller organ. For sentimental reasons, not wanting to see his masterpiece go into oblivion, our firm purchased the organ, with the thought in mind of modernizing it and disposing of it in the future for use in some other edifice. When calling Father Pellegrini's attention to this prospect, he immediately became interested. We submitted a plan of using the former St. Mark's organ, built by my father, and combining it with the Johnston organ they had into a divided organ on either side of the large rose window — modernizing it in every respect with a new 3 manual console and some further additions of pipes, making an instrument of 32 straight stops.

Rev. Constanzer, Pastor of the Church, agreed, a contract was signed, and soon a most imposing instrument took shape on the organ loft, with a tonal ensemble of a rich and beautiful tone adequate for the edifice. Father Pellegrini, a musician of note in charge of musical activities of this active community of the Salesians, was delighted with the new installation, and for us it was not only a matter of carrying out a signed contract, but a labor of love and affection in perpetuating the handiwork of our father for time to come in singing the praises of God, this time not in a Lutheran Church, but in a Catholic Church, which certainly would have pleased my father tremendously.

Since then further tonal additions were made to the organ, making this organ undoubtedly one of the show pieces of excellent pipe organs in San Francisco. Father Pellegrini, undoubtedly the donor of the greatest part of the organ to his Church, passed away recently.

SWEDISH EBENEZER LUTHERAN CHURCH

The Swedish Lutheran Church, before the fire of 1906, was located on the south side of Mission Street, between 8th and 9th Streets. I worked in this church only once, possibly during 1898 or earlier, assisting my father tune a large reed organ. The time and place impressed me because of a sinister fear I had while there in the church.

It was dark and gloomy. Adjoining the organ was a room, evdiently the living quarters of the janitor, or someone. I would hear voices and footsteps close to me, and yet as though they were trying to be concealed or covered. In my youthful imagination I undoubtedly thought of some murder mystery, or of something evil being concealed. Foolish, childish thoughts.

A new church was built on the southwest corner of 15th and Dolores Streets in 1904, and my father moved the large reed organ to the new edifice. A Mr. Eklund was the organist, or one of the trustees, and seemed to be a good friend of my father.

In 1913 the church secured a new Austin pipe organ, Opus 815 a pneumatic electric action organ of 10 stops, with detached console.

Heretofore it had been our privilege to install all of the Austin organs that came out this way. The installation of this organ, however, as well as one in Oakland and one in Marin County, were exceptions. Due to a misunderstanding we had with Mr. Fletcher Tilton, representative of the Austin Organ Company at the time, our relations were temporarily severed or strained, and he, therefore, directed this work to other parties. He found, however, that it was to his loss. The high excellence of our work was evidently not forthcoming from the new parties and he had difficulty in getting these new installations accepted. In all three instances our services were again demanded, as our reputation locally was established. Peace was again made. We brought the work on these organs to satisfactory completion and continued thereafter, as we had previously, to install the Austin organs in this territory. Mr. Tilton passed away a few years after this.

The large reed organ, used formerly in the old church and then in the present new church, was then sold on our recommendation, to Mission Dolores Church during 1919, and was used temporarily until, a few years later, when we installed the new and permanent three manual Hook and Hastings pipe organ in the new church. We then removed the reed organ and installed it in the chapel of the Notre Dame Convent on Dolores Street, opposite the Mission Dolores. We finally added a much needed blower to the organ and the instrument gave service for many years. In 1941 it was finally supplanted by a new Aeolian Skinner pipe organ. I remember seeing the reed organ later, dismantled and stored in the school yard, under a portico, and have been told it was sold again to some other party in Marin County, proving that almost invariably not only a cat has "nine lives", but that many an organ apparently lives on forever.

In due time, a set of chimes and a Vox Humana were added to the Austin pipe organ at the Swedish Lutheran Church. A new feature in this organ at the time was the Dulciana 16' in the Pedal, made of wood. It was a much welcomed and useful innovation, to have some other stop in the Pedal than the faithful, commonplace, old reliable Bourdon 16'.

The fire of 1906 did not destroy this church, although it reached to the opposite side of Dolores Street.

During 1953 the Swedish Lutherans sold the church, including the organ, and property to the First Southern Baptist denomination, the former moving to the new location in the Sunset District on Portola Drive.

MARCUS KOSHLAND RESIDENCE

Another residence organ of San Francisco was the Estey two manual and Pedal pneumatic organ in the Marcus Koshland residence on Maple and Washington Streets. Undoubtedly, it was placed in the mansion soon after it was built in 1904. It was installed on the upper floor near the main staircase, and faced a spacious rotunda from which many rooms lead. Light from above, through a skylight, suffused the whole court with a pleasant glow; below, potted ferns and a murmuring fountain in the center of the court gave added beauty to an exquisite setting. The organ case and exterior was of graceful design, blending harmoniously with its surroundings.

The specification of the organ consisted of 6 stops, which were controlled by the on and off stop key control arrangement, commonly used by the Estey Company at that period. The couplers were also mechanical. An automatic player of the old type was also a feature of the organ.

Mrs. Koshland, a patroness of the arts and music, a lady bountiful to many a struggling artist, also arranged for a musicale in her home, honoring visiting celebrities, artists and musicians. She had arranged for a musicale, a religious service commemorating the Feast of the Lighted Candles, one of the feastdays of the Jewish calendar. In addition to tuning and servicing the organ previous to the occasion, she also asked me to be present at the organ during the concert, to be prepared for any emergency that might arise. The house was filled with guests, every available space was occupied, and people were even seated on the broad marble stairs leading to the upper floor. Cantor Rinder of Temple Emanu-El conducted the services, and as was to be expected, Wallace Sabin presided at the organ. He was delighted to know that I would stay during the function and asked me to remain alongside the bench and turn his music for him. I did this somewhat reluctantly, as I remembered some previous occasion, in my zeal to turn the page on time, I upset the apple cart entirely by letting the book fall from the music rack. I noticed Mr. Sabin was unusually nervous, if not bewildered, and rather helpless. He inquired of me what to do next, when to play, etc. I, not having received any previous instruction on the program, could not be of much assistance to him on that score. I had never seen Wallace Sabin in such a mental state before, and after bidding him goodbye, on my way home I thought over the matter and mused that even the "great and mighty" have their day; that in the evening of life we all begin to slip. This occasion in 1937 proved to be the last time I saw Wallace Sabin alive. A week or two later he was mourned by hundreds of his friends, former pupils and confreres as he was laid to rest.

Mrs. Koshland passed away in 1959 and the mansion on Pacific Heights remained vacant for several years. The organ was then finally given to Temple Emanu-El by her heirs, and placed on the gallery of the Social Auditorium in memory of this philanthropic and generous benefactor of Temple Emanu-El. It was our privilege to install the organ in 1955. Several changes and additions were made at this time. A Trumpet 8' was added to the Great manual, a new modern concave radiating Pedal Board was applied. The old on and off manual key stop action was changed to the regular stop key type. With the installation of this organ, Temple Emanu-El can boast of the unusual fact of having three pipe organs in use in their institution.

PARKER HOLT RESIDENCE

Parker C. Holt, a pioneer and inventor of the caterpillar tractor, with a large plant at Stockton, California, manufacturing the tractor bearing his name, was also a resident of San

Francisco for many years.

Like all true American gentlemen, he enjoyed the pleasures and comforts of home and family life and, no doubt, with that thought in mind, he secured an Estey pipe organ with automatic player for his home at 2600 Vallejo Street, which was installed in 1912.

In 1928 Mr. Holt and his family left San Francisco and built a beautiful Spanish home on the pine-clad hillside of Pebble Beach, near old Monterey, overlooking the blue waters of the Pacific. We removed the organ from their former home and erected it in the new domicile. The occasion was a rather happy event for me, as I also made it a sort of summer vacation for myself and family, consisting then of my wife and five children. At that time I was the proud possessor of a Model T Ford, four door sedan. In this vehicle we packed our belongings and a quantity of provisions for a sojourn of about three weeks and merrily rode down the Peninsula to our destination.

On arrival, we rented a small cottage at Pacific Grove, near the public baths, a place on the shore of Monterey Bay. I shall always remember the kindness of my friends, Mr. and Mrs. Adam Kramer, who were living at that time in Pacific Grove. On learning that we intended to stay there for several weeks, they took us completely in charge. They secured the cottage for us and assisted my wife in every way in getting us comfortably settled, even supplying and cutting a formidable stack of wood to last us for the duration. My wife, and especially the children, found great delight and enjoyment in our sojourn there. For me it was, of course, mostly strenuous work every day.

One enjoyable feature of the job, however, was that it gave me the opportunity to travel over the scenic 17-Mile Drive twice a day to and from Pebble Beach to Pacific Grove. The appetizing lunch which my wife prepared for me each day was always enjoyed while sitting under the pine and cypress trees, looking out at the beautiful ocean. Mr. Kramer called frequently at the job, as the Holt residence was still in course of construction when I installed the organ. He was superintendent of construction for the firm of Rhule and Company, contractors who were builing the house.

While I was at work, my youngsters Lawrence, Bertam, Victoria and George were having one grand time and "made hay while the sun shone." The baby, Vincent, was mostly with his mother. One morning the two older boys left the house to play down on Sandy Beach. Looking out of the front window some time later, my wife observed two boys in a row boat a considerable distance out from shore. She was surprised at their youthfulness, but reassured herself that undoubtedly they were local boys and familiar with the sea. Nevertheless, she thought she would never let her boys engage in such dangerous sport unaccompanied. Her concern about those two boys was later turned to consternation, when, after several hours, our boys returned from the beach and jubilantly related all about the wonderful boat ride they had, all alone out on the Bay.

All told, our stay at Pacific Grove was most enjoyable. We attended Mass on Sunday at San Carlos Mission. In front of the entrance, alongside the grotto, we had a photograph taken of the family group, which I cherish to this day. On one occasion Mrs. Kramer took us in her car for an extended trip over the 17-Mile Drive to Mission Carmel, the burial place of the saintly Junipero Serra, the founder of the California Missions. To partake of our lunch, we selected a cozy spot on the white sands of the beach, alongside the remnants of an old wooden hull of a ship, probably an old Spanish galleon that had met disaster at this point in the early days.

Shortly after completion of the organ, the Holt family moved into their new home. It was some years later that I was called again to make some adjustments on the organ. I recall I was working rather late, as the next morning Mr. Holt, Jr., planned to drive to San Francisco in his car and had promised to take me along. I, therefore, wanted to complete my work that night. I remember the rooms were comfrotably heated, if anything quite warm, or perhaps I was somewhat overheated from the exertion of working so close to the ceiling. I was bathed in perspiration when I completed my work and was directed to my room for the night. Indeed, it was an exquisite room, with a splendid shower and bath. The shower beckoned me after the gritty, dusty work in the organ. I expected some warm or hot water to flow, but it was rather cold. I took a chill, but thought I would soon regain my composure and comfort under the warm blankets, but here, too, a dank feeling seemed to hold me in its grasp. I finally fell asleep, but the next morning on arising I had a severe pain in the small of my back. After a pleasant breakfast with my host, we were off to San Francisco in his car.

Before leaving home for Pebble Beach, I had promised Mr. Ross B. Ring, of Ferndale, California, to erect a Wicks organ in his home. Being somewhat delayed with my trip to Pebble Beach, he was getting impatient and insisted that I come as promised, without delay, as the organ and packing cases were cluttering up his home. Therefore, on arriving in San Francisco, I immediately made arrangements to take the night train to Ferndale, up near Eureka in northern California. On stepping out of Mr. Holt's car, I noticed my back hurt more than ever, but I thought it was due to the more or less cramped position and the long journey. On arriving at Ferndale I felt no better, but with my eargerness to tackle the job and make a showing, I had little time to think much of the pain that persistently remained with me during the day.

However, when evening came and bedtime, the pain was excruciating and I complained of my trouble to Mr. Ring, Sr., a kindly old gentleman who, incidently, was a pharmacist and had the leading drugstore in Ferndale, which was located in the store below the dwelling. He prescribed different lotions with which to rub my sore back, or rather, to call it by its proper name, to relieve the inflammatory rheumatism I had contracted when I got the chill in the shower bath. All rememdies seemed to be useless. Hard work and trying the forget the pain during the day seemed to be the best medicine, but I also needed rest and sleep. As a last resort, Mr. Ring brought up from the store an electric heating pad, a rather new gadget at the time, which I placed against my ailing back. This seemed to be the only means of relief and comfort that I could get and I was indeed grateful to my benefactor for this blessing.

ST. ANTHONY'S CHURCH

One of the most cherished and dearest churches to me, aside from St. Boniface Church where I was christened and attended the parochial school, is St. Anthony's Church. It is located at Army and Folsom Streets in the Mission District and is my own parish church. Both St. Boniface and St. Anthony's Churches are conducted by the Franciscan Fathers, the successors of the saintly Junipero Serra and members of the order founded by the patron of the City of San Francisco, the illustrious St. Francis of Assisi.

Previous to 1893, St. Boniface Church was the only German parish, but in 1893 it was decided to form a second parish for the German speaking people of the City, especially for the Swiss people engaged in the dairy business to the south of the City. With the approval and encouragement of the Archbishop, the Most Rev. Patrick W. Riordan, a warm friend of the German speaking people, necessary preparations were made for the establishing of a new parish under the title and patronage of St. Anthony. St. Boniface parish embraced that part of the City north of 20th Street, and St. Anthony's from 20th Street south to the County line.

The first services were held in the shoe store of George Holl on Mission Street, near 26th Street. Property was then acquired on Army Street, bounded by Folsom, Shotwell and Precita Avenue. A one story building was erected on the site consisting of four rooms. These were used on Sunday for divine service and during the week classes were held for the children, this being the nucleus of the present St. Anthony's School and Church. The Dominican Sisters from the Immaculate Conception Convent on Guerrero Street conducted the classes.

Scarcely had the school building been completed, when plans were made for a permanent church, as the need for it was obvious. The church was built partly of brick and of frame, and was erected on the Army Street frontage. It was substantially built of Romanesque design, with vaulted ceiling resting on rather generously proportioned columns. The facade of the church, with its pleasing tower and the exceptionally well executed masonry, especially the vaulting over the main entrance, gives it the stamp of genuine high class workmanship.

In 1894 the cornerstone of the church was laid. I remember the occasion distinctly, as I attended the celebration with my older brothers. The Rev. Peter C. Yorke, then Chancelor of the Archdiocese of San Francisco, delivered the sermon. Before the final dedication of the church, another celebration took place, at which I again was present. It was the blessing of the three bells that were eventually to ring out their joyous peals from the belfry high above the street. On this occasion they were temporarily placed on the stairs in front of the vestibule of the church. It seems significant that the charm of melody and music exemplified by these beautifully toned, melodious bells was to become one of the characteristics of this parish in future years. St. Anthony's parish is justly proud of having three bells in its belfry, as there is no other church in San Francisco that can claim this distinction. Ordinarily, only one bell is used. For Sunday services two bells are used and only on high feastdays are the three bells rung. No more elevating and inspiring thrill can be experienced than to hear these bells being rung - first striking intermittently, then rotating in even sequence, then striking in unison as they are swung on their axis. Many a time I have found inspiration in hearing the silvery notes wafted over the valley of the Mission District to my home a mile distant, on the hillside of the Southern Heights, especially with a favorable southwesterly wind blowing.

When the household heard "Die feierlichen Glocken" (the festive bells) of St. Anthony's ring, we invariably would go out on our rear porch overlooking the Mission District and listen to their peal. On many joyous occasions were they used. I recall when they were wedding bells for me, and again 25 years later, silver wedding anniversary bells. They also pealed forth on the occasion of the Golden Wedding anniversary of my parents. They also tolled in sorrow when they were laid to rest. As the ringing of the bells was a three man job, many an old parishioner prides himself on having at one time or other been one of the bell ringers.

Due to the large indebtedness incurred by the erection of the church and the school, and the making of necessary improvements, the thought of acquiring a pipe organ for the church had to be deferred for a long time. However, while this vital acquisition remained but a faint hope, church music was in no way neglected or subordinated to other essential activities of parish life. A modest harmonium served to furnish the necessary accompaniment and embellishment to an energetic and spirited volunteer choir that is an example, I may say, of devotedness and loyalty to the cause unexcelled in any other parish, several of the singers having served faithfully for over 50 years. Father Cletus, O.F.M., and Father Quirinus, O.F.M., were the first who, in addition to their priestly duties at the church, also played the organ and directed the choir.

In 1899, after the death of its first pastor, Rev. Leo Bruner, O.F.M., the parish was exceptionally fortunate in having appointed as its pastor the Rev. Raphael Fuhr, O.F.M, of Quincy, Illinois. He was a man of exceptional ability and accomplishments, a devoted priest, an inspiring pastor, and a musician and composer of no mean ability. Music and the church choir seemed to be his hobby. With his inspiration and his desire to provide his parish with the very best in church music, it was essential that a permanent organist be obtained. He was successful in securing the efficient services of Miss Lulu Curtaz, daughter of the late Ben Curtaz, of the well known piano firm of that time, a most charming young lady, with musical training and a fine soprano voice.

St. Anthony's Choir, under the guidance of Father Raphael Fuhr and the able organist, earned an enviable reputation for itself as producing only the finest music, suited to the liturgy of the church. The Gregorian chant and the more modern music of the Cecilian school, as exemplified by Jos. Singenberger, Gruber, etc., were rendered by the mixed choir, in its highest form of perfection. At different times, the choir also performed at concerts. At one time it made a visit to the Old Mission at Santa Barbara, to St. Mary's Church at San Jose, and to the Cathedral at Sacramento, on which occasions it joined in chorus with the local choirs.

At this time, under the regime of Miss Curtaz as organist, I could not resist the urge to join the church choir. My elder brother, Frank, and my younger sisters, Cecilia, and Helen, were also induced to do likewise.

I might state here that a few years after the dedication of the church, in 1896, our family moved into the parish, locating at 21st and Bryant Streets, and we considered ourselves thereafter loyal parishioners of St. Anthony's participating in its progress and development, sharing in its difficulties and unpleasant events, partaking of its blessings and fellowship, and always supporting it to the best of our ability in material ways, and especially offering it our loyal services wherever they might be needed.

With the foresight always shown by Father Raphael, realizing he would not always be pastor, he looked to the future to perpetuate the good work he had done in planting the seed for appreciation of only the highest in church music. As the organist also found it desirable to have a substitute to fall back upon at times, my younger sister, Cecilia, who had already been learning to play the piano and the organ, and who was also gifted with a good soprano voice, was induced to act as assistant organist. To prepare her more thoroughly in the fundamentals of music, Father Raphael, from his rich store of knowledge and musical experience, taught her harmony and the intricacies of the proper rendition of the Gregorian chant. Shortly after the marriage of Miss Curtaz to Joseph Ruegg, who was also one of the choir singers, my sister assumed complete charge of the choir and carried on the traditions implanted in the parish by its revered and esteemed pastor.

In 1904 Father Raphael Fuhr, O.F.M., was transferred to St. Joseph's Church at Los Angeles, much to the sorrow and regret of the parishioners. However, his spirit remained. The energy, the wholeheartedness, the cooperation and unity of purpose manifested by the parishioners to this day, it would seem, is the result, the fruition of those noble traits he so vividly exemplified, leaving a cherished motto to his memory, "Immer heiter, Gott hilft weiter"; "Ever cheerful be, God will help thee."

In 1913 it was found desirable to extend and complete the nave and transcept of the church to its full extent. This was done under the pastorate of Father Raymond Nolte, O.F.M., with the result that St. Anthony's is now certainly one of the most beautiful churches in San Francisco.

With the church completed, the discussion of securing a suitable pipe organ was again brought to the fore. Rev. Agedius Herkenrath, O.F.M., a most amiable and kind priest, was pastor at this time. With an organ builder in the parish, and the organist who had labored so faithfully for years on the harmonium, a member of the family, it was logical that he should take up the discussion of this important matter with us. After making visits with him and some of the parishioners to several of the local churches, which had organs of various makes, a price was determined upon and we were commissioned to procure a suitable organ.

As we were not in a position to manufacture one ourselves at the time, we had the contract awarded to the Hook and Hastings Co., of Boston, Mass., to build a two manual and Pedal electric pneumatic organ of 18 speaking stops, with detached console, and with the Swell, also part of the Great, enclosed in expression chambers. We designed the exterior of the organ and drew the specifications, adopting several suggestions offered by the builders, with the result that we believe a most satisfactory instrument was obtained for the money expended. Special features of construction were stipulated to its interior construction, such as a regulator for each division of the organ, an auxiliary bellows in the motor room, individually operated swell blinds, and ample bracing to make the organ strong and rigid.

In 1929, after 29 years of faithful service as organist and choir leader, Miss Cecilia Schoenstein accepted the position of organist at Mission Dolores Church, where there was a large 3 manual Hook and Hastings organ at her disposal, also a small sanctuary organ especially designed for the use of a vested choir consisting of young boys, mostly from the parochial school, augmented on occasion by men of the regular choir. With a limited quartet of paid singers, and the training of the boys choir, a new field was opened up to her, agreeable and interesting, but also tedious, as any director of a boys choir will understand. Her previous thorough training and experience in true ecclesiastical music, her voice training and culture which she had also acquired, were recognized and appreciated by the pastor of Mission Dolores, the Rev. Msgr. W. Sullivan.

After six years of efficient and harmonious work at Mission Dolores Church, her former position at St. Anthony's Church, which had become vacant due to the departure of her successor, Anna Madden, was again offered to her. To the delight of the former still loyal members of her choir, and of the congregation in general, she returned to her "first love", St. Anthony's Church and Choir. Cecilia Schoenstein and St. Anthony's Choir seem, after all, inseparable. One could not do without the other. A family spirit seems to prevail among the choir members - some of them have worked together harmoniously for nearly 50 years.

In 1944 the Golden Jubilee of the founding of the parish, which was also the jubilee of the church choir, was celebrated.

At about this time St. Anthony's Parish was again favored by having appointed as one of its assisting priests, Rev. Rayner Harrington, O.F.M., a newly ordained priest, a lover of music and an ardent and enthusiastic worker, whose special field was to organize and interest the young in the work of religion and in the services of the House of God. By forming a Junior Choir, which later amalgamated with the Senior Choir, and later still was called the St. Anthony's Choristers, he succeeded in reviving and stimulating a renewed interest in the singing of the church music, as well as in rendering several excellent concerts, the outstanding one being the oratorical pageant, the Passion of Christ, tendered in 1944.

On August 8, 1947, St. Anthony's Parish ceased to be a German National Church, but was given definite parish limits and was to cater to the English speaking Catholic people living within its boundaries.

May St. Cecilia, the patroness of church music, look benignly down upon those who did the pioneering work and planted the fine traditions of true church music in St. Anthony's, upon its loyal and efficient organist Cecilia Schoenstein, its energetic and jovial musical director, Rev. Rayner Harrington, O.F.M., and the faithful singers who unselfishly give of their time and talent, not for personal gain, but soley for the enhancing of the divine service and for the greater honor and glory of God.

ST. LUKE'S HOSPITAL CHAPEL

In 1914 St. Luke's Hospital had just completed some additions to the new hospital buildings, one wing of which was a charming little chapel in typical Gothic design for use of the nurses and patients who desired to attend their services. A contract was awarded to the Austin Organ Company to build a small suitable pipe organ of four stops duplexed, Opus 494, which we later installed during the month of May of the same year. The detached console was placed below, near the chancel, and the organ above on the east side of a gallery, filling a chamber especially provided for it. The entire organ is enclosed and is unusually effective. The blower room is on the floor above. In looking up to the organ loft from below, one observes two organ fronts; the one to the left, however, is only a dummy and installed to conserve the symmetry of the setting.

I recall that while I was erecting the exterior case, Mrs. Lydia Paige Monteagle who, I was informed at the time, was one of the donors of the organ and much interested in the chapel, called one day and immediately detected that the grills in the panels of the case, for emitting the tone of the organ, were not of Gothic design but were merely round holes bored through the oak panels. She insisted on the Gothic treatment, so the panels were removed and new ones made. Some alteration was also made to the console, but I know that on completion she was completely satisfied. I believe her objection to the console was that the color or finish did not match exactly with the surrounding woodwork of the chapel. To overcome this objection, I summoned my friend, **Joseph** Vogel, who was a color specialist and interior decorator, to do the necessary work.

It was while doing this work that one day he invited me to his home which was only a few blocks away, for lunch. It so happened that his younger sister, Josephine, whom I had previously met on occasions and of whom I had heard much favorable comment, especially from my mother, served us at the table. I must have been very susceptible to Cupid's darts that day. The sight of this charming lass performing her domestic duties in the sanctum of her own home must have appealed to me, and engendered thoughts that she would possibly make a good wife for me some day. At any rate, it was one of a few little incidents that finally culminated in a happy wedding for us on May 12, 1915.

We have serviced St. Luke's Hospital chapel organ regularly since we installed it. In tuning and playing on it while at work, we often wondered what effect it had on the patients lying in their beds. Invariably some nurses, and at times patients, or doctors appeared on the balcony to hear the music and see who was playing. Flattering compliments from them for our virtuosity was not unusual, but we often wondered if the patients enjoyed it or if it was annoying to some of them. Organ music, especially, may have quite different effects on the termperaments of ailing people. We, therefore, never play the organ any more than is absolutely necessary in our work.

I recall at one time we had a young man in our employ, then about 25 years old, a rather tall, slim, not too robust youth named Homer Hamlin. Unfortunately, he became ill and contracted pneumonia. He was brought to St. Luke's Hospital, unknown to us, and succumbed. The morning of the day he died, we tuned and serviced the organ. As was customary, we also played some music, on completion, to try it out. We were told later that he heard us play the organ and called the attention of the nurse to it, saying, "the boys are tuning the organ today." I trust the chords he heard then brought peace and comfort to his departing soul, and that they were an interlude to the celestial choir and harmony he is hearing in the heavenly courts above.

ST. AGNES CHURCH

I have a recollection from my boyhood days of a very disastrous fire that occurred in the Ashbury Heights District. Several blocks were consumed in the conflagration. I also recall visits we children made to the so-called frog pond, a deep declivity at Fulton Street and what is now Masonic Avenue, south of the McAllister Street cable car barns. In later years we also made visits to the Chutes, an amusement park located on Haight and Cole Streets, where a huge inflated balloon was sent up each Sunday afternoon to draw out the crowds. This territory around the old cemeteries was then sparsely settled, but it developed rapidly into a residential district and it was not long before the need for establishing a parish church in this district became evident.

In 1893 St. Agnes Church, a small frame structure, was built on the west side of Masonic Avenue, between Oak and Page Streets. I always admired its circular, canopied cupola resting on columns forming the facade of the church. When, in time, the need for a larger church became apparent, the small frame building was moved around the corner on Page Street and a larger, more commodious church was built on the former site. The old church was then used for a Sunday school and a social hall.

It was not until 1915 that the parish secured a pipe organ for the church. A two manual and Pedal electric pneumatic Johnston organ of about 20 stops was secured and was installed by my brother, Leo. I recall Mr. Bretherick, then organist of the Unitarian Church, was selected to judge and approve the organ when it was completed, which he readily did. It proved to be a very satisfactory instrument. I believe a Miss Mary Bumsted was the first organist.

In time, as the parish grew and it was found necessary to place chairs in the aisles to accommodate the growing Congregation, it was apparent that the church had to be enlarged. It was at this time that the Pastor, Rev. John A. Butler, engaged the services of the Architect Leo Devlin to draw up plans to extend the church, with the result that the forward part of the church containing the Sanctuary and Trancept was temporarily partitioned off and the permanent part of the new church was begun.

At this time, 1924, another young lady became organist, who, in the course of time through her proficiency at the organ and especially her activity with the Choir, was soon well known. It was no other than Miss Grace Marie

Compagno, who has now to her credit the composing and publishing of over 150 musical compositions, including four Masses, the "Missa Brevis" for mixed voices contrapuntal in style which was, incidentally, also sung by the Sistine Choir of Rome on one of their United States Concert Tours.

While the new Sanctuary and Trancept were being built we were awarded a contract to build a small Sanctuary or Antiphonal organ of five stops, in 1926, which was then installed behind a grill near the altar. When this part of the construction work was completed, the temporary dividing partition was removed and the completed Sanctuary and nave along with the old section of the church were used again for divine services for a number of years.

In 1949, after a period of twenty-five years, Miss Grace Marie Compagno relinquished her position as organist, choosing hereafter to be the wife of Mr. Alfred Groene, the proprietor of a Music Publishing establishment.

I conclude with an incident that occurred at the Christmas Eve Midnight Mass. The Church was crowded with Parishioners and a massed Choir was present on the organ loft. After a few opening chords, the organ petered out and gave up the ghost. Consternation prevailed for a moment, but the intrepid organist continued the number in acappella style until a convenient interval and then hurried, with the Choir enmass, down from the organ loft by a route outside along the church to the Sanctuary organ in front of the church, here singing another portion of the mass. The organist believed then she heard the motor of the gallery organ becoming active again and retraced her steps, with the Choir, to the gallery organ loft, but again found the organ inactive, again proceeding with the remaining mass sung in acappella. On conclusion of the mass the Pastor complimented the Choir and Organist for the beautiful antiphonal effect rendered and the acappella singing, not knowing the real cause of the disturbance. The following day when the electricians were called to locate the trouble they found the conduit containing the electric motor circuits, which were underground, had become filled with water and caused the short circuit. Why this trouble should occur on Christmas morning is one of those things that worries the organist and the organ maintenance man and begs for an answer.

Father Butler, the Pastor who was the instigator and the one who began construction of the new church, passed away in 1941, without achieving his dream of seeing the church completed. His successor is the Rev. Msgr. F. Millet.

Finally, in 1951 the completion of the unfinished part of the church was undertaken, though in a more simplified manner than originally planned. We were authorized to rebuild the old gallery Johnston organ, arrange it into two separate sections on either side of the gallery, all under expression, apply a modern new two manual console, new blowing plant and add several new stops. All told, the undertaking was most successful. This work was done by my son, Lawrence. The full organ ensemble in the enlarged and accoustically favorable edifice if overwhelming. Chester Farrell held the position of organist successfully from the time the church edifice was completed until recently when Leonard Fitzpatrick assumed the position.

ST. MATTHEW'S LUTHERAN CHURCH

St. Matthew's Lutheran Church, before the fire, was located on the east side of Eleventh Street, about fifty feet south of the Church of the Advent, nearer Mission Street. It was a little frame building. Its diminutive size and smallness seemed to appeal to me. The inside area was possibly no larger than 25 x 25 feet. Rev. Herman Gerhke was pastor at the time. I believe the congregation was an offshoot of St. Paulus Lutheran Church. There was no pipe organ in this church.

I recall being in the church with my father, tuning and repairing a reed organ. It was late in the day, probably autumn or winter of the year. The church was dark, aside from the small work light we were using. Suddenly, an unannounced and unwelcome visitor, unkempt and bedraggled, came strolling slowly up the aisle and accosted my father, asking him for some money. I did not like the looks of the intruder, as he appeared dangerous and vicious to me. I believe my father gave him something, and after he succeeded in getting rid of the man, he bolted the front door of the church through which the fellow had entered.

After the fire, St. Matthew's Lutheran Church located on 16th Street, near Dolores, where they built a larger, substantial frame building. It was dedicated in 1908. They secured a two manual Hinners organ, tubular pneumatic action of 8 stops. The tone of this organ is unusually good and I have often commented on its excellent Diapason tone. Although voiced on light pressure, its full and prevading tone is free from windiness, evenly regulated from bass to treble.

Rev. Gerhke passed away in 1936. He always spoke highly of my father who, in turn, had high regard for him. Rev. Herman Lukas succeeded Pastor Gerhke, until his retirement in 1961. Rev. Lukas was very popular with the German Lutherans of San Francisco and was highly respected and endeared by all.

STAR OF THE SEA CHURCH

The title of this church, "Star of the Sea", always intrigued me. It is quite fitting and appropriate, however, that San Francisco, on the brink of the west coast of the continent, a seaport of note, with a maritime background of historical charm and romance, should have one of her churches dedicated to the Virgin Mother under her title of "Star of the Sea."

The parish was established in 1894. I have a faint recollection of seeing the frame church standing in the almost vacant lots way out in the Richmond District. As youngsters we would take hiking trips to the top of Lone Mountain, then proceed a considerable distance farther out on Point Lobos Avenue, as Geary Boulevard was then called. Our goal was a race track that was out that way, but we never succeeded in getting there.

My first association with the church was in 1910 when the Vicar General, Very Rev. Philip O'Ryan, became pastor of the church. Msgr. O'Ryan had formerly been assistant pastor at Holy Cross Church, and while there certainly had occasion to become organ-minded and interested in the instrument as the pastor, Father McGinty, was an ardent lover and advocate of the pipe organ. Father O'Ryan secured an organ for the Star of the Sea Church from the successors of the Murray M. Harris Co., the Robert-Morton Organ Company of Los Angeles, a beautifully designed organ, well built and well voiced. It consists of three manuals and Pedal, a detached console, and 17 speaking stops. Part of the Great manual is unenclosed. I believe the organ was installed by my brother, Leo.

In 1930 it was decided to improve the facade of the church, heighten its towers and make other improvements to secure a more pleasing and harmonious whole. As this work entailed the adding and extending of necessary steel girders and much concrete work, it was deemed advisable to remove the organ in the interim.

We did this and stored it in one of the sacristy rooms for several months. One day while this remodeling work was going on, I happened to be passing the church and went in and up to the organ loft to see how the new structural work was progressing. Just then one of the workmen was pouring concrete into one of the moulds encasing a main upright supporting girder of the tower. The concrete was being poured from the top, but something must have given way below, and instead of filling the mould, it poured out into the small room alongside the choir stairs. The concrete was several feet deep before the mishap was discovered. After this alteration work was completed, we again erected the organ in its former location, with some rearrangement of the Pedal pipes. Marble altars, art glass windows, bronze doors, a redecorated church, have since been improvements made to the Star of the Sea Church. A Vox Humana, a set of Deagan chimes, have also been added to the organ, and a troublesome generator has been replaced by a new type rectifier, giving the organ the last word in assurance and dependability. Mrs. Alvara Gomez served as organist for twenty-three years and is now a Mrs. Zink, with a family, still interested in music.

CORPUS CHRISTI CHURCH

Corpus Christi parish was established in 1898. It is located out in the Mission District in the vicinity where once vegetable gardens and dairies flourished, and was especially established to cater to the needs of the Italian people, who were quite numerous in that district and was, therefore, one of their national churches. A modest church building and rectory were erected on the corner of Santa Rosa and Alemany Boulevard. Later on, a school, a convent, and further improvements were added.

With the traditional love of the Italian people for music, it was not surprising that at an early date, in 1914, they procured a splendid Kimball pipe organ of 7 stops, two manuals and Pedal. I believe the organ was purchased from the Eilers Music Company, who were the agents for the Kimball Organ Company at that time, and that it was installed by my brother, Leo, who was then in their employ.

After a period of some 25 years, the pneumatics in the organ needed to be recovered with new material. This we attended to, a procedure necessary in most organs, especially in a Kimball organ because of their use of a rubberized silk material.

I remember an incident that occurred one day when I had to repair a cipher due to a broken pedal spring on the pedal key. I had just removed the pedal keyboard, a procedure not often done. Naturally, a great amount of dirt and grit had accumulated under the keys. There were pencils, papers and what not lying there. As I could find no broom handy, I took a board nearby and scraped the debris to one side in a pile. To my surprise one of the dusty papers which I at first thought to be some old discarded music program or notice, and was unrecognizable due to the dust on it, turned out to be a good old one dollar bill. I dusted it off and instinctively put it in my pocket and continued with my work. Under ordinary circumstances, the finding of a little loose change is a pleasurable experience to the finder. However, this dollar bill seemed to be burning a hole in my pocket, and I had just about concluded that on the completion of my work I would present it to the pastor, as after all it was not my property, when he came up to the organ to see how my work was progressing. I could not resist telling him of my lucky find, and passed him the dollar bill. He at first hesitated to take it and told me to keep it. I, in turn, insisted that he take it as I considered it church property. After a few more "Alphonse and Gaston" gestures, he finally retained the spoils.

In the course of years, what was once vegetable gardens, nurseries and dairies, and what was considered the outskirts of the City, became what it now the thickly populated Excelsior District of San Francisco, with its lovely homes sheltering the families forming the backbone of San Francisco's citizenry. With this influx of many new people, the original Italian characteristics of the parish have greatly diminished, if not disappeared entirely. The Salesian Fathers of Don Bosco have had this parish in their charge from its inception and have been most successful in their work.

A new church with complete parish units was urgently needed. In 1953, after the second World War, when conditions were more normal, a building program was inaugurated. A new church was built alongside the old one. This new edifice created quite a stir in architectural circles, as also among the casual passersby, as something bizarre and out of the ordinary, a design certainly not fit for a church.

The entire facade is of a simple square outline, paneled off in square planes of glass of various contrasting hues. The side walls of the church were windowless, its illumination being through skylights from above. The Baptistry was on the floor above the vestibule, or on the choir loft. The Sanctuary received a very unusual treatment. The wall behind the Altar was of semi-circular shape, made of wood with a pattern of random pieces. The main Altar was simplicity itself, a black marble altar slab resting on two supports. The large Crucifix suspended over the altar was a wood carving of grotesque design and the 14 stations lining the side walls of the church were also wood. Its interior finish was of a high order.

Strange to say, that on first sight it was shocking for a conservative as I, to behold, but once inside one soon got reconciled to its appointments and, in fact, found laudable points . . . the indirect lighting system, the very successful accoustical sanctuary walls, the beautiful coloring of the paneled front windows, when looking out from the vestibule, etc.

After the completion of the new Church the old Kimball organ, which we had since electrified, was placed in the new church. The outline of its front pipes was altered to harmonize with the surrounding architecture. Front pipes, as well as the whole case, were redecorated and a set of chimes installed, resulting in a very satisfactory installation.

ST. VINCENT DE PAUL

Evidently when St. Brigid's parish became too populated, it was found expedient to form a new parish farther west, as the people were constantly moving in that direction. St. Vincent De Paul Church was established in 1901. It is located on the northwest corner of Green and Steiner Streets.

My first recollection of the church was in 1903, when my father and I were called upon to repair a large reed organ they had secured for their embryo church, as only the basement or lower floor of the church was then completed. On seeing the organ it looked familiar to us and we recognized it as the organ that had formerly been in use in the Gentlemen's Sodality Chapel at St. Ignatius Church, before we installed the old reconditioned pipe organ there that had been in use at Old St. Mary's Church years before.

This Peloubet reed organ was built on the pressure system, with individual valves for each reed, all accessible from the front of the organ, operated by long stickers from the tail of the key. This mechanism was well made, looked well and functioned satisfactorily. The stop action, however, worked pneumatically and was always wrong and unreliable and, for some reason, seemed to be unnecessarily complicated in design. We succeeded in making the necessary adjustments, so the organ was at least usuable temporarily.

Rev. Martin Ryan was pastor of the church, a pleasant, witty and, at times, as sarcastic an Irish gentleman as the Lord makes. I recall his small, sparkling eyes, his Irish brogue, and his delight in bluffing or getting one's goat. An old gentleman with the name of Powers, with silver white hair, was sexton at the time. I recall him as a very pious and saintly soul. After a few years of active service he passed on to his reward.

About this time, 1912, the talk of holding a World's Fair, or International Exposition in San Francisco in 1915 to commemorate the completion of the building of the Panama Canal, was heatedly discussed, especially where the site or location of the Exposition should be placed. After the Marina District was definitely selected, it evidently was also a clue for the Rev. Clergy of St. Vincent's Parish, the nearest Catholic Church to the Fair site, to take cognizance of the advantage and period of activity that would accrue to the young parish, to complete the church to be prepared for a period of much activity. In 1912 the completion of the church was begun.

On account of its proximity to the Fair site, it received the appropriate appellation of "The Exposition Church." It was well built, with a steel frame but with a wooden exterior. Its general type of architecture is French Normandy, and with its square tower its distinctive architecture makes a very attractive and imposing edifice. The exterior, made of redwood, is of excellent craftsmanship, and the fact that the wood was not painted, but varnished, was quite unusual. A large figure of its patron saint, St. Vincent de Paul, has a prominent place over the main entrance of the church.

The lighting system of the church was something novel at the time, and was designed by the expert, D'Arcy Ryan, who was in charge of the lighting effects at the Exposition. It consists of large leaded, opalescent glass bowls containing the electric bulbs. The light is thrown directly against the ceiling and reflected to the church below. It seems to throw a pleasant and sufficient glow over the entire church.

For the dedication of the church in 1913, a pipe organ was also included in the plan. Mr. Fletcher Tilton, agent of the Austin Organ Company, secured the contract for a two manual and Pedal electric action organ, Opusl 494, which we installed. This organ proved to be the first electric pneumatic Austin pipe organ installed in San Francisco, as all others heretofore installed were of the pneumatic type. A divided organ, on either side of the gallery, was decided upon. The organ actually occupied only the west end organ space, the east organ case was still only a hollow shell with front display pipes. The specification of the organ is the customary one adopted by the Austin Company. The organ consists of 6 stops duplexed, all enclosed or under expression except the Diapason in the Great, which is unexpressive.

The organ was adequate for the church and gave an excellent account of itself. Miss Ruth Austin, who was a friend of Father Ryan, played at the dedicatory services. Father Ryan invited us both to the reception that followed at the parochial residence, and had a word of praise for both of us for our accomplishment; to Miss Ruth Austin for the excellent music rendered, and to me for the satisfactory installation of the organ. As we were both young and unattached, and as the keen eye of Father Ryan evidently noted a rather mutual interest we unconsciously manifested toward one another during the weeks previous while working on the organ, with his Irish wit and chivalry he seemed to sense a romance budding, which he evidently wished to help along. Fate decreed otherwise, however, but the occasion always brings back pleasant memories to me.

Many organists in the course of the years functioned at the organ. Among them was Mr. Vincent X. Arrillga, who held the position for many years.

Referring again to Father Ryan, besides the other inherent traits he had, needless to say, he was also a shrewd and able business man. The fine school, convent, parochial residence, in addition to the church, all attest to this fact.

Back to the old Peloubet reed organ we worked on years ago; we moved it to a temporary hall alongside the church and advised Father Ryan to have the organ overhauled. We assured him this would make it dependable and then at some future time, the organ could be disposed of advantageously. He agreed to this, but stipulated he would not pay for the job until he sold the organ. This I know, the bill was never paid, and the salvaged material was undoubtedly our remuneration.

In later years, after I was a family man, having my wife and several children with me in a street car one day, on which Father Ryan also happened to be a passenger, I accosted him and introduced my wife and children. He spoke in high praise of me to my wife and complimented our firm on our loyalty and efficiency in the maintenance of the pipe organ at the church and stated it was against his policy to discharge a satisfactory employee, and that he believed loyalty and the faithful performance of one's duties warranted the assurance of continued employment. This policy he faithfully carried out. We have been servicing the organ since its installation 56 years ago. Rev. Martin Ryan passed to his eternal reward, beloved and respected by all, in 1941.

In 1946, the church was further improved by installing art glass windows throughout the edifice, giving its interior an entirely new appearance. Several years ago it was noticeable that a settling of the facade of the church was taking place, undoubtedly due to insufficient foundation to support its weight. After prolonged and extensive alterations this defect was corrected.

At the same time, to enlarge the seating capacity of the gallery, the organ, with both cases on either side, was removed. The organ was then placed in the tower room, or former blower room. The blowing plant was placed in the tower above. The organ, now concealed from view, placed as far back as possible with a screen in front of it, certainly has not improved the situation tonally. The organ has lost its prevading ensemble it once produced in its former unobstructed position.

ARRILLAGA MUSICAL COLLEGE

In addition to the privately endowed San Francisco Conservatory of Music, San Francisco has supported for many years another institution for the teaching and development of music. It was the Arrillaga Music College, located at Jackson and Fillmore Streets.

From a small beginning, through the untiring efforts of its founder, Mr. Leo de Arrillaga, a veteran in the musical profession, a pianist and a teacher of note, the institution grew and developed. In 1914 a somewhat extensive recital hall was added to the building on Jackson Street, in which an excellent Johnston two manual and Pedal pipe organ of 12 stops was installed. My brother, Leo, who was then employed by the Eilers Music Company, installed the instrument. The console was detached and was first located on the auditorium floor. Later we placed it on the stage proper. The organ had an excellent tone and would be considered a typical church organ.

Teachers of the organ were Vincent de Arrillaga, who, after the death of his father, conducted the College; Dr. Achille Artigues, Raymond White and others. About 1925-26 a second organ, a Wurlitzer, was installed on the upper floor. Apparently the institution enjoyed a prosperous period for some time, but with the approach of the severe depression of 1929, its succeeding years were not so roseate. Musical interests and institutions suffered the brunt of the depression's ill effects. Finally, the W.P.A. Project assumed charge of the college's many functions, with Vincent de Arrillaga acting only as nominal head. Mr. de Arrilaga, in addition to his many duties at the College, had been interested in conducting large musical choruses and had been organist of St. Vincent de Paul's Church for many years. Eventually the institution liquidated entirely. The Johnston organ has since been sold to the Mills College of Oakland, where it has been installed, and the Wurlitzer organ found a new home in the residence of Mr. Roehr of San Bruno, California. The Wurlitzer organ, placed in Mr. Roehr's residence in San Bruno, was never completed due to the shortage of help caused by World War II. Mr. Roehr sold his home, prior to moving to Menlo Park, and we again dismantled the incompleted organ, removed it and erected it in our shop. It was then sold to a party conducting a restaurant or resort on El Camino Highway, where it now provides the musical background for its patrons.

CHAS. E. GREEN SAN FRANCISCO RESIDENCE
Jackson Street near Walnut Street

It was in 1914 that Mr. Charles E. Green decided to move to San Francisco. I recall him saying that with the approaching opening of the Panama-Pacific International Exposition in 1915, he and his family wished to be in close proximity to the Fair, the better to enjoy its beauties and the many attractions it would have to offer. He located on the north side of Jackson Street, near Walnut Street, and had a large addition built to the rear of the house, which was to be the music room.

On completion of this addition, we moved his Murry M. Harris Organ from the San Mateo residence to its new abode on Jackson Street, San Francisco.

The organ was then placed in the organ chamber, built for it, occupying a space almost covering the entire width of the northern end of the music room. The case was of an elaborate design, made of mahogany, hand carved and beautifully finished. The console was attached. The bellows and blowing apparatus were in the basement below. Since the interior workmanship of the organ, the pipes, the voicing, were all of the highest standard of workmanship, we took special interest in keeping it immaculately clean, so that it could be displayed to his guests with just pride. Tonally, the organ had all those characteristics of a typical residence organ. Undoubtedly, the pipe organ and its music must have been Mr. Green's hobby and delight.

As fond and as interested as he was in music, to my knowledge Mr. Green could not perform on the organ or piano, and, therefore, naturally depended on the automatic player for his musical recreation and enjoyment. Therefore, in addition to the usual keyboard at the organ, with all the necessary stops and accessories, he also had a small detached console at the opposite end of the room for playing the organ automatically.

Evidently, the Aeolian Company would not countenance an arrangement of attaching their player to any other make of organ than their own. Therefore, Mr. Green's cherished hope for this acquisition seemed to be doomed. But the saying goes, "necessity is the mother of invention". We came to the assistance of Mr. Green and procured a used tracker board of an Aeolian organ and applied it successfully to his console, thereby making it possible for him to use their type of music rolls to his heart's content.

This console was not of the Duo-Art type of self-registering, however, the instrumentation had to be selected and arranged by the performer himself. Most music lovers and people possessing a pipe organ in their homes, even though not professional musicians, acquire in time a proficiency truly marvelous in interpreting the various moods, temperaments and aspirations of the composer. They perform with ease and with apparent satisfaction to themselves and to their listeners.

Not so, however, with Mr. Green. Maybe it was his self-consciousness, being aware that someone else was present who perhaps knew better how the organ should be operated. At any rate, he seemed to be most uncomfortable, apparently not enjoying the music that was being rendered, but being more concerned about its mechanical functioning. This impediment, of course, did not impart any sense of enjoyment to his listeners. Often I honestly pitied the poor man, prince that he was otherwise, for the apparent lack of enjoyment he got out of his organ. I hope that in quiet and secluded moments when Mr. Green was in his environment, either playing the organ himself or having it played for him, he found the pleasure and enjoyment in it that he so desired and richly deserved.

I do not know if the organ was used much for hand playing. Undoubtedly, visiting guests and friends were at times invited to play. Mrs. Green, a lovable, motherly woman, with a personality all her own, was always about and seemed to share equally Mr. Green's interest in the organ. I acquired a high regard and esteem for these people. Mr. Green, with an impulsiveness and irritability that at times made itself evident unintentionally, was again as desirous of being as kind and considerate as only a true, well-bred American gentleman could be. Both Mr. and Mrs. Green took a great interest in my aged father. At this time, in 1915, I married and built my future home, and one of the most cherished and welcome presents we received was a beautiful table lamp from Mr. and Mrs. Charles E. Green, which to this day I preserve and value as a token of real friendship and esteem.

Some time thereafter, when calling to work on the organ, I remember seeing Mr. Green confined in bed. The loss of his eldest son, Eldridge, from a heart attack while attending a dinner dance at the Palace Hotel, was a severe shock to him.

In later years he evidently did not use the organ much, as he found it expedient to sell it to Mr. George Cameron of Hillsborough, California, who, in 1935 or there about, added a large music room of Spanish medieval design to his mansion for the installation of the former Charles E. Green organ.

We, therefore, removed the organ from the Charles E. Green residence on Jackson Street, with the exception of the elaborate exterior case, and installed it in the George T. Cameron residence at Hillsborough. Here the organ was placed behind a grill, thoroughly modernized and rearranged. A new modern console of our manufacture was applied, several new stops added, consisting of a Tuba 8', Horn 8', Diapason 8', Clarinet 8', Flute d' Armour 4', and a set of Deagan chimes. The revised specification was made after consultation and with the approval of Warren D. Allen, Organist at Stanford University, and Dr. Humphrey J. Stewart, then organist of the outdoor organ at Balboa Park in San Diego, who was invited to play at the dedicatory concert.

Many years had passed since I last saw Dr. Stewart, and I was startled to see how age had taken its toll. White haired and dignified, he made a venerable appearance at the console, where this meeting took place. Mrs. Cameron also joined us at that moment, evidently seeing Dr. Stewart, her former friend and teacher of the organ, after a lapse of many years. Their greeting was most affectionate, sincere and genuine. This was the last occasion on which I saw Dr. Humphrey J. Stewart. He passed away shortly thereafter.

I was shocked when I heard of Mr. Green's death on September 16, 1933. Mrs. Green then returned to their old home in San Mateo, where I called on her one day to pay my respects. Later, I also learned of her demise. On a later occasion, in passing the old home in San Mateo, a place that recalled many happy and pleasant memories for me, I was sorry to see the structure being razed and leveled to the ground. Time, indeed, is fleeting and brings many changes.

ALL SAINTS EPISCOPAL CHURCH

I remember going with my father, for many years, to a

small church on Waller Street, near Masonic Avenue, called All Saints Episcopal Church. They had a large two manual and Pedal reed organ and we were called upon frequently to tune and adjust it. The reeds would frequently break, and we replaced many of them. The blowing arrangement of this organ was of the feeder type, driven by an electric motor.

In 1915, the church procured an Austin Chorophone two manual pipe organ, Opus 1214, which we installed. The large reed organ was disposed of. I believe it was sold to the Nineteenth Avenue Presbyterian Church, at the corner of 19th Avenue and Irving Street.

The Chorophone organ is a stock organ with a definite designed case. In this instance, the case, although part of the organ, was not finished as it was obscured behind the hinged panels. Evidently being aware of the psychological advantage of seeing a speaker or singer, as well as hearing him, this principle, was applied to the organ and a false, or dummy front, was provided with pipes across the organ chamber opening facing the congregation. This organ, therefore, had the unique distinction of having two complete organ fronts, one visible, the other not. The console is detached. All told, the organ has a pleasing, mellow tone, though held back somewhat in its confined surroundings.

Rev. Farlander was rector of the church at the time the organ was installed, and Miss Phoebe Cole, the faithful and efficient organist. I often think of a remark she made to me one day before the purchase of this particular Chorophone organ was made, when she, with a committee, visited our facoty on Bryant Street, where we had an old 2 manual tracker action pipe organ on display for disposal. During our interview, she remarked that her little parish church, All Saints Episcopal, was the dearest spot on earth to her. It would be wonderful if more people had such an attachment and affection for their church as this young lady unconsciously demonstrated.

Before Rev. Farlander was transferred to another field, thought was already given to enlarging the organ, but I believe that it was under the pastorate of his successor, Rev. Arthur Childs, that we added a set of Deagan chimes and a Vox Humana to the organ. These additions, I was informed, were made possible through the munificence of their devoted organist, Miss Phoebe Cole, and though they did not add more volume to the organ, they did prove very effective in enhancing the beauty of the service and of the music. Rev. Childs passed away in 1940 and with his demise the organist, Miss Cole, sought other fields for her musical endeavors.

With the advent of other Rectors, Rev. Little and Rev. Harris, with other ideas and plans, it was decided to move the organ and console from down below in the sanctuary to a small gallery over the front entrance of the church, where it now stands, concealed behind a gauze screen that apparently satisfies all their needs.

FESTIVAL HALL ORGAN
PANAMA PACIFIC INTERNATIONAL EXPOSITION 1915

During the period of 1912-1913, after the City of San Francisco had again arisen phoenix-like from its ashes and had astounded the world with its undaunted courage, will and determination to re-establish itself, and as the completion of the building of the Panama Canal, linking the two oceans at Panama, was drawing near, energetic and far-seeing San Franciscans conceived the idea of celebrating the rebuilding of San Francisco and the completion of the Panama Canal by holding a World's Fair, an International Exposition. The title selected for the fair was Panama Pacific International Exposition. The date set for the opening was February 21, 1915.

At this time Mr. Fletcher Tilton, a resident of San Francisco and a former salesman for the Murray M. Harris Organ Company of Los Angeles, was the western representative of the Austin Organ Company of Hartford, Conn. Mr. Tilton was a musician and an organist of some ability, a man of pleasant personality and easy approach, a conversationalist par excellence and, with these qualifications, proved himself to be just as efficient and able a salesman. During the period of 1908 to 1929, when he passed away, over 32 Austin organs were sold in this territory alone, through his efforts. Practically all of these were installed by our firm.

In preparing the plans for the Exposition, it was decided that a Festival, or Music Hall, should be among the main or central group of buildings, one suitable for holding indoor concerts, musical pageants, etc. And, it was also decided that a large and suitable pipe organ would be essential, one that would not only serve all needs to which it might be put, but one that would also be a drawing card and a credit to the Exposition. No sooner was this fact determined than steps were immediately taken to procure such an instrument, as time was of the essence. A Music Committee was appointed, consisting of Jacob Levison, Chairman, Wallace Sabin, Humphrey J. Stewart and Otto Fleisner, to draft specifications, draw plans and secure bids for the building and installation of such an organ.

Representatives or agents of the leading organ building firms of the country, in one instance the builder himself, soon arrived in San Francisco, all desirous of securing the coveted contract, using devious means of approach, influence, intrigue and salesmanship to win the prize. Excitement was keen, expectation high, but likewise disappointment acute to the unsuccessful bidders when the information was finally made public that the local representative of the Austin Organ Company of Hartford, Conn., Mr. Robert Fletcher Tilton, had secured the contract to build the organ. The contract was signed in 1914.

It was to be a four manual and Pedal, with echo organ, detached movable console with 114 straight stops, 7,500 pipes, costing the sum of $50,000 installed. It was to be erected in Festival Hall, which proved to be a large cupola-shaped building, specially arranged and accoustically treated for the holding of concerts, recitals, symphonies, etc., and was to be completed for the opening day, which was set for February 21, 1915. I remember well the occasion when I was called to Mr. Tilton's home, where the information that he was the successful bidder was given me. Usually, business appointments were held at his office. This achievement, however, deserved special consideration; therefore, the formal invitation to his home.

He placed before me on a table a huge roll of blueprints, which were those of the organ, and told me to look them over. Then he said, "Do you think you can do it?" I will say that the suddenness and the immensity of the job floored me momentarily, especially when I was made aware of the fact that a penalty of $100 a day was attached to the contract for each day overtime beyond the stipulated contact date for completion of the work. Knowing that the large organ at the St. Louis Purchase Centennial Exposition, in 1904, had never been fully completed, misgivings were not entirely out of order. However, "faint heart never won fair lady", so with a bold front and a determined affirmative reply, I gave my assurance that the organ would be ready for the dedication.

Meanwhile, frequent visits were made to the Exposition Grounds, with an especially watchful eye on the progress being made on the Festival Hall Building. This, we noticed in time, was not too favorable. The time for the opening of the Fair was approaching with lightning speed, or at least it seemed so to us, and our conclusions could not be otherwise than that the installation of the huge organ would be a rush job under trying difficulties, which it actually proved to be.

During October 1914, we received notice that the first carload had left the factory, and that three others would follow shortly thereafter. Tracers were put on the shipments and their progress across the continent constantly checked. Meanwhile, we made all arrangements, possible for the reception of the organ. Our visits to Festival Hall at that time were indeed discouraging. A forest of scaffolding filled the interior of the great dome, and we were informed that it would remain there for a month or two longer. Rough 3 x 12 planking, covered with a foot deep layer of litter and debris, was the uneven floor on which the organ was to be erected. No permanent lighting system was installed. Each contractor had to furnish his own light and pay for it. There were no steps or other access to the organ loft. Temporary roads to the building were removed as the landscaping and the leveling of the ground around the buildings was in progress.

Four huge furniture cars finally arrived in close succession at the Fair site. We had them spotted as close to Festival Hall as possible. However, the distance from the freight cars to Festival Hall was at least the length of a city block and a half, making it necessary for us to hire a team of horses and a flat body truck to move the material to the entrance of Festival Hall. In addition, we had to first lay our own planked way over the freshly graded sand to avoid delay or interruption in our work of installing the organ. All packing cases were numbered and, on removal from Festival Hall, were stored in a warehouse until the termination of the Fair, when they were again to be used in the expeditious removal of the organ.

We began the actual installation of the organ on November 7, 1914. I had the privilege of working only a few days on the organ when I had to leave to install another Austin organ, which had arrived in the meantime, for the Second Church of Christ Scientist of East Portland, Oregon, and a further visit to Spokane and Seattle for some minor work.

In the meantime, my four brothers and a crew of workmen had the greater part of the organ installed. On my return to Festival Hall, the air had just been turned on for the first time - the crucial moment for the organ builder - the first time the living breath is given the instrument. Naturally, there were many ciphers, adjustments to be made, wrong connections to be corrected, etc. The pipes were being installed preparatory to the first tuning.

As the day of opening was coming close, bedlam reigned in the huge building, all contractors striving to complete their particular work on time schedule, each one for himself, with the usual coarse slogan, "to hell with the other fellow."

A word of appreciation must here be given to Mr. Waters, acting superintendent of works under Mr. Connick. This gentleman, with all the multiplicity of untold detail, always reserved a special interest and consideration for us and our work of installing the organ. How one man could carry so much responsiblity and yet remain so pleasant and cheerful was always a wonder to me. However, our fears for his well-being were later fulfilled. Soon after the termination of the fair, he paid the penalty with a premature death.

It was soon made apparent to us, that under the conditions existing, the organ could not be properly tone regulated, voiced and tuned. Therefore, a double shift was arranged. During eight hours of the day we would work on the mechanical parts of the organ, and after quitting time of most of the other workers, when quiet was established, we would proceed through the night and early morning hours with the tuning, etc. About two weeks were spent at this work.

Finally, the day of the opening of the Fair arrived. The magic of Aladdin's Lamp could not have been more sudden and surprising than the work accomplished on the buildings and grounds of the Fair site during the last two weeks before the opening. Where a few days before there had been a deep declivity, there was now a beautiful lake, enclosed in a classicly designed balustrade. Grass plots and lawns seemed to be planted and grown overnight, flowers bloomed as if by magic, and finally at 7:00 a.m. on the morning of February 21, 1915, we called our job completed, removed our overalls and returned to our homes for breakfast, a cleaning up and a change of clothes.

Meanwhile, all San Francisco was surcharged with excitement, life and bustle. All humanity was moving out toward the Marina District, alongside the Golden Gate, where the Fair site was located. Whistles were blowing, horns were tooting, and the populace in a gay and festive mood. We arrived again at Festival Hall in due time for the official opening at 10:30 a.m. A memorable incident occurred at this time, which I shall never forget.

On the stage of Festival Hall, alongside the console of the organ, we had the pleasure of meeting for the first time John T. Austin, one of the proprietors of the Austin Organ Co., who made the trip from Hartford, Conn., especially to be present at this auspicious occasion. Beside Mr. Austin was Mr. Fletcher Tilton, their local representative, my father and his five sons, who had all participated in the erection of the organ. This is the only occasion, in my recollection, where father and we five sons were all present at one time and associated in one undertaking. Mr. Austin and Mr. Tilton complimented and congratulated us on our achievement. We, in turn, complimented them on their successful accomplishments.

Mr. Wallace Sabin, who had been appointed official Exposition organist, was seated at the console. A large chorus and orchestra opening up the Exposition with Handel's memorable Hallelujah Chorus, made a most impressive scene, never to be forgotten.

During the course of the Exposition, arrangements were made for sixty or so of the leading organists of the country to give daily recitals. As one of us brothers was present at every recital, we had occasion to observe the merits, qualifications and renditions of these eminent organists. Most of them were artists of high degree and deserving of the reputation they had gained. Some of them, however, failed dismally in coming up to our expectation due, undoubtedly, to nervousness in playing such a huge organ which, at the time it was built, was the seventh largest in the world, and the fact that they were playing for a critical and usually large audience at a World Fair exhibition.

Among the many who performed was also our local organist Uda Waldrop, whose fame at that time was equal, if not superior, to many of his confreres among the sixty visiting organists who performed. His recital, I believe, was outstanding. For one thing, he was the first organist to perform who had memorized his entire program; being thus relieved of the necessity of closely watching his score, his phrasing and instrumentation were exceptionally well done and his crisp and clean cut playing was remarkable. In fact, this performance was so superior to many previous ones given that the audience, not necessarily his local friends, but consisting of visitors from all over the country, gave him a tremendous ovation, which in our opinion was deserving and well merited.

Another incident may be of interest. It was on the occasion of the visit of the famous French organist and composer, Saint-Saëns of Paris. As previously stated, one of us brothers would be present at every recital for the purpose of stopping and starting the motors, putting the console in place, etc., and to be ready for any emergency that might develop. Aside from hurriedly connecting an extra wire alongside the console cable to replace a broken cable wire, which would cause a silent note, a frequent happening due to the bending of the insufficiently flexible cable, seldom any other unforeseen emergency occurred. However, on this special occasion when Saint Saëns was to conduct a large

augmented chorus with organ accompaniment, with Wallace
Sabin at the console, in one of Saint-Saëns own compositions, just such an unpredictable happening did occur. On
this particular occasion my father, after much persuasion,
had consented to be present in order that we three brothers
could attend some function which we, under no circumstances, wanted to miss. This was, as I recall, the first and
only time he attended. My two sisters were in the chorus and
related their experience as follows:

Festival Hall was packed with people. The chorus was
seated. Wallace Sabin at the console, was all in readiness,
albeit in a nervous tension waiting for the distinguished
composer and organist to begin. Behind the stage at this time
the organ motors had just been turned on, and an unearthly
roar from the organ bellowed forth. Evidently stops were in
an "on" position, by either the stop knobs being drawn,
crescendo or the sforzando pedal being on. My father,
hearing the uproar and seeing evidently nothing wrong at the
console, immediately dashed up to the organ loft, assuming
something had happened to the organ up there. Meanwhile
Mr. Sabin, in his faltering and hesitant speech, tried to
explain to the audience that the trouble was being corrected.
He likewise tried to reassure Saint-Saëns, but his limited
knowledge of the French language and Saint-Saëns inability
to converse in English only increased the tenseness of the
situation. It was then decided to abandon use of the organ
and to move the console from the stage. As some stage hands
began to move the console from its place, the organ
immediately became silent and docile, as it should have been
from the start. With quietude restored, and Sabin at the
console, it did not take long for the concert to begin. Due to
the incident, however, nerves were frayed and on edge and
the rendition did not get off to a good start, and suffered a
collapse shortly after its beginning. A fresh start was made
and the concert progressed satisfactorily from there on. My
two sisters, however, who were present, daughters of an
organ builder, realized the seriousness of the situation and
the unpleasant notoriety this incident would cause, and
concerned for the safety of their father climbing through the
organ, fearing he might stumble into the pipes or fall from a

ladder and do greater harm, were in a state of nervous collapse.

To one conversant with organ construction, especially the Austin console, it will be interesting to know that we found the trouble was caused by the Pedal contacts, which, on the Austin organ, are not directly under the pedal keys, as in most organs, but are permanently placed in the console opposite and independent of the key, but actuated by a lever from the forward end of the pedal key which, when depressed, engages the contact. In this case, the contact due to insufficient clearance had touched and made a circuit. In other words, the flooring of the stage was very uneven and rough, being 3" x 10" planks, and the console being placed in a different position from what it usually was for recital purposes, resulted in raising the back end of the Pedal board, though only a slight bit, yet perhaps enough to bring the forward end of the keys too close to the contacts, thus causing the ciphering. This experience taught us that whenever a movable console is desired, especially one with contacts applied elsewhere than on the key itself, both console and Pedal keys must be anchored firmly on a small platform as one unit, and that the platform should be equipped with castors for movability.

As interesting and exciting as the duration of the Fair was to us, the constant attendance at the organ recitals did become at times boring, depending of course, on who was the recitalist. On one of these occasions, at an evening performance, my younger brother, Erwin, was attnding the organ. Evidently tired from the day's work, instead of rambling around the stage and hall, he took his position inside the bellows, or pressure chamber of the organ, and amused himself reading a book. Sleep overtook him. The recital was long over and the stillness around him finally brought him to the realization that he was still inside of the organ. The motors were hurriedly stopped and a suitable explanation was made to the night watchman for his late departure from Festival Hall.

Indeed, 1915 was an eventful period of my life. Business was rushing, organs were being installed right and left in churches and theatres, and the installation of the Festival

Hall organ, now an accomplished fact, was well deserving of a feather in our cap.

Being in the prime of manhood, it was also logical that one's fancy inclined to other things than the prosaic duties of daily life. Love also had its inning. On May 12, 1915, I had the good fortune of leading my charming bride to the altar, claiming her as my own, where our vows of love and fidelity were pronounced until death do us part. St. Anthony's Church, our parish church, was the scene of the wedding. Josephine Reichmuth, a petite and charming lass became Mrs. Louis J. Schoenstein. Being very pressed for time in keeping up with our work and daily attendance at the Fair, I could not allow myself several weeks off for a honeymoon, so we contented ourselves with the evening of the wedding day at the Fair, and several days afterwards in arranging our new home located in "Southern Heights" overlooking the Mission District of the city.

Toward the close of the Fair, the announcement of the early arrival of the much heralded and famous English organist, Edwin H. Lemare, created quite a stir of anticipation. World War I was then in progress and Edwin H. Lemare, with his family, had to cross the submarine-infested Atlantic. We were forewarned to be prepared to have a severe taskmaster and critic to work for. Our fears, however, were soon allayed. We found Mr. Lemare a very charming gentleman, nevertheless, an artist who knew the organ, and a genius at the console fulfilling all those expectations and predictions of his virtuosity. Lemare was a great organist. True, he had his traits and characteristics and, as all Englishmen, he wanted service and recognition and got it. His recitals became so popular and the attendance was so large that, at great expense in the latter part of the Fair, Festival Hall was remodeled to increase its seating capacity.

Like all things made by mortal man, this wonderful Exposition, excelling all others in beauty, architecture, landscaping and natural setting, came to a close. Most expositions close their accounts on the debit side of the ledger, writing off a loss. This Exposition, however, was an exception. From the profits received on the investment, instead of returning them to the stockholders, they graciously consented to donate their interest to the benefit of the City of San Francisco by erecting the large auditorium in the Civic Center, and deeding it to the City. This building was originally known as Exposition Auditorium, now more commonly called Civic Auditorium. Here provisions were made to house the huge Festival Hall organ. This work was again entrusted to our firm.

After several months work, the organ was re-erected and ready for tuning. Meanwhile, arrangements had been made with Mr. Lemare, who evidently intended to become a permanent resident of San Francisco, and who also aspired to the position of Municipal Organist, to revoice and improve the organ tonally. During his tenure as organist at Festival Hall he had occasion to make observations and suggested certain tonal changes that should be made, especially with reference to its new environment in the large auditorium. When finally installed, these changes were successfully carried out.

Certain stops were returned to the factory for revoicing, others replaced with new stops of a more useful quality. Mr. King, voicer of the Austin factory, came out to San Francisco and, in connection with Mr. Lemare, did the final voicing and tuning. It was our unanimous verdict that the finished product was an improvement over the organ as orginally installed in Festival Hall.

The console at this time was located on the organ loft, immediately in front of the organ. Here I must record an episode that caused us great heartache. Being exceedingly proud of our work of originally installing the organ in Festival Hall, and of removing it and again erecting it in the Civic Auditorium, it was our hope and anticipation that thereafter this organ of our pride and affection would logically be entrusted to our care and maintenance. However, this was not to be the case. Mr. Lemare looked out for his own interest and succeeded in securing a contract from the city to give regular recitals as city organist for the fabulous sum of $10,000 a year, probably the greatest salary ever paid an organist anywhere. When we came to solicit the regular maintenance of the organ from the city fathers, we learned to our great disappointment and chagrin, that a Mr. Gallagher, a gentleman we had engaged to assist us with the installation of the organ, had secured the contract. We had been asked to hire him by Mr. Tilton, stating that he was from back East and an electrician, formerly in the employ of General Electric Company. We found out subsequently, however, that he was also an experienced employee of the Austin Organ Company. He serviced the organ for several years and eventually established himself in the organ maintenance business, which, however, did not survive for long.

Public recitals were held at the Exposition Auditorium on Wednesday and Sunday afternoons and proved very successful. Mr. Lemare's high ideals of classic and legitimate organ music, however, were not fully in accord with those of a fickle public, which wanted a lighter and more frivolous menu. Ideals clashed — discord and dissension made their appearance. Supervisor Emmet Hayden, chairman of the Music Committee of the Board of Supervisors, and Edwin Lemare were at loggerheads. The breach grew wider and discontent and public criticism were rampant. Lemare's princely salary of $10,000 was finally reduced to $8,750 a year. (Quoted in The Diapason, November 1, 1920, issue.) At the lowest ebb of his popularity and shortly before terminating his contract with the city, prior to accepting a new position as municipal organist at Portland, Maine, Lemare called me to his home, to my great surprise, to do a little work or favor for him. In the intimacy of his confession of his woes at City Hall, he confided to me that he did not have a single friend there and intimated that, after all, if he had been true to us he might have been better off.

Soon after Lemare's departure we received the maintenance of the organ through, no doubt, the interest and solicitation of Supervisor Emmet Hayden who, being concerned and responsible for the recitals and upkeep of the organ, noted that a change had to be made. Mr. Gallagher returned to the East and died a few years later, according to reports received from his former associates.

Mr. Lemare later took a position as municipal organist at the auditorium at Chattanooga, Tennessee. In the year 1921, Lemare made a return visit to San Francisco to play on his favorite organ at the Civic Auditorium once again. Much publicity was given the recital. Billboards emblazoning the name of Lemare, now famous in San Francisco, were displayed conspicuously throughout the city. An audience of from ten to twelve thousand people packed the auditorium. This, undoubtedly, was the largest organ recital audience that had ever assembled anywhere. This was Lemare's own statement after the recital, in which we fully concurred. Lemare was at his best; he had vindicated himself.

I recall that during the performance a cipher occurred. Lemare knowing, however, that we were present to take care of just such an emergency, nonchalantly stepped of the organ bench and in his typical English drawl used the intermission to tell the audience a little mishap had occurred to the organ, and that while it was being corrected he would make some comments and explain some of the numbers yet to be played. This was a habit of his, which he assiduously carried out at his recitals. Personally, we would have preferred that he continue with his playing, as the cipher would have been quickly eradicated.

About a year or so later, we also had a visit from the treasurer of the Austin company, Mr. Spencer Camp, a gentleman of high caliber. He was interested in seeing many of the Austin installations, and invited our candid opinion on matters relating to the interests of the Austin Organ Company. Aside from being the gentleman who signed and issued our pay checks, he also proved himself to be a competent and versatile organist, demonstrating to us his abilities on many of the Austin organs and proving his faith and interest in the organ he so successfully represented. His visit will be especially remembered by me owing to an invitation I extended him to visit our new home, which he graciously accepted. On this occasion I had the privilege of proudly showing him my first-born son, Lawrence, then a small infant peacefully sleeping in his crib. His quotation on gazing at him and referring to him as a "muted Viol", I thought was typical and symbolic of a true organ man.

Shortly after we secured the maintenance of the Exposition organ, we were authorized to remove the console from its fixed position on the organ loft and place it on a movable platform on the Auditorium floor, somewhat similar to the original arrangement at Festival Hall. This we did and applied a new flexible cable of 125 feet in length, with a coupling, so that the console could be entirely detached when occasion required. It might be of interest to state here that the cable was now the third cable that had been applied to the organ. The original cable from the factory was too solidly wound, and from the constant bending in pulling the console on and off the stage at the Exposition, the wire broke frequently, with the result that at the termination of the Fair, we had as many auxiliary wires temporarily attached and strung along the cable as there were in the original cable. When the organ was installed at the Auditorium, we replaced the original cable with a new one of shorter length. When we moved the console from the organ loft to the present movable platform on the Auditorium floor, we provided the 125 foot specially designed flexible cable, which has given wonderful service to the present day.

The movable console, built 49 years ago on the direct electric system, then in its infancy, with no air in the console whatsoever, was an achievement of the first rank. True, the setting of the combinations was not always infallible, and not being on the capture system, the console received some unfavorable criticism, to the effect that it could not be depended upon. However, about ten years ago when it became necessary to remodel the greater part of the console, due to a fire which had occurred in it, we replaced a lot of the mechanism with Austin's improved adjustable combination action, which has since functioned very satisfactorily. It is still, however, the ordinary adjustable type, pressing and holding the combination piston and setting the desired stop knob on or off.

The fire above mentioned had a peculiar origin. During period of non-use the console was detached from the cable, and the whole covered with a canvas covering and shoved to an unused corner of the Auditorium. For years not a sign of vermin was discernible in the Auditorium organ. However, when the plan for using the Auditorium more extensively than only for concerts and conventions was introduced, and the holding of fights, basket ball and other athletic events was permitted, we noticed signs of mice in the console. Food, chewing gum, peanuts and the like were left lying on the floor through the night until the janitors came in next morning to clean up, and we often found peanuts, chewing gum, and especially tinfoil carried by the mice into the quiet and undisturbed recesses of the console. On one occasion when the organ was to be used, my brother, Erwin reported for duty. The organist, Paul Carson, waited at the console, from which the canvas covering had not yet been removed. While my brother ascended to the organ loft to throw on the motor switches, which were still located in their former position on the loft in the wall formerly behind the console, to the consternation of the organist and my brother who, by that time had reached the Auditorium floor, a cloud of smoke was emerging from under the console covering. My brother made a hasty return to the organ loft to pull the switches, while the organist removed the canvas covering. My brother secured a fire extinguisher, some panels on the console were quickly opened and the fire extinguisher brought into play. Care was taken to use it judiciously and only where the fire was actually burning. On examination after the fire had been put out, it was discovered that it had started on the right side of the console, that the numerous wooden stop knob traces were consumed, and that the cause was a short circuit due to tinfoil wrappings having been placed by mice over two of the main leads which, although securely and permanently fastened, were exposed on the console bed under the stop traces. This damage was repaired. With the improvements made to the combination action, precautions were also taken to make it impossible for any mice to enter the interior of the console, either between the Pedal keys, the swell shoes, or any other opening, unless a hole were gnawed through the hard walnut case.

After Edwin Lemare's term as municipal organist came to a close, the local organist, Uda Waldrop, received the title of municipal organist. That was about the sum and substance of his appointment. However, he played at numerous functions, conventions, symphonies, etc., but a regular schedule of organ recitals was a thing of the past. Other organists also performed, depending on the occasion and the organist demanded by the organization putting on the program.

Among these events were, "The Hound of Heaven", Ben Moore at the organ; "The Miracle Play", when the organ was extensively used, the company having brought their own organist; the many national religious conventions, etc. However, some celebrities were specially featured by the San Francisco Art Commission, among these being Jos. Bonnet of Paris, Courboin, Dupre, Hollins, and Ramin.

Alfred Hollins, the blind Scottish organist, deserves a little special mention. Usually, on the arrival of some visiting organist we would explain the layout of the console and describe its functioning with regard to setting of combinations, etc. This advice is usually sought, regardless of former experience with many types of consoles. In Hollins' case, however, he being blind, we gave him, or thought we should give him, special consideration. After guiding his hand over the various divisions of stops, knobs and couplers, and stating their names, and directing his feet to the position of swell blinds, crescendo pedal, sforzando, and the many pedal tongues, reversible couplers, etc., under the manuals, all set and ready to play, he inquired of me hurriedly where the Great to Pedal coupler knob was. Although I was supposed to be familiar with the layout of the console, I had to look diligently for the desired knob. He, however, recalled the location and drew it before I could locate it.

An incident in Ramin's recital also bears repetition. Ramin arrived a day or so before his scheduled recital and applied himself most assiduously to the organ. The instrument received a merciless beating as his numbers seemed to favor the heavy, pompous style. His rehearsals passed off without event. On the night of the performance, however, before a crowded auditorium, in the latter part of the recital, I was shocked to hear a blasting, booming Tuba Magna, the loudest reed in the organ, on 25" pressure, bellowing out. I literally flew up to the organ loft, and recognizing from its sonority that it was the loud reed set, ascended immediately the tall ladder to the top of the organ where this stop is located, and soon hauled out the disturbing pipe. From behind the pipes I heard a loud applause from the audience, undoubtedly pleased that the recital could proceed. I, likewise, was elated that the trouble was so soon checked. I began descending the ladder, and Ramin resumed his number, but no sooner had he played a few chords when an unearthly rush of air made itself heard throughout the Auditorium. I do not know if Ramin or the audience knew what had happened, but it was the same note, the pipe which I had removed from its hole in the chest, and which now was silent tonally, was much alive due to the rushing of the high air pressure through the open pipe hole. Hurriedly shoving my handkerchief into the hole and placing the heavy pipe on top of it temporarily corrected this trouble.

With all credit to the City of San Francisco, I must say that the city never neglected the care and maintenance of its splendid organ. Although not now used as extensively as it should be, it is always kept in the best of tune and working condition by our firm, and our service contract is faithfully carried out by us for this purpose. May this organ, a gem in disguise, an asset to the city, once more come to the forefront as an entertaining, educational and cultural feature of our beloved city.

A $20,000,000.00 bond issue was voted on in 1962 and approved by the citizens of San Francisco to rehabilitate, reconstruct and modernize its Civic Auditorium. The organ will then, after 49 years, also receive a refurbishing, a thorough cleaning, releathering of all pneumatics, the furnishing of a new, modern console and the relocation of the Echo Organ, due to a new permanent ceiling being installed in the Auditorium. Tonally, we understand, the organ will not be altered, for which fact we will be very thankful, that we have at least one prominent organ remaining which is a true sample of the American Art of Organ Building and not an imitation of some European or Boroque instrument.

The following is the original specification of the organ when installed in the Panama Pacific International Exposition in 1915:

GREAT ORGAN

Compass CC to C4 — 61 notes.

1	Double Open Diapason	16'
2	Bourdon	16'
3	Open Diapason (1 large)	8'
4	Open Diapason (2 med.)	8'
5	Open Diapason (3 small)	8'
6	Viole de Gambe	8'
7	Dulciana	8'
8	Gemshorn	8'
9	Stopped Diapason	8'
10	Philomela	8'
11	Harmonic Flute	8'
12	Octave	4'
13	Gambette	4'
14	Flute Harmonique	4'
15	Twelfth	2-2/3'
16	Fifteenth	2'
17	Mixture 4 and 5 ranks.	
18	Double Trumpet	16'
19	Posaune	8'
20	French Trumpet	8'
21	Clarion	4'
22	Sesquialtra, 3 ranks	
23	Cathedral Chimes	

Swell to Great
Swell to Great Sub.
Swell to Great Octave
Choir to Great
Choir to Great Sub.
Choir to Great Octave
Solo and Echo to Great
Solo and Echo to Great Octave
Eight adjustable composition pistons
to control Great stops

SWELL ORGAN

1	Bourdon	16'
2	Double Dulciana	16'
3	Open Diapason (large)	8'
4	Open Diapason (small)	8'
5	Viole d'Orchestre	8'
6	Salicional	8'
7	Aeoline	8'
8	Voix Celeste	8'
9	Clarabella	8'
10	Spitzfloete	8'
11	Lieblich Gedeckt	8'
12	Principal	4'
13	Violina	4'
14	Flute Harmonique	4'
15	Wald Floete	4'
16	Piccolo Harmonique	2'
17	Mixture, 4 and 5 ranks.	
18	Contra Posaune	16'
19	Contra Fagotto	16'
20	Cornopean	8'
21	Oboe	8'
22	Harmonic Trumpet	8'
23	Clarion	4'
24	Vox Humana	8'
25	Unda Maris	8'

Tremulant
Swell Sub.
Swell Unison off.
Swell Octave
Solo and Echo to Swell
Eight adjustable composition pistons
to control Swell stops.

CHOIR ORGAN

1	Contra Gamba	16'
2	Open Diapason	8'
3	Gamba	8'
4	Concert Flute	8'
5	Hohl Floete	8'
6	Flauto Dolce	8'
7	Quintadena	8'
8	Dulciana	8'
9	Flute Celeste	8'
10	Octave	4'
11	Flute Harmonique	4'
12	Suabe Flute	4'
13	Harmonic Piccolo	2'
14	Dolce Cornet (3 ranks)	
15	Harmonic Trumpet	8'
16	Clarionet	8'
17	Cor Anglais	8'
18	Celesta	

Tremulant
Choir Sub.
Choir Unison off.
Choir Octave
Swell to Choir
Swell to Choir Sub.
Swell to Choir Octave
Solo and Echo to Choir
Solo and Echo to Choir Sub.
Solo and Echo to Choir Octave.
Eight adjustable composition pistons
　　to control Choir stops.
Echo organ also playable on choir manual by duplex action.

SOLO ORGAN

1	Tuba Magna	8'
2	Tuba Marabilis	8'
3	Tuba Clarion	4'

4	Viole d'Orchestre	8'
5	Viole Celeste	8'
6	Concert Flute	8'
7	Harmonic Flute	4'
8	Harmonic Piccolo	2'
9	Dolce	8'
10	French Horn	8'
11	Orchestral Oboe	8'
12	Corno di Bassetto	8'
13	Vox Humana	8'
14	Harmonic Trumpet	8'
15	Flugel Horn	8'
	Tremulant	

ECHO ORGAN

1	Lieblich Bourdon	16'
2	Small Diapason	8'
3	Gamba	8'
4	Dolce	8'
5	Cor de Nuit	8'
6	Chimney Flute	8'
7	Unda Maris	8'
8	Plauto Dolce	4'
	Solo and Echo Octave	
	Great to Solo and Echo	
	Solo "on", Echo "off"	
	Echo "on", Solo "off"	
	Solo and Echo "on"	
	Choir "on", Echo "off"	
9	Vox Humana	8'
10	Cathedral Chimes	
	Tremulant	

Echo organ stops are playable also from
Choir manual by duplex action.
Solo and Echo Sub.
Solo and Echo Unison off.
Echo "on", Choir "off"
Choir and Echo "on"

Eight adjustable composition pistons
to control Solo and Echo Stops.

PEDAL ORGAN

1	Gravissima, resultant	64'
2	Double Open Diapason	32'
3	Contra Violone	32'
4	Open Diapason	16'
5	Open Diapason	16'
6	Open Diapason	16'
7	Violone	16'
8	Dulciana	16'
9	Bourdon	16'
10	Lieblich Bourdon	16'
11	Gross Quint	10-3/8'
12	Flauto Dolce	8'
13	Gross Flute	8'
14	Octave Dulciana	8'
15	Violoncello	8'
16	Octave Flute	4'
17	Contra Bombarde	32'
18	Trombone	16'
19	Tuba	16'
20	Octave Trombone	8'
21	Posaune	16'

Great to Pedal
Swell to Pedal
Swell to Pedal Octave
Choir to Pedal
Solo and Echo to Pedal
Solo and Echo to Pedal Octave
Pedal Super Octave
Choir to Pedal Octave
The organ is voiced on 5-10-15 and 25
inches wind pressures

Six adjustable composition Pedals to control Pedal organ

Eight composition pedals duplicating the eight general pistons over upper manual

Four zero pistons affecting Swell, Choir, Great and Solo

Eight general pistons over upper manual affecting the entire organ including couplers, Adjustable

One zero piston over upper manual affecting the entire organ

ACCESSORY

Balanced Crescendo Pedal, adjustable, not moving registers

Balanced Swell Pedal

Balanced Choir Pedal

Balanced Solo and Echo Pedal

Great to Pedal, reversible

Solo to Pedal, reversible

Solo to Great, reversible

Sforzando Pedal

ILLINOIS BUILDING, P.P.I.E.

An excellent feature of the Panama Pacific International Exposition was the section devoted to buildings representing the forty-eight States of the Union.

As I recall the Illinois State Building, it was a rather large two or three story structure. Of special interest in the building was the Lincoln Memorial Museum, featuring Illinois' illustrious son, Abraham Lincoln.

The building had a two manual and Pedal, pneumatic organ of about 14 stops, and was built by the Hinners Organ Company of Pekin, Illinois. If I am not mistaken, our firm was asked to install this organ, but we reluctanctly had to refuse this offer as all our time and available resources were taken up with the installation of the large 114 stop Austin organ in Festival Hall, for which we had a contract with a severe penalty if it was not completed in time for the opening day of the Fair. I believe a representative of the Hinners factory finally installed it, and we later serviced it during the course of the Fair. Dr. Maurice O'Connell gave regular daily recitals on it.

The tonal qualities of the organ were unusually good. This was the largest Hinners pipe organ I had heard, and it certainly was a credit to its builders. I believe we removed the organ after the close of the Fair and shipped it back to the Hinners factory at Pekin, Illinois. Eventually, it was installed in St. Mary's Roman Catholic Church in Colorado Springs, Colorado.

SOUTHERN PACIFIC BUILDING, P.P.I.E.

One of the first buildings to be completed and occupied at the Fair was the Southern Pacific Building. It had a Kimball, 2 manual, pneumatic pipe organ, which was purchased through the Eilers Music Company in San Francisco. I believe the installation work was done by my brother, Leo. Concerts and performances were given, but not of a pretentious nature. After the close of the Fair, the organ found an abode in the T. & D. Theatre in Berkeley. I believe we later removed it from this theatre to make room for a large, rebuilt Robert-Morton organ.

We then installed it in the store of Turner and Dahnken, on Golden Gate avenue, near Leavenworth Street, where we applied an electric action to it and made the console detached. It was finally sold by Turner and Dahnken to St. Anne's Church in the Sunset District. This installation was done by Charles Geschoeff, then in the employ of Turner and Dahnken. We later acquired the regular servicing of the organ, and when the new basilica was built, we moved the organ to the new church where it has been giving excellent service ever since.

LIBERAL ARTS BUILDING, P.P.I.E.
American Steel and Wire Company Exhibit

One of the outstanding organs on display at the Panama

Pacific International Exposition was that of the American Steel and Wire Company in their exhibit in the Liberal Arts Building. It was a Wurlitzer-Hope-Jones organ, style 3, (7 ranks) shipped from the factory January 16, 1915. I do not know by whom this organ was installed, but I recall visiting the exhibit and listening to the very able organist, Mr. Spieler, who was engaged to play and demonstrate it.

On looking over the instrument I was surprised at the unusual type of construction. The unified chest, each pipe with its own magnet and primary, the numerous switches and couplers for the many unifications, the relay actions behind glass panels, all the pipes being rather congested, confined Swell boxes, the horseshoe console, the colored tablets the powerful, high pressured tones emanating from the effective swell boxes all seemed so new and different from the usual electric pneumatic organs I was familiar with.

This organ attracted considerable interest and was viewed by great numbers of visitors to the Fair. Its recitals were well advertised and the display of iron and steel parts, wire and the many other materials used in the construction of the organ were advantageously arranged so as to make this exhibit not only interesting, but of educational value as well.

After the Fair, the organ was removed and shipped to the factory, and re-sold, as Opus #67, to the Majestic Theatre, in Reno, Nevada, 12/ 21/18. In later years it was again brought to San Francisco and we were engaged to erect it in the Tivoli Theatre on Eddy Street. It was to be played in conjunction with a Kimball organ. Both organs were to be played at times simultaneously by two different organists. Mr. Gordon Bretland was the popular organist there at the time. Later both organs were removed to make room for a large Robert-Morton organ.

I do not recall what became of the Kimball organ, but the Wurlitzer organ that originally was installed in the American Steel and Wire Company's exhibit at the Fair, found its final resting place in the Mission Theatre at San Jose, California.

CREATION CONCESSION, P.P.I.E.

Another organ put to good use at the Fair was a Kimball organ used at the "Creation" concession. This scenic spectacle and stage presentation depicting the creation of the world, was awe inspiring, majestic and impressive. I recall the stentorian voice of the Creator calling out, "Let there be light," and from the gloom, darkness and chaos the radiant dawn of day emerged, ever brighter and more glorious to its zenith of beauty and grandeur. The organ music played continuously as an accompaniment and background to the majestic voice of the Creator, gave a reverent and solemn atmosphere to the whole scene, such as no other instrument or orchestra could have produced.

I did not have an opportunity to inspect this organ. After the Fair, it was moved, I was told, to the American Theatre in Oakland, where it was later displaced by a Robert-Morton organ. It was then installed in the Midgley home in Oakland where it was in use for a number of years. In 1943 we moved this organ from the Midgley residence and installed it in the Christian Brothers Novitiate at Mont La Salle, Napa, California, where it gave excellent service.

SECOND CHURCH OF CHRIST SCIENTIST

Second Church of Christ Scientist, as the name implies, was the second church of that denomination founded in San Francisco. Our first connection with the church occurred when they were located temporarily in the National Hall on Mission Street, near Sixteenth, during the year 1916.

During the course of the Panama Pacific International Exposition, the Hall Organ Company of West Haven, Conn., had one of its pipe organs on exhibit in the Liberal Arts Building. It was erected in the building by a Mr. Thompson. I was so well impressed with the neatness and high class finish and material of the interior of the organ, as well as with its smooth and pleasing tone, that I asked their representative, confidentially, if special care and attention had not been given this organ, due to the fact that it was an exhibit organ, or if all their organs were finished with the same high standard of perfection. He assured me that they were, and that the organ on exhibit was a true sample of their standard product. This in later years proved to be the fact, when several of their organs were sold out here.

At the close of the Fair, Second Church of Christ Scientist bought this organ. We installed it in the National Hall, where it remained for some time. Meanwhile, plans were being made for the new permanent church. A site was secured on the southeast corner of Dolores and Cumberland Streets, opposite the beautiful Mission Park, and in 1917 an imposing structure was standing there, crowned with a cupola, a landmark throughout the Mission District. In the new church, the pleasing front case of the organ and the display pipes were not seen as the organ in its entirety was placed behind a screen. The console, formerly attached to the organ, was now detached and placed to the left of the rostrum.

In later years it was placed in front in the center of the rostrum, on the auditorium floor, the organist now hearing the organ the same as the congregation does.

Mrs. Lizzie Spink, a most pleasant and agreeable lady and an excellent musician, was organist for many years, but has since passed away.

FOURTH CHURCH OF CHRIST SCIENTIST

The Fourth Church of Christ Scientist, located at Clement Street and Funston Avenue, in the Richmond District, put up a substantial edifice in 1915. They contracted for a three manual Kimball organ. I believe Mr. Gus Edwards installed this organ. As is customary in most Christian Science churches, the organ chambers are placed behind a grill. Originally only the swell and choir manuals were enclosed. In 1930, during the period when Philip Shinhan was organist, we received a contract from the church to make certain additions to the organ, to change several stops and to enclose the great division also in a swell box, thereby making the entire organ expressive. These additions and changes proved quite successful.

Mr. Shinhan was a most agreeable and interesting character, tall, lanky, with a foreign accent, most likely a Hollander. He was a most efficient and thorough organist, notwithstanding that he had put in many years at the consoles of theatre organs. I recall especially that he presided at the large Robert-Morton organ at the Liberty Theatre in Fresno. His limbs and frame were so large that he boasted of easily spanning twelve notes on the keyboard. A necessary part of his equipment at the organ was an auxiliary organ seat of about eighteen inches in width, which he would attach to the bench, giving him a more solid foundation. Mr. Shinhan, I believe, returned to Europe, and we have never had the pleasure of seeing him since.

ST. JOHN'S LUTHERAN CHURCH

In the heart of the Mission District, in close proximity to one another, are three Protestant churches. Grace United Church at 21st and Capp Streets, Trinity Center at 23rd and Capp Streets, and midway between, on 22nd Street, between Van Ness Avenue South and Capp Street, St. John's Lutheran Church.

It is a Gothic frame structure, substantially built, with the parsonage alongside. The St. John's Lutheran School has always been one of its proud accomplishments. Originally, the church catered to the German Lutheran residents of this part of the city and held its services in the German language, but like all the German speaking churches of the city, both Catholic and Protestant, this feature has gradually been eliminated.

I believe St. John's Lutheran Church at first had only a harmonium. In 1915 it secured its first pipe organ. It was built by Louis Schoen at his home on 26th Street, between Harrison Street and Treat Avenue. I recall at one time being invited by his father to see it, as it was installed in one of the rear rooms. Later he sold this organ to St. John's Lutheran Church. Considering that Mr. Schoen was not a professional organ builder, he certainly built an organ that was a credit to him. It was a two manual and Pedal tracker action organ, with attached console, and had 13 speaking stops. It had an oak case with two bays or towers containing the large 8' Diapasons. The front pipes were painted a pale blue. The organ made a good appearance upon the rear gallery of the church, and tonally was pleasing and adequate. Mr. Gruber, the school teacher, was organist for many years.

In time something more modern was desired, and a contract was made with the Moeller Organ Company of Hagerstown, Maryland, for a large modern instrument. My brother Leo, who at the time was the representative of the Moeller Company in this territory, made the sale and also installed the new organ, assisted by his son, Leo, Jr.

Through our efforts, the old organ was sold to The Albertinum, at Ukiah, California, a boys school conducted by the Dominican Sisters of the Holy Rosary. Mother Seraphin was the superior at the time, and Mr. Peter Derrick the director of the school. He also functioned as organist. We erected the organ in the chapel of the institution. Prior to moving it to Ukiah, necessary repairs were made and we also reduced the height of the case so that it would fit properly into the lower space available in the chapel. The organ proved to be very satisfactory in its new location and environment, and was a pleasure and delight for the nuns and children of the school.

After the Sisters of the Albertinum built a new modern chapel, the organ was removed and stored temporarily until the new chapel was erected on the same site. In 1931, the organ was re-erected in an elevated loft, placed behind a grill. The action was electrified and a new console provided, placed on the church floor level.

MISSION MASONIC TEMPLE ASSOCIATION

I remember even before the days of the fire of 1906 there stood a substantial brick building on the west side of Mission Street, between 22nd and 23rd Streets. The lower floor was occupied by the morticians, Bunker and Lunt. Mission Street was not always the business street it is now. Valencia Street had more claim to being the main business thoroughfare in the Mission District. The fire and earthquake, however, changed that overnight. The recovery of Valencia Street was retarded for a long time on account of the severe subsidence of the street level for several blocks between 17th and 20th Streets, caused by the earthquake, which had first to be filled in and brought up to grade again, and the subsequent conversion of the old Valencia cable car line to the electric system. Meanwhile, Mission Street, especially at 22nd and Mission, soon became the hub of business activity. The Bunker and Lunt establishment was not far distant from this corner, and undoubtedly found it desirable to locate in a new and more quiet neighborhood. The Mission Masonic Temple Association converted the lower floor to a more profitable use, by arranging the vacated space for retail stores.

The upper floor of the brick building was then already occupied by the Mission Masonic Temple Association in 1915, I was told by Mr. Fletcher Tilton, representative of the Austin Organ Company, that he had sold the organization a "Chorophone" Austin pipe organ Opus #672 and that we were to install it on its arrival. Heretofore, we had installed many of the Austin organs, which were all custom made. This organ, however, a new product of the Austin Company was to introduce a new venture on their part of also supplying the trade with a "stock" or ready made organ. We looked forward with much expectation to its arrival.

We found it to be a small two manual and Pedal electric pneumatic organ of four sets of pipes, unified and duplexed, applied with their patented Universal air chest, and a detached console. Each pipe is provided with its individual magnet and valve. The Open Diapason is played only from the Great manual and Pedal at 8' and 4' pitches. The Stopped Diapason unit is unified at 16' — 4' — 2-2/3' — and 2 ft., which also furnishes the wood stop for the Pedal and provides a pleasing mellow flute tone to the organ. The Viol Orchestra, a narrow, keen string tone unified at 16' - 8' - 4' pitches, gives in combination with the wood stop some wonderful tone coloring, and provides the organ with the needed brilliancy. The Dulciana unified at 8' - 4' pitches is serviceable mostly for accompanying the other stops and for soft playing. All these units are played from the Pedal also, and being duplexed, can be played from the Swell and Great manual as well, making the limited number of stops available as versatile as possible. The latter stops are, furthermore, in the Swell box, or under expression. Outside of the box is the Open Diapason and Octave 4 Unit, of which the front pipes are part and which are playable only from the Great manual. There are no dummy display pipes in these organs.

The available pressure for tone and action is 6", giving the organ a definite punch and an astoundingly snappy attack and repetition at the keyboard, a prerequisite of a well designed and well built organ. I must say that I know of no other organ at this time that exceeds this particular instrument in this attribute. I have on more than one occasion referred to its attack and response at the keys as, being "as quick as greased lightning."

Mr. Robert Burness was organist of this Lodge for a period of 57 years and served continuously until his death in 1945, passing away at the age of 80 years.

I also recall the old sexton in charge of the hall, whom we called Gus, with his sarcasm and smile. I had been married but a short time when we were installing this organ, and my charming young bride would drop in occasionally to see me at work. We both enjoyed these visits and Gus would help to make them still more pleasant for us. In later years he often inquired how the little bride was getting on. Finally he retired from his customary haunts to the Old People's Masonic Home at Decoto, California.

FIFTH CHURCH OF CHRIST, SCIENTIST

Fifth Church of Christ Scientist began its career in much the same way that the Second Church did, that is, they rented the Native Sons Hall on Mason Street. At first they had a large two manual Estey reed organ, with electric blower, to accompany the congregation during services. Here we met their able and most charming organist, Mr. Evelyn Lewis. He was a musician of rare ability, and a man of distinctive personality, in physique and bearing a second "Herman the Great", the magician. We enjoyed his good will and friendship until he was called by an untimely death.

With this fine musician, it was logical that they should want a better instrument for him to play upon. Again the Fifth Church followed the example set by the Second Church of Christ Scientist and procured an organ Opus #245 from the Hall Organ Company of West Haven, Connecticut in 1918. This was a three manual organ of about 18 stops. It was a divided organ placed on either side of the gallery alongside the stage. The oak case was of pleasing design, with decorated pipes, and the organ presented a fine appearance. My brother, Otto did most of the installation work, but before its completion he was called into the army to serve in the First World War. I completed the organ for the dedication.

Property was bought nearby, on the north side of O'Farrell Street, at the corner of Shannon Street. Here a stately building was erected and ample room was provided for the organ in three chambers concealed by grills extending across the entire north end of the building. By this method of having separate chambers, the whole organ was under expression, which made it more versatile than before. In addition, we added several new stops. One was a new Diapason. In the console some changes were also made, including a master swell arrangement to work all the blinds from one shoe.

The organ in the new edifice sounded very well and we received words of commendation for our job of removing and re-installing and enlarging the organ. With a new church and practically a new organ, and with the loss of their former organist, the late Evelyn Lewis, the services of Theodore Strong, a recent arrival in the City and a man of ability and active in musical circles, were secured.

Mr. Strong appreciated the organ very much, but found objection to the functioning of the console, considering it rather noisy, and especially objecting to the combination action as being uncertain and unreliable. It worked by direct electric action, and the large master solenoid used was somewhat noisy.

Mr. Strong prevailed upon the Church to secure a new console. My brother, Leo was at this time western representative of the Moller Organ Company of Hagerstown, Maryland, and having had some satisfactory business dealings with him previously, they awarded the contract to Moller.

After the Fifth Church vacated the Native Sons Hall and removed their Hall organ to their new edifice, the Seventh Church of Christ Scientist took over the Native Sons Auditorium for their use on Wednesdays and Sundays. They procured a three manual Moeller organ, formerly in use at one of our local theatres. Eventually, this Church also abandoned the use of the Native Sons Hall for their services, and the organ was finally disposed of and erected in the Native Sons Hall of Sacramento, California, where it is now in use.

ST. ANNE'S CHURCH

The Basilica of St. Anne of the Sunset is one of the well known churches of San Francisco. It is located at Funston Avenue and Judah Street in the Sunset District. It is a large concrete edifice, with imposing square towers. Its facade is beautifully ornamented with bas-relief, the work of one of the Dominican nuns of Mission San Jose. At this church the annual pilgrimage and novena to "Good St. Anne" are held, which are attended by thousands from all over the State. The first, original church was a frame structure and was located on the corner of Funston Avenue and Irving Street. Right Reverend William G. O'Mahoney was the popular and energetic pastor.

About 1917, Father O'Mahoney secured a two manual and Pedal Kimball organ of 8 stops from the Tivoli Theatre on Eddy Street, which he purchased from the Turner & Dahnken Circuit who, at that time, had their offices on Golden Gate and Leavenworth Streets. We modernized and electrified the organ and made the console attached.

In making plans for the new Basilica, provision was made for proper organ chambers, and these were built to provide for a large four manual organ suitable for the size and requirements of the Basilica. It was hoped to install such an organ at some later time. Undoubtedly, the depression and a heavy debt have to this time prevented the carrying out of this plan. However, we moved the Kimball organ from the old church and erected it in the Basilica in the center of the upper gallery, and made the console detached, locating it on the left side of the gallery. It is remarkable how powerful and sonorous this small organ sounds. In fact, it is so satisfactory that the need for a large and more imposing organ seems very remote these days.

Rt. Rev. Msgr. William G. O'Mahoney did not live to witness the dedication of the great Basilica for which he worked and planned so untiringly. He passed away in 1936. Rev. Msgr. Patrick G. Moriarity was appointed his successor.

ST. PAUL'S
GERMAN EVANGELICAL LUTHERAN CHURCH
(now - Orthodox Russian Congregation of Nicolas Cathedral)

On Howard Street, between 10th and 11th Streets, almost in the shadow of St. Joseph's Catholic Church, nestled in a little edifice formerly called St. Paul's German Evangelical Lutheran Church. Rev. Karl Struckmeier, a ruddy-faced, white haired, venerable looking gentleman, was the pastor for many years.

In 1920, they purchased a two manual and Pedal Hinners organ, tracker action, with about 7 stops. My father installed this organ with the assistance of my younger brother, Erwin. I believe this was one of the last organs erected under my father's direct personal supervision. This Hinners organ, as well as all Hinners organs, can justly be proud of their excellent tone, especially their unexcelled Diapasons.

After a number of years a consolidation was effected with the Bethel Evangelical Reformed Lutheran Church, located at 15th and Church Streets. The Howard Street church was vacated and was later occupied by a schismatic Hungarian Catholic church, and still more recently by a Greek congregation. The Bethel Evangelical Reformed Church was lacking a pipe organ, so the Hinners organ from the Howard Street church was moved there.

A friendly soul of this congregation was the treasurer, Mr. Shurman. Several musicians have held the position of organist at the church, among them Mrs. Jarboe. This small Bethel Evangelical Reformed Church changed again from its former status, by being taken over by a Spiritualist Congregation and, eventually, by the present Orthodox Russian Congregation of St. Nicolas Cathedral in 1960, under the pastorate of Fr. Mark. As the Russian Orthodox do not use any instruments in their Liturgy, the organ was sold to some local music house.

ST. CECILIA'S CHURCH

One of the early parishes to be established in the Sunset District was St. Cecilia's. It was founded in 1917, and the church, a small frame building, was originally located at Taraval Street and Twelfth Avenue. The district was one of the rapidly developing sections of San Francisco. It seemed particularly to attract newly married couples who moved out there in large numbers to build and establish their homes. It undoubtedly was a desirable district to live in, at least as far as increasing realty values were concerned, with its many new modern homes and a class of residents comprising our best people. This district is also noted for its exhilarating pure air coming directly off the mighty Pacific; also for the generous amount of fog it receives during the summer months. In this district my two younger brothers, Otto and Erwin, and many friends and acquaintances settled.

As the parish church follows the people, so St. Cecilia's was established and became the parish church of my two brothers. Here their children were christened and attended religious services, and later attended the parish school when it was opened. My brother, Erwin, especially interested himself in the early activities of St. Cecilia's, as he settled in the district before my brother, Otto did. Erwin joined the church choir, attended committee meetings with the pastor, Rev. John P. Tobin, and assisted and contributed in every way possible according to his ability. Being in the organ business, he was asked to repair a reed organ they wanted to use for services, which he gladly did without charge, devoting his evenings to the work to save the struggling parish any unnecessary expense.

With the steady influx of new parishioners, it was soon found necessary to secure larger quarters, and property was acquired on Seventeenth Avenue and Vicente Street. The old church was moved there and additions made to it. Later a permanent rectory, then a school and a convent were built. Again the talk of securing a pipe organ became more urgent and persistent. It was while my brother Erwin was working one evening on the reed organ that the pastor came to him in high spirits and informed him that it would not be necessary to bother further on the reed organ, as he had just signed a contract to buy a fine pipe organ for $2,000.00.

Father Tobin was aware that my brother was in the pipe organ business. It was my brother's belief that when the time came for a pipe organ to be purchased that he would be consulted. This was not the case.

Father John Harnet succeeded Father Tobin. After many years he was relieved by death, and was succeeded by the Rt. Rev. Harold E. Collins in 1946. The latter made many improvements to the parish plans and not least among them was to provide a new and more adequate organ for the church.

This time, our firm was authorized to build a suitable organ of four stops, which we did, in 1941.

With the amazing growth of the Sunset District, even with the enlargement of the temporary wooden church, it became very evident that the time had come to build the new contemplated, permanent church, that would take care of all their present needs as well as for the future. In 1955, work began on the new St. Cecilia's Church, located now at the corner of Eighteenth Avenue and Vicente Street. It is one of the most imposing church edifices in San Francisco. With the lofty tower dominating the surrounding dwellings, it is discernible from all directions. Its high altar, with baldochin, is massive and impressive. Its lofty nave, its art glass windows, its superb furnishings are all of the best. To top this outstanding accomplishment, the large three manual Austin pipe organ, Opus 2211, of 48 stops, installed in 1955, can be its crowning glory.

The organ is located in the gallery, placed on either side,

elevated above the choir floor, with exposed pipes now much in vogue. The organ is unique among the many organs of San Francisco in that it differs tonally from the organs the Austin Company built about fifty years ago. It is decidedly on the Baroque type, accentuating clarity and brilliance, though not lacking in foundation tone. My son Lawrence, installed this organ. The small organ we had built some years before has been put to good use in the large chapel of the lower Church. Besides this organ, there is also an antiphonal organ of four stops in a chapel to the left of the Sanctuary, part and parcel of the large Austin organ on the Gallery.

Leonard Fitzpatrick, organist since its installation, is doing credit to himself and his church.

DR. E. P. GENOCHIO RESIDENCE

In one of the elite neighborhoods of San Francisco, in an apartment house, overlooking the Golden Gate, the Bay, Alcatraz and the Marin Hills, is located a Robert-Morton organ. Judging from the exquisite setting and furnishing of this apartment deluxe, its owner, Dr. E. P. Genochio, must be a man of culture and taste, both musically and artistically.

The organ was a two manual and Pedal, with detached console, and automatic player, consisting of five units with harp, chimes, piano and percussion. It is all enclosed or under expression. I believe the organ was originally installed by my elder brother, Leo Schoenstein, in 1925, while in the employ of the Robert Morton Company, a very neat and beautiful installation.

We have made several visits since to service the organ. In these sumptuous surroundings where nature's scenic beauty vies with the paens of harmony from the pipes of Pan, music, beauty and art should be at their best.

CALIFORNIA PALACE OF THE LEGION OF HONOR

One of the outstanding organs of San Francisco is the large Skinner organ installed at the California Palace of the Legion of Honor, located on the heights in Lincoln Park, the western terminus of the Lincoln Highway, overlooking the Golden Gate and the mighty Pacific Ocean. This organ is outstanding for its size, its tonal appointments, its beautiful and impressive console, and also for its artistic setting in the museum.

The museum was built in 1924 by Adolph B. Spreckels and Alma DeBretteville Spreckels, and was donated by them to the City of San Francisco. It is, unquestionably, one of the most inspiring panoramic spots in the Country. Looking down from the summit in an easterly direction, one gets a magnificent view of the City with its hills, the San Francisco Women's College crowning old Lone Mountain, St. Ignatius Church with its spires and campanile atop Ignatian Heights, Sutro Forest, and the skyscrapers of Nob Hill. Close by is the lovely residential district of Sea Cliff, with its beautiful homes, and the green hills and cliffs of the Presidio, with the incomparable Golden Gate Bridge spanning the Gate.

Across the Golden Gate, on the opposite shore, one sees the Marin Hills, with beautiful Mount Tamalpais raising its lofty peak to the sky, and the abrupt cliffs of the Marin shore, with the endless breakers spilling their white foam over the beaches or breaking up in a fairy spray on the rocky crags. Farther out to the west one can see Point Bonita, with its lighthouse, Point Reyes and Drake's Bay. On the southern shore, directly below Lincoln Park, lies Point Lobos and the rocky cliffs leading on to the Sutro Baths and the Cliff House. Beyond them the famous Seal Rocks. In the channel about a mile out is the Mile Rock lighthouse, bearing the name of the rock on which it is built.

Whenever I gaze at this picturesque lighthouse, I recall the morning of Washington's Birthday, February 22, 1901, when my brother Frank and I and several companions set out to spend the day in making a circle tour around the confines of San Francisco. Starting out from our home in the Mission District, we rode directly to the Bay waterfront, then walked along the Embarcadero to Fisherman's Wharf and through the Presidio to Fort Point. Here we intended to continue on to the Cliff House and go along the Ocean Beach to what is now Fleischhacker's Zoo, then to Ingleside and back home to the Mission District. It was a foggy morning and when we reached the life saving station at the Presidio on the Golden Gate, about 10 a.m., the fog was just beginning to lift.

Noticing a group of people about the life saving station, a police patrol wagon and an ambulance, we concluded that something serious had happened and hurried on to the station to learn what had occurred. We were told that a ship coming through the dense fog had struck a submerged rock and had gone down with a loss of 128 people. Only 82 out of 210 survived.

The sad news had evidently not yet reached the morning papers when we left our homes. As the fog lifted, we observed flotsam still being carried by the tide through the Golden Gate into the Bay. We later learned that the ship was one of the Pacific Mail liners on the China run, the three-masted steamer Rio de Janeiro, inward bound from China with a rich cargo of silk and bullion aboard.

A remarkable fact of this tragedy is that to this day no trace of the huge hulk of the ship has ever been definitely found, although many soundings have been made in attempts to locate it. Some mail sacks and a little flotsam were the only relics of the ship ever to be procured.

Since this accident, a lighthouse has been built on Mile Rock to give warning to passing ships and possibly prevent a similar catastrophe. This sad happening, of course, marred our enjoyment of the day. Nevertheless, we proceeded on our way as far as Ingleside, but when we arrived there and again saw a street car, our determination to walk the complete circle weakened and we eagerly boarded the car and allowed ourselves the comfort of riding the rest of the way home, where we arrived tired and hungry.

The California Palace of the Legion of Honor is a replica of its namesake in Paris, France. It was built to commemorate and to honor the American heroes who sacrificed their lives for their country in World War I. A further motive of the donors in erecting this building was to cement the ties of friendship between the French and the American people and to foster and advance French culture, especially through the arts of music, sculpture and painting.

The Palace of the Legion of Honor, located on its

unsurpassed site, proved to be a gem of architecture and beauty. Here the choicest schulptures, especially a collection of the famous sculptor Rodin of France, with ancient tapestries, beautiful paintings, antique period furniture, specimens of pottery from past ages, found a fitting place. The art of music was also not to be overlooked. Through the beneficence of John D. Spreckels a worthy pipe organ, the King of Instruments, was a further gift to enhance the arts of sculptor, painting and music.

A contract was awarded the Skinner Organ Company of Boston for a four manual, Pedal and Echo organ consisting of 64 distinct stops, with a number of borrows and unifications. John Saul and Frank Astle, of the Skinner Organ Company of Boston, Mass., installed this organ.

The general design of the building is a letter U. After passing through an arch at the main entrance, one comes into a court flanked on all four sides by an arched colonnade. In the center is a lawn surrounded by walks and shrubbery. In the center of the lawn is the famous statue of "The Thinker" by Rodin. You are now facing the main portals of the edifice proper. Over the entrance is a large panel containing statuary in bas-relief artistically executed. It extends across the main center part of the building. Passing through the vestibule one enters the rotunda from which access is had to the main exhibit halls.

In the hall directly opposite the main entrance, which is devoted mainly to sculptures and tapestries, is located the huge 4 manual console of the organ. It is a masterpiece of fine woodwork, made of walnut, and its interior mechanism is the last word in high-class organ construction.

In servicing the organ, which we have been doing for the last 43 years, we find it necessary at times to remove the top cover and roll-top of the console. The first is so substantially built that it takes four men to remove and replace it. There are several nameplates on the console: one is the usual one of the builder, the Skinner Organ Company of Boston, Mass. A second one contains the inscription: "Designed by Marshall A. Geiselman." Mr. Geiselman was a young organist of great talent with, undoubtedly, a great future ahead of him. I believe he was a protege of the Spreckels family, which would account for his close connection with the donor. Mr. Geiselman, no doubt, did draft the original specifications of the organ, as he claims, but I am certain that Mr. Ernest M. Skinner, although then no longer the sole and guiding spirit of the company, had his say in the matter also. Then, last but not least, let me give credit where credit is due. Mr. Geiselman paid frequent visits to my brother Leo's home, with whom he was well acquainted, and worked with him and discussed the specifications of the organ over a long period of time, so we may say it is the brain child of several. Mr. Marshall Geiselman was the official organist from the time the organ was installed in 1924 to 1926. He passed away in 1942, still a comparatively young man.

There is yet a third inscription plate on the console. This one bears the name of our firm as custodians of the organ and reads: Felix F. Schoenstein & Sons, Custodians, San Francisco, Calif.

When this beautiful building was completed and endowed with its precious contents, it was graciously presented to the City of San Francisco for the future education, enjoyment and edification of the public. It was now a public institution, visited by thousands during the year, many attending the concerts that are given every Saturday and Sunday afternoon by one of San Francisco's leading organists, Uda Waldrop, who then was awarded the position of official organist, in 1926.

Uda Waldrop presided at the organ for 25 years until his untimely death in 1950. After his demise other arrangements were made relative to the position of organist. From here on two prominent organists alternated in playing the recitals, Richard Purvis, organist of Grace Cathedral, and Ludwig Altman, of the Temple Emanuel, which arrangement is in force at the present time.

On entering the main hall in which the console is located, especially on hearing the organ and seeing none of the organ pipes on display, the strange visitor invariably asks, "Where is the organ; where are the pipes located?" The organ chambers are directly over the entrance and the tone comes through the ceiling of the rotunda, which is made of a light gauze material, a sort of aeroplane silk, skillfully colored and lined to resemble the material of the surrounding plaster walls. The large opening over the arch into the main hall, as well as the opposite end of the hall containing the semicircular concave and convex arch, from which the tone of the Echo organ, located in a chamber over the ceiling, emanates, is also made of the same material. This simulation in the painter's and decorator's art has baffled many as apparently all the walls were made of solid plaster.

To the right of the main entrance, above the dome are the Choir and Solo divisions of the organ, and on the opposite side are the Swell and Great divisions. All these are under expression. In the large space between these right and left sections of the organ is the Pedal division, with its 32' full length pedal open Diapason, etc. The console is detachable, that is, by means of a junction plate the cable can be disconnected, and similarly the small air pipe for the mechanism of the console. The purpose of this was to permit the moving of the console at times out into the open court, weather permitting, for outdoor concerts. A similar junction box is concealed outside under an iron cover to protect it from the weather. The large panel in the facade of the building containing the bas-relief statuary, to which I have previously referred, is pivoted on the upper end. By operating a windlass up in the organ chamber, it can be opened in an outward direction, thus enabling the organ tone to be heard in the entrance court. At the same time, in addition to the ordinary expression shutters on the four divisions of the organ, there was one huge series of shutters whereby the entire area of the organ chamber ordinarily emitting the tone in the general direction of the rotunda and main hall, could be closed off. When the console was to be used in the court for an outdoor recital, the front panel with the bas-relief was opened and the large series of blinds behind it closed, thereby diverting the organ tone from inside the building out into the open court. These auxiliary shutters were controlled by a series of buttons placed in the console. In the forty-three years we have serviced the organ, at no time was the organ played from this outdoor position, to our knowledge.

Although this organ is an orthodox Skinner organ, it also contains the usual traps formerly found in theatre organs.

These were seldom used in the rather classic programs rendered by the organist, Uda Waldrop. These are two very effective sets of Deagen chimes in the organ, the one of the Echo organ being of a larger scale than the one in the Choir box. The Harp Celeste, one of very excellent quality, as all the Skinner harps are, was found to be rather soft and inaudible with the swell blinds closed, for the reason that it was located a considerable distance from the organist. We would say that the nearest manual pipes to the organist are a distance of about 75 feet, and the farthest about 150 feet away. This is not referring to the Echo organ, which might be a still farther distance away. We, therefore, brought the Harp out from its concealment and placed it over the rotunda in a separate enclosure. It is now very satisfactory.

Another unusual feature of the organ is a clarion 8' set of pipes on high pressure, about 30" wind, with its own blowing plant located in a chamber above the main arch at the entrance to the court. The purpose of this stop is for use as a fanfare, to announce to visitors and sightseers in the building and surroundings that the organ recitals are about to begin. In this chamber over the arch is also located an octave of the large Deagen tower chimes, operated electrically by large solenoids striking the chimes. It is played from either the main console or from a small miniature keyboard located in a closet in the organist room. The largest of these chimes weighs about 500 pounds. Their musical peal can be heard by the organist when playing them from either keyboard inside the building.

Now a few comments about the tonal appointments of the organ. The fact that it is a Skinner organ should preclude the necessity of my going into extended detail describing the beauties of its individual stops, the typical and characteristic reed sets that Skinner excels in, the beautiful strings and flutes, the sonorous and pleasing Diapason. All this is further enhanced due to its setup and environment, by a certain aloofness or indirectness of its tone floating over the air as if it were from nowwhere, recalling the adage that "distance lends charm and enchantment." The general ensemble of the organ is not, however, beyond criticism, as one must remember that the Skinner organ of 1924 is as different from those of our present time of 1969, as the Model T Ford of 1924 is different from those of our present time.

The super-brilliancy that is now the vogue in our classical organs, stressing the Diapason chorus, with its corroborating mixtures, etc., is decidedly lacking in the Palace of the Legion of Honor organ. True, on the Great manual there is a Mixture, a 12th and 15th in the Diapason chorus, also a Mixture in the Swell manual, but the available mutation tone is not in balance with the preponderant Flute and Diapason tone and the cloudy, heavy Pedal section, and criticism may justly be made on that score. However, if I were making a choice, I would prefer the pleasing, smooth, dignified round 8' tone to the sharp, brilliant, often shrill 4' and 2' tone so often predominating in our new organs.

At any rate, the organ at the Palace of the Legion of Honor, regardless of this criticism, is deserving of being seen and heard, and no San Franciscan worthy of the name should fail to make the trip to the heights in Lincoln Park to enjoy the organ recitals and the beauty and inspiration that this scenic spot affords.

Specifications of the
Skinner Organ
Of the California Palace of the Legion of Honor
San Francisco, California

Stop knobs in Console from top to bottom rotation:

GREAT ORGAN

Gt.	4'
Gt.	16'
Tremolo	
Gt. Unison off	
Clarion	4'
Trumpet	8'
Trumpet Profunda	16'
Super Octave	2'
Twelfth	2-2/3'
Octave	4'
Wald Flute	4'

Gemshorn Celeste	8'	
Dopple Flute	8'	
Gamba	8'	
Gross Flute	8'	(Ped)
2nd Diapason	8'	
1st Diapason	8'	
Diapason	16'	
Celesta	(Choir)	
Harp	(Choir)	
Chimes		
Aeoline Chimes		

SWELL ORGAN

Sw.	4'
Sw.	16'
Sw. Unison off	
Tremolo	
Clarion	4'
Fluegel Horn	8'
Vox Humana	8'
Posaune	8'
Posaune	16'
Mixture	4 RKS'
Flute Tierce	1-3/5'
Flute Twelfth	2-2/3'
Flute Super	2'
Gedeckt	4'
Flute Traverso	4'
Violina	4'
Viole d'Orchestre	8'
Vox Celeste	8'
Viole d'Orchestre Celeste	8'
Gedeckt	8'
Clarabella Celeste	8'
Stopped Diapason	8'
Violin Diapason	8'
Bourdon	16'
Open Diapason	8'

CHOIR ORGAN

Choir	4'
Choir	16'
Choir - Unison off	
Tremolo	
Corno de Bassetto	8'
Orchestral Oboe	8'
Piccolo	2'
Nazard	2-2/3'
Flute d'Amour	4'
Super Dolce	4'
Unda Maris	4'
Flute Celeste	8'
Dulciana	8'
Unda Maris	8'
Melodia	8'
Concert Flute	8'
Diapason Phonon	8'
Contra Dulciana	16'

SOLO ORGAN

Solo	8'
Solo	16'
Solo Unison off	
Tremolo	
Clarion	4'
Tuba Major	8'
Tuba Profunda	16'
Vox Humana	8'
English Horn	8'
Military Trumpet	8'
French Horn	8'
Gamba Celeste	8'
Chimney Flute	8'
Gamba	8'
Tibia Plena	8'
Stentorphone	8'
Celesta	(Choir)
Harp	(Choir)

Chimes   (Great)
Aeoline Chimes (Great)

ECHO ORGAN

Solo Playable Choir
Echo   4'
Echo   16'
Tremolo
Echo Unison off
Vox Humana   8'
Corno d'Amour   8'
Piccolo   2'
Flute d'Amour   4'
Viol Orchestre   8'
Vox Celeste   8'
Clarabella   8'
Stopped Diapason   8'
Echo Bourdon   16'
Chimes
Aeoline Chimes

TRAPS

Snare Drum P
Chinese Block
Triangle Roll
Gong Roll
Snare F F
Castanets
Triangle
Gong Leather Stroke
Bass Drum and Cymbal
Bass Drum
Tambourine
Gong Wood Stroke
Crash Cymbal
Chimes   (Great)
Aeoline Chimes (Great)
Celesta

Harp

COUPLERS
Sw to Ped
Gt to Ped
Ch to Ped
Solo to Ped
Echo to Ped
Sw to Ped 4'
Ch to Ped 4'

UNISON
Sw to Gt
Ch to Gt
Solo to Gt
Sw to Ch
Solo to Ch
Sw to Solo
Gt to Solo

OCTAVE
Sw to Gt   16'
Sw to Gt   4'
Ch to Gt   16'
Ch to Gt   4'
Solo to Gt 16'
Solo to Gt   4'
Sw to Ch   16'

Sw to Ch   4'
Solo to Ch 16'
Solo to Ch   4'
Sw to Solo 16'
Sw to Solo   4'
Gt to Solo 16'
Gt to Solo   4'

ARCH OVER MAIN ENTRANCE
Arch Clarion   8'
Large Chimes
Tremolo

PEDAL
Pedal Octave		
Clarion	4'	
Tuba	8'	
Trumpet	8'	(Great)
Trumpet Profunda	16'	(Great)
Trombone	16'	
Contra Posaune	16'	
Piccolo	2'	
Violin	4'	
Twelfth	2-2/3'	

Super Flute	4'	
Cello	8'	
Gamba Celeste	8'	(Solo)
Dolce Flute	8'	
Gross Flute	8'	
Flute	4'	
Bourdon	16'	(Echo)
Quintatone	10-2/3'	
Contra Dulciana	16'	(Choir)
Lieblich Gedeckt	16'	(Swell)
Violine	16'	
Second Diapason	16'	
Open Diapason	16'	
Bourdon	16'	
First Diapason	16'	
Gravissima	64'	
Bourdon	32'	
Tympany		
Echo Chimes		
Great Chimes		

At one time we were troubled by a severe vibration somewhere in the upper part of the main hall, especially when the pedal notes were played. I figured it might be some of the glass windows over a large overhanging cornice surrounding the hall, or some metallic vibration between the plaster walls. I began walking around the cornice, about 30 feet from the floor, trying to trace the location of the vibration. I was always a good climber, even tried out tight rope walking as a youngster, and therefore found no discomfiture up there as long as I could hold on to the frames of the windows. When I reached the end of the hall, however, where the cornice is reduced in width under the semicircular convexed ceiling where the Echo organ is located, and where the vibration proved to be, my courage failed me as I had nothing to hold on to, and a feeling of dizziness overcame me. I stopped, retraced my steps, taking a firm hold again, and descended. I then resorted to other means of entering the Echo organ over the roof, where I soon laid my hands on the metal which was vibrating between the plaster walls.

The tuning of this organ, with its several divisions in various locations and elevations, was a matter requiring consideration. Although four large steam radiators were located in the center portion or pedal division, the four chambers on either side of it would not benefit greatly from them. Finally, a series of ten electric thermostatically controlled Prometheus heaters was installed, and now I believe the temperature situation is taken care of permanently. The actual tuning and tone regulating of the organ also requires unusual skill, patience and endurance. The usual practice of the tuner shouting "next" to his helper below holding the keys is out of the question in this case as the distance is too great to make one's self understood, aside from the nuisance created by this method. Later we had a telephone system installed, but as the saying goes "practice makes perfect", and so in the matter of tuning this organ, we learned by experience.

It was usually my son, Lawrence and I who made the weekly visit to service and tune the organ. I would be seated at the console while he would go up in the organ. By a gradually evolved system of effective teamwork that we consistently followed at each visit, using a code of signals, we were soon able to dispense with the use of the telephone and now tune and regulate the organ to a nicety practically without uttering a word.

The management, guards and employees at the Palace of the Legion of Honor have always been most courteous and agreeable to work with. We have seen faces come and go. Some of the older employees I especially remember were Mr. Armand, Dick Paterson, Percy Cahill, Ed Klung, and Elmer Smith, the present manager, and several charming young ladies, and some not so young, who usually were stationed at the entrance or information desk. Two of the gardeners who would be the first to greet us as we approached the building, I cannot fail to mention. One was a ruddy Irishman, Mr. Sheehan, always interested in world affairs and the troubles of mankind, his loud voice echoing in the colonnade of the court. I think he would have made a much better philosopher than a gardener. Our chats were always interesting as we apparently were in accord in our ideas on many subjects we discussed.

Another lovable soul was the Scotsman, William M. Burns, namesake of the great Scottish poet, Robert Burns. His forte was God's great creation, the beauties of nature and the great outdoors. He was a poet doing the humble work of a gardener. One day he asked me if I was interested in poetry. I assured him I was. Leaning on the handle of his rake, he then recited a poem he had composed. I was so impressed with it that I asked him if he would give me a copy and if he would autograph it. Shortly thereafter I was informed of his sudden death. In his honor and loving memory, and to glorify one of San Francisco's famous visits, Lincoln Park and the Golden Gate, I herewith include his poem.

THE GOLDEN GATE
A Scotchman's Appreciation

There are pretty spots in Ireland,
That please the heart and eye;
And there's beauty in old Scotland's hills,
Her valleys, lakes, and sky.
But here in San Francisco
A fact I would like to state,
You'll seldom see a scene so fine
As our famous Golden Gate.

So take a stroll in Lincoln Park,
To see this lovely sight,
Go up any of its pathways,
To the Flagpole on the height;
And there by the Legion Palace,
Fair home to Honor and Art,
You'll see this place of beauty
That will please and charm your heart.

On the left is the Pacific Ocean,
To the right San Francisco Bay,
In front lies Golden Gate Strait,
A picture both pleasant and gay.
Gay with the Yachts of the sportsmen,
Sails filled with the balmy breeze;

Gay with the ships of all Nations
Whose home are the Seven Seas.

Gay with the smacks of the fishermen,
Coming home from their daily toll;
Gay with the cry of the sea gulls,
Swooping down to share in the spoil;
Pleasant the blue of its waters
Reflecting the Summer sky,
Pleasant the croon of its shore-line,
Dashing its spray so high.

Pleasant the view in the foreground,
With shadows on valley and hill,
Pleasant the view in the distance,
The mountains so silent and still.
To my heart it brings benediction,
And a joy I've tried to relate,
As I view this fair scene of Nature,
That's known as the Golden Gate.

W. M. Burns
Sept. 1930

Given to my Friend the Organ Tuner
By William M. Burns the Author Sept. 1936

Our trips to the California Palace of the Legion of Honor, located practically on the northwest end of the San Francisco Peninsula, were mostly made by Municipal Bus or by auto. Then followed a brisk walk up a rather steep hill to our destination, which, nonetheless, was always enjoyable. Midway up the path to the Palace of the Legion of Honor was a clearing between the trees and shrubbery from which a perfect view of the famous Golden Gate, with the huge bridge spanning its mile-wide expanse, was obtainable. Here we would halt to relax and take a breath of the invigorating air while evaluating the amount of work that had been accomplished in the preceding week on the bridge. From the very beginning of the work, when a barge was anchored over the pier sites taking the soundings for the foundations of the massive towers, until the day of its completion and dedication. Now that the bridge is completed, and the trees and shrubbery have grown, obscuring the view, we still halt at this spot as of yore to relax, but also to drink in the beauty of the scene before us, the unsurpassed setting of land and water and the mighty bridge spanning the Golden Gate.

SIXTH CHURCH OF CHRIST SCIENTIST

It was some time during 1915 when we first became acquainted with the Sixth Church of Christ Scientist. They had no permanent edifice of their own at that time, but held services in the Golden Gate Commandery Hall on Sutter Street, near Steiner, for a number of years. At the time they had a large two manual and Pedal Estey reed organ, driven by a motor. Mrs. Ella G. Ball was the organist, and our calls were frequent as she was very particular in having everything in the best possible condition.

As the congregation developed, the matter of procuring a permanent edifice was given attention. Mr. Grimm, the architect, prepared plans for a suitable structure, which was then built in 1924 at the southeast corner of Clay and Divisadero Streets. At about that time, in 1924, the First Church of Christ Scientist was also procuring a new organ, and their old 24 stop Austin organ, Opus 621, being available, was purchased by the Sixth Church of Christ Scientist for use in its new edifice. We secured the contract to remove the organ and also to rebuild and rearrange it into two sections to fit the new plans of a divided organ for the new church. At the same time, we also put in an entire new action, as the old action, which was one of thy first that the Austin Company had made, was becoming obsolete and was often in need of repair and adjustment.

It seems that previous to the consummation of our contract, the Sixth Church of Christ Scientist had already been in communication with the Kimball Company relative to a new organ. A motor and blower, which that company evidently had nearby, was installed in the church in preparation for the new organ they expected to install. However, the

Austin organ was secured instead, but the blower and motor which were to serve for the Kimball organ were retained. I believe Mr. Fletcher Tilton, the agent for the Austin Company, and Mr. Gus Edwards, who represented the Kimball Company, made the arrangements.

After we had the organ successfully installed and it had been in use for sometime, we observed that the old console, which had been left as it originally was, was the only source of complaint. It was built on the semi-tubular electric type. We induced the Church to procure a new modern console and in 1928 a three manual and Pedal Austin console was ordered from the factory at Hartford, Conn.

The Choir, or third manual, is now inoperative, except for the intermanual coupling, as the organ is only a two manual instrument, but some day it is expected that the Choir will be added. At the time the new console was installed, we also had the Church substitute the old cornopean in the Swell, one of a very raucous type, for a new smoother Corno d'Armour, which gives necessary brilliancy to the Swell, yet is a better blend in the full ensemble tone of the organ.

Mrs. Ella G. Ball had functioned as organist of the church for many years and, undoubtedly, had acquired a record for protracted service in a Christian Science Church. Mr. Harry Holland, a quiet, efficient worker, was sexton here for over 17 years, but has since found employment elsewhere. During the early part of September 1945, we were greatly surprised to learn one day of the passing of Mrs. Ella Ball, the faithful organist. A Mr. Popovich succeeded her.

MISSION COVENANT CHURCH

Having been in the organ business here for so many years, we thought we knew of practically every pipe organ that had been installed, regardless by whom or where located. We were, therefore, much surprised on our first visit to this church in 1929 to see and hear quite a good-sized two manual and Pedal Kimball organ of 12 stops, with a detached console and an imposing front. It was one of the latest built pneumatic action organs. Evidently, it had been installed by

Mr. Edwards, who did erecting work for the Kimball Company. Mr. Hurndahl, a piano tuner with undoubtedly some pipe organ experience, was our predecessor on the scene.

This organ, like most Kimball organs, possesses a rich, brilliant tone, with a somewhat higher pressure than ordinarily used. The full ensemble tone has a surprising punch to it. In 1939, through the generosity of Mr. and Mrs. J. A. Hultman and Mr. and Mrs. C. O. Wahlgren, gifts were made to the church which directly benefited the organ. The first couple donated a set of Deagen chimes, the latter couple a Deagen harp. We procured and installed both of these percussion instruments. At the same time we enclosed some of the stops of the Great manual that had heretofore been unenclosed, leaving only the Great Open Diapason unexpressive. The Chimes were placed in this new Great expression box. The Harp was placed in a separate expression chamber and placed over the original Swell box. Both of these additions to the organ were very welcome and serviceable. The dedication took place on Sunday, April 1, 1939. Louis Flint, as guest organist, presided at the organ on this occasion.

To make space for the new Great expression shutter, a rather novel expedient had to be resorted to, as the new blinds now rested upon the space formerly occupied by the Open Diapason pipes. We built a new chest for these pipes and placed them ahead of the expression shutters, and used the old pallets to work a relay to operate the new Diapason Chest valves electrically. Harp and Chimes also played electrically. As stated, the rest of the organ mechanism is operated pneumatically. We also installed successfully a rectifier instead of the usual generator. Mr. Roy Almquist has been organist at this church for many years.

FIRST ENGLISH LUTHERAN CHURCH

One of the older type church structures of the nineties that remained standing, unchanged, for many years is the English Lutheran Church on the brink of the Geary Street hill, near Octavia Street, with its pointed spire always noticeable on the skyline.

As far as my recollection goes, on passing this church I more frequently found it closed than open, and I often thought to myself, here is one church in San Francisco about which I know little. In 1929 I learned that the church had procured a two manual and Pedal, tubular pneumatic, Moller pipe organ of 12 stops. I believe it was installed by my nephew, Leo G. Schoenstein, Jr.

I remember how oldfashioned the church looked, with its ivy covered facade and its antiquated interior, and yet I admired the beauty of it. I recall the pleasant interview I had with the Rev. Pastor. He seemed to lament the laxity of his congregation in attending divine services, especially the younger generation, which apparently did not follow the example set by its elders. He also commented on the poor business policy of the Protestant denominations in dividing and scattering their interests instead of uniting and concentrating their efforts on one common purpose, for which, after all, they are all sincerely striving. He especially referred to the three Lutheran Churches, St. Mark's, St. Paul's and the English Lutheran Church, all located within a few blocks of one another, practically competing instead of combining in one strong Lutheran congregation. I admired his outspoken views on different subjects we discussed, his broadmindness, and sincere devotion to his church and religion.

In the latter part of 1945 the congregation sold its property and edifice to the Seventh Day Adventist denomination and the First English Lutheran Congregation secured a new site on the southeast corner of Geary Street and 30th Avenue, in the Richmond District, where they later built a new Church. Here they procured a two manual Wangerin organ. The organ was placed in the rear of the church to one side, and the choir and organist in the forward part of the church adjoining the Sanctuary, a basically unsatisfactory installation. The congregation in the rear of the church complained of being overwhelmed with the power of the organ and the choir and organist could not hear it directly, being placed in an alcove with a low ceiling to the side of the nave. Experiments were made in subduing the volume by covering the organ opening with a blanket and by using a P.A. system where the choir was located. The blower for this organ was placed inside of the organ chamber; objection was made to its noise. The minister, being practically inclined, took matters in his own hands and with sound proofing methods securely boxed the blower in an enclosure. When I remonstrated about the inaccessibility of getting access for oiling the motor, he stated the bearings were grease packed and did not need further lubrication. He evidently was right, as the blower, to my knowledge, has never been lubricated since.

ST. MONICA'S CHURCH

At Twenty-Third Avenue and Geary Boulevard, in the Richmond District, is located St. Monica's Church. Our first association with the church was around 1929 when we were summoned to repair and tune their pipe organ.

It was a two manual and Pedal tracker action organ with attached console, of about 12 stops. It evidently was a rebuilt organ. There was no name plate on the instrument. From the pipe work and the original chest that was retained, it could be assumed that the organ was of local manufacture, possibly a Bergstrom or Andrews organ. However, with a new bellows and case installed its exact identity could not be positively determined. I believe it was procured from one of the local music stores, which, in turn, had secured it from a church in the Mission District.

In 1939 the Rev. Edgar J. Boyle was appointed music director of the Archdiocese by the Most Reverend Archbishop, and took up his residence in St. Monica's Church. Being ardently interested in music, it was logical that his resident parish should be exemplary in demonstrating through a well-organized choir the type of liturgical music he endeavored to introduce. It was soon evident that the old organ which was located in the center of the choir loft, with the organist's back toward the singers, aside from its tonal and especially mechanical limitations, was not suited to the purpose of accompanying a large choir, so the question of procuring a new, modern divided organ was discussed. Miss Clare Harney was organist of St. Monica's Church when we first serviced the organ, later becoming the wife of Judge William Swigert.

The contract for the new organ was awarded to the Geo. Kilgen Company of St. Louis, Missouri, and was installed by their representatives. It is a two manual and Pedal divided organ of about 18 stops, with a detached console, electric pneumatic action. In addition, it has a second, duplicate console in the trancept of the church, which is used mostly for the children when attending mass Sunday mornings and for evening services. A set of Dulciana 8' pipes is located nearby to more readily establish pitch and tempo. The large gallery organ can also be played from the lower console. The organ being voiced on a slightly higher pressure than is customarily used, it sounded rather strident in full organ playing, and it was found necessary to soften some of the stops and trebles, especially the Trumpet 8' stop on the Great, which dominated the whole organ tone.

With the installation of the new organ, Mrs. Clare Swigert terminated her position as organist, and a prominent young man, Mr. Jos. Michaud, from Seattle, Washington, an able musician and a pupil of Mr. Lyon, organist of the Cathedral of Seattle, secured the position. He devoted much of his time to playing the organ, gave recitals, etc., and, in fact, I believe through his persistency made his tenure as organist unwelcomed. His services terminated at a rather early date. We have been informed he is now organist at the National Shrine in Washington, D.C. Mr. Joseph Stratcutter, a young and able musician of the City, was his successor and apparently carried on with complete satisfaction for some time. A Marcella Tosomey, a talented organist, also held the position for a time. The present organist is Gordon Wilson.

What became of the old organ I do not definitely know. Parts of it were lying in the basement of the Church for some time. Finally, they also disappeared. Possibly some amateur organ builder acquired the remnants.

In 1950, due to the increased attendance, the Church edifice was considerably lengthened. Rev. William Cantwell, a beloved and revered man, was pastor.

CHRISTIAN SCIENCE BENEVOLENT
HOME ASSOCIATION

It is not surprising that with the substantial growth of the Christian Science denomination in San Francisco from the year 1908, when the First Church of Christ was built, resulting now in a chain of about twelve established churches, that they also provided for the social and recreational well-being of their adherents. The Christian Science Benevolent Home Association was their answer to this apparent need.

The excellently designed Home, the work of Mr. Gutterson, the architect, nestling in a grove of eucalyptus trees out on Nineteenth Avenue, with its tile-covered, sloping roofs, its bay windows, its stately lines, reminiscent of some feudal castle, is most impressive. On entering the interior of the structure, one is struck by its high class finish and superb furnishing. I recall walking through it for the first time, marveling at the fine patterns of inlaid linoleum on the floors, the first of this material I had seen so used, exceedingly beautiful and in refined taste.

A building of this kind, and for the purpose for which it is used, would be incomplete without its chapel. Here, also, the architect was very successful in laying out a small but commodious assembly hall for the holding of religious services. An Estey two manual and Pedal electric pneumatic organ of 18 stops was secured in 1930, Opus 2896, which we installed. Mr. James B. Jamison, then agent of the Estey Company, made the sale. The console is alongside the reader's desk, and the organ proper, arranged in two chambers, is located on the floor above, placed behind two grills. The tonal qualities of the organ are excellent, typical of the general run of all Estey organs. I do not know whether the console of this organ was given particular attention as regards finish or not, but it certainly is a masterpiece in the wood finisher's or polisher's handicraft. Likewise, a grand piano standing alongside the console had a hard and smooth surface like glass, which always attracted my attention and admiration.

In playing the organ shortly after it was installed, a severe rattle or vibration developed, especially when playing on the deep pedal notes. This was most audible in the auditorium of the chapel. When we would go into the organ loft with the tone sounding to locate the vibration, it would apparently cease or disappear. This convinced us that it was not the pipes or any material in the organ chambers that was vibrating, but that it came from some other source. My brother Otto, who installed the organ, finally concluded that perhaps some metal lath above the ceiling and under the floor was causing the trouble. At an inconspicuous place in the organ chamber a hole was made through the plaster wall, through which we crawled with our extension cord, among wires, protruding pieces of angle-iron and rough plaster. The closer we crawled to the organ, the louder the vibration became, and unerringly we were led to the end of a dangling wire, which came in contact with a piece of angle-iron and caused the metallic vibration. It was an aural as well as an optical demonstration of a lesson in physics, demonstrating the effects of sound waves through space, causing vibrations of solid objects far distant from their source.

HELPERS OF THE HOLY SOULS

Shortly after the fire of 1906, for a few months, I worked with my friend, Joseph Maichen, as a cabinet maker in his small shop on Linden Avenue, between Franklin and Gough Streets. Incidentally, the shop was located just about on the property where the house in which I was born formerly stood. Work in the organ field after the fire had not yet gotten a start; however, carpentering and cabinet work was in great demand. I remember Mr. Maichen being called upon to make some repairs to an old flat on the south side of Golden Gate Avenue, between Fillmore and Steiner Streets. He told me it was to be used as a convent for some French nuns who were establishing themselves in San Francisco. It proved to be none other than the Congregation of Sisters known as the "Helpers of the Holy Souls", an order that came from France to participate in social service and religious activities of the

Diocese. I assisted Mr. Maichen in doing the necessary work in their new convent.

For several years thereafter I heard little of these Sisters, except for occasional notices in the papers. Later, I heard that they had secured a new location, a combination of several homes which, with some additions and alterations, were made into one unit, forming their present convent building at the corner of Haight and Laguna Streets.

As the heart and center of any convent is the chapel, the Sisters of the Helpers of the Holy Souls saw to it that they had a suitable chapel. Although small, yet adequate for their needs, it proved to be one of the most charming, reverential and edifying chapels in the City. At first they were provided with a two manual Estey reed organ. This, of course, was cumbersome and tiresome for the nuns to pump by foot, so they had us install a vacuum blower, which we did with good success.

As practical and economical as a reed organ may be, especially when funds are not available for the genuine article, the Sisters nevertheless sought for ways and means to secure a real pipe organ for their chapel. In 1925 we were given a contract to build a small pipe organ of three units, consisting of a stopped wood Flute, a Salicional and a conical metal Flute, unified on both manuals. This combination, with its related derivatives, proved quite satisfactory considering the limited number of stops. A very soft Dulciana, or Aeoline, would yet be desirable, but with the effective swell shutters it has, a fine pianissimo effect is procurable. Strange to say, the Tremolo, effective in many combinations if not overdone, was tabooed by the good Sisters as unliturgical and unbefitting the religious services. Another peculiarity of these good nuns, always so pleasant and cheerful, is a custom they undoubtedly brought from their beloved France. When we first tuned their reed organ, and again whenever we came to tune their present pipe organ, we always found the ivory keys covered with a piece of soft, white flannel the full length of the keyboard. It reminded me always of tucking the little keys to bed after their arduous day's work.

Several years ago the aforementioned soft accompanying stop, a Dulciana 8' stop augmented to a Dulcet 4', playable from both manuals, was installed. The chapel, as I have already remarked, is beautifully and harmoniously designed, and I regretted that the organ had to be placed on one end of the gallery and not in the center, thereby upsetting the proper balance or symmetry. Also, the organ front remains unfinished. Maybe some day some good benefactor will advocate and provide for these alterations. Meanwhile, I am certain that the fervent prayers and good deeds of these "Helpers of the Holy Souls" will be effective in releasing many souls from purgatory to the enjoyment of eternal bliss in heaven, regardless of whether the organ is located in the center of the gallery or at one end.

KPO
(Hale Bros and The Chronicle)

With the advent and development of the radio in the last decades, the pipe organ took a leading part as one of the mediums for providing musical entertainment broadcast over the ether waves allocated to the numerous radio stations. It was used either as a solo instrument, or as an accompaniment to singers, or in conjunction with an orchestra.

One of the most prominent of these radio stations on the west coast was Station KPO, for a long time sponsored by Hale Bros. and The Chronicle. KFRC, I believe, also had an organ.

KPO was located originally on the top floor of Hale's Department Store on Fifth and Market Streets. To broadcast organ music satisfactorily over the air seemed to require special care and preparation. As a general rule, the bass notes would be lost and the higher pitched tones or upper partials would predominate. Then again, any strong reverberation or echo would impair the transmission over the air. Special rooms were built at this station, with the walls heavily draped and padded and the floors thickly carpeted, all done to eliminate reverberation; just the opposite procedure from that followed in the ordinary installation of an organ in any other edifice, where just this quality in reasonable quantity is sought. It was even said that the specifications for these radio organs were specially drawn up to be more adaptable for this purpose, but personally I saw little difference in the voicing and selection of stops in these organs from what you would expect in a good concert organ.

Station KPO secured a Welte three manual organ of about 12 stops, with harp and chimes. It was a splendidly voiced organ, well built, and, I believe, was most satisfactory for its purpose. Its console, with the pianos and orchestra, were all in a separate room partitioned off by a large glass plate from the visiting public which was always present.

Somehow or other, I was never a great radio fan. My personal apathy for it, however, does not deny the fact that it is undoubtedly a comfort and blessing to many. I have always questioned the propriety of judging organ tone, the human voice, or any other musical sounds via the radio or ether wave. To hear them at their best, unaffected by mechanical devices, is to hear them at their source. Again, it amuses me to hear people rave over the rendition of certain organ numbers. Regardless of how painstaking and exacting an organist may be in interpreting the music to his own feeling, in putting soul and expression into his rendition of a composition, in observing his pianissimos and especially his fortes, at a grand climax his work may be undone by the "monitor" in the control room observing the dials, disregarding all musical values, to prevent any overload or shattering on the "mike."

To obviate this necessity, it was suggested and I believe it was tried, to place the organist at the console in a sound-proof case, so he would not hear the organ tone directly, but indirectly through the radio in his compartment, thereby being his own judge as to his volume of tone. Much ado was made about keeping the organ in tune with the orchestra, or vice versa, the orchestra with the organ. Due to the difference of temperatures, there seemed to be a constant variance. I always found it close and stuffy in the room, with insufficient ventilation. With all the heavy drapes and carpets about, with the full orchestra confined in the small room, it often became excessively warm. In the organ chambers and blower room it was always cooler. A heating system was then installed in the blower room and organ chambers to equalize their temperatures with that of the broadcasting room where the organist and orchestra were seated. In theory it should have worked out satisfactorily, but notwithstanding, I know that between the temperamental musicians and the over-harrassed organ tuner, the question whether the organ was above or below pitch was always a bone of contention.

Uda Waldrop opened the first engagement as solo organist, but the fickle radio audience soon demanded the lighter and more melodious type of music. Other organists followed, with varying success. In 1929, the Hale Bros.-Chronicle Association was discontinued - not the station. KPO continued over the air until some time about 1948. It is now KNBC. I am not certain what became of the organ, but believe it was shipped to Los Angeles.

KOHLER AND CHASE STORE

Fletcher Tilton, the accomplished and aggressive representative of the Austin Organ Company on the Pacific Coast, had his first office in the Clarke Wise Piano Store on Grant Avenue. Later he moved to the Wiley B. Allen Store on Kearny Street, and later to their new store on Sutter Street. Finally, he moved his headquarters to the Kohler & Chase Store on O'Farrell Street, near the Orpheum Theatre. Here I had my last business transactions with him. I noticed his health was failing; no longer did he have that indomitable energy and enthusiasm as formerly. The last organ he sold was for the Christian Science Church of Petaluma. He was a pitiable sight seated at the console while playing at the dedicatory service. Shortly thereafter he passed away.

While visiting him at his office, I recall that a Welte two manual and Pedal organ of about 10 stops was installed in the store, presumably for demonstrating purposes. It also had an automatic player. It was a very well voiced and toned organ, and mechanically functioned very well.

Kohler & Chase Company eventually retired from active business, or at least retired from the retail trade. The organ was removed from the premises and stored elsewhere and, in 1942, it finally was sold to the Ninth Church of Christ

Scientist on Sloat Boulevard, where it was erected in their new edifice by Chas. Hershman, a local organ mechanic.

ZION EVANGELICAL LUTHERAN CHURCH

Out in the Richmond District, on Anza Street and Ninth Avenue, was located a small Lutheran Church. Apparently, it was a thriving congregation. Its petiteness made it homelike and cozy, and everything connected with it indicated neatness and pride of ownership. Rev. M. H. Liebe, its pastor, radiated those traits and undoubtedly personified the ideals of his parishioners.

We first became aware of this little church when we were informed that they had purchased an Austin "Chorophone" pipe organ, Opus 1254, which we were to install, and I went out to see that the proper space was provided for the organ in the small gallery. Being quite busy at the time, we entrusted the work of installation to one of our trusted employees, James Heaton, who had been in our employ for many years.

Mr. Heaton was well under way with his work when, one day, we had an unexpected visitor at our office. It was Mr. John T. Austin, one of the founders of the Austin Organ Company of Hartford, Conn., who was visiting in San Francisco. He was accompanied by Mr. Fletcher Tilton, their local representative. During our conversation we mentioned that we were then in the process of installing one of their organs in the Zion Lutheran Church, and they stated that they would take occasion to drop in at the church during the day and see how the work was progressing.

Mr. Heaton later reported to us on the unexpected visitors he had had that day. He was personally acquainted with Mr. Tilton, but evidently Mr. Tilton did not immediately introduce Mr. Austin to him as the builder of the organ. What conversation took place or what remarks were made, I do not know in detail beyond Mr. Heaton's report to us, which was to the effect that while he was engaged in doing some particular piece of work Mr. Austin, his identity still unknown to Mr. Heaton, offered him some gratuitous advice, saying that if he were doing the work he would do it so and so. Mr. Heaton resented this unsolicited advice from an apparent stranger and let the party know it, although I am sure, in a gentlemanly way, but nevertheless in an emphatic manner, saying that he knew his business. When later he learned the stranger's identity, through a belated introduction, I am certain there was considerable embarassment on the part of the young mechanic. Later on, we added a Vox Humana to the organ with good effect.

In later years the gallery of the church was enlarged. Rev. Liebe, in the course of time, retired and a young and more energetic pastor by the name of Rev. F. A. Jacobson was his successor, with Rev. Liebe becoming the Pastor Emeritus.

In 1950 we were ordered to remove the organ from the church and store it, which we did, as the congregation planned to sell the church edifice and move it bodily from the present site to new owners, the Park Presidio Baptist Church, located on Tenth Avenue and Cabrillo Streets. A rear annex of the edifice was cut off, and the church proper, with spire and all, moved bodily in remarkably short time to its new location. A wandering building in San Francisco's streets is not an uncommon sight. It is indicative of the strength and durability of a well built frame building.

When the site was fully cleared, work began at once on the basement of the new church. The Chorophone organ was temporarily installed in this new location and was dedicated on Sunday, March 11, 1951. The church held services in this temporary church for several years until the super structure of the new edifice was finally completed.

S. H. KRESS DEPARTMENT STORE

We have heard much of the great department store of Wanamaker in New York and Philadelphia and of the huge pipe organ in the latter place, used for the entertainment of its patrons.

San Francisco also had its "Wanamaker" Store in miniature in the S. H. Kress Department Store, on Market Street near Fifth Street. Here, for a period of fifteen years, daily recitals were given on an excellent Aeolian pipe organ. Glen

Goff, the popular organist, presided at the console for over twelve consecutive years, giving recitals twice daily and catering mostly to the more popular tunes and airs, as requested by the audience. For some years music from this organ was also broadcast over Station KPO.

It was a three manual organ with chimes and harp, originally installed by Mr. A. P. Martin. The Choir and Great stops were mostly duplexed, except the Open Diapason and the Clarinet. It was divided into two sections and located on a mezzanine floor behind a grill, the Swell, Great and Choir on the West side of the store and the Pedal division on the opposite side. The console, rather large in size, was conspicuously located on a raised platform between both organ chambers, in full view of the public. The organ also was provided with a duo art player which, however, to our knowledge was never used. The relay, coupler stack and automatic mechanism, of which there was a generous amount, with the blower and generator occupied a special room on the floor above.

We serviced this organ monthly for many years. This work was, of course, done evenings after the store had closed for the day. For some reason or other, this work seemed to fall to my lot, undoubtedly because I was living nearest to this establishment. At best, it was a hard organ to tune. Conversation between the tuner in the organ and the one holding the keys at the console was difficult. Accessibility to the mechanism under the Chest was almost impossible on account of limited space. Access to the rear of the console was also very limited, as the console was close to the wall. The only access to the organ chamber was by a freight elevator. Often this had to be used also by the night shift of janitors and employees stocking the store for the next day's business. On these occasions we would be brought to the organ chamber door and on entering would have to close the fire door behind us so that it could be used by the other employees. While thus securely locked in this exitless chamber, the thought often occurred to us, what would we do should there be a fire or earthquake? Fortunately, we were never confronted with such an emergency.

The tuning of this organ was not easy, as stated, and I soon began to teach my son Lawrence the required procedure so that he would be able to assist me. He was still attending high school, but had an inherent ambition and desire to become an organ builder, and had a fine ear for music and the art of tuning. Under my guidance he soon became accomplished and proficient. The pipes were excellently voiced and were of the finest quality. Especially noteworthy in the organ was its smooth Tuba 8', its fine Diapasons, Strings and Flutes. A fine balanced ensemble was the crowning glory of this organ and I often singled it out as one of my favorite toned instruments.

In 1941 an unexpected order was issued from the main office in New York that further use of the organ should be discontinued. Mr. Glen Goff, who for the twelve years previous had apparently pleased and satisfied the patrons of the establishment, was shocked and dismayed at this unwelcome news. He bestirred himself and had a petition sent to headquarters signed by hundreds of enthusiastic organ fans who had regularly attended and applauded his renditions, but to no avail. Glen Goff took this blow very seriously. To help him offset to an extent this enforced idleness, and in an endeavor to help him find a new position, we engaged him to dedicate a new organ we had just completed for the Danish Lutheran Church, on Church and Market Streets, San Francisco.

He officiated at the new console at the dedication of the organ at the morning services, and after returning to his home in Burlingame, he worked a bit in his garden in the afternoon, when he suffered a heart attack which resulted in his death. I attended his funeral. Glen Goff was a changed man after he was informed that he was no longer needed to play the organ he had so faithfully and successfully presided over for twelve years.

In 1942 the organ was donated to the College of the Pacific, located at Stockton, California, for their beautiful new chapel. It was removed from the store and placed in its new abode.

ST. FRANCIS EPISCOPAL CHURCH

In the Ingleside District of San Francisco there is an Episcopal church named after the beloved and popular saint of the Catholic Church, or rather the beloved and revered saint of the whole world. St. Francis Episcopal Church is located at the corner of Ocean Avenue and San Fernando Way. The first unit of the permanent church was built in 1930. It was a rather low stucco structure on the Mission style, with tiled roof, deep recessed windows, and an arched portico facing what was later to be a garden court which would, eventually, according to the general plan, be practically enclosed by the additions yet to be built. This first unit served temporarily for church services and as a social hall.

While it was being built, we were advised that a fine two manual Farrand & Votey pipe organ of about 18 stops, which was then standing in the residence of the late Mrs. De Witt Kittle, formerly the Willis Davis residence, located at the northwest corner of Pacific Avenue and Scott Street, would be available as the old residence was to be razed, and that arrangements had been made by St. Francis Episcopal Church to acquire this organ. We accordingly made our plans to properly house the organ in its new location.

We recall our experience with the architect, a rather obstinate and uncompromising individual. In planning the organ for this new location, its interior parts were all to be rearranged from its original pattern, and he was insistent that we tell him what the minimum width of the organ would be so that he could provide the space for it. We, of course, always recommend some margin of space, the more the better, for general accessibility, convenience, etc. However, as he had certain limitations of measurements in his mind to conform to his plan, space for the organ seemed to be at a premium, at least from the architect's standpoint, which always seems to be the case, and he insisted on the minimum width. Reluctantly, we gave him this measurement.

As we installed the organ, which work was mostly entrusted to our faithful employee, James Heaton, the minimum width proved to be just that and no more. Not a quarter of an inch of marginal space was available; in fact, when placing the main chest in position, the freshly plastered walls were scraped on either side to permit it to enter.

The lack of accessibility was a handicap ever after, but fortunately the organ was well constructed and drastic repairs were not necessary for many years, until the steel springs on the Pedal chest pneumatics began to break, due mostly to corrosion.

This organ chamber, consisting of three plastered walls and ceiling enclosing the entire organ, with a light set of single Swell shades controlling the sound output into the church, is most remarkable for its effectiveness, considering the light material of which the shades are made. From a rather diminutive exterior front, one is surprised at the volume of tone coming from the organ. The voicing and scaling of the pipes is excellently done, and the high grade workmanship on the organ throughout is commendable. The electric action used in the organ is of the standard used in 1898, when it was built, and it is still giving good service, barring a few magnets which in time have been replaced due to short circuiting.

In 1942 a new social hall at the corner of the property was erected, with the necessary annexes connecting the church with the social hall. The part of the building which was used previously for both church and social purposes was hereafter used only for church services. A new altar, communion rail, choir stalls, pulpit and pews were installed, transforming the former hall into a strictly church edifice. Even the beautifully finished mahogany case of the organ received attention by subduing its color, bringing it in harmony with the color scheme of the other furnishings of the church. The motor and blower are in the room adjoining the organ and are very quiet in operation. This is one of the few electric pneumatic action organs that has an individual motor to operate its generator.

Robert Sproule, their accomplished and energetic organist, was in charge of the choir and music.

Originally, the console was attached to the organ, not to favorable a situation for an organist to lead and direct a divided choir in the chancel. Later on this situation was altered by installing a new modern console and placing it on the opposite side of the organ.

Incidentally, this work was just being completed when the American Guild of Organists, or Organists National Association, were holding their annual convention in San Francisco. This organ was selected as a typical two manual organ suitable for demonstrating its possibilities.

SAN FRANCISCO CONSERVATORY OF MUSIC

With the interest San Francisco has always shown in the arts and music, it is logical that among her institutions there should be an organization devoting its special efforts to the development of music in its many branches. Such an organization is the San Francisco Conservatory of Music, originally located at Sacramento and Locust Streets in the Richmond District. It was founded by Mr. Bloch and is endowed and managed by a Board of Directors.

Although its headquarters in the past were of rather modest proportions for a city of San Francisco's culture and importance, it has now changed that situation by securing a new and excellent building, some years ago, at 19th Avenue and Ortega Streets in the Sunset District. There are ample practice rooms and also a suitable recital hall where their 13 stop Kimball pipe organ, acquired in 1930, has been put to good use.

In both buildings the demand for organ instruction and coaching have always been in demand. Pupils were taught by some of the most prominent organists. Among these were Wallace A. Sabin, Warren D. Allen, Phillip Shinham and, more recently, Harold Mueller. At times recitals are given by the pupils. The organ is an excellent small instrument, with an action that is very responsive and expression shutters unusually effective.

ST. JOHN'S CATHOLIC CHURCH

Out on what was once called Mission Road, where stood the old St. Mary's College, a street intersects Mission Street bearing the name St. Mary's Avenue. Here is located St.

John's Catholic Church, a well designed and pleasing structure. Two beautiful towers grace its facade, and an imposing colonnade supports a portico over the entrance, which gives it a classical appearance.

For many years the church contented itself with a small harmonium. Finally, the day came when the securing of a pipe organ was in order. We had interviewed the pastor on several occasions in regard to it and felt from all indications we had the matter well in hand, awaiting only the final okay and signature on the dotted line.

At the time, 1930, we were quite busy with various other jobs, and I was away for several weeks on and off at Stanford University installing a new Skinner 4 manual console and a new action on the organ there. On one of my weekend visits to the City, I called at St. John's Church, with the firm hope of securing the contract to build their new organ. To my surprise and disappointment, however, I was notified that due to my protracted absence, the contract had been let to an eastern firm. Their local representative, a man of action, with persuasive qualities undoubtedly outclassing my abilities as a salesman, secured the contract. A small two manual 6 stop Estey pneumatic action organ was secured and is giving the church unusually good service, judging from the few occasional visits we are called upon to keep it in tune and repair.

PRESIDIO POST CHAPEL

Besides the Old Mission Dolores, there is probably no other spot in San Francisco as historic and romantic as the Presidio in the northern part of the City, abutting the ocean, the famous Golden Gate and San Francisco Bay. Here the oldest building in San Francisco remains, though modernized and reconditioned. It now serves as the Officers' Club and is located on the south end of the parade grounds.

Built of adobe, its exterior contour is almost concealed by modern trimmings. Not far from this venerable building, a little to the west on the knoll overlooking the Bay and skirting the walls of the National Cemetery, is the new

Presidio Post Chapel. It is a substantial edifice, built of concrete, of Spanish architecture, with an impressive tower and a red tiled roof. The interior is rather dark, its beautiful art glass windows permitting but little sunlight to enter. With its heavy beamed ceiling and its walls draped with the flags and pennants of many military organizations, with many memorial plaques and tablets encased in the walls, one readily perceives the martial aspect of the chapel. A simple altar with candles and crucifix, and the sanctuary light glowing over the chancel, would give one the impression that he were in an Episcopal church. It is non-denominational, however, and serves for the holding of religious services for all Protestants at the Post. The Catholic chapel is located near the parade grounds, and has no pipe organ.

This Protestant chapel is equipped with a pipe organ. The contract to build it was awarded to the Oliver Organ Company of Berkeley. The organ was built and installed in 1930. It consists of two manuals and Pedal of 8 stops and a set of chimes, all enclosed in one chamber elevated about twelve feet above the church floor on the left side of the chancel. The console is located on the right side of the altar on the church floor level, behind the choir stalls and set in a recess. Unfortunately, set in this alcove, with a low ceiling over the organist, he cannot hear the organ to the best advantage. There are very pleasing tones in the organ and, from the nave of the church, the organ sounds well.

As the Oliver Company was of recent origin and had been organized shortly before the building of this organ, we were interested in observing its outcome. The maintenance of the organ was entrusted to us shortly after its installation, and I must say that no organ could have been more neatly built or with better materials than were used in this organ. Oddly enough, after the completion of this organ, the firm liquidated.

In this connection, I might relate an interesting occurrence which perhaps might also throw some light on the possible cause of the dissolution of the Oliver Organ Company. During the course of construction of the chapel, we received from the United States Government specifications and an invitation to submit a bid to build a suitable organ for the chapel. Undoubtedly, other organ builders throughout the country received similar invitations to bid. The time and place were clearly stipulated where and when the bids would be received and opened. We entered into the competition wholeheartedly, had necessary plans drawn, blue prints made, and had all our papers presumably ready. The vital day and hour on which the bids were to be opened were marked on a desk calendar pad, and a further memorandum thereof was written in an order book to make sure there would be no slip-up. I, being the senior partner, the handling of the transaction was left mostly to me; yet my two brothers, junior partners, were also deeply interested and concerned. In addition, we had a charming and most effective office girl who had saved the day more than once by reminding us of a fixed appointment, etc. With all the precaution taken and concern not to be late in presenting our bid, with four bright and intelligent minds to keep tab and remind one another, at 10:00 o'clock on the morning on which the bids were to be opened at the Quartermaster Depot at Fort Mason, and the complete office staff slipped up on the matter.

It was about 9:40 A.M. when I happened to glance at the desk calendar pad and noted, to my horror, that this was the day on which the bids were to be opened at 10:00 o'clock. In my concern about the prospect, which we had received about two weeks previous, and which received our prompt attention, I had somehow let the erroneous date, for the following day, enter my mind which caused my Waterloo. I hastened with all speed with my plans, specifications and bid to the Quartermaster Depot, but arrived panting and excited, a few minutes too late — the bids had been opened. Discouragement, chagrin and sad disappointment were not my lot for long, however, as a kind and courteous official, seeing my apparent discomfiture, asked if I would care to seé the results of the bidding. I assured him I most certainly would. Heading the list as the successful bidder was our local competitor, the Oliver Organ Company of Berkeley. Midway down the list of about ten bidders was our bid, if it had been on time. With this information, that our figure was not the lowest, nor one of the highest, my ruffled feelings were somewhat appeased.

Unbelievable as it was to me that a small local builder

could successfully outbid all the larger and older eastern firms, this doubt was fully answered by the early liquidation of the firm, a short time after the installation of the organ. To the credit of the builders of the organ, however, it must be stated that they delivered an organ to the letter and spirit of the specifications.

On my return to the office and informing my partners and our office girl that I was too late to enter the bid and of the various ratings of the bidders, I expected, and probably justly deserved, a panning for my negligence. However, that did not happen and to this day I still wonder what kept their wrath in check. Possibly it was the human element that they considered we all make mistakes, or did they feel they were equally at fault in letting father time sneak up on us to be a few minutes past the deadline for the opening of the bids!

ST. THOMAS CHURCH

What I know of the life of St. Thomas the Apostle is the fact that he was not only a fisherman in his early years, but that in later years in carrying out the mission appointed to him in preaching the Gospel of Christ, his journeys were made mostly by sea. It is, therefore, fitting that in selecting a name for the church within sight of the vast Pacific Ocean, considered at the time it was built to be the most westerly located Catholic church in San Francisco, it should be named after the great apostle who traveled the then known routes of the sea extensively.

St. Thomas Church is located in the Richmond District on Balboa Street and 43rd Avenue. It is in Normandy design, with buttressed walls and dormer windows. Its slate roof mates its gray walls. Over the nave is built a rather broad-pointed tower. The interior of the church is extremely simple, but pleasing and harmonious in color and design. What attracts the eye, however, immediately on entering the church is the simple but most devotional and strictly liturgical altar. I believe this is the first of its kind that I saw in any of our local churches, and its genuine orthodoxy appealed to me strongly — a decided contrast to the over-ornate high altars that have gradually found their places in many Catholic churches.

In keeping with the simplicity and the religious reverence with which this church inspires one, it was logical that the completing touch should be a strictly typical church organ. This was acquired in time by securing the two manual and Pedal Whalley tracker pipe organ that was formerly used in Sacred Heart Church on Fell and Fillmore Streets. We were, at this time, in 1935, installing in Sacred Heart Church their new Hook & Hastings organ and, as their old organ was thus available, we induced Rev. James P. Moran, pastor of St. Thomas Church, to purchase it. Rev. Norbert Feely of Sacred Heart Church joined in advocating the purchase of the instrument, and so it was acquired by St. Thomas Church. We installed the organ in the choir gallery, which, fortunately, was just large enough to accommodate it. A better-toned organ could not be procured, and although mechanically old-fashioned, it answers all requirements of the church.

SEVENTH AVENUE PRESBYTERIAN CHURCH

I recall working several times on a reed organ in the old church, and I remember urging on different occasions the desirability of procuring a genuine pipe organ. I was always told, however, that they were planning to build a new church and that at that time they would give the matter consideration.

The pumping by foot of the large reed organ was the bugaboo in this situation. I made them an estimate of the cost of installing a standard vacuum blower to operate the organ, but some clever mechanic of the church applied a fan of a vacuum cleaner to it. This did the work in a way, and for the time being eliminated the need of a standard blower.

In time, the long contemplated construction of a new, permanent church materialized. The old structure was moved to the rear and in front of it, and annexed to it, the new edifice was erected. Dr. Markel and Mrs. Madden, the organist, were appointed on the music committee and interviewed us on the building of a pipe prgan. We submitted a bid and specification, and felt that we had made a good presentation and had about won the coveted prize. However, negotiations got into a stalemate and no progress was being made either way when, finally, we were informed that the contract had been let to the Estey Company, owing to our reluctance to reduce our price by $500. Friendly relations were still maintained, however, as evidenced by the fact that we eventually installed the new organ for the Estey Company. It proved to be a very satisfactory instrument. Rev. Walter Carl Subke was the amiable pastor of this church.

CHRIST LUTHERAN CHURCH

Christ Lutheran Church is one of the smaller churches of the Sunset District, located at Sixth Avenue and Irving Street. Our first connection with the church was when we were summoned by the pastor, Rev. Pieper, to see what we could do with their pipe organ to make it more satisfactory.

We found a sweet-toned Whalley organ, but one that, due to its mechanical design, was unreliable and gave much trouble. The organ was designed on the electric pneumatic system, mostly direct electric, and in addition, was planned on the Universal Air Chest system. Workmanship was of the highest order, but due to the delicate adjustment of its direct electric individual chest valves, its relay action, and an unnecessarily complicated wiring system, it was continuously out of order.

With great patience and much skill, we thought we had the difficulty mastered but as the years progressed, we found our efforts were futile. We, therefore, urged the congregation to rebuild the organ, replace its original faulty action with a standard electric pneumatic action, and put in an entirely new console. As the organ was a gift from Mr. Frank Werner to the church, it was desirable for his sake that its functioning be a credit to the donor. Our suggestion to rebuild was, therefore, followed. After this rebuilding, the new console was placed at the opposite end of the church, while the choir still remained in the chancel near the altar - a rather unusual arrangement, but from all indications it works out well. The organ has proven to be very reliable and gives good service since this alteration work was done.

Organ maintenance men are often put to many inconveniences in performing their work. This organ had a combination of them. Among others, each time we had to repair or adjust something, the motor had to be shut off before entering the air chamber where most of the mechanism was located, as there was no air lock or vestibule applied. Also, we had to leave the church to get into the Universal air chest from an outside door. Once inside the air chest, it was difficult to make oneself heard and understood on the outside. To get up into the pipes of the Swell box for tuning, we first had to enter the minister's residence, adjoining, disturb his privacy by entering his bedroom, from which, through a closet door, we could then enter the organ chamber. All this we changed by placing the blower in an accessible location in the Sunday School room and made access to the organ chamber through the front of it from the chancel side. I believe this was the most recent organ Whalley built, at least for San Francisco, and in its rebuilt condition it is a credit to his memory. We have been informed that recently the Congregation has secured new quarters and that the edifice, including the organ, has been taken over by the Newman Club, a Catholic Organization.

ST. EMYDIUS CHURCH

I recall very well the old Ingleside District in the southwestern part of the City. A race track was located out there in the neighborhood of Ocean Avenue and Sloat Boulevard, back in the 1890's. I remember riding out to this district on the Mission Street car, which at that time terminated at Sloat Boulevard, and did not proceed to the ocean beach as at present. The whole section was beautifully wooded with an abundance of fir trees covering the hillside and vacant lots. With the development in this district of Westwood Park, St. Francis Wood and Ingleside Terrace, for residential purposes, the beautiful trees had to give way and they were ruthlessly and probably unnecessarily uprooted. I recall how my father and mother, both lovers of nature, deplored their removal. A deep ravine called "Trocadero", leading off from what is now Westwood Drive and terminating with a lake and famous resort with laid out gardens at the western end of the gully, now Sigmund Stern Grove, was one of the favorite spots for a Sunday afternoon outing for the family.

With the completion of the Twin Peaks Tunnel, this entire western section of the City rapidly developed. As the population moves, the churches follow, and St. Emydius, the saint whose protection we implore against the ravages of earthquake, was chosen as the patron saint of the first Catholic church in this district. In 1913 a temporary church was built. Later, in 1930, a new, permanent edifice was built of concrete, with two imposing towers, a pleasing facade and a well-designed interior. Rev. John J. Doran was pastor at this time.

St. Brigid's Church at this time, was securing a new pipe organ so their old 2 manual and Pedal Kimball pipe organ of 7 stops was available. This organ was purchased and we had it removed and installed it in the new St. Emydius Church. For transporting and hoisting the organ, we engaged the services of a professional rigger as the organ parts were large and very heavy, the Chest containing all the pipes already planted over their pipe holes. The rigging concern was admirably equipped with the necessary paraphernalia, such as power-driven windlass direct from the truck, etc. This made the moving and installation job one that was a masterpiece in quick and efficient procedure.

The organ supplied the needs of the parish quite satisfactorily although, of course, an organ of larger proportions would have been better. To give the organ a more imposing appearance on the gallery, we altered the front design by removing the rounded corners of the case and arranging them in a straight line, thus making it appear broader.

Father Doran passed away in 1940 and was succeeded by Father Edmond J. Motherway, who had formerly been pastor at All Hallows' Church. In recent years, a large school has been added to the parish unit, making the parish facilities still more complete. At a later date a new altar was installed, and the whole sanctuary was refurbished and improved. Like all Kimball organs built on the tubular pneumatic system at that time, using rubberized silk for their pneumatics, pouches and coupler stacks, after a period of time this crystallized and became hard, causing persistent ciphering. We insisted that the organ had to be modernized or an entirely new organ procured. Since the church had never had an organ adequate for its size, and the parish seeming to be in a more favorable position than ever before, the time to secure a new organ was at hand.

Several years before, we had installed a moderate size three manual Estey organ in the residence of Robert Watt Miller of Hillsborough, San Mateo County. We had made many additions to the organ, while in his home, but for some good reason he decided to abandon his mansion. Realizing the opportunity of making an advantageous transaction between Mr. Miller and Fr. Edmond J. Motherway, arrangements were made and the organ purchased, in 1957. Some alteration had to be made in the church to prepare suitable organ chambers on either side of the gallery. This being completed, the 36 stop organ was installed and after months of work the dedicatory concert was given by Fr. Robert Hayburn, who was also instrumental in suggesting certain changes in the stop list. The organ is a most desirable acquisition to the church — as if to the Manor born.

NINTH CHURCH OF CHRIST, SCIENTIST

The Ninth Church of Christ, Scientist, located on Sloat Boulevard in the Ingleside District, was for many years without a pipe organ. The first structure was built for temporary use only, until a permanent building could be erected. In the meantime, they got along with the ever-ready standby, a reed organ. I remember being at the church one time to take measurements for a proposed organ they seemed to be interested in at the time. However, the acquisition of a pipe organ had to wait until later, when the new church was completed. We again made plans for a suitable organ, in collaboration with the architect, Mr. Gutterson. However, the church selected a Welte pipe organ that was for many years installed in the Kohler & Chase Music Store on O'Farrell Street, alongside the old Orpheum Theatre. I remember working on this organ for Mr. Tilton, representative of the Austin Organ Company, who had his office in the building at the time. It was an excellently built organ with a fine tone, and in its new location should make a very satisfactory instrument for the church. Mr. Charles Hershman installed the organ in 1942.

THIRD CHURCH OF CHRIST, SCIENTIST

One of the several substantially built Christian Science churches of the City is the Third Church of Christ, Scientist, located on the north side of Haight Street, near Lyon Street. Built of buff brick, its facade makes a most pleasing and impressive appearance. This church secured an Edwin A. Spencer two manual and Pedal organ of about 12 stops from Los Angeles. It was exceedingly well built; the interior woodwork was made mostly of cedar wood.

The organ was placed on the north end of the Church behind an ornate grill. The console was placed in a pit to the left of the reader's desk. Due to the generously proportioned scales used in the organ and a preponderance of heavy flutes in the specification, the tone of the organ sounded rather thick or tubby. A further defect was that the grill was too solidly built, preventing much of the tone from entering freely into the auditorium, and subduing and beclouding an otherwise excellently toned organ. In 1925, to counteract this defect, we added several stops, which helped eliminate this drawback. We also added an Echo organ of several stops, which was placed in the gallery on the opposite end of the church, making the organ a total of 30 stops. The Echo stops were made playable from the Swell manual by use of a cutout switch. I would have preferred a better selection of stops of a more ethereal nature.

I do not know who installed the organ originally, but it could have been Mr. Spencer, the builder. Mr. Whalley of Berkeley was called on the scene soon thereafter, as he applied a new relay action. Undoubtedly, this was installed to replace an action that was not completely reliable. Soon, however, this new mechanism also, though professionally well made, began to give trouble and show defects. We were finally called in and after observing its functioning and noting its weak points, we were able, by making a few minor alterations to make it work reliably and satisfactorily. The piston combination action of the console was also quite troublesome. The aforesaid improvements were made to the organ during the period when Chaplain Bayley was organist. He was a fine man, a Christian gentleman, a good musician, a former organist of Grace Cathedral. He passed away in the prime of manhood. After his death our service was discontinued. Still another relay mechanism of the direct electric type was installed by others and the console was placed in a pit in the center in front of the reader's desk.

Sometime later, our firm was again entrusted with the maintenance of the organ and were authorized to make further improvements to the organ as follows: we replaced the Spencer draw knob Console with one of our own stop key type, substituted the fan Tremolos for the bellows type, releathered all the chest pouches and pneumatics, installed a rectifier in place of the belt driven generator, added an Octave 4', a Mixture and bright Trumpet 8' to the Great Manual, on the Swell manual converted the Swell Cornopean 8' to a Clarion 4', brightening the ensemble tone of the organ considerably, and then we did needed revoicing of the organ. Mrs. Gladys I. Marley was organist at the Church for many years previous and during this period of renovation, and we appreciated her patience and forbearance.

TEMPLE METHODIST CHURCH

In 1929 a movement became active in San Francisco to consolidate several Methodist churches and to form one congregation under the title of Temple Methodist Church. A supplementary object of the project was to combine the church with a hotel unit. This plan was consummated by the consolidation of the Wesley M. E. Church, formerly located on Hayes and Buchanan Streets, the Central Methodist Church, formerly at Leavenworth and O'Farrell Streets, and the Howard Street M. E. Church, formerly located at Howard and Harriet Streets.

I believe the properties of these churches were then sold and their assets merged in the William Taylor Hotel Company, an organization financed to carry on the venture until all the indebtedness incurred had been paid off.

Property was then acquired at the northwest corner of McAllister and Leavenworth Streets and plans were drawn for a huge skyscraper hotel of 26 stories, with a church annex. In 1930 the building and church were completed and opened to the public. The church was of Gothic design, rather lofty, but somewhat short for its height. Beautiful art glass windows graced the facade and a large rose window adorned the north wall. A large gallery was placed on the south end of the church.

Due to its favorable central location and having all the qualifications for becoming one of the prominent churches of the City, the question of a suitable pipe organ for this edifice was soon a topic of interest to all organ builders. I recall that I had drawn quite an elaborate ornamental Gothic case, as a suggestion for the committee, for a divided organ in the front part of the church, in chambers which were planned by the architect, Mr. Hobart. Unfortunately, quite a debate ensued between the architect, the pastor, and the church people as to the location of the organ, and the choir, on which of course depended the final arrangement of the interior of the edifice. As I recall, the minister, Rev. Walter John Sherman, D.D., favored the more liturgical plan of having an altar as the central feature with choir stalls on either side, with console and lectern to the left and pulpit to the right; the organ to be placed in the chambers above in alcoves provided on either side of the chancel. Since the location of the organ could not be definitely decided upon at the time the church was being built, and the plastering had to be completed, the walls in which would ordinarily be the openings, or grills, through which the tone would enter the church were plastered shut. Should a decision be reached later to make use of these chambers, the plaster walls could have easily been opened.

As the church structure drew near to completion, the vexed question as to whether the organ should be placed in the chancel or in the choir loft in the rear, became quite heated. I was invited by the pastor to attend one of the meetings. I knew the pastor cherished the liturgical plan of an altar as the central or focal point, and in support of his idea, he stated that it is just that that makes the Catholic edifice distinctive without a doubt — the altar of sacrifice centrally or conspicuously placed. I doubted at the time whether he would win his point, for his plans were decidedly contrary to what one would expect in a Methodist church.

Decision was finally reached to place the organ and choir on the rear gallery; the organ to be divided, part on either side of the gallery. A contract was then awarded the Skinner Organ Company of Boston to build a four manual and Pedal instrument, consisting of 40 stops. When the organ was installed the Choir and Solo were located on the east side of the gallery and the Swell and Great on the west side.

Although speaking and ornamental pipes filled the openings of the organ chambers, no attempt whatever was made to make them an architectural embellishment. It was a sad disappointment to me, especially as I had dreamed of a beautiful Gothic case, highly ornamented with filigree-work, etc. The organ was installed under the supervision of one of Skinner's employees, assisted by local help and was dedicated on August 31, 1930. It was a gift to the church in memory of Rolla Vernon Watt. The organ, tonally and mechanically, as usual, was a credit to the Skinner Organ Company. It was frequently played upon by visiting recitalists and received much well-deserved praise. Miss Harriet Beecher Fish was appointed permanent organist, which position she filled very satisfactorily.

Soon after its completion, we received the regular maintenance of the organ. Unfortunately, with the coming of the depression and hard times, the financial status of the William Taylor Hotel Company became impaired, and likewise that of the Temple Methodist Church. Obligations to the bond holders could not be met and finally foreclosure proceedings were instituted. The hotel was turned over to other hands, and the name changed to Empire Hotel, and instead of catering, as formerly, to a selected clientele of church people, it was now opened as a commercial and transient hotel, with its skyroom atop the building more popular than its church nestling at its side under the same roof. Finally, the Temple Methodist Church also closed its doors. The congregation then made a merger with the First Congregational Church at Post and Mason Streets, under the title of "The Temple Church", with their respective pastors, Rev. Jason Pierce Noble and Rev. Lowther, functioning as co-pastors.

The beautiful art glass windows of the former Temple Methodist Church were then removed, being replaced by plain amber glass window panes, and finally were set into place in the beautiful Gothic chapel on the campus of the College of the Pacific at Stockton, California.

The organ, now silent, remained standing for some time until it was sold to the Occidental College of Los Angeles, in 1963. We were awarded the contract to remove and pack the organ, which we did, thinking how short-lived is the existence and fame of many human institutions.

During the hectic days of World War II, Uncle Sam commandeered the entire hotel building, and the space that was once the Temple Methodist Church is now equipped as a large office used by the Federal tax and income departments.

GLIDE MEMORIAL M. E. CHURCH

I have referred to the great success achieved by the late Mr. Fletcher Tilton, who was local representative of the Austin Organ Company, in selling their organs in this vicinity. I think no agent could duplicate his record. However, a good runner-up in later years was Mr. James B. Jamison, then representative of the Estey Organ Company of Brattleboro, Vermont. He sold many of the Estey organs, among them several large ones in this section.

One of these was the large three manual and Pedal Estey organ, Opus 2943, of 21 stops for the Glide Foundation, or Memorial Church, on the northwest corner of O'Farrell and Taylor Streets. The edifice was just being completed when the organ arrived. The organ was erected by my brother Otto, in 1930. It was arranged in two sections placed on either side of the rostrum and located behind grills. It proved very satisfactory and met with universal approval.

I recall the day the maintenance work was entrusted to us. Usually, there is no question of who is to do the work. It is logical and a common practice that the party who installs the organ also services it in the future. In this instance, however, other parties seemed to be interested in securing the work, among them Mr. Fred Wood, an organ maintenance man thoroughly proficient, and one for whom we always had a high regard. We both happened to meet at the same time at the desk in the church office, to make our bid for the work. The gentleman who interviewed us, and who was in authority, evidently was in a quandary, but the gallant action of my competitor in standing up and recommending that after all, the work should be given to us, certainly made our regard for him so much the greater. Many organists of prominence have played on this organ, among them Glen Goff and Louis Flint. Rev. McPheeters was the pastor at this time.

PARK-PRESIDIO COMMUNITY CHURCH

The Park-Presidio Community Church is located on the south side of Geary Boulevard and Sixth Avenue. Shortly after the church was completed they secured a pipe organ. I do not know whether it was new or used. This was a Tellers Kent organ, two manual and Pedal electric pneumatic action, with about 4 or 5 stops. The console was placed in the chancel to the left of the pulpit, and the organ on the floor above, the tone entering the church through a grill. Fortunately, it is a very well voiced sounding organ. However, its original installation was far from satisfactory.

We were called to the church to help a one-legged organ man complete his work. I do not recall his name to this day, nor have I ever seen him again. In all deference to his handicap and physical affliction of having only one leg, I must say I never saw an organ erected in such unprofessional manner. He must have had a poor sense of the fitness of things; everything was on the bias and out of square. Electric wires dangled in all directions, temporary expedients were used to stop serious air leaks, etc. But, with all these shortcomings, I always had a sympathetic feeling for the unfortunate man and I admired his grit. What he lacked in professional experience or technique, the organ makes up for by its fine tone and good behavior. I believe in later years a new Wicks organ replaced the Tellers Kent organ.

N. GRAY & COMPANY –   Morticians

N. Gray & Company, the oldest established morticians in San Francisco, were organized in 1850. At present they are located at the southwest corner of Post and Divisadero Streets, where they have a well-equipped establishment, with two chapels. It was about the time they moved to this new location, in 1924, that we were informed by our friend, Mr. Otto Fleisner, then organist at the First Presbyterian Church, that they were in the market for a small pipe organ for their large chapel. The use of pipe organs in the chapels of mortuary establishments was then in its infancy. We interviewed the proper authorities and, with the collaboration of Mr. Fleisner, prepared plans and specifications for a small suitable organ, and were awarded the contract to build it.

It was a three stop organ, unified, of two manuals and Pedal, with a detached console, all enclosed or under expression. It was placed in an alcove above the chapel floor. The units consisted of a wood flute, Stopped Diapason, a string or Salicional, and a reed or Vox Humana stop, making a desirable and practical combination of tone. This was further augmented with an effective tremolo and a very efficient expression shutter. The organ proved to be satisfactory in all respects and received many encomiums from organists who played it.

My sister, Cecilia, in addition to her position as organist at St. Anthony's Church, served as organist for N. Gray & Company for several years. To my knowledge this organ was the first pipe organ installed in a mortuary in San Francisco. Several years later, a second organ was installed in the smaller chapel. This, however, was a Wicks organ. The contents were about the same as the organ in the larger chapel, except that it had a set of chimes.

N. Gray & Company, during the long years of its establishment in San Francisco, has served many a family in their hour of sad bereavement, including our own when my parents passed away. An outstanding figure who came unexpectedly under their charge, was the late President of the United States, Warren G. Harding, who passed away in San Francisco while visiting here on a tour of the United States.

GANTNER, FELDER, KENNY CO.
Morticians

Years ago, while attending school at St. Boniface, I recall that when funerals were held in the church, which was then located above the school, the undertaker conducting the funeral was invariably from the firm of Gantner & Guntz. The use of the old Calvary Cemetery in the Western Addition was, about this time, 1898, discontinued and the new cemetery at Holy Cross was used hereafter. Those were the horse and buggy days when a trip to Holy Cross Cemetery and back over the macadamized Mission Road took practically the better part of a day. It was then one of the most coveted privileges of an altar boy to be selected to accompany the priest to the cemetery and thus get a ride in a horse drawn carriage.

After the demise of both Mr. Gantner and Mr. Guntz, two familiar figures in St. Boniface parish, the business was taken over by Mr. Gantner's sons, who later took in as partner our jovial friend, Louis Felder. The old-established connections, plus the genial disposition of the new partner could not help but bring a larger and more satisfied clientele, especially among the German speaking people. Their business sagacity and foresight was no less successful than their apparent ease in making loyal friends, so to still further expand their field of activity, they added as a third partner, Mr. Denis I. Kenny, a pleasant gentleman of Irish ancestry. With this combination, their business apparently flourished still more and soon made it necessary to move their quarters on Guerrero and Sixteenth Streets to their well-established and beautiful parlors on Market Street opposite Duboce Avenue.

Having progressive ideas, our friends were not slow in seeing the need of having a suitable pipe organ for their new establishment. True to their loyalty, our friend Louis Felder and his partners, after but perfunctory investigation, in 1934, and with complete confidence in our integrity, entrusted us with the building of thier chapel organ. This we undertook with the greatest of pleasure, and, I believe, we have built them one of the finest organs we have ever made. The organ consists of four stops unified and is most pleasing in tone and satisfactory in operation. It is placed on a gallery in the chapel.

I recall that while the organ was under construction, the question arose as to whether they wanted chimes or a Vox Humana, and Louis Felder in his humorous vein replied: "I don't know anything about pipe organs, but for the love of Mike don't put any chimes in this organ. I am sick and tired of hearing them." Even an undertaker can rebel at overdoing a good thing. We put in a Vox Humana, and a good one at that.

As the environs of a mortuary establishment are not too cheerful, it does happen to be a place nevertheless where friends and acquaintances, lodge and church members meet more often than they probably care to. However, invariably when the boys get together and "Louie" springs one of his anecdotes, in an off moment, the seriousness of the environment is, momentarily, forgotten. One of his stories ran something like the following: He had conducted a funeral at a cemetery. The lowering of the casket had just taken place and solemnity of the occasion had left its mark on the faces of all the mourners. Quietness reigned supreme. The pallbearers were removing their boutonnieres from their coat lapels and taking off their white gloves to toss them upon the lowered coffin when one of them accidently missed his footing and slipped into the open grave. The serenity and solemnity of the occasion was suddenly marred; to injury was added profanity when one of the gravediggers standing nearby as was their custom, shouted to the man below, "Come up, you fool. What in hell are you doing down there?"

It is a strange coincidence that at this establishment many an old acquaintance, friend or schoolmate, was warmly greeted after a long lapse of time, performing his last respects to the memory of some other fellow traveler.

LEONARD BUCK RESIDENCE

The Aeolian Organ Company of New York must have sold many an organ to its well-to-do friends in all parts of the country. California and San Francisco and environs also had their share of them. One of these organs was installed in the home of Leonard Buck, then residing on the seventh floor of the apartment building on California and Franklin Streets. A large room fronting on California Street was used as the music room. Here on the east side of the room was the organ, a large two manual and Pedal Aeolian duplex organ of about 22 stops. The entire organ was enclosed behind expression shutters. These, in turn, were gracefully and artistically concealed with beautifully arranged drapery. At the opposite end of the room were two consoles. One was the usual two manual and Pedal console with automatic player attached; the other, standing nearby, was for use only with the Duo Art playing device. Needless to say, the organ was made to the high standard of the Aeolian Company, and the voicing and tonal qualities of the various stops were of the utmost refinement. Yet with all, there was nothing lacking in the full ensemble of the organ.

We serviced the organ quite frequently. However, a few years ago Mr. Buck decided to give up his apartment and make his home in Marin County. We were asked for a bid to dismantle the organ and move it to its new location, and submitted the requested data. Evidently our figure was not the lowest and other parties were entrusted with the work. After this we had no occasion to work on the organ again, for several years. Late in 1945 we were again summoned to work on the organ and to service it regularly. We found it now erected in a beautiful mansion at Ross, Marin County, an instrument to again furnish joy, musical appreciation and entertainment to its esteemed owner.

SHERMAN CLAY & COMPANY STUDIO

On the eighth floor of the Sherman Clay & Company building on Sutter and Kearny Streets, in what was known as their recital room, there was formerly installed a beautiful Aeolian pipe organ of two manuals and Pedal and an Echo organ. This room, or studio, was unquestionably one of the most beautiful and artistic I have ever seen. A heavy, soft carpet covered the floor, rich velvet draperies hung in artistic folds on either side of the windows. The ceiling was paneled and a massive chandelier with soft glowing lights was suspended therefrom. In the center of the room was a large library table, with a table lamp and books and photographs on it. There was also a grand piano in the room, a large music cabinet of medieval design, and some select pieces of upholstered furniture. Two oil paintings adorned the walls and at the southern end of the room hung a beautiful tapestry. Behind this tapestry was the organ chamber. On the north end of the room was the console with its automatic player.

On entering the studio through a massive door, the effect was most bewitching, yet restful and inviting. In this environment prospective customers could hear their favorite pieces played on the Aeolian organ or from the duo art rolls on the grand piano. It was also a rendezvous for musical celebrities for recitals, concerts, etc. The organ had about 21 stops and was of the usual high type of craftsmanship, both mechanically and tonally, always turned out by the Aeolian Company. I believe a Mr. L. C. Smith, one of the employees of the Aeolian Company, installed this organ, as also most of the other Aeolian organs that were erected in this vicinity. We serviced the organ for a long time.

One noteworthy feature of the organ was the Echo organ. It consisted of several stops and was placed in a room behind the main organ. The tone, however, was led through a duct over the entrance to the hall. It sounded very distant and ethereal and was put to good use in bringing out some wonderful musical effects.

In time, interest in the organ seemed to wane. Changes in management also took place, and due to the altered economic and social conditions among the wealthy clientele who formerly took so much pride in the owernship of one of these marvelous instruments, they now turned to the radio and other entertainment. Home life with its problem of domestic help was becoming increasingly difficult, with the result that many of the wealthy gave up their mansions and moved to apartments less difficult to maintain, and sought their entertainment in other places than at home. What was once a wealthy gentleman's object of pride — the ownership of a pipe organ — lost its attraction. The organ at Sherman Clay & Company, after standing idle for some time, was, I understand, finally disposed of and sent to Southern California.

DR. JOHNSON RESIDENCE ORGAN

Out in the Westwood Park District there was a neighborhood theatre on Ocean Avenue called the Balboa Theatre. They had a small Lethurby Smith organ of about 8 stops which had a pleasing tone and gave quite satisfactory service. The theatre was opened as a drawing card to attract business around it and establish a shopping center in the district. The aim of the promoters having been achieved and the neighborhood finally established, the little community theatre was not longer found profitable, and so it was abandoned.

The organ was purchased by Dr. Johnson, who had a young son, a very brilliant young chap of high school age, a musical prodigy. He was very much interested in the lighter type of music, but it was evidently Dr. and Mrs. Johnson's idea to give him opportunities to learn the study the more classic type of music and, by purchasing the organ and having it established in their home, they felt that he would have every opportunity to thus improve and develop musically.

About 1930 we removed the organ from the theatre and

installed it in Dr. H. H. Johnson's home on San Leandro Way. The installation was quite unusual. An excavation was made in the basement to house the organ. Through an opening in the floor of the living room, the tone entered the upper floor. Swell blinds were placed in the opening to control the volume of tone, and a wood grill of sufficient strength was placed over the opening, which at times was partially covered with a floor mat or rug. The console was in the living room.

Certain changes and additions were made by us to the organ while erecting it. At the time we were in possession of a fine three manual Estey console which had been replaced by a larger console of our own make on an installation job down the Peninsula. This console Dr. Johnson bought and we installed it in place of the original Lethurby Smith console. We also added a Tuba 16-8-4 unit and made some other minor changes.

I recall the first winter the organ was installed we were greatly shocked one day to be informed that the organ pit or chamber was flooded with water. Although the walls and floor were of about 8" thickness, the water from the severe rains prevalent that winter seeped through the concrete and had risen to about 2' from its floor. If I am not mistaken, the fire department was called to pump out the pit. Oil stoves were temporarily placed around to dry it out. However, immediate action had to be taken to avoid a similar occurrence at the next heavy downpour. It was finally decided to again dismantle and remove the organ temporarily and resurface the pit with some waterproof cement. This was done. The organ was then reassembled and put back into place, and since then has been free from further trouble from moisture or dampness.

Soon thereafter, however, the Johnsons sold their home with the organ, to other parties. We called occasionally to service it. I have often wondered if the young son for whose interest and cultural advantage his parents had installed the organ appreciated their efforts, and if he developed his musical taste and talents in the direction of the better class of music rather than along the lines of jazz and the frivolous type of music his parents objected to.

LINCOLN PARK PRESBYTERIAN CHURCH

Out on 31st Avenue and Clement Street in the Richmond District is located the Lincoln Park Presbyterian Church, a well built, imposing structure. I believe for some time after completion of the building the congregation functioned without a pipe organ. Later a used Johnston organ was secured. I do not know from where it originally came, or who installed the organ but, as frequently happens, we were later summoned to put the organ in tune and good working order. The organ consists of 12 stops, all enclosed in a swell chamber located behind a grill over the chancel. The detached console was to the left of the rostrum. In recent years a set of chimes was installed. Several years ago drastic changes were made. The console was removed from the Sanctuary in the front of the church to the gallery in the back where the choir was also located. Also the console was reconditioned. Evidently, the church finds this arrangement satisfactory.

TARAVAL TEMPLE

Taraval Temple Association is one of the outlying Masonic Lodges located in the Sunset District, on the corner of Taraval Street and 16th Avenue. Our first association with the Temple was when we were summoned by a Mr. Wright to repair a reed organ they had and which they intended to dispose of. This led to our making the suggestion that they secure a genuine pipe organ for their Lodge room. We submitted an estimate for a small, adequate organ suitable for their needs, at a fair and reasonable price. The gentleman above referred to, however, having business connections with one of the large banks of the City, was aware of the fact that one of the clients of the bank, The Nogert-Morton Company, was in default of payment of certain loans but had in its possession a number of used organs. He, therefore, worked out a deal in which the indebtedness would be liquidated, at least to an extent, by disposing of one of their organs to the Taraval Temple. We, not having previously seen the organ he contemplated procuring, or knowing any of the details of its construction, were engaged to erect it.

It was a four stop organ with automatic player attachment, evidently formerly located in a residence. At the outset we found it lacked a Swell box, apparently having previously been placed in a plastered room or enclosure. The Swell shutters that were sent along were of small dimension, far too inadequate for an effective swell effect. We also learned that it was voiced on the rather high pressure of 6" wind. This high pressure required a correspondingly stronger motor. Instead of a one-half or three-quarter h.p. motor that would have sufficed for a normal pressure, a three h.p. motor was required. This high powered motor made it necessary to put in a heavier circuit in the building to carry the load. Then another difficulty developed. In the Los Angeles area, where the organ was formerly located, 50 cycle current was used, whereas the San Francisco area had 60 cycle current. This necessitated the exchange of motors. After this exchange was made and heavier wiring installed, and the motor and blower were finally running, there developed an excessive vibration on the concrete floor on which the blower was placed, due undoubtedly to the blower being out of balance. This again had to be corrected by a machinist at considerable cost and worry. The whole blowing plant was then enclosed in a sound-proof room. As the organ was lacking a swell box and a proper case or exterior front, these also had to be applied.

After all these extra items had been finally attended to, we know the cost of the organ far exceeded the price we submitted originally for a suitable new organ build for their particular needs and requirements, and built right here in our home town. Nevertheless, the organ sounded well, and I presume as far as the rank and file of the Lodge members were concerned, they knew little of the many shortcomings and difficulties that had been encountered before the organ was satisfactorily installed and in playing condition.

We serviced the organ for a number of years after its installation. Finally, with the advent of the electronic organs, the pipe organ was dispensed with as the latter instrument seemed to lend itself more suitably to the needs of their lodge meetings. The pipe organ then found its final abode in the new Dominican Novitiate of St. Albert the Great in the hills of Berkeley.

CHURCH OF THE LATTER DAY SAINTS

One of the new churches of San Francisco, and also of a denomination of more recent origin, is the Church of the Latter Day Saints, located at 23rd Avenue and Lawton Street in the Sunset District. In 1940 they built their present new church, a structure of some proportions. I recall the completion of the edifice was somewhat delayed, either for want of material, labor, or cash, or some other reason.

A contract was made with the Austin Organ Company for a suitable pipe organ, Opus 2027, and our firm was entrusted with the installation, which work was done under the direct supervision of my brother, Otto. We progressed with the installation of the organ as far as conditions would permit. Then there was a long delay. When we were instructed to again proceed with the work, it was found that the uncompleted church had been burglarized in the interim; the generator for the organ and a lot of building material had disappeared. This again caused further delay, until a new generator could be procured.

The blower room was unfinished and the blower was standing on the loose ground. The organ, which had been erected months before in the unfinished church, did not fare any too well from this experience. We were plagued for some time thereafter with ciphers and all sorts of annoyances, due to the moisture the organ had absorbed, and the prevalence of grit, plaster and cement dust around the organ and blower room. Eventually, we succeeded in overcoming these troubles, and the organ is now functioning with the utmost satisfaction and reliability.

I might add that this organ is one of the newer type Austin organs, with a very pleasing tone. An innovation in reed construction was introduced to San Francisco in this Austin organ. The ordinary lead blocks of the reeds are reinforced with an additional support or block, adding about double the weight at the source of tone where the reed is fastened on the eschalot, producing a firm, resonant tone, a decided improvement on the customary procedure.

Unfortunately, the organ is located in a chamber to the left of the rostrum or choir loft, behind a grill, the openings of which are far too small for the full and satisfactory egress of the organ tone. Being located at the extreme left end of the choir loft, it completely upsets the symmetrical balance of the front part of the church, which is an annoyance to anyone with a sense of balance or symmetry. The organ consists of two manuals and Pedal, and has seven sets of pipes. A detached console, located a few feet beyond the organ, is of the usual Austin type. Tonally, the organ is of a most pleasing character, and undoubtedly it fills all the needs and requirements of the church.

MR. LOUIS DU MOULIN RESIDENCE

It is strange how events take place or come across one's path. In writing this book I have noted that practically every pipe organ, or at least every prominent one erected in San Francisco, most certainly in recent years, was listed, at least so I thought.

The early part of January 1946 we received a summons from a Mr. Emanuel Alvernaz, to inspect a dismantled Robert-Morton Theater Organ he intended buying, that was formerly located in the Harding Theater; also to inspect his home where he contemplated locating the organ permanently. Mr. Alvernaz was unfortunately afflicted with blindness, and on that account desired our evaluation of the Harding Theater organ and the practibility of its planned installation.

Being born in San Francisco and traversing its various districts continuously, I thought I knew about every locality worth knowing. I was advised to take a No. 6 bus, ride to the end of the line, walk one block west and one block south. I was soon made aware that I was riding in a district I had but seldom frequented, ascending the hills of Clarendon Heights. On leaving the bus a lady in an automobile hailed me, inquiring if I was Mr. Schoenstein. On stating that I was, she introduced herself as Mrs. Alvernaz who, in a few minutes, whisked me to a still higher elevation to their beautiful home overlooking this city and environs.

Two plate glass windows of huge dimensions, encompassing an unsurpassed view of Golden Gate Park, the Bay and the Golden Gate, with the Marin Hills opposite, were advantageously placed in the living room where the console was to be located. After looking over the basement, or lower floor, where the organ proper was to be located and finding it all satisfactory, they suggested driving me to the home of a friend nearby. This friend visited was Mr. Louis Du Moulin, who had a Wurlitzer organ in his so-called den or cocktail lounge. Soon the owner and his charming wife appeared, he attired in a Naval Officer's uniform evidently stationed at nearby Treasure Island. The organ was played, and indeed there were many novelties about it and the surrounding room with its bizarre lighting affects.

The instrument was satisfactorily installed, considering the work was done by an amateur. Its functioning seemed to be beyond criticism. The most unusual feature that caught my eye was that many of the pipes inside of the organ were painted. Some of the Diapasons in crimson red, some of the Tibias in a gaudy blue, some large open Basses were painted in jet black. By pushing a number of buttons fantastic lighting effects transformed the room into a weird place. Other unusual novelties consisted of a "Chrysolglot", cleverly camouflaged behind and abutting the console. Its closeness to the performer would ordinarily be condemned, but for the purpose for which it was evidently used, it was perfection. Another surprise was to hear and to see the chimes played. They were in two groups on either side of the organ opening. When a chime was struck a concealed colored light illuminated the chime struck, a most unusual and intersting effect. To make the setting more true to form, the host inquired graciously if I ever took a drink. I told him I never refused a good drink, whereupon we gentlemen toasted the gallant host and his charming wife on their typical jazz organ and wished the new owners of the Robert-Morton organ a satisfactory deal.

Had I not had the summons from Mr. Alvernaz to inspect this former Harding Theater organ that day, I should not have known of this unique installation in an otherwise unassuming home far out in the Sunset District.

OUR STUDIO ORGAN

About the year 1929, the influx of new organ installations seemed to be subsiding. The urge to do more constructive work ourselves took firmer hold on us, and realizing the need of more spacious and inviting quarters than those of our small shop at the rear of our premises at 2306 Bryant Street, where we had been located for almost 35 years, we looked about for a new site. We finally selected and bought the 25 x 104 corner lot on the southwest corner of Alabama and Twentieth Streets. An architect was consulted, who designed a suitable factory of three stories, with studio, offices, erecting room and lofts especially arranged to suit our needs. Mager Bros. were the contractors.

After its completion we soon decided and agreed that the studio would not be complete without a demonstrating pipe organ as a specimen of what we could build. It could further be used for practice purposes, musicals, etc. We, therefore, built an organ of six stops unified, all enclosed in a general swell box. The console was detached and placed in the opposite corner of the room. There was no exterior case to the organ, excepting the walls of the swell box. We concealed the latter by hanging a beautifully draped sateen curtain in front of it. Monks cloth drapes were placed on the numerous windows facing on Twentieth Street. A large mirror was placed on the wall. Two large pictures depicting scenes of Yosemite Valley, autographed photographs of celebrities and an assortment of other pictures found a place in the collection. A grass rug, wicker furniture and a large floor map completed the furnishing of the room.

From the outset the studio was much in demand, and was a mecca for organ students desiring a place to practice on a good organ, undisturbed and without many prohibitions and limitations. A charge of fifty cents an hour was made. At times, especially on Saturday afternoons, it was in great demand. The organ held up remarkably well, and received many favorable comments from all who played on it. Invariably when church committees called for a prospective new organ, a demonstration on the instrument was more conclusive than many words of super-salesmanship. In fact, several offered to buy the organ if it were for sale.

In time we further improved it by adding a Vox Humana 8', a Deagan harp and a set of chimes. We also later added an oak case with display pipes to it and discarded the beautiful turqoise blue curtain. Then an automatic player was attached. This, however, was not put to much use. The excellent swell expression in the organ, with its well voiced stops, and the otherwise pleasant and agreeable surroundings make the organ a much sought for instrument to play on.

During the year 1930 the organ was used to broadcast over Station KYA, with Dolla Sargeant at the console. Later, for a long period, the less prominent station KSAN used it for their broadcast under the supervision of Rev. Mildon. On one occasion we invited the Northern Chapter, American Guild of Organists to our factory, and the organ was used in giving a concert number and a description of it by Uda Waldrop. The business meeting also took place in the studio under the chairmanship of Mrs. Estelle Swift, the presiding Dean of the Northern California Chapter at that time. The outstanding event of the evening was the social gathering that followed in the adjoining loft. About seventy-five guests were seated at a table for a light repast. Sociability, oratory and music filled the fleeting hours. A pleasant and impressive incident of this event was the fact that my father, founder of the business, then 81 years old, and his four sons who all followed in his footsteps were present.

As stated, the studio organ is rented out for practice purposes to anyone desiring to avail himself of the privilege. Our most loyal and steadfast customer has been the well-known and one time child prodigy, Birdie Cohen. Young and old, sailors, soldiers, Salvation Army lassies, teamsters, teachers and organists of proficiency and accomplishment have found pleasure in practicing on the organ.

The most persistent and sacrificing student was a Miss Wallace, who often was waiting at the front door for it to be opened at 8:00 a.m. for her half hour of practice before going to her work downtown.

Other organs were also available at the factory and some customers preferred them; one a large two manual 21 stop Bergstrom organ, another a large Wurlitzer, formerly a theatre organ. Our studio seems to fill a need for those desiring a pleasant and convenient place to practice undisturbed.

ST. PHILIP'S CHURCH

St. Philip's Church on Elizabeth and Diamond Streets is one of the more recent established parish churches in the Noe Valley District. I recall in 1922 when the first temporary structure was built on Elizabeth Street. Rev. Jerome B. Hannigan was pastor at the time. Like all beginnings, so also the founding and development of this parish unit meant work and sacrifice. Having resorted to the holding of large whist parties as a means of parish income, St. Philip's parish soon ranked as the outstanding proponent of this medium for raising funds, and their card parties were attended by people from all over the City. Their example was followed by practically all other parishes since, with more or less success.

It was our privilege to sell Father Hannigan a large two manual Vocalion reed organ which had come into our possession. I believe it was originally in Judge Treadwell's residence on San Jose Avenue. At the church we installed a kinetic blower for the organ. Father Hannigan passed away in 1925. The organ, I believe, finally found its way, in 1927, to St. Paul's Episcopal Church on El Camino Highway in Burlingame. Meanwhile, St. Philip's Church built their new edifice at the corner of Diamond and Elizabeth Streets. Rev. Cantillion was appointed pastor in 1925 to succeed the late Rev. Hannigan. The church functioned without a pipe organ for many years. Knowing that the parish carried a heavy debt, we did not consider it as a likely prospect for a new pipe organ for a long time to come and therefore spared them the annoyance of frequent soliciting.

My brother, Leo, and his family had settled meanwhile in this neighborhood in 1916, and were faithful and devoted members of the parish. In time, the pastor became organ-minded and a pipe organ was purchased, which proved to be a very excellent Estey two manual and Pedal organ. In discussing the matter later with the pastor, he made the statement to us that the Schoensteins must have been asleep, as he was not aware that he had an organ builder and his family residing in his parish, or he would most certainly have done business with him. We, at the office, excused our apparent lack of alertness, stating that we felt that my brother being on the ground and a member of the parish would be summoned. Undoubtedly, his loyalty to the parish was of the genuine kind, in which religion was not mixed with business. My brother's son, Leo, Jr., serviced the organ for many years thereafter and it is now being serviced by our firm.

The organ at St. Philip's is a two manual and Pedal Estey, all enclosed, with two expression chambers. It has 12 straight stops. Bass notes are telescopic. Its tonal characteristics are typical of the Estey organ, a rich, pleasing tone. The organ occupies practically the full width of the choir loft. The console is located on the right side of the loft at right angles to the organ. The organ proper is concealed behind a partition with openings covered by grills. Over the organ, on either side of a beautiful art glass window, are two clusters of display pipes. The whole arrangement is unique and distinctive.

Being the parish church of my brother and his family, several outstanding events occurred there which will always remain fresh in my memory. The wedding of my nephew, Paul Schoenstein, to Madeline Costello in 1927, a happy and joyous event; the wedding of my niece, Helen, and Vincent Kelley in 1937; the funeral of my sister-in-law, Sophie Schoenstein, the wife of my brother Leo, who passed away in Honolulu, T.H., on February 16, 1943, the funeral taking place at St. Philip's several weeks later on March 15, 1943. Leo Schoenstein, Sr., followed Sophia, his wife, in death in 1951.

GENEVA AVENUE COMMUNITY CHURCH

Undoubtedly through the influence of Rev. Busher of the First Methodist Church we were recommended to Rev. Reneau as a reliable and competent concern to build a suitable pipe organ for their small church, on Geneva Avenue in the Crocker-Amazon District. A contract was awarded to us in 1937 to build a two manual and Pedal six stop, electric pneumatic, duplex action organ. The console was attached. A simple Philippine mahogany case was designed with a group of large display pipes. The pressure used on this organ was somewhat higher than we ordinarily used, due to the fact that we wanted to use several sets that we had on hand that were voiced on a higher pressure. This gave the organ a somewhat fuller and more pervading tone, resulting all told in a very pleasing and satisfactory instrument. The motor and blower were placed, as directed, in the room alongside the organ, but a better choice would have been made if they had been placed further away on the lower floor. The organ certainly meets all their requirements, and at some future time when a larger and more commodious church is built, the organ will still be adequate and serviceable. Rev. Herril, the present pastor, a young and most likeable clergyman, will undoubtedly be the means of bringing to fruition these plans for the future development of his congregation.

MILTON SCHWABACHER RESIDENCE

One day we were summoned by Mr. Schwabacher to his store, Schwabacher-Frey Company on Market Street, relative to the installation of a large Orchestrelle he had at that time stored in a warehouse. The organ was to be erected in his residence at the northeast corner of Clay and Gough Streets. After visiting the warehouse to look over the organ, the next move was to visit the residence to see how the organ could be brought into a certain room where Mr. Schwabacher wished it installed. On calling, I was graciously received and had the pleasure of meeting Mr. Schwabacher's mother. I recall with what loving affection and high esteem the son, well in middle age, spoke of his aged mother. After meeting her and being charmed myself with her motherly, sympathetic bearing, I understood the reason for the filial devotion of her son. I believe it was his purpose to install this automatic organ for her special pleasure and entertainment.

On being introduced to Mrs. Carrie Schwabacher and on hearing my name, she made further inquiries regarding my religion and nationality. When I told her that I was a Catholic and of German ancestry, the conversation drifted to the persecuted Jews in Germany, and she asked me what I thought of Hitler, just then looming up menacingly on the horizon. I assured her I did not approve of the persecution of any people on account of race or religion. With her motherly interest, she soon learned in the course of our conversation that I was the father of quite a family. Before leaving her home that day she gave me a large package, neatly wrapped, and said, "Something for the wife and children." On opening the package at home that evening, we found it contained, to the great delight of the whole family, a box of the choicest candies. And more than that, many of the morsels contained some deliciously flavored liqueur. It might have been at the close of the prohibition era, I do not remember, but no scruples were had in consuming the complete contents of the box.

Now a few words about the organ. I soon discovered that there was no way of getting the organ up into the particular room on the second floor of the residence where it was to be installed, due to its bulky size. After consultation with Mr. Schwabacher, it was decided to remove a window and cut an opening through the wall large enough to permit the organ to pass through. Mr. Irvine, the contractor, was soon on the job and the aperture was made. The next day a van with the organ arrived. A large jin pole was rigged up and in short order the organ was high up in the air and drawn into the room. The opening in the wall was then closed and the window replaced and everything restored to its original appearance. I called but once or twice thereafter.

I doubt if the mother ever played the organ as, after all, its manipulation did require some experience. Regardless, this incident left a deep impression on me, especially the thoughtfulness, the love and affection shown by a son for his aged mother. Mrs. Carrier Schwabacher, the charming woman above mentioned, was a native of California, and passed away at the age of 87 on May 24, 1945.

NAT C. MANEELY MORTUARY

It is strange how some organs do travel around. It was during the depth of the depression period, in 1933, when new jobs were few and far between, that a young gentleman, Mr. Vezina, called at our factory and asked if we could build him a small organ containing stops of a flute quality that would blend well with a jazz orchestra he was conducting evenings in his leisure time. He wanted something that was also portable and not too heavy. He paid a deposit and we set about to meet his requirements. Beauty of design was of no consideration — utility and quality of tone were what was wanted.

A one manual organ containing a flute and tremolo was designed, all enclosed in a swell box, with electric key action and a motor and generator. The organ was delivered to his home and he was greatly pleased with its performance, giving his jazz band something others could not brag of. The organ did not remain long in his home, however. I believe the depression finally got to him, too, and the organ found its way back to our shop.

Then, one day, Mr. Nat Maneely and his wife, proprietors of the Nat C. Maneely Mortuary Company, called on us looking for a small pipe organ for their establishment. They admired the mellow tone of this organ as it was so different and superior to the usual reed organ, and decided to buy it provided we could make a more artistic case for it, suitable for their chapel. This we did, designing and building an appropriate case of gumwood to conform to the finish of the chapel, and added a group of ornamental front pipes to further improve its appearance.

Miss Harriet Fish was organist for some time and liked the organ. The owners were also satisfied. However, for the purposes of a mortuary chapel, the organ should have had a softer stop, also a Dulciana or Salicional. Then the fact that it was a one manual organ with only a tenor C pedal was a cause of criticism from the organist as well as from others who occasionally played it. These critics, however, forgot that the organ was not originally made for mortuary chapel purposes, notwithstanding its prosaic, church-like organ front. The organ was again sold to a mortuary in Los Gatos, California. Whether further needed improvements were made, I do not know. The Maneelys, in turn, secured a new organ, A Wick's, one of not much greater content, but one containing a necessary soft stop and a standard console.

Harriet Fish, who, in addition to her duties as organist at the mortuary, was also organist at the Temple M.E. Church and the Portalhurst Church, was suddenly called by death. I attended the funeral services held for her at the chapel. The organ, accompanied by a select orchestra, played beautifully. The finesse with which the musicians played together, the expression and feeling put into their music, was touching. Mr. and Mrs. Maneely, as well as their successor after Mr. Maneely's death, have always been fine people to work for, appreciative and considerate.

HALSTEAD & COMPANY — Morticians

Halstead and Company, morticians on Sutter Street near Polk, were undoubtedly one of the first morticians to secure pipe organs for their chapels. I remember calling there to make some repairs on a small pipe organ. Later on, an opportunity presented itself to bid on supplying a second small organ or enlarging and modernizing the organ we had worked on previously. However, not being successful in our bidding, other parties did the modernizing work at that time.

Later, a small Wicks organ was acquired. I remember a not too pleasant occurrence happening to me on this organ. In climbing to a high spot in the organ, to the stoppers on the Pedal Bourdon, I believe, to get a support for my foot I stood on the rail holding the twenty note chime. This rail was not shouldered or screwed sufficiently and became dislodged. With a clang and din most unmusical, it fell on top of me.

Fortunately, I was not hurt, nor was any injury done to the organ. I replaced the frame, fastened it with more screws and put the chimes back in place. I was never deludged before with such unwelcomed music than on this occasion.

Another experience we had with these two organs was with their blowing plant. Each had a complete unit of blower and generator. One of them, either old or extensively used, was becoming worn out, noisy and ready all round for discarding. Instead of buying a complete new plant, we advised the use of the larger and better blower for both organs, with some slight change in the air pipes. This change was satisfactorily accomplished.

DR. MARKEL RESIDENCE

During 1930 when the Seventh Avenue Presbyterian Church was building their new edifice in the Sunset District, I had the pleasure of becoming acquainted with Dr. Markel, a physician and surgeon of note in the city, who was then acting in the capacity of chairman of the music committee with the definite purpose of selecting a suitable pipe organ for the new church. He and other members of his church visited our factory. We had submitted a proposal at his request for building an organ and our prospect of being awarded the contract seemed bright. However, we did not get the contract, as it was awarded to another firm, the Estey Organ Company. On interviewing Dr. Markel shortly thereafter to learn the reason for their rejection of our proposal, we learned that if we had not been so reluctant about making a reduction of several hundred dollars in our estimate, we would have had the contract. However, our business relations remained friendly. We eventually installed the new Estey organ he had selected and serviced it thereafter.

Evidently having had some experience in buying pipe organs, he later purchased a Robert-Morton theatre organ for his own home, located on Maywood Drive on the western slope of the Forest Hill District, overlooking the ocean. The organ consisted of about 6 stops, with chimes and a xylophone. It was placed in a room on the lower floor, and the tone entered the living room above through a grill. The console, as well as a beautiful grand piano, adorned this living room. The first time we were summoned to his home we found the organ in a deplorable condition and in urgent need of the services of an experienced organ mechanic. After a few days work, we had the organ tonally, as well as mechanically, in fine and satisfactory condition again.

While we were doing this work we had the pleasure of meeting Dr. Markel's charming little wife and learned that it was for her especial benefit and pleasure that the organ had been procured. We soon found that Mrs. Markel was quite proficient on the ivory keys and had a special fancy for the light, fantastic music typical of the Spanish people, from whom I believe she descended. This also explained why the xylophone was retained for a residence organ and one day, when she performed for us on the organ, I marveled at her skill in manipulating this percussion so efficiently in conjunction with the rest of the organ.

On a later visit we found Dr. Markel at home, an invalid. This was during 1945, I believe. Shortly thereafter the malady that afflicted him claimed his wife. Since then we have called only a few times to service the organ.

JAMES B. JAMISON RESIDENCE ORGAN

In 1925 the organ field in the West evidently seemed promising to some of the old-established organ builders of the East. Several of them found it advantageous to have a resident representative in this field of activity. The Estey Organ Company of Brattleboro, Vermont, selected Mr. James B. Jamison, the noted organ authority, as their representative. Being endowed with a pleasant personality and unusual ability as a successful salesman, his home company further enhanced his capabilities by erecting in his beautiful home he had built on Monterey Boulevard, in the St. Francis Wood District, a two manual and Pedal pipe organ with automatic player for demonstrating purposes. Thus equipped, Mr. Jamison made his mark hereabouts in disposing of a considerable number of Estey organs, among them some large four manual instruments.

It might be noted here that the home above referred to won the award from the American Institute of Architects as one of the best designed and most artistic residences built during the course of that year. Its gabled, slate-covered roof, its beamed and semi-plastered walls, its large leaded glass Tudor window through which one gets a glimpse of the beamed-ceiling living room, make a charming picture indeed. This was made more complete by the house being set back somewhat in a rustic garden, with tall eucalyptus trees as a background.

The organ that was installed was an Estey of two manuals and Pedal, of 9 sets duplexed, with harp and chimes, all enclosed in one expression chamber. The organ is built practically on a double deck plan. The chest and most of the pipes are on the upper level, the harp, chimes and mechanism on the lower level. A rather heavy drapery concealed the swell blinds. This drapery, of course, very definitely reduced the volume and reverberation of tone, but evidently it was satisfactory to the occupants of the house, probably desiring a more subdued ensemble. An automatic player was also applied to the console.

Mr. Jamison lived here for several years, but I believe with the approach of the depression he found it desirable to make other business connections. The home was vacated and Mr. Jamison moved to a new location in the hills at Los Gatos, California. From this beautiful but rather secluded spot, he continued to interest himself in the organ. He has written many interesting articles for "The Diapason", and other publications. He has also written a book in 1959, entitled "Organ Design and Appraisal".

Mr. Jamison later took over the agency of the Austin Organ Company of Hartford, Connecticut, and is again living up to his reputation as an untiring and efficient salesman. His knowledge and experience in the art of tonal design are being given some wonderful demonstrations in his new connection with the Austin Company, which is producing an organ now of more classic design, a drastic change from the Austin organ of years ago.

The Estey organ in Mr. Jamison's former home in San

Francisco has since been sold to the East Oakland Church of the Nazarene, where we have installed it and where it is in frequent use.

In 1957 Mr. Jamison's health seemed to decline rapidly, suffering a malignant illness and he passed away shortly thereafter. Our firm has since taken over the West Coast Agency of the Austin Organ Company of Hartford, Conn.

SEVENTH DAY ADVENTIST CHURCH
California and Broderick Streets

A Murray M. Harris organ was originally installed in the California St. M.E. Church and subsequently moved to the Grace United Church at 21st and Capp Streets. The church building at California and Broderick Streets was then acquired by the Seventh Day Adventists. Some alterations and improvements were made to the edifice; the pointed spire on the corner tower was removed.

For some time they carried on without a pipe organ. During the pastorate of Elder Sage, however, they seriously took up the matter of purchasing a pipe organ. We had a particular organ available at the time, which, however, would have required considerable alteration to make it fit into the chambers they had provided. Therefore, a more suitable and practical organ for their purposes was acquired, a Robert-Morton, a former theatre organ, and this was installed by the parties selling the organ. Evidently, it is satisfying all their needs and giving good service.

PORTALHURST COMMUNITY CHURCH

One of the more recent churches built in the Sunset District is the Portalhurst Community Church, located on Taraval Street at 14th Avenue. During the time the church was selecting an organ, we had a visit from their organ committee. Their final choice, however, was a small Wurlitzer organ of 3 sets unified. It was placed up in a loft in a rather large room on the left side of the chancel, behind three small openings covered by a grill. Evidently the tonal volume of the organ, placed in this location, was not up to their expectation, as arrangements were later made to partition off the large vacant space behind the organ so that all the tone would be directed out into the auditorium of the church. The console was placed on the left side of the chancel and is decidedly of the church organ type, and not of the usual theatre type. Miss Harriet Fish was organist of this church.

We serviced this organ regularly for some time. Later the church was enlarged, conforming to a plan originally layed out. Aware of the inadequacy of the small Wurlitzer organ, they now sought a larger and more suitable instrument. A two manual Moller organ was selected.

HAMILTON SQUARE BAPTIST CHURCH

In the early 90's while we lived in the neighborhood of Turk and Fillmore Streets, I recall neighbors of ours, named Robinette, attending services at Hamilton Square Baptist Church. At that time it was a small wooden structure, situated at the same location where it now stands, Post and Steiner Streets near Hamilton Square, a public park, from which it undoubtedly received its name.

In 1911 a new brick edifice was built and it was shortly thereafter, or during 1912, that we assisted Stanley W. Williams, associated with the Murray M. Harris Co. of Los Angeles, to install and complete the organ. It was a two manual and Pedal, electric pneumatic action, Murray M. Harris organ, with detached console and ten stops, a fine sounding organ as all the Murray M. Harris organs were. I thought the Diapason 8' on the Great manual was especially rich in harmonics, with that so-called "bloom" giving it life and richness in good measure. Other stops were of equally excellent quality and I believe it was in this organ that I saw pipes made of redwood for the first time. The organ was a gift of the women of the church, under the inspiration of their President, Mrs. Richard Bayne, a most charming person.

As excellent as the tone of the organ was, we immediately experienced difficulty with the mechanism. Many notes would not speak, or showed a tendency of speaking slowly, or with difficulty. The trouble was traced down to the unusual fact that the pouches of the pallet rails were surfaced with leather that was too thick, and which offered so much resistance, that the pouches were unable to open the valve discs. The pallet rails were then all removed, sent to the factory in Los Angeles and resurfaced with a leather of a lighter grade. Since then no unusual experience was had with the organ.

We serviced it regularly. Miss Orrie E. Young was organist for 25 years and knew better than anyone how to get the most out of this well liked organ. Rev. Louis J. Sawyer, D.D., was the revered and beloved pastor of the church until he retired.

We added a Vox Humana 8' stop, a gift of Mrs. William H. Barnes, and a set of Deagan chimes, a gift of Mrs. Clara E. Gentle, to the organ. Also a new motor driven fan Tremolo, which further improved the instrument.

In 1940 Miss Orrie Young, after many years service, relinquished her position. Several other pastors succeeded Rev. Sawyer, and it seemd that during depression years the congregation had hard sledding. In recent years, especially under the pastorate of Rev. Arno I. Weniger, D.D., it seems a new lease on life was obtained.

With the outbreak of World War II, however, and the resulting changes, especially with respect to new residents in the immediate neighborhood of the church, it was found desirous to sell the property to some other congregation and to buy elsewhere. Instead of following the usual procedure of going further west to a new section of the City, property was purchased further downtown, on the northwest corner of Geary and Franklin Streets. Here the foundations and basement for a modern edifice were built, the church meanwhile using the crypt for services until some future day when the edifice was fully completed. The old Murray Harris organ was left in its old abode for the use of the new congregation that took over the property, now called Jones Methodist Church.

In 1948 the new Hamilton Square Baptist Church was occupied. A two manual Wurlitzer organ was acquired and installed by other parties. Very shortly thereafter, we were solicited to put the organ in good working order and to service it regularly in the future.

LETHURBY STUDIO ORGAN

When the theatre organ was in its heyday, we became acquainted with a Mr. George Lethurby, then western representative of the Wurlitzer Organ Company. He was a suave, pleasing gentleman. On one occasion he invited me to come to his office, at that time located on the upper floor of the Eilers Building, to discuss some theatre organ installations with him. Sales of the Wurlitzer organs were being made at a rapid rate, everything seemed to be rosy, the future bright and promising. They were in need of experienced and expert help. Not being satisfied that we were installing organs for them, they wanted to have us in their direct employ, and as a feeler I was offered the tempting salary of $10.00 a day, a flattering offer at that time, to take over the work of installing the Wurlitzer theatre organs then being sold to many of the theatres. Having had too much experience in the ways of the world and knowing how short-lived are many of these prosperity flurries, and having too much regard and esteem for the work my father had done in past years in establishing his business which we were carrying on to the best of our ability, I declined the offer. Later on, my younger brother, Erwin, accepted an offer from them temporarily, and spent some time in their employ helping them out of an evident dilemma.

After the boom of theatre organ installations had subsided, Mr. Lethurby established himself in business and opened a store on Golden Gate Avenue and Leavenworth Street. He specialized in the sale of mechanical musical instruments, was agent for the Seaburg-Smith pipe organ and later became agent for the Everett Orgatron, an electronic rival of the Hammond electronic organ.

He had a Seaburg-Smith two manual and Pedal organ installed in his studio, which he used for demonstrating purposes and also rented to students for practice purposes. In

1941 Mr. Lethurby died, at a rather early age, and the business is carried on by his brother, Clarence Lethurby. The organ that had long been standing in his studio was finally sold to the Catholic Church in Salinas, California.

GRACE LUTHERAN CHURCH
Bayview

During the balmy days when the popularity of the theatre organ was at its height, many mechanics were drawn into the pipe organ field, some very efficient and some not so good. Among the very efficient ones was a Mr. Chas. Geschoeff, an Austrian of the old school, a good mechanic and a hard worker, and an all around pleasant person. As the boom subsided, and having accumulated considerable theatre organ material from the many jobs he worked on, he evidently decided to make a small pipe organ out of this material and eventually disposed of the organ. He succeeded in selling it to the Grace Lutheran Church in the Bayview section, on Brussell and Silliman Streets. We heard glowing reports of it at the time of its dedication, and apparently it came up to the expectations of its purchaser.

A year or two thereafter, however, we were called to service the organ and found it in need of a thorough going over. Having the makings of a good organ if its mechanical functioning was adjusted to work reliably and dependably, we hoped at some future calls to complete this work, as only the most necessary adjustments were made at the time of our first visit. However, we were never called to finish the job until in 1945, when my son, Lawrence, spent considerable time on it and greatly improved it.

Chas. Geschoeff apparently never seriously entered the church organ field as a builder. His greatest contribution was in the theatre organ field, where he did many rebuilding jobs, some of quite extensive proportions, while in the employ of the Turner and Dahnken Company, and later the West Coast and Fox Theatre Circuits. The organ referred to above is the only church organ in use in San Francisco built by Chas. Geschoeff that we know of.

This organ was built of parts of several makes of organs,

with varying types of magnets used, each with their troublesome peculiarities, with pipes of exaggerated scales, voiced on the high pressure the theatre organs were formerly voiced to. These pipes were altered and revoiced for a 3½" pressure, which made the organ difficult to tune and keep in order. The blowing plant was located in a cramped space on the ground under the organ with a motor belted to a Kinetic blower and another motor belted to a generator. One took his life in his hands to first lift a heavy soundproof door to get access to the blower and to navigate safely between these whirling belts and apparatus. On several occasions the organ was seriously soaked from bad leaks in the roof over the organ. In time, the congregation found it necessary to build a new and larger church. Property was secured at the corner of Woolsey and Somerset Street and a very substantial and functional church plant was built. The old church, with its organ, was sold to some other denomination. For the new church they secured a modernized, electrified two manual and Pedal Kimball organ from our firm.

FRED SUHR & COMPANY – Morticians

One of the most popular mortuaries in the Mission District, if it is proper to so designate a mortuary, is undoubtedly that of Fred Suhr and Company on Mission Street near 25th Street. Our first business with the firm was some years ago when the establishment was being rebuilt. We installed a set of Deagan chimes and placed them over an arched glass ceiling. They were played from a small movable keyboard which we applied alongside a reed organ in a loft on the opposite end of the chapel. Distance lent charm to these chimes and beautiful effects were obtained in conjunction with the organ accompaniment. We had always urged upon the management of this concern the desirability of securing a pipe organ for their chapel, but our urging seemed to go unheeded. However, in 1941, with surprising alacrity a Wicks pipe organ was secured and installed, undoubtedly filling a much felt want.

DR. CECIL E. NIXON RESIDENCE

Previously I have referred to several residence organ installations. Usually they were in the homes of the wealthy and elite, homes and mansions whose exteriors bespoke the beauty and grandeur that was within. However, the home of Dr. Cecil Nixon, a dentist, had none of these attractions to offer, rather the opposite. It had the most depressing and uncanny appearance on the outside, and brought thoughts to the visitor of a haunted house, a forsaken and abandoned home. Such was my impression when I first called at Dr. Nixon's home on Broadway, near Van Ness Avenue.

Previous to this visit, possibly some time in 1930, Dr. Nixon called at our factory relative to securing some material to build an automatic player pipe organ for his home. I was absent from the office at the time and he was directed to St. Peter's Church nearby, at 24th and Alabama Streets, where I was working on the organ. Here Dr. Nixon explained to me what he was after. I found him a most pleasant and affable gentleman, a tall, slim figure, bespectacled, with drooping moustache and a rather luxuriant crop of long, unkempt hair. In his presence one was aware that one was not speaking to an average person. Intellect and scholarship seemed to stamp his every mannerism. He invited me to his home to better describe and explain to me what he desired for his contemplated organ.

I had heard of Dr. Nixon frequently in the past and had read articles in current magazines and papers about his achievements in the realm of mechanical design; about his creation of the famous lifelike robot, the Egyptian Princess Isis, who played three thousand tunes on a zither at a spoken command; about the many mysterious appliances he had in his home, of doors opening automatically at a given word, of magic notes of a silver flute floating through the air when ordered, and of many other uncanny things happening at the most unexpected moments. With Dr. Nixon's natural bent for mechanical development and his fondness for music, it was not surprising that he should eventually turn to the great and enthralling possibilities of the pipe organ.

With this in mind, I called on him. We were able to offer

him the so-called tracker board of a former Aeolian pipe organ, and with this and other parts that he acquired from some theatre organs, he was able in time to assemble and construct a sizeable organ, which he erected in the basement of his house. The console was placed on an alcove on the upper floor and the sound came up through a duct into the living room.

A word or two about the interior of the home may be of interest. There is undoubtedly no other home in San Francisco so unique. The forlorn appearance of the exterior of the house, with its almost blackened walls and unwashed windows, with the shades invariably drawn, is no indication of what one finds inside. Though rather gloomy, no finer specimen of architectural beauty and high clsss workmanship in woodcraft, carving, and finish can be found. Practically all the doors, walls and ceiling are adorned by richly carved panels, friezes, mouldings, etc., in costly woods with finish of the highest excellence. The floors are layed in beautiful parquetry.

I doubt if Mr. Nixon himself was the creator of all this beautiful craftsmanship. But knowing that he was a lover of anything that is beautiful, and one who can appreciate true art and craftsmanship, I believe he acquired many of these choice pieces of woodcraft from some of the famous old mansions in the City that were being razed to make room for modern structures. Regardless of where he acquired the many superb pices, the fact of his assembling and fitting these pieces together and making a homogeneous architectural unity out of this varied assortment, if such an achievement is possible, is to me a most remarkable fact.

I do not know anything of the private life of Dr. Nixon, but would assume that it is that of a recluse and bachelor. On leaving his home I thought the only thing lacking was the feminine touch of some charming woman, someone to tidy up, hang some curtains on the windows, place some fragrant flowers about and, above all, let a bit of our glorious California sunshine into those darkened rooms. Then art, beauty and music could really thrive there and come into their own.

Dr. Nixon, a national figure, is deserving of a little further introduction to my readers, who, perhaps, have not heard of his achievements in recent years, as he seems to be less in the limelight today than he was several decades ago. Dr. Nixon was born in the Virgin Islands, his father an Englishman, his mother an Austrian. At the age of five he was brought to America. His father was a teacher and professor and planned for his son a similar career, a life of culture and refinement. However, through a sad and regretable incident, his father met an early death and the necessary means to put the son through college and in the upper strata of elite society were not forthcoming. Young Nixon was thus put on his own resources and at the age of 19, through the influence of some wealthy friend, secured employment with the Pacific Steel Rolling Mills of San Francisco as assistant draftsman. Here his natural bent for the mechanical, a talent his parents recognized in him and never discouraged, notwithstanding their hope for a more intellectual career for him, stood him in good stead. He soon proved his ability and gained valuable knowledge of the many intricacies of ship and bridge building, of structural design and of electricity and the mechanical crafts connected therewith. He used his spare time to gain further knowledge at home in experimenting with his pet theories and hobbies, and in time he had many interesting inventions to his credit. He also became an accomplished magician and was admitted to membership in the Society of American Magicians.

The thing that undoubtedly contributed most to bring him into the limelight was the creation of his famous robot, or automaton "Isis", to which he, or the public, ascribed almost human capabilities. This became the object of much debate in the public press. In an article describing his creation, the author claims that "Isis possesses all human qualities." Dr. Nixon in his articles also refuted the much heralded claims of communication with the spirit world made by the late Conan Doyle and other psychics, and countered with the statement that, while he believed in the spirit world, he could reproduce through mechanical and scientific devices all the spirit manifestations which they claimed.

I expected in the near future to be called upon to tune and adjust his excellent pipe organ, as undoubtedly with all his skill and ability, as above referred to, there are still some unsolved mysteries in a pipe organ which even a magician of his exalted position has not conquered. Here the humble organ tuner with his years of specialized experience comes into his own. I had the pleasure of putting his organ in tune. I feel certain that had Dr. Nixon in his early youth been fortunate enough to become intrigued by the mysteries and intricacies of the pipe organ, he would have become an even greater magician and wizard of the apparently impossible, than he is today.

ST. JOSEPH'S HOSPITAL CHAPEL

On the heights of Buena Vista Park, overlooking the city, is the popular and much patronized St. Joseph's Hospital, conducted by the Franciscan Sisters of the Sacred Heart. Formerly they conducted a home for old people, where the folks bought themselves in and resided until they passed away.

In time beautiful new fireproof buildings were erected, a nurses' home was built, also a beautiful chapel. For many years the nuns contented themselves with a small harmonium. Services at the chapel were popular, and were attended by the patients when possible, by the nurses and the nuns and by the many visitors who frequented the institution. In years past, the institution was especially popular with the German-speaking people of the City, as originally most of the nuns were of that nationality, and the chaplains were mostly furnished by the Franciscans from St. Boniface Parish.

The hospital has been up on the hill for 74 years. I recall an incident of my early youth that occurred about 1894, that I always think of with pleasure. My mother was an ardent lover of nature. Owing to the fact that she was always busy about the home attending to the needs and wants of her large family of ten children, she had little opportunity to enjoy the outdoors or see the countryside. On this occasion she had expressed a desire to witness what she hoped would be a beautiful sunrise from the top of the hill at St. Joseph's

Hospital. We then lived at Turk and Fillmore Streets in the Western Addition. The night before she told my brother Frank, then about 13, and me, about 10, that she wanted us to accompany her on the outing the next morning. It must have been during the spring or summer months. We arose very early. The weather was ideal. It was on a Sunday morning. After partaking of a very light repast, as we expected to be back again at the usual breakfast hour, we started out while it was still dark and walked up to the hill, which required about a half hour's brisk walk. Mother seemed to be a bit worried at being out at that hour of the morning and of possibly being accosted by strange men roaming the streets. But then she had her two stalwart bodyguards, so everything seemed to be okay, until we started climbing through the underbrush and trees covering the hill. At that time it was still in the wild, primitive stage as nature had made it. It was not yet laid out as a city park, with beautiful pathways leading to the summit. As dawn was breaking and the rays of the sun had not yet come up over the horizon, we were not too sure of our footing and had to climb cautiously. Suddenly what my mother most feared, occurred. A drunken man was lying under a bush, evidently sleeping off his over-indulgence of the night before. Our approach awakened him and he mumbled some incoherent words about our disturbing his sleep, but did not molest us otherwise. We hurried on to leave him behind us, also to reach a higher level and to get an unobstructed view of the eastern horizon, with the hills of Oakland across the Bay, and Mt. Diablo in the distance dominating all, the glistening waters of the Bay, and the downtown section of the City, South of Market, the Western Addition and the Mission District still in peaceful slumber. The sky that morning happened to be dotted with numerous small, fleecy clouds. We had arrived none too early at our destination. The gradual awakening of the dawn, unfolding entrancing colors and hues on the beautiful scenery as the sun came up, finally tinging every cloud with color ever changing, until the mighty golden sphere rose over the hills in full view, was a sight I shall never forget in all my life. I have seen some sunrises from a mountain top over the clouds since then, and many a gorgeous sunset from the rear of my modest home, which has a western exposure, but I cannot recall seeing a more magnificent and beautifully colored sky, with its tinge of gold, than the sky on this particular morning.

Added to the beauty of the heavens was the beauty of awakening nature around us. The birds greeted us with their happy song, the dewdrops on flowers and foliage sparkled in the sunlight, the air was fresh and fragrant, all combining to make this an unforgettable experience of my childhood. Having achieved our desire of witnessing this wonderful spectacle, and I am sure in our hearts we gave praise to the Creator for his glorious works, our thoughts returned to earthly things and we began to feel hungry. The half hour's hike and the climb up the hill had intensified our appetites considerably. Being Sunday morning, and as we were close to St. Joseph's Hospital, my mother suggested that we attend mass in the Sisters' chapel there, instead of going to St. Boniface Church, as we usually did on Sunday morning. We arrived at the hospital in time for the 7:30 a.m. mass. I recall the nuns singing the familiar German hymns that we, as children, sang at St. Boniface Church, and I was delighted to find that these beautiful hymns were being sung in other places and not alone in St. Boniface's.

Evidently breakfast was also being prepared at the hospital for soon we perceived the fragrant aroma of freshly made coffee permeating the chapel. My hunger became intense. I was almost famished, and yet I had to wait for my breakfast until we arrived home again. I shall never forget as long as I live the keen desire I had at that time for a cup of coffee and a piece of toast, or something else to eat. No wonder my fondness for coffee follows me through life.

St. Joseph's Hospital has been the rendezvous and place of refuge for many a friend, relative and sick member of our family in the years gone by. It also has been the birthplace of several of my children, and the final scene in the departing life of several of my relatives. One of these relatives, especially dear to me, was an aged uncle, F. B. Schoenstein, who passed away at the age of 85 years. A short time after his death I had the privilege, as his executor, to present the institution with a substantial check, carrying out a bequest he had made to the hospital in his will. St. Joseph's Hospital has been the recipient, no doubt, of many larger bequests, and from one of these, if I am correctly informed, the new organ that now adorns the Chapel was secured.

Our firm had always hoped and expected that when the time arrived to supply the Hospital Chapel with a pipe organ we, as local manufacturers and as friends of the institution, would at least be considered. This was not the case, however. We were informed that when the time had come to select an organ, a prominent member of the clergy and a leading organist in the City were consulted and their advice sought as to which was the best pipe organ manufactured. Their verdict was the Aeolian-Skinner organ, apparently. "No sooner said than done," a Skinner organ was ordered. Hearing rumors that an organ was to be secured, we inquired and were given the information that the contract had already been let, and that the best organ obtainable was going to be installed. We, ourselves, were always great admirers of the Aeolian-Skinner organ, and had recommended it as the best on several occasions. Yet we did not consider their product and reputation so all-inclusive, as to exclude other builders entirely from consideration.

The Aeolian-Skinner organ installed is a two manual and Pedal instrument, with electric pneumatic action. The console is detached and the entire organ is under expression. It has 9 stops. The organ was installed by an Aeolian-Skinner representative in 1939. It was placed in a specially built chamber. The tone of the organ is typical of the recent Aeolian-Skinner organs, over-rich in the mutation stops, especially for so small an instrument. However, the organ has its admirers who speak in praise of its tonal resources.

HERBERT LAW RESIDENCE

Nestled among the sumptuous mansions on Nob Hill was an apparently modest residence, at least so it appeared on the outside, having a frontage of no more than 25 feet, two stories in height, of gray sandstone finish. It was located on the south side of California Street, between Taylor and

Mason Streets. Like many of the residences of the wealthy in the gay '90's, this residence was also equipped with an organ, true, not a pipe organ, but an Aeolian Orchestrelle. The organ at that time had the old 58 note single manual music spool and a one manual keyboard, with an ornate case. My father was called upon to repair the organ, so I had the privilege of accompanying and assisting him. Although the building was only two stories high in front, in the rear it counted four stories as Nob Hill at this point precipitately declines to the south. Inside, the home was sumptuously furnished with exquisite carpets, rugs and draperies, period furniture, objects of art and paintings. As the location of this residence was practically in the center of the fire area of the great conflagration of 1906, it quite naturally was expected that it would be consumed and destroyed by the fire along with the many other residences surrounding it. But such was not the case. The structure remained unharmed, possibly due to some change of air current or draft, and the fact that on the adjoining property to the east and west there were tall stone buildings which, however, were destroyed, offering a sheltering protection to this house. It thus shares the distinction of being one of the few buildings that were thus spared and unharmed, though completely surrounded by fire. Nob Hill has since been rebuilt, not with the homes and mansions of the wealthy as of yore, but with an imposing Cathedral of the Episcopal Church, apartment houses and hotels of worldwide fame. The residence above referred to still nestles between two tall apartment houses. However, its former owner disposed of his equity and no new residents have occupied the home.

The last time we serviced the Orchestrelle for Mr. Law was in 1914. I often wondered on passing the house in later years, what had become of the Orchestrelle. Thirty-one years had passed by when one day during 1945 we received a telephone call from a Mr. Stevens Heershey of 1015 California Street asking us to call relative to the moving of a Vocalian organ, and to quote a price for the purchase of it. On calling, I found it was none other than the former Herbert Law residence, and the Aeolian Orchestrelle, wrongly named, that I had worked on as a youngster.

The home had all the grandeur it had in the past, but the organ was not the same any more. Its original beautiful case had been removed and the interior of the organ was placed in an alcove, just leaving the keyboard protruding from the wall. This was artistically done; the keyboard was removed from the front and placed at the narrow end of the organ. The old 58 note single tracker bar was removed and replaced with the modern double tracker board. Robert-Morton pipes and associated equipment had been added to make the organ a real pipe organ. All pneumatics were releathered and the organ retubed. In place of the foot treadle, a kinetic blower was applied and placed in the basement. This work was done presumably during 1923. We bought the organ and removed it to our factory. It is remarkable how organs persist in surviving, almost outdoing the cat's proverbial nine lives.

AMBERG HIRTH RESIDENCE

On the brow of Telegraph Hill, an old landmark of San Francisco, just opposite a deep and threatening declevity, a former quarry, a modern but unpretentious apartment house of several stories was located. We were called upon to build and install a pipe organ there. The owner of this apartment, Mr. Amberg Hirth, an art and antique connoisseur, apparently knew what he wanted and it was our good fortune to build it for him.

It was a small, unified organ, of three units of exquisite tonal quality. As the organ was not to be boisterous and unduly loud and annoying to other tenants of the building, every precaution was taken that its tone would not penetrate beyond the confines of the owner's own apartment. Incidently, the motor and blower were also located within the organ. The object sought, to prevent the organ music from penetrating beyond the confines of the apartment, was admirably achieved. The organ proper was concealed behind a light drapery and only the keyboard was exposed, the latter being finished in a light cream shade, with an egg shell finish, conforming with the most charming color scheme of the apartment.

My brother, Otto, in 1943, installed this instrument. I

recall, in assisting him moving the material up into the apartment, how I was impressed with the unusual vista that greeted one. Directly below was a steep embankment, then one looked over the roofs of warehouses and just beyond them to the broad Embarcadero from where the piers of San Francisco's famous waterfront jut out into the Bay. With World War II in the throes of its greatest activity, every pier was occupied with vessels waiting to be loaded for their voyage to the Orient. The Embarcadero was teaming with activity, with moving vans and trucks, the Belt Line Railroad switching and shuttling its freight cars on the network of spur tracks. Out in the stream more ships were anchored awaiting docking facilities. Although born in San Francisco and knowing the City well, this view was unexpectedly new and fascinating to me. I thought what a contrast. Below, the hill, activity, bustle, commotion and thriving industry and shipping; above, in the apartment, quiet and an ever changing panorama of the Bay through the spacious windows.

SOKOL HALL

In 1920, we were called upon to tune and adjust a Kimball pipe organ of two manuals and Pedal, pneumatic action, of the usual stock type, with 6 sets of pipes, in a hall located on Page Street in the Western Addition. The party who summoned us was a gentleman of foreign birth or extraction, with a decided foreign accent in his speech and I, therefore, presume the hall was a rendezvous of possibly a Polish or Slavic organization. Who originally installed the organ, or what eventually became of it, I am not able to record, as I never had occasion to work on the organ again. The hall is no longer there, the organ evidently having been moved.

CENTRAL METHODIST CHURCH

On the corner of 14th and Belcher Streets there is a three story building which I thought was a flat or apartment house. One day we were directed to tune a large Estey reed organ on

14th Street, and discovered that it was the Central Methodist Church, the building I previously thought was only a flat. The Church auditorium is located on the lower floor, the Sunday School adjoining, with windows facing on Belcher Street. The upper floors are living quarters.

After the depression years, when the congregation evidently came into better financial standing, persistent discussion was had about securing a pipe organ. It was under the pastorate of the Rev. Arne O. Nielsen in 1943 that the contract was finally signed with our firm, to build a small two manual and Pedal electric pneumatic unified organ of three units. The organ was placed to the right of the chancel, behind a grill, the detached console placed a short distance in front of it.

This small organ was a stock organ of which we had built quite a number. It had a well designed case made of Philippine mahogany, consisting of two large Gothic panels on either side and a group of decorated gold pipes in the center. The minister approved the design of the organ front and would have preferred to have the organ, with its ornate case, placed directly behind the altar. However, since no space was available he had us install it in the alcove to the right of the chancel and placed behind a grill. The original organ front, however, with its gold pipes, was placed as he desired, in back of the altar and incorporated in the cabinet work, making it a very impressive background, possibly also deceiving many as to where the organ tones came from.

ST. STEPHEN'S EPISCOPAL CHURCH

In the Western Addition, on the west side of Fulton Street near Fillmore Street, stood a typical old fashioned church of frame construction, called St. Stephen's Episcopal Church. I recall passing it often as we lived in the immediate neighborhood as children.

It seems that the life blood of St. Stephen's gradually ebbed away, for what reasons I do not know. At any rate, the congregation disbanded and the edifice was taken over by some Orthodox Russian or Greek Church. As there was no need for a pipe organ, their singing being done in acapella style, they wished to have it removed. This was the motive of my first visit to the church.

We did not secure the contract to remove the old organ and as there was no name plate or identification of the builder on the organ, I do not know who the builder was. It was an old two manual and Pedal tracker organ of about 10 stops and was certainly not built by any local builder. It evidently came from the Atlantic Seaboard and could have been an Appleton or Simmons organ.

From reliable sources I later heard it may have been secured by the Federated Community Church of Santa Clara, California, who undoubtedly used the pipes in an organ being constructed for their church by one of their own parishioners.

GLAD TIDINGS TEMPLE

About 1939, the Glad Tidings Temple and Bible Institute built a large edifice on Ellis Street near Buchanan Street, with adjoining structure used as a College and living quarters for its students. I was impressed with the size of the auditorium, seating about 2000 people and always considered the Institution as a prospect some day for a suitable pipe organ. However, during the ten or twelve years of the depression period the outlook became less hopeful. During the interim pianos, reed organs and an electronic organ were tried, but it seems with unsatisfactory results.

With the approach of World War II and a general prosperity again prevailing, reflecting its affect on many a religious institution in a more satisfactory financial status than for many years previous, the thought of obtaining a suitable pipe organ came up again.

In 1944, we received a summons from a Mr. Douglass to inspect a large Wurlitzer residence organ at his country estate in Menlo Park, California, and to advise on its removal and disposal. Upon arrival we were astounded at the vastness of the estate. We were impressed with the verdant grandeur of its parklike landscape, at the size of the home, its stateliness, with its covered carriage entrance, its broad marble stairs leading up gradually to the main entrance. On opening the massive doors we entered a large reception room. Directly opposite was a spacious living room, abutting this room was the music room in which, upon entering, the console of an organ was discernable at once, made of walnut finished in gold, in Louis XVI design. This former home was now unoccupied and was under the supervision of a caretaker; it was also unheated and its chillness and claminess, notwithstanding its architectural beauty and the luxurious furnishings, affected me visibly. How short lived was this luxury and abundance. These marble halls, once the scene of gaiety, joy, laughter and hospitality were now as silent, cold and dismal as a tomb.

The organ was located in two chambers in the basement and the tone was lead through a duct into the music room above. Although we found the organ in apparent perfect condition, an accumulation of spider webs and nut shells, evidently carried there by field mice, indicated that these uninhabited precincts were not tread by anyone for many a day. As no current was available in the building, the organ could not be tried, but from the high class workmanship that was plainly evident and the well preserved condition of the organ, we made a proposition to remove it from the mansion, store and erect it temporarily in our factory until a purchaser was found for it. The organ was a typical Wurlitzer instrument consisting of 13 sets of pipes. These were voiced expressly for residence use and were not of the extreme theater type. Therefore, we had every confidence that in a reasonable time we would readily dispose of it.

It so happened that shortly after the organ was installed in our factory and in playing condition, representatives of the Glad Tidings Temple called relative to the purchase of a pipe organ. On hearing this Wurlitzer they immediately became interested and considered acquiring it for their use. Satisfactory terms were made, the organ purchased, certain minor alterations and improvements were made, an automatic player with which the organ was originally equipped was removed. Two excellent, spacious chambers were built at the church on either side of the choir gallery to house the organ and the instrument was then erected. It more than satisfied the needs of the institution in furnishing dignified church music, also the lighter type of music for religious pageants, dramas and cantatas.

BETHEL AFRICAN METHODIST CHURCH

Bethel African Methodist Church was located on the west side of Powell Street near Pacific. To my knowledge they had no pipe organ in their church before the fire. After the fire, on or about 1907, they rebuilt on the same site and we installed a two manual and Pedal electric action, detached console, Austin Chorophone organ, Opus 1328. In addition to the usual front case that accompanied the Chorophone organ, a second case was also provided and erected on the opposite side, filling up a corner to a very good advantage.

The church, in 1944, sold the old site and moved to its new location on the East side of Laguna Street, between Golden Gate Avenue and McAllister Street, occupying an old church that was built in 1875, and was formerly used by various denominations. The Chorophone of the old church was installed in this new location by my brother, Otto, with some slight alterations in the case design, and is giving excellent results.

ROSCOE OAKES RESIDENCE ORGAN

The many years we have been actively engaged in the organ business in San Francisco would naturally imply that we were thoroughly familiar with the pipe organ field in our own city, that we knew of every pipe organ existent, its history, when installed, etc. This knowledge we thought we had at our disposal, the natural result of many contracts, inquiries by mail and phone and the indirect means of the grape-vine route. However, notwithstanding these aides, we were surprised to learn one day from a sexton of one of the churches we serviced, of a neighbor of his living in an apartment house, having an Aeolian pipe organ. It was news to us. I made note of the party and intended at some future time, when work was more slack, to look him up for possible future business opportunities.

However, a few months later, we unexpectedly received a phone call from the gentleman, Mr. Roscoe Oakes, residing at 2600 Washington Street, near Gough, on the tenth and eleventh floors, in possibly one of the most picturesque sites in San Francisco, directly opposite Lafayette Square, to call and inspect his pipe organ and see if we could dispose of it for him. The organ had been installed in 1926. It was an Aeolian, two manual and Pedal organ of 11 stops, with Harp and Chimes and was placed on one side of the music room. Its opening grill was partly concealed by a tapestry, with clusters of display pipes placed in heavy oak paneled doors on either side. On the opposite side of the room and to one end, was the console containing a Duo Art Player. The motor and blower were in the penthouse on the roof. The organ was practically all enclosed with the exception of the Pedals, Harp and Chimes. On the floor on which the organ was located, but ahead of the expression blinds, an opening to the floor below was made, covered with a grill, to permit the organ to be heard and enjoyed on the lower floor also. For reasons unknown to us, this beautiful instrument of exceptionally fine workmanship and exquisite tonal color was no longer wanted.

Fortunately, we had a client interested in the purchase of an Aeolian Organ. This happened to be the nuns of St. Mary's Hospital, San Francisco, the Sisters of Mercy whose Mother-house is at Burlingame, California. Years before they had purchased the estate of the late Frederick Kohl with its beautiful medieval mansion, containing a rather large Aeolian organ. This mansion was converted to a high school and the Aeolian organ was then transferred by us to their new Convent building, erected a short distance therefrom. So pleased and satisfied were the Sisters with this organ that it was a foregone conclusion that no other make of organ would be acceptable for their beautiful chapel at St. Mary's Hospital. Being on the lookout for this type of instrument we realized our opportunity and informed the Sisters of the prospect, arranged for an inspection and demonstration. A price was agreed upon and the organ was purchased. This occurred in 1948.

It was now our task of first removing it preparatory to erecting it in its new location in St. Mary's Hospital Chapel. After a casual examination we soon discovered that we were up against several difficulties. Only the front portion of the console was finished and visible, the back portion was built securely into an alcove. In its new location it would be entirely exposed and would therefore have to be completely enclosed. We at once realized the removal of the pipes and large organ parts would be a problem. There was a rather large service elevator that went only to the tenth floor and a small automatic passenger elevator terminating at the eleventh floor. The latter was the only one that could be used. It was during vacation season, however, when many of the tenants were away so the interruption of the elevator service would not inconvenience anyone.

We could not bring our packing cases, stored meanwhile in the basement, up to the organ as they were too bulky for the elevator. Therefore, all pipes had to be carried down in small lots and packed in the cases in the basement below. After removing all the smaller pieces, the pipe chest, which was made in one whole piece measuring about 7' by 8' by 28" remained. After carefully examining all possible exits, stairways, even the possibility of moving the chest to an adjoining roof through a window or French doors, we were stymied on account of the iron bars on the window casement. We finally made a templet of light wood of the size of the chest and experimented whether we could lower the chest on the top of the passenger elevator to the basement floor. After making the necessary trial we decided on this procedure. A strong temporary platform was built on top of the elevator cage, two experts from the elevator company were engaged to operate the elevator manually. With a crew of other necessary help, the bulky chest, weighing about 800 pounds, was skillfully placed on top of the elevator cage, with little margin to spare, diagonally across the elevator shaft. We lashed the chest to the cables and three of us made the descent down the deep shaft. During my many years of experience in the organ business, this was my first experience of this nature. The removal of this large piece, it seems, was not only our worry but everybody about the place seemed to be concerned. The owner of the apartments conveniently arranged to be absent and especially to have his wife elsewhere. The two maids were concerned whether the cables would hold the heavy load. The carpenters who already had begun alteration work where the organ formerly stood were anxious until word was passed around that we had arrived at the basement safely. A sigh of relief seemed to go up from all, especially the maids. I must say I felt greatly relieved to be closer to Mother Earth again. The elevator was now resting on the floor of the sub-basement but we found that an additional drop of about two inches was needed for the chest to clear the basement door. By skillful work on the part of the elevator experts, including reducing the tautness of the cables, the cage settled that amount and by some dexterous juggling and heaving, by a hairs breadth, we succeeded in getting the chest through the elevator door into the base-ment. As we were just emerging from the shaft, greasy and grimy from the oily cables, perspiration on our foreheads and breathing heavily, Mr. Oakes appeared on the scene, delighted to see the crisis had passed. He congratulated us on a good piece of work.

The removal of the blower from the penthouse on the highest part of the building was also no small matter. Although the motor was removed and all fans and baffle partitions were taken out to reduce the weight to a minimum, it still was a heavy piece to handle. After removing it from the penthouse onto a small roof we had to ascend a parapet of about five feet and then descent another fifteen feet to a story below. This was done on skids, with a block and tackle to hold it back. This job was also successfully accomplished, aside from a broken roof tile caused by the skids shifting and the weight resting on the tile.

While making these preparations and doing this work, we certainly enjoyed the vista from atop this lofty apartment house. The view was superb and inspiring. I have always been a great admirer of the romantic and picturesque setting of San Francisco, but the unobstructed view from this vantage point, embracing the ocean, the Golden Gate, Alcatraz and

Angel Island, the beautiful Bay, the docks and the ever-changing vistas of beautiful San Francisco, gave me further pride in the City of my birth and its justififed claim of being the Queen City of the Pacific Coast.

Previous to the dismantling and removal of these heavy parts of the organ, I inquired of Mr. Oakes just how they were originally brought up, but never received a clear or satisfying answer. I assumed that the building was in course of construction at the time and that the elevators were not installed, allowing an unobstructed lift through the empty elevator shafts. Neither Mr. Oakes or others about the place seemed to remember, until we finally had it in the basement. One of the employees of the building attracted to the scene by the interruption of the elevator service, remembered that all the organ parts were hoisted outside of the building by a steam donkey engine to the eleventh floor and the penthouse above. So our planning to do the work in a different way, possibly more laboriously and with some doubt of success, was rewarding after all.

CHURCH OF THE EPIPHANY

One of the beautiful and impressive edifices built in the Crocker-Amazon District, is the Church of the Epiphany, on Vienna and Amazon Streets. When the present, permanent church was built, its revered pastor, Rev. Maurice J. O'Keefe, a most amiable gentleman, was also desirous of getting a suitable pipe organ.

At about this time the First Congregational Church of Berkeley, California, had built their new church and were using the organ formerly installed in the old edifice, which we had subsequently enlarged and electrified. They now wanted a new and more modern instrument and bought a large Moeller organ. The old organ, therefore, was available and for sale.

We advised Father O'Keefe to purchase this instrument, provided a new console and other necessary improvements were made. Who the actual builders of this organ were still remains a doubt to us, as the organ never had a name plate.

We believe, however, it was built by Thomas Whalley of Berkeley, and his erstwhile partner, Mr. Edwin A. Spencer. The name of a Mr. Klann was also frequently mentioned when questioned who the builders were.

The organ was built in 1907 and consisted of three manuals and Pedal, with 30 ranks of pipes of excellent tone. In 1951 we installed this organ in Epiphany Church in lofts provided on either side of the gallery, Swell and Pedal on the left side, Choir and Pedal on the right side. These lofts are located one story above the gallery floor. The unenclosed Great section, however, was placed in the center on the gallery floor against the front wall of the church, with the console facing the organ. The pipes of this unenclosed Great section are all visible, arranged in symmetrical order and, I believe, it was the first organ in San Francisco, so treated. It is now almost the universal custom of organ builders in laying out the modern church organ to have all interior pipes, or as many of them as possible, visible.

Several new stops of a more pungent character were added to this organ at this time, giving the organ added brilliance, more on the baroque type. My son Lawrence, with needed help, did a splendid job of installation.

ST. PAUL'S LUTHERAN CHURCH

In 1947 we built a small four stop, two manual and Pedal electric action organ for the St. Paul's Lutheran Church on Sloat Boulevard, near Nineteenth Avenue. All stops were enclosed excepting an Open Diapason 8' from Tenor C, which was outside of the Swell box. Although of excellent tone, they found the organ in time inadequate in supporting the full congregational singing. We then completed the Diapason 8' its full octave to the bass and added an octave of pipes to the treble, unifying the whole set as an Open Diapason 8' and Octave 4', making both available in the Pedal also. This improvement added more volume and also brilliancy to the organ, with very satisfying results.

BETHEL LUTHERAN CHURCH
Alemany Boulevard

In 1948 Bethel Lutheran Church, at the corner of Alemany Boulevard and Huron Street, secured a small organ of four ranks from our firm, all under expression, which was placed in a chamber behind a grill. A detached console was placed immediately in front of the grill, with the organist's back toward the latter. The Dimimuendo and Forte effects from this organ were remarkable, in fact so much so that the organist later complained about it and had the console removed farther to the center of the gallery where we originally recommended it be placed. After several years, when the financial status of the congregation improved, further additions were made by adding a Trumpet 8' and a set of Chimes.

CHURCH OF THE VISITATION

Near the Southern County line of the City and County of San Francisco is Visitation Valley, of historical interest as it was the camping site of the early Franciscan Missionaries when enroute to establishing Mission Dolores in 1784. Located in this valley is the recently built Church of the Visitation. In this district, for many years previous to this time, there existed a small scarcely known church, surrounded mostly by vegetable gardens, nurseries, railroad yards and a power substation. However, with the expanding population of San Francisco with its limited ground area, this countryside within the city limits soon was occupied with houses of people of the middle or working class. The need for a larger and more modern church was soon evident, so rose the Church of the Visitation.

Our firm in 1952, received the contract to install a suitable organ. Soon after it was in use we experienced trouble with frequent ciphering, which perplexed us, as it was evidently built from the same material and of the same construction as many a previous successful installation. We soon established the fact that the motion of the armatures of the electric magnets, supplied to us by some eastern supply house, did not have sufficient clearance, either due to a variance in height from the former bases used, or because the thickness of the armatures varied. As this motion was not adjustable and as the armatures were covered on one side with an insert of blotting paper to quiet the clicking sound when in action, we were convinced that the absorption of moisture by the blotting paper in this foggy valley, especially in the summer months, was the cause of the trouble. By ordering a new lot of properly spaced magnet bases with more clearance, gladly sent by our suppliers, our troubles were permanently ended.

ST. PAUL OF THE SHIPWRECK

The Church of the Immaculate Conception, an Italian National Church located on Folsom Street, on the north side of Bernal Hieghts, had for many years a large two manual and Pedal Vocalion reed organ, hand pumped. It had an excellent tone, probably the nearest approach to a genuine pipe organ. But, being hand pumped and very hard to play, especially when using the couplers, it was not surprising that some energetic electronic salesman soon induced the Pastor to secure an electronic organ.

The Vocalion organ was then secured by St. Paul of the Shipwreck Church, also conducted by the Franciscan Fathers, located in the Bayview District on Oakdale Street, near Third Street. We installed the organ in the new location and applied a blower to it. With the organ put in good condition, albeit with its heavy action to play, it was used many years thereafter with satisfactory results.

In time the old church also became inadequate and in 1961, a new edifice was built a few blocks farther south, on Jamestown and Third Streets. Here we secured the contract to build and install one of our small pipe organs, similar to those previously quoted. This installation has also been very satisfactory.

OTHER PIPE ORGANS NOT LISTED

In the foregoing chapters I believe I have referred to and commented on practically every pipe organ that has been installed in San Francisco since its founding. Let me amplify this statement by adding that it applies most certainly to the pipe organs erected in San Francisco up to the year 1930.

Since the Depression, when the cost of a pipe organ became all but prohibitive for many a struggling church burdened with heavy debt, the pipe organ builders of the country, including the older and well-established firms, conceived the idea of building smaller pipe organs to meet the financial situation of the times — also to meet the competition of the electronic organs that were then entering the pipe organ field.

Possibly there were some small pipe organs built and installed in local churches during this period and after, which were not mentioned that would be entitled to be listed, if for no other reason than to make my statistical report complete. But in deference to the patience of my readers I will conclude with the statement that in the foregoing chapters I have described the names and places of 87 distinct pipe organ installations in San Francisco. Forty-seven of these organs were destroyed in the great fire of 1906.

I might also mention that in my father's notes I find reference to a two manual Bergstrom organ he erected in the residence of a Miss Delany. As no further comment is made thereon, I am in the dark as to who the party was or where the home was located.

There is also a reference in my father's notes to a one manual Mayer organ, originally installed in the old Presbyterian Church in the Potrero District, and evidently later removed again to Mayer's shop. This, also, I am unable to comment on for lack of personal knowledge.

Chapter V

FOUNDING OF THE FIRM

Felix Fridolin Schoenstein was a native of Germany, born in Villingen, Baden, in the Black Forest on February 23, 1849. He traced his ancestry back to the Sixteenth Century when, in feudal times, the head of the family, who was the owner of the vast estate, was known as "Freiherr von Schönstein."* With the advent of the Thirty Year's War, 1617-1648, waged in the time of Gustavus Adolphus, their estate was confiscated, and the family reduced to penury. Thereafter, the former family title was abandoned.

Of this family, Leo Schönstein, my grandfather, was the only male offspring. He was born in 1811 and later begot a large family, one of which was my father, Felix Fridolin Schönstein. Mr grandfather Leo, held a government position as forester and Custom Collector in the Black Forest and devoted himself, in his spare time, to the fabrication of cuckoo clocks and pipes for orchestrions, industries popular in that district in Germany. In later years, his five sons worked with a local Orchestrion maker, named Hugo Blessing. In 1864, they established themselves in business, with marked success, exporting Orchestrions (see Chapter III)

Referring to the aforementioned title my forbearers carried, I might add that for many years it appeared to us that our family name "Schoenstein" comprising our immediate family here in California and our relatives abroad in Germany, were the only ones bearing this name. However, in recent years we were made aware of the fact, from different parts of the United States, there were others claiming this name, coming from different ranks of life with diversified trades and professions, claiming other countries than Germany as their origin, and professing other than the Catholic faith. An article in the San Francisco Chronicle, under date of December 19, 1928, referring to a recent wedding of the "Countess Hatsfeld", the adopted daughter of the late Collis P. Huntington, referred to her husband as a "Schoenstein" whose ancestral forbears had a castle in the "Rhine" country, the remains of which are still standing. The wedding was solemnized in the Brompton Oratory of London amidst great splendor and impressiveness.

to foreign countries. Lucas P. Schönstein, the eldest brother, operated the business.

My father, after attending school in his home village, began to serve his apprenticeship with his brothers. At this time, the Schönstein brothers received an order from distant San Francisco to build and install two large Orchestrions for the then famous music halls of "Bottle" Mayer and "Bottle" Koenig. These men conducted their business on Jackson Street near Portsmouth Square and were the first purveyors of bottled beer in San Francisco. Young Felix, then nineteen years old, disliked the idea of military service under the Prussian regime which, at this time, had its heavy heel on the Duchy of Baden. Filled with love of adventure, he grasped the opportunity of emigrating to America to install these instruments and to establish his future destiny in the New World. (From this point the name was spelled Schoenstein.)

After a stormy voyage, Felix F. arrived in New York and met his elder brother, F. Berthold, who had preceded him, and together they set out for California, via the Isthmus of Panama. From the small port of Acapulco on the Pacific side of the Isthmus, they embarked upon the S.S. Sacramento, a sidewheeler of the Pacific Mail Steamship Company, and arrived in San Francisco on October 19, 1868.

The two brothers successfully installed these instruments. F. B. Schoenstein then established a business importing and selling Orchestrions.

My father worked in a furniture factory for some time, finally offering his services to California's first organ builder, Joseph Severin Mayer. This was in 1869, and for eight years he worked with Mr. Mayer as his foreman, living with him in his home, and was treated as his son. On August 4, 1877, my father established his own business at 512 Birch Avenue, in the Hayes Valley district, where he arranged music on cylinders for Orchestrions, which were being imported frequently from Europe. To all evidences, he was the only person West of the Rockies who was competent to do this work. Orchestrions installed at this time, aside from the two previously mentioned, were the following: one at the Cliff House, the large one at Seal Rock House, one at Woodward's Garden, another at San Luis Obispo, and others mentioned in

Chapter III of this book. In the course of time, this type of instrument was superseded by a less cumbersome and more convenient perforated music-roll device, which was driven by electric power. As the original Orchestrion had become obsolete, my father adjusted himself to this change and thereafter devoted himself almost exclusively to the building of church organs, and to their maintenance and repair.

In 1878, Felix married Magdalena Hofmann, a native of Bavaria, Germany, after a courtship of several months. They were married at St. Boniface Church in San Francisco, and were blessed with ten children, six of whom are still living. In 1928, they celebrated their Golden Wedding Anniversary, surrounded by nine surviving children, at that time, with thirty-one grandchildren and one great-grandchild. To the end, my father maintained a keen interest in the construction and maintenance of organs. He was of an inventive mind and had two patents to his credit: one, a pneumatic action for pipe organs, and the other an automatic player device to enable one to play one or more manuals simultaneously. In his later years, aviation captured his fancy, and he drew many a unique design for a self-propelled apparatus which was to enable an individual to fly in bird-like fashion. Scientific theories, also, usurped his attention, and Darwin's Theory of Evolution, which was causing a great uproar at the time, provoked stern objections from my father. A local newspaper was the recipient of his vehement protestations.

Felix Schoenstein was a devout Catholic, a devoted father to his family, and a loyal and respected citizen of his adopted country, putting to shame many native Americans for their laxity of interest in the welfare of their country. Although he held a genuine affection for his native land, he never made a return visit. In his later years he feared for Germany's future, under the dictatorship of Adolf Hitler, then looming on the horizon. He was a great lover of children and earned the sobriquet of the "Ding-Dong Man", especially throughout the Mission district of San Francisco, where he was known for his jovial nature toward children. Characterized by his flowing beard, then whitened with age, by a walking cane which he constantly carried with him, and a Homberg hat he always wore. He was also called "Santa Claus" by the throngs of children who pressed about him, clamoring for a somersault, a swing, or a pat on the cheek. His pockets always contained gadgets from the organ shop, which he would pass out generously to his little followers.

On June 18, 1931, Magdalena Schoenstein, his devoted wife for over fifty years, passed to her eternal reward. Five years later, on March 29, 1936, at the age of eighty-seven, Felix F. Schoenstein followed her to Eternity.

The first organ my father built was for St. Mary's Church, Stockton, in 1881. (See autobiography in Appendix for details.) His next organ was for a Mr. W. F. Smith for a private home, consisting of two stops and a Pedal. This organ was built in 1882. The next organ was built in 1884 for a Mr. S. W. Parrott, an artist from Portland, Oregon. This evidently was also a residence organ, though larger than the former, consisting of two manuals and Pedal and about five stops. My father evidently journeyed to Portland, Oregon, to install this organ. I am certain the organ proved to be satisfactory, but I note from his records and from his statements made to us later, the financial outcome of this contract was not so satisfactory, that in lieu of receiving his full stipulated amount in cash for building the organ, he finally, by mutual consent, accepted two beautiful oil paintings, one of Mt. Hood and the other of Mt. Shasta. These paintings are still in the family as valued heirlooms.

After building another organ in Stockton (see Appendix) and two more in San Francisco, in 1894 he built a two manual and Pedal organ, six to eight stops, for the German St. Paul's Lutheran Church of Sacramento, California. In 1899 he built still another organ for St. Agnes Convent in Stockton, California. It was a one manual of four stops. In my youth I recall tuning it a few times with my father. When the Convent was moved from its location on San Joaquin Street, near the Santa Fe Station, it was dismantled. In later years, 1946, I was informed that the Baumgarten family of Stockton had the organ stored in their basement. It was finally sold to a Mr. Sandin of Fortuna, California, an organ enthusiast who was building an organ for himself.

In going over my father's old account books, evidently his first helpers, or employees, were a Mr. Robrecht and a Mr.

Ruperich. Possibly his next helper was his old friend, Peter Mueller, a bachelor, whose name I find frequently recorded. He also mentioned Herman Partman and a boy helping him by the name of Copp. In later years, when I was about thirteen, during an absence of my father from the City, I went with Peter Mueller a few times to service some organs. He evidently did have organ experience, as previously stated, but at that time he certainly proved awkward and inefficient. Some of my experiences with him are still vivid in my mind. I recall my father stating that one day he sent him to repair and tune a reed organ in a certain church across the Bay. When evening came he returned; my father questioned him on how his work had progressed. Dismayed, he reported that he could not even find the reeds, much less tune or adjust them. Nevertheless, he must have been, at least in his younger days, a conscientious and efficient worker or my father would not have employed him.

In 1889 my father moved his shop from Birch Avenue, in Hayes Valley, to 1202 Fillmore Street, near Turk, out farther in the Western Addition, evidently to have his home and work shop under one roof. I recall this event vividly as my brother, Frank, and I were finally perched on top of a well-loaded express wagon containing the household furniture, eating soda crackers en route to our new home. A block before reaching the destination at Turk and Webster Streets, the expressman, Joseph Feldhaus, with his helpers, tied up the horses at a watering trough for the thirsty animals to quench their thirst while the men entered the saloon to refresh themselves before starting the arduous task of unloading their heavy load. The ordeal of moving from one abode to a new location is usually dreaded by the grownup folks. To us youngsters, however, it was a delightful experience to move into a new place, explore the neighborhood and get acquainted. The car barns and stables of the old Omnibus Railway Company which was running horse cars on Turk, Eddy, Fillmore and other streets in this locality, and the intersection of Turk and Fillmore Streets, with these terminal headquarters and facilities, was a thriving business section. Catering to the car crews and car barn help, were restaurants, cigar stores, saloons, grocery stores, drug stores, and all needed facilities for an up-to-date business center. In one corner of the car barn buildings was the horseshoeing shop, where we youngsters spent much of our time. All in all, it was a great neighborhood to us, with plenty of life and commotion about it.

Soon my father's shop was established. At about this time I often heard of a Mr. Wilhem and his brother, who worked for my dad for some time. They befriended me often bringing me small trinkets and goodies to eat. Later on they worked for themselves and rebuilt the Odell organ at the Church of the Advent on Eleventh Street, somewhat to the chagrin of my father who, undoubtedly, expected to receive this work himself.

In 1890 my father received the contract to build the large organ for St. Markus Lutheran Church and, as he required all available space obtainable on the premises, the family moved from the rear of the house and found a new home around the corner on Turk Street, between Webster and Fillmore, opposite the car barns.

As may be expected, we youngsters soon struck up friendships with many car drivers. One we were particularly friendly with and nicknamed him "McGinty", recalling the ditty popular then, "down went McGinty to the bottom of the sea." I especially remember this driver because of his short stature and a black goattee he had, and an incident that occurred which was both chivalrous and amusing to us small children. Those were the days before San Francisco had bituminized streets. Cobblestones and basalt blocks were the pavements in the older parts of the city, in the downtown district, but out in the Western Addition red macadam was the material used, dry and dusty in the summer and wet and muddy during the rainy season. It was during one of these exceedingly wet spells, the rain was coming down in torrents from the adjoining hillsides, and the water accumulated in the low section of Turk and Fillmore Streets. The gushing waters lifted the heavy iron lids from the manholes, soon flooding the streets and sidewalks. Mother happened to go downtown early that morning undoubtedly not anticipating the stormy weather, and left us youngsters in charge of one of the older children.

As it was wet and miserable outside, we were confined indoors and found our delight in the front room with our faces against the window panes looking out to the street that was now transformed into a lake, watching the horses pulling the cars throught the water, wondering when and how mother would come home. Many a car, with its tinkling bell attached to the horse's harness, had passed and our vigil seemed wasted and unrewarded. Finally, a car came along and stopped directly in front of our house. It was our friend McGinty driving the car and his lone passenger was our mother, standing bewildered and gesticulating on the rear step, wondering how to get to the sidewalk. Mother and the driver both spied us at the window. Our joy and delight that mother came home again must have been vividly expressed in our faces and actions, softening, no doubt, the heart of our "Romeo", the car driver, who then without faltering, left his front platform, waded through the water, and with a manly grip lifted mother high and dry and carried her to the front steps of our home, where he was profusely thanked by a rather embarrassed lady, but cheered by the glee and laughter of us children.

In constructing the St. Markus organ, my father had Peter Mueller and Herman Partman again, and a young man named Edward L. Crome assist him. Young Crome had just recently come from St. Louis, Missouri, and I believe was a member of St. Markus Lutheran Church, for whom the organ was being built. He took a fancy to me and I to him. I recall his taking me out to the Cliff House one Sunday afternoon, on the old steam train skirting the southern fringe of Golden Gate Park. Of course he furnished me with the essential bag of peanuts and popcorn, which were consumed while riding through the sand dunes out to the beach. After visiting the Cliff House we went to the Seal Rock House to listen to the large orchestrion built by my uncles, formerly in Bottle Maier's resort, and later installed here by my father. I believe this was my first visit to the ocean beach. While listening to the music, Ed Crome ordered a cooling draught of beer for himself and permitted me to sip off the foam. This was my first taste of beer.

Peter Mueller, my father's old trusted employee, died on

November 20, 1904. Some time during 1894-1895 Ed Crome left for Los Angeles and joined the Murray M. Harris Organ Company.

Another faithful employee comes to my mind, a Mr. Kellner. I recall he lived in the southern part of the City. One Sunday afternoon my father evidently wanted to re-engage him, so he made it a family outing to visit him. He lived on the northern side of Bernal Hieghts and the trip was an enjoyable one for us children.

After the St. Markus organ was completed, the family again moved back to the old place on Fillmore Street, but not for long. As we children were growing up and it became evident that larger quarters for the family were needed, we moved to 2614 Bush Street, between Divisadero and Broderick Streers. We had a beautiful little cottage all to ourselves, which we greatly enjoyed, with a garden in the front and rear of the house. Organ work must have been at a standstill then, as the small basement of the home answered all the needs for the repair work my father was doing at that time. I recall some of the happiest days of my youth during this period, although they were the hardest years for my parents. At this time the youngest of our family, my brother Erwin, was born, the last of ten children.

The old location at Turk and Fillmore Streets must have had some attraction for my parents, and the former landlord, Mr. Donovan, who also knew who were desirable tenants notwithstanding the large roster of children my parents had, made an offer to them which was accepted, to again rent them the entire lower floor of 1206 Fillmore Street for father's shop and the entire upper flat, 1208 Fillmore Street, for living quarters. This proved to be very satisfactory for a number of years, until, in 1896, through the urging of a friend of my mother's, Mr. William Knopf, who was a builder and contractor and interested in real estate, my parents were induced to buy their own home, a very desirable place in the warm belt of the Mission District at 2306 Bryant Avenue, near 21st Street. Although the shop was again located, this time in a spacious basement, father had little need for it as he only built one organ here. That organ was for the Scandinavian Lutheran Church on Howard Street, opposite Thirteenth

Street.

However, he was always occupied. Organ maintenance and repair work kept him busy. From 1898 on, after leaving school, I worked with my father while my brother, Leo, went to New York to work with the Muller and Abel Organ Co. He returned in 1902 and worked as partner with my father again for some time, until the earthquake and fire of 1906 which terminated, as it were, the partnership and certainly made it incumbent on many to turn a new leaf in their lives and plan a new future.

Shortly before and for some period after the fire, Fred Mayer, son of the vereran California organ builder, Joseph Mayer, worked for us. In 1907 I went to New York. My younger brother, Otto, and later my brother, Erwin, who had been assisting my father since 1906 continued in this capacity. My brother, Leo, made other business connections, working extensively for the W. W. Kimball Organ Company of Chicago, Illinois, in the San Francisco Bay Area.

In 1909 I again returned to San Francisco at the urgent request of my father, to assist him with his organ work and the installation of the many new organs now arriving, mostly from Eastern builders, to replace those that had been destroyed in the fire and earthquake. On April 9, 1909, I joined my father in business, forming the partnership of Felix F. Schoenstein & Son. In 1913 my elder brother, Leo, again worked with us for a time. Work seemed to be plentiful, especially the installation of new pipe organs for Eastern manufacturers, as well as others from Southern California.

As we younger men felt the urge to not only install and erect pipe organs for other firms, but were determined to do something constructive ourselves in the line of new work, we built, in 1913, a sizeable shop in the rear of the property at 2306 Bryant Street, and were favored with much activity in the line of modernizing old organs, rebuilding and maintenance work.

As my younger brothers, Otto and Erwin, were now maturing into young manhood and the prospect for continued prosperity seemed promising, they were also added to the partnership in or about 1911, forming the present partnership of Felix F. Schoenstein & Sons.

Here again we found it necessary to hire outside help — Mr. A. C. Burnham and George Mundinger. We later secured the services of Robert and Shield Toutjian and their father, expert cabinet makers and experienced organ men, former employees of the Murray M. Harris Company. Several others who were in our employ at this time in 1909 were John Olderler, John Oston, Mike Towey and Mr. Lindsey. Albert Jestadt, Gus Abeling and a boy helper named Joseph Lee helped us in 1911. On or about this time Richmond H. Skinner, the son of the well-known organ builder, Ernest M. Skinner of Boston, was in San Francisco and was employed by us for a short time.

With the constantly increasing number of new church organs arriving here, due largely to live and energetic agents and representatives of Eastern firms who made their head-quarters here, and with the theatre organ now in its heyday, we required quite a crew of maintenance men. Some of the first of these helpers were: Edward Hause and Frankie Farren who began work in 1914, also his friend Harold Wright; Frankie Fassler, Willie Nessier, John O'Neil and Charles Sweeney. It might be of interest to note here that Frankie Farren, a rather quiet, reticent lad, followed on the side as his private avocation, unknown to us for a time, the manly art of self defense (pugilism) and, to our surprise, we later learned that he received the title of "Pacific Coast Amateur Light-weight Champion" of his class.

Another interesting helper we had was Harry Doyle, a graduate of the University of California. He helped us erect several organs. His ambition was to become a professional organ builder. He finally decided that the East offered better opportunities for advancement and left our employ. Through a recommendation we gave him he succeeded in getting employment with the A. Gottfried Co. of Erie, Pennsylvania, later working also with other firms.

In 1920 we secured the services of a young lad, James Heaton, who proved very loyal and satisfactory and remained with us for twenty-one years. In close succession, about 1921, we also secured the services of our nephews, my older brother's sons, Leo, Junior and Paul Schoenstein, and then Alex Schoenstein, grandsons of my father, the third generation of Schoensteins. This pleased my father very much, who at this time at 72 years of age had retired from active work.

In time we hired other outside men to assist us. Among them, Frank Roberts, Murray Knowlton, Paul Beckwith, Martin Donant, William Dahl, John Strathaus and Gilbert Crosby. The services of Julius Peterson, Frank Cusak and Homer Hamlin were added to the cabinet making force and, finally, Fred Walti, a young and efficient worker who gave us valuable assistance at the bench and whenever needed. Frank Schoenstein, Jr., another nephew also worked with us during intervals while attending the University of California.

Having a roster of about thirteen permanent employees now, the need for a bookkeeper became urgent. In 1914 we first secured the services of a part-time bookkeeper, Mr. C. A. Stewart, a faithful, honest and efficient man who served us for a number of years. However, with the increasing work and voluminous correspondence, which I found I was not able to cope with satisfactorily any more, we finally, in 1925, secured the services of a full time bookkeeper and office girl, in the person of Miss Stella Lazzaroni, now Mrs. John Bufalini, who has been with us now for forty-four years, doing the work most satisfactorily.

In 1928 we found the urgent need of securing still larger and better quarters and facilities for our ever-increasing business. There seemed to be no lack of work. Fifty-one previous years of efficient and honest dealings in trying to serve our customers seemed to bring their reward. So after years at the Bryant Street location, a suitable larger site was sought, with the result that the property on the southwest corner of Alabama and 20th Streets was purchased, and a three-story factory, with office, lofts and studio was erected. It was specially designed for our work and has a floor space of 7500 square feet. A considerable debt was incurred in this venture, but we felt in view of our past reputation and experience that the move was warranted.

We feel that we made a prudent move. Many an organ has been erected in it. Many a time we have found it none too large when all space was occupied. We have permanently erected in our studio a demonstrating organ, which we also rent out for practice purposes, to the pleasure and advantage of many an organ enthusiast. Notwithstanding the depression, we finally paid off the mortgage and now, after many years of hard and sacrificing work, take pride and joy in the sole ownership of the property and building. Our factory has been most favorably commented upon by all who visit it and it is usually a surprise to most visitors, as they do not expect to find such an establishment out here in the West. We may modestly add that to our knowledge it is the largest and best equipped organ factory west of Chicago.

Before moving into the new quarters, however, Leo, Jr., and his helper, John Strathaus, decided to leave our employ.

No sooner had we established ourselves in our new building, in 1928, than the disastrous depression overtook us, along with so many others similarly situated. We noted immediately a drop in our work. On top of this setback, the theatres, once a great boon to the organ business, almost overnight, with the introduction of the vitaphone, or "talkies", abandoned the silent pictures and made the once indispensable theatre organ also as silent as the speechless films of its day. Layoffs of our employees were inevitable. In following the rule of seniority, we tried to do justice to all but evidently hurt the feelings of our young nephews who, due to circumstances, had to look elsewhere for employment. Fred Walti, sensing the lack of work, left us for a more lucrative position. James Heaton remained with us. Our faithful bookkeeper, Stella, remained.

As the depression gradually passed, we again needed a good, steady cabinet worker, whom we found in the person of Andrew Rosberg. We also found a very faithful and efficient woman worker with experience in other organ firms, Helen Houston, who did the finer work for which a woman is best suited, such as making pneumatics, wiring, etc., and is still with us.

During these latter years, my son Lawrence, and later Erwin's sons Robert and Leonard, also worked with the firm. However, with the coming of World War II, my nephews Frank, Robert and Leonard joined the Army and Navy. My son Lawrence, went over to defense work, making diesel engines instead of pipe organs. Finally, James Heaton, who was with us for the longest period, twenty-one years, also found it more profitable to work in the shipyards than to do organ work, and left us. Fred Wood, an experienced and loyal worker, gave us his valuable aid when we needed it, but found the daily commuting across the Bay undesirable and accepted work on the East side of the Bay. Finally during the labor troubles that the country experienced shortly after the cessation of hostilities in 1946, my son-in-law, Ernest Berlo, a machinist by trade, a mechanic par excellence, also worked for us a short time and in short time acquired the qualifications of an experienced organ maintenance man. He again returned to his former job when the labor situation was adjusted.

On September 22, 1946, my younger son, Vincent, joined our firm. For two years previous he was in the Armed Forces in the European field, having served in the Infantry in the Seventh Army under General Patch, returning home with his English bride, Moira Wootton, whom he married in Liverpool, England. After a year of happy association with us, to my regret he also found it expedient to secure work elsewhere. Shortly after his leaving we secured the services of Richard Trafny, an experienced organ mechanic.

Other employees who worked for us and were not previously listed and to whom we are grateful, are the following: Chester Wiltse, Donald Black, Ted Crawford, Gus Minch, Victor Kinkella, Frank Reichmuth, Peter Derrick, Thomas Rhodes, John Ogle, West Jorgensen, Robert Sproule, Bradford Morse, George T. Limacher, Ed M. Stout, Jon Johnston, and my grandson, Robert Berlo. We also secured the services of an excellent cabinet worker, named August Sustaric. In mentioning all the names of employees, to the best of my recollection, who worked for us in the past years for a long or short period, I do so for a reason. I felt they would feel honored to have worked for our firm and to have their names recorded in this book.

An event that occurred in our factory and which has often been referred to since, was the occasion when our firm acted as host to the Northern California Chapter of the American Guild of Organists. It was on September 26, 1933. Mrs. Estelle Drummond Swift was the Dean. About seventy-five guests, in response to our invitation, were present in our establishment. After a short business session, a recital was given on the Studio organ, at which Wallace Sabin performed. This was followed by a talk on some selected topic by a guest speaker whose name I do not remember. As a fitting climax to the evening's entertainment, the guests were seated at a festive table arranged in the middle section of the top floor. Here speech making, joviality and good fellowship brought the event to a happy close. On this occasion my father, founder of the business, and four of his sons were all present, evoking many laudable comments from the assembled guests.

It was my father's hope and expectation that his sons and grandsons would carry on when the oldsters had passed out of the picture. This was also my hope and ambition and I was, therefore, delighted to see my oldest son Lawrence take interest, after graduating from the Lick-Wilmerding School, in following the organ building profession. I hoped and expected in time he would automatically step into my shoes and carry on but that, in time, proved not to be the case. Outside interests undoubtedly observed his background, capabilities and personality, and being better financially situated than we were, offered him a flattering proposition to represent and to work for their firm. As opportunity, it is said, comes knocking only once at your door, the offer was irresistable. I was sadly disappointed in the frustration of my dreams for his future, and as our personal relations nonetheless remained most cordial, I could not restrain myself from complimenting him on his selection as the "West Coast Representative" of undoubtedly America's outstanding organ builders, the Aeolian-Skinner Organ Company of Boston, Mass. I am pleased that his son, Terrence Schoenstein, the fourth generation, is working with the firm at the present time. I also wish to express my gratitude to Paul Schoenstein, my nephew, who is and has been working with the firm for many years carrying on the old tradition with his uncles Otto and Erwin Schoenstein.

At this point I may state that after working practically continuously with the firm for 64 years, since 1898, I found it expedient to retire on June 30, 1962 from active participation. With 79 years behind me I felt a relaxation from responsibility and the bustle of daily life was in order and have sought the quietude of Paradise (Northern California) as my rendezvous, where I and my loving wife hope to spend the summer months, and the winter months in our old established home, in my beloved native city, San Francisco.

Now after 92 years of continuous operation, surviving periods of wars, depressions and other adversities, I hope our firm of Felix F. Schoenstein and Sons can still look forward with trust to the future that we and our progeny may carry on to serve our clientele to build, modernize and maintain their pipe organs, the instrument best suited to elevate troubled souls and to sing Divine praises — the Pipe Organ, the King of Instruments.

Chapter VI

MY SOJOURN IN NEW YORK AND BOSTON

498

After the turmoil and excitement of the great fire and earthquake of 1906 had subsided and after we had the organs that were left remaining and again entrusted to our care rehabilitated and in playing condition, a little lull seemed to occur in our otherwise busy careers. I then worked temporarily for a few months as a cabinet maker with my friend Jospeh Maichen, while my younger brothers assisted my father.

Being then 23 years of age, young, ambitious and to an extent adventurous, I harbored the desire to travel a bit, to go to New York to work for some of the larger organ concerns in the East, to acquire first-hand knowledge in the art of organ building and a broader general organ experience, intending later to return to San Francisco to continue in business with my father. It so happened at this time that a representative of the Reuben Midmer Organ Company, of Brooklyn, New York, visited us. I told him of my plans and he unhesitatingly encouraged me, telling me there would be no difficulty whatever in securing work as young men of my experience and background were sought. He also suggested that I write to his firm, which I did.

His roseate picture of the promising prospects that awaited me, coupled with my own dream picture of what a wonderful experience it would be, made it easy for me to reach the decision to leave home at an early date. My father was much in favor of the plan, and gave me his blessing. My younger brother Otto, who already had been working with us and at times also my youngest brother Erwin, could be his assistants in my absence. I arranged my affairs accordingly, and after enjoying some farewell parties given by my family and friends, I left San Francisco on October 21, 1907. My mother, sister and brother accompanied me to the train. The many farewells, leaving parents, sisters and brothers for a rather indefinite period (I then planned to be away for about five years), launching out to make my own way in the world, all had an emotional effect upon me. A lump in my throat, moist eyes, with few words spoken, we boarded the ferry and saw the beautiful skyline of San Francisco with its myriads of lights fade in the distance. I boarded my train, a last farewell, and I was on my way to an uncertain future in the great City of New York.

I might mention here that about two days before my departure I received a reply to my letter to the Reuben Midmer Organ Company of Brooklyn, stating that unfortunately they had just put on some new help when they received my letter and, therefore, could not offer me a position at the present time, but that if I decided to come to New York to call on them, as possibly in the future there would be an opening for me. Naturally, I was disappointed, but not discouraged and did not let this interfere with carrying out my plan.

I enjoyed a good night's sleep in my Pullman berth and when I awoke in the morning we were going through the snowsheds in the Sierras. Then on to Reno, Ogden, and Salt Lake, finally arriving in Chicago. There I engaged a room at the Bismarck Hotel for the night, as I intended leaving for Manitowoc, Wisconsin, on Lake Michigan, the next morning to visit two of my sisters who, six years previously, had left home together to join a Franciscan Sisterhood whose Mother-house was at Alverno, a few miles north of Manitowoc. I was the first one of the family to see them since they had left home and, needless to say, it was a happy reunion. On arrival at the convent, after riding in an open buggy on the seat next to the driver, I was about frozen stiff so that I could not talk for some time. Although there was no snow on the ground, it was bitterly cold. After a stay of a few days at Manitowoc, I continued my journey to New York.

Having an uncle and aunt with seven little cousins living in Brooklyn, New York, whom I had never met before, I intended staying with them for a few days, as we had previously arranged. When I got to Syracuse, New York, I sent them a telegram, saying I would arrive at the New York Central Station in New York City at 10:30 p.m., expecting that someone would be there to greet me. However, on my arrival at the station, finding no one around looking for an expected arrival, and finally being practically left to myself, I concluded I would find my way alone to my aunt's home at that late hour of the night. Receiving directions from a policeman I approached on the sidewalk, I soon found myself crossing the Brooklyn Bridge. I got off at the Fulton Street Station, as directed, and again inquired of a policeman how to get to Beresford and Bergen Avenue. Following his direction I soon espied the house where my aunt lived. I had often seen a photograph of it at home and always admired it very much. It had a brownstone front, circular bay exterior and white marble steps. It was about midnight when I arrived and the first ring of the bell at the main entrance remained unanswered. Repeated ringing on the lower entrance, however finally brought a response and my aunt appeared at an upstairs window in night attire and inquired who was at the door. The mention of my name and the sight of my traveling bag was sufficient to identify her late caller. I was most cordially welcomed by my aunt and three of the older cousins, who were awakened from their slumber to greet their cousin from San Francisco. Refreshments were quickly prepared and we spent several happy hours together until we finally retired, about three a.m. I learned then they had not received my telegram from Syracuse announcing my arrival as the Telegraph Company's employees were on strike at the time.

The next morning it was my pleasure to meet the other younger cousins, all little pink-cheeked blondes, born in Germany. The family, a year or two previously, had come to America to take possession of the beautiful home that had been bequeathed to them by another aunt who had died without offspring. The next day the older cousins accompanied me to New York City to see the sights and to acquaint me with the general layout of the metropolis. I remember at that time the Singer Tower was the tallest structure, and the Metropolitan Tower was in course of construction. I soon felt at home in New York City and readily found my way about, using both subway and elevated railways. I remained about two weeks with my relatives, enjoyed their company and hospitality immensely, and was royally entertained by them.

During this time I did not give the matter of securing employment any serious consideration. I thought that would be quite a simple matter; all that would be necessary would be to show my credentials and mention my name, as my dad was known to most of the old-established organ firms, and the rest would be easy. Not wanting to impose on my relatives any longer, I then seriously began looking for work and called on the organ fraternity to see if there was any opening for me. I called on the Odell Company, as my brother Leo had worked for them at one time, on Hook & Hastings Company's representative, and the Reuben Midmer Organ Company of Brooklyn. All were most courteous, apparently pleased to see me and inquired about my father, but regretfully informed me that they had just hired help and there was no opening for me at present, but they would call me if an opportunity should present itself. All this was, of course, discouraging to me, and I came to realize that it was not so easy, even with the background and training I had, to secure a position. I then began to look for the real reason why I was unable to secure employment. It was obviously the lack of work in the organ field. I had not realized that we were going through a financial depression. This was forcibly and unpleasantly brought to my attention one day while I was walking through Madison Square when I saw hundreds of people standing in a long line waiting patiently to make withdrawals at a bank.

Anxious to secure a position, as my ready funds were beginning to dwindle, and with no immediate prospect of securing work in New York, I decided to go to Boston where a number of large organ factories were located, and try my luck there. Having no relatives or acquaintances there, I realized I would be entirely on my own.

Before leaving San Francisco, Mr. Charles E. Green, then manager of the Crocker Estate, who had a pipe organ in his residence in San Mateo and for whom we often worked, on hearing of my plans to go back East, asked me to call at the Geo. Hutchings Company in Boston, should I be going to that City, and make some inquiries about an automatic two manual player in which he was interested. Incidentally, he presented me at the time with sufficient funds to pay the traveling expenses from New York to Boston. With this obligation to fulfill, as a further incentive to visit the Hub City, I left New York on the steamer "Yale" going to West Haven, Connecticut, an enjoyable ride up the Sound, and took the train from there to Boston. On arrival I registered at the United States Hotel and immediately set out to look for work.

Before I left San Francisco, my friend Joseph Maichen for whom I had worked as a cabinet maker for a short time, and who had lived for many years in Boston, gave me the names and addresses of some of his relatives there, asking me to call on them in the event I should get to Boston. Visiting and sightseeing, as interesting as it may be, was not for me then, while roaming the streets, going from factory to factory in search of work. My most cherished hope of securing some work with the Hutchings Company also fell through. I was not a little dissatisfied and disappointed, especially on seeing my ready cash disappear rapidly. I realized that I had to terminate my stay at the hotel at once and seek lower-priced quarters. The inner man also had to be content with less costly menus. I still had a reserve fund in a San Francisco Bank, which I hoped to hold intact for a nest egg. In my financial stringency, however, I finally decided to go to a bank, hoping I might be able to draw on my San Francisco account. However, in this move I was also unsuccessful as the bank notified me that they required a month's notice before the withdrawal could be made.

By this time I was feeling quite desperate and finally decided to call on one of the relatives of my friend, Joseph Maichen. Swallowing my pride, I told them of my dilemma, of looking for a job without success, and of my funds running dangerously low, and asked them if they could house me temporarily until I secured a position. They welcomed me graciously and I was happy to be domiciled with the William Berlo family in Roxbury, a suburb of Boston. It was getting exceedingly cold. Daily I would make the rounds, visiting the different plants in the City and in the outlying districts.

One day I visited Mr. Searles of Methuen, Mass. He remembered my father. Again I went to the Hook & Hastings plant at Kendal Green, Mass. Here I was hospitably received by the elderly Mr. Hastings, who finally offered me some work but the remuneration was so ridiculously low I did not accept it. About two weeks passed thus, and my spirits were about as low as they possibly could be.

The Berlo family, however, made my stay with them as

agreeable as possible. I enjoyed their home life. Sundays I attended services at the Holy Trinity Church on Shawmut Avenue, was invited to join the choir, attended some of the young men's meetings, and could have made myself right at home in this new environment. However, the securing of a permanent job was the all-absorbing question.

Up to this time I had heard little of the Ernest M. Skinner Organ Company. I had called at the Mason & Hamlin factory without success, and my only remaining prospect to my knowledge was the Ernest M. Skinner Company. It was late on a weary winter afternoon when I arrived in Dorchester at the brick factory bearing the company's name in large letters.

I was prepared to receive the usual reply that had been given me on all previous applications. However, on being admitted to Mr. Skinner's office I did not have much time to explain my mission, except to say that I came from San Francisco, had organ experience and would like to secure a position in Boston. Without much questioning or hesitancy, he asked me if I was married and if I cared to work in New York. I told him I was not married and that I would be more than delighted to work any place, if I only secured a permanent position. The deal was made. That same evening I was to call at the factory and go with some of his men and some material on a late train to New York to begin work on the organ of Grace Episcopal Church on Broadway and Tenth Street, the next morning. Needless to say, a heavy burden was lifted from my mind. Quaint old Boston looked good to me then, and I vowed I would revisit the City again at some more auspicious time to really enjoy its many historical landmarks and places of interest. I hastened back to my friends, had supper with them, borrowed some money for my railroad fare to New York, and departed thanking them for the many kindnesses and hospitality.

With a permanent job ahead, life seemed to take on a different aspect entirely. I again found welcome domicile with my aunt in Brooklyn for a short time until I found my own permanent quarters. At Grace Church I was introduced to a Mr. Fred Wilck, who was to be my future boss.

Work on the large organs in New York was most interesting. We worked for a considerable time on the chancel organ at Grace Church, built by Hilborn Roosevelt in 1880, releathering the pneumatics and giving the organ a general tuning and overhauling. The little chantry organ was also modernized, and some work was done on the large Skinner gallery organ. Mr. Skinner would call quite frequently, and would stop at the St. Denis Hotel nearby. We also spent considerable time at St. Bartholomew's Church on Madison Avenue; called at the Tompkins Avenue Presbyterian Church, Brooklyn, also a large Skinner organ, where Clarence Eddy was then playing; also at Columbia University Chapel, the Sloan Residence on Fifth Avenue, and visited many other churches in and about New York. Finally, the installation of Skinner's great organ at the City College of New York was started, on which I was engaged for a considerable time, especially in tuning and voicing with Walter R. Birkmaier, the flute voicer, and Walter Brockbank, the reed voicer.

The dedication of this grand and imposing organ in the great hall of the City College of New York was an outstanding event both musically and socially. A large number of the prominent people of the country were present. Mrs. Grover Cleveland, wife of the former President of the United States, was the guest of honor. Mr. David Bisham, the famous basso, was the soloist. Samuel D. Baldwin functioned at the organ and was the regular organist for many years thereafter.

The days passed by too quickly. I spent two winters and one summer in New York and would have stayed much longer, as my status with the Ernest M. Skinner Company seemed to be most satisfactory. At the earnest request of my father, however, to return to San Francisco to assist him and to assume the practical management of our established business, which was them becoming quite active as many of the churches that had lost their organs in the fire were beginning to replace them, I decided to terminate my stay in New York and return home. In taking leave of Mr. Skinner, he remarked: "What do you want to do in that earthquake town, when apparently everything is satisfactory here and the prospects good for your future."

Mr. Skinner's readiness to give me work when I needed it so badly will always be thankfully remembered my me. His skill and genius in organ building makes him in my opinion America's outstanding organ builder.

On my trip home, which I made quite leisurely, I stopped off at Niagara Falls, visited Boston again and my good friends who had been so kind to me. I also paid my two sisters another visit, one now stationed at Quincy, Illinois, and the other at Brillion, Wisconsin. In Chicago I called at the Kimball factory to visit with Mr. Frank T. Milner, their former representative in San Francisco, who, however, was absent at the time. Then going by way of Los Angeles, I finally arrived home April 9, 1909. I was not long getting back into business again, joining in a partnership with my father as Felix F. Schoenstein & Son.

In 1936, after not seeing them for thirty years, the kindly couple, Mr. and Mrs. William Berlo of Boston, who had befriended me, paid a visit to San Francisco to see their relative, Joseph Maichen. Accompanying them was their young son, Ernest, who had not yet been born when I visited them. As they desired to have him remain out West to attend aviation school, it was my turn to reciprocate the kindness they had shown me. Young Ernest became our guest and boarder and, eventually, became my son-in-law.

After 46 years, in 1955, it was my privilege to visit New York again and to look up the old haunts and places where I worked as a young man. Being interested in a local Church organization, the German Catholic Federation of California, and having served the organization as Secretary for twenty-one years, my wife and I were elected delegates to represent our State Organization at the National Convention of the Catholic Central Union (Verein) convening at Rochester, New York, for its Centenary celebration. We decided to take our youngest son, Edward along and, after attending the Convention, to hire an auto and have him chauffeur us to visit friends in Boston and as far south as Washington, D.C., and then back to New York. We flew to Rochester, New York, and, after the Convention, again to Boston, Mass. The latter trip was a rough flight as we were just trailing the Diana Hurricane that was blowing up the Atlantic Coast. At Boston we rented an auto, met our friends who invited us to visit Situate in the Cape Cod Country. Even with the inclement

weather we enjoyed the New England countryside immensely.

On returning to Boston we visited the Aeolian Skinner
Organ Factory where we were cordially received; also visited
the Christian Science Mother Church and other landmarks.
At Hartford, Connecticut, we called at the Spencer Turbine
Company, manufacturers of the "Orgoblo", with whom we
had had business dealings for many years. We then visited the
Austin Organ Company factory, for whom we installed most
of their organs on the Pacific Coast, and were most graciously
received. Mr. Marks, the treasurer of the company, invited us
to a splendid lunch, at which many reminiscenses were
recalled of some of their many installations and of Mr. John
T. Austin's visit to San Francisco in 1915.

Chapter VII

AROUND THE BAY

Some of the Pipe Organs Erected and Serviced
Beyond the Confines of San Francisco.

Notre Dame Convent, San Jose

Behind a high brick wall over which protruded a mass of rich foliage of palms, trees and greenery could be seen the walls of the three story Notre Dame Convent building. It was located on West Santa Clara Street, west of Market Street. As a youth of about sixteen years, I had to go with my elder brother, Leo, to tune and service the organ. Later, I recall I again went with him to install an additional stop to the organ that was made in the shop. I believe it was a soft Viola Dolce 8' stop and a Tremolo. It was a small two manual 7 rank Farrand and Votey organ.

Strange to say, some years later my younger sister, Clara, as also a second cousin of hers, Pauline Burhans, entered this Convent as novices, receiving the names of Sister Louise, N.D., and Sister Gertrude, N.D. Unfortunately, Clara was not privileged to become a full-fledged nun as, in time, she contracted a malignant ailment and later died in a Health Sanitarium in Colorado Springs, Colorado.

When the nuns decided to secure a new location closer to San Francisco, they established themselves in Belmont, on the Peninsula, where they secured the old estate of the millionaire, William Chapman Ralston, owner and builder of the famous Palace Hotel of San Francisco. On this spacious estate soon new College Buildings were erected and the old mansion was used for the Convent. Although it contained a sumptuous ballroom, with parquet floors and mirrored walls, which ornamentation was removed, it was not adequate in size, especially if the old pipe organ was erected therein. It was, therefore, decided to store the organ in a shed nearby, where it remained for many years. About 1937, the nuns decided to build a new Novitiate in the hills of Saratoga, California, and here in their ample sized Chapel we erected the Farrand and Votey organ again, that was laying almost forgotten and not in use for many years in the Belmont shed. I believe it is still in use at the present time.

ST. MARY'S CHURCH
Stockton, California

The organ at St. Mary's Church, Stockton, California, was

the first organ my father built. It was built in 1881 and I recall, as children, we had a photograph of this organ at home (see my father's autobiography with appendix for details). In 1899, my father modernized it by applying his patented pneumatic action and was engaged on this work for several weeks, with my brother, Leo, assisting him. Then I heard more of St. Mary's Church and of their frequent trips to Stockton on the river boat and of the successful conclusion of their work. At this time, I believe, the facade of the church was improved by adding the graceful Gothic spire that adorns the structure. Advantage was taken of this space in the tower room behind the organ, I was informed, by placing a large 16' Pedal Open Diapason and Bourdon 16' pipes there, thus making decidedly more space in the organ proper.

It was in 1898, or thereabouts, that I was privileged to go with my father to Stockton for the first time. I do not recall whether we went by train or boat, but I do remember the weather was exceedingly hot and most uncomfortable to me when we got there. We stopped at a small, two story, gable-roofed hotel or lodging house, called the San Joaquin Hotel, opposite the Court House square on the northwest corner of Weber Avenue and San Joaquin Street. It was conducted by a friendly German couple, the proprietor being of extremely heavy, rotund proportions. I recall their persistency in trying to force me to eat my breakfast, intimating my father would have to pay whether I ate or not.

My first view of St. Mary's Church and the organ impressed me very much. I at once recognized the organ from the photograph I had seen so often at home, and with a feeling of veneration and affection I admired the handicraft of my father. On entering the organ, there came to my mind thoughts of the trials, diappointments and ultimate triumph this, his first organ, had brought to him and I wondered what it would say were it able to speak. It was also my privilege on this visit to be introduced to the venerable pastor, Rev. William B. O'Connor, who had originally given my father the order to build the instrument. He retired shortly afterward and passed away at St. Joseph's Hospital, Stockton.

At the time of my first visit, the organ was blown by an electric motor, operating a crankshaft engaging four feeders.

In addition to these there was an auxiliary bellows furnishing the high pressure for the pneumatic key action which was applied to the organ when it was changed from its original tracker action to pneumatic. This blowing device was rather noisy and the blowing of fuses was an annoying occurrence, undoubtedly due to an overloaded motor. The organ then showed signs of age and usage and was covered with church dust, an acquisition in most church organs after a few years installation. A large, frame building or pavilion occupied the greater part of the square opposite the church at the time of my first visit to Stockton, but this was later consumed by a fire in 1902, that seriously endangered the church and the organ.

Mr. Carl Bruck was the organist for many years. He was an admirer of the organ, but also a very severe and unreasonable critic at times, especially if something with the mechanism did not function satisfactorily, which happened occasionally and, of course, at the most inopportune times. This was nothing to be surprised at in a climate that can get as warm and sultry as it does in the San Joaquin Valley during the summer months, but it led in time to an estrangement between Mr. Bruck and my father, and for a number of years we did not service this organ.

In 1913, under the pastorate of Rev. William E. McGough, we were again summoned, and made some major repairs to the organ, replacing rubber tubing that had dried out, and discarded the troublesome blowing arrangements which was inside the organ, for which we substituted a modern Kinetic blower, placed in an alcove under the choir stairs on the lower floor of the church. This installation proved to be eminently satisfactory and gave the organ a new lease on life. After this improvement, we serviced the organ only intermittently. Calling after one of these intervals, we found to our regret that during the intervening period some other maintenance man had altered some of the original voicing of the organ by discarding the free reed brass resonator trumpet set my father had imported from Germany, and of which he was exceedingly proud; also by changing the cut-up on some of the Swell stops, especially some delicate wood strings and flutes.

In time, the district in which St. Mary's Church was located became less desirable for a parish church, due to its close proximity to Chinatown and the business center, and the moving of its parishioners to the more desirable residential sections of the city. In 1942 a new St. Mary's Church was planned and built by Msgr. William E. McGough, in the College Park District. At first it was planned to move the old, faithful organ to the new church, modernize and electrify it, but after due deliberation it was decided to leave the organ in its hallowed environs, where it had functioned for many years, as the old church was to remain and serve the Mexican population that had meanwhile settled around it, and those of the old parishioners still living nearby.

In 1946, however, under the pastorate of Rev. O'Connor, a namesake of the first pastor, Rev. W. O'Connor, when a general rejuvenation of the old church plant was undertaken, it was finally decided to purchase a new pipe organ and the contract was awarded to the Moller Organ Company. The old organ, the first pipe organ my father built, in 1881, was then dismantled and stored in the church basement, where it lay for several years. In 1953, through the kindness of my friend, John C. Swinford of Redwood City, I was informed that the Holy Trinity Episcopal Church of Menlo Park, California, had secured the organ and they would incorporate the pipes of the old organ, which my father had originally made, into a new modern instrument for the aforementioned church. Mr. Swinford was assisted in this work by Mr. Charles Fisk, a member of the Choir, and other volunteer workers. Additional stops were added to the organ, making it now an organ of 26 stops.

Mr. Swinford presented me with some of the manual keys of the old organ as a keepsake of the handiwork of my father, which I cherish greatly. An interesting program was issued at the dedication of the organ, giving the specification of the new and enlarged instrument, with an historical background of the organ and its original builder, Felix F. Schoenstein, for which I extend my sincere thanks.

CATHEDRAL OF THE BLESSED SACRAMENT
Sacramento, California

In 1880, when St. Rose's Church, the former name of the Cathedral, was located on K and Seventh Streets where the old Post Office building now stands, my father installed an Odell organ Opus 170, built in 1879, in the edifice. In later years, when the new Blessed Sacrament Cathedral was built a few blocks further east on K and Twelfth Streets, a structure said to be the largest church in California, my father removed the Odell organ to the new Cathedral and installed it in the upper gallery.

The organ had two manuals and Pedal, tracker action, and 21 stops. Up in its high location, it is almost unseen from below in the church, yet these limited stops answer their purpose admirably. An organ three times its size would not be too large for an edifice of the proportions of this Cathedral. Miss Lizzie Griffen was the organist for many years. She was holding this position when I first called with my father, and it seems a warm friendship always existed between them. This was also one of the first out-of-town jobs that I attempted to do alone. My father had received a call to come to Sacramento. The organ was reported to be in terrible shape and needed attention immediately. He was in a dilemma as he could not readily respond. The call appeared to be urgent — the organ was to be used for the Christmas or New Year's services. I must have been feeling quite ambitious and confident in my ability to tackle the job, for I boldly offered my services. My father was only too pleased to see me show some sign of confidence and self-reliance, and let me go. When the organist, Miss Griffen, saw me alone, she was surprised, but she was no more surprised than I was when I found the organ in apparently good condition. She was profuse in her apologies when I found that the organ was not in the terrible condition she claimed it was, saying that evidently the trouble had corrected itself, or that possibly a cat might have been in the organ. However, a few Oboes were raspy or buzzy, which she asked me to improve. Without the proper tools, and not actually having done any reed voicing before, although often observing my father do it, I tried to oblige her. I had a hard time of it, and I doubt if I greatly improved them. At any rate, I finally, through diplomacy more than accomplishment, received her okay that everything was all right and I was only too glad to leave the organ until our next regular visit.

However, the experience taught me how super-sensitive some musicians are, what strong imaginations some have, and what diplomacy one must use at times not to hurt or ruffle their feelings, and yet not make a fool of one's self.

During our visits to Sacramento, which were made quarterly and at which times we also serviced other organs, we invariably stayed at the new William Tell Hotel on J Street. It was run by Swiss people named Wunder, and it was a popular place in its day, especially with the foreign element. When I think now of the accommodations we received compared with any moderate-priced hotel today, it indeed was pioneering. It was mostly patronized by workingmen. After returning from work in the evening, it seems the first routine was to blow the steam off a portly stein or two of Rhustahler beer. Then a walk to the rear of the establishment followed, where public wooden washtrays were located, with Sacramento's muddy river water flowing from the faucets. One or two roller towels were provided, mostly damp from frequent use. Then at a signal, the huge dining room was thrown open. A series of long tables, seating about twenty each, were soon occupied. The tables were laden with platters and bowls filled with food; a big soup tureen or two to each table. Coffee, milk or wine could be had. As new boarders arrived, they would take the next adjoining table that meanwhile had been prepared in the same manner, so by the end of the meal practically all the tables in the dining room were occupied. Food was plentiful, varied and well cooked, and one could always take a second helping. In the evening after supper, especially in summer, the armchair brigade would line up outside on the sidewalk, smoking their cigars or pipes. At bedtime one would find a clean bed in one's room, but none too soft, also the usual bureau or dresser with a large wash bowl and a pitcher of water on it. Prices were reasonable and the house was always filled. The management was respectable and everything was well ordered.

While staying at this hotel I had my first bicycle ride. Ben Steinauer, the barkeeper, had a fine racing bicycle. He asked me one evening if I wanted to ride it. I told him I was afraid to, as I hardly knew how to ride and if I were to fall off, I might injure his bicycle. He insisted, however, as traffic was not so heavy at that time of the evening. I managed successfully to straddle the bicycle and rode out as far as 26th and K Streets to the last electric light on the street. Beyond that it was dark and apparently open country, so I retraced my route. Meanwhile, however, instead of enjoying my experience, which had been successful so far, I began worrying about how I would stop and get off without falling, as I had not mastered that trick yet. Furthermore, I knew that in the downtown section of the City there would be plenty of spectators even at that time of night. Finally, I had to make the supreme effort of getting off the bicycle without falling, and lo and behold, the curbs I always criticized in the town as being too high, now came to my rescue. I rode up slowly and carefully against the curb and gracefully and professionally, as it were, stepped onto the sidewalk, alighting with ease. I returned the bicycle to my friend, and thanked him for his kindness, but must admit I did not enjoy the ride.

Heretofore, to tune the organ at the Cathedral, it required an organ pumper. Mr. Bender was the official pumper and for a little extra recompense he gladly assisted me. I recall observing the floor where he stood. In the course of time a noticeable depression had been worn into it. When my brother, Leo, later induced the pastor to install a blower for the organ, the pumper resented this modernization as it apparently deprived him to an extent of a means of livelihood. It was a Sturdivant blower that my brother installed, belted to a motor that was placed high up in the tower. It gave satisfactory service for many years. Rev. Quinn was pastor at the time and served until his death.

Later, during Msgr. Horgan's long pastorate, there was talk of enlarging the Cathedral organ, getting a new one, or modernizing the present one. Meanwhile, the organist, Miss Lizzie M. Griffen, after 35 years of faithful service, retired. I noted her hearing was definitely failing her, and several times she had us make visits in close succession, insisting there were many notes in the organ that were not speaking. We were convinced that they were. Miss Griffen was the last person in the world we would want to come in conflict with, as our relations with her had always been so amicable. However, her insistence that we were not properly servicing the organ as of old, also her complaining to the pastor about it, jeopardized our position and induced us finally to have him and the organist present the next time she summoned us. It was soon evident to the pastor and to me that the notes she claimed were silent (on the softer stops and treble notes) were very audible and plain to us. A knowing nod from the pastor, substantiating our claim that everything was okay, was sufficient for us and we then departed. I believe that was the last time I saw Miss Griffen. She retired, highly honored and beloved by everyone, after completing a most useful life as school teacher and Cathedral organist. On June 30, 1943 she passed to her eternal reward. Miss Griffen was the sister of Judge Frank Griffen of the Superior Court of California.

Mr. Howard Scott, a young and brilliant organist, succeeded Miss Griffen as organist and it was during his occupancy of the position that the question of modernizing the organ was diligently carried forward to fruition. After going over many plans, some of them entirely out of the range of possible fulfillment, and receiving bids from various concerns, the decision was finally reached to leave the organ where it was and make a few additions to it, apply a detached console with a complete electrification, and install a new blowing plant. We were commissioned to do this work and satisfactorily completed it. This modernization was done in 1940. A dedicatory recital on the modernized organ took place with Mr. Warren D. Allen of Stanford University presiding at the console. After a long and successful term as pastor of the Cathedral, Msgr. Horgan asked to be transferred to St. Joseph's Catholic Church in Marysville, where he is now continuing his good work.

ST. FRANCIS DE SALES CHURCH
Oakland, California

One of the first jobs in which I helped my father while I was still attending school, was at St. Francis de Sales Church in Oakland. It seemed to be customary to have the organ serviced before Easter and Christmas. It was about 1896. I recall a Miss McNally was organist, and we children at home made a little jingle about her name, shouting: "Miss McNally, she lived in an alley." However, our poetry seemed to end about there.

I recall the streets of Oakland were mostly macadamized at that time. Grove Street and San Pablo Avenue, near the church, were a mass of red mud in the winter. Opposite the church, on a triangular block between San Pablo Avenue, Grove and 22nd Streets, where now the Key Route office building stands, was a power-house for one of the cable lines of Oakland. I remember the large, empty cable drums that were stored there.

St. Francis de Sales organ was built by the Odell Organ Company of New York, Opus 306 - 1892, and my father assisted their representative in installing it. I remember my father related that in hoisting the organ one of the heavy chests slipped from the sling and fell. The effects of this fall are to be seen on one corner of the chest, where it came in contact with some other hard object and was severely dented. Father McSweeney was pastor here for many years. He was called to his eternal reward in 1915, and was succeeded by Father Keane, who later became Bishop of Sacramento. During his pastorate, in 1909, we removed the large, heavy wheel which operated the crank for pumping the organ and put in a direct current motor, with belt drive and a rheostat, to operate the original feeders, which worked quietly and most efficiently. In later years the church had to dispense with the direct current, so a single phase A.C. motor and a modern kinetic blower were installed. Mr. Tailliander was organist at this time and for a number of years thereafter.

In the earthquake of 1906 the organ fared well, but nevertheless received a severe shaking. Several cracks were made in the brick walls of the church, and the upper portions under the gabled roof were thrown down. One of the largest dummy pipes of a series over the front speaking pipes was also thrown down and landed directly on the organ bench. The latter was made of hard ash wood, but nevertheless the seat was split in two, necessitating replacing it with a new seat. Surely a fortunate break for the organist that she was not there when it landed.

Msgr. Richard Gleason followed Father Keane. After 45 years, the organ began to show signs of wear and tear. The large bellows were in urgent need of repair, the leather links for the pull-down wires frequently broke. Some delicate springs on the Swell to Great coupler were always breaking, making it necessary often to take the whole console apart. We, therefore, urged the Monsignor to have the whole organ thoroughly overhauled and, at the same time, to modernize and electrify the mechanism. As the organ was now being used more frequently than formerly, for accompanying a large chorus of children at their mass, choir space and a detached console were almost indispensible. We, therefore, submitted a plan for a re-arranged organ and loft, using the full width of the choir loft for the organ, with console in the center, organist facing the choir, now to be located between the organ case and console. By this change the dark, useless corners formerly on either side of the organ would be utilized by the rearranged organ itself, and the choir would be all together, mostly in the center with no valuable space sacrificed. Furthermore, a beautiful art glass window that was almost completely hidden by the organ would then be brought into full view again, admitting additional light. Our plan and proposals were finally accepted in 1937. We at this time also added a new Trumpet 8' to the organ in place of a Clarinet 8', and a Gemshorn 8' on the Great and a Vox Humana 8' on the Swell. Useful octave couplers that were not in the organ before were also added, making the organ modern, complete and serviceable again for many years to come.

Mrs. Gregory was organist for many years before the organ was renovated and for some time after. Msgr. Gleason passed away in 1942 and since then many changes occurred. The most recent change took place in 1962, when the extensive Archdiocese of San Francisco was dissected into three dioceses and St. Francis de Sales Church of Oakland became the Cathedral of the Oakland Diocese, with the Most Rev. Floyd L. Begin the presiding Bishop.

So time marches on, from boyhood days with fond memories lingering in my mind of working with my dad on this organ to years later remodeling it with my son, Lawrence. The organ, built in 1892, being rejuvenated, has become young again but we, now with whitened hair at 85, fading gracefully into oblivion. So be it. God be praised.

CHARLES E. GREEN SAN MATEO RESIDENCE

One of the first jobs I worked on with my father was in 1898 when we erected a small one manual, pneumatic action Farrand and Votey pipe organ for Mr. Charles E. Green, in his San Mateo residence. A Mr. Green, not related to Charles E. Green, a representative of the Aeolian Organ Company and located with Kohler and Chase Music Store of San Francisco, interviewed my father relative to the installation of this small residence organ, and he agreed to make the installation.

Mr. Charles E. Green was at that time manager of the Charles Crocker Estate. He was a kind, estimable gentleman, exceedingly thoughtful and considerate of others, but of a rather irritable nature when caught off his guard, undoubtedly the result of overwork and mental strain. His country home was located on Tilton Avenue and El Camino Real in San Mateo. It was a rustic, shingle covered building, surrounded by trees and a garden. To the rear of the home were stables and other utility structures. At the time the only means of transportation between San Francisco and San Mateo was the Southern Pacific steam train. The Interurban Electric Line had not yet been built.

Burlingame, Hillsborough and San Mateo were the suburban towns adjacent to San Francisco where the wealthy made their homes. These towns and surrounding country always made me think of England and the English countryside, from the description I had read of that country. San Mateo's many stone walls and green hedges, its old mansions and estates, its venerable and rather luxurious growth of trees along its streets, the almost ever-present aroma of burning logs from the many inviting fireplaces, the many beautiful horse-drawn carriages, with their liveried attendants, that one would see driving along the streets, always entranced me when I was there.

The Farrand and Votey organ we installed in Charles E. Green's San Mateo residence was a one manual instrument, with divided stops of treble and bass, about six sets, with automatic player. It had a beautifully carved mahogany case, ornamented with decorated display pipes. I believe that previous to the arrival of the organ, Mr. Green had the living room where the organ was placed, specially enlarged to house it. It was a cheerful, homelike room. The organ was on the west end, with windows on the opposite end looking out into the garden, flanking a huge fireplace. On another side were large built-in cabinets with an extensive array of books. On the walls hung some choice Keith paintings, and a large rug covered the floor. A billiard table was set in one corner, and some large easy chairs and several pieces of period furniture completed the furnishings.

Mr. Green was exceedingly interested in and concerned about the organ. The organ chamber was given special consideration to make it sound reflecting, dry and damp-proof. A Ross water motor, vertical piston type, was placed in the basement under the organ to pump the bellows. I recall my father had considerable trouble in designing and applying a suitable hook in pedal starting device and automatic bellows control to govern the water motor. One day, returning from our noon meal, I remember we halted at a corner a few blocks from the Green residence, father with his pad and pencil in hand, designing the arrangement he would apply, so as to be certain how to proceed when we arrived.

I also recall the occasion when the organ was completed. Charles E. Green and his wife were always charming and delightful hosts. On this occasion we were invited to stay for dinner. Those present were Mr. and Mrs. Charles E. Green, Mr. Green's aged mother, the Mr. Green of Kohler and Chase

Company, and my father and I. The table was beautifully set with an immaculate white linen tablecloth and shining silver, and I recall the white-aproned and white-capped maid who waited upon us. I greatly admired the home life of the Green family, which I had occasion to observe intimately while working at their home. Often, in later years, in retrospect I recalled the fine impression it made on my young life. Charles E. Green was a prince of a man; between him and his devoted wife there seemed to be perfect harmony and understanding. The aged mother of Mr. Green, reclining in a rocking chair, always friendly and interested in what we were doing, was the center of devotion of all in the home. Mr. Green's three sons, Eldridge, Allan, and Arthur, then young lads about my age, were attending the Belmont School, in Belmont, California. Refinement and culture, respect and affection for their parents marked their every action.

While working on the organ, we usually traveled back and forth on the train each day. However, one evening we worked very late and missed the last train to the City. Being thus obliged to remain in San Mateo overnight, we made our way to the Union Hotel near the depot. Here it seems everyone had retired early, as would be expected in a small town. After repeated ringing of the night bell, the proprietor came down to the office in his nightshirt and slippers, rather disturbed, but nonetheless welcoming new customers. It was also here that I later experienced my first night away from home alone, in a hotel. Father had some important appointment in the City the following day, so he left me behind. I recall the feeling of loneliness that came over me when I heard the train whistle blow and watched the train depart for the City. At other times, when we were obliged to stay overnight, we went to Buckman's Hotel, alongside the rushing waters of the creek, at that time open and exposed, running through the town. This hotel was nearer the Green residence.

Mr. Green was an ardent smoker, and when he arrived at home from the City, at about four p.m., the fragrant aroma of a good cigar filled the air. He would usually inquire of my father what had been accomplished on the organ during the day, and invariably complimented him on the progress being made. One evening when my father had completed a particularly difficult task, he invited us to remain a little longer to listen to his music. After bidding us to sit down, he passed some of his fine cigars to my father and rather strongly insisted that he smoke one with him, then and there. My father was no smoker; I had never in my life seen him with a cigar in his mouth before. Ill at ease and somewhat embarrassed, possibly on my account, as I also did not smoke, he gingerly fingered the cigar and placed it between his lips, Mr. Green lighting it for him. This unusual sight of my father pretending to smoke a cigar almost brought me to laughter, but I quickly checked the impulse. Whether Mr. Green was aware of the embarrassing position in which he placed my father, I do not know.

After using the small organ above described for some years, Mr. Green desired a new and more pretentious organ, and had the small Farrand and Votey organ installed in the Crocker Estate at "Uplands", Hillsborough. In later years it was given to St. Catherine's Church, Burlingame, where we again serviced it at intervals. In 1939 my son, Lawrence, and I moved and installed it in the new Chapel of St. Joseph's Military School, formerly St. Mathews Military Academy, Belmont, where it was in use for several years, until the institution was dissolved. On July 29, 1955, it was removed by our firm and temporarily stored in the basement of St. Mary's Hospital Nurses' Home, San Francisco. Finally, it found a new home in a private residence in San Rafael.

Referring again to Mr. Green's desire to secure a new and larger organ, around 1902, he authorized the Murray M. Harris Co. of Los Angeles, California, to build him an organ of two manuals and Pedal, with an attached console, consisting of 26 stops, all enclosed in a specially built chamber and equipped with a separate detached automatic player console, consisting of two independent spools and other necessary gadgets. At the time, the organ was being build and installed for Mr. Green, the Aeolian Organ Company was advertising and introducing its patented two manual player, with two rows of perforations, one alongside the other on only one and the same tracker board, using only one music roll, with smaller and larger perforations. Mr. Green evidently cherished this idea better than the two spindle arrangement he had and was also impressed by the complete and extensive library of music one had to choose from, compared with the very limited choice of music rolls available on the double spindle arrangement. Having in mind using these Aeolian music rolls, he had the company construct a similar single tracker board with two rows of perforations similar to the Aeolian tracker board, for him.

As I recall, a critical situation developed. The builders of the automatic player must have imitated the Aeolian player to a marked degree, with the result that some legal action was threatened, possibly a law suit, against the company for infringement of their Aeolian patent, and the player device had to be removed from the organ.

Since Mr. Green did not play the organ manually, he did, however, invite his organist friends to do so for him. One organist I recall especailly was Professor Smith, an elderly English gentleman who was at the time, I believe, organist at St. Mathew's Episcopal Church in San Mateo. At one time Mr. Green arranged for a musical to be held at his home. It was quite an elaborate social affair and received considerable attention in the newspapers. The then famous organist, Clarence Eddy, was guest organist presiding at the organ. I was asked to be present to take care of any possible trouble that might occur. Everything, however, went off beautifully and it was a glorious event. The elite of the Peninsula were present. Clarence Eddy, tall and stately, with his white hair and flowing beard, was the center of attraction. He gave a most delightful program, after which he was encircled by his many admirers, and his charming and gracious manner seemed to capture the fancy and interest of all present. During Mr. Eddy's recital and the reception which followed, I, of course, made myself as inconspicuous as possible, and when the time came for dispensing refreshments I excused myself as I still had to make connection with a late train for the City. I intended leaving unobserved, but my attentive host and hostess sought me out and invited me to stay and thanked me kindly for being present. Needless to say, I told them the pleasure was all mine, and the memory of that evening still lingers with me.

Possibly at this time, Clarence Eddy made some comments

about the tonal qualities of the organ and some suggestions for further improving it. I recall Mr. Green later had a Mr. John W. Whitely, a pipe voicer who recently came from England and who was employed by the Murray M. Harris Co. to revoice many of the stops. I was requested to assist him, which I did with great pleasure, spending about two weeks at the undertaking. This task, needless to say proved to be very beneficial to me as I had the opportunity to watch and observe at close range the many artistic results achieved by this genius. Our two weeks of collaboration were also very interesting and entertaining to me, as Mr. Whitely amused me with many a fine story and anecdote of his past experiences as a voicer in England.

F. M. SMITH (BORAX SMITH) RESIDENCE
Oakland, California

Shortly after the large 4 manual Farrand & Votey 84 stop organ was installed in St. Ignatius Church, San Francisco, 1898, by Colonel William D. Wood and Mr. Whitehead, representing the Farrand & Votey Company of Detroit, Michigan, my father was commissioned by them to install a small Votey organ in the residence of F. M. Smith (also known as Borax Smith, in connection with the 20-Mule Team advertising of Borax chips and soap), at Eighth Avenue and East 24th Street, Oakland. On the first visit I made with my father, I believe the organ was already placed in the residence, but not erected. Mr. William D. Wood of the Votey Company, Mr. Benham, the architect of the residence, and my father were discussing the installation of the organ. I recall especailly Mr. Wood giving my father the necessary instructions for the wiring of the organ, as previous to this installation my father had never erected an electric pneumatic organ.

Due to lack of space for the console, and as its accessibility was mostly from the back, the air pipe supplying it had to be made flexible. To leave the console movable if needed, in fact, the whole organ was compact and crowded. I assisted my father in erecting this organ, which required about two weeks time. I will never forget, when the vital moment came to give the organ its "breath of life", it would not respond but remained inanimate. Realizing the handicaps under which it was erected, this first setback was not too discouraging. First the blowing apparatus, located in the basement, a three crank belt-driven feeder pump and bellows arrangement, was operated by a friction drive Pelton waterwheel. The water pressure was derived from their own tank. If the pressure was lacking, or the friction device too loose, there would be insufficient air. Then the low voltage current for the organ was obtained from three storage batteries. These had to be charged in Oakland and then brought out to the residence by horse and buggy, often spilling much of the liquid enroute. However, neither of these two annoyances was the direct cause of the organ failing to respond at our first test.

After trying and changing various connections, without success, which apparently had been made according to instructions as my father understood them, he finally engaged the services of some electricians. They, too, fumbled around for some time studying the circuits, etc. I was too inexperienced then to offer any suggestions myself, but I suffered with my father the embarrassment and agony of putting up an organ that we could not get a sound out of. Accidently, I believe, rather than by design, someone operated a cutout switch of the automatic player manually, which completed the circuit, the organ gave a yelp and was from then on very much alive. Undoubtedly my dad and I learned much from this experience, the first electric pneumatic organ we had installed. It took much of the mystery out of this new type of organ action that eventually was to become the pattern for practically all future organs.

A few remarks on the organ proper might be of interest here. It was a two manual and Pedal instrument with automatic player in the detached console, all enclosed in a Swell box except the Pedal Bourdon. It had six or eight stops, all typical of the high standard of the Votey Organ Company. It had only one reed, a Trumpet, a free reed similar to a reed organ reed arranged in the boot of the pipe. I recall this stop gave us much trouble, it was far too loud and blatant. We put it in a separate enclosure, but the difficulty then was to get at it to tune it. It did not stay in tune. The tremolo, a beater tremolo, was fastened to the wall of the Swell box. It thumped like a bass drum. My father, always resourceful, conceived the idea to fasten it on a long iron rod, about six feet long, attached to the floor, and so free it from all contact with any object. It solved the problem of the annoying thump. The exterior case of the organ was made of oak, beautifully designed in three bays with grilled panels, on which were fine carvings of oak leaves and acorns. The front pipes were tastefully decorated in a pastel shade of blue and gold, with the oak leaf again used as the motif. The case was made by a cabinet maker in Oakland.

Here I might relate my impressions on this first visit to the Smith residence, also called Arbor Villa. Leaving the train at Seventh and Broadway Station of the Southern Pacific in Oakland, we took an electric car at Franklin and Eighth Streets. This went out to Eighth Avenue and East 15th Streets, where we would transfer to the 8th Avenue car. From Eighth Avenue, looking toward East 24th Street, the tall water tower of the Smith estate was visible. Arriving at the main entrance, a well paved macadam road led directly to the mansion, some several hundred yards ahead. It was like entering paradise. The scent of violets and roses from a nearby hedge filled the air with fragrance. Large maple shade trees and palms paralleled the road leading to the house. To the right was an orchard. The house was a large building, several stories high, of stone foundation and frame super-structure, partly shiplap and shingle exterior finish, painted a brown color and varnished.

Before reaching the house which, I believe, was on the highest knoll of the estate, one passed a small crude shack with a large cauldron lying alongside of it. I wondered why this apparent misfit in such sumptuous surroundings was permitted. Later I learned that it had been the living quarters of Mr. Smith while he was prospecting in Death Valley, California, and came across the rich borax deposits that made him a wealthy man. Somewhat to the right of the house was the stable, a quite pretentious building for horses and carriages. The wide stairs leading to the main entrance of the residence were flanked on either side by palms and tropical plants. Usually a white-coated Chinese, or at times a maid in white apron and cap, responded to the doorbell. On entering one would step into the reception room or court, octagonal in shape, two stories high, the second floor being the balcony. Opposite the entrance was a conservatory, glass enclosed, filled with choice plants and beautiful flowers. Above it on the balcony and opposite the main entrance was the organ. A large, broad stairway, covered with thick, soft carpet led to the balcony. Bronze statuary was placed on the inner corners of the balcony railing. All the interior was of polished oak, the floor in parquet design with costly rugs lying about. The furniture, likewise, was in keeping with the sumptuous surroundings. Mrs. Smith whom we saw at times, although always pleasant, did seem somewhat severe. White-haired and dignified, she reminded me of Queen Victoria. More frequently we did see and have occasion to converse with Mrs. Smith's secretary, Miss Ellis. Mr. Smith we would see later in the afternoon at times, and he was always gracious to my father.

I recall that while we were working on the organ I was anxious to see as much of the grounds as possible, without intruding on the owner's privacy. Opposite the residence was a deer paddock, and a little beyond a rather tempting little nook with some fruit bearing trees, which we singled out as a good place to eat our lunch. Heretofore, we had eaten in the carriage house. The little nook in the orchard was almost too good a place to be true. In addition to eating our own lunch, which we brought along, we helped ourselves to delicious red apples from the trees above. Possibly being forbidden fruit made them taste so much better. Mr. Frohnmueller, the general manager of the place, was helpful and obliging to us at all times.

Park Boulevard was the northern limits of the estate. Beyond that were vacant hills and pasture land. However, two large buildings adorned the hillside. They were, I believe, philanthropic endeavors of Mrs. Smith, homes for young girls, to which she gave much of her time and attention. Another familiar figure about the house at that time was the adopted daughter, Evelyn, a beautiful, auburn-haired girl who, I believe, later became Mrs. Oliver. Some time later Mrs.

Smith passed away and we did not call at the Smith residence for a considerable period thereafter. To our surprise, on our return trip in 1907, Miss Ellis, the former Mrs. Smith's secretary, was now the mistress of the house, the new Mrs. F. M. Smith. Several children, in time, were born of this marriage. On our subsequent visits a new life seemed to pervade the home, in fact, that is what the beautiful mansion seemed to have become, a home, in every sense of the word, with frolicking children, not merely a palatial residence.

In the latter years of Mr. Smith's life, ill fortune seemed to pursue him. Bad investments, or manipulation of his assets to his disadvantage, caused a rapid decline in his exalted financial position and his great wealth soon dwindled and disappeared. About this time Mr. Smith also passed to the great beyond. His estate was sold to meet the demands of his creditors, and the beautiful home with all its luxurious furnishings was sold for a fraction of its worth.

We removed the organ to our factory and eventually sold it for the Smith heirs to the St. Andrews Episcopal Cathedral at Honolulu, Hawaii, where it was installed in their Chapel by my brother, Erwin Schoenstein. The elaborate case, however, was not desired, as it did not harmonize with the surroundings of the Cathedral and was, therefore, left at our factory. In time we built a small organ for the Drake Catering Company of Berkeley, and this case was used to good advantage on this installation.

Misfortune again seemed to be the lot of the organ. The catering firm met with financial difficulties and dissolved. We then were fortunate enough to find a ready buyer for the ornate oak case and organ and it was sold to the St. Aloysius Catholic Church at Delano, California, in the San Joaquin Valley. It is strange what fates befall even the inanimate though faithful pipe organ. This beautiful case, the finest a millionaire could afford to adorn and enhance the beauty of his home, now does that equally so, but not in a mansion of the wealthy, but in the House of God.

FIRST CONGREGATIONAL CHURCH
Berkeley, California

One day, in the spring of 1907, my father was called to the First Congregational Church of Berkeley by a Mr. Bradley, one of the trustees of the church, to inspect their pipe organ which had but recently been installed and evidently did not prove to be satisfactory. It was a rather large three manual organ of 34 ranks, with detached console, mahogany case and gilded front pipes. As far as we were able to learn, the organ was originally built by a Mr. Klann, a stranger in the organ business hereabouts, who apparently had come from one of the eastern states. From the design of the mechanism of the organ, and its construction, he was evidently a very progressive and up-to-date builder. Yet, with his apparent general knowledge, he seemed to be lacking in practical experience, as the sum total of his work was not satisfactory.

The mechanism of the organ was not reliable; there was much ciphering; stops failed to work, couplers failed to function properly; and some unified stops especailly were practically useless. The mechanism of the organ was the tubular pneumatic type. Undoubtedly, the weakness of the organ was the complex design of its mechanism. It was a combination of supply and exhaust action, a type of action I had never seen before. The tubes connecting the console with the organ were supplied with air by the key when depressed. This supplying of the tube was not accomplished by the ordinary method of a supply and exhaust valve disc, or by a supply and exhaust pallet, or by a simple exhaust valve at the console end, with the bleed vent on the opposite end. The manual keys operated pallets, or ventils, under which were the holes for the main tube and the several holes supplying the couplers on the manual. However, a fine skiver leather was glued over the pallet chest holes on which the keys rested. When a key was depressed or the pallet lifted from its seat, air pressure from a general supply, or depending on what coupler was on, would lift the leather acting as an enclosed diaphram, permitting the air to enter its respective tube. The Great manual having had about six of these apertures or couplers, exerted a lifting pressure against the key valve, inclining it to speak or cipher when not wanted. The only remedy the builder had for this was to increase the tension on the key spring to counteract the pressure from under, with the result that the organ had the stiffest key touch I had ever felt, surpassing even that of some old tracker organs. This also applied to the other manuals in lesser degree. Another fault that developed, due to this peculiar type of key supply, was that when the manuals were coupled together they would eventually work backward, i.e., instead of coupling Swell to the Great manual, one could also play the Great from the Swell manual.

The organ was a conundrum, and from the outset my father concluded that it would be my job to solve the many problems that seemed to plague this otherwise well-built and good-sounding organ. Based on an estimate my father made, not realizing however, the amount of work involved, the church agreed to a stipulated price which was mutually acceptable.

I do not know how long Mr. Klann was engaged on the organ, but evidently he gave up in despair. Mr. Thomas Whalley of Berkeley was also given an opportunity to try his skill in correcting some of the many mistakes. I was not told and do not know how long they worked on the organ, but it was following their attempts to set things right, which did not prove successful, that we were called on the scene.

At the time I was about twenty-three years of age, ambitious and eager for the opportunity to solve just such a problem. I systematically tackled each item that was faulty, studied its design and functioning, and soon found its weak points. These were then corrected, one item at a time. In the case of the Unified Bourdon 16'-8'-4' on the Swell manual, which was also borrowed on the pedal, I made an entire new mechanism. The intricate lead tubing of the console was removed and a check valve arrangement provided for each tube, so that the air could no longer travel backward as heretofore. In time, and I should say a considerably longer time than we had anticipated, order was brought out of chaos, and everything was made to work dependably and satisfactorily.

I recall riding home on the train every evening with a pad and pencil in my hand, on which I would sketch the particular part of the action that was giving trouble, making my deductions and conclusions, thus preparing myself for the next day's attempt to rectify the trouble. As stated, the organ was finally satisfactorily completed on September 19, 1907, and we were highly commended by Mr. Bradley, the trustee, and Mr. Frederick Wolle, who was then director of the choir. Mr. Harahan, I believe, was the organist. From then on the organ was no longer a "child of sorrow", but a valuable asset to the church. Owing to the fact that we had greatly exceeded the estimated time it would take to put the organ in condition, we made concessions in our financial arrangement with the church which was also satisfactory to both parties.

As this particular job gave me pleasure in solving the difficulties that beset this organ, it also gave me much confidence in myself and spurred my ambition to greater achievement. I had dreams of going back east to New York or Boston to work in some of the large organ factories, there to acquire more and varied experience and then, after a few years, returning again to San Francisco to work with my father and brothers. This I eventually did.

Meanwhile, and for many years later, the organ at the Berkeley Cengregational Church functioned satisfactorily. Mrs. Mabel Hill Redfield succeeded Mr. Harahan as organist and held the position until 1946, when she passed away. Frederick Wolle, the former choir director, moved to Bethlehem, Pennsylvania, and has since become famous with his annual Bach Festivals.

In 1915 the old church was razed to make place for the new structure of Colonial design which now occupies the site. We removed the organ and reassembled it in the new edifice as a divided organ on either side of the choir loft. We electrified the action throughout and installed a modern blowing plant. We also added a Trumpet 8' and Viol d'Amour stop to the Great manual, and a Clarinet to the Choir manual. The Choir manual was enclosed, to make it also expressive, and a set of chimes was added to the Great manual.

I recall with pleasure one of my first successful achievements in the organ profession, the salvaging of an organ that was practically given up as hopeless. Yet this organ has given forty-one years of faithful service.

In 1948, with the object in mind of making improvements to the Choir end of the church, the thought of a new organ was projected and finally consummated by acquiring a new 4 manual Moller organ. Mr. Black, a new arrival from Boston, occupied the position of organist at the time. The old organ was put in storage for a time and was finally sold to the Epiphany Catholic Church in San Francisco, where we installed it.

STANFORD UNIVERSITY
Palo Alto, California

In 1901, a 57 stop, three manual Murray M. Harris electric-pneumatic organ was completed as scheduled, in fact before Stanford was ready to receive it. So by mutual consent it was temporarily erected in the Mechanics Pavilion in San Francisco, for a Christian Endeavor Convention, which was held there in 1901. After the convention, the organ was removed and erected in Stanford Memorial Chapel, where we serviced it at frequent intervals.

It was in 1906, a short time after the cataclysm of April 18, when the territory from San Luis Obispo, in the south, to Santa Rosa, in the north, suffered the severe effects of the earth's convulsion, which destroyed the works of man in a few fleeting moments, that we were again summoned to Stanford University by the comptroller, Mr. Lathrop, to clean out and safeguard from further injury the famous Murray M. Harris organ.

The Memorial Chapel, built of marble and stone, with its costly mosaics, marble statuary and art glass windows, was a scene of desolation when we beheld it on our first visit to the campus on June 25, 1906. Several other buildings were wrecked beyond repair, stones and debris littered the adjacent lawns and roadways and marble statues were toppled from their pedestals high up on the facades of buildings. The large Memorial arch was in ruins and innumerable arches in the corridors showed gapping fissures. The central tower of the church, spanning the nave and trancept, layed in a heap of debris on the floor, the front or facade of the church with its famous mosaic, the Sermon on the Mount, was a heap of debris strewn about the quadrangle. The side walls and roof over the organ, fortunately, remained intact, shielding the organ from a severe rainstorm that followed a few days after the earthquake.

The first task of reconstruction on the Memorial Chapel was to build a temporary wall at the back and at the front of the organ loft, completely enclosing the organ and separating it entirely from the rest of the edifice. We then removed every pipe in the organ and took out buckets of plaster and debris from within the organ. Fortunately, the Swell and Choir manuals had the extra protection of the Swell boxes over them. The Pedal pipes adjoining the front wall and the open Great section were buried in debris. However, aside from some broken pipe racks and a few severe dents in the front display pipes, which were of pure English block tin, the damage, after some effort, was successfully repaired. No permanent or serious injury was done to the organ. My father and I, with a helper, Mr. Beale, supplied by the University, worked for over a month in restoring the organ to its former state of perfection.

I remember, during this period, the long, tedious walks every day from town to the campus. I believe, due to the temporary suspension of classes at the University, the electric cars were not running at this time. Eating our lunch together under the palm trees in the quadrangle was a welcome intermission in our work each day, and in the evening after dinner we would often enjoy a walk to the base of a large redwood tree on the edge of San Francisquito Creek. I recall a heart to heart talk I had with my dad one particular, beautiful evening at this tree. My decision was then and there definitely made to remain with my father and follow in his footsteps as his successor in his business.

The restoration of the Chapel was resumed almost immediately after the disaster. The tower above the Chapel was, however, eliminated in the new plan. Also, the mosaics on the facade of the Chapel were not replaced until later.

However, every effort to restore those of the interior of the nave were made.

Soon after we had finished cleaning out the organ it was found that the period of reconstruction and restoration of the Chapel would be protracted, and as it was felt that this work would interfere too much with the religious services in the Chapel, it was then decided to remove the organ entirely and temporarily install it in the Assembly Hall on the campus. Here it remained for some time, until the work in the chapel was far enough advanced to again use it for Divine services. The organ was again erected in its former place by the Murray M. Harris Company successors. At this time a harp was added to the organ, and an echo organ and chimes were installed high up near the ceiling in the west transept. These improvements were very successful and added to the beauty of the organ.

The restoration of the mosaics did not progress so favorably. Ill fortune seemed to follow the carrying out of this work. The mosaics, which were made in Italy, were, by some process or other, glued or fastened to squares of paper or cloth. Due to absorbing moisture while aboard ship enroute from Italy they became loosened from their backing and when the artisans opened the cases they found a jumble of countless pieces of colored glass and small stones, utterly useless for the purpose for which they were intended. A second order had to be made, delaying for months the completion of the interior of the Chapel. During this period of waiting for the arrival of the new mosaics, and during the long period of placing the mosaics on the walls by the two skilled artists who came from Italy to do the work, the Chapel was filled with huge scaffolding. The herioc marble figures of the Twelve Apostles which had formerly occupied niches on either side of the altar were not replaced after the restoration, an omission I always regretted.

During this trying time of restoration, services were held in the Chapel and the organ was used frequently. Professor B. C. Blodgett, an amiable, lovable old soul played the organ up to this time. After his death, Professor Louis Horton Eaton presided at the organ, but being of a high strung temperament he complained bitterly of his inability to practice during the day on account of the constant tapping of the hammers of the artisans working on the mosaics, and of the unsightly scaffolding obstructing his view of the altar and the congregation. He longed for the day when the work would be completed. But like Moses of old, who could only view the Promised Land from the mountain top, Louis Eaton, bearing the annoyances and irritations of this construction period, had to content himself with visualizing what the completed Chapel in its final serene quiet and calm would be like. He passed away on November 15, 1918.

Dr. Gardner served as chaplain of the University for many years while we serviced the organ and our relations with him were most pleasant. Following the death of Louis Eaton, Warren D. Allen was selected as his successor. He held the position of Dean of Music at the University.

In 1928, shortly after his engagement, consideration was given to improving and enlarging the organ and, in 1930, a contract was entered into with the Skinner Organ Company of Boston to furnish a new 4 manual console, complete and adequate for all future additions that were contemplated for the organ. The organ, already equipped with the electric pneumatic action of the Murray M. Harris type, beautifully made and designed, proved nevertheless to be inferior in comparison with the modern electric actions of more recent design. A Skinner electric magnet and a primary were applied to the chest operating the old secondary valve of the grooved chest. In addition, a new chest in the Choir section was installed for future additions, a Diapason 8' and Tuba 8' were added to the Great. An entirely new, modern and larger blowing plant was installed, one that would be adequate for the Solo division or fourth manual that was to be installed at some future time.

Our firm was entrusted with this work and for several weeks we bacame regular boarders at the campus until our work was completed. The outcome was very satisfactory. I recall an incident that happened to me while boarding and lodging at the Student's Union, where I was assigned a room for the time we were engaged in this construction work. I had already been occupying the room for about a week and felt quite at ease. A teachers' convention or institute was being held at the University at this time. One evening on returning to my room, tired and possibly not appearing too neat and tidy after the day's work, I was surprised to find it occupied by several professors. I do not know who was the most startled, whether it was I who justly considered the right to the room mine, on account of prior possession, or the surprised professors who, from all indications, considered me an intruder. I remonstrated with one who seemed to be the most indignant, and was most haughtily informed, that I was talking to Professor so-and-so, one of the prominent professors of the University, as I learned to my surprise later. Nonetheless, I did not admire his attitude for a cultured gentleman. I removed my belongings. The intruders held the fort and I was finally assigned to another room.

As so often happens, nothing seems to be permanent in this world of ours. Having always taken great pride in our care and maintenance of this organ during the many years previous, and in the installation of the various improvements, it was indeed a shock to us to be notified one day that our services were no longer needed. Other parties were entrusted with the work and also finally installed the Solo or fourth manual, completing the instrument and making it undoubtedly one of the outstanding organs of this territory. Recitals are frequently held Sunday afternoons, and tourists and visitors make this renowned Chapel and campus a mecca for enjoying the beautiful in art and music.

GORDON BLANDING RESIDENCE
Belvedere Island

Gordon Blanding was a Southern Pacific Railroad attorney by profession and a relative of the Loyd Tevis family, a philanthropist and patron of the arts, a most esteemed gentleman. He resided in his home on Franklin Street, San Francisco, for some time before the fire and earthquake of 1906. Although his home was on the fringe of the fire limit and was not consumed, he chose to move his estate across the bay to Marin County, on the southern tip of Belvedere Island.

My brother, Leo, had made several visits to service the organ prior to my first visit there, in 1914, so I was somewhat prepared by him to see a wonderful place and to meet a prince of a gentleman, the sire of the house, Mr. Blanding. My expectations were more than fulfilled. The trip to Sausalito by ferry, in view of the Golden Gate, is always fascinating. On arriving at the Sausalito slip, we boarded the little steamer "Marin" and in a short time disembarked at a landing on the Island. A series of steep steps, with a few cutoffs through some private gardens, soon put us on the road to the Blanding residence. Later on, changes were made in transportation facilities and we were obliged, on arriving at Sausalito, to board another ferry which went direct to Tiburon. Invariably, Mr. Blanding would have his faithful chauffeur, Mr. George Place, in his car waiting to drive us up to his residence along the beautiful, scenic road with its artistic homes nestling on the hillside and the rustic moss and vine covered walls and embankments. The higher one ascended, the more beautiful did the scene become. Opposite, toward Tiburon, glimpses were had of the little island containing the Corinthian Yacht Club, with its many yachts at their moorings. Finally, Raccoon Strait, with its strong current, said to be the deepest water in the Bay, separating Belvedere Island from Angel Island, came into view. Soon we were atop the Island of Belvedere, at the stone wall with a heavy ornamental iron gate enclosing the Blanding estate. The view through this gate of charming San Francisco in the distance, with the bay intervening, I often thought, would make a wonderful painting or photograph. In entering the gate one could not help but admire the beautiful flowers and foliage that abounded in this delightful place. From this vantage point I also saw a panorama of San Francisco, the bay, Sausalito to the Golden Gate, Alcatraz and Angel Island that I had never seen before. My first impression was that of being in some foriegn port on the Mediterranean, with the blue waters of the Bay, the dream city opposite, ships of all nations passing in and out of the Golden Gate.

Soon Mr. Blanding, a man well on in years, still spry, jovial and with a ruddy complexion, would appear to greet us, often wearing a white yachting cap, blue jacket and white trousers. The organ was, of course, the purpose of our visit, but nothing seemed to please Mr. Blanding better than to find others who took equal pleasure and genuine delight in admiring the beauty of this favored spot. So a little jaunt through the paths of his garden usually was a preliminary to our real task of tuning and servicing the organ. There were three large buildings on his estate — the colonial mansion on the highest point, with its old-fashioned veranda always freshly painted in immaculate white; then the lower house where the organ was located in a large music room, which also contained two grand pianos and the automatic player console, and an invaluable collection of Keith paintings adorning the walls. This California artist, Mr. Blanding idolized. The third, or lowest house, he called his cottage. Why, I do not know, as it had two stories in front and was quite pretentious in size.

On occasions I had taken my aged father with me, to give him an opportunity to see this beautiful place and to meet Mr. Blanding, who was of his same age. On these occasions Mr. Blanding was most gracious and at noontime invited us to join him at his table for luncheon. We enjoyed his hospitality, although accepting under protest as we had only come to tune the organ. I recall my father's wonderment at the service given us, seated at a perfectly appointed table covered with an immaculate linen cloth and laid with beautiful silverware, the liveried butler, Edward Eicholtz, standing at our back ready to serve as the meal progressed. Mr. Blanding was always a most gracious host and an interesting conversationalist. He wrote several books or essays on subjects of timely interest and was also a frequent contributor to the "Pulse of the Public" or "The Safety Valve" of the San Francisco papers. He was a great patron of the arts, a sponsor of the San Francisco Symphony Orchestra and a lover of the pipe organ.

During the course of the years Mr. Blanding had his original Aeolian organ greatly enlarged, resulting finally in a three manual instrument of 54 stops. The console was attached. On the opposite end of the room from where the organ stood was the self-player console, with stop and other controls only, which Mr. Blanding skillfully manipulated with a high degree of perfection. In a cabinet alongside the attahced console was the Duo-Art Player. Usually on the completion of our two days work tuning the organ, which time he insisted must be spent on the organ even if we could have done it satisfactorily in less time, he would give us a little recital with the Duo-Art, so we could hear how our work turned out. Invariably, after several beautiful and exquisite numbers, he would finish with "The Storm" by Lemmens, taxing the capacity of the organ to its utmost. Mr. Blanding valued his Aeolian pipe organ, and no needed expense was denied it. I recall on one occasion I told him of another gentleman whom I considered rather well-to-do, who had a pipe organ in his home but was rather disconcerted at the expense it entailed. Mr. Blanding's comment on this was, that a pipe organ in a man's home is only a rich man's privilege and that the gentleman should have known better.

I had never seen Mr. Blanding play at the keyboard, but was informed by his faithful butler that when seemingly unobserved and unheard by anyone, it was one of Mr. Blanding's greatest delights to extemporize at the organ, trying out the many tone-color combinations. With old age creeping gracefully upon him, he retired to his city domicile at the fairmont Hotel. The estate at Belvedere was sold, each house with sufficient grounds about it, separately.

Fortunately, the house where the organ was located was sold to the Kretchmer family, also devotees and performers on the pipe organ. The beautiful Keith collection was removed and finally found a deserving place in the exhibit halls of the Palace of the Legion of Honor and another large marine view window was installed. The dummy front of display pipes and the ornate case were dispensed with, although it was an artistic piece of workmanship. In fact, the room was transformed from a rather sedate music salon to a cheerful homelike living room.

The organ still gives forth its melodious music and is possibly as much admired by its new owners as it was of yore, but something had definitely left it, the soul of Mr. Blanding that breathed into it during the many years that it was his comfort and delight. Mr. Blanding died September 11, 1945, at the Fairmont Hotel, which he made his home in recent years. He reached the age of 95 years. His faithful butler, Edward Eicholtz, in his employ for almost 40 years, also passed on. His chauffeur, George Place, found other employment and the two charming housekeepers who so cheerfully waited on us, Anna Anderson and Emma Scott, also found employment in other homes. The former we had occasion to meet one day in the apartment of Roscoe Oakes, when we were arranging to remove his Aeolian organ.

MISSION SANTA CLARA
or
SANTA CLARA UNIVERSITY
Santa Clara, California

Mission Santa Clara was one in the chain of twenty-one Missions built in California by the early Franciscan padres. The adobe mission church at Santa Clara was originally built in 1777. In 1850 the facade of the Mission was modernized by adding two towers. A story was also added to the adobe walls of the building adjoining the Mission to the south, which served for many years as the priest residence. An organ loft and vestibule were also added to the Mission Church at that time. Lenzen Bros., of San Jose, I was told, were the architects who designed these improvements.

Back in 1884 Joseph Mayer built an exhibit organ for the Mechanics Pavilion in San Francisco, and this organ was eventually bought by the Jesuits and was erected by Mr. Mayer in the Santa Clara Mission. According to data I have from my father the organ was erected in the front of the church, placed to one side in the Sanctuary. It was a two manual and Pedal tracker action organ of about 16 stops, and from a description given me by an old Jesuit Brother who was there for many years, the blowing arrangement consisted of an unusual type bellows, consisting of two large boxes which would telescope one into the other and force the air into the organ. These boxes were raised and lowered by foot power.

The organ was later moved from the Sanctuary to the gallery, or opposite end of the church, over the entrance vestibule. A new bellows of the conventional type was then installed, and a well designed oak case was made for the organ by one of the Brothers. I was informed a man from Oakland did the organ work at this time, evidently Mr. George Andrews, as the new bellows indicated his handiwork.

Sometime thereafter, in 1900, my father was called to make some alterations on the organ, and I accompanied him. Rev. Kenna, S.J., was Pastor of the parish. I believe the Andrews bellows, with its feeders, were taken out of the organ at this time and placed in the tower room for the purpose of applying an electric motor to it and to make the blowing arrangement as quiet as possible. A new auxiliary bellows, without feeders, was substituted by us in its place and located in the organ. I recall the rickety stairs on the outside of the building up to the organ loft, its only entrance, which many a time we ascended.

Behind the organ was a large clear glass window offering an inspiring view of a portion of Santa Clara, with the hills on the Eastern horizon mellowed in glowing colors and shadows as the sun sank in the western sky. Directly below the window, about 50 feet forward, stands the original Mission cross, now encased in a protective covering, with its significant inscription: "He that shall persevere to the end, he shall be saved. Mission founded 1777." The thick adobe walls of this Mission Church, the ceiling decorations, painted by the Indians, as also the handmade tiles covering its roof, the altars and statuary of typical Spanish design, the former made in Mexico and brought in sections of about 2 x 3 feet on the backs of mules to the Mission and erected there, the musty, peculiar odor permeating this hallowed place, all helped to lend a charm of romance and reverence. I recall the first evening we were there at the ringing of the Angelus bell. This bell was one of three that was presented to the Missions by the King of Spain in 1799 with the priviso that it be rung every day, which promise has been faithfully kept ever since.

As the work we were doing on the organ required about a week or two to complete, my father and I were temporarily domiciled at the Mission, and we slept in one of the old adobe buildings, then used as an infirmary. I recall evenings after work reading some interesting books that were lying about. The chief work we were doing on the organ was to place the old bellows with feeders in the tower room and connect it with an air pipe to the new auxiliary bellows placed in the organ in its stead. A large hole for the air pipe had to be cut through the thick adobe walls. I recall cutting this hole, how I almost venerated every particle I dislodged. I took a sample home as a souvenir. My fancy wandered back to the early days of California when the good Franciscan padres, with their Indian neophytes, made and laid these very bricks one upon another, that I was now disturbing. (Evidently my reverence for venerable old Missions was not shared by others as I was informed that at the time the facade of the old Mission was modernized the original side walls and the Sanctuary walls of the Mission were removed, for what purpose I do not know excepting possibly for being unsafe and were substituted with new ones, and the material was strewn on the field in front of the Mission.)

As the entire organ, the front excepted, was to be enclosed within a wooden enclosure, the priest in charge, Father Raggio, S.J., told us to tell our needs to one of the Brothers who was a carpenter, who would attend to our wants. It was not long before a tall, intellectual looking man in plain working clothes came up to the organ loft for further instructions. After a few words of greeting, it was soon evident that Brother "Joe", as he was called, was of German birth and thereafter all conversation between him and my father was in the German language. I recall that evening after supper my father and I worked a little overtime on the organ. It was in the twilight, approaching darkness, when we were startled by the approach of a tall, distinguished-looking clergyman wearing a black habit, scrutinizing the work that had been done. We thought it was one of the priests, but it proved to be our friend the carpenter, Brother Joe, who a few hours before had been working in his crude carpenter outfit, now wore the simple but dignified black habit of the Jesuit Order. An intimate friendship sprang up between Brother "Joe", (later better known to us as Brother Joseph Maichen, S.J.), my father and myself, which survived for many years until their passing away.

The partition enclosing the organ was part of a scheme

recommended by one of the professors of the College, a Mr. Carl Buehrer, who evidently was also an organist or musical director and who played the organ at St. Joseph's Church in San Jose. In addition to the enclosure around the organ he had a large roller shade applied in front, which was to be drawn down to the front pipe sill when the organ was not in use to prevent any dust from entering the organ. I often thought of the impracticability of his scheme. With all his concern, dust did enter the organ nevertheless.

The installing of the motor in the tower room to operate the feeders required the work of some electrician, so again as in the case of the carpenter work, the priest said he would send one of the professors over who would arrange for it. The gentleman was John J. Montgomery professor of physics. He applied and arranged the necessary wiring and apparatus for the operation and control of the motor. The only current available at the time for this purpose was from the 500 volt line which supplied the street car which passed the Mission. The necessary rheostat to control the motor was made and designed by Professor Montgomery. I recall being told at the time that Professor John J. Montgomery was also interested in aeronautics and had developed a flying machine or glider. In later years I learned that these experiments were made at Otay Messa, California, south of San Diego, in 1883, with his brother James. Since the Wright Brothers of Dayton, Ohio, developed their glider seventeen years later in 1900, Professor Montgomery might have had prior claim to being the originator of the glider, predecessor to the modern airplane. While further experienting and developing his glider, he met with death in a crash in 1911 in Evergreen Valley, Santa Clara. A monument is now being planned to be erected on the site of his first flight to commemorate the event and the inventor.

Returning to the subject of the old Mission Church, the regular organist was an Italian, Mr. Martinelli. He was a rather stout, slow-spoken gentleman with a decided accent. In addition to his musical position as organist, he was also the cook of the institution. I recall one beautiful evening after supper with my father, I decided to take a walk to the next community, which was the City of San Jose. There was a trolley car running between the two towns but we preferred the pleasant walk. It was my first visit to San Jose and so my introduction into this beautiful "Garden City" was not by train or car, but by foot. It was a most enjoyable walk of about three miles in the cool evening air on the broad Alameda, with its tall shade trees and beautiful homes on either side. On completion of our work on the organ, Brother Joseph and the pastor invited us into one of the small dining rooms, the woodwork and finishing of which, incidentally, was also the handiwork of Brother Joe, and served us a refreshing drink and some eatables to show their appreciation for the work we had done.

Santa Clara College, in time, became the University of Santa Clara and has received wide acclaim for its notable teachers, professors and scholars that direct its destinies. Among them were Father Careda, S.J., Prefect of Studies; Father Robert Sesnon, in charge of music and dramatics; Father Thedor Bell, S.J., Mathemetician and Scientist. An outstanding dramatic presentation given by the students of the University, which received much acclaim, was the Passion Play, written by Clay M. Green, an alumnus of the University. Another priest of Santa Clara who received recognition was the "Padre of the Rains", Father Jerome Rickard, S.J., who acquired a national reputation as a long distance weather prophet and forecaster, and the famous "Glacier Priest", Fr. Hubbard, S.J.

In addition to the old adobe Mission Church, Santa Clara University also had its student Chapel, a substantial brick building, designed and built by a Mr. Clinch. Here we installed a small two manual and Pedal Farrand and Votey organ that had previously been in Holy Cross Church in San Francisco. One day in 1911 or sometime thereafter, I believe, the Chapel building and its contents were consumed by a fire and completely destroyed. During the passing years we called intermittently to service the old Mission organ. However, our old friend, Joseph Maichen, was no longer there; other priests were in charge.

Improvements were made and modern buildings have been erected, forming the University campus around the old gardens of the Mission. A new parish church has also been built in the town for the special use of the town's people, leaving the old Mission Church for the exclusive use of the student body. The old Mayer organ was removed from the Mission, enlarged and modernized by the Artcraft Organ Company of Southern California, and then erected in the new St. Clare's Church, where it is giving good service.

At about this time, after the organ had been removed, a disasterous fire also destroyed the old adobe Mission. With difficulty the old Mission bell, the gift of the Spanish king, and other relics of the old Mission were rescued. If I have been correctly informed, the Mission bell was put on a temproary support to be rung that evening at the Angelus hour, in order to maintain the unbroken record and uphold the tradition connected with it, that it be rung every day.

A new, substantial edifice has since been built, a replica, as nearly as possible, of the original Mission building, although somewhat larger. The original tiles were again used on the roof and the interior decoration was duplicated as much as possible. All in all the new edifice is a worthy successor to the old Mission Church.

In 1927 a splendid Moller organ, hidden behind a typical Spanish screen, was acquired and now furnishes music for this interesting and famous landmark, one of the twenty-one Missions adorning our glorious State of California.

ST. JOHN THE BAPTIST CATHEDRAL
Fresno, California

Sometime in 1912 my father received a request from Rev. J. McCarthy, of St. John the Baptist Church, Fresno, California, to call at the church and look over a pipe organ he was having installed, but which was not yet completed, as the builder, a Mr. Heatherington of Watsonville, California, had died, leaving the unfinished organ on his hands. It seems Rev. McCarthy had other parties also working on the organ before calling us, with not very satisfactory results. From a record I note, my elder brother, Leo, also called to inspect or work on the organ, but apparently did nothing drastic to improve the instrument as he evidently thought it a hopeless case.

Eventually arrangements were made that I make the trip to Fresno for the purpose of finally putting the organ in condition, if it were possible.

It was my first trip to Fresno. I found it a charming little city, rather warm in summer, with the fragrant odor of drying raisins filling the air. After securing lodgings in the old Grand Central Hotel, in the business section of the city, I set out for the brick church with its two spires, on Mariposa Street. There I met Father McCarthy for the first time. In later years he told me of his surprise on meeting me, as he had expected to see a matured, baldheaded, or possibly gray-haired gentleman, similar in appearance perhaps to my father and elder brother, and my youthful appearance rather startled him. However, in a most kind and courteous manner he told me the history of this organ, of his disillusionment, and dissappointment, that after all his expense and high expectations, the organ was not complete, was not reliable and was seemingly a failure. I promised that if he would give me a few days time to familiarize myself with the peculiar type of mechanism used, make some tests and see how things responded to treatment, I would give him my verdict and an estimate of the probable cost of putting it into good shape.

I found a two manual organ of 21 stops, pneumatic action. It proved to be a combination of systems, exhaust at the manual key, and a pneumatic relay, partly exhaust and supply. The grooves were in the chest table proper, with small removable panels below for access. A unique type of individual valve was applied, with two unified stops on the Great, an Open Diapason 8' and Octave 4' unit. And on the Swell a 16' Bourdon and an 8' Stopped Diapason unit, also used as a 16' Lieblich Bourdon in the pedal. These unifications made the mechanism rather complicated. The Great was unexpressive. The wood and pedal pipes were undoubtedly made by the builder, the metal pipes very probably by some old-established pipe maker. The bellow was a peculiarly designed affair, a square box about 4 x 4 feet and one foot deep, covered with a leather covering, with a floating top panel like a huge diaphragm pouch or pneumatic, which was loaded with weights and which would rise and fall like the usual type bellow, as wind was supplied or consumed by the organ. A pumping arrangement was in the tower room, consisting of three feeders connected to a crank, belt-driven by an electric motor. It was exceedingly noisy and distracting to listen to and was the first item that drew my criticism. The case was made of oak but showed the effects of excessive heat by warped and split panels. The front pipes were numerous and lavishly decorated.

After donning my overalls my first task was to remove the debris and leavings which the former organmen had strewn about, not only in the organ proper but outside also; even in the tower room above I noted old discarded organ parts, indicating that undoubtedly the latter was their workshop, and from the leavings accumulated there, I concluded that much experimenting had been done. At this particular time, just as I had my broom in hand, Father McCarthy came up and saw me thus engaged. Undoubtedly his anxiety as to what my verdict on the condition of the organ would be could not be longer restrained. Though I could not tell him anything definite, as the cursory examination I had made of the mechanism was not yet conclusive, yet it indicated that the type of action used was very progressive indeed and that the general workmanship indicated that the organ had been designed and built by someone familiar with organ construction, in fact by one with very advanced ideas. After experimenting with the couplers, for instance, that would not respond, I found it was a matter of adjusting a vent peculiarly made with a piece of lead tube which was to have an aperture of the proper size, but which aperture was lacking. In other cases felt or leather gaskets were not cut through, impeding the air flow. Adjusting vents and regulating springs on the manual primary valve stems corrected other sources of trouble. I was soon able to tell the pastor definitely that the organ could be put in good order and what the probable cost would be. He commissioned me to do the work and I had my younger brother, Erwin, come from the City to assist me. This was in September 1912. For several weeks we were thus employed.

A Mr. Spence, employed on the Fresno Republican, was the organist. The Balthis Sisters, Catherine and Marguerite, were active in the choir; the former possessing a beautiful soprano voice, was director of the choir, her sister singing contralto. An energetic and enthusiastic choir was available, which was easily understandable with Father McCarthy, an able performer on the organ and a good musician, spurring them on to higher perfection for the beautification of the church service.

Our work was finally completed and the organ has since been in continuous service. I had never met the builder of the organ, Mr. Heatherington, due to his death, but after viewing his unfinished work, I am certain that, had he lived, we would in time have heard much to his credit in the organ profession. I believe he also built an organ for the Calvary Episcopal Church at Santa Cruz. He came originally from Australia and worked on the large Town Hall organ in Sydney, Australia.

During our sojourn in Fresno, Father McCarthy made our stay most pleasant. When we were about to leave he told me, that he had questioned my ability to do the work when he first saw me because of my youthful appearance, but when he saw me with broom in hand cleaning up the rubbish left behind by others, and beginning with a clean slate, he immediately took heart and figured that the young fellow has the energy and determination and, undoubtedly, will prove his skill, given a chance.

One of the most impressive religious rites and the first of its kind I was privileged to witness was the investiture of Rev. J. McCarthy as a Domestic Prelate. Cardinal Dennis Dougherty of Philadelphia, a friend of Father McCarthy, was the officiating prelate. I was there to see that the organ functioned perfectly. It was a Red Letter Day for Rev. McCarthy and for the City of Fresno and the Diocese. I recall the impressive entry into the church, the organist playing the processional "The War March of the Priest", by Mendelssohn. After the services a reception was held in the parlors of the priest's house, where Monsignor McCarthy received the felicitations of his firends and especially his faithful choir members. After a few words of thanks and appreciation, the new Monsignor requested those present to sing his favorite song, "When You Come To The End Of A Perfect Day." So indeed, it was, a beautiful, memorable day.

Sometime later St. John the Baptist Church was enlarged and beautifully frescoed. Also, a chapel was built in the basement. Having organized a vested boys choir, after the organ in the gallery was put in condition, and now having a spacious sanctuary, Msgr. McCarthy dreamed of further improvements, of a sanctuary organ close to the choir boys to accompany them — also to be used on Sundays for the children's mass and, eventually, as an Echo organ from the organ in the gallery.

We were, accordingly, commissioned by him to build a five stop organ, all enclosed under expression, and to place it behind the high altar where it would not be seen by the congregation, yet leaving a passageway under it to permit the altar boys to pass through to either sacristy, as heretofore. The console was to be placed out in the transept of the church. The passageway behind the altar was only two feet wide, so it required much study and an unusual design to lay out the organ. It proved to be about fifteen feet wide and two feet deep. The swell blinds were on the ceiling of the Swell box. The organ contained an Open Diapason, Tibia, Gamba, Dulciana and Flute, the Tibia serving for the extended pedal. The organ proved to be very satisfactory and received the highest praise from Msgr. McCarthy for its excellent tone. We then set to work to arrange for playing the sanctuary organ from the gallery organ. The new organ being operated on the electric action and the gallery organ on the pneumatic, we had to apply the necessary contact and duplicate stop keys on the gallery organ to operate the sanctuary organ. Finally, everything was completed, both organs were in fine condition, deserving of a proper and fitting dedication.

Msgr. McCarthy arranged for the church services, and it was our good fortune to secure the services of the famed, veteran organist, Clarence Eddy, who at the time was sojourning in San Francisco, for the dedicatory recital. It took place at an evening service before a packed congregation. The church choir also did its part as the services terminated with Benediction of the Blessed Sacrament. Clarence Eddy played several numbers on the large organ in the gallery and some additional numbers on the small organ from the console below. It was an inspiring occasion. This sanctuary organ, to my knowledge, was the first of its kind installed hereabouts.

Shortly after this, Msgr. McCarthy was transferred to St. Andrews Parish in Pasadena, California, presiding over what I consider one of California's most beautiful churches. Soon thereafter the Fresno Diocese was formed, with Very Rev. McGinley its first bishop. A very substantial rectory had meanwhile been built and many changes took place thereafter. The sanctuary organ, so close behind the high altar, was objected to by some of the new clergy while saying mass, and was sold in 1932 to St. Aloysius Church at Tulare, California, where we placed it on the gallery and where it is giving good service today. However, another pastor was later assigned to St. John the Baptist Church, Msgr. MrGrath, formerly of Santa Cruz. He was an ardent lover of the pipe organ, also, and seeing the advantage of having a small organ again for use in the church below, secured a two manual and Pedal organ with chimes from a firm in Los Angeles, and had it erected in the right transept of the church. Msgr. McGrath has since been transferred.

We occasionally called at the church to service both organs and were especially surprised at the tenacity and endurance of the old organ on the gallery that was once given up, almost as a failure, but which has proved its merits by many years of fruitful service under the most severe climatic conditions possible. Although there was no name plate on the organ, this little testimonial to undoubtedly a forgotten organ builder, should keep the name of "Heatherington" in respectful memory.

With a new Bishop in the Diocese of Fresno, The Most Rev. Willinger, and with improvements being made to the gallery of St. Johns Cathedral, with the object of securing more seating space, it was decided to dispose of the old Heatherington organ. An opportunity presented itself at that time to purchase a large three manual Kimball organ that had previously been electrified and had been in use at the First Congregational Church of Oakland, California, since 1899. The latter church, in turn, had secured a new Moeller organ.

The Kimball organ was then installed in St. Johns

Cathedral gallery in or about 1961, after many drastic alterations were made, and by utilizing the additional space of a large tower room adjoining, once used as the blower room of the first organ.

Through much effort on our part, we were fortunate again to find a new abode for the Heatherington organ which, tonally, we always considered of excellent quality, and sold it, in 1953, to the St. Mary's Catholic Church at Sacramento, California. We used only the pipes and blower of the old organ; all the other parts and mechanism are new. We made it a divided organ, all under expression, with several new stops added, among them a Trumpet 8', to give the organ more brilliancy. The organ that undoubtedly was doomed to oblivion had we not intervened for its preservation, and which held so many dear memories for us, has again received a new lease on life, sounding better than ever before, and is appreciated and revered by its new owners.

ST. MARY'S COLLEGE
Moraga, California

Several years ago Calvary Presbyterian Church, on Jackson and Fillmore Streets, was the recipient of a considerable sum of money, given by Mr. John McGregor, for the special purpose of purchasing a new organ. Since their present Murray M. Harris organ was to be disposed of, and had to be removed at an early date, so the church edifice could be extended to house the new organ and make other necessary additions, we were fortunate in interesting the Christian Brothers, who were building the new St. Mary's College at Moraga, California, in purchasing the organ for their beautiful and imposing new chapel. The sum of $3,500 was paid for it and we were soon engaged in erecting it, in its new abode. I might say that we considered it a furtunate buy for the college. We always admired its grand and impressive church organ tone, with its three manuals and Pedal and as fine a specification as could be desired. Its workmanship was of the finest, and with its classic and artistic case it looked as if it were "to the manor born."

It might be of interest to recall that the old organ was a tracker action, built by Erben of New York, and was located in the old Calvary Presbyterian Church, where the St. Francis Hotel now stands. In 1901 the church moved to its new edifice erected at Jackson and Fillmore Streets. At that time, Murray M. Harris of Los Angeles built a new organ, on the pneumatic system, for the new church, but retained the Diapason sets, several of the wood stops, the large scale wood Open Diapason of the Pedals and the exterior case, along with the front pipes of the old Erben organ. All the remaining pipes and mechanisms were new.

At St. Mary's College we installed a modern blower, still further improving the instrument. The installation of the organ took some time. The ride to and fro each day across the Bay to Moraga, the hoisting of the large, heavy chest and bellows, which required special rigging equipment, all took time and a great amount of energy. I recall it required a large van and a second truck to carry the complete instrument. As we reached the old tunnel, formerly part of the old tunnel road, the driver realized that his load was too bulky to permit a second vehicle to pass him in the narrow tunnel, so a scout ran ahead to prevent anyone from entering at the opposite end until the truck had passed through.

The dedicatory service of the new St. Mary's College was a great event. We were present on the occasion. Another great celebration was "Charlemagne Day." The well-known musician, Rev. Ryberon, in charge of the music and the choir at the College, with additional outside talent, prepared an unexcelled program of Palestrina music for the occasion. With an augmented choir and Warren D. Allen of Stanford University at the organ, an unforgettable program was rendered, severe and classical to the utmost, yet entirely in keeping with the occasion and the intellectual setting and environment.

Here I might mention a little amusing incident that occurred anent the fact of a Catholic Institution buying an organ from a Presbyterian Church. Many years later I happened to be working again at Calvary Presbyterian Church, this time on its new Aeolian organ, when I was introduced to Rev. Van Nuys, its Pastor. After indulging in some pleasantries, I reminded him that we were the party who sold the old Murray M. Harris organ to St. Mary's College and he said, "Quite so, but it took Calvary Church to put a Protestant note in a Catholic Institution."

In later years we called only intermittently at St. Mary's College to tune and service the organ. In time, moths caused considerable damage to the swell pneumatics, which had to be releathered. The lead tubing began to corrode and split. An electrification of the mechanism of the organ, with a new detached console was strongly advocated by us at that time, which would be the crowning glory to this otherwise excellent instrument. Undoubtedly the material and financial status of St. Mary's College, after building this great institution, was not one of ease and plenty. During the period of depression, their lot was indeed not one strewn with roses but, from all indications, better times lie ahead.

On one of my visits to the College to repair the large chapel organ, above referred to, I was also asked to tune and repair a large two manual reed organ in one of the Brothers' assembly rooms. I hoped to complete my work the latter part of the afternoon and make connections with a certain train that would bring me to the City about nightfall. I was, however, delayed with my work and did not get away until after six o'clock, and so missed the train I expected to take. The next train was scheduled to pass Moraga at about 10 p.m. Anxious to get home and not wanting to stay at the College overnight, I hied myself to the highway skirting the College grounds in the hope of at least thumbing a ride to Oakland. However, the automobiles passing on this country road were few and far between, and as darkness had meanwhile set in, I knew I had no chance whatever of being picked up enroute. My first attempt at thumbing a ride was a failure. I thereupon walked to the adjoining town of Moraga, a little junction consisting of a shed for the railroad station, which by the way was unlighted, a general merchandise store and a few barns and dwellings. I entered the general store, ordered a sandwich and drink for my supper and told the proprietor of my predicament. He informed me the next and last train that night would pass Moraga about 10 p.m. and if I would flag it they would undoubtedly stop, provided they saw me in time in the darkness. I enjoyed my little repast and was told I was welcome to remain in the store until 9 p.m., when he would close up and retire for the night. I made myself comfortable and by leisurely reading the papers, the time passed quickly enough. At 9 o'clock I walked over to the lonely station, which was still unlighted. Because of the darkness, and not having any matches with me, not being a smoker, I could not see the time on my watch and therefore, I feared that if I should lie down on the bench for a much desired nap I would miss the train and then be compelled to pass the night in true hobo fashion on the cold bench of the station. Accordingly, I kept alert, my eyes glued to the track in the distance for the beam of the headlight, and listening intently for the clickity-click sound on the tracks, indicating the approach of the train. My vigil was finally rewarded. I saw and heard the train approaching. Running out to the track, I waved my hands frantically, hoping that the engineer would see me in time to stop, and yet, should he fail to do so, that I be off the track in time not to endanger my life. I heard the brakes squeak and the speed of the train was being checked. He had seen me and was stopping. The conductor, on alighting, was surprised to receive another passenger at such an unfrequented station and at that hour of the night.

With the outbreak of World War II, St. Mary's College underwent a transformation. The United States Navy took over the institution as a Pre-Flight School for its naval cadets. The regular curriculum of the College, however, was continued. What a transformation from previous years, what life and commotion, young stalwarts training with grim determination to put themselves into good physical shape and to master the art of aeronautics, to be pilots in the air. The chapel and organ was used now more than ever. In the morning the Catholic youths attended mass, in the afternoon the non-Catholic cadets had their religious services. It was indeed inspiring to see the chapel filled to the last seat. War may be abhorrent, but it also has its compensations. It certainly brings young men nearer to their God and Maker.

In or about 1962, the modernization of the organ was undertaken and further additions made thereto. The work was entrusted to the firm of Swain and Kates, Inc., of

Oakland, California.

BOHEMIAN GROVE ORGAN
Monte Rio, California

Undoubtedly one of the most pleasant out-of-town jobs we had was installing the Austin pipe organ at the Bohemian Grove, a timbered country of redwoods, consisting of 2,000 acres abutting the Russian River near Monte Rio. In 1920 Mr. Fletcher Tilton, representative of the Austin Organ Company, and a member of the Bohemian Club, contracted with the organization to install a three manual and Pedal electric action Austin organ, Opus 913, of 21 stops for their outdoor theater at the Grove. He arranged a trip to the Grove, with several officers of the Club, for the purpose of selecting a location for the organ and to make recommendations for the building of a suitable structure to house it, consisting of Mr. Joseph Redding, then president of the Club, Mr. Farquarth, the architect, Mr. Tilton and myself.

On arriving at Bohemia, which was one station before Monte Rio, a service bus was waiting to take us, and a number of other gentlemen, who were also going to the Grove, to our destination. I recall the beautiful scenery on the trip along the banks of the Russian River, and the happy, carefree people who had gone there to enjoy their summer vacations. Because of its convenient accessibility by automobile, over good roads built in recent years, this section had become a very popular vacation spot. On entering the Grove itself, with its majestic Redwoods, dating back as many as 1200 years, some as high as 301 feet, with its scented fragrance, its stillness and entrancing charm, with the rays of the sun stealing through the lofty trees, there came to my mind the words of the disciple at the Transfiguration on the Mount, "Lord, it is good to be here."

Passing what are called the civic center buildings, the bar, indoor restaurant and Camp Fire Circle, we came to the amphitheater. From here I had my first view of the stage built at the base of the hill. A cluster of large redwoods on the right and left confined the width of the stage and looked as though they were planted there for the purpose. The stage floor itself is made of smooth pine and inclined slightly as though they were planted there for the purpose. The stage floor itself is made of smooth pine and inclined slightly towards the foothills. The background and general scenery of the stage setting is nature's own work. The high hillside, with its winding roads, ferns and shrubbery, clusters of redwood trees, especially one group referred to as the Three Graces, presents a background for the stage no artist could improve upon. Floodlights set to direct their rays on the stage proper were placed behind the huge trees and out of view of the audience. Under the stage are the dressing and make up rooms.

For certain types of plays, scene sets of castles, ruins, or whatever the play required, are still built and erected to fit into nature's setting, always made to blend and harmonize perfectly with the natural surroundings. The so-called auditorium of the theater, or space out beyond the stage for the audience, consists of an orchestra pit, seating about sixty musicians, and an incline toward the rear of about one hundred feet. Redwood logs, about twenty-four inches in diameter, laid in rows on the turf, constituted the seats for the audience. This outdoor auditorium is again encircled by high redwood trees. An entrance to this auditorium, almost directly opposite the stage, about ten feet wide, was flanked on either side by two huge trees, again giving the impression that they were placed there for that particular purpose.

It is the custom of the Bohemian Club each year to have one of its literary members write a play or pageant, and one of its musicians compose the music for it, for presentation at the Grove during the summer encampment of the Club. Needless to say, with the literary and musical talent available in this famous Club, in which a true democratic spirit prevails, where art, culture and good-fellowship are the guiding lights regardless of wealth or position, truly marvelous and stupendous productions and pageants have been presented. A few of these may be mentioned: "The Kings of Tara", words by Frederick S. Myrtle, music by Wallace Sabin; "Montezuma", music by Humphrey J. Stewart; "Nec-Netama" in 1914 and "Golden Feather" in 1939, music by Uda Waldrop. These plays were presented as the climax of the encampment, on High Jinks night.

Coming back to my subject of the organ, a favorable site was located for it, to the left facing the stage, behind the stage proscenium. It was to be built of concrete, with hollow tile lining and plastered, its outer surface camouflaged to blend with the surrounding foliage. Every precaution was taken for proper drainage and to guard against dampness. The entire front was to be open to direct the tone out toward the stage and the auditorium; closed, however, securely with wooden panels when the season was over and kept at an even temperature by electric thermostatic controls. The console was applied with a coupling and detached after the season was over and placed in a warehouse for safe keeping.

After attending to these essential preliminary matters, we were the guests of the caretaker of the Grove and his wife, Mr. and Mrs. Dow, who had prepared luncheon for us at the Lodge, located at the entrance to the Grove.

Several months later, when the organ chamber was completed and the organ had arrived, I returned to the Grove to install it. I took my wife and two small children with me on this trip and we secured accommodations at the Riverview Inn. I also brought a helper along, Harry Doyle, who was familiar with our work. This was in the spring after the heavy rains. The organ was to be ready for the opening of the encampment in July. As only the regular employees of the Grove were there at the time, my wife and children would occasionally walk from the Hotel to the Grove to visit me, taking this opportunity to see the wonderful spot as, during the encampment, women are not allowed within its confines.

On arrival the organ was temporarily stored under the stage in the dressing rooms while the installation work was being done. However, one night a severe rainstorm visited the place and in the morning we found our packing cases soaked with water, due to the leaky roof above. The main parts of the organ were already in place in the organ chamber and were, therefore, safe from damage and, fortunately, no serious damage was done to the pipes as we detected the water in time. Eventually the work was completed and the day of the dedication of the organ arrived. It was a pleasant, sunny afternoon. After a few dedicatory remarks by the president, Mr. Joseph Redding, accepting the organ on behalf of the Bohemian Club, its veteran organist and member, Samuel D. Mayer, opened up the organ with Handel's incomparable "Hallelujah Chorus", followed by other exquisite and appropriate numbers, to the delight of his audience. The encampment of the season 1920 was now opened.

I recall at this time the wives of Harry Perry and Uda Waldrop were also staying at the Riverview Hotel in Monte Rio, and were most friendly and gracious to my wife and children. Many celebrities of national and world renown have been visitors at the Grove. An outstanding one that I recall was the Crown Prince of Sweden, in whose honor special events and ceremonies were conducted. He took the puns and jokes coming his way in a most jovial and democratic manner.

All in all, with the many pleasant and agreeable happenings, friendships made, and happy memories to cherish in connection with the installation of this organ and the annual visits thereafter, it is one of our jobs that we always recall with pleasure. There is also a little pathos connected with it, as each year some new face would be there to greet us, taking the place of an old-timer who had finished his life's work.

I might mention that previous to the installation of the organ in 1920, any attempt to modernize the Grove; to introduce electricity, for instance, was strictly banned. Illumination of the stage, the camp in general, the large outdoor dining room the tents and cabins, was by acetylene gas. With the advent of the organ and the need for electricity to operate the organ motor, however, a power line was run underground into the Grove and electricity was used extensively thereafter on the stage and wherever it was of advantage to use it. No overhead electric wiring was permitted, always bearing in mind the ideal of preserving the forest in its primeval stage of beauty, was a fast rule.

Mentioning primeval forest reminds me of an incident relative to Bohemian Grove. In one of the many visits I made to "Bohemia" to service the organ while the Northwestern Pacific was still operating, one of the passengers on the train was the beloved "Uncle John McLaren", creator, if one might use that term, or planner of the famous Golden Gate Park in

San Francisco. I recognized the little Scot, introduced myself and, as I was soon made aware that he was headed for the same destination as myself, we engaged in a congenial conversation. Our topic was the beauties of the majestic redwoods of the Grove, the outdoor stage, organ, etc. We also talked about "Golden Gate Park", his life's achievement, the work of his hands and skill. I told him how greatly I admired its beauty, its superb setting, its lawns and trees, and recalled its development from early childhood days. I also expressed the one regret I had, that among the hundreds of species of trees and plants growing there, the California Redwood, Sequoia "Sempervierens" aparently seemed to be neglected or overlooked, and wondered what the reason was. A startled and reprimanding glance greeted me, and I was informed that was not the case, that two large successful groves of Redwoods had been planted some years ago, one called "Redwood Memorial Grove" and the other "Heroes Grove." My surprise of the fact and the pleasure it gave him to assert that nothing was overlooked, compensated him. I thought I knew all the interesting points of the Park, but realized I was· mistaken. A later visit to Golden Gate Park in search of the aforementioned Redwood Groves proved to me I had yet much more to explore and see. At the time of this writing, 1946, the trees had reached a height of forty to fifty feet, but have centuries yet ahead of them to match the height of the trees at "Bohemia." Since then, Uncle John McLaren has passed on, after reaching the age of 96 years. His monument in bronze in his beloved Golden Gate Park, erected by the citizens of San Francisco, is but a cold reminder of the esteem and affection in which he was held. The redwood trees, however, which he planted will be a living and breathing testimonial to him for centuries to come. True, "Only God can make a tree", but Uncle John McLaren was the means to plant and nourish them.

Returning to the subject of the organ at the Grove, about 1928 it was decided that it would be desirable to have the console of the organ available not only in its location near the organ in the Grove Theater, but also at the Camp Fire Circle, some distance beyond. The cable was extended underground to the Camp Fire Circle Platform, where a junction board was placed. The console can now be moved there whenever desired for performances.

As previously stated, when building the organ chamber, every precaution was taken to prevent dampness from attacking the organ. The only wood used in its construction was the wooden floor, which was nailed to wooden sleepers embedded in the concrete. These sleepers and the concrete base were coated with asphaltum, with space between floor and concrete. However, in time we noticed that the floor was beginning to get soft or soggy in places, as though its underpinning were giving away. We then decided to investigate. Upon removing the canvas carpet of the air chamber and making an opening in the floor, we were surprised to find a great portion of the sleepers rotted away, either from dry rot or from moisture that had finally penetrated the asphaltum on the concrete floor, or from lack of circulation between the sleepers. We removed large portions of the floor piecemeal, jacking up the organ overhead, and provided openings on either end of the organ chamber so that air could circulate between concrete and wooden floors more freely.

Another improvement made to the organ was the replacing of the air driven fan Tremolos with the newer type bellows Tremolo. This required separating by means of panels the Swell and part of the Great chest, from direct supply of the Universal air chest. A Saxophone stop was also removed and exchanged for a Clarinet stop.

I believe every organist of prominence who ever came to the Bay Region has visited the Grove and played on its organ. A photograph taken at the Grove that remains fresh in my memory is one showing four distinguished organists grouped about the console of the organ — Edwin Lemare, Dr. Humphrey J. Stewart, Wallace Sabin and Benjamin Moore.

A word of appreciation is due Mr. Odell and his sons, caretakers of the Grove, for their many courtesies and attentions shown us while working there.

In the shade of these majestic redwoods, may gay Bohemia carry on. May its emblem, the wise old owl, and its motto, "Weaving spiders come not here", bar all that may mar the peace and tranquility of this beautiful spot.

In conclusion, I want to single out my dear, late friend,

Uda Waldrop, who undoubtedly was the Club's favorite son. The fact that he was the only member to be privileged to have his wedding ceremony celebrated at the Club, November 4, 1919, is proof of this assertion. I especially recall his courtesy and obliging kindness while erecting the Grove organ, the interest he and his charming wife took in my two children we had there for a vacation. Also the many years of association we had with him on the various positions he held and in recalling his last telephone call, before his demise in 1951, in which he nostagically confirmed our mutual friendship of many years. Uda Waldrop, although not a Catholic, was honored by receiving a Doctorate Degree from the Rev. Henry Woods, S.J., representing the University of San Francisco, in the Opera House in 1934.

STANLEY PAGE RESIDENCE
Los Gatos, California

During 1914, when the Panama-Pacific International Exposition was in course of construction, several of the leading organ builders of the country came to San Francisco with the purpose in mind of capturing the coveted award to build the huge pipe organ which was to be housed in Festival Hall on the Exposition grounds. Ernest M. Skinner was one of these, and as it behooves every successful business man to use all fair means to sell his product, so also Mr. Skinner had his friend and admirer, Mr. Jacob B. Struble, of Oakland, a noted inventor and engineer, use his good offices and influence with the "Powers that be" to help sway their decision Mr. Skinner's way. Events turned out otherwise, and the contract was awarded to the Austin Organ Company.

Mr. Strubble had his domicile on the top floor of the Hotel Oakland, and in his living room he had a splendid two manual and echo Aeolian organ, with a detached console with automatic player. He would invite his organist friends and lovers of music to perform on the organ or to enjoy the music he so artistically rendered from the player mechanism. Mr. Struble undoubtedly was an authority on the pipe organ and a lover of music. Being an admirer of Ernest Skinner, he had the latter install four sets of his choice stops in his organ, a conical Flute Celeste of his Erzaehler type, a French Horn, a Saxaphone and an English Horn. At the time of Mr. Skinner's visit to San Francisco in September 1914, Mr. Skinner and I installed these pipes and tuned and tone-regulated them, to the great satisfaction and delight of Mr. Struble, who prized them very highly.

Adjoining the Struble apartment at the Hotel, resided Dr. W. A. Clark. He, too, was a lover of music and possessed an Orchestrelle reed organ with player, an Aeolian product. They exchanged visits frequently as they were good friends. Dr. Clark had a patient, a middleaged man named Stanley Page who, at times, was among the guests present at the Struble gatherings. Because of ill health, it had been suggested to Mr. Page that he live in the hills of beautiful Los Gatos, to rest and absorb the invigorating sunshine amid the gardens and orchards of this delightful section to the south of San Francisco. Here he had a lovely, cozy home, and a workshop where he could spend his time as he desired, as Mr. Page, like his friend Mr. Struble, was also of an inventive mind.

While staying at Mr. Page's home, as his guest one weekend, Mr. Struble suddenly passed away, to the great sorrow of Mr. Page. After Mr. Struble's passing, I believe Dr. Clark took over his apartment at the Hotel Oakland, giving up his own. The Orchestrelle that was his found its way to the home of his friend Mr. Stanley Page at Los Gatos. I was commissioned to install it, and that was the occasion of my first visit there and becoming acquainted with Mr. and Mrs. Stanley Page. While installing the Orchestrelle, tuning it and putting it in good working order, the soothing charms of music found a sympathetic response in Mrs. Page, and, combined with the pleasure of solving the mechanical functioning of the organ, which interested Mr. Page equally as much, it was not surprising that in time his ambition musically was whetted for something better.

Mr. Page remembered the arrangement of the detached console on Mr. Struble's organ and expressed a desire to have a similar arrangement for his organ if it could be done. We told him it could, and later built a detached console for the automatic player on the Orchestrelle, applied electric primary boxes and otherwise made the entire organ function electrically. The player console was then placed opposite the organ and in a rear corner of the living room. Since the one manual keyboard was removed from the Orchestrelle, and it could no longer be played by hand, and as the ornate case was interfered with by this alteration, the organ was placed in a chamber behind the wall, concealed from view entirely.

Now that the Orchestrelle had an electric action, we soon added three sets of pipes to it, consisting of a Vox Humana, a Gemshorn and a Dopple Flute. These were placed in a chamber in the basement, the tone coming up through a duct into the living room. The tone of the Orchestrelle as well as of the pipes was controlled by a general swell before it entered the living room. On the whole, it was a charming installation, refined and pleasant, and gave the Page's much pleasure.

About this time, 1933, Dr. Clark passed away and the Aeolian organ which had originally belonged to Mr. Struble was bequeathed by Dr. Clark to his friend Stanley Page who, with the passing of years, appeared to be regaining his health. The organ had to be removed from the Hotel Oakland apartment on rather short notice, as the rooms had to be made available for new tenants. We dismantled and packed the organ and, piece by piece, removed it from the top floor to the basement of the hotel, awaiting an opportunity to move it at one time on a truck to Mr. Page's residence where it was to be stored in his workshop awaiting installation. The removal of the organ from Dr. Clark's apartment was no small matter. All large pieces had to be taken on dollies through the long corridors to the passenger elevators, and then await an opportunity when they could be spared to take the load to the basement. There the organ was in everyone's way, and the day it was finally hauled to the sidewalk to be transported, it rained in torrents, making it necessary to take extra precaution to protect the instrument from damage.

At Los Gatos, due to the wet road, the truck and trailer could not negotiate the slippery road up the steep hillside, so the trailer was detached and hauled up separately. The organ was safely stored for a number of years in Mr. Page's workshop. He had first planned to have it erected in his home, but as it resolved itself into the situation of "build the home to suit the organ", as the chambers were very high, he abandoned the idea in time and decided to dispose of some of the stops for which space could not be provided.

We tried to assist Mr. Page in disposing of the stops which could not be used and had several prospects, but with the depression years then prevailing, not many organs were being bought or sold. Finally, Mr. Page had an opportunity to make a bargain with a certain organ mechanic, who then took over the job of installing the organ. We wished Mr. Page well and concluded this was the end of our dealings.

At later periods, when in the neighborhood, I telephoned occasionally to inquire how the Page household was faring and, on one occasion, was glad to be informed that Mr. Page had completely regained his helath, was again working with the Union Diesel Engine Company of Oakland, in which firm he was interested. War conditions undoubtedly made this move necessary, as Mr. Page's skill and genius as a designer and mechanical engineer were now very valuable.

Correspondence from Mr. Page regarding the peculiar behavior of his free reed Clarinet, that would not respond to the treatment given it by the organ mechanic, and a general complaint of the condition of his organ, finally resulted in a request from Mr. Page in 1951, that we visit him and look over the organ to see what might be required to put it in order. We finally made a date and prepared to give Mr. Page several weeks of our time, if necessary, to put his organ into satisfactory condition. Mr. Page kindly put a small summer cottage, located in the prune orchard on his estate, at our disposal. My son Lawrence, his wife and child, and I were then the happy occupants of the cottage on the hill. While my daughter-in-law busied herself with the baby and household tasks, my son and I, with Mr. Page an interested onlooker, delved into the many problems that confronted us.

Tonally, the organ was abominably out of tune. Then the sound of rushing air coming from the organ chambers sounded more like the noises in a boiler room. The swell blinds did not function satisfactorily, having only two positions — full open and completely closed, so they were disconnected and rearranged. The Harp stop was badly out of regulation. Some incorrect connections in the automatic player brought the octave in the Pedal continuously on, outbalancing the Pedal in proportion to the other manuals. In fact, there were too many discrepancies apparent to enumerate. In addition to it all, regretable to state, was the slipshod, amateurish way in which the work had been performed. The console, as we found it, was placed on the side of the living room in an alcove, and behind a jog in the wall, making it extremely difficult for the player to hear the organ properly.

We induced Mr. Page to have it placed on the opposite side of the room where originally the console of his Orchestrelle had stood, and where no obstruction interfered with properly hearing the organ. The excessive noise from the rushing air was next tackled and corrected by placing a regulating valve in the blower room near the motor, instead of in the organ chamber. The trouble experienced with the free reed Clarinet, which would eventually turn into an annoying squeal if held for a length of time, we corrected by increasing the tone pressure to its proper degree. A metal Flute of generous scale was altered and revoiced to a Diapason, to give that section of the organ some semblance of Diapason quality it sorely needed. The two weeks at our disposal passed with lightening speed, but in the meanwhile a new organ was being created, harmony and music were evolving from former discord and noise, and Mr. and Mrs. Page again saw hope of enjoying their organ, and of possessing an organ they could be proud of.

During this period we also had the privilege of enjoying some demonstrations of Mr. Page's scientific ability. The question of the theory of tone as produced by an organ pipe was discussed and debated. We maintained that the air stream vibrated in and out of the mouth of the pipe; Mr. Page held that it was mostly outward. His stroboscope was, therefore, hooked up for an optical demonstration. By applying some very light fuzz at the edge of the wind way, also at one time the thread of a spider web, and letting it wave freely to and fro, reducing the rapid vibration to slow motion, its path of in and out, passing the upper lip, could easily be followed. Again, with the discussion veering to harmonics of a given tone, in fact the theory of sound waves, he clearly demonstrated their peculiarities by the illuminated graph on his oscilloscope, a most interesting and scientific demonstration, making frequency and amplitude characteristics of sound waves plainly visible, which heretofore had to be deduced and reckoned by mathematical calculation and other tests.

Mr. Page was a man of few words, but nevertheless possessed a good bit of humor, which he would use effectively at the opportune time. The many days I spent at his place were as instructive to me as I hope they were pleasant for him. Mr. Page was never satisfied with a vague or indefinite analysis of any mechanical wrong. He wanted to know the reason why a thing was wrong and wouldn't work. The trouble had first to be correctly analyzed before a remedy could be prescribed. His workshop was his sanctum, and only if one knew how to use tools and had the good sense to put them back in the place where he found them, was one welcome therein. ·

Mr. Page's talent for designing mechanical devices was demonstrated to me more than once, but his piece de resistance to me was the expression shutter he devised for one of the organ chambers which had but a small opening on the narrow end of the chest, possibly only 3' x 3'. This opening was further reduced by a number of thick swell shades, and the latter at that, only part open. Mr. Page eliminated the usual multiple type organ expression shades and substituted therefore one larger shade or lid fulcrumed at the lower edge of about 2" thick material, thus obtaining a 100% effective opening to the chambers. This was operated by the swell shoe at the console, but its motive force because of the size and weight of the single shade was compressed air, created in advance by a small air compressor. In addition, he applied a baffleboard to direct the sound upward into the living room, as the organ was in the basement below, and an additional triangular-shaped baffle which made the initial opening very easy to control. I have never heard a more gradual, effective, or more responsive swell mechanism. Regardless of whether the shoe was moved slowly or full speed ahead, it caused the shade to absolutely follow the movement of the foot, and that with perfect quietness. There were no fixed stations as in most electric swell actions. I complimented him on his masterpiece, told him he should have it patented and thought to myself what a God-send he would be in an organ factory, instead of designing gas engines.

In the art of music, Mr. Page's accomplishments were equally remarkable. He always gave one the impression that he knew nothing about the technique of music, of harmony, etc. I do not doubt that he could not perform on the keyboard, but I do know he was very proficient on the automatic player, using excellent phrasing, diminuendo and registration. I did observe that he had a keen sense for tuning, but it was only recently when we could not give him the time we would have liked to, that he also acquired the skill to tune the organ himself. True, he made some bad misses we had to adjust, but practice makes perfect, and I do not doubt he finds this sphere of the organ work just as alluring as the mechanical end of the organ.

I am happy that the organ, the "King of Instruments" can yet beguile men of means, men of learning and skill, to give of their valuable time and money to learn and enjoy the charms of its music and to perfect and improve those mechanical means, that make the music possible.

To Mrs. Page should go a great amount of appreciation for quietly enduring organ mechanics so frequently in her home, and for the encouragement she gave Mr. Page, especially when his health outlook was discouraging. May they, and their entire household, who were always so hospitable and considerate of us, find untold pleasure and enjoyment in the organ that is their great delight.

On October 5, 1964, Mr. Stanley Page, to our sincere regret and surprise, was called to his eternal reward. Even after his departure from this life, his memory, as also a happy association with his widowed wife, remain a cherished legacy. We also feel deeply rewarded that we were privileged to have Mr. Stanley Page write the excellent "Foreword" to this, our humble effort in writing.

CHRISTIAN BROTHERS NOVITIATE
Mont La Salle
Napa, California

During the spring of 1943, with World War II in progress and the production of the implements of war for our armed forces requiring all mechanical skills, the organ builders of the country converted their plants from organ building to supplying needed equipment for the army and the navy. Previous to the war, the organ profession was slowly emerging from the effects of one of the severest depressions the country had ever experienced. Now, however, due to the war no new organs could be manufactured and those desiring to procure one began to look around for good, used organs. These were mostly found in former residences and institutions. It so happened that within a few months six pipe organs hereabouts, that had been available for many years to anyone who wanted one, were sold in short order. The two manual and Pedal Kimball pipe organ of 13 stops, with automatic player, formerly in the home of Mr. Van Midgley of Oakland, was one of these. This organ, evidently a used one, was installed in his home, in or about 1936, evidently by Mr. Gus Edwards, their Western representative. Due to lack of space and also considering it had a large scale Pedal Open Diapason 16', rather unnecessary in a small residence organ, he disposed of the latter. We were unaware of this transaction, its purchaser or its destination. The Van Midgley organ was erected in the lower floor of his home, the organ divided into two chambers. The tone then entered into a mixing chamber and finally into the living room, a floor above, through a grill. The console, with an automatic player, was located in the living room upstairs. After several years of use, Mr. Van Midgley, for reasons of his own, wished to dispose of his pipe organ. Since the Christian Brothers, at Mont La Salle, Napa, were interested in securing a pipe organ for their chapel, we suggested and recommended the Van Midgley organ. The instrument was purchased and it was my good fortune to install it.

Shortly after Van Midgley had his organ installed in his home, a retired Lutheran minister called at our office and offered to sell us a set of 18 large Pedal Open Diapason 16' pipes with its valve chest. This material was stored in the basement of the Oakland Theatre and the smaller pipes in the basement of his home. We purchased these pipes, brought them to our factory, made new pipes for the twelve missing treble pipes and stored them in our erecting room awaiting an opportunity when we could use them advantageously on some other modernization job.

When we began dismantling the Midgley organ, in preparation for its installation at Mont La Salle, Napa, we were surprised to find the 12 treble pipes and their chest stored in an unfrequented room in his basement with the same telltale shipping notation (San Antonio, Texas) thereon, the same as were on the other pipes we had stored in our factory. So, after about seven years, the divergent parts of the organ that were distributed at different locations, finally found themselves united and were installed as a whole as originally built, in their new location at Christian Bros. Novitiate.

Referring again to the dismantling of the organ and its installation, with labor scarce due to the war situation, I had my two sons, George and Vincent, and my brother-in-law, Frank Reichmuth, assist me in dismantling the organ and packing the pipes. It was a pleasant task, and yet one with a little pathos attached to it, as I knew it would be the last time my son George would assist me at work. He had just completed five years of study at St. Anthony's Seminary in Santa Barbara, where he made his preliminary studies for the Franciscan priesthood and was home for his last vacation, as he was to enter the novitiate the following week.

At the Christian Brothers Novitiate at Mont La Salle, the organ was again divided but placed on the organ loft, chambers having been built to accommodate it, and the console was placed on the church floor below in the rear of the church. The automatic player was removed from the console and a roll-top cover was applied.

When the organ was ready to be moved, I rode along with the driver of the large van to its future home up in the hills of Redwood Canyon, the Christian Brothers Novitiate at Mont La Salle, Napa; a most picturesque location, the former estate of the famed wine merchant, Theodore Gier, with vineyards adorning the hillsides and in the shadow of the trees, the old ivy covered winery. The Brothers' novitiate, a little way up the hill, is a most modern institution, built of steel and concrete, with a lofty tower on the chapel building. Adjoining the chapel on one side is a wing of the Juniorate, and on the other side the novices quarters, with the Brothers section abutting in the rear; arched walks connecting all buildings. With their buff colored walls and tiled roofs, and rustic gardens between the buildings, they make a beautiful setting. A glimpse of the landscaping around, still further enhances the picture. Directly behind the institution, the wooded hillsides, containing a variety of trees as well as some tall redwoods, ascends several hundred feet higher. The surrounding hillls, mostly wooded, are interspersed with vineyards wherever there is an open space, and the scenic Napa Valley lies in the foreground.

When I arrived at the Novitiate with the organ, I was consigned to a neat room with an unparalelled panorama to enjoy. The item of help was again a question. It was to be furnished me when needed. I soon learned that at an institution where everything moves at the stroke of a clock, I would also have to arrange my work accordingly. When I needed a crew of men for some heavy lifting, 1:30 p.m. was the time for that, and a score of husky young lads would be available. Soon all the heavy parts were in place and only the lighter and more tedious work of applying air pipes, which on account of a new arrangement of parts had mostly to be altered, the fastening of cables, and lastly the placing of the pipes on the chest and the first tuning and voicing of the pipes remained to be done. In addition to the help given me by the young men of the Novitiate, when needed, I was privileged to have the assistance of Brother Benedict, the organist, much of the time. He was also a teacher of physics and mathematics, a most able and interesting man to work with. Indeed, in the line of physics and applied electricity, I learned some valuable lessons from him.

Recalling the old saying, "When in Rome, do as the Romans do," I soon arranged my daily routine in a monastery to conform to the general schedule — arise early, meals at stated periods, go to bed early, everything according to schedule. As I was never in the habit of retiring very early, I found it very trying to remain in my room after supper, being quiet, especially after 9 p.m., so as not to disturb those in the rooms adjoining, as from that time on absolute silence reigned until early the next morning. Fortunately, I liked to read and write and this was my diversion during the long evenings when I was alone.

The organ installation progressed slowly, due to many obstacles, but satisfactorily, and in due time the "breath of life" was given the instrument. I had assumed it to be an excellent sounding organ due to the generous scales and weight of material used in the pipes, and the fine and resonant acoustics of the chapel, and so it proved to be. Having heard the organ only once previously in the Van Midgley residence, and then for only a short period, and there being rather subdued and muffled, the organ in its new ideal location at the Novitiate sounded like a different instrument. Its tonal qualities were superb. Both chambers being under expression, it lent itself to wonderful expression from the softest pianissimo to a grand and vibrant full organ cathedral tone, that rolled with pleasing effect through the rafters of the lofty nave of the chapel. Seldom was I more pleased or gratified with the tonal effects of an organ, yet it had but a limited number of stops, all voiced on 4" wind pressure, but of generous scales and superb voicing, the Great Diapason being of #40 scale (low CC 7" diameter).

Becoming a regular boarder of the institution, as it were, I soon observed and got to learn, if only by sight, the novices and juniors that would visit the chapel daily at regular intervals, noted their fine community singing, their devout recitation of their office and their general demeanor about the institution, which made a very favorable impression upon me, especially as my own son was at the same time entering the Franciscan Novitiate at San Luis Rey, Southern California.

Living in a monastery, where quiet reigns supreme and one is away from all bustle and excitement, every sound or noise seems more noticeable. As stated, I was domiciled in the Brothers' quarters. Near my room Brother Benedict had his room. I recall the welcome calls of his cuckoo clock calling out the hours, also his pet parrot cawing, breaking the silence about the place. Evenings, after supper, and especially Sundays, musical sounds from many instruments and from various sources would greet my ear. Opposite my room I heard an embryo Flutist, from a room on the lower floor a Pianist doing fairly well, also a Clarinetist blowing squeaks in an attempt to master the scale, and from another direction a Trumpeter blowing blue notes. This conglomeration of harmony and discord at one time would ordinarily be a distraction, but here, as a contrast to the deadly quietness during the ordinary routine, it was most welcome. However, the Flutist opposite my room interested me most, as at one time I also played the Flute in an amateurish way. One day Brother Boniface entered my room upon finding my door ajar. I showed him some of my literary work and, incidently asked him who the Flutist was. Upon being informed that it was he, I soon was trying to teach him the scale and proper fingering of the instrument. Unfortunately, his Flute was not the usual type, held horizontally to the lips, and which requires considerable skill in securing the proper embrochure, but the other type held forward with the tone produced by a labium and not by blowing over an apurture. At a later visit, Brother Boniface had secured a modern Boehm Flute and, therefore, I, his erstwhile teacher, was now left in the shadow by my progressive pupil. The flute I played was only a simple Mayer Flute with about half the clappers and ventils of the Boehm Flute.

Another character I will never forget was old Brother Raphael, a retired monastic, who spent most of his time alone in the chapel before the Blessed Sacrament. I admired his faith and perseverence. We soon got to be good friends. One day he asked me if I believed in Anti Christ. I said I believed he would appear in due time. He thereupon gave me a book to read dealing with the prophesy of the end of the world, of Anti Christ and the final judgement day. Needless to say, it made a deep impression on me, so much so in fact, that evenings after work in looking out of my window over the extensive valley below, I could almost visualize the gathering of all nations in the Valley of Jesophat, awaiting final judgement. The last evening before I left he asked if he would visit me in my room and relate to me how he found his vocation of being a Brother, renouncing the World and devoting his life to the good of others. We had a pleasant hour together. This proved to be the last time I was to see him — on my next visit to the Novitiate I was informed of his passing to his eternal reward.

I might say here that the matter of properly concealing, or rather decorating, the exterior of both organ chambers, measuring 13' x 13' x 18', was a matter of importance. The organ, in its previous location in the residence in Oakland, was entirely hidden from view; here it was exposed to its fullest extent. As there were no display pipes, and the procuring of any, or the building of an ornate case during the war period, was out of the question, Brother Celestine, the Director of the Juniorate, a most practical and energetic worker, secured draperies made of Silesia of an amber shade and hung them gracefully in front and on the sides of each chamber. A crown moulding was fastened to the top from which the curtains were suspended.

In the quiet of my room in the evenings I was glad of the opportunity to apply myself undisturbed to the writing of this book, my first literary attempt. At times after a specially strenuous day a knock at the door would announce Brother Benedict or Brother Celestine, bringing a little refreshment, possibly a bottle of some of their famous wines. This was always enjoyed and appreciated. At other times I would find some choice fruit placed on my dresser. On several occasions, to break the monotony of the daily routine, I was invited to attend some movies that were being shown in the school auditorium. Eating in the workmen's dining room became sort of a family affair. In time the first shyness gave way to more familiarity. A generous variety of well cooked food was provided, and the meals were always enjoyed.

Returning again to the organ, one afternoon while working alone quietly on the instrument, I heard someone playing the harmonium in the chapel below. I realized at once that it was an artist, a real musician, who was playing. His repertoire was extensive, and included many a tune and melody of the lighter type of music familiar to me. "In a Monastery Garden", and "The Lost Chord", were among some of my favorites that he played. After listening to the beautiful melodies, as excellently played on a Harmonium as I had ever heard them played before, curiousity induced me to quietly look over the choir railing to see who was playing. It was Brother Chrysostom, who had all this time been playing from memory. It was a surprise to me, as I was not aware that he could even play. At my first opportunity I complimented him and invited him to play the same music on the pipe organ when my work on it was sufficiently advanced. This he soon did, in a most masterly way, giving all those who heard the organ a preview of its fine tonal qualities and musical possibilities.

At about this stage of the work, Mr. Hans Hoerline of Napa, organist at the chapel at Mare Island, called with his wife one evening to give an impromptu organ recital on the organ. For several hours he delighted us with a rather classic program, mostly of Bach fugues, etc., a decided contrast to the romantic music played by Brother Chrysostom, demonstrating beyond a doubt that the organ was equally responsive to both types of music. With a promise to invite him again to play on the finished organ, he left at a late hour.

On All Saints Day, November 1, 1944, with solemn services conducted by Father Olsen, O.P., chaplain of the Novitiate, the organ was dedicated. Brother Cyril of Sacramento performed at the organ. I was not able to be present on the occasion, however. Letters of praise and appreciation were received from those responsible for the purchase of the organ, which indeed was gratifying.

Shortly after, I met Brother Columban, principal of St. Peter's School in San Francisco, an accomplished organist, one who often played the large Exposition Auditorium organ in the Civic Center at San Francisco, as well as the St. Mary's Cathedral organ. It was gratifying to also hear his expressions of praises of the fine organ at the Novitiate.

Mention of the Chaplain, Father Olsen, O.P., brings to my mind a little remark he made while we were at lunch one day. Father Olsen knew my father well, as he had serviced the organ at the old Benicia Monastery for many years. On hearing my name, Father Olsen looked at me and then said: "Yes, I knew your father well, and if you wore a beard as he did, you would resemble him greatly."

My work in erecting the pipe organ in the Christian Brothers Novitiate at Mont La Salle was a most interesting and pleasant experience, leaving happy memories and a great respect for the Christian Brothers and their noble calling.

In 1958 I received the reliable report that the use of the pipe organ had been discontinued and that an electronic organ was being used. After an interval of nine years, through the instigation of Brother Columban, now residing at the Monastery, the Murray M. Harris organ formerly installed in the Grace Methodist Church of San Francisco, now dissolved, was purchased by the Christian Brothers. It was erected by my brother, Otto, on the rear gallery, with the console in the chapel below. It makes an imposing sight with its beautiful, richly carved Oak case, and its rich pervading tone is a pleasure to hear.

ST. DOMINIC'S CHURCH AND MONASTERY
Benicia, California

As a youngster, I recall my father often mentioning the town of Benicia and in later years learned that it was the servicing of an old Mayer organ at St. Dominic's Monastery that brought him there. Early in my organ building career I went with him to service that organ, as well as the one at St. Paul's Episcopal Church.

I do not recall now how we approached the town, as it was off the beaten path, but I presume it was by the Southern Pacific main line train to Martinez, where we boarded a ferry and crossed the Carquinez Straits to Benicia. I recall the large tannery buildings near the waters edge, the walk up the main street, seeing St. Dominic's Church, with its two towers and rather classical facade, standing prominently on a slight elevation to the right on the outskirts of town. To get to the church an inlet of water had to be crossed by a trestle or boardwalk. I often wondered why this site for the church, so isolated from the heart of the town, was selected.

The organ at the monastery was a one manual Mayer organ, hand pumped, consisting originally of seven stops, with a pleasing front with keyboard attached. It was an old organ when I first worked on it. It seems someone at one time built an addition of three stops by extending the pallet grooves on the chests. These new additions were wood pipes and judging from their construction were made by an amateur. The organ served the purposes of the Dominicans, who were in charge of the monastery.

I may add that the institution was originally planned as a Novitiate for aspirants to the Dominican Order. The general layout of the church and adjoining monastery building clearly indicated that, but in time the Novitiate was located elsewhere and it was used only as a local parish church. The edifice is outstanding for its simple but classic design, its impressive Corinthian columns and especially its sanctuary and altar, the former occupying more space than in most churches, containing the monk's stalls on either side of the sanctuary and facing each other, partly concealed by an iron grill from the nave of the church.

I recall one visit especially, while working with my father. We were invited to lunch at the noon hour. I can picture the refectory vividly. Two long tables were located on either side of the hall with seats built against the wall, designed at one time evidently to be large enough to accommodate a considerable number of religious. On this particular occasion, however, there were only five or six present. In the center of the hall, somewhat elevated, was a readers desk. Here, during the meal, one of the Fathers read aloud some spiritual book. The sight of these Dominican Friars with their cowled white, woolen robes, the large crucifix adorning the wall, the medieval setting and the spiritual atmosphere impressed me.

We made regular visits to service the organ for many years but in time, due undoubtedly to the inaccessibility of the place and other urgent calls made for our services elsewhere, and as the organ had become decrepit with the passing years, we advised them not to spend further money on the organ but to get a new one in time.

With the outbreak of World War II and with the location of the Benicia Arsenal of the U.S. Government but a few miles distant, and with a general influx of new residents to this otherwise quiet and romantic town, a new life seemed to open up for the church. It seems a Mr. Arnold, an attache at the Arsenal and a man interested in church music, induced the Fathers to do something to the organ to improve it. Presumably, due to our labor shortage and impossibility to serve them promptly, a piano tuner named Mr. Mass was engaged to releather the worn out bellows and rehabilitate the organ. The bellows was thus releathered and the greater part of the organ was removed to get it out for repair but, unfortunately, he died while thus employed. About this time the severe explosion at Port Chicago, an ammunition supply depot for the Government, occurred doing great damage, not only in loss of life and property in the immediate vicinity, but also opposite the Strait, and damaged the roof of the church.

After this damage was repaired and the church given a general rejuvenating, it seems a last urgent appeal was made to us by the Fathers to put the organ in condition again. I made the trip to Benicia via Greyhound Bus to Vallejo and over the Carquinez Bridge, then by another bus to Benicia. I did not know that the organ was practically dismantled, expecting it was just a matter of installing a few new pipes which had been, meanwhile, ordered from the factory.

On seeing the organ again after many years and this time looking more forlorn and hopeless than ever, I recalled my former verdict of the futility of spending further funds on it and told the present Rector, Father Gabish, O.P., my candid opinion. "Well," he said, "I am glad you have told me so because I have an opportunity of buying a good two manual Estey reed organ with a blower, in town, for a reasonable sum. Let's go and look at it." Arriving at the place I at once saw its value and superiority over the old hand pumped organ and advised the purchase of the reed organ. The deal was made, and then and there an expressman was readily secured, incidently doing business under the name of "lively Express." I had never seen such quick action and response to a summons before. The expressman lived up to his name and the organ was delivered within an hour at the church.

Here, also, decisions were quickly made as to placing the organ and other details. We decided to retain only the old organ front, mostly for sentimental reasons and to appease the old timers, as it had a pleasing appearance with its gold pipes, making a perfect architectural setting for this end of the church. We then removed the remaining mechanism from behind the case, cut a necessary opening in the case where the keyboard would appear and set the new Estey reed organ behind the old organ front. A neat and pleasing trans- formation took place. The organ sounded well. Temporarily it had to be hand pumped, as I had to make another trip to install the blower in the attic later.

I recall, in removing the insides of the old organ, seeing a notation written on one of the case panels that the organ was erected by John Bergstrom of San Francisco in 1890. Another shipping mark inside the organ was: Rev. O'Neil, O.P., Benicia, California. In mentioning these inscriptions to the Rev. Pastor, Fr. Gabish, O.P., he informed me that the original St. Dominic's Church of Benicia was first built in the heart of the old town where the former State Capitol building still stands . . . California's first State Capitol. The latter inscription was undoubtedly the shipping directions from Mr. Joseph Mayer's shop in San Francisco to its destination when built, which coincided with his biography, page 5, enumerating a list of organs built, their location, year, and cost. He listed the organ of St. Dominic's, Benicia, as built in 1875. The organ evidently remained in the old church until 1890, when Bergstrom installed it in the present St. Dominic's Church. The organ then, with its further usefulness ended, was 79 years old.

Two weeks later I returned to install the blower and remove the remaining parts that were still left lying on the organ gallery to some storage room in the monastery for turure disposal. It was apparently doomed to be discarded as useless material.

Incidently, my stay at the Monastery during this work was made most pleasant by my host, the Prior Father Gabish, O.P., and his assistants, Father Mueller and Father Mitchell, O.P., also an old retired priest and the Brother, especially so when we all assembled at meal time in the dining room. The last day I was there the old retired priest, Father Branigan, O.P., who the day before was apparently well, passed to his eternal reward. The organ I had just completed was then used for the first time officially, for his funeral.

The only adverse comment heard regarding the procuring of the reed organ and the abandoning of the pipe organ was one reluctantly made by Father Mueller. He had, at some previous time through the generosity of an old lady, accepted some money for the restoration of the old organ, which he had subsequently begun by the removal and releathering of the bllows. Therefore, he had some mental qualms about the money thus far expended being wasted and not being used for the purpose for which it was donated. To ease his mind I agreed to remove what was left of the old organ, erect it in our shop, supply it with new metal pipes, add a new case and sell it for a nominal sum, so that we both could come out even in the venture. Shortly thereafter I had to go to Eureka, California, to install and complete a modernization job on the organ of the Presbyterian Church. One day a visitor called on me, Mr. George Sandin, who I had met at our factory before when he was buying material for an organ that he was building for his home. He asked if I knew where he could secure some old organ pipes. Immediately, the Benicia organ, stored in the Monastery came to my mind. I mentioned the fact to him that they were old pipes, that many needed doctoring, that there were some new substitutes for the decrepit ones, but in no way did I glorify the prospect. Evidently being desperately in need of the pipes, he bought them for the price asked, thereby settling the priest's objection to the sale of the old organ, and brought them to his home in Fortuna, California. I was agreeably surprised one evening shortly thereafter upon being invited to his home for supper to see all the pipes neatly laid out in rows on the floor, looking better than I had ever seen them before, and ready to install in his house organ.

This deal again verifies an oft repeated observation I have made, that it is a rare occurrence when a pipe organ, as long as tone still emanates from it, is definitely discarded. May the spirit of the old Benicia Monastery organ remain in its new environment for many more years to come.

ST. PAUL'S EPISCOPAL CHURCH - Benicia

In the early days of my apprenticeship, I tuned and repaired this organ with my father, on one or two occasions. Later, others of our firm called at intervals. At the time I called I was in my teen years, with youth in its bloom and I had other topics and dreams to occupy my mind than to delve into the history of the old organs I had occasion to work on.

I recall calling for the keys of the Church, asking for a Mr. Knauck, who conducted the old Brewery at Benicia, and being presented with the keys by his charming daughter, whose beauty and charm lingered long in my memory.

Though always having a reverent and sentimental attitude for things of antiquity or of another age than my own, it was only through the fact of writing this book, in later years, where one historic, interesting fact from the past lead to another, that I concluded the old organ at St. Paul's Episcopal, Benicia, deserved some special mention. Its builder is unknown, possibly Erben. It was a one manual and Pedal tracker action organ of about four stops. Strange to say, there was no Swell box to the organ as we usually understand it, consisting of an enclosure with louvres or shutters, operated by a foot pedal. However, provision was made to obtain a certain degree of piano and fortissimo effect by opening or closing two large glass hinged panels, or doors, which encase the entire upper part of the organ. The quaintness of this arrangement reminds me of a popular picture one often sees in art stores or picture galleries of a Franciscan monk, seated at a small pipe organ, with a gaze of ecstacy looking heavenward, rays of sunlight streaming through a Gothic window and, in the background, a group of angels forming the celestial choir. Also, the picture of St. Cecilia, often depicted at a similar organ, will help my readers visualize the old organ at St. Paul's Episcopal Church, Benicia. Needless to say, that the tone of the organ was delightfully pleasing. The church is a frame structure and was dedicated February 12, 1860. Its interior fittings and furnishings seem to have a hallowed reverence of their own, befitting the old town that was once California's capitol. On

June 30, 1955, my brother, Otto, visited the church and found the organ removed and stored in the basement of the church.

Chapter VIII

IN THE NORTHWEST

Organs which we have installed in the Northwest

According to my father's records, in 1884 he built a six stop pipe organ for a Mr. Parrott of Portland, Oregon. From all accounts he went to Portland to install the organ. Some years later, possibly around 1890, he again made a trip to the Northwest. It was a sort of speculative venture in search of work. I recall his return home after several months absence, describing the beauties of the trip, the marvelous scenery of the Northwest, especially his impression on viewing the mighty Mt. Shasta, and showing us circulars with photos depicting the cooling mineral waters gushing out of the rocks of Shasta Springs, where his train stopped enroute. His trip extended as far as Victoria, British Columbia, where he tuned the Cathedral organ and gave it a general servicing. Returning, he called at Seattle and Vancouver, Washington, and at Portland and Salem, Oregon, where he tuned and serviced many organs. I remember my father stating that the trip all-told was successful and that he was well repaid for his trouble.

Good organ mechanics in those parts of the country were far and few between, and I remember my father advising us in later years, during slack periods, to make similar scouting trips for work. He did not realize, however, that times had changed since his trip and that most of the larger cities now had their own experienced organ men.

It was in the early part of 1910, however, that we received an inquiry from the Moeller Organ Company of Hagerstown, Maryland, asking if we would install an organ for them in St. Mary's Church in Portland, Oregon. Shortly thereafter, during the month of June, I was on my way to make the installation. I had never been in that part of the country before, so I looked forward to this trip to Portland with much pleasure and anticipation. I took passage on the Steamer George W. Elder, a small passenger steamer in the coastal service. It was my first ocean voyage.

I recall having lunch aboard ship with my sister Cecilia, who accompanied me to the dock to see me off. Finally, sailing time arrived. She took her leave and we pulled away from the dock and headed for the Golden Gate, then took a northerly course up along the Coast. I enjoyed my meal, felt in the best of health and spirits, and was very pleased with

the view of San Francisco from other than the customary
hilltops, or ferry boats crossing the Bay. Gradually the City,
the Golden Gate, with Fort Winfield Scott guarding its
entrance, the Cliff House, and the Seal Rocks faded from
view.

I now noted that the calm waters of the Bay had given
place to giant swells, and the ship, which until now had
proceeded on an even keel, began to roll and pitch. All this
time I was on the upper deck. Somehow the rolling of the
ship and the fatty smell from the kitchen, which it seemed I
could not get away from, suddenly made me feel ill. I had
heard of seasickness, and remembered being told to chew
gum or suck on a lemon as a means to overcome it. I resorted
to these purported remedies, but with the best of intentions
and will power I could not avoid finally making a beeline for
the railing. No question about it — it was a case of "Mal de
Mer." I remained a constant occupant of my cabin for several
days, avoiding the dining room at all cost, until we arrived at
the bar of the Columbia River at Astoria, Oregon. The trip up
the coast was a very rough and stormy one. At times the bow
would dip into the briny deep, with the water splashing over
the deck and rails; again the propeller would emerge from the
water, causing the ship to vibrate violently. After crossing the
bar and docking at Astoria, I took advantage of the
opportunity to leave the ship for a short time and to get a
little tonic drink to settle my disturbed stomach, and to walk
again on terra firma. As if by magic my seasickness left me,
though I did feel a little unsteady in my underpinnings. The
remaining part of the trip, up the beautiful Columbia and
Willamette Rivers was most enjoyable.

I arrived at Portland about sunset. The western sky was
beautifully illumined and colored. I crossed the bridge for
East Portland and soon found my way to St. Mary's Catholic
Church on Williams Avenue. Rev. W. Daly was the pastor, a
tall, amiable and pleasant gentleman, who greeted me
cordially. The organ to be erected was a two manual,
pneumatic organ of about 12 stops. It had a rather large
bellows with two feeders. A Ross water motor was placed in
the basement and a long reinforced connecting rod actuated
the feeders in the organ above. I noticed from the outset that

the arrangement was cumbersome and unyieldy, due to the heavy weight of the long connecting rod which, especially when going fast, thumped and made a considerable noise.

(About a year later, during July 1911, while on a second visit to Portland in connection with some other work, I removed the feeders from the organ and placed them alongside the water motor in the basement below, thereby eliminating all noise in the church above and making it a very satisfactory installation. Joe Maier, the sexton, with whom I became very friendly, was my able assistant.)

I returned to San Francisco again by steamer, but this time it was a larger, more luxurious steamer, the "Bear." The trip was most enjoyable, especially as I did not become seasick and could enjoy the meals that were served.

During May 1911, we also received an order from the Hook and Hastings Company of Boston, Mass., to install a large manual electric action organ for the First Church of Christ Scientist in Portland. On this trip I took my younger brother Erwin with me. The organ had 31 stops and was the first Hook & Hastings electric organ our firm installed. It proved to be a very satisfactory installation.

On this visit we got acquainted with Mr. Lucien E. Becker, who then was organist of a large Kimball organ in the Presbyterian Church. We made some adjustments on this organ and I remember how delighted we were when he played the William Tell Overture for us. Lucien Becker passed away in the East in 1943.

While at Portland we made the acquaintance of Frederick Goodrich, who also played a Kimball organ, Opus 382, at the Catholic Cathedral. We serviced his organ a few times while there and frequently attended services at the Cathedral on Sundays. He seemed to enjoy the prestige a Cathedral position gives an organist, and was quoted with respect and authority wherever his name was mentioned.

During April and May 1912, we installed an organ for the Austin Organ Company of Hartford, Connecticut, in the United Presbyterian Church of Spokane, Washington. It was a two manual organ of 10 stops, pneumatic action. On this occasion I had my brother, Otto, assisting me.

I recall one night at the Boga being awakened from a

sound sleep by an unearthly roar and rumble, which increased in intensity as it came nearer. Finally, a company of firemen with their apparatus passed the house, and, to our surprise, we learned that it was a motorized fire apparatus, the first we had ever seen. This induced us, at our first opportunity the next day, to visit the nearest firehouse to inspect this modern innovation. The fire apparatus of San Francisco at that time was still horse-drawn, so we were obliged to give this far Northwestern City great credit for its progressiveness and initiative.

In the course of our work on the organ at the United Presbyterian Church we discovered that the Austin Company had inadvertently overlooked installing the Tremolo tablet in the console. I applied a temporary gadget, which would answer for the time being, but knew that eventually it meant another trip to Spokane to install the proper Tremolo tablet. I knew that it would not be difficult to arrange this, as there were then several new organ installations in the Northwest in prospect for the immediate future.

It so happened that we were called, during the same year 1912, to install a new Vox Humana in the Echo organ of the large four manual Austin organ, Opus 181, at the First Presbyterian Church in Seattle, Washington, where the Rev. Matthews was the popular preacher. On this trip I had my brother, Erwin, along. While there I also visited the new edifice of the First Church of Christ Scientist, then in course of construction, to take necessary measurements for the new 3 manual Austin organ, Opus 354, we were to install later. We also did some work on the Skinner organ at the Plymouth Congregational Church, and the Hutchings organ at the Catholic Cathedral for Dr. Franklin Palmer.

On the return trip I again visited Spokane to install the Tremolo tablet. It was during the winter and I recall the beautiful scenery passing through the Cascade Mountains, with snowbanks on either side of the railroad tracks, and snow a foot deep on the gable roofs of the houses and sheds, with icicles hanging glittering in the sun. At Spokane I witnessed the first outdoor ice skating I had seen. I had spent two winters in New York City, but never saw any ice skating on the ponds or lakes of Central Park. Evidently they did not freeze thick enough to make them safe for the public to use for skating. This winter scene in Spokane, the ground covered with snow, frolicking people in winter attire skating over the smooth ice, a fire burning nearby, fascinated me and I always recall the picture with pleasure.

In 1912, we also installed an Austin two manual pipe organ, Opus 408, in Portland, at the Globe Theatre on Washington Street. My brother, Erwin, accompanied me on this trip. It was the first theatre organ we had installed. It consisted of about 16 stops, with an Echo organ on the rear balcony. The case of the organ was made of birch wood, placed high up from the floor, and its main overhanging feature was made in one piece. It was with extreme difficulty that I succeeded in getting it into place, as there seemed to be no satisfactory way of attaching it to a suitable block and tackle for hoisting it. And, after it was in place, its overhanging weight was a constant worry to me as I could not secure it to the adjoining walls to my full satisfaction. Messrs. Goldstein and Cohen were the managers of the theatre. This organ was removed from the theatre in 1942 or 1943, and it is now installed in St. Joseph's Church in Portland. This organ was the first electric action Austin organ we installed, outside of San Francisco.

We enjoyed our sojourn in Portland very much; our associations with the people connected with the theatre were most friendly and agreeable, leaving only pleasant memories. We became quite familiar with the film operator and often visited him evenings high up in his booth, where we could observe him while in action. We nicknamed him "See Raeuber", the German name for "Sea Pirate", from a picture he was then showing. He being interested in knowing the meaning of the title in German, we interpreted it for him. I also recall the pleasant times we spent in a certain restaurant we frequented. The proprietor, a foreigner, took a fatherly interest in us. On one occasion, not knowing what to have for dinner, and wanting to break the monotony for us of the usual Friday fish order, he suggested that we take an order of crawfish. We did not know what it would be, but assumed we would get a substantial plate of some fried fish, such as sole or some other fried fish. To our surprise, however, he brought us two heaping plates of red shellfish, a sort of miniature lobster, a seafood I was never specially fond of. He was amused at our surprise and showed us how to tackle the dish set before us by breaking the bones and sucking out their contents. It proved to be a tasty dish, but I thought not satisfying or filling enough for the work involved. We left the restaurant still feeling a desire for a real dinner.

In the latter part of the same year, 1912, we made another organ installation for the Globe Theatre of the Circuit Amusement Company of Salem, Oregon. It was Opus 412 of 12 stops. It was also electric action, but had the addition of an automatic player. When the organ arrived, which was in the early part of October, the theatre was not quite completed. Plastering was in progress. With the incessant rains that had been prevailing, it seems difficulty was experienced in getting the theatre auditorium sufficiently dried out to warrant proceeding with the painting, etc. Large smudge pots were, therefore, placed in the auditorium for about a week, delaying the installation of the organ some-what, but also no doubt proving beneficial to it, by having a thoroughly dry environment.

To operate the automatic player, vacuum was required. I recall the ingenious device the Austin Company applied to produce a vacuum. No additional motor or blower was required; a Venturi Tube was resorted to which furnished a small but adequate amount of vacuum to operate the player mechanism. Mr. Davenport was the manager of the theatre. My brother, Otto, assisted me in installing the organ.

Following the installation of the organ at the Globe Theatre in Salem, we had a final installation to complete for the year 1912, and that was a large Austin organ of 19 stops, pneumatic action, Opus 420, for St. Francis Church of East Portland, Oregon. The church building was a huge frame structure with two imposing towers, a landmark on the east side of Portland. Its exterior was plastered to resemble stone work. Unfortunately, this covering, applied to metal laths, disintegrated in time and fell off in large pieces. The church was massive, but always gave me the impression that someone in his zeal and enthusiasm had exceeded the bounds of good judgment and practicability. I was rather surprised when we were informed that we were to install a pipe organ there, when apparently so many other vital improvements were necessary.

The organ was to be completed for Christmas Day, 1912. My younger brother, Erwin, assisted me in this installation. I remember early in December, the day before a church holy day, the good pastor, a venerable, dignified gentleman, Rev. Father Black, approached me and notified me that we could not work the following day. I said, "Yes, I know, it is the Feast of the Immaculate Conception, and we do not intend to work tomorrow." He seemed very much surprised at my answer and asked if we were Catholics. I assured him that we were, and he then admitted that he had thought we were of the Jewish faith because of our name.

The organ was dedicated at the early mass on Christmas morning. I remained for the occasion, but let my brother, Erwin, return home to celebrate Christmas with the family, as there is no place like home to enjoy this happy feast. As for me, aside from the solemn church services, which to a true Christian are always inspiring, this was about the most dismal Christmas I ever spent, away from home, a stranger among strangers.

Another job that took my brother Otto and I to the Northwest was during 1913 for the installation of the Austin organ, Opus 422, 2 manual, 11 stops, for the First Presbyterian Church at Albany, Oregon. After all the pipes were unwrapped and removed from the packing cases and placed in their respective pipe holes on the chest, I found I was missing four small pipes. After looking diligently all over the place, I was just about to give up the search and order new ones, when the thought occurred to me to look in the furnace where the sexton had put all the loose wrapping paper. Carefully it was all removed and, sure enough, to my great relief, the package containing the four small missing pipes was found among the discarded wrappings. Had I not found the pipes, it would have meant another trip to Albany as I could not have installed the organ complete without them.

Another installation in the Northwest shortly thereafter, in 1913, was for the Humphrey Memorial Church at Eugene,

Oregon, an Austin Opus 455, a three manual, 26 stop organ. The outstanding incident I recall about this installation was that the organ was too large for the space provided. As we had nothing to do with the measurements, it was of course not our fault. All I know is that it was up to us to fit the organ into the space. Here was a case where practical experience came in handy. It meant rebuilding or rearranging the layout of one end of the organ. We succeeded with this work and it turned out to be a very satisfactory installation.

On most installations where we required additional help, besides that which we frequently brought along with us, we procured any available labor and paid for it at the rate prevailing in the respective locality. On this installation, however, one of our helpers was a member of the church. I believe he was recommended to me by the Austin Organ Company's representative. On stipulating his pay he protested and demanded a considerably higher wage than offered him, although he did no more work than others. However, he gave us to understand that his employment by us in the erection of the organ was his compensation for the part he played in having the organ contract awarded the Austin Company. We reluctantly met the pay he demanded, however, assuming it was correct as we did not know the commitments he had made personally with the sales agent of the Austin Company. My brother, Erwin, was with me on the job. While in Eugene we stopped at the Smede Hotel.

Before leaving San Francisco, a brother-in-law of mine, Joseph Hirth, upon hearing I was to be in Eugene, Oregon to install an organ, informed me, he had a friend named Nick Rhoder working in a lumber camp in the mountains near Eugene, and that he would ask him to call on us. I throught this was just a friendly gesture and forgot about it entirely. However, one evening after dinner while my brother and I were in our room enjoying some relaxation and leisure, there came a sharp knock at the door. I responded, thinking perhaps we were to be reprimanded by the hotel management for being too loud; we expected no visitor and knew no one in the town. Upon opening the door I was surprised to see a huge, powerful man, a typical lumberjack, bearded and ruddy face, clad in heavy boots, plaid shirt and topcoat, standing in the doorway. Undoubtedly, our startled look surprised him as he was slow to speak and was hesitant in stating who he was and what he wanted. I noticed a German accent in his speech, and when he finally mentioned his name, Nick Rhoder, and referred to my relative in San Francisco, I made the connection and bade him enter and be seated.

After a little conversation we soon found that under his rough exterior he carried a most charming personality, that he was exceedingly intelligent, a devout Catholic and a religious man. Learning that he had gone to considerable trouble to visit us, having ridden in the cab of the locomotive of a logging train, and that he intended to stay in town a day or so, we arranged with the management of the hotel for him to stay in our room, which was very spacious. The following day, Sunday, we attended mass and then set out for a little trip into the country, which proved very enjoyable. We had many interesting discussions and talked on every conceivable subject. Later, as we became better acquainted, we asked him why a man of his intelligence and culture would accept work as a lumberjack in a forest, among rough and uncouth men, far from civilization, when he could get more agreeable work elsewhere. His answer was that 'someone had to do the work, so he was doing his part.' I have often thought of Nick Rhoder, on the outside a rough stone, but on the inside a polished gem.

Eugene, Oregon, and the country thereabouts impressed us very much. Especially tempting were the luscious and appetizing cherries that are produced in that vicinity in such abundance.

The last trip I made to the Northwest was to install a two manual and Pedal, 24 stop, Austin electric pneumatic organ, Opus 530, for the Second Church of Christ Scientist in Portland, Oregon. It was during the latter part of 1914 and the early part of 1915. The installation of the organ proceeded without any special incident. We stayed at the Grand Union Hotel and I recall how anxious I was to receive letters from home, or rather from my fiancee who, in my absence, was supervising the construction of our new home, which was to be ready for occupancy following our wedding in May. On my return, I found our future home almost completed.

There were few organ maintenance men, as far as I know, permanently located in the Northwest at that time. I believe a Mr. Longmore, a representative of the Kimball Company, was located in Seattle, but I never met him as my stays in Seattle were mostly of a short duration. At Portland, there was a Mr. Ferry, I believe, doing organ maintenance work but I never had occasion to meet him.

Chapter IX

THEATRES OF YESTERYEAR

Some of the Theatre Organs Erected in San Francisco

Undoubtedly it would be interesting to know in which city and in what theatre the pipe organ was first introduced. The West Coast is where I have every reason to believe that, with the birth and development of the silent picture industry, the theatre organ, a prerequisite of the silent movie, also had its beginning.

I have been informed that a theatre in Seattle was the first to introduce successfully the organ as an accompaniment to the silent picture, and that several theatres in the Northwest were making much of their pipe organs before the theatre organ was introduced in California. I recall installing, in 1912, a straight Austin pipe organ of 10 stops, with Echo, in the Globe Theater of Portland, Oregon, for Messrs. Goldstein and Lesser Cohen, the managers. We then installed another Austin organ with automatic player in the Globe Theater in Salem, Oregon.

About this time we began hearing of the American Photo Player Company and their factory in Berkeley, California, conducted by the Van Valkenburg Brothers, specializing in the so-called Pit Organ. These organs were placed in the orchestra pit and consisted of a piano in the center and two sections of the organ on either side. Two automatic player mechanisms were provided in the piano to give continuous music. Some of these pit organs also had harmonium reeds, and for the purpose of tuning these, my father and I made frequent visits to the factory in West Berkeley. These Photo Player organs were also equipped with every imaginable percussion device (or so-called traps), bass drums, snare drums, bells, gongs, whistles, castanets, etc. A series of pull knobs controlling these devices hung within easy reach of the performer. Further, there were the knee swells affecting both organ chambers. I recall hearing and seeing Hal Van Valken-burg give a demonstration on one of the organs at the factory. Being the builder of the organ he may have been exceptionally expert at manipulating it, but I do not recall hearing anyone since who could match him in agility, or in following the music roll and interpreting the music so perfectly. The mechanism of these organs was tubular, on the exhaust and pressure system and were readily assembled.

I remember working on a Photo Player organ, which I was told was one of the very first introduced, at the Palm Theater on Sixth Avenue and Clement Street, San Francisco. A little later the Van Valkenburg Brothers had us assemble a pipe organ, evidently made by an organ supply house in the East, for the Broadway Theater in Oakland, at Broadway and Fifteenth Street. This theater boasted of having a revolving stage, with several stage settings and scenery all prearranged for use as needed. I believe the theater shortly thereafter failed. I never heard what became of the organ.

Another of the early Photo Player Company organs was installed, in 1913, in the Strand Theater in Alameda. It was not long thereafter, in about 1918, when the name "American Photo Player Company" disappeared from the scene, and the name of Robert-Morton, of Van Nuys, California, loomed up prominently. At the same time the name Wurlitzer was a close rival in the theater organ field. Undoubtedly other builders of legitimate church organs, such as Moeller, Austin, Seeburg-Smith, Kimball, followed suit, but most certainly the two outstanding firms that specialized in the theater organ were the two first mentioned.

The evolution, development and improvement of the theater organ tonally and mechanically was very marked. After but a short space of time the noisemaking appliances customarily associated with the first theater organs were dispensed with or used in a more conservative way. At one time this phase of musical noise production, if I may so call it, was specialized in by a Mr. Carney of the Imperial Theater, and received much attention. He had his own air compressor and produced the most realistic steam whistle, locomotive bell and whistle effects. He also had many other kinds of gadgets worked by air enclosed in a cabinet with swell box to control their effect.

The unified type of organ with its many unifications playable from all manuals, making untold effects possible, was universally adopted. High pressures were invariably used, exaggerated pipe scaling from extreme narrow strings to tubby Tibias and Diapasons were applied. Orchestral reeds, such as Clarinets, Kinnura's, Orchestral Oboe's, English and

French Horns and Brass Trumpets were mostly used, also bright Flutes and Piccolos, evidently imitating the orchestra as much as possible. Effective swell boxes, possible of great diminuendo effects, were sought; the never ending throbbing tremolo was absolutely indispensable; a rapid, spontaneous key action was an absolute necessity, as a new style of music evolved, called jazz. This type of organ developed its own type of organist, so much so that a legitimate organist was entirely at sea in the theater.

The theater organist was in a class of his own, requiring great versatility, agility, a good ear for rhythm, music and harmony, a gift for memorizing and extemporizing, and interpreting the silent screen picture into a living scene, with feeling and pathos, fear and awe, love and romance, as the scenes on the screen demanded. A fine technique was developed. I knew one organist, not content with the superb action of the Wurlitzer organ he played on, with its prompt attack and repetition, sprinkled talcum powder over the keys to further facilitate the movement of his fleet fingers gliding over them. There is no question but that the general public enjoyed, preferred and demanded this type of musical accompaniment for the silent picture in preference to an orchestra, the cost of which, barring possibly some of the largest theaters, would have been prohibitive. Organists were paid good union wages.

The organ in the silent picture theaters seemed to be a permanent and established institution. However, quite suddenly and unheralded, the movie theater profession was confronted with the new invention, the Talkie, or sound producing film. Within two weeks time thereafter, as if by magic, the theater pipe organs were abandoned. Organists lost their lucrative positions as one theater after another installed the silver screen with the huge loudspeaker behind it, amplifying the spoken word as well as furnishing suitable music as recorded on the celluloid film passing through the projector.

There is no doubt that the talkie movie is an improvement over the silent picture, although at first, sound and picture did not always synchronize; but that has now been brought to a high point of perfection. Musically, however, I maintain that the blatant noise we now often get as music — canned music — is inferior to what was provided the public formerly. I believe the greater majority of movie goers do not listen to the music now or realize it is being rendered at all, and consider it as a mere preliminary or by-product or background to the picture.

As I personally was never particularly enthusiastic about the theater organ, or better said, about the working conditions that prevailed about the theaters and their organs, I have not followed their history, development or their records very closely. On the other hand, my brothers with whom I was associated in business, as well as other organ artisans, of whom there were many at the time, consider that period of the organ profession the heyday of the organ builder's career. Working eight hours a day in the organs of churches was perhaps "heaven", speaking literally and figuratively, depending on the faith that was in you, but I could never get any joy out of working, invariably after eleven p.m. when other people were enjoying their night's sleep, in the dark, smelly theaters where no ray of sunlight had ever entered the building since they were constructed; crawling around in dusty organ chambers, orchestra pits. basements and backstage, which often seemed not to belong to the theater so far as the janitorial service was concerned. The work would be done before the show opened in the morning, and it was always a case of rush and hurry. Added to these difficulties was the endless testing of circuits, broken cont acts, etc., as these organs were put under terrific strain, being played uninterruptedly, often from 11 a.m. to 11 p.m., making the life of a new theater organ only about seven years. However, the following references to some of the important theater organs of San Francisco might be of interest to my readers.

The Tivoli Opera House, during 1913-1914, undoubtedly was one of the first theaters that went into the use of the pipe organ in a big way. It originally had a two manual Kimball pipe organ. Later a Wurlitzer organ from Reno, Nevada, was used. I recall we were making arrangements to play these two organs from the Wurlitzer console, or of having two organists play both organs, but synchronize their playing as to appear as though it were one organ. The venture, however, did not prove satisfactory and they finally procured a large Robert-Morton organ with its huge console. I do not doubt that in number of pipes, this was the largest theater organ in the city. Charles Gechoef was mostly connected with the installation of this organ. Two of the organists were Uda Waldrop and Gordon Bretland.

The Polk Street Theater, under the management of Nassar Bros., had a Robert-Morton organ. Mr. Bolton, an ingenious mechanic and musician, seemed to have complete control in organ matters here. His young daughter, a prodigy at the organ, was featured as soloist with great acclaim. This organ never impressed me favorably. It was a hodge-podge of additions and units added together, crowded into inaccessible corners and alcoves. It was installed sometime in 1913-1914.

At the New Mission and New Fillmore Theaters were Robert-Morton organs of no small proportions, with three manual consoles. They were well built and well installed and were typical examples of the Robert Morton product. These theaters were operated by the Golden State Theater Circuit. Dick Arndt was organist at the New Mission for a long time.

The Rialto Theater had one of the first Wurlitzer organs. It was featured extensively with the then popular C Sharp Minor at the console.

The Imperial Theater first had a two manual Kimball organ, then a Wurlitzer. John Allen (Jack) Partington was the manager of this theater, a gentleman as fine as you make them, a lover of the pipe organ. The organist here at one time was Jesse Crawford, who later became quite famous. The organ was badly damaged by fire at one time. This fact was generally unknown to the public and to the regular patrons of the theater. The fire occurred one evening after the show. The next day the movie show continued as usual. The asbestos curtain was dropped and a piano used instead of the organ; a generous supply of disinfectant applied to dissipate the odor of charred and burnt wood, and the show went on. Behind the asbestos curtain the whole stage floor had been burnt out. This meant that the organ cables connecting the console located in the pit with the two organ chambers on either side of the stage had also been destroyed. The flames had just about licked at the console in the pit when it was brought under control. It was our job, a night and day job, to put in a new cable or splice the old one where damaged. I thought this procedure typical of the theatrical business in general. Before the curtain, tinsel and gold, sham and subterfuge; behind the curtain, chaos and disaster, but still the show must go on.

The St. Francis Theater, Geary and Powell Streets, had a Johnston two manual, a typical church organ. The theater venture was a failure and the organ was removed and installed elsewhere.

At the American Theater, Fillmore and Turk Streets, there was a Kimball two manual organ. This was later removed to a Catholic Institution.

The California Theater, Fourth and Market Streets, had a large four manual Wurlitzer with Echo organ. Eddie Horton was the popular organist at the console. The organ was extensively featured. Sunday Symphony concerts, given under the direction of Mr. Heller, created quite a stir among music lovers. Emil Breitenfeld, composer and organist, also held the position of organist here for a long time. Mr. Roth was the manager of the theater. The organ was installed by Mr. Coxroft, and serviced by us for many years. The organ was located in five distinct places in the theater. On either side of the stage were sections of the organ, two sections were over the proscenium, the Echo organ was over the ceiling in about the center of the theater, and a large glass-enclosed room in the basement contained the relays, switches, etc. The organ chambers and especially the relay room were equipped with suitable thermostatically control-led heating units. We serviced the organ weekly at this time and the instrument was kept in the best possible condition, considering the terrific use it was put to. However, on a special visit we made, the organ was exceptionally ill behaved and out of order. Notes were ciphering in all sections of the organ, stops and couplers would not respond or release; in fact, we had never seen the organ in such a condition. As there was nothing unusual about the console, and the trouble seemed to be general all over the organ, we decided before going to any particular chamber or doing anything else, to take a look in the relay room in the basement. On approaching this room, which was partitioned off with glass paneling from the rest of the basement, we noticed a haze or smoky atmosphere in its enclosure. Approaching closer, we felt that the glass panes were hot. On opening the door we were overcome by a wave of intense heat. Immediately we realized that the thermostat controls were not working and that the heaters were on full blast, and for how long a time we did not know, undoubtedly due to some maladjustment. We threw off the switch, opened the doors for circulation, and after a considerable cooling off period when normal temperature was restored, the organ again functioned properly, none the worse for the ordeal it had gone through. We had possibly arrived just in time to avert a serious conflagration.

The Granada Theater, now the Paramount, had a large four manual Wurlitzer with Echo organ that was exceedingly popular in its day. On its arrival the organ was loaded onto fourteen trucks and paraded through the streets of the city before being erected. It was advertised as the world's largest organ. Oliver Wallace, organist par excellence, also highly advertised and petite Iris Vining, a charming bit of feminity, were at the console. The organ was voiced and erected by James Nutall, Fred Wood, my brother, Erwin, and others. Miss Vining passed away in 1943.

The new Orpheum Theater had a large four manual Robert-Morton organ. It was well spoken of and popular with organists and music lovers. Don George was the favorite organist here. The organ was erected by Gail Seward, Paul Schoenstein and others.

The Fox West Coast Theater on Market Street, between Larkin and Polk Streets, one of the latest theaters built, was unquestionably the largest and finest theater in San Francisco. It had a large four manual Wurlitzer organ, outclassing all others in size, with two consoles. Also a Moller two manual with automatic player in the lobby.

At the Golden Gate Theater there was a two manual Moller organ. Numerous organists performed here. The Moller organ was later replaced with a Wurlitzer. Mr. Clift was the manager at this theater.

At the Warfield Theater on Market Street, opposite Sixth, the first organ installed was also a Moller two manual organ.

This, likewise, was later removed to make place for a Wurlitzer organ.

The Coliseum Theater, at Ninth Avenue and Clement Street in the Richmond District, was one of the first large and imposing neighborhood theaters. It first had a Robert-Morton organ, which was later moved to the Metropolitan Theater. The theater was operated by Samuel Levin, who possibly was the originator of the idea of utilizing pipe organs in theaters in this locality. His first venture was tried out in a small theater in San Mateo. After removing the Robert-Morton organ from the Coliseum Theater, they secured a Wurlitzer. This Wurlitzer organ was later erected in our factory and remained there for a number of years and was finally sold to Mr. Merlyn Morse of Oakland, where he installed it in his residence. An organist at the Coliseum for a long time was Leslie Harvey.

The Castro Theater, Market and Castro Streets, had a Robert-Morton organ. Samuel Levin was also the manager of this theater.

The El Capitan Theater in the Mission District had a Wurlitzer organ. The popular Mel Hertz was organist here for a long time. He passed away in 1952.

Many other theaters had organs, too many in fact to enumerate and comment on here. With the sudden disuse of the theater organs they remained idle and undisturbed for some time, evidently awaiting the reaction of the public to the new type of movie, the vitaphone, or talkie. Gradually indifference and abandonment seemed to be the verdict. In many cases consoles were merely boarded over or removed from the orchestra pits by cutting the cable in two; motors and generators were removed for other useful purposes. Invariably the chimes, drums and traps disappeared and what was not destroyed or removed with intent, was often put to final disuse by malicious boys and vandals, who removed the organ pipes or wantonly destroyed them. Several of the organs, however, were carefully preserved and quite a few found their places eventually in our local churches.

To enumerate the large roster of names of theater organists who played on the organs in San Francisco's theaters, or those in the larger theaters of the Bay Region and as far south as Fresno, would be beyond my powers of recollection now. Some of them not mentioned in my foregoing brief notes were: Dr. Bruce Gordon Kingsley, Henry B. Murtah, Gordon Bretland, Irma Falvey, Albert Hay Mollott, Floyd Wright, George Wright, Tim Crawford, George Nycklicek, Eddie Seller, Alta Wadsworth, Philip Shinahan, Rae West, Kenneth Loomis, Dolla Sargeant, Charles Wilson, Christine Decker, Henry La Belle, Charles E. Anderson and others.

The most striking episode relative to the theaters of San Francisco was the demolition of the sumptuous "Fox West Coast Theater", in 1963. The last performance was scheduled and much publicity was given to it to make it a gala event. Movie celebrities from Hollywood were invited. City officials were present. George Wright, the popular theater organist did justice to the "mighty" Wurlitzer. Fantastic admission prices were charged and a jovial, yet nostalgic audience, with moistened eyes, bid farewell to one of the city's famous landmarks. The organ was finally sold to a party in southern California.

Chapter X

OLD PIPE ORGANS OF CALIFORNIA

These are some old instruments located in places some-what off the beaten path that I am certain would be of further interest. I will, mention first the pipe organs I consider the oldest in the State of California.

During the month of September 1907, my father and my younger brother, Otto, were called upon to erect a small tracker action pipe organ of several stops, two manual and Pedal, for the Unitarian Church in Palo Alto, California. I did not see this organ personally, but heard of an unusual notation they found inscribed on some of the organ pipes. As the incident received considerable publicity in the local press of the town, I herewith print the account in full:

FINDS ANCIENT PIPES IN ORGAN HANDEL PLAYED
Expert Deciphers Writing Which Says
Washington Heard the Instrument

Palo Alto, Calif., Sept. 28, 1907. Has Palo Alto the oldest organ in the United States? From the discoveries made by Felix F. Schoenstein, an organ expert of San Francisco, yesterday, while setting up the organ, it certainly looks so. The organ is a gift to the youngest Unitarian Church in America at this place from the oldest at Scituate, Mass. In unpacking the instrument Schoenstein found that two of the small wooden pipes were of different material and workman-ship and that one of them was covered on both sides with almost undecipherable writing. On the C pipe in writing of many flourishes were the following words: "Put up by Gilbert & Woodbridge, organders to his honor"; and also the following inscriptions: "Put up in South Reading, April, 1832" and "This pipe was made by Johan Snetzler in London about 100 years ago and has been made to sound by Handel and was heard by George Washington when Commander of the American Army at Cambridge." The last two notations are in different handwriting and the phrase, "about 100 years ago", is of no value in determining the age of the pipes. If Handel played the organ it must have been constructed in the middle of the eighteenth century, for Handel died in 1759, and the organ probably is nearly 200 years of age. The organ in question was without doubt made for use in London and after some years of use, with the installation of a new organ, found its way to America and after numerous wanderings a final resting place for some years at the parish at Scituate. To have been heard by Washington it probably was installed at Cambridge, where Washington took command of the American Army, July 2, 1775. The organ will be ready for use at the services in the Unitarian Church next Sunday. Schoenstein has found its construction to be of the best.

Another ancient organ now located in California, also one that came originally from England and has an interesting background, is the small pipe organ at the Old Mission of San Juan Bautista, one of the twenty-one Missions of California. Although not a manually played organ and being an organ of very diminutive size, it is still considered a pipe organ. I refer my readers to a book written by Will Connell, entitled the "Missions of California", page 92, where the author refers to a "Barrel Pipe Organ" and, also, shows a photo of it. It is claimed to have been presented to Friar Lausen, O.F.M., of the Mission, in 1793, by the voyager "Vancouver" on his visit to these regions as a peace offering for his permission to trespass Spanish territory. The organ is of a portable type, used in the large Cathedrals, to be moved readily to different chapels. A group of twenty secular tunes is arranged on its barrel and the book further states that, although its wooden cogs are badly worm eaten, it still delivers some music. Legend has it that an early Indian insurrection was quelled when Father de la Cuesta played the organ in the plaza in front of the Mission.

Another old, legitimate pipe organ is the instrument in St. Joseph's Catholic Church, Marysville, California. This church was at one time the Cathedral church of Bishop Monogue; later the Bishopric was situated at Grass Valley and then, eventually, at Sacramento, California. The Rev. Monsignor Thomas Horgan, an elderly and amiable churchman, was pastor of this church.

The organ is in constant use at present. It was originally a two manual and Pedal tracker action organ of seven stops, attached console, with a walnut case and ornamental front pipes. A number of years ago it was electrified by Toutjian

Bros. of Berkeley, California. A Vox Humana was added to it and a modern blowing plant was installed. We had serviced it on several occasions since, but it was during the month of March, 1946, that we were summoned to give the organ a thorough overhauling, due to damages done by water, the result of a fire that was started in the spire of the church by lightning. This work was entrusted to my elder son, Lawrence, who was engaged several weeks in correcting the damage. In the course of his work, he noted an inscription on the inside of the bung board which read, "J. G. Moulton, Maker, August 30th, 1876." St. Joseph's Church was erected in 1855.

From the biography of Jos. Mayer, California's pioneer organ builder, I learned that he, then a resident of Marysville, established himself in the organ business there and, in 1856, built the first pipe organ made in California, for which he received an award from the State at the State Fair in 1857. His biography further states that the instrument was later purchased by the Roman Catholic Church of Marysville. Statements my father made to me, and data I since received from Rev. Monsignor Horgan, indicate that a second Catholic Church or parish existed in Marysville in its early history. The German Catholics of the town had founded a church under the name Immaculate Conception, and a Rev. Mailer was Pastor. In what year this German national church was founded and what year their church was built, and whether the above mentioned Mayer organ was installed in the former or the latter church, I do not know. However, it would be logical to assume that the small national church, dependent almost entirely for its financial support on its own nationals, would not have been in a position to build their church and, at the same time, invest in a pipe organ. This assumption would be further born out by later developments, as the congregation finally disbanded and amalgamated with St. Joseph's parish.

It is, therefore, logical to assume that the Catholic church Mayer refers to was St. Joseph's Church and that the first pipe organ built in California by Mayer found its abode in this edifice; presumably the "Moulton Organ" was installed some years after. It is also possible that the "Moulton

Organ", now in St. Joseph's Church, was installed by Jos. Mayer himself. It is also possible that a firm by the name of Hall and Labagh, organ mechanics, which name I remember my father mentioned at times, and briefly referred to in his Marysville notes, might have installed the organ. However, the notation stating the builder's name and the evident date of construction establishes it as the third oldest pipe organ in California.

As most of the pipe organs, that were erected in early San Francisco and other towns of California before the advent of Jos. Mayer in 1856, came from the Atlantic Seaboard and from Europe, it is most likely that the Moulton Organ came from England. Certain telltale marks in the voicing and design of the pipes, also the fact that the writer of the inscription used the word "Maker" in preference to the word "Builder", more commonly used in this country, might indicate foreign origin. Also the fact that the name "Moulton" was never heard heretofore by the writer in the category of American organ builders, would indicate it most probably was built in England, then shipped to the Atlantic Seaboard and finally transported by ship to California. A further shipping mark on one of the large pedal pipes read: "Mr. M. C. Ellis, Marysville, Blue Line, C.F.F.L." As Marysville at that time was the terminus of the Sacramento River boats, and all water transportation to the gold mines in the Sierras, it most likely was carried to Marysville by a boat of the Blue Line.

That Marysville was organ-minded in those days and showed possibilities of development, would be further substantiated by the fact that California's pioneer organ builder, Jos. Mayer, established himself in business there. His shop was located at 175 Yuba Valley, between 6th and 7th Streets, according to the Marysville Directory of 1857.

Marysville can claim another old pipe organ, the one formerly in the old First Presbyterian Church. It was originally a two manual and Pedal tracker action organ. Some years ago it was modernized and electrified, and somewhat enlarged, by Toutjian Bros. of Berkeley. It had about 11 stops, was well built and of excellent tone. The console was originally attached, but was then detached. A peculiar feature of this organ was that the Swell blinds were visible above the front pipes. They layed horizontally and were decorated with a pattern to match the decoration on the front display pipes. The front case was made of heavy black walnut, was beautifully designed and made a fine appearance. The builder of this organ was E. G. Hook, Opus 491, 1869, of Boston, Mass.

When the old brick church was razed and the congregation moved to their new church, further out in the suburbs, the old organ was removed and reinstalled in their new church by John Swinford. Here the organ was divided and placed in two separate chambers. A group of large 16' Open Diapason metal front pipes filled in the open space facing the congregation, but were never made to sound, and some changes were made to the stop list. The Toutjian console from the old church was not used, but a used console of another make was installed. The entire piston combination action was removed, however, for some reason and lay in a confused and hopeless mess in an adjoining room above. Undoubtedly, some misunderstanding or disagreement developed with the church authorities and the organ expert.

Our firm was then engaged to put in a modern piston combination action and also add a Trumpet 8' to the organ, a 4' coupler to the Great manual and otherwise bring the organ to its final completed condition. Although the organ seemed to be a source of woe and discomfort for those entrusted with its installation and completion it, nonetheless, is a fine sounding and an adequate organ, being used regularly at the present time.

The Episcopal Church of Marysville was also interested at an early date in pipe organs. From the Marysville directory I again noted that the church was established in 1854 and purchased a pipe organ in 1861. No mention is made of the builder.

In 1918 we installed an Austin Chorophone in the old church, which was later removed to the new edifice by other parties. In 1946 and 1949, we again spent considerable time in rejuvenating this instrument and, finally, in 1951, we placed the organ in the forward end of the church near the Chancel, in close proximity with the Choir. Here we added several new stops to the organ, improving considerably its tonal quality and added a well-designed, pleasing facade of display pipes to the organ front. This work was under the pastorate of Rev. Tamblyn, Rector of the Church, and the installation mostly by my son, Lawrence.

Trinity Episcopal Church of San Jose had an old two manual and Pedal tracker action organ of ten or twelve stops that certainly has claims of being one of California's old organs. It was built by William Stevens of Boston, Mass., in 1836. In 1863 it was procured by Trinity Episcopal Church of San Jose. It was shipped by boat from Boston via the Isthmus of Panama. Who installed the organ I do not know. Nor did my father ever mention working on it.

During 1924 Trinity Episcopal Church of San Francisco had purchased a new four manual Skinner organ for their favorite son, their organist, the late highly esteemed Benjamin Moore. Their old three manual Hook and Hastings organ, installed by our firm in or about 1898, was then available for disposal and was secured by the Trinity Episcopal Church of San Jose. The removal and installation of this organ in Trinity Church, San Jose, was done by Thomas Whalley of Berkeley, at which time he also made some additions and alterations.

Before the installation of this Hook and Hastings organ could be made, their old Stevens tracker organ had to be removed to make room for this new instrument. The latter then found a new abode at St. James Episcopal Church in Paso Robles, where it is now in constant use. Some time after its installation in St. James, I had occasion to visit the town and called on the Rector, Rev. Thomas, with whom I became acquainted while working on his organ when he was stationed at Trinity Episcopal Church in Oakland. He requested me to check over their old Stevens organ, which I did and while thus engaged noted a plaque applied to the organ reading as follows:

"Mrs. Hayes visited with Stevens' daughter of Boston when he built San Jose Trinity organ later removed to St. James Ep. Church, Paso Robles, Sept. 15 — 1924.

Erected in Trinity Ep. Church 1863
Came via Isthmus of Panama.

The San Jose Mercury and Paso Robles press archives contain interesting additional material on the above instruments.

Other old organs of California are: A one manual, tracker action organ at the Catholic Church in Centerville, the Lutheran Church of Napa, the "Hook" organ at the Methodist Church in Ferndale. Incidentally, a Mr. Sandin, an amateur organ enthusiast of Fortuna, evidently, in making some alterations to the latter mentioned organ, removed the Dulciana 8' set, with the intention of using them in a house organ he was building. My son, Lawrence, in turn, secured this set for an organ he had partly completed for our own home. This organ has since been sold and installed in the Redeemer Lutheran Church, now called Mission Covenant Church, in Redwood City, and is in constant use. The Presbyterian Church of Chico had an old "Hook" two manual tracker organ. Some fifty years ago I rejuvenated the instrument.

An old two manual and Pedal tracker action organ was installed in the former St. Stephens Episcopal Church on the north side of Fulton Street, between Fillmore and Webster Streets, in San Francisco. We do not know its age or the builder of the instrument, but know it was not of local make. I believe the congregation disbanded and the edifice was taken over by a Greek Orthodox congregation. The organ was put up for sale and finally found its way to the Federated Community Church of Santa Clara.

Chapter XI

GREMLINS AND THE PLAGUES OF THE ORGAN TUNER

611

WHILE THE CAT SLEPT, THE MICE PLAYED

During the month of February 1914, we were called to an old estate down the Peninsula that had a large pipe organ in a beautiful music room. The squire of the house was a composer and a performer on the instrument. It was a two manual Bergstrom tracker action organ. On starting the organ, which was blown by a revolving water-wheel in the basement of the house, we heard nothing but a great gush of air. On closer inspection we found that mice had chewed off all the gussets on the bellows. These invariably are made of soft alum-tanned sheep skin leather, which proved a tempting morsel to the uninvited visitors. With the bellows punctured at all corners, it leaked like a sieve. We also noticed that most of the keys were lying down limp and inactive. Investigating further, we found that the mice had chewed off all the glue and thread used in binding the threaded wire on the end of the tracker. Evidently the glue had some tasty ingredient in it that satisfied their hunger. This entailed quite an extensive repair job, for in chewing the glue and thread, they also chewed off the wooden tracker. The latter had to be spliced again with a new piece and extended.

With this damage to tracker and bellows repaired, the organ was again serviceable for many years. About 35 years later I helped remove the same organ from the old estate, as the property was being subdivided and sold for modern home sites.

I recalled with amusement the escapades of the mice, which undoubtedly during many quiet moments, were roaming through the organ mechanism satisfying their appetites, while on the other side of the organ case, well-dressed ladies and society folk were entertaining and having their tea.

WANTED! A "PIED PIPER"

An old tracker action organ in the San Joaquin Valley had its trouble from vermin. Several pipes failed to speak. On investigation, we found that rats had nested on the pipe chest, between the pipe racks and top of the chest, and wherever a pipe foot interferred with their living quarters, they gnawed off the obstruction. These rats must have been exceedingly hungry, as I had never before, nor since, seen rats gnaw off metal. Maybe they were very particular just how their living quarters were arranged, and if there was anything to interfere with their comfort, the shortest and quickest way was to eat the obstruction, be it wood or metal.

LITTLE CREATURES IN GOD'S COUNTRY

One of the outstanding organs in California, due in this instance to its location and environment, is an Austin organ located outdoors at Bohemian Grove, Bohemia, California.

The organ itself is placed in a concrete building, with proper openings made to emit the tone, but safe, dry and thermostatically heated during the winter months. When the season in which the organ is used is over it is practically hermetically sealed (or so we thought), as there is then no opening except a small two inch hole through the wall through which the cable enters, and after that is removed it is securely closed with a plug, and a ventilator opened high near the ceiling for circulation of air.

On entering the organ chamber for the first time one season, I was startled by the gyrations of a small water snake trying to make a getaway. Up between the trackers field mice had made a nest, but caused no serious damage. On another occasion the Swell engine failed to work properly. To muffle the exhaust of the Swell engine the exhaust pipe was made to discharge between the wooden floor and the concrete floor upon which it was laid. On removing the Swell engine from the floor, we found its interior stuffed with fine wool and cotton, the work undoubtedly of field mice who had made it their domicile.

A LIFE CRUSHED OUT

When theatre organs were in their heyday and the movie

organists were in their prime, we received a phone call one day, not exactly to repair a certain theatre organ in Oakland, but to remove a terrible stench around the console which defied the efforts of the house manager and the janitors, plus all sorts of disinfectants, air purifiers, etc. We removed the pedal board and movable panels, and not finding any foreign matter we decided to open the key boards one by one. It was a three manual organ. After opening the Swell and then the Great manual keys, just in the center of the manuals between the Great and Choir keys, a dead mouse was found crushed between the keys. Probably during some "agitato" movement, when the fair lady organist's fingers were more forceful than sensitive, she crushed the life of the little creature while he was passing between the keys.

ONLY THE SKELETON REMAINED

Another incident of a theatre organ may be related here, if you are still able to take it after these rodent recitals.

We had occasion to remove an organ from a theatre in the Western Addition. The organ had been out of use for some years. Having previously worked on it we took this work reluctantly, as there had always been a disagreeable odor about the place. In fact, this particular theatre caused me to have a dislike for theatre work in general. The confined, enclosed places, never touched by the benevolent and health giving rays of the sun, the night work after theatre performances, with the air thick and stuffy from the crowded audiences, held no attraction for me. The cause of the unwholesome odor in this theatre was discovered to be the decomposed carcass of a large rat lying under some organ parts, and which could not be seen or removed until the organ was later dismantled for removal to a new location.

THERE IS NOTHING PERMANENT HERE BELOW — ORGANS INCLUDED

Fortunately, in San Francisco and the Bay Region we are

not troubled with insects or borers that destroy the wood of the organ. True, of late, we have heard much and seen evidence of termites destroying wood in building construction, but I do not recall any case where local wood, be it redwood, cedar or sugar pine, the most commonly used woods in organ construction, became subject to the ravages of beetle, borer or termite. A most common pest, however, is the moth, which enters and destroys the felt which is used quite sparingly in pipe organs as compared with piano work. Unaccountable reactions to the effects of moths in organs can be noted. We know of some organs 35 to 40 years old where the felt is as good as when it was first applied. Others, after a few years in use, are literally eaten up by moths. Undoubtedly, the process of manufacture of the felt, and whether it is made of wool or cotton, has much bearing on the matter; also the other materials it comes in contact with. We have noticed that felt glued on leather often lasts indefinitely, as for instance the pallet valves on some of the old tracker organs, whereas the newly manufactured zephyr leather, although in itself non-porous, pliable and very serviceable, if it comes in contact or close proximity to felt, is invariably soon punctured and consumed by moths.

Surroundings and conditions in close proximity to organs often have much to do with the preservation of the organ material. In a church in San Jose the organ had given good service for 35 years and never a complaint was made on account of damage done by moths. This situation was quickly changed by new conditions surrounding the organ. An old carpet that had given service for many years in the sanctuary, and had been replaced with a new one, was deemed good enough to give some further service on the choir loft. From that time on we had trouble with moths destroying the felt in the organ.

Bellows leather we also find subject to deterioration, dependent, no doubt, on the process used in tanning. One of the larger organs of San Francisco, built over 50 years ago, still has its original bellows and the leather is still soft and pliable and with sufficient strength to last many more years. On the other hand, we have used the thin, pneumatic leathers in certain work which had to be replaced after three years use, as the material had completely dried out and become lifeless. Rubberized silk material used in pneumatics gives perfect service when new, but in the course of time it hardens, cracks and defeats the purpose for which it is used and becomes a source of grief and trouble.

One organ in particular I recall, where aluminum valve discs were used on the pneumatics, instead of the ordinary fiber or cardboard discs that gave us much trouble. The aluminum discs were fastened to the pneumatics with small alum tanned leather washers and iron screws to permit it to oscillate. The combinations of the three substances, through chemical reaction, ate a large hole through the aluminum discs, causing all the pipes to cipher. All aluminum discs had to be removed and cardboard or fiber discs with felt, instead of a leather washer was substituted. This procedure solved our problem, and the organ is giving good service ever since.

In another organ in one of our Coast cities, which used a peculiar type individual valve system, we had much trouble from corrosion. The valve itself was a piece of galvanized iron suspended on one end, acting as a hinge, the other end being actuated by a tracker, and the valve covered by a thick, soft piece of alum-tanned leather to make a soft seat. The combination, soon after installation, proved unsatisfactory. Grains of salt formed under the leather on the surface of the metal, making the valve seat uneven and unreliable.

A summary of our experience would be, keep organs and organ lofts clean, free of all eatables, rubbish and unnecessary accumulations. Have as little carpet around as possible, use moth balls or disinfectants where signs of moths are present. Use high grade genuine leather in all organ work where possible, and avoid the combination of alum-tanned leather and iron coming in contact with one another.

VANDALS AT WORK

One day we received an emergency call to tune one of the large Skinner organs in the city, being informed that the organ was horribly out of tune. As we called monthly to service this organ we could not imagine what had caused the complained of condition. However, as we learned long ago never to argue with an organist, we called, perhaps somewhat dubious, surmising that at worst an individual note had gone badly off pitch.

When we tried the organ we were appalled, as it actually did sound like a bunch of wild cats. In climbing up to the Swell and Solo divisions we saw large pipes laying criss cross over others, pipes lifted out of their places and inserted in the tops of other pipes, many pipes in their wrong holes, also quite a few pipes were missing. Fortunately, none of the pipes was abused.

We notified the church authorities of what had happened, informing them that someone had been in the organ, exchanged the pipes and committed general devilment. To our surprise the authority we spoke to was not over excited or alarmed on what we had to say, as though he had expected it. He advised us to immediately put things back in order and repair or replace any damage that had been done. The incident was hushed up as much as possible. The reason for this secrecy was later made known to us. The perpetrators of this hoax were some of the teenagers of prominent members of the church who thought, that by mixing up the pipes in the organ they were playing a smart joke on the congregation. Their dads paid the bill.

At another smaller organ which we also service monthly, the organist went to the church for her usual afternoon practice and also found the organ terribly out of tune. Having played the organ for a morning's service, at which time everything was in the best of condition, she was confounded and notified us to call. Here we found that someone had entered the Swell box. Every metal pipe from about tenor C was crushed tightly shut on top. The wooden flute stops that had metal tuners on top were completely rolled shut. The stoppers of the Stopped Diapason and the Bourdons were shoved down as far as possible, the tuning wires of the Oboe were pulled up and down. Fortunately, none of the mouths of the pipes was tampered with or pipes taken out of their holes or exchanged. Here, also, we repaired the organ, none the worse off for its experience. The culprit was evidently someone familiar with organ pipes, one who knew how to put an organ pipe badly out of tune, but still not damage it. Authorities of the church were baffled to know how the party got into the organ unobserved. He must have worked in the dark and very quietly, and left as cunningly as he had entered. Who the intruder was or what his motives were in manhandling the organ have not been solved to this day.

VAGARIES OF CHANGING TEMPERATURE

One of the plagues that affronts the organ tuner almost all the time is the variance of temperature. This occurs daily, also seasonally, and at times when churches and auditoriums are heated artificially. In our favored locality of San Francisco and the Bay Region, sixty to sixty-two degrees Fahrenheit is considered normal temperature during the greater part of the day. Indeed, I think there are few such spots on earth where the temperature varies so little as it does in San Francisco. Maximum cold in winter may strike thirty degrees or thereabouts, and some unusual hot days in summer may reach ninety degrees, but these extremes are usually of short duration as the sharp cold of the winter months is usually dissipated by the warm Japanese current, and the warm spell of summer is dispelled by the cooling fogs which invariably roll in from the Pacific. Therefore, with this normal temperature of sixty degrees, more or less, the pipe organs are indeed fortunate and when once put in tune and not tampered with usually remain in tune for a long time. For this reason we claim that the pipe organs around this area, especially those that are regularly serviced, are the best tuned organs anywhere in the country.

I have personally observed this in making comparisons of the stay-in-tune qualities of many of the large organs of New York City and other cities, of comments of some of the leading organists while touring the country, also from comments I have heard from organ authorities visiting Europe, stating that in getting within close range of some of the large Cathedral organs many tonal discrepancies are noticeable, especially in tone regulating and smoothness of reeds, which indeed sounded mediocre compared with the fine standard demanded and maintained in the organs of this area.

Despite our favored locale organs go out of tune, depending on environment and natural conditions, such as a divided organ located on the east and the west side of the church; different elevations of chest levels, some near the floor and others close to the ceiling, faulty wind distribution, or robbing of chests. The greatest difficulty is to tune an organ in an edifice artificially heated, particularly if the system is of the type which just forces hot air into the building, resulting in different temperatures in each organ chamber. Often, on Sunday morning after doors have been opened frequently, a noticeable drop in temperature takes place, with a resultant out of tune situation, annoying to all musical ears, but certainly not the fault of the conscientious Organ Tuner. To tune an organ under such conditions is often worse than not to have tuned it at all. Even when termostatic heating units are applied to organ chambers I have still to find an installation as satisfactory as where nature favors a locality with an even temperature, as in and around the San Francisco area. Organ pipes being made of different alloys of metal, also of wood, and not being affected exactly alike by heat and cold, go out of tune. Reed stops, especially those in which different metals are used for tongues, eschalots and resonators, with insecure tuning wires, frequently go out of tune. Also the scales, the design of the pipe and the weight or the gauge of the material used in their construction have an influence on their staying in tune. Topping these points is the natural tendency of the small or treble pipes to go out of tune more readily than the larger or base pipes. Also too great a variance between blower room temperature and temperature of the air surrounding the pipes is another cause of organs going out of tune.

As a rule, we recommend a general tuning when the temperature is normal. First we set our bearings from a pitch pipe, tuning fork, harp or chime or some medium which is agreed upon. Then we lay the temperament on a clear, audible stop such as an Octave 4', Diapason 8' or keen string and copy the middle tuning C on the different manuals or chests so that all divisions of the organ synchronize. Then from these, as standards, we proceed to tune the entire organ. That is all an organ tuner can do. Possibly by evening a waiver will be noticed between different manuals. This condition is the result again of a slight change in temperature, and it will correct itself. The organ will be in tune again when the temperature returns to that point at which it was when the organ was tuned. Even with all this care, due to temperature changes beyond the control of man, different chambers of the organ may be out of tune with each other, although each is in tune with itself. This natural condition must be endured; it is permissable and is not unmusical, though the organ tuners ideal is always a perfect blend. Individual pipes, however, which are out of tune with their own octaves, due to wrong tuning, effects of dust at the languid, shifting or accidental moving of the tuning slide or roll, or any other cause, is not permissable and should be put in tune.

It is strange how one bad note, or one out of tune, will mar a whole ensemble. The good notes, or those in tune, bring no comment, they are taken for granted, but the bad one, just like in human society, is conspicuous and brazen. In human society again we ostrasize such a character and try to nullify his bad behavior, however, many an organist seems to be helpless and knows not how to pick out the offending stop or pipe or make it at least temporarily impotent, until corrected by the organ tuner. In such cases he should try to locate the offending stop or note. Most frequently it may be a reed. Meanwhile, he should avoid using the Crescendo Pedal or Sforzando Pedal. If the offending stop cannot be taken off the combination pistons readily, registration should be done by hand.

In coming in contact with some of the world's famous organists virtuoso and being obliged to serve them in tuning the organs on which they were to perform, we invariably found them the most considerate and lenient when it came to finding fault with notes being out of tune. The lesser lights, however, made a furor if the organ was out of tune, claiming they cannot play their program — "it is terrible, unbearable, nerve racking." etc. No one is more desirous of having an organ in tune than is the organ tuner, especially after his tedious work and effort spent in trying to achieve his goal. Cooperate with him. Be fair and reasonable. Do not expect the impossible or hold him responsible for the vagaries changes of temperature will cause.

TIN FOIL IS A CONDUCTOR

In one of the largest organs on the West Coast, in the Civic Auditorium of San Francisco, we had an eventful occurrence . . . a fire that, fortunately, turned out less harmful than it could have been. The incident was the result of a short circuit in the console, caused by vermin.

At the time Edwin Lemare was Municipal Organist. The Civic Auditorium was only used for cultural purposes, such as organ recitals, symphonies, dramatic pagaents, lectures and conventions. Evidently, the financial returns did not cover the outlay for upkeep. It was then decided to put the Auditorium to general use, including sports of all kinds. A crew of janitors were daily at work keeping the huge building in shipshape condition.

Up to the time of this change of policy we had never been annoyed by any vermin, not even a mouse. However, thereafter, in time, we frequently found leftover food morsels in the corners of the interior of the console — peanuts, popcorn, chewing gum and tin foil wrappers. There were two heavy #6 gauge bare copper wire leads, positive and negative, for making the many necessary connections to their respective terminals on either side of the console. Undoubtedly, some of the above-mentioned tin foil eventually found its resting place across these two terminals, making a direct short circuit.

One afternoon thereafter we had an appointment to connect the organ cable to the console. The console, when not in use, was disconnected from the cable and rolled to an unfrequented corner of the Auditorium and covered with a tarpaulin for protection. My brother, Erwin responded, met the organist, connected the cable and then proceeded to the organ loft where the starting switches for the motors were located. All of a sudden a cloud of smoke issued from under the tarpaulin. He quickly pulled the starting switches open again and, on his way to the console, seized a fire extinguisher, removed the tarpaulin and movable panels on the left hand side and by careful and judicious use of the fire extinguisher put the blaze out.

This Austin console, being of the draw stop knob type, the latter being connected with a frail wood connecting trace to the rear mechanism, proved to be excellent kindling wood to start a real fire, had it not been checked immediately. There could have been serious consequences had not someone familiar with the opening of the console been on hand at the time. The console was rat-proofed thereafter, especially the openings for the expression shoes and the Crescendo Pedal, the openings through which, undoubtedly, the rodents entered the console.

INEVITABLE DEATH

In the many years that I have worked on organs I have never had an experience such as I encountered in a certain residence organ which we serviced monthly. I found several of the Oboe reeds silent, not an unusual occurrence. Usually due to some foreign matter that has dropped into the pipe, very often a large moth, a fly, or loose plaster falling from the ceiling. In this organ, however, just to prevent this possibility a light gauze was securely fastened on the tops of each resonator to intercept any matter falling into them.

In the process of removing the silent pipe to clean the reed, I noticed that the gauze on the adjoining smaller pipe was deeply depressed, as though someone had accidently or clumsily shoved his fingers into it. In lifting the dead pipe from the chest it seemed to weigh more than it should. On removing the boot I noticed that a heavy coating of verdigris had formed on the eschalot and the reed of the pipe, in fact so much that the reed could not vibrate at all. The toe of the boot was also clogged by some scum, preventing any air entering the boot. In other words, this Oboe pipe was as dead as a Dodo.

When I first entered the organ chamber I thought I

detected a strange, unpleasant odor and when I got my sensitive nose close to the opening of the silent pipe I definitely smelled a foul odor. I secured a long, thin curtain rod and used it as a ram rod to force out whatever was lodged inside of the pipe. Being prepared by this time for an unpleasant surprise and being almost overcome by the putrid odor emanating from the pipe, I placed a paper on the floor on which to discharge the contents of the pipe, whatever it might be, and to avoid handling it. With one or two rams of the rod, which I passed through the narrow end of the resonator, a cracass of a dead mouse fell out, which had been securely wedged midway in the conical resonator. The ill smelling remains of the dead mouse were hurriedly removed from the building, the resonator washed out, eschalot and reed cleaned and burnished and the pipe toe reopened. The heretofore silent Oboe that had become a death trap to an undoubtedly lively mouse, functioned again.

Observing the antics of mice in pipe organs I have noticed that they do not make a practice of climbing over the tops of metal pipes. The slick surfaces, with meager foothold, offer too little security. However the soft netting fastened over the tops of these reeds provided a neat little nest. The depression made in the top of the pipe adjoining the one in which I found the dead mouse indicated that it was used for that purpose. Evidently, from this vantage point, which was just about opposite the open tuning scroll of the next larger pipe, the mouse must have entered to explore the immediate surroundings, slipped and then become wedged in the narrow tapering section of the pipe.

I might add that this organ chamber was always kept immaculately clean and that the presence of vermin was not due to untidiness, but rather to its secluded and undisturbed privacy. The organ was, furthermore, thermostatically maintained at an even temperature, which made desirable living quarters for the little creatures.

Chapter XII

ORGAN TONE
My Views on the Much Discussed Question
of Mixture Stops and Organ Ensemble Tone

In the December 1, 1944 issue of *The Diapason* its editor, the late Mr. Gruenstein, recalls the various cycles and transitions that took place in the organ field. Among others, he refers to the period when the organ pumper was a mighty important personage, who was replaced by the present electrically-driven centrifugal blower. He witnessed the tracker and pneumatic action replaced by the electric action. He recalled when Hope Jones was at the peak of his popularity and when his revolutionary type of organ was a topic of general discussion. He remembered when the most colossal as well as the smallest pipe organs were built. He witnessed a decided change in the tonal design of the organ, followed by a revolutionary movement, or better said, a renaissance to the old traditional type of tonal design. "We saw Mixtures go and return." This latter statement struck my eye, as it has always been a moot question with me how to evaluate the Mixture stops in an organ. Are they a necessity? Are they desirable? Is an organ complete without them? Are organs that have them in abundance better organs than those in which they are but sparingly used? Who is the authority, vested with infallibility, to dictate which is right and which is wrong on this question? Is there but one inflexible rule by which to judge, or is a resonable compromise possible?

Without a doubt, the fundamental theory of a Diapason Chorus in an organ is correct. No experienced or well-versed organ builder would deny its need and the logical sequence of building the entire tonal structure on this basic element, as nature had implanted it in the formation of tone and harmony. There is, and justly so, a decided cleavage of opinion, however, as to the prominence, or the amount, of Mixture tone desirable in an organ. There are those who can conceive of no other organ nowadays than the Baroque or classic organ, with at best a feeble representation of 8' tone. But there are others of a more moderate school who realize the fundamental theory of harmonic structure and the proper sequence of building up organ tone on an 8 foot foundation. They advocate using Mixtures certainly, but conservatively, or by adding stops of a natural, rich harmonic content, less pronounced than by the direct application of Mixtures obtaining, after all, the same result, though in a modified form.

After all, I still believe that the 8' pitch should be the predominant pitch of any organ. When the Mixtures (and Mutation) stops acquire the ascendency, brilliancy and clarity is substituted for body or substance, I believe we have missed our goal of making a well voiced, balanced organ ensemble. Following a natural instinct in me, even when I was a lad and knew little about organs, I have always decidedly disliked sharp or shrill, high-pitched tones. During my apprenticeship in assisting my father tuning and repairing many makes of organs, I had an excellent opportunity to hear and judge what I thought to be the best and most pleasing sounding organs.

One of the very first organs I worked on with my father was a large three manual 64 stop German-built organ by Ibach, of Barmen, Germany, installed in St. Patrick's Church, San Francisco, in 1869. This organ had a rather large-scaled Mixture and a mounted Coronet on the Great Manual, with its Octave 4', a wood Flute, possibly a Gamba 8', 12th and 15th, etc., in addition to a loud, snarling Trumpet 8'. Its open Diapason 8', beautifully voiced, made of English block tin was, however, greatly subordinated by the Mixtures and the Cornet and the loud Trumpet. I recall I definitely and instinctively disliked the Ensemble of this organ.

Another organ that received a lot of recognition was the organ built for St. Mary's Cathedral, San Francisco, by Hook & Hastings Company of Boston, in 1890, consisting of 43 stops, 3 manuals and Pedal. This organ was also voiced and designed on the old traditional line, but also had on the Great manual a 16' and two 8' Diapasons, Octave 4', Twelfth, 2-2/3', Fifteenth 2' and a Mixture, Acuta and Quint. It also had a Cornet on the Swell manual and the usual complement of reed and flute stops. The Choir manual had a Violin Diapason 8'. The general Ensemble tone was rather brilliant, notwithstanding that the organ was voiced on the 3½" pressure. I preferred the St. Mary's Cathedral organ to the German-built organ at St. Patrick's Church, due to a more solid foundation tone of the 8' registers.

Most of the organs built during the period of 1860 to 1900, among them Johnsons, Hook-Hastings, Simmons,

Appletons, Odells, etc., were voiced on the old traditional plan, that is, with a Diapason chorus, with its corroborating Mixture and Mutation stops. In most of these organs I thought the upper work was over assertive in the full ensemble. I will admit that at the time I did not know the theoretical reason for their use. All I knew was that they did not suit my taste; they did not sound as I thought they should.

Now, possibly dislike of an overabundance of Mixture and Mutation tone was experienced by other organ builders also, as it became evident that in organs built around 1900 less tress was placed on the necessity of Mixture and Mutation stops. Hutchings, Skinner, Austin and others almost eliminated them entirely in their organs. Hope Jones decidedly rejected them.

I recall erecting a Hook & Hastings organ in the Methodist Church of Pomona, in Southern California, in 1909 and noting to my satisfaction that for once the Octave, Twelfth and Fifteenth on the Great were moderately voiced and, in fact, were of a flutey quality, which I thought blended in nicely with the Diapason and other stops of the Great. This also applied to the 2' and 4' stops on the Swell and, for once, I found an ensemble that was pleasing where all stops combined and where the high pitched pipes did not stand out or penetrate, but blended in to the general whole. I recall I was so pleased with this organ that I expressed my satisfaction in a letter to the company, believing that finally some other people had tastes similar to mine.

About 1909 I heard my first large Austin organ, which we helped install in the First Church of Christ, Scientist in San Francisco. The tone of the Austin organ was distinctive, outstanding and different from any other organ I had heard heretofore. First, it was the solidity of its tone, there was not a waver or fluctuation in the pitch. Of course, the Universal air chest with its unlimited air supply under the pipes accounted for this. Also, a decidedly higher pressure was used than ordinarily resorted to, namely 6" to 10", compared with the usual 3½" pressure. I noted its keen string tones, a superfluity of sub and super couplers, rather bright reeds, but still with body and substance, but not a Mixture or Mutation stop at all. It was a different tone. At first it seemed bold and overpowering, but in time I came to like it.

In 1909 Ernest Skinner installed a large 3 manual organ in the First Unitarian Church in San Francisco. This organ was also highly acclaimed by most organists of the City, also criticized by a few for its unique specification, especially that of the Great manual, which contained a Diapason 8', Octave 4', Philomela 8', Bourdon 16', Erzaehler 8', Gamba 8', but no reed, Mixture or Mutation stop. The full Swell furnished the brilliancy, with its full complement of chorus reeds and a moderate Mixture. The Choir contained, among other essential stops, some of Skinner's choicest reeds, a Clarinet 8', English horn 8', Orchestral Oboe 8' and a Vox Humana 8'. Yet the ensemble of this organ if excellent, well balanced, pleasing in all respects, and is one of my favorite organs.

Another excellent organ of this type, built by the Hutchings Company, is installed in the First Presbyterian Church, San Francisco. Its general ensemble is more brilliant and richer than the organ of the Unitarian Church. It has, however, only one Mixture or Cornet on the Swell manual. The Hook & Hastings organ of Old St. Mary's Church, consisting of 43 stops, has always been one of my favorites for quality of tone, build up and full ensemble. Voiced only on 3½" wind, with only a Cornet in the Swell and a moderate 8' Trumpet on the Great, its ensemble tone is perfect. St. Markus organ, consisting of 21 stops, the organ built by my father, was also a good example of a well balanced organ, with the exception that the free reed Trumpet of the Great had brass resonators. If these were replaced with reeds of modern design, of the striking reed variety, even possibly retaining the brass resonators, I believe its ensemble would be ideal. Incidentally, my father installed in this organ a three rank Mixture on the Great manual of copious scale obtained from Toepfers Organ Book. It completed the Diapason chorus, or harmonic structure perfectly, however, still a little too pronounced on the brilliant side for my liking. In fact, one could almost dispense with the Trumpet on the Great when the Mixture was drawn.

In 1912 or thereabout, Hope-Jones installed a large three manual organ of 30 stops in St. Luke's Episcopal Church, San

Francisco. It was the talk of the town, as Hope Jones had at this time about reached the zenith of his popularity. All bowed before him, as it were. His ideas of tonal structure, though revolutionary, were supposed to be correct because Hope-Jones, the oracle, so ordained. On hearing the organ for the first time, I was amazed at its volume of tone, its pervading fullness, its reeds, round and resonant, that seemed to completely fill the entire church. Its keen strings narrow scaled and biting, its Chimney flutes and Quintedenas with pronounced harmonic content, Diapasons full and sonorous, round full toned Flutes, and yet, with all these extremes the tone seemed to combine and one could not say that the full ensemble was not pleasing. With all this volume from large and narrow scaled pipes, on pressures from 10" to 25", but with Swell chambers and blinds that could effectually control and balance the tone, the general effect was surpisingly good. Yet there is not a Mixture or Mutation stop in the while organ. This organ, at that particular time, was hailed by the elite of the organ fraternity as the organ of the future.

All the pipe organs hereabouts built by Thomas Whalley, although none of large content, have, in my estimation, well balanced, yet rich and vibrant organ tone. The Murray M. Harris organs of Sherith Israel, San Francisco, Stanford University, Palo Alto, California (as originally built), the original Calvary Presbyterian and Holy Cross Church of San Francisco suited my ideal of full organ tone. The large Austin organ of 114 stops at the Civic Auditorium in San Francisco, after being revoiced under the supervision of Edwin Lemare is, according to my view, a well balanced organ.

Having mentioned some of my favorite-toned organs, I will also mention some of those to which I cannot give my whole-hearted approval, of course basing my criticism solely on the full ensemble tone. The Skinner organ of Trinity Episcopal Church, San Francisco, I consider over-brilliant and rich. The Austin organs at St. Paul's Episcopal Church and the Unitarian Church, Oakland are, in my estimation, entirely out of balance. Grace Cathedral's Aeolian Skinner organ, San Francisco, well supplied with many Mixtures and corroborating stops, is sparkling and brilliant in its ensemble, due undoubtedly to the huge size of the building, is agreeable but verges on the border line of over-sufficiency in the upper harmonic work. The Temple Emanuel Skinner organ, in San Francisco, was also originally on the brilliant side in its Ensemble. But since the accoustical treatment of its interior vaulted dome and walls was applied and the organ's resonance over subdued, this brilliancy has again been restored by adding several new Mutation stops and a more assertive Trumpet 8' to is specification. The large Skinner organ at the California Palace of the Legion of Honor, San Francisco, is one organ, on the other hand, predominantly of the 8' pitch and due possibly to location, is urgently in need of brightening up in general. Here is a patient in which an injection of the Mixture and Mutation virus would put new life and virility into its murky veins.

Having divested myself of my likes and dislikes of full organ tone or Ensemble, from which standpoint after all we judge or condemn most organs, regardless of their many other fine total points and qualifications, and having mentioned specific instruments as illustrations, I now want to state that if I had the opportunity to build a large three manual organ according to my tastes and ideals, my dream organ would contain the following specifications: I certainly would follow the traditional type of organ, but would keep the *upper partial work subordinate to the 8' pitch* by all means, and not follow the procedure as seems evident in most of the larger instruments of recent vintage. The Diapason chorus, and some Flutes would be voiced on the light pressure of 3½" wind. The Great manual would have a complete Diapason chorus of 16'-8'-4', 12th and 15th, and a well selected Mixture of three or four ranks to carry on, build up and corroborate with the 8' Diapason tone. Strings and reeds I would voice on somewhat higher pressures.

The Swell manual, aside from the usual solo and accompanying stops, would also contain an 8' Diapason Chorus of a lighter intensity than that of the Great manual. It would further contain the customary reed chorus, full and brilliant, yet pleasing, and subordinate to the while, with its Cornet or Mixture. The Choir would also have a Diapason 8' and its soft accompanying and orchestral stops. The Pedal, of various pitches, would be commensurate with the rest of the organ, but not tubby or cloudy. We would avoid the use of snarling, nasal, penetrating 4' reeds, as also high pitched 2' string tones. (We readily admit that the use of these exotic tone qualities used in conjunction with suitable Flute stops can produce quaint, piquant orchestral effects, but we doubt if they add to a majestic, impressive and inspiring organ tone or ensemble). Reed tones should be characteristic of the instruments they represent, but that should not exempt them from also having body and substance to blend with all the flue stops.

If the full ensemble builds up evenly and gradually to a beautiful, rich and majestic climax, there is no question but that its individual stops will all be tinged with the same blessed attribute of being pleasing and agreeable components of the whole, resulting in a well balanced, harmonious ensemble, unlike some of our more recent instruments which have such a flare for brilliancy and clarity that the fundamental 8' organ tone is submerged entirely.

I might recall an experience I had while seated in the center of the Civic Auditorium on the occasion of one of the National Conventions of the American Guild of Organists, held in San Francisco, when Virgil Fox was performing at the console in one of his inspiring and dramatic Organ Recitals. I tried to determine if I could distinguish what quality of organ tone was most predominant, whether it was Diapason foundation and flue tone, Mutation, Mixture, or Reed tone. I was made aware that this was impossible, as none of the above seemed to predominate, but blended all into a harmonious whole of typical organ tone which only the King of Instruments, the pipe organ, can produce. When any one type of tone is predominent and heard for a long duration, as is the case at many organ recitals, it is not surprising that it becomes boring and monotonous to many an audience who, with a sigh of relief, if probably only in thought, are inclined to say thank God it is over, instead of regretting its termination. If the tone of a pipe organ blends harmoniously and is well balanced, there is no instrument or combination of instruments, as Brass Bands or Symphony Orchestras, that can produce the sustained tone, the great range of pitch and volume of majestic tone as the ensemble of a well balanced pipe organ.

I recall the occasion of the visit of *Karg Ellert,* who was on a tour of America in 1931. While preparing for his recital at St. Dominic's Church, I interviewed him regarding the specifications, tone and ensemble of the German organs. I expressed to him my regret that at that time I had not yet been to Europe to see and hear some of their large Cathedral organs, and stated that judging from their specifications, with their abundance of Mixture and Mutation work, the organs must sound shrill and piercing. He, however, said such was not the case, that they were proportionately balanced, pleasing to listen to, that their tones were as clear and harmonious and blending as the tones of a large bell. Since then I had the privilege of visiting Europe, especially Germany, twice, and must conclude that my preference still holds good for the typical American built organ, as designed by the late Ernest M. Skinner, and other of his time, in preference to the European, Baroque or Classical organ, lacking sufficient foundation tone.

I thought that the bell analogy, however, was a well balanced ensemble tone for a pipe organ. Shortly thereafter, while tuning the organ at St. Mary's Cathedral, the Angelus bell rang in the tower. Karg Ellert's analogy of the bell and the organ tone came to my mind. My natural impulse was to try to find what the ground tone note of the bell was and try to locate it on the keyboard. I was bewildered in not being able to readily determine the ground tone. Being rather close to the bell, the many harmonics and upper partials were rich and pronounced, and each key I touched seemed to harmonize and was present in that glorious harmonic ensemble, yet it evidently had a fundamental or ground tone. From a more distant location possibly it would have been easier to detect it. However, it proved that nature's own admixture of harmonics and corroborating tones is generous, but yet proportionately balanced and blended. However, if our advocates of the Baroque organ with their superabundant Mixtures had their way, they would undoubtedly also advocate the adding of additional bells to ring with the master bell simultaneously, akin to the Mixture stops in the organ, say at the fourth or fifth interval to bolster up or improve the already perfect tone of the master bell, nature's own product. I believe the over-emphasis of Mixture tone in an organ ensemble can be likened to gilding the lily.

In tuning a certain Aeolian residence organ, I noticed it had a five-rank String Mixture. Playing the stop singularly it was of pleasing quality and strength. The varying harmonic intervals could be readily discerned. In drawing the stop in conjunction with a group of other stops, mostly 8' and 4' pitches, the Mixture stop tone seemed inaudible and to disappear. We know the latter not to be a fact. The pipes were still sounding but were blending into a homogeneous whole. The same experiment I noted on an Ernest Skinner organ with a Mixture on the Swell manual. Singly used, it certainly was plainly audible, but drawing the stop on against the full Swell it appeared as though no additional sound was forthcoming. I believe this is as it should be, "small children should be seen but not heard." Our augmented harmonic or corroborating stops, should and must be utilized to produce a rich tone, but in proportion or balance to the other 8' pitched stops in the organ.

My favorite way of describing my taste for Mixture tone, is to compare it with the preparation of food. If insufficient seasoning is applied, the food is flat, tasteless and uninviting. If too much is applied, it is equally unpalatable. If applied in proper proportion, not enough to repel and not so little as to be missed, we pronounce the dish well seasoned. This would be my guide also in judging the proper or improper amount of Mixture ingredients to be used in the dish I am serving — "Pipe organ ensemble tone."

Chapter XIII

EPISODES HERE AND THERE

In My Career as an Organ Builder

IF AT FIRST YOU DON'T SUCCEED
TRY, TRY, AGAIN

This is an occurrence that will indicate that we are always under the guidance and direction of a Higher Power, which invariably results to our good if we follow the promptings of the inner voice. In one of the larger cities of California where we make our quarterly visits, it happened that there were three buildings adjoining one another, each having a pipe organ. We installed two of them and practically completed the installation of the third and had the regular maintenance of all three. After some years, with the approach of the lean, depression years, regular care on one of them was discontinued. Finally, the second church, thinking they could make a better bargain, secured the services of another concern, so only the one institution between the two others, retained our regular quarterly service.

One day while at work tuning the organ there, it being the noon hour, the sexton told us he was going home for the day and asked us to be kind enough to see to it that the door was locked, that the lights were out and that everything was in shipshape condition before we left. This we promised him we would do. Meanwhile I was waiting for my helper who had gone to lunch, therefore, I did not lock the front door immediately, but left it open for him to enter. No sooner had the janitor left than a young lady entered the place unannounced, and acting as though she were quite at home, seated herself at the piano on the stage and began to practice. Since I could not proceed with my art of tuning the organ without my helper anyway I let her continue her playing and finally she left. Immediately I locked the door behind her. At last my helper came and I opened the door for him. It has been a rule of mine when working in a building, institution, or home, to refrain from answering the telephone or responding to anyone knocking at the door or ringing the door bell.

I then proceeded with the tuning of the organ where I had left off at noon. I had scarcely begun work when I heard a heavy pounding on the rear alley door, near where the organ was located. My helper at the console, hearing the commotion, thought I was causing it, but I told him it was some stranger at the door and I did not care who it was or what he wanted, I was not going to open the door. The caller, however, persisted and increased his knocking, making it louder by using some heavy tool on the door to make himself heard. His persistence and determination finally made me go to the door, as I could not make progress with my work anyway, to see who it was and what he so urgently wanted.

It was the sexton of the church next door, a stranger to me, with a monkey wrench in his hand, which he had used to good advantage on the metal door to attract my attention. He excitedly told me that the janitor of the place where I was working had phoned him to call me and to let me know that he had accidentally left the gas flame burning in the kitchen stove in the basement, and he was afraid it might cause a fire, and asked if we would please put it out. Thereupon, we both went to the kitchen and, on approaching it, smelled hot iron and gas fumes. A large kettle had been left on the gas stove and the water had evaporated. Had it been left over the open flame long enough a hole would have been burnt through the kettle and possibly caused further damage as nearby some newspapers were lying on the surface of the stove.

Had I not followed the voice within me to open the door, despite my determination not to do so, undoubtedly a conflagration would have ensued. This little episode gave me the opportunity to get further acquainted with the sexton of the church next door, the organ of which we had formerly serviced, and the information I received from him gave me every indication that before long we would again be called to service that organ. Evidently the connection they had made after discontinuing our service proved to be unsatisfactory.

A NOCTURNAL VISITOR

An amusing incident, not directly connected with churches or organ tuners, occurred to one of my elder sons, Bertram. It was the second night of his wedded life in his new apartment in Sacramento, when his wife was suddenly awakened from a sound sleep by hearing him shout frantically "I got a bird"; "I got a bird." Assuming his disturbance was possibly the aftermath of a rather late and hearty supper, she tried to arouse him from his sleep to interrupt the dream that was troubling him. He insisted, however, he had a bird in his hand and was not dreaming. His frightened wife then turned on the light. My son had definitely awakened by then and they saw that he was holding in his clenched fist a live bat, twitching and biting and trying to escape.

The young wife was horror stricken, having heard of bats getting into women's hair, but this bat must have hovered very close to her husband's head. Unconsciously, in his sleep he must have been annoyed by the bat, and caught it literally on the fly. While tuning organs I have seen bats flying in dark churches, but this was the first time I had heard of bats in a bridal chamber.

There might be some significance connected with this bat story and this young couple. Bertram was very fond of the violin and played remarkably well, considering the few lessons he had. He belonged to two amateur orchestras and enjoyed playing his favorite, the overture to "Die Fledermaus", (The Bat), with them. It was at one of these orchestras' rehearsals that he became acquainted with his bride, who is a very proficient violinist. No doubt in the future whenever they may be playing the "Fledermaus" overture they will recall the incident of their nocturnal visitor in their bridal chamber.

EFFICACY OF PRAYER

Christmas Eve had always been a happy, eventful time in my life. The eve before Christmas, with that indescribable joy, a reminder of innocent, happy childhood days, with that spirit of good will and peace to all permeating as it were the very atmosphere we breathe. Fortunate indeed is the individual, who, on this evening, can gather around the fireside with his family and friends, or enjoy the hospitality of others. Peculiar to the organ tuner's life, Christmas Eve and the day before Easter are the busiest times of the year. The church pipe organ comes into its own on these holidays.

Every organist and choir director wants his pipe organ in good tune and working order.

One year, on the eve before Christmas, I had several jobs in the East Bay cities assigned to me for servicing. The last one on my list was the two manual Kimball organ at St. John's Presbyterian Church on College Avenue in Berkeley. Naturally, being anxious to be home at a reasonable hour on this evening for our traditional Christmas Eve celebration, especially for the sake of my children, we lingered none too long, yet realized the importance of having everything on the organ in shipshape condition for the Christmas services. After tuning, I checked over all the mechanism, finally trying the combination pistons. There was an adjusting device for setting the stops on the desired piston. This in some way had jammed, with the result that the draw stop knobs were rigid and would go neither on or off — a fine situation for an organ to be in the night before Christmas.

A hasty scrutiny of the situation, with the hope that it was only a temporary disarrangement that could be readily adjusted, proved not to be the case. Serious and persistent study of the mechanism, in the hope that I might lay my finger on the sore spot, also proved unavailing. Meanwhile, the desire to be at home with the family was growing more persistent. Noticing that I was not solving the mystery that was perplexing me, but rather was getting more bewildered than ever, my youthful helper, Frankie Fassler, conceived a bright idea. He was as anxious as I was to get to his home and, as he could offer me no technical advice that would help solve the difficulty he, in his boyish simplicity, said, "I will say a prayer to the Christ Child that you locate the trouble and correct it." It seemed no sooner said than done. To my surprise I found some other valves in the lower part of the console near the floor, unobserved until then, one of which was stuck tight and which had caused the whole combination action to become inoperative. With a few adjustments, quickly made, the organ was again functioning perfectly and we were soon on our way home to celebrate Christmas Eve.

MY ELDEST SON – LAWRENCE

It has been the custom, more so in former years than in our present age, that the eldest son of the family follows in his father's footsteps. It was so in our family, where not only the eldest son, but several of the younger brothers took up our father's profession. Now my own son, Lawrence, was following suit. I observed early in him a decided interest in the organ. This pleased me greatly, and especially my aged father, who was delighted to know that his grandson, one of the fourth generation bearing his name, would carry on and so gave him every encouragement in his power.

After graduating from the Lick-Wilmerding School, where he was especially interested in physics and acoustical phenomena, he entered our employ — although during his school years he had already helped whenever he had free time.

When he was 21 in 1936, he conceived the idea of building a small pipe organ. The fascination of this venture took complete hold of him, and developed into an ambitious hope to build a permanent 2 manual electric-pneumatic action pipe organ for our home. I gave him my blessing and every encouragement, but decided that it should be his own individual handiwork and the child of his own brain. In many items we did not agree, especially in the conventional design of the console, the pedal keyboard without an exterior framework, the type of coupler contacts used, etc. He planned the organ to be placed in a small room alongside the garage in the basement below. The console was to be placed in the bay window in the living room above, and the blower in the basement below. The tone of the organ was to come through a grill in the ceiling of the basement, into the living room above. To his credit, I must say he worked every spare moment at his disposal, on holidays and often late at night, on his pet hobby, his pipe organ.

Soon things began to take shape, and a motor blower and generator were acquired. At another time used pipes were procured at a reasonable price but in great effort in hauling them over a distance of 150 miles. The bass and larger wood pipes were made by him. Other necessary material was purchased from time to time, and every bit used in the organ was paid for by him personally, giving him that sense of ownership one appreciates when working and paying for things one's self. The exterior finish of the walnut console was done by his brother Bertram, a painter and decorator by trade. It was sprayed with a lacquer finish and rubbed down.

Finally, the organ was completed and was played upon by many, who seemed to enjoy it. The fine appearance of the console, and the novelty of the organ tone apparently coming from nowhere, if its location had not previously been disclosed, intrigued everyone and earned the young builder deserved praise and commendation. Tonally the organ was pleasing and of just sufficient volume for a moderate sized living room.

The organ was voiced on 4½" pressure. One of the sets, the Violin 8, was not the customary metal stop, but was made of wood, still preserving a keen string tone with more body than the ordinary string tone has. The original set began at tenor C 4' pitch. This stop Lawrence extended down an octave to CC 8' pitch. He made and voiced these pipes himself, a most difficult tone and character to carry down. No better string-toned Cello effect could be obtained. He also made the lowest octave of the Pedal Bourdon, which proved very satisfactory.

After the organ had been installed about a year and his great ambition to build an organ had been achieved, I noticed his interest was gradually being directed to other channels. In the spring of life, a man's thoughts usually drift to the romantic and he lives in a land of dreams and expectancy. My son was no exception, visions of his own home were in his mind. The organ he had built would probably some day fittingly adorn this home of his, or perhaps the disposal of it would help to feather his nest.

About this time a committee from the Redeemer Lutheran Church down the peninsula visited our factory to see about the purchase of a small pipe organ. The committee was undecided as to whether they should buy an electronic or a genuine pipe organ. We showed them a small pipe organ, electric pneumatic action, of three units that we had available at our factory, but apparently it was too small and the cost more than they cared to pay. As they were about to leave, and feeling certain that we were going to lose them as a customer, I mentioned that my son had built an organ for our home, which he might be interested in selling and asked them if they would care to hear and see it. They accepted my invitation and I took them to my home. The organ made an immediate and favorable impression. A set of chimes that my son had also made appealed to them strongly as that was something they also wanted. The full power of the organ was listened to from the living room as well as from the garage, and it satisfied all their expectations. A deal was made, the organ purchased and we installed it in the church. Some very fortunate circumstances favored the installation throughout. The organ could not have fitted more perfectly into the space already provided if it had been specially built for it. The color of the console exterior could not have been a better match with the interior finish of the woodwork of the church. I might say here that the organ sounded decidedly better in the church than it had in our home. A larger opening was made and a new set of expression shades was installed.

Installation progressed satisfactorily and the opening date was set for Thanksgiving Day, November 24, 1939. Harold Mueller of St. Luke's Episcopal Church, San Francisco, was organist for the dedication service. One thing the pastor insisted on when making the arrangements for the purchase of the organ that it should not cipher, as that was the strong point made by the advocates of the electronic organ, i.e., that the usual type of electric-pneumatic organ frequently ciphered and caused trouble, whereas the electronic organ could not go wrong. With this request, or demand, ringing in our ears, the word "cipher" was anathema to us. I assisted my son with the installation of the organ as the time set for the dedication was coming close and I felt a personal responsibility in the matter after recommending its purchase. During its installation a few ciphers developed, which is no uncommon occurrence in any new organ.

The day of the dedication went off without mishap. However, we noticed that the more the organ was played the more tendency developed for notes to hang on. This struck us as unusual, as seldom had a cipher occurred while it was in our home. We looked, without success, for springs on the pneumatic that were weak, or valves which did not seat properly. The trouble seemed to become aggravated. We feared what would happen if the organ should cipher on the following Sunday, what the defeated advocates of the electronic organ would have to say if the organ should squeal continuously and disrupt the service, and what others would say of buying an organ made by an inexperienced youth. I admit that the thought of this happening made my head swim. My son worked away feverishly and tried to reassure me, for I could find no reason why the organ should act up as it did. It was apparently designed and built properly. Much less could I suggest a remedy to correct the trouble.

I admitted defeat and, in my own insufficiency, resorted to divine help in prayer. I said a fervent prayer to the Mother of God to help me in this dilemma, as she had often done before. I was at the console at the time, my son inside of the organ. On the left side of the console was a small hinged panel behind which was the starting switch for the motor, and a meter indicating the voltage of the generator. I recalled my son stating that while the organ was erected in our home it operated on about 9 or 10 volts — here I observed the volt meter indicated over 12 volts. At once I realized the cause of our trouble. The magnets were being overcharged, causing the armatures to cling to them because of residual magnetism. The more the organ was played, the more they were getting saturated. I immediately informed my son of this, to his great relief and mental comfort. I, in turn, said a devout "thank you" to Mary, "The Helper of the Afflicted." The generator speed was reduced, bringing the voltage to its proper point, the polarity changed and, as if by magic, our nightmare was over. Prayer was efficacious.

In 1952 the Redeemer Lutheran congregation moved to their new Church in Redwood City, for which our firm built a larger organ. The former Church edifice, including the pipe organ, was taken over by the Mission Covenant Church.

THE PRAYERS OF AN OLD NUN

I was called at one time to tune and repair a large reed

organ in the Catholic Church at Rio Vista, a town up along the Sacramento River. What it required most was replacing of the moth-eaten felt between the leather and the long stop ventils controlling the stops. It was quite a job and necessitated my remaining for two nights in the hotel. On the last day, just as I was about completing the work, the pastor asked me if I would be so kind as to look at a reed organ in the chapel of the Sisters' Convent nearby. As I recall, connections with the main line of the Sacramento Northern Electric Railway were not too frequent in those days. A small bus met the trains and brought the passengers to Rio Vista. It was late in the afternoon when I called at the convent, and I was anxious to get home.

On examining the organ I found that a note was continuously sounding. To correct this properly I knew it meant taking the organ apart, although there are expedients that can at times be resorted to temporarily to correct this trouble. Being short of time and very anxious to make connection with the next train, which would be the last one that day, I debated with myself whether I sould do a thorough job or an emergency operation only. An old nun who evidently played the organ, was with me and urged me to do a complete job while I was there. I finally agreed to do so. The old nun remained with me to give me any assistance she could.

Never before did I make my hands work more swiftly, or make every move count to save precious moments. It was a rather large reed organ and, as it seems there are no two alike, I had also to use my head as well as my hands. The old nun, seeing that she was getting into my way and that she could not be of much assistance, finally sat down and, taking out her rosary, began to say her beads, saying: "I see I can't help you, but I will pray that you have success."

When I finally got to the inside of the organ I found a piece of dirt on the valve. I removed this and hurriedly began to reassemble the organ. Meanwhile, the Sister had an automobile waiting for me at the front entrance to whisk me off to the station.

The ride to Rio Vista Junction was made at breakneck speed. We arrived at the Junction just as the headlight of the approaching train loomed up a short distance from the station. It was a record job done in record time. I am sure I would not have been sitting comfortable in the train on my way home that night if the good nun had not assisted me with her prayers, while I was doing the work.

PROFANITY AND IRREVERENCE
IN THE HOUSE OF GOD

"Patience is a Virtue" is a trite saying with which we are all familiar, but it is only when we are called upon to practice it that we come to realize its full import, and often find that in addition to being a virtue, it can also be a blessing. If there is any profession that calls for a generous amount of patience, it is certainly the organ builder's profession, or rather, the organ tuner's and maintenance man's work. The following story, having a bearing on this subject, was told me by a Mr. John W. Whitely, an English voicer, years ago. Mr. Whitely was then in the employ of the Murray M. Harris Organ Company and was revoicing the organ in the residence of Charles E. Green in San Mateo. I was assisting him in holding the keys and in tuning and tone regulating the pipes as directed by him.

The story, as he related it to me, was about an organ tuner who was engaged in tuning some large cathedral organ in England. This man was rather erratic and hot tempered by nature, and evidently, in pursuing his vocation as organ tuner, this natural disposition was intensified. His vocabulary was not always the most refined. However, working in churches and sacred edifices, he realized his obligation to be at all times respectful and reverent. This he tried to be, but realizing his human weakness for a ready use of profanity and cuss words, he admonished his boy helper before entering the organ that should he get ill-tempered while at work and resort to his usual habit of cursing and swearing and, should the boy see the parson approaching, he should give him a signal by tapping a few of the highest treble notes as a warning for him to desist.

The work started out satisfactorily and agreeably; tuner

and helper were understanding one another. Finally, however, some recalcitrant pipe needed special attention. The go
back signal was given, then again, next, next, etc., try it
again, etc. The boy helper at the keyboard, becoming
confused, could not distinguish the tuner's shouts or demands, the tuner could not hear the apologies of the boy.
The tuner shouted back, louder and louder became the
barrage of shouting, sparks began to fly, profanity filled the
air. At this stage the parson entered the church. The boy
remembered his instructions to signal the master up in the
organ by tapping the highest treble notes. This he did
repeatedly, only aggravating still more the irate tuner up
among the pipes, who further increased his brand of
profanity to the breaking point. Forgetting his instructions
entirely he rushed down to the frightened lad at the console
to see why the orderly progress of their work was being
interruped, when, of course, he suddenly encountered the
indignant parson. Apologies were made, but as the story
went, word was left at the organ factory never to send that
man again.

HEEDING THE INNER VOICE

Working frequently in Catholic churches, and being a
Catholic myself and aware of the Divine Presence in the
tabernacle, when entering a church and finding it vacant, not
a human soul present, the small flickering sanctuary lamp
apparently the only sentinel on watch, my thoughts would
turn in reverence and love to the hidden Lord. On such
occasions I have thought myself privileged, as an organ tuner,
to be the only visitor to the King of Kings in the tabernacle,
and as a token of oblation I would offer up to the greater
honor and glory of God all the crosses and burdens of the
day, all the aggravations and irritations that would beset me
in tuning and repairing the organs, acknowledging the futility
of my own frail efforts without His Divine assistance.

This assistance from above has helped me often to
overcome spells of temper and impatience. In many instances, though the happening may have been trivial, I have

certainly felt that the hand of providence was guiding me. One time I left one of my tools behind on a job. It was only a tool, and we could have picked it up at some other time. However, a voice within me kept urging me to go back right then and get it, or I might forget where I had left it. I did so at some inconvenience. On entering the organ, I found the tool, but also became aware of the fact that I had left the motor running, and oversight that could have had serious consequences.

On another occasion, after closing up the organ I noticed that I had left a light burning in the Swell box. In this particular organ the lights were not controlled by a master switch, but each light had to be turned out by hand. In another case, checking my irritation at being obliged to retrace my steps and unlock doors again to turn off the light, I found on entering the swell box a number of tools that I had left on the walkboard.

Possibly you may say rewards for good deeds done on earth may be expected in the life to come. I firmly believe I have had some rewards already here on earth.

MAN PROPOSES BUT GOD DISPOSES

I remember an incident that occurred while working with my father shortly before the fire. He had sold an old tracker action organ to another church and agreed in its new installation and modernization to put in a new pneumatic action. Although he had successfully made several before, and also had a patent on an action he had invented, he nevertheless allowed himself to be persuaded by another party, who was supposed to have considerable experience in modern organ construction, to use a different type of action than he favored.

All plans were drawn and apparently worked fine on paper. The workmanship was excellently done, but when the air was put on and the organ was to function, due to an error in design, the Swell to Great coupler would not work. Needless to say, my father was embarrassed and humiliated. He had never, he said, gone through such an ordeal, such a feeling of embarrassment and mortification in trying to explain why the coupler would not function. I believe a mechanical coupler was finally resorted to, as a temporary expedient.

I remember in this dilemma I also resorted to prayer, as the matter involved not only the mechanical aspect of the organ, but a strained relationship between my father and the party whose advice he followed whose design failed to function properly. I wondered what the final outcome of the situation would be. I was not kept long in suspense.

The fire and earthquake of April 18. 1906 came along and totally destroyed the church and the organ included. After all, it was only a small material matter that caused so much mental anguish and strained friendly relations. Divine Providence, however, chose His own methods and His own time to efface a disagreeable situation.

NEVER TOO OLD TO LEARN

While we were at work on a reed organ owned by Mr. Allen Taylor, he arrived home and with the great interest watched us reassemble the organ. Noting how many parts there were in an organ he jokingly remarked to his wife, "Wouldn't it be funny if the organ man, like the doctor, were to sew up a sponge or something in the patient's stomach." The organ was unusually intricate and required care and caution to get everything back in proper sequence and into its right location.

Finally everything was in place and we screwed on the cover, panels, etc. In gathering up the tools I missed a long, slim screwdriver which I definitely recalled I had shortly before been using. My son Vincent, as well as Mr. and Mrs. Taylor, looked everywhere for it. Finally I gave it up as lost. While I was putting away the balance of my tools Mr. Taylor sat down to try the organ and give it is final approval. After playing a bit, he drew on the Great to Pedal coupler and a discordant shriek marred the beautiful harmony he was producing. Several notes kept ciphering. Something was decidely wrong. Whatever it was it had to be corrected, so out came the tools again, and the panels reopened. My son then looked at me and said, "Dad, could it be the lost screwdriver?" On removing the lids he reached into a space where I had previously worked and, sure enought, there it was.

On informing Mr. Taylor that we had found the screwdriver and that it was actually in the inards of the organ, I realized the laugh was on me.

WAITING AT THE DOOR

In the early part of 1943 we built a small chapel organ for the Jesuit Sacred Heart Novitiate at Los Gatos. Several months later we were called to make some extensive repairs and adjustments on the Aeolian pipe organ in the country home of Mr. Stanley Page, in the foothills of Los Gatos. There was considerable work to be done and it took longer than we anticipated. My son, Lawrence, and I set out to do this work and we took my son's wife and child along on this little trip. Mr. Page kindly put at our disposal a guest cottage out in his orchard for our temporary domicile. We found the outdoor life, the fragrant country air, the birds, the unsurpassed scenery, a great boon and delight.

Sunday came along, so we all attended mass at the Catholic church in Los Gatos. Having my son's car with us, after services we thought it would be nice to take a little ride to see the town. I suggested a trip up the hillside to the Sacred Heart Novitiate where I had recently installed the new organ. The suggestion was readily accepted as both my son and daughter-in-law had never been there.

In climbing the wooded hillside and on coming in sight of the vineyard adorning the property behind the monastery, I first gave the thought consideration that perhaps the hour was inopportune to go visitng, especially when calling unannounced. I had particularly in mind to call on Father Reinhold Doerge', S.J., Minister of the Novitiate, with whom I had become quite friendly while installing the organ.

We soon arrived at the portals of the Novitiate, alighted, and went up the front stairs and were about to ring the front doorbell when I noticed a sign above the bell stating, "Visiting hours between 2 and 4 p.m. only." As it was close to the noon hour for one thing, I hesitated to ring the bell, but after reading the sign I was doubly doubtful and turned to my son and his wife to ask their opinion. While standing there debating, I heard footsteps approaching the front door. Soon it opened and the very party I hoped to see welcomed us in graciously, without our even ringing the bell. I asked him how he knew we were there. A knowing smile was his only answer.

My son and I, with Father Doerge', visited the chapel and tried out the organ we had recently installed. After a little walk through the grounds and a pleasant leave taking, we again entered our car for the return trip to our guest house at Stanley Page's home at Los Gatos.

EDWARD GREGORY — MY YOUNGEST SON

As in all families, so also in my own family, there is a last arrival. In my case it was the ninth child, a boy, whom we named Edward Gregory. A fine lad he was, and judging from very noticeable traits, it would not have surprised me if one day he also followed the organ profession as his vocation and worked with his elder brother, Lawrence. At an early age he showed great aptitude for drawing and sketching; he is fond of music and likes to sing, and is naturally interested in my work.

To satisfy his frequent pleadings to take him along to a job some day, I took the opportunity that presented itself one Sunday afternoon, when I had to make an emergency call at the University Christian Church in Berkeley, and took him with me. The ride across the Bay over the new San Francisco-Oakland Bridge was in itself a treat for the youngster, then only 8 years old. To help me and to get his first glimpse inside of an organ, to let him tune a pipe or two, added further to his enjoyment and pleasure. It also afforded him the privilege of writing his name on the wall inside of the organ chamber alongside others who apparently wanted their names to be remembered.

Edward Gregory has since grown to maturity. He is now married and making his mark, not in the organ profession, but as a Draftsman and Designer. He graduated from the Lick-Wilmerding School, spent some time at City College in San Francisco, and graduated from Chico State College, where he taught architectural drawing, drafting, and designing on a part-time basis. He also established himself in business, catering to architectural designing, drafting and its kindred branches. He has since earned his M.A. Degree and taught in the Bakersfield, California, Junior College, and more recently accepted a teaching position in the San Mateo Junior College. His love and interest in the pipe organ, its construction and maintenance is still keen and deeply rooted.

DO YOU BELIEVE IN SIGNS?

In the course of our work, humorous and ridiculous notes are often left for us at the consoles, specifying adjustments to be made to the organs, or notes written on the walls of the choir lofts. One left on the console of the Bohemian Grove organ at Monte Rio read as follows:

"Felix F. Schoenstein & Sons, any or all of them; the C# on the Pedal is stuck. I put a broom in the pipe and cut off the primary valve in the Chest with a screw. Will see you as soon as the rehearsal is over, about 1:15 p.m. Am going down (to the City) right after the play. Will try to thumb a ride for you, too."

I recall another incident related by one of our employees servicing an organ. He had a few spare moments on his hands and jokingly wrote on the lid of a Vox Humana box that had to be lifted each time the pipes were tuned: "Do not open until after Christmas."

In another organ where all tuners during the years had written their names with given dates on a nearby wall, one concluded the list by adding the phrase: "Poor boys."

Still another church, where the pastor seemed to be rather cantankerous and fussy about the upkeep of the edifice, the walls were adorned with numerous "don't" signs. A few of them read as follows: "Don't lean against the walls",

evidently meant for the sheiks with their slick, greased hair.
Another: "Do not throw rice on the church property." Also:
"Be sure to turn off the motor." In the pathway alongside
the church, "No bicycles permitted" and another one "None
but choir members allowed." He certainly believed in signs.

In a rather secluded corner of a certain organ loft were
printed on the walls the following admonitions — "This is the
house of God" — "The Master is here." Some other
significant mottos listed in a choir loft were: "Vocal prayer is
the highest form of prayer, Sung prayer is twice prayed."
One evidently to check those undoubtedly too glib with their
tongues, "The choir loft is still part of the church. In church
we worship, not whisper."

One of my nephews, who was in our employ for some
time, also left his name inscribed on a wall, but due evidently
to the length of his name (eleven letters), he abbreviated it as
follows: Bob Sch. etc. 3/10/50.

At St. Peter and Paul Church, after crawling into a tight
corner to make some adjustments which required much
agility, I found written on a wall before me — "He was a
brave man." And, as usual, "Kilroy was here." An item, one
of many complaints, on an organist trouble sheet — "B flat
speaks silently."

Organ Tuner — "C below middle C doesn't sound in either
Bourdon or Open Diapason in the feet."

THE INDISPENSABLE MAN

"Cleanliness is next to Godliness". Especially should this
be so in the house of God, and I wish here to put in a good
word for the "Indispensable Man", the church sexton. In past
years there seemed to be no particular difficulty in securing
reliable and efficient sextons. We have met many of them in
the churches we visit who have given long years of faithful
service, some of them with proud records of over forty years.
Uniformly the churches and institutions with this sort of
dependable and conscientious help reflected the good work
that was being done. Everything was in its place and work
was done on a schedule. More often than not we found the

sexton at work when we made our regular visits.

But how this situation has changed since World War II, with the scarcity of manpower and the ever-increasing rise in salaries. Now, one seldom comes across a regularly appointed sexton. All sorts of makeshift help have been resorted to. High school boys working part-time and in some cases women, but more often than not there is no one about to do the work regularly. Even high dignitaries have been helping out by locking the church doors at night, and in some places I have seen the clergy sweeping the sidewalk in front of the church to tidy things up a bit before a funeral or wedding took place. The organ lofts, I have noted, have been especially neglected for long periods, as though they were not a part of the church, and the situation is not improved by the carelessness and untidyness of choir members in throwing papers and rubbish on the choir floors. Accumulations of discarded and unused materials take the shortest route into some corner, closet or basement.

Let us hope that when normal times return again, the loyal, dependable sexton will also again be with us. Possibly a living wage and proper recognition of his worth will bring about this much-to-be-desired consummation more readily.

Some of the Sextons I have known and deem to be deserving of special mention are: Mr. Westfield and Mr. John Goman, Trinity Episcopal Church; Mr. Radcliff, Calvary Presbyterian Church; Mr. Pedro Gomez, St. Mary's Cathedral; Mr. Casey, Old St. Mary's Church; Mr. Jim Maher, St. Patrick's Church; Mr. Millet, Mr. Frank Rhodes, and Mr. Charles McCusker, Temple Emanuel; Mr. Blanchflower, St. Luke's Episcopal Church; Mr. Doyle, St. Peter's Catholic Church; and Mr. Tom Moran, St. Paul's Catholic Church.

A COMBINATION LOCK

In many cases instructions are left at our office where keys to organs can be found, as not always the same tuner makes the visit, and to remember all the numerous hiding places would be taxing one's memory too much. There was one church, however, that seemed to outdo all the others. We had a key for the exterior door of the church but in order to make sure that no one but the organist herself and those authorized by her had access to the organ, she conceived a very intricate routine for securing the key for the motor switch. The process reminded me of the procedure in operating a combination lock on a safe. It was: 1) Pick lock on door of music cabinet in hallway behind organ with a knife. 2) Find large key in cabinet on nail at left side to open door into organ. 3) After opening door, find motor switch key on ledge directly before you. 4) Open motor switchbox under keyboard and start motor.

A CASE OF MISTAKEN IDENTITY

From early youth I had always taken my share of responsibility in the business activities of my father. I recall one day while I was still attending school, it was probably a Saturday morning, my mother received a message from some church asking that my father service their organ that same day. It was an emergency call. We lived at that time on Turk and Fillmore Streets. My father has just left the house and I was directed to try to locate him at St. Patrick's Church.

My father frequently used the horsedrawn omnibus down Turk Street, and at times in order to make a quicker connection he would take the Ellis Street cable line. I concluded he had taken the latter route and, therefore, proceeded to that street, a few blocks North of Turk Street, hoping to intercept him. A car had just passed and in catching up with it I definitely thought I saw him sitting inside, his back towards me. At times I got a glimpse of his familiar black beard and was convinced it was he. The task was now to draw his attention. I ran along the side of the car calling to him, as I had no carfare to board the car, gesticulating, tapping on the window, trying to attract his attention, but with no apparent success. I was almost exhausted and about to give up when finally I got the attention of another passenger, who beckoned to my father. He turned around and looked out the window to see what all the excitement and commotion was about. Getting my first glimpse of his face, I realized at once it was not my father, although he did resemble him greatly. Embarrassed and exhausted, I hurried to the sidewalk to regain my breath and composure and then disappeared as fast as I could.

DO YOU PLAY THE ORGAN?

One of the annoying questions often put to me when tuning an organ, by bystanders around the console, was: "Do you play the organ?" I thought that a silly question, especially after their having just heard me play, if not a Bach fugue, at least some melodious chords or harmony. I have never claimed to be an organist, as I have never learned to play professionally. However, working around organs and being associated with them all my life, and knowing their tonal structure and possibly having a good ear for pitch and harmony, in time I learned to play some chords, modulate, extemporize, and move my feet with agility on the pedal-board.

On many occasions my apparent virtuosity seemed to impress my listeners, and I was the recipient of undeserved praise, as no one knew better than I, how little I knew. Yet, on others, my so-called organ playing apparently made no impression whatever, for after I had played my usual stereotyped rendition of my limited repertoire, they would ask naively, "now please play something on the organ for us." Before giving them an answer, I would invariably ask myself the question, "Well, what do they think I was just doing, washing dishes or sawing wood, when I thought I was performing creditably?"

So, my conclusion was, that my reputation as an organist rested indeed precariously on an insecure pedestal.

NO SOLO STOPS IN THE ORGAN

A frequent criticism made by organists, especially of small and limited organs of eight to ten stops, is that they have no Solo stops to play on. Notwithstanding that all the essential and commonly used stops of an average organ are available, such as Open Diapason, Melodia, Stopped Diapason, Dulciana, Gamba, Harmonic, Flute, Octave, Clarabella, etc., and further realizing that an organ of 10 to 20 stops has more variety of color, pitch, etc., than a smaller organ, this criticism impelled me to ask, 'what is considered a Solo stop?' I am inclined to believe that any stop in the organ, with the possible exception of the Mixture stops, could be considered a Solo stop, if used as such with a suitable and proportionate accompaniment.

Why should not a Diapason tone be as musical as an Oboe tone, for instance; or the tone of the Gamba or the Stopped Diapason equally as effective as a French Horn, if accompanied by properly selected accompanying stops. To illustrate this point, I recall a visit to San Francisco years ago of Mr. Champ Clark, treasurer at the time of the Austin Organ Company of Hartford, Conn. In addition to the position he held in his company, he was also an accomplished organist. In visiting several of the Austin organs we had installed for his company he asked us if we realized what beautiful effects could be obtained by using the treble notes of the Pedal Bourdon 16 stop. After giving us a demonstration of some clever manipulation of the pedal in a region of the pedalboard, seldom used and often found dust covered from non-use, accompanied by suitable accompanying stops on the manual we were astounded and surprised to find out that out of this lowly, commonplace stop a Solo stop could be made.

I believe that the more justifiable and correct criticism of small or medium sized organs would be, that they lack sufficient accompanying stops and not Solo stops.

BLOOD WILL TELL

Two of my sons were called to the service of our country during World War II. Both were mechanically inclined and during school vacations and other free times frequently assisted me. Bertram, then 28 years old, followed the painting and decorating trade, while Vincent, 18, had just graduated from high school and had scarcely had an opportunity to choose his future career when inducted into the service. At the outbreak of hostilities, Bertram had already worked for the government for two years at McClellan Field, Sacramento, at his calling, with the hope of eventually finishing and spraying airplanes, work he had done previously at Mills Field, San Mateo County, before the war.

When the draft regulations became more drastic he was finally inducted into the service and aspired then for the Aviation Cadet Service, having a pilot's license, but due to a physical handicap and other reasons he was stationed as crew chief of a ground crew at several aviation centers in Texas and the Far West. Being musically as well as mechanically inclined, it was not surprising that one day he found himself trying to repair and give a breath of life to an old automatic piano, evidently donated for the use of the soldiers in a ward in the hospital, but standing there only as a silent ornament. His letters were amusing describing his difficulties in detecting the reasons why it would not work and the remedy he had to apply to correct it, also the odd materials and tools at his disposal to work with. He succeeded in getting the automatic player working, to the pleasure and entertainment of his buddies.

On another occasion, just prior to the Christmas feast, the organ, apparently a new model Estey reed organ, in the barracks Chapel in which he sang in the choir, completely failed to function Christmas Eve at rehearsal. As he was known by the chaplain and his buddies as an organ builder's son, he was again importuned to use his skill and luck in correcting the trouble. He related that from all outward appearances it was the usual type reed organ, so he concluded it was something wrong with the bellows. In opening up the organ he was surprised to see a generator in addition to a motor and blower that furnished air. Here his limited knowledge of organ building and experience came to the fore at once, and for the first time he realized that the key action of the organ functioned electrically instead of mechanically. By cleaning the brushes of the generator, which had become sticky and failed to function, the organ worked better than ever and was ready for the Christmas service. It took this incident to inform me that notwithstanding my 47 years of organ building experience at that time, to learn that there was such a thing as a reed organ with electric action.

Referring again to my younger son, Vincent, after 15 weeks of training in various camps in Texas he was ordered to Maryland. Enroute there, he spent a few days at home in San Francisco. After this visit he was stationed briefly in a camp in Maryland, and a few weeks later we received his APO address in New York. We realized then that he was on his way across the Atlantic. Finally, we received word from him across Alsace-Lorraine, France, where he informed us he was in the 7th Army, under General Alexander M. Patch. For almost three months the poor lad was out of touch with home; although we received his letters, he did not hear from us.

In one of his letters he related the following incident: He was stationed in a town that had been severely shelled in driving the Germans out of Alsace. The tower of St. Francis Catholic Church was struck by shell fire and crumpled, the debris falling into the organ. The falling material threw a set of large 16 foot Open Diapason pipes from its mooring into an open section of the Great, adding to the damage and injury by bending many pipes. The pipes of the Swell manual being enclosed in a Swell box were not badly damaged. It was a German made tracker action organ of two manuals and Pedal with about 21 stops, driven by an electric motor. The latter, however, due to the shelling of the edifice, or possibly to lack of current in the town, could not be used. The organ was built by "Die Gebruder Links, Orgel Baumeister, Wurtemberg." Knowing that my younger son was always devoted to his religion, and evidently no stranger to the chaplain, he was asked by the latter, who apparently had learned he was also an organ builder's son, if he would not kindly try to repair the organ and get it back into its former condition.

His letter was most interesting in describing his anguish and trepidation in tackling a job of such magnitude without much previous experience. Cleaning out the debris, repairing broken trackers, regulating the action, straightening out damaged pipes and getting them to speak again, cleaning out the Trumpet reeds, substituting some pipes from the Mixture stop, that was hopelessly wrecked, to replace some equally badly damaged Diapason pipes and using some left over Oboe reeds to fill out and complete the Trumpet set, the organ was finally ready for tuning.

Realizing that my son had actually never done any work of this sort before, although he had often been with me and observed the general practice of tuning and repairing, I think he took on a big job for himself. In spite of obstacles and lack of experience, he was successful, and got the organ that was silent for months to function well again.

For the reopening of the organ a daughter of the Lutheran minister of the town was engaged to play, evidently she being an accomplished organist as my son mentioned that she played the Bach Toccata and Fugue in F. As the motor could not be used and a foot pump arrangement was available, the village blacksmith was engaged to pump the organ. My son stated that the service went off without a hitch, the organ did not cipher and everybody was happy and delighted to hear the instrument played again.

This sense of achievement and gratification in knowing that his undertaking was a success elated my son immensely and he said that it was his happiest moment since he left home. As a memento of his experience he wrote his name in the organ as follows: "Tuned and repaired by Pfc. Vincent Schoenstein of the firm of Felix F. Schoenstein & Sons, of San Francisco, California."

Possibly some day "Gebruder Links of Wurtenberg" may call again to complete this organ or some local French builder from Strassbourg, France, will have the privilege, and I hope they will communicate with the young American lad who at least gave temporary aid to an ailing organ in a period of much travail.

WHAT'S IN A NAME

I have often wondered how certain people receive the names they have. Of course, we know at times it is to honor or perpetuate the name of some favorite friend or relative or, more often, to honor some hero or prominent personality or to recall some place or event that left an indelible impression on our memory.

I recall on one occasion in the early years of our married life when a prominent official of the Austin Organ Company accepted an invitation to visit our home. On showing him our first born son asleep in his crib he used a professional term to express his delight in the sleeping babe, by alluding to one of the organ stops in referring to him as a "Muted Viol." I thought it a good analogy and often recalled it. In fact, some twenty seven years later when this same "Muted Viol" grew to young manhood and became the father himself of a small brood of three children, the latter two of which proved to be identical twin girls, he also resorted to his professional background, and out of its vocabulary selected the two charming names of Viola and Celeste for his daughters. Since two similar scaled and voiced pipes make the best etherial stops, such as a "Vox Celeste", "Unda Maris, "Flute Celeste", etc., I hope these twins, with similarity of appearance, termperament and character will continue in this oneness which is so baffling to their grandparents.

A PIGEON ON THE LOOSE

I have often heard and seen pictures of the pigeons of St. Mark's Square, Venice, a sight recommended for tourists to see, which I in later years had the privilege of doing. I believe the pigeons of the Civic Center Plaza and Union Square in San Francisco can give the pigeons of Venice a good run for their popularity. So numerous and tame have they become that eating out of one's hand or perching themselves on one's shoulder or arm are commonplace sights. Even after official cognizance was taken of their untidy effects, and edict to exterminate them had been issued, they still persist in patronizing Union Square and the Civic Center and other favored haunts, but also still have their advocates and friends who go out of their way to feed them, all of which may help to give these locations their charm and old world atmosphere — although to the chagrin of the City officials. That some of these pigeons may stray from their beaten path is also probable.

It so happened that one day one of these pigeons fluttered around the tower of St. Boniface Church, on Golden Gate Avenue and Leavenworth Street. In seeking a resting place it then perched on an open window and eventually decided to investigate the interior of the church. Services were going on, but that of course did not bother the bird, except for the fact that it finally realized it was confined and could not reach the open space. I was told that it was a prisoner for several days as attempts to corral it proved futile. Finally, its antics became annoying and unbearable, flying hither and yon, ascending at times high toward the vaulted ceiling, then again sweeping down close to the congregation it caused quite a bit of merriment and distraction. I have heard of pigeons being released at lectures and sermons at psychological moments, for religious effect, impersonating the descent of the Holy Spirit. However, this pigeon, being univited and unscheduled, did as it pleased and made of itself a general nuisance.

Undoubtedly becoming tired and not being able to find an exit, it finally perched itself on the top of one of the tallest front pipes of the organ, a pipe about 6" in diameter and about 16 to 18 feet long. The organ was being used for the High Mass and when the organist possibly played the pipe on which the bird was resting, it became frightened and fell into the pipe. Choir singers on the organ loft who had been observing the pigeon all the time in its maneuvers, noted it made a brave attempt to extricate itself, but naturally it gradually fell or sank to the languid at the bottom of the pipe. His fluttering seemed to cease for a time. Feathers were flying about, especially when that particular pipe got a puff of air which again stimulated the bird to try to extricate himself through the mouth of the pipe. This being narrow, however, only his head would protrude or, at times, his tail, but he remained a hopeless prisoner.

As the pipe was large and heavy and, therefore, dangerous to handle alone, especially for an inexperienced person, a telephone call was sent for us to call immediately to extricate the bird. I was not at home at the time so my son, Vincent, responded. On arriving and sizing up the situation, realizing that many people were still in the church and that no additional disturbances would be permissable, he decided against removing the pipe. He climbed to the top of the dusty organ, finally reaching the top of the front pipe. He then dropped a long extension cord, which I always carried in my tool kit, into the pipe until it emerged at the open mouth below, drew it out and attached to it a small sock containing felt and leather. This he then shoved into the mouth of the pipe. The pigeon evidently sensed that a rescue attempt was being made and cooperated by standing on top of the sack. My son again ascended to the top of the pipe and slowly but steadily drew up the sack with the pigeon on it until it reached the top, carefully grasping the frightened bird before he could again make his getaway. A sorry sight of a pigeon appeared, exhausted and minus the greater part of his feathers, docile, but yet with the urge to live. He was gently brought to an open window and given his liberty, and was last seen flying in the direction of the Civic Center where more freedom was assured.

I complimented my son on his good judgment and mode of rescue. He lamented a good Sunday suit being messed up in clambering over the front pipes, but then it was all in a day's work for an organ maintenance man.

EPILOGUE

Philosophizing on life is usually expected of one terminating a career, completing a cycle of life, or preparing for the great adventure of embarking into the unknown realms of eternity. Possibly these thoughts may justify my extemporizing on life's purpose and destiny, possibly one or the other may claim prior right, but the fact is that I am at the outer threshold of a period of sixty-four years of faithful, diligent and whole-hearted effort in carrying out my allotted task or profession. I am, therefore, halting and evaluating the heretofore unabated desire and striving for the elusive something. A final consciousness seems to say, reflect, pause, and let other more adventurous and daring souls push on in endless endeavor to achieve that elusive urge that fortunately nature has planted in every human breast. It is, therefore, a pleasure, a comfort, to relax, to think and ponder more on the deeper meanings of life, to be probably less active physically but more alert and interested in the many spiritual things leading us closer to our one and final goal, the alpha and omega of our very existence, God.

With this thought in mind retracing my pilgrimage in this mortal vale of tears, I first want to express my thanks to an Almighty Providence which singled me out from untold millions to be privileged to be born into this world, by my esteemed and respected parents. I was favored to be baptized as a child of God and had, as my parents, devoted and practical adherents of that great faith, the Catholic Church. All my actions and aspirations of life, therefore, were nurtured with that saving grace to know one's destiny and to live and work for achieving its goal, the final salvation of one's soul and the attainment of a final and everlasting happiness in the life to come.

Therefore, in following that pattern of life in my youth, I can say, they were happy childhood days. The first cloud that marred my joy was when I went to school and had to be separated from my parents, sisters and brothers, and especially my elder brother, Frank, who brought me to school. Alas, I had to associate with strange children. Undoubtedly my shyness or backwardness was the weakness which I had to combat in later years. Fortunately I was ambitious, industrious and willing to learn, but I was not endowed with special gifts of intelligence and had to learn and acquire knowledge the hard way. Being one of a large family and not being raised with a golden spoon in my mouth, I was content with the simple things of life. In my boyhood days I gladly helped my father in his work when needed, acquiring at an early age a sense of responsibility and seriousness of life. In my adolescent years I thank God that, through my earlier school and church affiliations I was fortunate, with other members of my family, to associate with young people of my own belief, station in life and traditional background, forming friendships and acquaintances that have endured to the present time. Those days of my youth were happy and apparently carefree days. Were I to live them over again I would not choose to live them otherwise.

Fortunately, as I felt it but a natural duty to assist my parents as I grew to manhood, I seemed to have been Providently led into the career I was to follow as my profession and livelihood, that of an organ builder. I was interested in it from the start, enjoyed its fascinating and always interesting requirements and to this day would be unhappy, were I not associated with it in some way. Enjoying my work made it not labor, but pleasure. Being thus absorbed in this my profession, and always assuming more responsibilities, instead of romancing and being swayed by the frivolities of a lovelorn "Galahad" when most men seemed to be overcome by the darts of Dan Cupid, I had my nose too much to the grindstone to notice or even seriously think of him. However, when I was thirty, I fully realized the desirability of a good wife and helpmate, and here again a kind Providence led me to a good choice. My dreams of a happy family life were abundantly realized. I participated in the joys and happiness of the married state and well may it be so, for in later years memories of the happy days serve as a comfort and consolation when the crosses and burdens that all must carry patiently to our final goal to gain our reward, seem at times to overwhelm us. I was blessed with good and devoted children, nine of them, all of them the crown and joy of my life, one of them now a Missionary of the Franciscan Order stationed in the Philippines, a daughter, a Nun, a Superior in the Dominican Order at Oakland, California, and all my other children happily married. We were also privileged to celebrate our Golden Wedding Anniversary in 1965.

As no one can expect to receive reward without sacrifice, or a crown without valor and suffering, so I have experienced my share of setbacks, disappointments and heartaches. In the course of years, death has taken its toll from among our dear ones. Father and Mother passed on leaving a wonderful heritage to us children. Graciously, my own family was spared the losses by death suffered by many other families. Of the ten children of my parents family, after a period of 91 years, six are still living in the best of concord with one another. Three of my sisters entered the Religious Life. The youngest of them died while in her Novitiate. A second one passed away a few months before celebrating her Golden Jubilee, and the third, now in her 88th year, is still with us. Two of my brothers also died during this long interval.

After 92 years, the business my father established, and in which his sons loyally supported and sustained him, is still being carried on uninterruptedly, with just pride in our past achievements and with assurance for continued success. With grandsons nobly and gradually taking our places, following their grandfather's footsteps, as he wished them to do, I feel that after sixty-four years of active service, I am now justified in making a graceful bow and stepping out of the spotlight.

In 1962, June 30th, I definitely retired and, with my dear, devoted wife, had a small home built in Paradise, Northern California, where we resided for six years, spending the summer months there, and the winter months in our home in dear old San Francisco.

In 1968, we moved to the old historic town of Sonoma, California, closer to the city of San Francisco, to share more conveniently our company with our children, grandchildren, of whom there are thirty-four, and three great-grandchildren.

With this effort of mine in writing this book, I hope I can leave to posterity some interesting historical data, reminiscences of the past, and some data on my life.

APPENDIX

EARLY NORTHERN CALIFORNIA
ORGAN BUILDERS

Author's Note

Undoubtedly, some of the early pipe organs installed in San Francisco, not built by local builders, were transported here via the long circuitous route, by tramp steamer, around the Horn. The veteran California organ builder, Joseph Mayer, first established himself in San Francisco in 1860, and it is definitely known that several pipe organs were already in use here at that time. The Cape Horn route around South America, and possibly later the Panama route, were the only available ones for transporting such bulky material.

Among the great concourse of people who flocked to San Francisco in the early days were, I am sure, many of musical talent and ability. To cater to their musical wants, several large music stores were established. Among this clientele were some professional organ mechanics with former experience at their trade, competent to erect these pipe organs that arrived in San Francisco. It is logical to presume that from the Atlantic Seaboard it would have been prohibitive to furnish transportation for organ mechanics, when local help was available.

Two outstanding firm names frequently mentioned by my father in this respect were those of Shellard and McGrath, and Hall and LaBabagh, the latter possibly residing at one time in Marysville, California. He always mentioned the names of the former in conjunction with one another, so I presume they were partners in business. My father was personally acquainted with Mr. Shellard. Mr. John McGrath (or McGraith) resided in 1858 at Broadway and Hyde Streets, in the neighborhood of Meiggs Wharf. Mr. B. Shellard in 1859 lived at Montgomery and Green Streets, in the Telegraph Hill district.

In an attempt to definitely establish the age of the oldest pipe organ in San Francisco, and lacking data as to whether they were used organs or new organs built for their destinations when they arrived, I am inclined to believe they were the former, prior in use in some city on the Atlantic Seaboard, being displaced for new and large instruments there and deemed good enough for a further extended period of use in the new and growing Wild West.

In point of age, I would conclude from the evidence of the large three inch hand made, wood screws in the organ at Old St. Mary's Cathedral, California and Dupont Streets, that this organ, possibly a Willcox, was the oldest organ of its kind in San Francisco when installed.

Other organs installed in San Francisco before the advent of Mr. Joseph Mayer, in 1860, were the organs in Howard Presbyterian Church on Mission Street between Third and Fourth Streets; Calvary Presbyterian Church, Powell and Geary Streets; First Congregational Church, California and Dupont Streets; St. Joseph's Church, Tenth and Howard Streets; the African A.M.E. Church on Powell and Jackson Streets; the Howard St. Methodist Church on Howard and Second Streets; Trinity Episcopal Church on Post and Powell Streets; St. James Episcopal, later called St. John's Presbyterian Church on Post near Mason Street; and the Church of the Advent Episcopal on Howard Street, opposite New Montgomery Street.

Last, but not least, a small organ was erected in the brick Mission Dolores Church at 16th and Dolores Streets, along the side of the old adobe mission, which possibly was also installed and in use already in the old adobe mission itself.

Since all of the above mentioned organs and edifices, with the exception of the organ of Howard Presbyterian Church, now at Oak and Baker Streets, have been destroyed in the great conflagration of 1906, the Howard Presbyterian organ has the distinction of being the oldest organ in San Francisco today.

More recently several organ builders established firms in Northern California. In the contemporary list of local organ builders, I respectfully include the names of E. A. Spencer and the American Photo Player Company, Oliver Lowe and the Oliver Organ Company, and Smith and Sons, who have built creditable instruments, some of which are still in use.

On the following pages are biographies and work lists of

early builders listed alphabetically.

GEORGE NORTON ANDREWS
and
CHARLES BACKUS ANDREWS

GEORGE NORTON ANDREWS was born in Waterville, Oneida County, New York, October 12, 1832, son of Alvinza Andrews and Mary Norton Andrews. As a young man Mr. Andrews worked for his father who, in 1834, had founded a business for the manufacture of pipe and parlour organs, in the home town of Waterville. Later, in 1854, father and son moved their organ factory to Utica, New York, where they built and shipped organs into many states. On September 25, 1856, George N. Andrews was married to Mary Backus, daughter of Judge Talcott Backus and Nancy Root Backus, all of Cazenovia, Madison County, New York. Mr. Andrews brought his bride to the home which had been built by his father on Rutger Street, near the organ factory. (A note in passing: The Organ Factory in Utica, which was built on Seymour Avenue, was later occupied by the Buehl Organ Factory.)

CHARLES BACKUS ANDREWS, only child of George and Mary Andrews, was born May 26, 1858, at the family home in Utica, New York. Both George and Charles Andrews were proud of their ancestry, which they trace back to the Pilgrim Fathers and then to England, back to the time of William The Conqueror, since 1066.

In January of 1886, Mr. George Andrews and his son Charles, having been assured of a large field for church organs in the West, moved with their families, including Mrs. Alvinza Andrews, to Oakland, California. Having found a suitable home and building for their use at 620 Sixteenth Street, they began their business in the new location. They had great success in this field. Mr. Andrews specialized in small organs and, although Mr. George Andrews has long ago passed on, his work and that of his son stands as a memorial to honest, efficient and faithful service.

After the death of George Norton Andrews, on September

17, 1904, his son carried on the business of building, repairing and tuning organs. During the earthquake of April 18, 1906, many of the churches in which Mr. Andrews worked periodically were destroyed; and having had a desire for many years to become a rancher in a small way, Mr. Charles B. Andrews, with his wife, moved to Los Gatos, Santa Clara County, California, where they have lived happily for many years.

Author's Note

The writer of the above lines, Miss Alice J. Andrews, youngest daughter of Mr. and Mrs. Charles B. Andrews, recently visited Utica, New York, and found organs, built long before 1886, still in constant use. The most interesting organ and the oldest which was found, was in the Trinity Episcopal Church in Newton, Fairfield County, Connecticut, an organ which was erected in the year 1854 by Mr. Alvinza Andrews. The name plate is still on the organ as evidence of its manufacture, with an additional plate noting that the organ was rebuilt in 1896 by George Jardine and Sons of New York City, November 25,

The first organ Mr. Andrews built in California was in partnership with Mr. Whalley. The organ was erected in St. Luke's Episcopal Church in San Francisco and completed April 24, 1888. After the building of this organ, the partnership was dissolved, but Mr. Andrews continued servicing the organ until it was destroyed in the fire of April 18, 1906.

ORGANS BUILT BY
George Norton Andrews and Son Charles Backus Andrews
From April 24, 1888 to Aug. 27, 1904 Inclusive

October 5, 1888	Church of the Advent, East Oakland, Calif.	$1,500.00
May 8, 1889	Mrs. N. J. Brittin, Redwood City, Calif.	1,800.00
August 31, 1889	1st Methodist Church, Washington Territory	2,480.00
April 17, 1890	1st Universalist Church, Oakland, Calif.	975.00
June 27, 1890	1st Methodist Church, Los Gatos, Calif.	2,249.20
November 7, 1890	Deaf, Dumb and Blind Asylum, Berkeley, Calif.	2,500.00

January 7, 1891	Crocker Old People's Home, San Francisco, Calif.	1,000.00
April 22, 1891	Masonic Temple, Oakland, Calif.	1,590.00
October 22, 1891	Church of the New Jerusalem, San Francisco	1,500.00
February 25, 1892	1st Baptist Church, Santa Cruz, Calif.	1,600.00
May 20, 1892	1st Unitarian Church, Santa Barbara, Calif.	2,975.00
June 23, 1893	St. Mary the Virgin, San Francisco, Calif.	1,800.00
March 17, 1894	St. Peter's Episcopal Church, San Francisco	1,950.00
October 23, 1894	Church of the Ascension, Vallejo, Calif.	600.00
July 19, 1895	1st Baptist Church, Alameda, Calif.	900.00
December 9, 1895	Centennial or Chester St., Methodist Church, Oakland, Calif.	965.00
March 11, 1896	1st Congregational Church, San Jose, Calif.	1,575.00
June 6, 1896	St. Anthony's Catholic Church, East Oakland	2,500.00
November 18, 1896	All Hallows Church, San Francisco, Calif.	900.00
November 8, 1898	Rev. Louis Metsger, Albany, Oregon	2,060.00
September 18, 1899	1st Presbyterian Church, Santa Rosa, Calif.	2,350.00
November 5, 1900	St. John's Episcopal Church, Oakland, Calif.	2,900.00
June 4, 1900	1st German Lutheran Church, Alameda, Calif.	1,129.00
December 12, 1900	First Unitarian Church, Oakland, Calif.	1,925.00
May 29, 1901	Christ Church, Eureka, Calif.	1,925.00
January 4, 1902	Pilgrim Congregational Church, East Oakland	700.00
September 8, 1902	1st Swedish Lutheran Church, Oakland, Calif.	900.00
August 27, 1904	Cathedral Mission, San Francisco, Calif.	1,200.00

JOHN ERIC BERGSTROM

John Eric Bergstrom was born in Gotenborg, Sweden, March 1, 1826. In his youth he served his apprenticeship with an organ builder of his native country. In the course of time he married, and a daughter was born to the couple. In common with many of his countrymen, in 1850 he migrated to America, arriving in New York, where he stayed but a short time, eventually moving to Boston, where he worked at his profession as organ builder.

Here he married a second time, taking as his wife Miss Elizabeth Ann Gibbons. From this union seven children were born, three sons and four daughters, the former being James and Hector, twins, and Jack Bergstrom. Three of the daughters passed away a few years ago, elderly women. Mrs. Emma M. Hedemark, now also well along in years, resides in Oakland, California, and is the last suriving member of the family.

In 1854, Mr. Bergstrom decided to move with his family to California, and made the journey by way of Panama to San Francisco. He first accepted work as a carpenter and cabinet maker and finally, in 1874 or 1875, established his own business as organ builder and located his establishment at the southeast corner of 24th and Mission Streets. Here he built quite a number of organs, among them his largest and most important instrument, the $10,000 organ for the Metropolitan Temple, located then on Fifth Street, opposite the United States Mint. About this time, some merger was entered into with Sherman Clay & Company. Being unsatisfactory, the affiliation was soon terminated. At this time he also found it expedient to move to a new location, farther south on the west side of Mission at 29th Street.

Being in a receptive mood at this time for a plan to better his condition, and listening too trustfully, no doubt, to well-intentioned but ill-advised suggestions from his friends, he was inveigled into abandoning his local field and casting his lot in an entirely new environment in a strange city. In 1891 he moved, with his family, to Minneapolis, Minnesota, where he established an organ business. The roseate picture of a promising field and unquestionable success did not materialize and, disillusioned, he returned to San Francisco in 1893, this time establishing his business on California Avenue in the Bernal Heights district, now Coolidge Avenue. Here several organs were built.

His sons, James, Hector and Jack, by this time grown to young manhood, faithful workers with their father for many years, undoubtedly perceiving a decline and a period of inactivity approaching in the organ building industry, moved to Honolulu, Hawaii, and established the Bergstrom Music Company which functioned successfully for many years. Later, the name was changed to the Honolulu Music Company.

Mr. John Bergstrom, at that time well along in years, gradually retired from active business and, on September 9, 1907, at the age of 81 passed to his eternal rest. In the course of the following years his three sons also died.

All of the many organs John Bergstrom built during his career were of the tracker action type. The tone and specifications of his organs exemplified the typical church organ quality, pleasing and satisfactory. In construction and finish they were fashioned after a standard pattern, easily distinguished and identified, durably but simply and economically made. Mr. Bergstrom built a considerable number of organs, and for diverse locations. One was built for Guatemala, Central America, four for the Hawaiian Islands; these organs were installed by Mr. Bergstrom personally. From my father's records, I note Mr. Bergstrom also built a two manual residence for a Miss Deasy, on Post Street, near Franklin.

ORGANS BUILT BY
JOHN ERIC BERGSTROM

Catholic Church, Guatamala, Central America
Kawaiahao Church, Honolulu, Hawaiian Islands
Chapel of Kahmeamea School, Honolulu, Hawaiian Islands
Old Music Hall, Punahou School, Honolulu, Hawaiian Islands
Haile Church, Hilo, Hawaii
First Methodist Church, San Francisco, Calif.
Metropolitan Temple, San Francisco, Calif.
St. Francis Church, San Francisco, Calif.
St. Peter's Catholic Church, San Francisco, Calif.
Presentation Convent, San Francisco, Calif.
Third Congregational Church, San Francisco, Calif.
Lebanon Presbyterian Church, San Francisco, Calif.
Sherith Israel, San Francisco, Calif.
Beth Israel, San Francisco, Calif.
Spanish Church, San Francisco, Calif.
Bethany Congregational Church, San Francisco, Calif.
Grace Methodist Episcopal Church, San Francisco, Calif.
Wesley Methodist Episcopal Church, San Francisco, Calif.
Emanuel Baptist Church, San Francisco, Calif.
St. Mary's Hospital, San Francisco, Calif.
St. Matthew's Catholic Church, San Mateo, Calif.
Parrott Residence, San Mateo, Calif.
Episcopal Church, Sausalito, Calif.
First Methodist Church, Oakland, Calif.
Tenth Avenue Baptist Church, Oakland, Calif.
Presbyterian Church, Napa, Calif.
Congregational Church, Santa Clara, Calif.
Community Church, San Pablo, Calif.
Congregational Church, Sonoma, Calif.

JOSEPH SEVERIN MAYER

Joseph Severin Mayer, first organ builder of California, was born in Wurttemberg, Germany, May 27, 1823, in the village of Schomberg. He was reared on a farm and received his early education in the district school. Later he worked on his father's farm for a short time, when he decided to further his education; and at the age of eighteen he went to Stuttgart, there to study and later to become a cabinet maker.

When he had mastered his trade, he went to Duesseldorf and started to work as an apprentice in an organ factory. He concentrated on pipe organs and later worked in different establishments in Strassburg, Duesseldorf and Stuttgart, and studied music in the evenings, taking lessons on the violin, piano and organ.

He emigrated to the United States in 1853, leaving Germany in August. Upon his arrival in this country, he worked in several organ factories in New York City. After eighteen months he left for California to try his luck in the gold fields. He prospected throughout the Mother Lode Country, the district that was, at that time, the attraction of fortune hunters during the gold rush days, but fortune did not favor his quest and, in 1856, he settled in Marysville.

He opened a small workshop there, where he constructed the first pipe organ ever built in California, and for which the State awarded Mr. Mayer a diploma at the annual State Fair in 1857. This instrument was later purchased by the Roman Catholic Church of Marysville. Encouraged by his success, he constructed an organ for exhibition at the State Fair in 1858, for which he received a Gold Medal Award.

He was a progressive and industrious man, with faith in the development of California industry and saw great possibilities lying ahead for an organ builder. In 1860 he went to San Francisco. He found room and board in a residence at 25 Dupont Street (now Grant Avenue), which was conducted by Mrs. William Schultz. Soon after his arrival he established a factory at 728 Montgomery Street. The demand for pipe organs soon exceeded his wildest expectations and he was obliged to enlarge his plant from time to time, first by taking over more floor space at 730 Montgomery Street, then later, in 1861, he moved to a large building at 7 First Street.

Mr. Mayer's reputation as an organ builder soon became widespread, and, as business increased, he opened a spacious plant at the southeast corner of Post and Stockton Streets, and took up living quarters on Sutter Street near the German Roman Catholic Church (St. Boniface), in which church he served as organist and choir master for sixteen years, without remuneration. In 1865 he invested in real estate, which was located on the south side of Page Street near Octavia, and there established a sizable factory, employing a number of assistants, and manufactured pipe organs extensively.

On July 28, 1868, he married Miss Barbara Weigand of Buffalo, New York, with whom he had carried on a correspondence courtship. The ceremony was performed at St. Boniface Church, which was at that time located on Sutter Street near Montgomery. Mr. and Mrs. Mayer made their home at 127 Page Street, adjoining the business establishment. In 1884, Mr. Mayer again built an organ expressly for exhibition purposes and was given a Gold Medal Award, his second, this time by the Committee of the Mechanics Fair, a yearly event held in the Mechanics Pavilion.

The following year, Mr. Mayer retired from active life and moved with his family, consisting of two sons and two daughters, to Santa Clara, Santa Clara County, where he remained for six years.

In December, 1899, he returned to the family home on Page Street, in San Francisco, and resumed business in a small way, repairing and manufacturing organs, more as a hobby than as a commercial enterprise.

About 1894-95, when over 70 years of age, he finished two small parlor organs, which he later disposed of, one to Rev. Father McNaboe, erected in the Catholic Church in Mission San Jose, the other to Rev. Father McQuaide, which Mr. Mayer erected in Holy Redeemer Church after his 82nd birthday.

He died on October 15, 1909, after a short illness, when 86 years of age, with twenty-nine instruments of his manufacture sold throughout the State of California.

The above was written by Joseph Mayer's daughter, Josephine. From my father's notes, I noted a high regard my father had for Mr. Mayer for his kindness in giving him employment in his young manhood days; for the high regard he had for him for his fine Christian and manly qualities and the respect and dignity in which he valued his calling, the art of being an organ builder. As he took this attitude literally and considered himself only a master, or builder, and would not condescend to do patching or repairing, as he called it, he undoubtedly, in time, paved the way for his dissolution.

ORGANS BUILT IN CALIFORNIA
by JOSEPH SEVERIN MAYER

1857 for Catholic Church, Marysville	8	Stops	$1,200.00
1858 for Catholic Church, Shasta	8	"	1,200.00
1858 for State Fair (Gold Medal Award)	8	"	1,000.00
1859 Repairing organ for H. Cramer	10	"	600.00
1860 for Sisters of Notre Dame, San Jose	4	"	500.00
1862 for German Catholic Church (St. Boniface), San Francisco	8	"	900.00
1862 for Grace Cathedral (rented for years, later sold for)			1,000.00
1864 for St. Patrick's Catholic Church, San Fran.	16	"	1,400.00
1864 for First Congregational Church, San Fran.	10	"	1,000.00
1864 for Unitarian Church, San Francisco	24	"	3,350.00
1864 for Church in Mexico, Mexico	3	"	400.00
1865 for Temple EmanuEl, San Francisco	28	"	4,650.00
1866 for Odd Fellows, San Francisco	10	"	1,000.00
1867 for Third Baptist (Black) Church, S.F.	10	"	1,000.00
1867 for German Protestant Church, S.F.	16	"	1,500.00
1867 for Free Masons — Post and Montgomery, San Francisco	16	"	1,500.00
1867 for St. John's Church - Rented and later sold for			1,200.00
1868 for Second Congregational Church, S.F.	16	"	1,500.00

1868 for Odd Fellows - 7th and Market Streets, San Francisco	5	"	750.00
1869 for Catholic Church, San Jose	24	"	2,420.00
1871 for Catholic Church (German), Marysville	5	"	400.00
1872 for Jewish Synagogue, San Francisco	16	"	1,500.00
1875 for Catholic Church, Benicia	7	"	750.00
1875 for French Catholic Church, San Francisco	18	"	2,500.00
1876 for Chapel, Sisters of Notre Dame, S.F.	16	"	1,200.00
1880 for Catholic Church, Los Angeles	16	"	1,600.00
1884 for Catholic Church (Gold Medal), Santa Clara	16	"	1,600.00
1894 for Catholic Church (Parlor), Mission San Jose	6	"	400.00
1894-95 for Parlor Organ (rented for years), Holy Redeemer Church	12	"	600.00

THOMAS W. WHALLEY

Thomas W. Whalley was born in San Francisco, California, February 2, 1856, on Stockton near Clay St., one of six children to Christopher and Emily Whalley. His father came to California from around the Horn from Boston in 1849, bringing with him a supply of crockery and chinaware to open a store in Sacramento. He later moved to San Francisco and operated a store on Mongtomery Street, near Bush.

Thomas W. Whalley had a keen ear for music, and during his early life worked at various jobs to earn money to study music, so that he might satisfy a desire to play the pipe organ. While an apprentice in a lumber mill, an accident, resulting in the loss of two fingers, ended that phase of his intention to become a musician. But, not to be deprived of his chosen musical instrument, he turned from one form of its musical expression to another, that of making pipe organs. No record is available of his early apprenticeship to the organ-making trade, but prior to 1890 he entered into a partnership with someone named Genung, starting business in what is now the heart of downtown Oakland. This partnership, operating under the name of Whalley and Genung, did not last long. At least two manual tracker action organs were built; one was sold to St. Paul's Episcopal Church, Oakland.

In 1890, he married Eliza Bousefield, an English-born

woman who had emigrated from England, via Canada, with her parents. During the next eight years three children were born, two sons and a daughter, Christopher, the oldest, Ralph and Mary.

In 1892 after the partnership had been dissolved, the shop moved to Berkeley, at that time a wide expanse of hay fields and vegetable gardens. From 1892 to 1905, Mr. Whalley operated a business of building, tuning and repairing pipe organs under his own name. Quite a few were sold, one in the State of Washington, and one in Nevada, as well as several around the San Francisco Bay Area. All were of the conventional mechanical tracker action, two manuals and a pedal organ. Outside of the ivory keys and metal pipes, all parts of the organs were made in Berkeley. Mr. Whalley was very keen on the tonal quality of his instruments, doing a great deal of the voicing himself.

By 1905 business had grown and expanded and, in order to take care of the increased work, a partnership was formed with Mr. E. A. Spencer, who came from Southern California. The firm of Whalley and Spencer built four organs, with several more on order when the earthquake and fire of 1906 disrupted the business to such an extent that the partnership was dissolved. During this period, the tracker action type of organ was given up, and the tubular pneumatic action was manufactured. Pipe organs were installed in San Francisco, San Rafael, Oakland and Alameda.

From 1906 until 1931, when death came, Mr. Whalley continued to build pipe organs, changing from the pneumatic type to the electro-pneumatic type, developing the universal air chest and other improvements. Most of the mechanical developments during this period were worked out by his foreman, Mr. C. A. Anderson, Mr. Whalley devoting his time to the tonal part of the work. During one period of this era trouble was experienced in getting an adequate supply of metal pipes from eastern organ supply houses. To alleviate the condition, a metal pipe shop was installed, so that both quality and quantity could be controlled. Mr. James Bolton operated the pipe shop, turning out pipes for the trade, as well as those for Mr. Whalley. Some exceptionally fine Open Diapason sets were produced by Mr. Bolton, Mr. Whalley being a firm believer in the theory that there was no substitute for these pipes to secure real Church organ music. Once having secured the necessary pipes, he felt it was safe to augment them with mechanical aides in the form of couplers, unification of key stops and the use of separate expression chambers.

Refinements were incorporated in some later organs, such as duplex chests, console adjustable combinations, pneumatic swell shutters.

During his life he enjoyed music and had many friends in musical circles, chief among these was one of San Francisco's greatest organists and teacher of pipe organ playing, the late Mr. Wallace A. Sabin, whose advice and criticism Mr. Whalley valued highly.

Since his death in 1931, the business has been carried on by his widow, who died in 1941, and by his son Ralph up to the present time.

Mr. Whalley was a member of the Masonic Order and the Knights of Pythias.

Author's Note

These notes were written by his son — Ralph Whalley.

ORGANS BUILT
by THOMAS W. WHALLEY

*Reno, Nevada	Episcopal Church	2 manual tracker action
*Oakland, California	St. Paul's Episcopal	2 manual tracker action (removed)
Virginia City, Nevada	Episcopal Church	2 manual tracker action
Port Angeles, Washington		2 manual tracker action
Cloverdale, California	Congregational Church	2 manual tracker action
Santa Rosa, California	Roman Catholic Church	2 manual tracker action
Santa Rosa, California	Episcopal Church	2 manual tracker action
Petaluma, California	Episcopal Church	2 manual tracker action (rebuilt by others)
San Francisco, California	Church of the Advent	2 manual tracker action (destroyed by 1906 fire)
Berkeley, California	St. Mark's Episcopal	2 manual tracker action
Santa Clara, California	Methodist Episcopal	2 manual
Berkeley, California	Masonic Temple	2 manual tracker action
**Oakland, California	First Christian Science	2 manual tubular (electrified by others)
San Leandro, California	All Saints Episcopal	Single manual and Pedal
Sonora, California	St. Patrick's Roman Catholic	2 manual tracker, pneumatic pedals
**Alameda, California	First Congregational	2 manual tracker action
Alameda, California	Christ Episcopal	2 manual tubular (electrified by others)
San Francisco, California	Grace Cathedral Chapel	2 manual tracker action (removed)
San Francisco, California	Sacred Heart Roman Catholic	2 manual tracker action (removed)
San Francisco, California	Church of the Advent	2 manual pneumatic
San Francisco, California	Christ Lutheran Church	2 manual electro pneumatic
**San Francisco, California	Albert Pike Temple (Masonic)	2 manual tracker, pneumatic pedals

**San Rafael, California	First Presbyterian Church	2 manual tracker, pneumatic pedals
Lodi, California	Methodist Church	2 manual electric action
Berkeley, California	2nd Christian Science	2 manual electric
Berkeley, California	Private Home (Mr. Rose)	2 manual electric (now in Lomita Park)
Oakland, California	Shattuck Avenue M. E. Church	2 manual electric, duplex chests
Oakland, California	Lutheran Church	2 manual electric
Santa Cruz, California	Episcopal Church	2 manual electric
Santa Cruz, California	Congregational Church	2 manual tubular
Ontario, California	Episcopal Church	2 manual pneumatic
Palo Alto, California	Episcopal Church	2 manual pneumatic

Organs Rebuilt:

Oakland, California	First M. E. Church	2 manual electrified, new console, new open diapasons (3) high pressure reed and chimes.
San Jose, California	First Baptist Church	New pipes and action
Oakland, California	Mills College	Electrify, new console
Oakland, California	St. James Episcopal Church	Electrify

*Whalley & Genung; **Whalley & Spencer

FELIX F. SCHOENSTEIN

"I, Felix F. Schoenstein, am the youngest son of Leo Schoenstein, of Villingen, Baden (Black Forest), Germany, who was born in 1811 and followed the art of clock making, assembling and constructing the complete clocks by hand-work. In the revolutionary period of 1848 he lost his means of livelihood in following the clock making profession, and had to take up some other work. He succeeded in getting the position of Foerster, "forest ranger", and moved, consequently, into the forest house called "Salfest" in the forest, with a few acres of land around it. This house was formerly the economy building of the "Burg Kernek", the ruins of which are still standing. I recall my father relating that when he took possession of the house it was occupied by a Prussian patrol of four or five soldiers on the lookout for fleeing rebels.

My father, Leo Schoenstein, had seventeen children, of which five sons and three daughters reached adulthood. I was the youngest of the sons. After living eleven years in the forest, father and mother moved back to Villingen, and once again worked at clock making, constructing musical clocks and orchestrions, etc., in a more commercial way. The two oldest sons, Lucas and Karl, in 1852, entered into an apprenticeship with Hubert Blessing of Unter Kirnach, nearby, learning the manufacture of Orchestrions and each stayed with the firm for twelve years. By 1862 the two Blessings and the Welte's of Foehrenbach had developed the orchestrion from the humble beginning of a musical clock that played a little folk song at every hour's striking, to the grand orchestrion. The music was produced by inserting a wooden cylinder into the orchestrion from five to eight inches in diameter and from six to twelve feet long, into which thousands of brass pins of various lengths were inserted, operating the keys which controlled the valve supplying air to the pipes, drums, cymbals, etc.

Hubert Blessing, the younger of the two brothers, had a factory employing about twelve men; half of them were engaged at wood work, the other at metal and mechanical work. All work was done by hand until 1862. Working time was from 5 a.m. to 6 p.m. All men had board and lodging in the same house. The table was set in the shop itself and the meals passed through a window from the kitchen. The "Meister", or head of the house, and all the men were Catholics, so the youngest apprentice said the table prayers aloud. All workmen had to take part in the brass band organized by the shop. The Meister, Hubert Blessing, himself directed the music and rehearsals, which also occurred in the shop around the same dinner table. If one could not afford to buy an instrument, the Meister would furnish one for him and deduct it from his wages. All had to go to church on Sundays. The Meister was also organist. During church time no one was allowed to stay at the house. The brass band also furnished church music at times and during the summer gave concerts at Fuerst von Fuerstenberg, and at other places and outings. All employed stayed together for a long period and lived harmoniously like one family. At free times they went to the "Roessle", a hotel or "Wirtschaft". They sat together as a club, having a fine time, but always orderly under the guidance of Blessing, who was looked upon as their "Hausvater". Hubert Blessing died early in life, at the age of 50 years. By chance he had just finished an order for a cylinder containing a funeral march on one of his large orchestrions, which was then played when he was carried out of the house for his own funeral.

The demand for these early orchestrions came mostly from Russia's leading cities, St. Petersburg and Odessa; also some from Bombay, India. They were not merely considered as commercial products, but as works of art. As regards construction, design, quality of tone, arrangement of music, and in appearance, they could not be excelled. They were made for royal palaces and residences. About 1862 I frequently came to the factory and saw one, then being finished for the King of Spain. I found there great inspiration for that kind of work. At this time, 1862, the factory of Hubert Blessing installed the first steam engine.

In 1864, my two brothers started in business for themselves. Lucas, the oldest, located in his home city, Villingen, and Karl went to Odessa, Russia, as agent for the Blessings and his brother. I, at that time fourteen years old, took apprenticeship with Lucas for five years, without wages, as was then customary, and under contract to stay full time. Working hours were from five a.m. to six p.m. for everybody, under a city law. Mechanical apprentices had to attend a "Gewerbeschule", trade school, where they were taught geometry, mathematics, drawing, etc. At five o'clock every morning, summer or winter, the apprentices had to arise and apply themselves to their studies, then followed breakfast and the usual routine of the day to six p.m.

During my apprenticeship with my brother Lucas, in 1865, he made an orchestrion of about 6 stops for Bombay, India. This played the overtures from Traviata, Semiramide, etc. The case was covered with leaf gold, the mouldings and carvings were burnished to a bright luster, the lower panels were glass mirrors. The orchestrion was packed in cases of one and a quarter inch lumber, with dovetailed corners. No screws or nails were allowed to be used on it, only wedges were used. Finally, the whole case was lined with metal, and joints soldered, to make it water-tight for shipment. This was Lucas' greatest job. In 1868 Lucas Schoenstein built an orchestrion for Mr. J. Wittmeir of San Francisco, California, U.S.A., for a large resort on Jackson Street, near Kearny Street.

As I had finished my apprenticeship at this time and was ambitious to see the world, and felt competent to make my own living and, at the same time being desirous to avoid military service, I, being 19 years old, emigrated to America and went along with the above mentioned orchestrion directly to San Francisco, by way of Bremen, New York, Panama and arrived in San Francisco, California, October 19, 1868, two days before the big earthquake (the most severe one antedating the catastrophe of 1906).

As there was little opportunity here to engage permanently in my original profession, I went over to the church organ field. This work, however, appeared crude to me compared with the high standard followed in the orchestrion business. In 1869 I accepted employment with Joseph Mayer, on Page Street near Gough, California's pioneer organ builder, and served with him as foreman for eight years. Board and lodging were given to me and, in general, I was treated as a son of the family. Shop and family were in the same house, the same custom as was followed in Europe.

In the meantime, two other of my brothers entered the orchestrion business, Erwin Schoenstein in Odessa, Russia, and F. B. Schoenstein in San Francisco. The latter took over the agency of Lucas' firm in San Francisco and I occasionally made the cylinders containing the new music for his trade. I had a special machine for this purpose and was able to make any size cylinder according to sample, without having the orchestrion directly before me for which the music was being made. I was the only man in California who could make these musical cylinders. I had to make the pins myself by hand, also arrange and rewrite the music from piano or other scores to conform to the scale and instrumentation of the orchestrion for which the cylinder was being made. In later years, the perforated paper music roll was invented, which gradually supplanted the cumbersome wooden cylinders heretofore used in orchestrions.

On August 4, 1877, I started organ building for myself on Birch Avenue, near Octavia Street, in San Francisco. I was in good health, had ambition, a capital of about $500.00, and the ownership of a vacant lot on Seventh Street, Oakland, at Market Street Station. Although organ building was not very prosperous at the time, 1878, at the age of 29 I married and, in the course of years, became the proud father of ten children, five sons — Leo, Frank, Louis, Otto and Erwin, and five daughters — Frances, Marie, Cecilia, Clara and Helen, losing none of my children in childhood. All ten children proved to be healthy and intelligent, naturally gifted for music, and inclined for work, thrift and religion. All were trained on established European principles applied to our practical "American way of life." Each and all of them proved to be the pride of their parents. The boys all started early making use of their opportunity of being allowed in the shop, preferring this to the field of sports, or associating with questionable company, thus learning with pleasure the handling of tools and the forming of mechanical and practical ideas. They became, in time, expert organ builders and helped to establish the present business by remaining at the profession.

About 1899, Leo, the oldest son, went East to work for the organ firm of Müller & Abel of New York. He later came back and in 1903 joined me for a short time before starting independently in San Francisco. The next son, Frank, took up mechanical or machinist work. Louis went East for a time and worked for Ernest M. Skinner. Otto was drafted in the army in World War I, but came back unharmed. Erwin, the youngest, stayed with me. The latter three, Louis, Otto and Erwin, together now conduct the business at the present time, 1925, in fine harmony and with success.

Referring again to the beginning of my business career in 1877 and the following twelve years thereafter, I attended mostly to organ tuning, rebuilding, and making music cylinders for the orchestrions. I also filled the position of baritone in the paid choir of St. Patrick's Church, and was leader of the Kolping's Verein Singing Section and the Cecilia Band.

My first important job was to completely revoice the large 60 stop imported organ from Ibach of Barmen, Germany, installed a few years before in St. Patrick's Church, during Mr. John H. Dohrman's term as organist and under the pastorate of Rev. Father Grey. In 1878 I received the regular maintenance of the organ.

In the year 1881, I built the organ for St. Mary's Church, Stockton, California, for Rev. W. O'Connor, consisting of 20 speaking stops, three couplers, a concave Pedal board of 27 notes (the first one to be built in California) horizontal bellows with double folds, with four feeders on a crankshaft, two manual keyboard, with rosewood veneering, having one piston coupler, 2 combination Pedals, a balanced Swell and a complete Gothic case. All display pipes were speaking pipes. The console was attached.

A few of the tonal features introduced were a Violin string tone stop made of wood, a Dolcan, not a Dulciana, also made of wood, wider on top than at the mouth, a Clarinet free reed, also a Trumpet free reed with brass resonators, a Piccolo 2' made of maple wood the full 58 notes throughout, a Flute 8' with round labium, and a Pedal Violin 8' with double lips, a strong double bass quality. The action was of a new design, eliminating the customary roller board. The chest was of the usual draw top slider type with pull-down pallet valves. These, however, rested on a bed plate of brass to prevent shrinking and unevenness. The pipe table being wider at the bass than at the treble end was so built to give the large bass pipes more speaking room. The pipes were chromatically arranged. The swell blinds were made of double thickness lumber filled with a deadening material standing vertical, oscillating on a pin located at the left end of the blind. All blinds were connected by a general trace operating all at one time. Each blind could be lifted out of place independently of the others for ready access for tuning. I made all of the metal and wood pipes in the organ and every part of the mechanism myself, including the keys of the manuals. It was blown by hand power operated by a crankshaft, to which later an electric motor was applied. In building this organ, I did so primarily to prove that I had ideas of my own and was not merely copying someone else's ideas, and in that sense, it was somewhat of an experiment. Rev. William O'Connor was pastor of the church and Mr. F. W. Schmidt was organist.

The next organ I built was for the Baptist Church of Stockton, in 1887. It was also a two manual of 18 stops with a concave pedal keyboard. Considerable discussion developed regarding the location of the keyboard. If it were applied to the front of the organ, it would interfere with the baptismal tank behind and under the pulpit. The older members of the church would rather have no organ than to move the tank. The younger folks wanted the organ regardless of where the keyboard was placed. So I placed the keyboard on the right side of the organ and therefore had to design a special tracker action to fit the unusual arrangement. The case of the organ was made of black walnut, of Roman design with three round towers of pipes in the facade of the organ. The bellows were pumped by two foot treadles, and arranged so that the pumper was behind the organ out of view.

Authors Note:

This brief autobiography was written on August 10, 1925 at age 76. For a more complete and accurate record of the organs built by Felix F. Schoenstein see the following list and Chapter V.

ORGANS BUILT BY FELIX F. SCHOENSTEIN
and subsequently by
THE PARTNERSHIP OF FELIX F. SCHOENSTEIN & SONS
(1877 to 1969)

1881	St. Mary's Church, Stockton, California
1882	W. F. Smith (Residence), San Francisco, California
1884	Parrot's Residence, Portland, Oregon
1887	First Baptist Church, Stockton, California
1890	John Schoen (residence), San Francisco, California
1890	Sacred Heart Church, San Francisco, California
1891	St. Markus Lutheran Church, San Francisco, California
1894	St. Pauls German Lutheran Church, Sacramento, California
1899	St. Agnes Convent, Stockton, California
1904	Scandinavian Lutheran Church, San Francisco, California
1912	Cathedral St. John the Baptist (Sanctuary), Fresno, California
1924	N. Gray & Company Mortuary, San Francisco, California
1925	Helpers Holy Souls Convent, San Francisco, California
1926	St. Francis Assisi Church, San Francisco, California
1926	St. Agnes Church (Sanctuary), San Francisco, California
1928	Hull & Durgin Mortuary, Berkeley, California
1928	Mission Dolores Church (Sanctuary), San Francisco, California
1929	Columbarium (Mortuary), Oakland, California
1929	Felix F. Schoenstein & Sons (Studio), San Francisco, California
1929	First Presbyterian Church, Sausalito, California
1930	Maneely (Mortuary), San Francisco, California
1932	Parks M.E. Chapel, Oakland, California
1934	Gantner, Felder, Kenny (Mortuary), San Francisco, California

1932	Albert Engel (Mortuary), Oakland, California
1937	St. Brendans Church, San Francisco, California
1937	Geneva Avenue Community Church, San Francisco, California
1938	St. Aloysius Church, Delano, California
1939	St. Vincent Church, Vallejo, California
1939	Redeemer Lutheran Church, Redwood City, California
1940	Church of the Nativity, San Francisco, California
1940	St. Augustin Church, Pleasanton, California
1941	Sacred Heart Novitate, Los Gatos, California
1941	St. Cecilia's Church, San Francisco, California
1943	Central Methodist, San Francisco, California
1943	St. Pauls A.M.E. Church, Berkeley, California
1943	Amberg Hirth Residence, San Francisco, California
1943	Bethel Lutheran Church, Berkeley, California
1944	O.J. Wohlgemuth (Residence), Walnut Creek, California
1946	Community Church, Pleasanton, California
1947	West Portal Lutheran Church, San Francisco, California
1947	Orinda Community Church, Orinda, California
1947	St. Gabriels Church, San Francisco, California
1948	Bethel Lutheran Church, San Francisco, California
1948	St. Peters Lutheran Church, San Leandro, California
1949	Brigham Young University (Studio), Provo, Utah
1950	St. James Episcopal Church, San Francisco, California
1950	Immaculate Conception Church, Sacramento, California
1950	St. Joseph's Church, Pinole, California
1951	St. Rose Church, Sacramento, California
1951	Holy Cross Church, San Jose, California
1951	St. Eugene Church, Santa Rosa, California
1952	St. Francis Episcopal Church, Turlock, California
1952	Church of the Visitation, San Francisco, California
1953	Redeemer Lutheran Church, Redwood City, California
1954	St. Joachim's Church, Hayward, California
1954	St. Philomena's Church, Sacramento, California
1954	Trinity Lutheran Church, Burlingame, California
1954	Queen of All Saints Church, Concord, California
1954	C. P. Bannon Mortuary, Oakland, California
1955	Holy Names Convent, Los Gatos, California
1955	Latter Day Saints Church, Walnut Creek, California
1956	Griffith Bratt Studio, Boise, Idaho
1957	Latter Day Saints Church, Vallejo, California
1959	Carmelite Monastery, Mount Carmel, California
1959	Dominican Convent, Mission San Jose, California
1960	Josef Schnelker Studio, Salem, Oregon
1960	Modesto Junior College, Modesto, California
1960	Puget Sound University, Tacoma, Washington
1960	Immanuel Lutheran Church, Boise, Idaho
1961	St. Paul of the Shipwreck Church, San Francisco, California
1963	First Methodist Church, Moscow, Idaho
1963	Sacred Hearts Convent, Honolulu, Hawaii

In addition to the foregoing list of new organs built by the firm during the last ninety-two years of its existence, an equally impressive number of old tracker and pneumatic action organs was successfully electrified, often entailing more skill and ingenuity than the building of new organs. In addition to these and kindred activities, we installed many new organs built by various Eastern Manufacturers throughout the Western States and Hawaii.

INDEX

Note: The editors have prepared a cross-index of organ builders mentioned in this volume. Space did not permit it to be printed; however, the publisher will gladly help researchers with reference information on request.

Craftsmen at work circa 1932 in the assembly shop at the Felix F. Schoenstein & Sons factory, Twentieth and Alabama Streets, San Francisco.

In 1931 San Francisco's oldest pipe organ, oldest active organbuilder and oldest living organist. Mrs. Elizabeth Fotheringham, organist of Howard Presbyterian Church, is seated at the 1852 Simmons organ with Harandon Pratt (left) and Felix F. Schoenstein (right).

1876 pencil study from the sketchbook of Felix F. Schoenstein.

Four stop organ built in 1964 by Lawrence L. Schoenstein (the author's eldest son) using pipes — the 8' wood Flute and the 2' tin Principal — made and voiced by Lukas Schoenstein (the author's uncle) in Villingen, Germany.

Felix F. Schoenstein's Opus 7 (1891) St. Markus Lutheran Church, San Francisco, California.

Orchestrion built by the Schoenstein firm in Villingen, Germany. The case was made in San Francisco by Felix F. Schoenstein.

Felix F. Schoenstein's Opus 1 (1881) St. Mary's Church, Stockton, California.

Copies of this volume are available from the publisher at 3101 Twentieth Street, San Francisco, California 94110. Tel. (415) 647-5132.